UNDERSTANDING LAW
IN
A CHANGING SOCIETY

Bruce E. Altschuler
Celia A. Sgroi
State University of New York—Oswego

Prentice Hall, Inc., *Englewood Cliffs, NJ 07632*

Library of Congress Cataloging-in-Publication Data

Altschuler, Bruce E.
    Understanding law in a changing society / Bruce E. Altschuler,
Celia A. Sgroi.
        p.   cm.
    Includes bibliographical references and index.
    ISBN 0-13-934134-X
    1. Law--United States. 2. Courts--United States. 3. Justice,
Administration of--United States. I. Sgroi, Celia A., (date)
II. Title.
KF385.A4A45 1992
349.73--dc20
[347.3]   91-8841
                                                           CIP

Editorial/production supervision,
    interior design, and pagemakeup: ELIZABETH BEST
Copy Editor: ANDREA HAMMER
Cover Designer: MARIANNE FRASCO
Prepress Buyer: TRUDI PISCIOTTI
Manufacturing Buyer: BOB ANDERSON
Supplements Editor: JENNY SHEEHAN

 © 1992 by Prentice-Hall, Inc.
A Simon & Schuster Company
Englewood Cliffs, New Jersey 07632

Printed in the United States of America

10 9 8 7 6 5 4 3 2 1

0-13-934134-X

Prentice-Hall International (UK) Limited, *London*
Prentice-Hall of Australia Pty. Limited, *Sydney*
Prentice-Hall Canada Inc., *Toronto*
Prentice-Hall Hispanoamericana, S.A., *Mexico*
Prentice-Hall of India Private Limited, *New Delhi*
Prentice-Hall of Japan, Inc., *Tokyo*
Simon & Schuster Asia Pte. Ltd., *Singapore*
Editora Prentice-Hall do Brasil, Ltda., *Rio de Janeiro*

CONTENTS

Chapter 2: How Courts Differ from Legislatures   38

Chapter 3: Due Process of Law   72

Chapter 4: Precedent   93

Chapter 5: Limits on Courts   115

Part 2: Substantive Law

Chapter 6: Property   145

Chapter 7: Contracts   200

Chapter 9: Equity 334

Chapter 10: Remedies   374

PREFACE

INTRODUCTION

To most Americans, the law, especially non-criminal law, is a mystery that only someone with a law degree can solve. This text is an attempt to show that an undergraduate student with little or no previous knowledge of the law can understand the basic elements of the subject. This book will not make you a lawyer, but after reading it you will understand a great deal more about the substance and language of the law and how courts interpret them.

This text has three main purposes: 1) to introduce you to the basic concepts and processes of American civil (non-criminal) law; 2) to acquaint you with the analysis and interpretation of judicial opinions as a major source of American law; and 3) to provide some insight into the way law and social change affect one another. The text is divided into two parts: the first deals with **legal process**, focusing on the institutions and rules by which cases are heard and decided, whereas the second part deals with **substantive law**, emphasizing the concepts and rules which establish legal rights and obligations. The primary material of the text is judicial opinions and readings from various legal commentators.

As the title indicates, one major concern of this text is to acquaint you with law within its social context and, specifically, within a context of political and social change. In other words, in many instances we will be looking at law both in terms of how changes in society affect the law and how the law effects changes in society. For example, when the Court of Appeals, the highest court in New York State, rules that two homosexuals living together in a rent-controlled apartment are a "family" for purposes of New York City's rent control law, such a change in the way the court interprets the concept of "family" stems in large measure from changes in the way society views "alternative" sexual practices, as well as changes in the traditional view of the family. Once such a precedent is established, it can pave the way for subsequent changes, so that other non-traditional groupings of unrelated individuals may in the future be regarded as a family for the same or other purposes. For example, New York City has subsequently passed a law permitting "cohabiting couples," whether heterosexual or homosexual, to qualify for certain benefits, such as bereavement leave.

People in society generally believe in progress; therefore, they expect to see changes occur. Moreover, most people believe in what is called an "instrumental" theory of law. That is, they see law as a means of doing things that need to be done. This view is an active one that leads to change. Additionally, people have come to expect the government, including the legal system, to be deeply involved in change, reform, and improvement of conditions. Generally, the effect of social forces on law and of law on society is best seen in the workings of the legislature, but courts are not immune from these forces. Courts do have significant limitations as instruments of social change, however. Civil litigation, for example, arises from demands of private individuals. These demands largely condition the work load of the courts and the law that will be made. If no one is disputing about trade secrets in a given year, that legal subject will not be addressed by the court. Because the court rules specifically on the issue(s) raised by the particular case before it, it cannot make law in a comprehensive fashion, the way a legislature can. Moreover, the operation of our courts is by nature conservative, because courts generally look to past precedents to decide the cases before them. Therefore, the court is always looking to the past as it considers present and future problems, which is not exactly conducive to change. Courts have their own jurisdiction and rules of operation, which are distinct from those of the legislature, and they may not usurp legislative functions. But even though the court and its actors, the judges and lawyers, follow the internal rules and logic of the legal system, they do so in response to the demands of litigants from the "outside world," with their own interests and agendas. The courts and their decisions cannot deviate too greatly from external social forces and demands without being looked on as wrong, outdated, or dysfunctional in some way. For individuals and groups who lack significant political power, civil litigation—selective, conservative, slow, and uncertain as it often is—may be the only opportunity to effect social change. For example, the National Association for the Advancement of Colored People (NAACP), from its inception, used the courts as a means to achieve equal rights for blacks. In the 1950s and 1960s, when filibusters in Congress blocked action on civil rights legislation, civil rights groups took to the courts to secure relief, such as in *Brown* v. *Board of Education*, the landmark school desegregation case. Another tactic frequently used by those lacking political power is to bring a so-called test case—that is, to support financially a litigant who brings a lawsuit challenging a particular law.

This is not to say that using civil litigation as a tool to effect change is easy or straightforward, no matter how necessary it may be for some people. As is the case with the legal system as a whole, the use of civil litigation is sometimes encouraged and often discouraged, and decisions about relative costs and benefits will certainly deter a great many marginal users of the system. The cost of litigation is high and the system is slow and cumbersome, posing serious barriers to its use. Nevertheless, in some situations a means of circumventing the barriers is created, such as the use of the contingent fee in tort cases, many of which could not be brought if attorneys' fees had to be paid "up front."

We could give many examples of how changes in society affect law and, how society is, in turn, affected by changes in the law. To give just a few illustrations, the so-called sexual revolution has led to many changes in matrimonial and family law. Those legal changes have, in turn, affected the institutions of marriage and the family. Similarly, changes in social and economic status of women have led to changes in family law, property law, wills and estates law, and labor law. Concern with the environment has led to changes in property law, health and welfare laws, and criminal law. Changes in technology have required a great many legal responses from the courts—without changes in medicine, for example, we would not be litigating about the "right to die" or whether a frozen embryo is property.

Nevertheless, effecting social change is only one function of civil law, and often not the most important one. People use civil litigation as a means of dispute resolution. Through civil litigation people are compensated for the loss or damage of things of value and determine to whom valuable things belong. Civil law and litigation help to facilitate certain activities, particularly economic ones, such as owning property, making contracts, passing on property at death, establishing standards of safety and quality for goods and services. Law can be both conservative and innovative. We will see instances in which the law effects change, but we will also see many instances in which the law protects and preserves the status quo. You will see that the substantive legal subjects covered in detail by this text are property, contracts, and torts, a kind of conservative triumvarite of the law, the core of the first-year curriculum in every law school in the United States, subjects that appear to be the province of the nineteenth century more than of the twentieth. Yet even here the process of change is evident, and not just in torts (the law of civil wrongs), where it has become quite commonplace. In these subjects we will see the civil law in both its conservative and innovative aspects, and be able to observe the frequent tension between the two.

One of the first things you will notice is that this book does not emphasize so-called black letter rules of law that must be mastered and memorized. That is not because legal rules are unimportant—quite the contrary—but because they are not always easy to discover and rarely permit themselves to be "listed" comprehensively. Moreover, legal rules change over time. They may be replaced by other rules, or, equally likely, the rule appears to stay the same but is applied differently. Even rules that have apparently been replaced can later reappear to carry out a new function or to place limits on the rule that replaced them.

If there are no lists of rules, however, how will the reader learn the law? Although we will sometimes refer to legislation, the primary material of this text is judicial opinions. When judges decide significant points of law, they write opinions to explain and justify their rulings. These opinions, called "case law,"[1] are a major source of our law because the way judges interpret and apply law to specific factual situations determines to a great degree what the law actually is. In fact, it is a prevailing belief in our contemporary legal system that the real focus of the law must be on what the judge actually does with it. Oliver Wendell Holmes, Jr., expressed that belief in a now famous formulation: "Prophecies of what the court will do in fact—that and no other—is what I mean by the law."

This belief that the *process* of legal decision making gives us the most accurate view of the nature and substance of the law also explains why American law schools continue to use judicial decisions and the "case method" to teach the law. In addition, exploring judicial reasoning in particular cases can be interesting, intellectually challenging, and, we hope, sometimes even exciting. Another reason for focusing on analysis of judicial decisions rather than learning lists of rules is that our law is as extraordinarily complex as the society it helps to regulate. Today we rely heavily on law to order and regulate our relationships to other people, often to the exclusion of other means. Our legal system's response to this complexity is to concentrate less on articulating ultimate rules and more on developing and refining a *method* of dealing with problems. For that reason, as we look at decisions in various subject areas of the law we will be as concerned to identify *how* the court arrived at its decision, and what implications that may have for future cases, as what rule it applied.

---

[1]Case law is also sometimes called "common law," although common law is, strictly speaking, a term that should be restricted to the body of case law rules and precedents that formed English and American law in the days before legislation played a major role as a source of law in these legal systems.

Like most other skills, reading and understanding judicial opinions takes time and effort. The first cases you read may seem to have been written in another language, the language of the law, and, in fact, they are. Our highly professionalized and exclusive legal profession has maintained its complicated style and "foreign" vocabulary at least in part as a means of discouraging access to the law by the uninitiated. Fortunately, some time and practice can make judicial opinions more understandable, because there is a relatively simple technique that anyone can use to understand the format of these cases. This technique, known as "briefing a case," involves breaking the opinion down into its basic elements. This allows you to concentrate on what is most important in the case.

The first point you will notice in reading a judicial opinion is its heading. By way of example, we can take the first decision in Chapter One:

CASE

Ezell v. Bowen
849 F.2d 844(1987)

The first line indicates the names of the two parties to the case. In this particular decision Ezell, the plaintiff, is appealing the lower court decision won by Bowen, the defendant. Ezell is called the appellant; Bowen the appellee. The abbreviations following the title of the case tell you how to look up the decision as it was originally published. In this text, nearly all of the opinions are excerpts; that is, they contain the most important parts of the decisions but eliminate some details that are important to the parties to the case and their lawyers, but not to us. If you wish to examine the entire case, the abbreviations tell you where to find it. Not all judicial decisions are rendered in the form of written opinions, and not all written opinions are reported, but the opinions of all significant decisions are published. The abbreviation in the center of the example above (F.2d) tells us which of the publications to look in—the Federal Reporter, second series.[2] The number on the left tells us to look in volume 849; the one on the right tells us to turn to page 844. Thus anyone can go to a law library and find this or any other case in a matter of a few minutes. After the title, the opinion will also list the court that heard it, the date (in this case 1987), and the name of the judge who wrote the opinion.

Once past these preliminaries, we can brief a case by breaking it into the facts, legal issue(s), holding, concurring and dissenting opinions (if any), and significance. Let us examine each of these.

Facts. Every case presents a distinct set of facts. In general, someone has a grievance against someone else that he or she is bringing to court. The facts in the opinion explain the nature of the controversy and how it got to court. Cases often present many interesting facts, but in your brief you should only record those that are essential to understand the case. What exactly are the two sides arguing about? What remedy is being sought? What happened in the lower court?

Issues(s). Each of the cases in this text illustrates one or more significant legal points. In the section of your brief dealing with issues you should explain the nature of the legal argument. For example, in *Ezell* v. *Bowen*, one of the issues is whether the statute in question violated the constitutional requirements of due process because it was vague and ambiguous. The issues generally concern arguments over points of law.

---

[2]In our legal system, with both federal and state courts rendering important decisions, there are publications that report federal opinions and others that report state opinions.

Holding. The judge, or a majority of the judges if there is more than one, not only determines the outcome but must explain his or her reasoning. This is called the holding. In your brief you need first to state who won, then explain how the court arrived at its decision. In other words, you need to include both the outcome and the rationale for it.

Concurring Opinion (if any). Most appeals are heard by more than one judge. If one of the judges agrees with the result but disagrees with some or all of the court's reasoning, that judge may write a concurring opinion explaining the nature of the disagreement. Such a concurring opinion may be based on a major disagreement on interpretation of the applicable law or may simply reflect a desire to give a slightly different emphasis to one or more points. Unlike the holding, a concurring opinion does not have the force of the law. Instead, it is an attempt to persuade future judges to reconsider or the legislature to change the law.

Dissenting opinion (if any). When the judges vote on the outcomes of the case, the result may not be unanimous. The minority judge(s) will often write a dissenting opinion, explaining why the result of the case should have been different. Because dissenting judges are in the minority, dissenting opinions have no value as precedents but, like concurring opinions, are efforts to persuade. Indeed, over time the position taken in a dissenting opinion may become the majority view of that particular court.

Significance. What does this case mean? Of what importance is it? What precedent did the case set? What will future readers of the case, whether students, lawyers, or others, learn from it?

For the first cases you read, you may wish to write these briefs out to use as an aid to class discussion. Of course, your instructor may require you to brief all the cases you read, but even if not, at the least you should organize your thoughts along these lines. (You will find that the discussion questions following each case will help you to identify the important issues and significance of the cases.) You should also make a list of the legal terms used and be able to define them. The results, although they represent quite a bit of work at first, should make these cases as understandable to you as material in other courses.

The law is and must be responsive to competing interests and to the need for change, yet it must still provide for stability and a substantial degree of consistency if people are to have confidence in the legal system. If you ask people about their ideal of law and the legal system, most will be likely to tell you that they expect it to be impartial, consistent, disinterested, evenhanded, and fair. Those, however, are the qualities we expect of *judges*, but not of legislators, lawyers, or even most of the public (except when they serve on a jury). We acknowledge that legislators will be influenced by politics and that lawyers are interested primarily in advocating on behalf of their clients. They would not be doing their jobs properly if they acted otherwise. The litigants themselves, of course, are motivated by their own self-interest rather than by any abstract concept of law or justice. That leaves the judges to be guardians of the integrity of the legal system. Some people firmly believe that this is the case, but others believe just as firmly that it is not.

As you read this text, you will find that much of what judges do is a subject of controversy. Are judges too active? Do they rewrite or distort statutes instead of applying them as written? Are they too creative? That is, do they invent, or at least recognize, too many new rights or extend old ones further than they should? Conversely, do they stick so close to old habits that they fail to correct mistakes or change with the times? The readings that accompany the cases in the text are intended to help you explore the questions of how the law is made and changed in the courts and the implications of these changes both for the legal system and for society as a whole.

ACKNOWLEDGMENTS

No text is solely the product of its authors. Our teaching not only provided the impetus for writing this book, it also allowed us to benefit from the wisdom of others. We would especially like to thank the students at SUNY Oswego who showed us what it takes to make legal concepts clear to undergraduates. Over the years our students made it very obvious when they found materials interesting and useful and when they did not. We would also like to thank our colleagues in the Public Justice Department—Linda Campbell, Irwin Flack, Luciano Iorizzo, John Maceri, and Norman Weiner—for the many discussions we have had about how to teach law to undergraduates, as well as the more specific discussions on most of the topics in this book. Additionally, we wish to thank the staff of Penfield Library for their assistance in research, and the Director and staff of the Academic Computing Center at SUNY Oswego for help in preparing the manuscript.

We would like to give special thanks to the Prentice-Hall reviewers: Professor Arlene Schubert, University of North Dakota; Professor Sandra N. Hurd, Syracuse University; Professor Walter Giles, Georgetown University; Professor Nancy R. Mansfield, Georgia State University; Professor Patrick J. Cihon, Syracuse University; and Professor George Felkenes, Claremount Graduate School. All of these reviewers provided criticism and suggestions that have greatly improved the final version of our text.

We also wish to thank all those who did the often unglamorous but exacting work of actually producing the book. Karen E. Meany typed much of our manuscript with her usual combination of efficiency and good humor. And we would like to express our particular gratitude to Elizabeth Best, who was in charge of production of the book, and who was especially helpful at keeping us and our project under control.

Finally, we would like to offer our thanks to our families, friends, and colleagues, whose patience, support, and concern contributed to the successful completion of this text.

1

THE
AMERICAN
COURT SYSTEM

INTRODUCTION

Although we are often told (and sometimes experience) how important the American court system is, the public is surprisingly ignorant about how the courts work. A 1978 survey found that 30 percent of those questioned thought that the district attorney defends poor defendants, 37 percent believed that the governor must approve state court decisions, and few could distinguish between the different types of courts.[1] In this chapter we will provide an introduction to these different courts, explaining what they do and how they do it. The following chapter will explain how courts differ from the other branches of government.

Sources of Law

The law itself comes from several sources: constitutional law, treaties, statutes, executive orders, administrative regulations, and common law. The U. S. Constitution is the supreme law of the land that takes precedence over any of the other categories. Each state also has a constitution that similarly takes precedence over any other state law (within its own state, of course). The federal government can enter into treaties with other countries that also have the force of law. The president negotiates these treaties, which must then be approved by two-thirds of the Senate. Statutes, laws passed by legislatures, are the type of law most of us are likely to think of when we are asked about sources of law but sometimes the executive (president or governor) is permitted to issue regulations that have the force of law. A common example of such an executive order would require that government

---

[1]*The Public Image of Courts*. (Williamsburg, Va.: National Center for State Courts, 1978).

contractors make every effort to hire women and minorities. Failure to do so could result in loss of current or future contracts.

Often, administrative agencies are given the power to make regulations that have the force of law. For example, the Federal Communications Commission has the power to license broadcasters, but Congress left it to the commission to issue regulations to determine which stations best serve the public interest. Such decisions can mean the gain or loss of millions of dollars. As government has grown, Congress and state legislatures, lacking the time and resources to go into every detail, have more and more left the power to make these regulations, known as administrative law, in the hands of regulatory agencies. This has been a major change in our legal system since the Constitution was first adopted.

Despite all these sources of law, situations can still arise that are not covered by any of them. When this occurs, it is up to judges to determine the law. In doing so they turn to a body of past cases setting out rules for handling such problems. These rules, based on precedents dating back to precolonial England, are known as the common law. This means that judges not only interpret the other types of law but can also make law. That is a major reason we will emphasize change in this text. As new problems arise, courts need to reconsider their rules and interpretations to determine whether they are still appropriate to solve today's problems.

Court Structure

The United States has a dual court system with separate state and federal systems, each primarily interpreting its own laws. This means that there are actually fifty-one court systems, one for the federal government and one for each of the fifty states. Fortunately for us, despite a variety of names for the different courts, the structure of each system is basically the same.

The courts we are most likely to come in contact with are trial courts. In these courts the two sides present their arguments and evidence with a judge serving as a referee on points of law. In a bench trial, the judge also decides the outcome. In a jury trial, the judge explains the law to the jury, which then interprets the facts presented by the two adversaries and delivers a verdict. In our adversary system, the court depends on the two sides to present information rather than going out and determining the facts for itself. The judge, applying the rules set out by law, determines what evidence may or may not be presented by the two sides. For a trial to have a fair result, the judge must give each side a chance to present its case, and each of the two sides must make its arguments as strongly as the law permits.

Cases may be civil or criminal. Criminal cases draw the most attention; however, this text will focus on civil law, which has a greater impact on our daily lives. As a general rule, civil cases involve private wrongs while criminal cases involve those acts serious enough to be outlawed by the government. This points to several important differences between a civil and a criminal case, beginning with the title. Because a civil case is most often a dispute between private parties, it will usually have a title naming them—for example, *Jones* v. *Smith*. Conversely, a violation of criminal law is an offense against society, so government or the people will always represent the prosecution—*People* v. *Jones* or *United States* v. *Johnson*. To prove someone guilty of a crime, the prosecution must show that the defendant is guilty beyond a reasonable doubt. To win a civil case, the person suing (called the plaintiff) need only show a preponderance of the evidence—in other words, the greater weight even if it is only slightly greater than that presented by the defendant. Most crimes are deliberate actions usually requiring proof of intent, whereas mere negligence can make a defendant liable in a civil case. Criminal offenses are misdemeanors or felonies; civil cases usually involve, but are not limited to, torts (breaches of legal duty) or disputes about contracts or property, all of which will be discussed in detail in later chapters. Finally, convicted criminals can be punished by fines, probation, incarceration, or even death. Civil defendants may be ordered to pay damages to the plaintiff or to obey an injunction, a court order to perform or refrain from performing a specified action. For example, an injunction might command striking workers to return to their jobs. It is also important to note that civil and criminal actions are separate and independent. Even if someone is found not guilty of the crime of assaulting me, I can still sue him for damages in a civil case without violating the double jeopardy provision of the Constitution. The not-guilty verdict in the criminal case would have no effect on the result of my civil suit.

If either of the two sides is dissatisfied with the result of a trial, an appeal can be filed. In most states there are both intermediate appellate courts and a highest appellate court. The latter is frequently, but not always, termed the state's Supreme Court. On the federal level, the primary trial courts are the ninety-four U. S. District Courts, although there are also specialized trial courts such as the U. S. Claims Court and the U. S. Tax Court. Cases from these courts can be appealed to one of the thirteen U. S. Courts of Appeals, also known as circuit courts, then to the U. S. Supreme Court. Figure 1–1 shows the structure of the federal court system. Because illustrating the court system in each of the fifty states would be beyond the scope of this text, Figure 1–2 shows a typical state court system. Remember that there are slight variations in this structure in each state and a variety of names for each court.

Most intermediate appeals are heard by a panel of three judges although particularly important cases may be heard by all the judges of the court, sitting en banc (sometimes as many as fifteen). The appellate judges do not retry the case. Instead they rely on the trial transcript, written briefs from the two sides, and oral arguments. Because they do not see the witnesses and evidence first hand, appellate judges will only overturn the trial court's judgment of a factual question if it is "clearly erroneous." Therefore, most appeals argue that the trial court made a mistake in interpreting the law, not the facts. An unfavorable result at this level can be appealed to the highest state court or, for the federal system, to the U.S. Supreme Court. In addition, rulings of the highest state courts can be appealed directly to the U.S. Supreme Court but only if they present a federal question.

Figure 1–1   Federal Court System

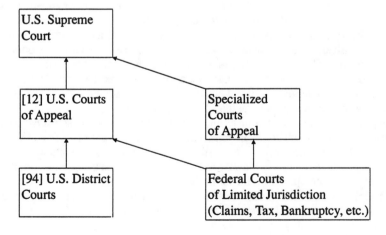

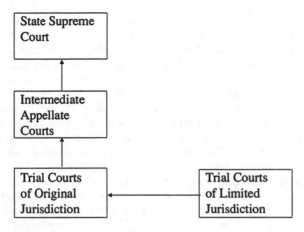

Figure 1–2   Typical State Court System

Jurisdiction

To hear a case, a court must have jurisdiction, the power to rule on that case. The court must have jurisdiction over the parties in the case and its subject matter. The federal courts have subject matter jurisdiction over two types of cases. Federal question cases present a dispute primarily involving federal law. Diversity cases involve suits between citizens of two or more different states for more than $50,000. Diversity cases require the federal courts to use the laws and precedents of the state in which they are heard rather than federal laws and precedents. Such state issues are tried in federal court to prevent state courts from favoring their own citizens over those from other states. As Alexander Hamilton put it in *Federalist 80*, written during the debate over whether to adopt the Constitution, these disputes are best handled by "that tribunal which, having no local attachments, will be likely to be impartial between the different States and their citizens." Many judges today, however, argue that such local prejudices are no longer a serious problem in today's courts and that diversity cases should be returned to the state courts rather than remaining in federal court. After reading the material on diversity jurisdiction in this chapter, evaluate the arguments on both sides and decide whether you believe that conditions have changed enough so that such a reform would be wise.

In addition to subject matter jurisdiction, a court requires in personam (personal) jurisdiction, jurisdiction over the parties involved. This may be gained in one of three ways: (1) **Compulsory process.** If a defendant is served with a summons, which notifies the defendant of the suit and requires an appearance in court to respond, within the court's state it gains jurisdiction. (2) **Residence or business in the state.** (3) **Consent.** An appearance in court without objecting to in personam jurisdiction is considered consent. Thus, the court always has jurisdiction over the plaintiff who has consented by bringing the case. In contrast, subject matter jurisdiction cannot be gained simply by consent.

To protect their citizens from unscrupulous out-of-staters, some states have enacted long-arm statutes. These grant courts in personam jurisdiction over people from other states who have had at least minimum contacts within the state. Without such statutes, a citizen of Wyoming might have to travel to Delaware to sue a company with headquarters in the latter state. Another way states protect citizens is through small claims courts. The television program "People's Court" has made the format of a small claims court familiar to most Americans. These courts handle disputes over relatively small sums of money (typically

$1,000 or less) in an informal way. Because lawyers are not necessary, the cost to both sides is kept down, allowing poor and middle-class citizens to bring cases they could not otherwise afford to. The results can be appealed to more formal courts, however.

At the opposite end of the judicial spectrum is the country's highest court, the U.S. Supreme Court. It consists of nine justices, each holding office for life. They are appointed by the president with the advice and consent of the Senate. Cases brought to the Supreme Court are heard by all of the justices.

We have all heard someone say, "I'll take this case all the way to the Supreme Court," but in practice only a small percentage of cases goes that far. The high cost in time and money causes most of those who lose in lower court to give up along the way. Nor is there any guarantee that those who do not give up will be heard by the Supreme Court, which grants full review to fewer than two hundred of the nearly five thousand cases appealed to it every year. The main method of asking for such a review is a request for a writ of certiorari. An appellant (the person seeking appeal) needs to convince four of the justices that the case is worth their attention to get this writ. Because the Supreme Court deliberates in secret and does not explain why they decide to review one case but not another we can never be certain of their reasons. Observers, however, can infer some reasons from such clues as the cases granted review, leaks from those close to the Court, and accounts given by the justices years later in interviews or autobiographies.

Alternatives to the Courts

Much has been written about the large growth in court case loads. For example, from 1964 to 1984 there was a 200 percent increase in cases filed in Federal District Court. Between 1952 and 1982 the increase in the Courts of Appeals was more than 800 percent.[2] That was a major reason for the suggestion for eliminating or reducing diversity jurisdiction. Although this would help unclog federal courts, it would do so at the expense of the states whose courts would have to rule on most of the former federal diversity suits. Thus, attention has turned to alternative methods of resolving disputes. The most important has been arbitration. When two parties agree to arbitration, they are bound by the arbitrator's decision. Courts can review these decisions but will only overturn them if they violated public policy or exceeded the authority granted by the original agreement. Arbitration has become particularly popular in labor agreements. Those readers who follow baseball are aware of the yearly salary arbitration hearings. Mediation differs from arbitration because it is not binding. The mediator seeks to bridge the gap between the disputants, helping them to resolve their conflict voluntarily. Because mediation and arbitration are quicker and less formal than the courts, many disputes that would previously have resulted in lawsuits are now being settled through these alternative methods. Even in divorce cases, some parties find that the adversary system stresses conflict too much so that they prefer, at least for relatively amicable divorces, the more cooperative atmosphere offered by mediation. It is likely that the expansion of alternatives to courts will continue.

LAW, JUDGES, AND CASES

The following case illustrates several of the sources of law discussed earlier. The court is called on to review an administrative law judge's ruling, decide a claim of constitutional law, and interpret several statutes. In briefing the case you should note each of these legal

---

[2] Roger J. Miner, "Federal Courts at the Crossroads," *Constitutional Commentary,* 4 (Summer 1987), p. 252.

issues and how the Court of Appeals resolves them. You may also wish to review the concept of subject matter jurisdiction to understand how the court applies it here. When a court lacks jurisdiction, it is without power to hear a suit and must reject it no matter what it thinks of the merits of the case.

This is a per curiam opinion. *Per curiam* is Latin meaning for the court. Such an opinion represents the views of the court but, unlike most written opinions, is not signed by any single judge.

CASE

Ezell v. Bowen
United States Court of Appeals, Fourth Circuit (1987)
849 F.2d 844

PER CURIAM.   Sheryl Ezell appeals the district court dismissal of her complaint challenging the decision of the Secretary of Health and Human Services prohibiting her from representing claimants seeking benefits pursuant to the Social Security Act. We affirm.

Section 206(a) of the Social Security Act provides that non-attorneys may represent claimants if "they are of good charcter [*sic*] and in good repute." Ezell, a non-attorney representative of claimants, was notified in August 1984 that the Secretary was initiating proceedings to suspend or disqualify her from further representation of claimants. The Secretary's actions were based upon Ezell's September 1983 felony conviction of two counts of filing false claims for job-related expenses.

Following a hearing an administrative law judge suspended Ezell from representing claimants for a period of five years. The Social Security Administration's Appeals Council affirmed that decision, but found disqualification rather than suspension to be warranted. Ezell then filed suit in district court challenging the constitutionality of section 206(a) and the statutory authority for her disqualification. She contended that in addition to the lack of authority for the disqualification, the standard of good character and reputation required of non-attorney representatives denied her equal protection and due process. She based her equal protection argument on the claim that the good character requirement unconstitutionally distinguishes between attorneys and non-attorneys. Due process was allegedly denied because the requirement was ambiguous and vague.

The district court dismissed Ezell's complaint, finding that the court lacked subject matter jurisdiction. The court held that judicial review of the Secretary's decision was precluded by Section 205(h) of the Social Security Act, which provides:

> The findings and decision of the Secretary after a hearing shall be binding upon all individuals who were parties to such hearing. No findings of fact or decision of the Secretary shall be reviewed by any person, tribunal, or governmental agency except as herein provided.

The district court rejected Ezell's argument that section 205(h) does not foreclose judicial review of the action due to the presence of her constitutional questions, stating that Ezell's "constitutional claims [were] 'inextricably intertwined' with her challenge to the Secretary's decision to suspend her."

As the district court noted, the regulations implementing section 206(a) do not provide for judicial review of the disqualification decision. One administrative action which is not subject to judicial review is "[d]isqualifying or suspending a person from acting as [a] representative in a proceeding."

These regulations do not absolutely foreclose judicial review because federal courts are always free to examine whether the Secretary has acted arbitrarily or exceeded his authority. However, before subject matter jurisdiction arises for review of the propriety of the Secretary's actions, there must be more than a bare allegation of unconstitutional action. *Thomason* v. *Schweiker*, 692 F.2d 333 (4th Cir. 1982). The court in *Thomason* determined that the district court had properly dismissed an action for lack of subject matter jurisdiction where there was no "colorable" claim on constitutional, statutory, or regulatory grounds. This result is consistent with the Supreme Court's declaration that a "substantial" constitutional claim is required for invocation of federal subject matter jurisdiction. *Hagans* v. *Lavine*, 415 U.S. 528 (1974).

Ezell's contentions fail to meet these requirements. She entered a guilty plea for two counts of filing false claims for expenses following her dismissal from employment with the federal government. The action of the Secretary disqualifying Ezell for lack of good character was clearly warranted in light of this felony conviction and Ezell failed to assert a colorable statutory challenge to this decision. Further, her claims of violations of constitutional protections are clearly unsubstantiated.

Affirmed.

FOR DISCUSSION

1. Congress required that nonattorneys who represent Social Security claimants be of good character. Why do you think they did not specifically require this of attorneys?

2. In this case, the court concluded that it lacked subject matter jurisdiction. What do they mean by this? On what basis did they come to this conclusion?

3. According to the court, "These regulations do not absolutely foreclose judicial review." Can you think of a situation when judicial review of a decision to disqualify a nonattorney from representing claimants would be appropriate?

4. Why do you think Congress limited the authority of the courts to review certain administrative decisions concerning Social Security? If you were a member of Congress would you have voted for the portion of Section 205(h) quoted by the court?

5. Overall, was Ezell treated fairly?

In the following essay, federal judge Marvin Frankel explains some of the problems that face a trial judge in criminal cases. Because most of the cases in this book are civil cases, you should keep the differences between the two types in mind, especially the different standards of proof, the different penalties, and the fact that the civil defendant is not being prosecuted by government. Conversely, both civil and criminal cases are adversary proceedings with each side doing all it can, within the limits of the law and legal ethics, to win.

READING   **The Adversary Judge**
                    By Marvin E. Frankel*

One need not be a working poet, let alone the greatest of them, to be conscious now and again of how all the world seems a stage and all of us players upon it. Along with the playwrights, the sociologists have taken particular note of this phenomenon. From watching us and spreading us on their statistical tables, they have evolved a considerable amount of observation and speculation in the now established specialty of "role theory." They have taught us how the sundry roles we all play—as student, parent, doctor, lawyer—are defined by the play of expectations. They have studied and somewhat illuminated problems of "role conflict" resulting from disparate or inconsistent expectations. They have given us insights into the causes and qualities of "role strain"—the conscious or unconscious difficulties in fulfilling the obligations of, or finding satisfaction in, the effort.

Provoked by the sociologists, among others, and working at one of the jobs in our society that commonly calls for donning a costume for public appearances, I have been led to think a little self-consciously about the role of the trial judge in our legal system as I have over the years watched others and myself trying to fulfill it. To be more specific, as signaled in the title of this essay, I mean to discuss the essential quality of adversariness in our trial procedures and some of the effects of this characteristic upon the trial judge's behavior and perception of himself or herself.

THE ROLE AS WRITTEN

There is an unhappily wide consensus that excellent trial judges are not in long supply. While we fail too regularly to people the bench ideally, the ideal is not itself very uncertain. The trial judge ought to be neutral, detached, kindly, benign, reasonably learned in the law, firm but fair, wise, knowledgeable about human behavior, and, in lesser respects as well, somewhat superhuman. Here and throughout, especially as the discussion grows more concrete and specific, the vision I have in mind is the judge presiding over the trial by jury of serious criminal cases, which is perhaps the crucible model and the one in which our failures are most frequent and notable.

Whatever the variations, a central core of agreed standards defines the trial judge as the neutral, impartial, calm, noncontentious umpire standing between the adversary parties, seeing that they observe the rules of the adversary game. The bedrock premise is that the adversary contest is the ideal way to achieve truth and a just result rested upon the truth. In the quest for truth through the clash of contradictions, which is, of course, the only reason in theory for having trials, the judge does not care where the chips may fall.

These are banalities. Like many fundamental propositions, they are thought to be self-evident. Nevertheless, the fact is that these professed ideals, like others, seem not to be designed, under our practice, for consistently effective pursuit. The tension between the ideals and some insistent realities triggers the conflicts, or potentials for conflict, that constitute my central theme.

THE ADVERSARY PERFORMANCE

Much of the time, the script, cues, and setting of the courtroom drama support the judge in performing his role as impartial arbiter between the parties and faithful guide of the jury toward the truth. The prescribed role has been learned by the judge during a (usually) long course of training and observation. The two sides, in the well, are physically equal. The judge sits between them, usually on a raised bench, and is called upon to reaffirm more than once the equality of the contestants before the law. The jurors are enjoined, over and over again, to be impartial, and the judge is both their mentor and their colleague in this effort. The usual pressures to conform encourage and drive the judge to be neutral.

But there are contradictions, powerful pressures in a different direction, that constitute the focus of this essay. The very nature of our accepted trial procedures generates forces that work against the judge's efforts to be neutral and detached. I find these factors subdividing into two categories, those that cause the judge to take on combative qualities and those that serve to frustrate or impede or visibly depreciate his duty of leadership toward the truth.

The Judge Embattled

The supreme concern of the parties on trial, and therefore of counsel, is to win. Of course, the battle should be fought by the rules, but the goal is victory—not the triumph of "justice" viewed in detachment, but triumph. The high objective of the defense lawyer on trial is acquittal—not an acquittal because the client is innocent, just an acquittal. The preeminence of the concern for victory is less total for the prosecutor, but it is not a subordinate matter either. Prosecutors seek convictions. Under the rules, which seem increasingly to be obeyed, they have other, broader obligations. But their goal on trial is a guilty verdict, and their behavior in court is oriented accordingly.

With partisan counsel fighting to win, and with the judge as an umpire to enforce the rules of the fight, there might seem a priori no reason in the nature of the contest why the judge should himself be, or seem to be, or perceive himself as being, drawn into the fray. The adversary trial, however, happens to be a game in which the role of umpire includes unorthodox features. Although it has no instant replays of particular events, its participants have a large stake in increasing the probability that the whole game may have to be replayed. This probability depends largely, of course, on whether the judicial umpire himself commits fouls—"errors," as we say—in the regulating of the trial. And this element is liable to cause the detachment of the trial judge to be tested, threatened, and sometimes impaired, if not entirely lost.

Judges and lawyers both have written about this combative aspect of their relationship to each other. The confrontation can be tense and wearing. When the crucial question has been asked, or almost asked, the courtroom explodes as people spring up at the several tables shouting objections, usually loudly because they are in some haste and heat to cut off forbidden answers. All perhaps look somehow menacing from combined effects of tension, hostility to the questioner, and anticipated conflict. The judge is pitted against the objector, who dares him to rule adversely.

Nobody doubts the range of adversary implications in our description of the judge as being "on trial." Among the more explicit references to trying the judge are the usually proper things lawyers must do or say "for the record." But propriety or no, the statement may have a cutting edge. When the lawyer says, "Just for the record, judge," depending upon the degree of the judge's self-confidence, the phrase may seem to mean simply "to preserve our rights." Or perhaps it means, "This is too much for you, judge, but it is to be your undoing up above." And the lawyer may in fact intend that it be heard either way. Judge-baiting, if not one of the approved techniques, is, after all, not an utter rarity, although perhaps less common than some judges perceive it to be. Whether it is done—and how well it is done—is seen often to depend upon the wit and agility of the judge.

The contending lawyer, "making a record," plays well within the rules of the game as they are practically construed when he scores points against the judge by urging views that he actually wishes and expects to have overruled. A seasoned lawyer in the largest of the Watergate trials, it is reported, responded to adverse rulings by observing repeatedly that he was keeping an "error bag" of misdeeds by the trial judge to be exploited in a higher, better court. The judge, also an old hand, was described as replying in bantering good cheer. But it was the reply of the confident gladiator, not of an uninvolved referee.

The thorough adversariness of our system—again as contrasted with others—has been noticed as a corollary of our limited faith in officials generally and judges most particularly. Where a society places more trust in officialdom, judicial responsibility for the process—for gathering the evidence, running the trial, moving toward the result—is greater. In our system the mistrust results in control by the contending parties, a more thoroughgoing and unmitigated adversariness.

How do trial judges handle the battle with the defense? Some, very few I hope, play it safe by keeping the scoring down: They rule doubtful points for the defense, leaving the prosecution with grinding teeth but no right of appeal. Some, another minority one trusts, enter the fray with hot enthusiasm. They bait, resist, and strive to defeat the defense. The majority of judges—again, I express a hope derived from years of unstructured observation, not a "scientific" report—stay on the prescribed course because the pressures for that are overriding. The long history of acculturation, the professional standard, the powerfully conditioned ego, all mark as failure the deviation from rigorous neutrality. But, maintaining neutrality is a strain, however it is managed.

The Judge Discomfited

Apart from the threats to his detachment and neutrality, the adversary battle before the jury is frequently conducted under conditions that entail a potential sense of frustration, even stultification, for the presiding judge. Each of the contestants seeks to win. For either or both, in part or in whole, the goal of victory may be inconsistent with the quest for truth which represents the public goal the judge is commissioned to pursue.

A whole class of examples arises in courts where plea bargaining is practiced. The bargaining, in which the judge frequently participates, starts from an understanding that the defendant has done approximately the wrong with which he is charged. In many cases, however, no deal is made. The defendant goes to trial. In the trial, the defense, by cross-examination and otherwise, fights to prevent demonstration of facts that were conceded before trial and are thus, in a sufficient and meaningful sense, known by the judge and counsel to be true.

How does it all look and feel to the impartial judge, regulating the contest, waiting to see whether the jury arrives at findings he knows to be correct or is successfully kept from doing so? Judges vary, of course, so there is no single answer, not even for any single judge. My own survey—much self-analysis plus amateur polling—discloses several:

1. Trial judges are, preponderantly, ex-trial lawyers. The game is still fascinating. Participating, even as referee, is still fun.

2. The broad interests protected by the trial process are vital in themselves, and their furtherance day in and day out is a worthy form of service. The result in any single case is a matter of relatively lesser consequence.

3. It is galling to stand by helplessly while facts are obscured and distorted as part of the professional contribution to truth-seeking. The satisfactions of the cases involving genuine, good-faith contests are nullified by such travesties.

4. The judge's role as teacher, along with the citizen-juror's role in the administration of justice, is warped and diminished when the jurors become the unwitting butt of a joke, launched on a chancy hunt after answers known to all the participants except themselves. The jurors, who should leave the courthouse more appreciative than they were of themselves and the laws they helped vindicate, too often receive an unedifying demonstration that trickery and low cunning may be permitted to defeat the ends of justice.

Of course, a majority of cases are tried responsibly, respecting the judgment and credulity of jurors and judges. But these are not my subject just now. The judge's problem of unease, embarrassment, and frustration arises from the substantial minority of cases in which, only after long struggle and with good fortune, the jury may come to see that members of the bar and litigants have been committing impositions in the service of winning, not in the service of truth.

THOUGHTS FOR THE CRITICS AND ROLE THEORISTS

If judges take, or are provoked to, adversarial stances, all of us, not least the judges, should be conscious of this circumstance. If the loss of impartiality is an evil, as all would agree, the awareness of its happening, or of the possibility, is a key first step to improvement. If we feel distress over some of the artificialities or visible devices for thwarting the search for truth, it is good that we acknowledge this feeling explicitly and not leave it to fester as an unacknowledged or unconscious source of irritation and possibly injudicious behavior on the bench.

If powerful forces tend to drag judges away from the neutral middle, we should acknowledge and face them. One of my favorite true stories concerns a judge who was asked to declare a mistrial and step out of a case after he had heard and stricken from the record an item of evidence said to be grossly and ineradicably prejudicial. "Counsel," he declared, "may be assured that I have utterly erased that testimony, both from my conscious mind, and from my unconscious mind." Whether or not that judge was right in his ruling or in that rationale, most of us lack both the power and the insight he announced. But we must do our best to regulate ourselves with such candor as we can muster.

NOTES

*Published originally in 54 *Texas Law Review*, 465–87 (1976). Copyright © 1976 by the *Texas Law Review*. Reprinted by permission.

FOR DISCUSSION

1. According to Frankel, "There is an unhappily wide consensus that excellent trial judges are not in long supply." Explain why this is so. What could be done to increase the number of capable trial judges?

2. Frankel suggests that the adversary system creates considerable role conflict for the trial judge. Discuss this conflict. How can a good trial judge overcome it?

3. Frankel writes from the perspective of a trial judge. How would the views of an attorney differ?

4. This article concentrates on serious criminal cases. Review the differences between civil and criminal cases. How would you expect the problems facing a judge in a civil trial to be either similar to or different from those pointed out by Frankel? When you have completed this chapter see if your answer has changed.

5. In many European countries, judges receive specialized education rather than, as in the United States, being selected from experienced attorneys. Would such a system reduce or increase the problems discussed by Frankel? Would you prefer such a system?

6. We often speak of having a "government of laws, not men." Do you think Frankel would agree? Explain.

APPEALS

In the following case, Centroplex Ford, having lost in state trial court, takes the next step, appealing the case to Texas's intermediate appellate court. Centroplex Ford is termed the appellant, and Kirby is the appellee. In a criminal case, double jeopardy prevents the prosecution from appealing a not-guilty verdict, but the defense can appeal a guilty one. In a civil case, conversely, either side is free to appeal an adverse decision. Most states require the intermediate appellate court to hear all cases properly appealed to them. In this appeal, Centroplex Ford charges that the trial court made seven errors, hoping that the appellate court will agree with their arguments on one or more that would overturn the trial court's verdict against them. The loser in this case could appeal to Texas's highest court, which would have discretion as to whether or not to hear the appeal.

CASE

Centroplex Ford, Inc. v. Kirby
Court of Appeals of Texas , Austin (1987)
736 S.W.2d 261

BRADY, Justice.   Centroplex Ford appeals from a judgment awarding damages for breach of warranty arising out of an auto repair. The suit was brought under the Texas Deceptive Trade Practices and Consumer Protection Act (hereafter referred to as DTPA) and was tried to a jury. The jury awarded appellees David Kirby and his wife $28,500 plus attorney's fees. Appellant argues seven points of error asserting that there were both jury and judicial misconduct, that an incorrect measure of damages was applied, and that there was insufficient evidence to support both the finding of breach of warranty and the awards of damages for mental anguish and attorney's fees.

In July of 1985, the Kirbys' new Ford automobile was damaged and taken to appellant's dealership for repair. The dealer represented that the vehicle could be repaired and back in service in six weeks. In actuality, the car was not repaired for nearly six months. As a result of this delay, the Kirbys filed suit seeking damages for breach of warranty, the cost of a rental car and mental anguish.

At trial, the jury found for the Kirbys. Specifically, the jury found that appellant represented that the repair would take six weeks and that the failure to complete the work in this time was a producing cause of the damages to the Kirbys. The jury also found the representation and failure to complete the repair timely was an unconscionable course of action. Finally, the jury found that the appellant expressly warranted that the repairs would make the Kirbys' car "like a new one" and that the car was not restored in the warranted fashion nor was the work done in "a good workmanlike manner."

Appellant's first point of error complains of jury misconduct. Appellant asserts that one of the jurors, a psychologist, gave his professional opinion that one of appellant's witnesses was lying.The evidence also showed that the offending juror was admonished by the foreman for indulging in that sort of discussion. In order to obtain a new trial on the basis of jury misconduct, the appellant "must establish not only that the misconduct occurred, but also that it was material misconduct, and that based on the record as a whole, the misconduct probably resulted in harm to the complaining party." *Strange* v. *Treasure City*, 608 S.W.2d 604 (Tex.1980) Whether an act of jury misconduct occurred is a question of fact for the trial court, and if there is conflicting evidence on the issue, the finding of the trial court is binding on appellate review. Giving the conflicting nature of the evidence as to whether the juror's attempt to offer an improper opinion was harmful, we must defer to the trial court's determination and affirm the refusal to order a new trial.

Appellant also complains of judicial misconduct asserting the judge called his attorney a liar in front of the jury and threatened him with contempt. However, no record of this event appears in the statement of facts before us; thus no error is preserved for review. This point is overruled.

Appellant further charges the court reporter with nonfeasance for allegedly failing to make a record of the bench proceedings. Again there is nothing in the record before us to demonstrate that such error or misconduct occurred. If the court reporter refused to perform his duty, appellant had other means to bring a record of such error before this Court, including perfection of a formal and/or "bystander's" bill of exceptions. Without a record, there is nothing to review.

In its second point of error, appellant asserts that the trial court charged the jury on the improper measure of damages when he allowed them to consider the amounts expended by the Kirbys in renting a replacement car. The recent case of *Kish* v. *Van Note*, 692 S.W.2d 463 (Tex.1985) held that the DTPA permits an injured consumer to recover actual damages caused by a deceptive trade practice, including related and reasonably necessary expenses. Furthermore, although this particular type of loss of use damages has not been directly approved by the Texas Supreme Court, the cost of renting a car has been held recoverable as actual damages under the DTPA by other courts of appeals. We hold the reasonable expenses incurred in procuring alternative transportation were properly recoverable under the DTPA as actual damages for loss of use.

Appellant's third point of error attacks the jury's findings on breach of warranty and unconscionable conduct on grounds that appellant "was not ultimately responsible for delays and made a good faith effort to repair the automobile." We assume this point of error challenges the sufficiency of the evidence to support the jury's findings. In determining an "insufficient evidence" point of error, the reviewing court must consider and weigh all the evidence, both in support of and contrary to the judgment, and may set aside the judgment only if the findings are so against the great weight and preponderance of the evidence as to be manifestly unjust.

The evidence presented at trial supports the jury's findings. Although there was some evidence of appellant's good faith and inability to obtain parts, the jury had before it evidence that appellant repeatedly asserted the car would be repaired in six weeks, that the car was not repaired for six months, that appellant warranted the car would be repaired "like a new one," and that the work eventually performed by appellant was not done in a good workmanlike manner. As trier of fact, the jury is the sole judge of the credibility of the witnesses and may accept or reject the evidence presented to it. Because the jury found both breach of an express warranty and an unconscionable course of action, they apparently elected to reject appellant's allegedly exculpatory evidence. From a review of the record, we cannot say that these findings were unsupported by factually sufficient evidence. Appellant's third point is overruled.

In its fourth point of error, appellant complains the trial court erroneously awarded damages for mental anguish because there was no showing of "an intentional tort, gross negligence, willful or wanton misconduct, or accompanying physical injury." At the outset, we recognize that damages for mental anguish have been allowed under the DTPA. Secondly, the jury found that appellant engaged in an unconscionable course of action which, under appellant's asserted requirements for mental anguish damages would surely qualify as wanton misconduct. Finally, the Texas Supreme Court has recently held proof of physical injury is no longer required in order to recover for infliction of mental anguish. *St. Elizabeth Hospital* v. *James Garrard*, 730 S.W.2d 649 (Tex.1987).

Appellant's fourth point of error is overruled.

Appellant's fifth point of error complains there was no evidence to support the award of attorney's fees. In reviewing a "no evidence" point of error, the reviewing court considers only the evidence which, when viewed in its most favorable light, supports the finding; all contrary evidence and inferences must be disregarded. The evidence on attorney's fees consisted of the testimony of attorney David Fernandez. He stated that thirty hours of work and a fee of $100 per hour would be reasonable for a DTPA case such as this one. He further stated that $3,000 was a reasonable amount for an appeal to the Court of Appeals, and that an additional $3,000 would be a reasonable fee for further appeal to the Supreme Court of Texas. The jury awarded attorney's fees in these amounts. We hold there was sufficient evidence to support the award.

The sixth point of error complains of the award of prejudgment interest because the rate was contrary to statute. Appellant complains that the award of 10% interest was improper. We note, however, that the appellant made no objection to this award at the trial level. Because this alleged error was not brought to the attention of the trial court, any error in applying this rate of interest was waived.

Finally, appellant alleges that the trial court erred in allowing a post-verdict trial amendment which permitted appellees to add a prayer for mental anguish. Evidence of mental anguish was presented and the issue was submitted to the jury without objection by the appellant. It appears from the motion that the amendment was intended merely to conform the pleadings to the verdict. Since the issue was tried by consent, we see no error in permitting this amendment.

The judgment of the trial court is Affirmed.

FOR DISCUSSION

1. Some of Centroplex Ford's arguments were rejected by the Texas Court of Appeals because they were not raised at the trial. Explain the reasoning behind this position.

2. What standard does the appeals court use to determine when the jury's findings of fact should be overruled? Discuss how this standard is used.

3. Frankel argues that the trial judge should try to ensure that the trial is a quest for truth. Discuss whether the trial and appeal in *Centroplex Ford* v. *Kirby* succeeded in this task.

4. Appellate judges rely heavily on the trial transcript. How did the transcript play a part in the outcome of this appeal?

5. Frankel writes that after a case, jurors "should leave the courthouse more appreciative than they were of themselves and the laws they helped vindicate." Do you think they did in *Centroplex Ford*?

JURISDICTION

In discussing the history of the federal courts, Charles Clark, Chief Judge of the Fifth Circuit Court of Appeals, emphasizes just how much change there has been during the 200 years the court system has evolved. He argues that these changes have made diversity jurisdiction (which was explained at the beginning of this chapter) "a concept with roots in the Constitution but whose time has gone." Keeping the original goals of diversity jurisdiction in mind, evaluate his proposals for reducing or eliminating it.

READING   **The Role of National Courts in 200 Years
of Evolving Governance**
*By Charles Clark**

INTRODUCTION

The greatest debt we owe the founding fathers is not due to their creation of a federal republic but to their enshrinement of the spirit of liberty in our charter. History teaches that necessity, not virtue, dictated the choice of federalism as our form of government. America was not settled as a unit; separate colonies became independent and sovereign states. In the constitutional convention, each state insisted on preserving its individual constituency and autonomy. Events controlled ideals then, as now.

In the period from 1787 to 1987, the environment of America moved from pen and ink to laser-jet printers, from Middlesex village and town to a small world. Under the press of changing events, our federalism evolved from thirteen independent states barely bound together by a limited cession of collective powers to a parental central force controlling most of the critical functions of governance in what are now fifty sibling states. Events that occurred over these 200 years, including the passage of the sixteenth amendment [authorizing the federal income tax] and the emergence of Russian bear, wrought a transformation in the form of our federalism that would astound even Alexander Hamilton.

National courts and their concepts of constitutional power changed apace. History shows no mean spirit at work; rather, here too change has been driven by events. Political predilections of individual judges have also played their parts, to be sure. The outset of the period saw Chief Justice Marshall use the case at hand to incorporate broad concepts of a strong federal judiciary in the body of the law. He was succeeded by Chief Justice Taney, whose decisions consistently cut back the breadth of the Marshall legacy.

Subsequent years have seen the national government, through taxing power, grants-in-aid, and subsidies, become the pervasive regulator of agriculture, commerce, communications, energy, finance, health, military, labor, transportation, and welfare. Meanwhile the courts of the central government—with a few pauses, such as striking down the income tax and begetting the sixteenth amendment—have moved apace to authenticate most efforts to centralize power, sometimes in innovative ways. When the problem demanded a broad-based solution in the area of racial desegregation, federal courts treated their judgments, not like traditional case resolutions, but like general edicts, legislative in nature.

This evolution has not been without accommodations, both legislative and judicial, in favor of state power. Statutes have long limited the injunctive power of the federal courts and required deference to state law. Courts developed the doctrines of abstention and deference to state criminal prosecutions to protect important state civil interests. This process of backing and filling has continued throughout the past 200 years. But, the net effect has been that, in the courts, as in the other branches, the flow in Washington's direction has exceeded its ebb.

Do modern times dictate different federal-state relations from those intended by the founders? Or are such relations controlled by the mission provided for states in the text? It is easy to say that the resolution of this argument affects the balance of power between the federal government and state governments and their respective roles in our future. Ignorance, however, requires that I leave such esoteric deliberation to my betters.

DIVERSITY JURISDICTION

I would call up diversity jurisdiction, a concept with roots in the Constitution but whose time has gone. In *The Federalist Number 80*, Alexander Hamilton stressed the need to relieve the hazard of provincialism through the device of concurrent jurisdiction in diversity cases. As the nation has become more centralized, and communication, transportation, and economic competition have made our country more homogeneous, the justification for diversity jurisdiction—that a party from another state would be denied justice in a local court—has evaporated. Nevertheless, lawyers who want the luxury of choosing between alternative forums have defeated every effort to remove this insult to federalism from our law.

The United States has both a fiscal and a federal interest in seeing diversity jurisdiction abolished or limited. Preliminary estimates by the Federal Judicial Center indicate that abolishing diversity jurisdiction entirely would save over $120 million a year in expenditures by the federal courts. That is equivalent to 192 district judges and 22 court of appeals judges, plus support personnel, spending all of their time on diversity cases. These costs divert scarce judicial resources from true federal interests, and, in my view, are alone enough to justify eliminating diversity jurisdiction. A piece-meal approach would result in unproportionately smaller savings.

The time has long since passed when diversity served a useful legal purpose; such usefulness clearly ended with *Erie Railroad* v. *Tompkins* (304 U.S. 64 [1938]). Prior to *Erie*, under the reign of *Swift* v. *Tyson* (41 U.S. [16 Pet.] 1 [1842]), federal courts developed and applied theories of national law in diversity cases. At least then, the litigant's choice of forum carried substantive legal significance. In 1938 the Supreme Court in *Erie*, sua sponte, overruled *Swift* and decided to apply the substantive law of the forum in diversity cases. The *Erie* Court declared that "[t]here is no federal general common law." By making the availability of a federal forum superfluous to every concern but systemic honesty, the change from *Swift* to *Erie* should have assured the early demise of diversity. Instead, *Erie* (with the added twist of allowing federal courts to certify questions to state courts) has become part of its lingering strength.

To this date, the cited justification for the preservation of diversity jurisdiction is the risk of bias against residents of other states. The unvarnished truth is that the provincial bias feared two-hundred years ago has long been dissipated. In my experience as a practicing attorney and during my tenure as a judge, I have seen even small-town trial court bias against nonresidents evaporate. The risk of bias has effectively disappeared because businesses and individuals have become more mobile and the world has become smaller. States wish to attract industry and commerce from other parts of the country, not discourage it by fleecing nonresidents. Tourism is a major business in many states. Even fools know biased local courts would do much to discourage visitors and the money they spend. Moreover, over thirty percent of Americans live in states other than the one in which they were born. This increased homogeneity furthers the national or at least regional outlook of the population. From a consideration of these factors, it is apparent that the risk of local bias is far outweighed by the damage that the premises for diversity jurisdiction impose on federal and state relations.

The irrationality of diversity jurisdiction is well illustrated by two limitations on that jurisdiction, both of which are justified on grounds of federalism. The first is the domestic relations exception. Federal courts decline jurisdiction given them under the diversity statute in various marital and child custody disputes. The asserted justification for this exception is federalism, but states have interests and expertise in the administration of all state laws, not just laws on marriage and divorce. If federalism justifies this exception, it should also justify doing away with all diversity jurisdiction.

Furthermore, consider the practice of certifying questions to state supreme courts. Certification is also justified in the name of federalism; it is said to foster a "cooperative judicial federalism." Numerous states have authorized federal courts to certify questions of state law to the highest state court. Courts praise the practice as vastly superior to abstention, which they decry as time consuming and wasteful. But for diversity cases involving solely state law issues, it would be even more expeditious to bring the case in state court in the first place. Moreover, the justification for certification—that state courts are best able to provide an authoritative statement of what state law is—counsels against federal court diversity jurisdiction and its concomitant "*Erie* guess" at state law.

It is a cruel irony that in the name of furthering federalism we continue to let lawyers choose to bring state cases in federal courts that then ask state courts how to decide them. Yet, the subliminal basis for perpetuating this charade is that state forums are not honest enough to fairly decide such controversies—a basis that masked lawyers whisper about in dark places. This dead hand from the past is even held out when the parties bringing the suit in the federal forum are residents of the state which was denied the right to handle its own cases. Some federalism!

The political prospects for abolishing this anachronism are poor. Attempts to date have failed for the most part because of strong opposition by the bar. Past legislation has corrected only the abuses of diversity, and the benefits of the amount in controversy requirement [the minimum dollar amount required] have dissipated as lawsuit recoveries have risen. Because the health of federalism demands it, we should redouble our efforts to move national courts out of diversity cases entirely.

CONCLUSION

Our federalism has changed as the world has grown smaller and the national government has grown larger. As the governance of America evolves, the process of give and take between the states and the central government constantly changes the weights in the delicate balance that keeps our federalism viable.

Not even a consummate federalist can reasonably argue that the paramount purpose of the Constitution—to form a more perfect union to better serve the people of this country—is advanced by reflexively aggregating power in the central government or its courts. It is time that ideals exert more influence over events. Nothing less than a deliberate effort to restore state power and prestige will suffice. There is no better time than this bicentennial to acknowledge that the future of true constitutional federalism is in our hands.

NOTES

*Published originally in *Cumberland Law Review*, 18 (1987), 95–109. Reprinted by permission.

FOR DISCUSSION

1. Clark points out that before *Erie Railroad* v. *Tompkins* (1938), federal courts developed a body of national common law to apply to all diversity cases. *Erie* changed that, requiring federal courts to follow the common law of the state in which the case was heard. Discuss the advantages and disadvantages of each of these two approaches. Which do you prefer?

2. Why was diversity jurisdiction originally given to the federal courts? How valid does Clark feel that rationale is today? Explain whether or not you agree with him.

3. Even though Clark is one of many federal judges who favor the abolition of diversity jurisdiction, he notes that "the political prospects for abolishing this anachronism are poor." Explain who opposes abolition and why.

4. While on vacation you are driving through another state where you have a serious automobile accident. Would it matter to you whether you are sued in state or federal court?

5. In 1989, two years after Clark's article appeared, Congress raised the threshold for diversity cases from $10,000 to $50,000, which they estimated would save $44 million per year. Would Clark be satisfied by this? Can you think of any objections to this increase?

The following case is an example of how federal courts handle diversity cases. In this case the court needs to determine whether there is indeed diversity of citizenship between the parties. The judge relies on the distinction between domicile, a person's permanent home, and residence, where a person is living, which may be his or her domicile or merely a temporary living place.

CASE   **Carter v. Flowers et al.**
United States District Court (1987)
664 F. Supp. 1002, M.D.La.

POLOZOLA, District Judge.   The issue before the court is whether there is diversity of citizenship between the parties in this case. It is clear a federal court may, on its own motion, question the court's subject matter jurisdiction. The court finds that complete diversity of citizenship does not exist among the parties and, therefore, this court lacks jurisdiction over the subject matter. Therefore, this case must be dismissed.

It is uncontroverted that the defendant James Boren is a citizen of Louisiana. Therefore, plaintiff must prove by a preponderance of the evidence that the plaintiff is not a citizen of Louisiana.

The plaintiff is presently incarcerated in a prison located outside the state of Louisiana. The parties agree that the place of incarceration is not the domicile of the plaintiff. The plaintiff's pre-incarceration domicile will determine his citizenship for diversity jurisdiction purposes.

Plaintiff contends he is a citizen of the State of New York. In support of this contention, the plaintiff has introduced only four documents: (1) a rental car agreement dated June 9, 1980, listing a New York address for the plaintiff; (2) a letter addressed to plaintiff at a New York address from Trans Freight Lines dated June 12, 1980; (3) a lease agreement with a term of ten years beginning May 1, 1980, which purports to lease basement space at 2 Bond Street in New York City; and (4) an affidavit from the plaintiff's sub-lessor which states that New York is plaintiff's "principal domicile."

These documents do not prove that plaintiff's domicile is New York rather than Louisiana. Both the rental car agreement and the letter are almost seven years old and do not tend to prove plaintiff's domicile one way or the other. These documents only show that plaintiff rents property in New York and receives mail there. The affidavit is also insufficient because it only states a legal conclusion and does not set forth an adequate basis of knowledge of the affiant.[3]

---

[3]An affidavit is a sworn statement made in writing to an officer of the court or notary public. The person who makes the statement is termed the affiant (editor's note).

It must be noted that the plaintiff has failed to submit his own sworn statement or any sworn statement from members of his family. In his brief, the plaintiff argues that he and his family live in New York and that this is their domicile. The evidence filed with the court shows that the plaintiff has been divorced twice. Therefore, it is unclear which family members the plaintiff speaks of in his brief. It is possible that plaintiff's former wife now resides in the New York apartment. It is also possible that other family members of the plaintiff reside there. However, no evidence has been introduced to prove these facts one way or the other.

The plaintiff also argues in his brief that he has had insufficient time to prepare the evidence to support his contention that the court has subject matter jurisdiction. This argument is without merit. A United States Magistrate in the Eastern District of Louisiana recommended that this case be dismissed for lack of jurisdiction on March 20, 1986 and the plaintiff filed an objection to this report on April 2, 1986. Therefore, plaintiff was aware that there was a question as to the existence of jurisdiction over one year ago. Plaintiff has had more than ample time to collect and present evidence to this court. However, plaintiff has failed to do so.

The defendant has introduced convincing evidence that the plaintiff is in fact a citizen of Louisiana. The defendant has introduced sworn statements of the plaintiff given during a recent criminal proceeding in which the plaintiff states that he lived at 930 North Street and at a Main Street address which is also located in Baton Rouge. Plaintiff also testified that the location he had lived the longest in the past five years was Denham Springs, Louisiana.

The plaintiff also stated in a sworn act of sale with mortgage, which was passed before a notary, that he was a domiciliary of Baton Rouge. Plaintiff also had a Louisiana drivers license.

Therefore, it is clear from evidence presented by the defendants that the plaintiff at the time of his arrest had an apartment in Baton Rouge in which he had lived for the past eight months. He also had a Louisiana drivers license and owned property in Louisiana. Plaintiff conducted business in Baton Rouge according to paragraph 9 of his complaint. Plaintiff has introduced virtually no evidence to controvert the evidence introduced by the defendants. Plaintiff argues in his brief that he maintains several residences including Louisiana, Alabama and Florida, but his domicile is New York. However, plaintiff has not carried his burden in persuading this court that such is the case.

From the evidence now before the court, plaintiff has failed to carry his burden of establishing the court's jurisdiction. In fact it appears from the evidence that plaintiff is now and was at the time his suit was filed a citizen of Louisiana. Thus, the court finds there is no complete diversity of citizenship between the parties. There being no diversity of citizenship, the court lacks jurisdiction herein.

Judgment shall be entered dismissing plaintiff's suit with prejudice.

FOR DISCUSSION

1. Diversity jurisdiction requires that the plaintiff and defendant be citizens of different states. What makes a person a citizen of a state?
2. What evidence does the plaintiff use to show that he is not a citizen of Louisiana? Why does Judge Polozola disagree?
3. If you were the plaintiff's lawyer, what would you advise him to do now?
4. Does this case provide evidence for or against Clark's arguments favoring abolition of federal diversity jurisdiction?

5. Although this case does not discuss the substance of Carter's suit, he obviously went to a great deal of trouble to try to demonstrate diversity. Why do you think a plaintiff would so strongly prefer to try a case in federal rather than state court?

Some states have enacted long-arm statutes that give their courts in personam jurisdiction over out of state parties who have had at least minimum contacts within the state. The following case shows how courts determine whether such minimum contacts have occurred.

CASE

Sherburne County Social Services v. Kennedy
Court of Appeals of Minnesota (1987)
409 N.W.2d 907

RANDALL, Judge. Appellant Kevin Kennedy appeals the trial court's denial of his motion to dismiss this paternity action. Kennedy's motion asserted that the court lacked personal jurisdiction over him because he is a resident of Montana, and because there are insufficient contacts with the State of Minnesota concerning the issue before the court.

Appellant, while a resident of Minnesota, engaged in consensual intercourse with Jean Pouliot, a Minnesota resident, on July 30, 1983. Thereafter appellant moved to Montana and still resides there. Over the Thanksgiving holiday and between November 20 and November 26 [1983], Pouliot and a friend visited appellant at his Montana home. Pouliot and appellant engaged in intercourse approximately two or three times during this visit.

On September 5, 1984, Pouliot gave birth to a son. The County of Sherburne subsequently brought this action in Minnesota to determine paternity, to assign responsibility for medical expenses relative to the birth, and to set child support. Appellant did not answer, but moved to dismiss based on lack of personal jurisdiction. The trial court denied the motion.

Minnesota served appellant under the long arm statute, Minn.Stat. 543.19 (1984). Appellant argues he has insufficient minimum contacts with Minnesota for this state to exercise jurisdiction over him. He claims that his July 30 act of intercourse with Pouliot is insufficient basis to assert personal jurisdiction over him because the child was not conceived then, and he has no other Minnesota based contacts. He contends that if he is the father, the act of intercourse leading to conception must have occurred during Pouliot's visit to Montana in November 1983. Pouliot gave birth thirteen months and one week after the intercourse in Minnesota, and approximately nine and one half months after the intercourse in Montana.

Before Minnesota courts can exercise long arm jurisdiction over nonresidents, two tests must be met: (1) the long arm statute must be satisfied, and (2) plaintiff must show minimum contacts between defendant and his state such that asserting jurisdiction does not offend due process. *Howells* v. *McKibben*, 281 N.W.2d 154 (Minn.1979) and *State* v. *Hartling*, 360 N.W.2d 439 (Minn.Ct.App. 1985).

Minnesota's long-arm statute permits a court of this state having subject matter jurisdiction to exercise personal jurisdiction over a nonresident individual if that individual "commits any act outside Minnesota causing injury or property damage in Minnesota." Paternity is a tort cause of action, within the scope of 543.19.

In *Howells* the supreme court found that, even though conception may have occurred in Wisconsin, the "injury" to the plaintiff occurred in Minnesota. The court defined "injury" as the mother's physical and emotional suffering caused by having to raise the child alone, the resulting medical expenses, and those expenses incident to raising the child. Here, although conception occurred outside Minnesota, the birth is inside Minnesota. For the purposes of appellate review, the first part of the long arm statute has been satisfied. We now turn to whether or not the burden placed on the appellant by being brought under the state's jurisdiction would violate fairness and substantial justice.

Appellant argues he does not have sufficient minimum contacts with Minnesota to be compelled to defend a paternity suit here. Due process, the basis of the minimum contact test, is served only where there exists a "sufficient nexus between Minnesota and defendant so that it is both fair and reasonable to require defense of the action in this state." *Howells* at 157. Minimum contacts must be determined on a case by case basis. The pertinent factors to be considered are:

(1) the quantity of defendant's contacts with the state;
(2) the nature and quality of the contacts;
(3) the connection of the cause of action with those contacts;
(4) the interest of the state in providing a forum; and
(5) convenience to the parties.

A. Quantity of appellant's contacts with Minnesota

Appellant formerly lived in Minnesota. One isolated sexual incident with Pouliot occurred here. Appellant's contacts with Pouliot in Minnesota are minimal. If medical science is to be believed, their act of intercourse on July 30, 1983 did not result in the September 5, 1984 birth. "When the quantity of contacts is minimal, the nature and quality become dispositive." *Hartling* at 441.

B. Nature and quality of the contacts

Appellant argues the quality of contacts between him and Pouliot does not support exercise of personal jurisdiction over him, because the act that resulted in her pregnancy, if he is the father, did not occur in Minnesota. Respondent argues appellant knew he was having intercourse in Montana with a Minnesota resident who would eventually return to Minnesota, and thus, jurisdiction in Minnesota is proper. Respondent cites *Hartling* as controlling on this issue.

In *Hartling*, a paternity action, the father was a resident of Wisconsin, the mother a resident of Minnesota. The child was conceived in Wisconsin, and born in Minnesota. The court held that the quality and quantity of contacts of the father with the State of Minnesota and the mother, a Minnesota resident, were sufficient to permit Minnesota to exercise personal jurisdiction. There, the couple met in June and began a relationship of social activities and sexual intercourse in the Duluth, Minnesota/Superior, Wisconsin area. Most of the incidents of intercourse, including the intercourse leading to conception, occurred in Wisconsin. The relationship continued from June until mid-October.

This court found that the continuous, four month social and sexual relationship bore a direct relationship to the cause of action, and that it was not constitutionally impermissible to require Hartling to come to Minnesota to defend on the paternity suit. This court concluded that Hartling's contacts with Minnesota and a Minnesota resident were such that he could reasonably anticipate being hailed into Minnesota court for child support.

On the other hand, here Pouliot concedes that there was one isolated act of sexual intercourse in Minnesota in July 1983. Thereafter she voluntarily traveled to Montana in November 1983, and engaged in sexual intercourse there with appellant. Pouliot does not dispute that if appellant is the father, the act of intercourse leading to conception took place in November 1983 in Montana. Appellant's contacts with Minnesota are minimal, and the limited quality and quantity of contacts in Minnesota are dissimilar enough that *Hartling* is not controlling on this issue.

C. Source and connection of the cause of action with those contacts

Appellant argues this element has not been proved because Pouliot did not have a continuing relationship with appellant, her contacts with him were isolated incidents, and the couple had more contacts in Montana than in Minnesota. Since we accept the parties' statements that the sexual contact that led to the cause of action, if appellant is the father, arose in Montana, appellant prevails on this element.

D. Interest of Minnesota in providing a forum

In *West American Insurance Co.* v. *Westin, Inc.*, 337 N.W.2d 676 (Minn.1983), the Minnesota Supreme Court noted that "the critical focus in any jurisdictional analysis must be on 'the relationship among the defendant, the forum, and the litigation'.... This tripartite relationship is defined by the defendant's contacts with the forum *state*, not by the defendant's contacts with *residents* of the forum." Here appellant has no contacts with the forum state, other than the allegation he has fathered the child of a Minnesota resident.

E. Relative convenience of the parties

In *West American*, the Minnesota Supreme Court held, "this factor is irrelevant unless the defendant also has, as a threshold matter, sufficient contacts with the forum state." Appellant argues that since the element of "sufficient contacts" has not been met, convenience is not dispositive. We agree, and do not decide this case on relative convenience. We note the availability of legal redress in the State of Montana for Sherburne County and Pouliot under the Uniform Reciprocal Enforcement of Support Act.

We hold appellant's contacts with Minnesota are insufficient to require him to come to Minnesota to defend this paternity action. The trial court erred by finding personal jurisdiction over appellant.

Reversed.

FOR DISCUSSION

1. Can you think of any reasons why the Social Services Department did not sue Kennedy in Montana where the state courts would have had in personam jurisdiction?

2. What factors does Judge Randall consider in deciding whether Kennedy had sufficient minimum contacts in Minnesota to give the state courts in personam jurisdiction? Would you come to the same conclusion?

3. The County Social Services Department cites *State* v. *Hartling* as a precedent supporting jurisdiction. What was the holding in that case? How does the Minnesota Court of Appeals compare the two cases?

4. If Sherburne County Social Services sued Kennedy in federal court in Montana would that court have had subject matter jurisdiction?

5. Suppose the County Social Services Department had argued that the public interest in establishing a child's paternity and determining who should be financially responsible for its upbringing outweigh the interests underlying the "minimum contacts" rule. Would you find that argument persuasive. Explain thoroughly.

Small claims courts provide a less formal and costly alternative for cases that might not otherwise be brought to court. However, their decisions can be appealed to higher courts, requiring lawyers and more formal procedures that result in increased costs. Note how such an appeal is treated in the following case.

CASE

Miner v. Bray
Appellate Court of Illinois, Third District (1987)
13 N.E. 530

Justice HEIPLE delivered the opinion of the Court. The plaintiff, Stephen E. Miner, a chiropractor, sued the defendants, Sharon Bray and State Farm Mutual Automobile Insurance Company, for his professional fees. The trial court granted the plaintiff judgment against both defendants for $1,879. The defendants appeal.

Bray was injured in an auto accident and went to the plaintiff for treatment. Prior to receiving treatment, she signed a contract assigning to the plaintiff, to the extent of her bill, any benefits claims she might have under a State Farm insurance policy. Both defendants later refused to pay the plaintiff, resulting in the instant small claims action.

On appeal, the defendants first argue that the trial court abused its discretion when it allowed the plaintiff to amend his complaint after he had rested his case. At the close of the plaintiff's case, the defendants moved to dismiss Bray from the suit. The defendants argued that the plaintiff had brought suit under the physician's lien statute and that Bray was not a proper party in such a suit. The plaintiff's counsel, though stating that he believed the complaint was sufficient, moved to amend the complaint to add a cause of action against Bray personally. The trial court denied the defendants' motion, without specifying whether it found that the complaint was sufficient or whether it was allowing the plaintiff's motion to amend.

Supreme Court Rule 282 provides that a small claim may be commenced by "filing a short and simple complaint setting forth (1) plaintiff's name, residence address, and telephone number, (2) defendant's name and place of residence, or place of business or regular employment, and (3) the nature and amount of the plaintiff's claim, giving dates and other relevant information." If a complaint in a small claims action clearly notifies the defendant of the nature of the plaintiff's claim, it states a cause of action.

In the instant case, the plaintiff's complaint named Bray as a defendant and stated that "I, the undersigned, claim that the defendant is indebted to the plaintiff in the sum of $1,879.00 plus costs for enforcement of a statutory lien pursuant to Chapter 82, Sec. 101.1 et. seq. and that the plaintiff has demanded payment of said sum; that the defendant refused to pay the same and no part thereof has been paid; that the defendant resides at .... " The address given was that of Bray, not State Farm. Further, an attached notice of lien, which was also served upon Bray, stated that she was liable to the plaintiff for $1,879.

The plaintiff's complaint provided all the information required by Supreme Court Rule 282. It clearly alleged Bray's personal liability for the amount claimed. While it cited only the physician's lien statute, under the relaxed pleading standards of small claims court, the complaint and attached lien provided sufficient notice to Bray that she was required to appear and defend the action. Accordingly, the trial court properly denied the defendants' motion to dismiss Bray.

The defendants' second argument on appeal is that the trial court erred in entering judgment for the plaintiff, because the plaintiff's services were rendered on a "no out of pocket expense" basis. Specifically, the defendants' point to the language in the contract assigning Bray's insurance benefits to the plaintiff. It states:

I recognize that payment for services rendered by Doctor is due upon receipt of the services but that Doctor has agreed to accept this assignment as an accommodation to me and that Doctor may revoke this assignment at any time.

The defendants contend that the plaintiff never revoked the agreement and Bray is not therefore personally liable for her chiropractic bills.

When the terms of a contract are clear and unambiguous, they will be given their natural and ordinary meaning. The natural and ordinary meaning of the contractual clause in question empowered the plaintiff, at his discretion, to hold Bray personally liable for his services. The plaintiff's filing of the instant lawsuit, naming Bray as a defendant and providing her with the appropriate notice, clearly indicated that he was holding her personally liable for his services. The assignment does not limit notice of revocation to a specific procedure. Accordingly, we find that the plaintiff's actions in suing Bray provided her with sufficient notice that he was revoking his accommodation to her.

The defendants' third argument on appeal is that the plaintiff did not prove any contractual relationship between Bray and State Farm, nor the terms of the alleged policy.

A defendant in a small claims case need not file an answer to the complaint; its appearance is considered a denial of the allegations in the complaint. While certain procedures are relaxed in small claims court, the use of short and simplified complaints makes it more compelling that a plaintiff prove his case at trial. The existence of coverage is an essential element of an insured's case against his insurer; the insured has the burden of proving that his loss falls within the terms of his policy. An assignee stands in the shoes of his assignor, acquiring no greater rights than were possessed by the assignor.

We have examined the record in the instant case and find that the plaintiff's case consisted almost entirely of evidence proving the assignment of Bray's rights and the value of plaintiff's services. The plaintiff did introduce a letter from State Farm asking him to complete a standard report of the services he had rendered to Bray. The plaintiff offered no other evidence of why State Farm could be held liable to Bray.

We find that the letter from State Farm merely asked for more information on the plaintiff's claim for services rendered to Bray and did not admit that State Farm insured Bray. Further, the plaintiff's testimony that State Farm was Bray's insurer is insufficient by itself to establish a contract of insurance between Bray and State Farm, let alone the coverage of such a contract. Accordingly, we find that the plaintiff failed to establish a prima facie case that his services to Bray were covered by a State Farm insurance policy.

The judgment of the circuit court of Rock Island County finding Sharon Bray liable to the plaintiff for $1,879 is affirmed. The judgment of the circuit court finding State Farm liable to the plaintiff is reversed.

FOR DISCUSSION

1. Small claims courts use less formal rules than other courts. List the legal technicalities raised by defendant Bray but dismissed by Justice Heiple. Would the result have been different if the trial had not been held in a small claims court?

2. Watch an episode of the "People's Court" on television. Compare it to the small claims court procedures outlined in this case. These courts are open to the public so you should visit one and observe the proceedings.

3. Do the problems faced by a small claims judge differ from those outlined by Frankel?

4. The award of $1,879 in Miner v. Bray is greater than is permitted for a small claims action in most other states. Explain what monetary limit you would set for small claims cases.

5. Does allowing small claims cases to be appealed defeat the purpose of small claims courts? Explain.

THE U. S. SUPREME COURT

The nine justices of the U. S. Supreme Court cannot possibly hear all of the thousands of cases appealed to them. To allow them to manage their work load, Congress has given them the authority to select only the most important cases for review. A person seeking Supreme Court review asks for a writ of certiorari, known in legal slang as cert. Because the Supreme Court grants less than 5 percent of these requests, it is important for appellants and their attorneys to understand how best to convince the required four justices that this particular case should be one of the few favored with cert. Unfortunately, the Court does not explain why it does or does not grant certiorari in specific cases. However, it does provide some general guidelines, especially its Rule 17. In the following essay, Edward Leahy attempts to figure out some of the Court's criteria so as to suggest strategy to litigants.

Note: The following is reprinted with permission from the *ABA Journal*, the Lawyer's Magazine, published by the American Bar Association.

READING **The Ten Commandments of Certiorari**
By Edward Leahy*

Although every case has some chance of making it to the U.S. Supreme Court, that possibility is slim. This term [1985], approximately 4,100 cases will be presented for Supreme Court review. Of this number, the Court will give full review to approximately 170 cases—fewer than one in 25. How do you increase those odds?

To begin, there is no druidic incantation or secret formula that guarantees the Court will hear your case. An unparalleled team of Supreme Court practitioners could prepare your petition for certiorari, yet the Court may enter a simple "Certiorari Denied" on its order list. It is trite, but true, that you cannot make a silk purse out of a sow's ear.

On the other hand, many cases for which counsel seek Supreme Court review contain the seed of an important, far-ranging issue that deserves the Court's attention. It is up to counsel for the petitioners to uncover that seed of constitutional dimension, analyze its significance and package it so that its importance will be at once apparent to the Supreme Court.

Although there is no simple formula for success in the certiorari process, I have outlined a few fundamental rules that if followed, should greatly increase the odds of having the Supreme Court agree to hear your case.

COMMANDMENT NO. 1

Make an honest assessment of your case.   Better cases have a better chance of being reviewed. The first rule of any certiorari primer, therefore, is to take a good, hard look at your case. If you do not have a colorably cert-worthy issue, you should not petition for certiorari.

Supreme Court Rule 17 sets forth the considerations governing review of certiorari. Certiorari review is discretionary and granted only for "special and important reasons," such as (1) the existence of a true and significant conflict, or (2) when the lower court has decided an important question of federal law that should be settled by the Supreme Court, or (3) the federal court of appeals "has so far departed from the accepted and usual course of judicial proceedings, or so far sanctioned such a departure by a lower court, as to call for an exercise of this court's power of supervision."

When you have a genuine circuit conflict or a "hot" issue, your chances of success increase significantly. Most attorneys who petition for certiorari, however, feel that their case falls in the third of the above categories. Having lost, you may think that the lower court was clearly in error, but can you dispassionately conclude that the court's decision was so far a departure from accepted judicial proceedings as to justify Supreme Court review?

Your petition, to be successful, ultimately must convince the Court that you fit within the letter and spirit of Rule 17. If you do not think your case is arguably within the rule, you have an obligation both to your client and to the Court to reassess the advisability of seeking review.

There is one additional point to keep in mind. Rule 49.2 provides that the Court may award "appropriate damages" for frivolous petitions and appeals. This provision has been largely ignored until the current term, when some justices have indicated in off-the-bench comments that the Court should invoke this power.

COMMANDMENT NO. 2

Determine whether you really want a dispositive, national policy on your issue. Institutional litigants and public policy organizations often have a luxury not available to most individuals. They can look at the big picture and consider not only the immediate best interests of their client in a particular case but also can consider how their individual case affects the development of the law. You may have lost below, but your client or similarly situated litigants may be better off ultimately with one adverse court of appeals decision than a possible adverse Supreme Court (and national) decision. Many institutional defendants deliberately elect not to petition for Supreme Court review, although their case contains a cert-worthy issue. If you have this luxury, consider carefully what is the best case and the best court to push the law in the direction you wish it to go.

COMMANDMENT NO. 3

Read the Supreme Court Rules. Court rules are a starting point for attorneys in all forums, and the Supreme Court is no exception. The rules provide a wealth of essential information, including the mechanics and time requirements for filing petitions and the factors the Court considers in addressing its docket. The numerous additional procedural questions not covered by the rules usually can be answered by the Office of the Clerk of the Supreme Court, or from *Supreme Court Practice*, an excellent guidebook.

COMMANDMENT NO. 4

Make your "Question Presented" simple, succinct, informative. Framing the "Question Presented" is one of the most important tasks you do in preparing the petition. You must present a clear and crisp picture of the issue to the Court. The more deeply involved we become in our cases, the more likely we are to dwell on the nuances and vagaries of our particular facts. Step back from your case and frame the issue in the simplest and clearest terms possible. The Court has not lived with your case for several years; you have a great deal to convey in a very limited space. It is critical that you formulate and reformulate the question presented until you have provided a favorable, accurate and succinct characterization of the issues involved in your case.

The question presented should tell the Court in one sentence what the case is about. The question should be brief, readily understood and identify the substantive areas of the law involved. Avoid the general: "Did the court of appeals err in affirming the clearly erroneous decision of the district court?" "Whether the court of appeals erred in refusing to review the district court's failure to hear all of petitioner's evidence," and my all time favorite, "Whether the court of appeals erred and violated federal law in failing to adhere to the decisions of other courts by unconstitutionally denying petitioner due process of law."

Contrast these with the question presented in a recent successful petition from the U.S. solicitor general: "Does Fifth Amendment privilege against compelled self-incrimination protect contents of individual's voluntarily prepared financial records." When you read that question you know what substantive area of the law is involved and what subset of that area is at issue.

If the Court gets the impression that you cannot frame the issue intelligently, why should it trust you to brief and argue one of the few cases it review each year?

COMMANDMENT NO. 5

Show why your case should be reviewed. After the question presented, you should clearly and succinctly explain the issue and why the Supreme Court should review your case. Do not expect a justice or law clerk to make your case for you. Each certiorari petition must be a self-contained unit. Justices and clerks simply do not have time to undertake independent research to dissect the case for the "angle" you missed. There is very little percentage in submitting a pedestrian petition in the hope that someone in the Court is going to see something in the case that you failed to develop.

In the court of appeals, and frequently in state supreme courts, attorneys spend a great deal of time distinguishing similar cases from other jurisdictions. Supreme Court opinions do not analyze the unique twists and turns of lower court opinions and try to distinguish them. They look almost entirely to their own opinions or legislative history. The Supreme Court in many instances decides what the law ought to be.

You should emphasize why your case is the appropriate vehicle for determining what the law should be. Emphasize policy considerations, why the issue is ripe for review, why courts need the guiding light of the Supreme Court. Any conflict should be clearly stated. In addition, it never hurts to add that the result in your case is unfair and that the unfairness is likely to be repeated in other cases.

COMMANDMENT NO. 6

Maintain your credibility. At the trial court level, an attorney sometimes can present a factual argument in a shaded light and succeed because the opponent fails to point out misstated or ignored facts. This tactic is less likely to succeed at the appellate stage and can be fatal if attempted in the Supreme Court. The Court has little time to review your petition. If you unfairly shade your facts in an effort to attract the Court's attention, your opposing counsel will undoubtedly pick up your characterization and create a purely factual dispute, which will weigh heavily against review. More important, the Court may not and should not put the responsibility for briefing a precedent-setting case in the hands of someone who cannot be trusted to state fairly the strong points of the case. The court will deny a petition in a close case when the attorney has overstepped the bounds of fair presentation.

Just as you should not shade the facts, you should not shade the law. The most frequent sinning ground is in the discussion of conflicts. Direct conflicts among the circuits on matters of constitutional importance are rare. Yet it seems that virtually every petition claims that the lower court's decision is contrary to decisions in at least one other circuit. Most of these purported conflicts are trumped up—and the Court knows it. Look for a conflict. If it exists, explain it clearly and briefly. If the area of law is incoherent, say so. If there is not a clear conflict, however, do not try to create one.

COMMANDMENT NO. 7

Review the justices' positions in similar cases. Know where the justices stand on your issue. If your case is important enough to be taken to the Supreme Court, it is important for you to know how each of the justices treated similar or related issues in earlier cases.

It is frequently possible to pinpoint concerns of individual justices by reviewing not only the majority and dissenting opinions in Supreme Court cases but also by reviewing dissents from denials of certiorari. Certain justices are known for their concern about conflicts, or federalism, or judicial activism, or limited appellate review or the historical significance of selected issues. Pick up those points if they are relevant to your issue. You have volumes of written work by your intended audience. Take advantage of this benefit.

COMMANDMENT NO. 8

Do not overlook your allies. By the time you have an adverse decision from a court of appeals, you may have identified your natural allies. Trade associations, city or state leagues, and civil liberties groups frequently maintain legal staffs who review and monitor precedent-setting litigation. Rule 36.1 allows for the filing of amicus briefs, with the consent of the parties, to support petitions for certiorari. Motions for leave to file when consent has been refused are not favored at this stage. So you have the ability to exercise considerable control over the presence of amici during this initial presentation to the Court.

If another organization or group corroborates your assertion that an issue is important, it may help your petition. The amicus should have some independent point to raise to the Court, such as explaining the financial or practical effect of the decision on its own interests. Proceed with caution, however, before inviting or consenting to an amicus brief. Be absolutely certain that your amicus does not put forth an argument that will be detrimental to your client or that distorts the case for its own advantage.

Your strongest potential ally is the solicitor general, who carries tremendous credibility with the Court. If you think the solicitor general will support your position, you can make the approach either through the specific governmental agency or department that would have an interest in your case or directly to the Solicitor General's Office. The solicitor general, however, is unlikely to appear voluntarily in support of your petition unless a truly important issue is presented.

COMMANDMENT NO. 9

Consider creative dispositions. Your first choice, presumably is to have a full briefing of your case before the Court. Realistically, however, you may want to present to the Court the equivalent of a compromise verdict. Review the current and prior terms of the Court for any cases that have been decided since the decision of the lower court in your case. If the Court has issued a decision that could change the result in your case, petition the Court for a summary reversal. Or, at a minimum, recommend that the Court grant your petition, vacate the judgment of the lower court and remand your case in light of the subsequent decision.

In addition, check whether the Court is considering any case containing an issue similar to yours. Hitching your petition to a case in which certiorari has already been granted will sometimes cause the Court to "hold" your case and dispose of it once the case under consideration has been decided. Playing for a "hold" and remand, however, has the obvious disadvantage that the issue in your case will be decided on the basis of another counsel's argument.

Finally, if the decision in your case was based on a statute, check whether Congress has amended the statute. Subsequent legislation often causes the Court to remand for reconsideration in light of the new legislation. Beware, however, of pending legislation. If the Court thinks that pending legislation will take care of the problem presented, you petition likely will be denied.

COMMANDMENT NO. 10

The final check—anticipate your opponent's response.   The brief in opposition will take a negative stand and will succeed simply by pointing out any excuse to the Court for not considering your case. A good opposition will point out jurisdictional and similar defects; improper or incomplete recitation of the facts; uniqueness of the case or likelihood that the case will not recur; the issues are not significant; the conflict is illusory; decision by the Supreme Court is premature; or the case was correctly decided and is consistent with public policy and the Court's prior decisions.

MAYBE 20 COMMANDMENTS

These commandments are not meant to provide an exhaustive analysis of how to prepare a petition for certiorari. There could easily be 11 commandments or maybe even 20. These rules, however, touch on some of the most important considerations that go into a successful petition.

NOTES

*From Jesse Choper (ed.),The Supreme Court and Its Justices, (Chicago: The American Bar Association, 1987), pp. 246–53.

FOR DISCUSSION

1. In the case of *Idaho Dept. of Employment* v. *Smith*, 434 U.S. 100 (1977), Supreme Court Justice John Paul Stevens wrote that he did not "believe that error is sufficient justification" for granting certiorari because the Court is "much too busy to correct every error that is called to our attention in the thousands of certiorari petitions that are filed each year." Comment on this statement in light of Leahy's article. What other factors do the justices use to decide whether to review a case?

2. The Supreme Court decides whether to grant certiorari in secret and does not give reasons for denial. Can you think of any reasons for their doing this?

3. Leahy suggests that some people who lose in lower courts may not wish to have the Supreme Court review their cases. Explain why not.

4. Leahy suggests that the Court may start enforcing the rule awarding damages for frivolous appeals? Is this a good idea? How would you judge whether an appeal is frivolous?

5. Because of the large number of cases appealed to the Supreme Court, some justices and others have suggested a new court whose job would be to screen out relatively minor cases not worthy of the Supreme Court's attention. Would you favor such a change?

In the following case, the Postal Service is asking that a Court of Appeals order to reinstate a fired employee be postponed until they have a chance to convince the Supreme Court to hear their appeal to reverse that decision. In order to decide whether or not to stay the order, Supreme Court Chief Justice William Rehnquist, acting as a circuit judge (a practice less common today than in the early days of the court), must evaluate the likelihood that the Supreme Court will grant a writ of certiorari.

CASE   **U.S. Postal Service v. National Association of Letter Carriers**
(1987)
107 S.Ct. 2095

Chief Justice REHNQUIST, Circuit Justice. Applicant United States Postal Service asks that I stay the mandate of the Court of Appeals for the District of Columbia Circuit, enforcing an arbitrator's decision that applicant reinstate Edward Hyde as a postal worker. In 1984, Hyde was convicted of unlawful delay of the mail by a postal employee after postal inspectors found more than 3,500 pieces of undelivered mail in his possession. The Postal Service discharged Hyde for dereliction of duty. Respondent filed a grievance against applicant on Hyde's behalf, seeking arbitration. The arbitrator ordered that applicant reinstate Hyde after a 60-day medical leave of absence. Applicant filed suit, seeking to set aside the award as contrary to public policy. The District Court set aside the arbitrator's decision, finding that the Postal Service must retain the power to remove employees who breach the public trust and hamper the strong public interest in ensuring prompt delivery of the mails. The Court of Appeals reversed, holding that a Court may set aside an arbitrator's award as contrary to public policy only when the award itself violates established law or compels unlawful conduct.

The standards for granting a stay pending a petition for certiorari are well settled: a Circuit Justice is required "to determine whether four Justices would vote to grant certiorari, to balance the so-called 'stay equities,' and to give some consideration as to predicting the final outcome of the case in this Court." *Heckler* v. *Redbud Hospital District,* 473 U.S. 1308, 106 S.Ct. 1 (1985).

In my view, the applicant has satisfied these requirements. There is a reasonable probability that four Justices will eventually grant certiorari in this case. The Court has already granted certiorari in *United Paperworkers International Union* v. *Misco, Inc.,* 107 S.Ct. 871 (1987), which raises the identical issue: the scope of the public policy exception to enforcement of arbitration awards. Although that case presents the issue in the context of a private employer, applicant presents a stronger case for setting aside the arbitrator's award because it operates under a statutory mandate to ensure prompt delivery of the mails.

Moreover, I find that the stay equities favor the applicant. Even the temporary reinstatement of Hyde, a convicted criminal, will seriously impair the applicant's ability to impress the seriousness of the Postal Service's mission upon its workers. While Hyde does have some interest in returning to his position, he has not worked for the applicant for almost three years. Continuation of the status quo will not work an irreparable harm on Hyde, but it will preserve the applicant's ability to carry out its legal obligations.

The application for a stay of the Court of Appeals' mandate pending the filing and disposition of a petition for certiorari is granted.

FOR DISCUSSION

1. In this case, Chief Justice Rehnquist is required to determine whether the Supreme Court is likely to grant certiorari. Compare his reasoning to Leahy's rules. Do you think Leahy would come to the same conclusion?

2. The Postal Service is asking Rehnquist to stay the order of the Court of Appeals requiring Hyde's reinstatement as a postal worker. In other words, they are claiming that they will be irreparably harmed if they put him back on the job then win their appeal. How does Rehnquist balance this against Hyde's rights? Explain whether you agree.

3. What will happen if the Supreme Court fails to grant certiorari in this case?

ARBITRATION

In the next article, Judge Judith Kaye discusses one of the major alternatives to bringing a lawsuit. She explains when and why arbitration is preferred as well as how courts handle arbitrations that are appealed to them.

READING   **Arbitration: A View from the Bench**
                                        By Judith S. Kaye*

From my vantage point on the New York Court of Appeals, it appears that the courts of this state have, for a very long time, furnished a receptive climate in which domestic as well as international arbitrations can proceed in accordance with the agreement of the parties, without undue judicial interference. One of the most settled policies of this state has been the policy favoring the voluntary arbitration of disputes and the enforcement of predispute arbitration agreements. This is most evident in the court decisions upholding agreements to arbitrate, as well as the fact that judicial review of arbitration awards has been highly circumscribed. Our court has often stated that it would set aside an arbitration award on the ground that it is wholly irrational, but the fact remains that we have yet to come upon such a creature. It is undoubtedly because the policy favoring arbitration is so well known and ingrained in our substantive law that few arbitration cases even reach us. The significant cases during my own tenure on the court have uniformly supported the arbitral process.

As a former commercial litigator, I have followed with particular interest the issues now being litigated in the federal courts concerning arbitrability of claims under the Securities Exchange Act, particularly investor-broker disputes. That is a controversy into which the New York Court of Appeals has not been drawn. But I am reminded that just last year we did decide that a dispute between a brokerage firm and its former employees should be arbitrated under the Federal Arbitration Act. In so doing, we rejected the conclusion of the federal court of appeals of this circuit, and we recognized the *federal* policy—consonant with our own state policy—supporting consensual arbitration and resolving all doubts in favor of arbitration. In short, there can be little question that arbitration agreements and the voluntary, contractual arbitration process are strongly favored in the state court system.

My second observation is that this is hardly altruistic. Given the crushing burdens borne by our court system, a policy strongly favoring voluntary, binding arbitration is not only rational but also prudent—in our own self-interest. I do not intend to recount the statistics on case filings in the state courts. The numbers are truly staggering—in the millions. As a society, we seem to have developed a mind cast that courts should resolve every crisis in our lives, and the escalating state court filings show that there is no relief in sight. Indeed, in a recent *New York Times* article reporting on the investor-broker arbitration case I mentioned, the investors complaining about churning and excessive fees are quoted as describing a jury trial as "the American way." Images are evoked of John Peter Zenger and the American Revolution; I think this is a popular belief. But we hardly need to be reminded of the choking court dockets or the costs, delays, and inefficiencies of litigation in order to recognize and appreciate the enormous value of arbitration and other alternative dispute resolution (ADR) mechanisms as an integral part of the justice system.

My third observation is that for several decades now we have gone far beyond questioning the utility of alternative dispute resolution. No one asks any more whether ADR is a good thing. We are instead well into an era of searching out new and innovative applications for procedures we know are fundamentally sensible and can work well. One of the nice things about having an interest in the burgeoning subject of alternative dispute resolution—as I do—is that an unbelievable quantity of material is being generated. There seems to be an outpouring of studies, newsletters, and journals, and I'm delighted to receive them. Just recently, for example, I received clippings about the thriving operation of the "rent-a-judge" program in Albany; I learned of formal negotiations as an adjunct to litigation in connection with a land dispute between the Oneida Indians and the State of New York; and I read in the *New York Law Journal* of a Queens County felony case involving arbitration. I hear of all sorts of hybrids and experiments with mediation, mini-trials, impartial experts, neutral case evaluations, and a host of other techniques to supplement litigation and settle disputes.

Because we, as a society, are so inherently court-oriented—because a courthouse disposition is still viewed by many as "the American way"—to my mind, the most fascinating experiments just now are taking place at the courthouse, or under the umbrella of the court system. New York State Chief Judge Sol Wachtler, in his State of the Judiciary message this year, reaffirmed the belief of the State Unified Court System that alternative dispute resolution methods will continue to be of great value in the operation of the courts of this state. It is alone significant, and symptomatic of this new era, that a discussion of alternative dispute resolution has become a substantial segment of the Chief Judge's State of the Judiciary message to the legislature.

Chief Judge Wachtler spoke specifically of two programs. First, the state-funded Community Dispute Resolution Centers are now in operation in just about every one of the state's 62 counties and annually handle tens of thousands of case referrals from courts, district attorneys, and others. These neighborhood centers deal principally with disputes involving families, neighbors, and coworkers, where substantial justice can be rendered—and in a true sense possibly can only be rendered—outside the adversarial system, giving the participants a chance to work out their grievances quickly and get on with their lives. I was somewhat surprised to learn that these centers regularly handle not only civil matters but also criminal cases and, since November 1986, even felonies—for example, cases of harassment and assault among friends and family members—that need never become criminal court statistics. Indeed, in 1986, 75 percent of the business of these centers involved criminal matters, and nearly a half-million dollars in restitution was awarded. The best evidence that the system works well is its continuously enlarging responsibility. As my colleagues, Judges Wachtler and Bellacosa have repeatedly acknowledged, a great public service is accomplished by these neighborhood centers in caringly and expeditiously resolving the type of disputes that benefit from a nonadversarial setting and, simultaneously, offering some relief to the court system.

The second ongoing program mentioned in the Chief Judge's State of the Judiciary message was the compulsory arbitration of small civil cases, with the right of either party on demand to a de novo jury trial following an arbitrator's determination. This is nonvoluntary, nonbinding arbitration. The program thus far has also been highly successful—with dispositions of about 15,000 cases annually and a very low de novo demand rate. Efforts are afoot to expand that program by increasing the size of cases within its reach. In the federal courts of New York City, cases of far greater magnitude are today being routinely referred by individual judges to panels of lawyer/arbitrators or to the American Arbitration Association for the purpose of exploring *resolution* of the controversies or simply *streamlining* the cases, as by factfinding, mini-trials (to narrow controversies or dispose of collateral issues), summary jury trials, and advisory arbitration. In the state system, we even have a *third* program functioning within the courts—the small claims assessment review program—whereby homeowners can procure expeditious review of real estate assessments before hearing officers.

By no means do I suggest, or even support the idea, that we must search out new and different ways to close the courthouse doors to the public, or simply funnel more and more cases elsewhere for hasty disposition. We all recognize that cases are much more than numbers and statistics. They represent flesh-and-blood controversies often profoundly affecting people's lives. Moreover, court judgments throughout the history of this nation have shaped and defined matters of great societal significance. But however much one might believe that access to the courts should be broadened, not restricted—as I do—and however much one may believe that many of our complex, costly procedures are necessary to assure fairness within our legal system—as I do—still there are hard realities about the litigation process today that cannot be ignored. One is that our swollen criminal dockets, with speedy trial constraints, necessarily cast the civil disputes in a new light. Another is that many cases in the courts—particularly those involving disintegrated personal relationships—probably do not belong there at all; indeed, keeping such disputes in a formal litigation mold may oftentimes actually exacerbate the human tragedy. And yet another reality is the plain fact that so often court proceedings serve as but a framework for striking a bargain and are not in any sense a test of principles or an engine of reform.

It seems to me, therefore, essential that we find the cases and the noncases that are needlessly distorting and misshaping our adversary system and resolve them in other ways. Chief Administrative Judge Albert Rosenblatt recently noted that, by expanding ADR, we simplify and disencumber the judicial process, and we "express optimism." I join wholeheartedly in this sentiment. The enlarging application of ADR to court controversies is indeed an expression of optimism about the future of our justice system and is appropriately celebrated today.

NOTES

*Previously printed in the American Arbitration Journal, 42 (Sept 1987), 3–5. Reprinted by permission of the author and the publisher.

FOR DISCUSSION

1. Judge Kaye speaks of state and federal policies "supporting consensual arbitration and resolving all doubts in favor of arbitration." Do you agree with this policy? On what grounds can an arbitrator's decision be challenged in court?

2. *USPS* v. *National Association of Letter Carriers* involved an arbitration that was challenged in court. Does that case show any weaknesses in the arbitration process?

3. Would any of the other cases in this chapter have been handled better by arbitration than by the court system?

4. Kaye suggests that cases "involving disintegrated personal relationships" may not be best handled by the courts. Explain whether you think arbitration is a better way to handle divorces than litigation in court.

5. Another alternative to the courts is mediation. Because the mediator, unlike an arbitrator, cannot issue a binding decision, he or she tries to bring the parties to a voluntary agreement. Is mediation preferable to arbitration? What types of disputes are best handled by mediation? By arbitration?

6. What qualifications should an arbitrator have? Compare them to Frankel's view of what makes a good adversary judge.

The next case provides a practical example of how arbitration works in what is probably the most common type of dispute handled by an arbitrator, one between employer and employee. Because the collective bargaining agreement provides for the arbitration of certain disputes, the result can be appealed to the courts if one side believes that there is a violation of that contract or a violation of the law or public policy. Otherwise, courts are reluctant to second guess the judgment of arbitrators.

CASE

School Committee of Waltham v. Waltham Educators Association
Supreme Judicial Court of Massachusetts, Middlesex (1986)
500 N.E. 2d 1312, 398 Mass. 703

NOLAN, Justice.   We reverse the judgment of the Superior Court, which vacated an arbitrator's award in favor of Samuel Poulten (the teacher).

The teacher was serving with the benefit of tenure at Waltham High School when, on January 17, 1984, during a class in social studies, he struck a student with his hand. Immediately before the incident, he had escorted a student from the room. During his absence a student (not the object of the blow) had put a tack on the teacher's chair. When he returned and sat down, the tack penetrated his testicle. He jumped from his chair and hit a student. Whether he struck the student intentionally or as a result of the shock from the tack's penetration is important and will be discussed later. When he realized that the student whom he hit was not the student who had ambushed him by placing the tack on his chair, the teacher offered a pointer to the victim of his blow and suggested that the student hit him. The student declined. The teacher reported the incident immediately to the authorities at the school but subsequently referred to it as an accident. Ultimately, the school committee, after a hearing, voted unanimously to suspend the teacher for ten days without pay. The teacher then filed a grievance and exercised his rights to arbitration under the collective bargaining agreement.

The arbitrator conducted a hearing at which several witnesses testified, including some of the students and the teacher. The issue for arbitration was framed as follows: "Whether or not the School Committee violated Article 1.2 of the Collective Bargaining Agreement when it suspended/disciplined for ten days without pay, the grievant, Samuel Poulten? If so, what shall the remedy be?" In relevant part, Article 1.2 provides: "No tenured employee in a classification covered by this agreement will be discharged, disciplined, or reprimanded or reduced in rank or compensation without just cause; just cause including, but not limited to inefficiency, incapacity, conduct unbecoming such employee, or insubordination."

The arbitrator ruled that the committee had violated Article 1.2 when it suspended the teacher because the suspension was without just cause, and made an award ordering the committee to reimburse the teacher for the loss of pay for ten days and noting that the committee, "if it so desires [may] issue a letter of warning to Mr. Poulten" regarding the incident with the pointer.

The defendant, Waltham Educators Association, moved to confirm the award. A judge of the Superior Court denied the motion and entered an order vacated the award for a variety of reasons which will be treated as they surface in the issues raised by the association's appeal.

1. *Inconsistent and contradictory findings in award.* The judge ruled that the "arbitrator's award is unfounded in reason and fact." A careful reading of the arbitrator's findings lends some support to this conclusion. The arbitrator seemed at first to imply that the teacher's act in striking the pupil was the result of shock to his nervous system. However, he also appeared to retreat from that by finding a time interval between the teacher's contact with the tack and delivery of the blow, indicating, perhaps, some reflection. Finally, the arbitrator returned to his first premise, finding that the act was not intentional but the result of "shock." The judge's criticism is well-founded but his action in vacating the award is error.

Judicial review of an arbitrator's award is governed by G.L. c. 150C (1984 ed.) which provides for a very limited scope of review. Whether we view the judge's criticism of the award as a charge of error of law or of error of fact is not important, because an arbitrator's award may not be vacated on either ground.

Absent fraud, the court's inquiry is confined to the question whether the arbitrator exceeded the scope of his reference or awarded relief in excess of his authority. The fact that an arbitrator has been found to have committed an error of law does not, by itself, mean that he has exceeded his authority.

Clearly, this award is squarely within the reference which raised the issue whether the committee violated Article 1.2 of the collective bargaining agreement. The award was entirely responsive to that issue in finding a violation.

As to whether the award exceeded the arbitrator's authority, we must consider the provisions of the statute which authorize establishment of a grievance procedure in collective bargaining agreements between public employers and their employees. This case clearly falls within language which provides for resolution of grievances and the election of arbitration in matters involving "suspension, dismissal, removal, or termination" of public employees.

Finally, in connection with the arbitrator's interpretation of the agreement, we have conceded only that "[c]ourts do consider whether an arbitrator's award draws its essence from the collective bargaining agreement." *Concerned Minority Educators of Worcester* v. *School Committee of Worcester*, 466 N.E. 2d 114 (1984). The award here manifestly meets this test.

2. *Corporal punishment.* The judge ruled that "[t]he award violates the state's prohibition against corporal punishment." This is simply not so. Despite the arbitrator's ambiguous and apparently contradictory findings related to the teacher's striking the student, we do not view his award as derogating from the statute which prohibits corporal punishment. Corporal punishment, if it means anything, must be intentional. It is difficult to conceive an unintentional

act, however forceful, as corporal punishment. The arbitrator, despite his linguistic failings, found the teacher's act to be unintentional. Therefore, it could not qualify as corporal punishment.

3. *Nature of arbitrator's hearing.* The committee argues that the arbitrator should not have heard the evidence and decided the case de novo. The committee argues that the arbitrator's review of the committee's action should be no broader than judicial review. We disagree. The Superior Court judge's inquiry is whether the committee's action in disciplining the teacher is justifiable, which has been interpreted to focus on whether the action was "arbitrary, irrational, unreasonable, in bad faith, or irrelevant to the committee's task" of operating a good school system. *Springgate* v. *School Comm. of Mattapoiset*, 415 N.E. 2d 888 (1981).

The subject of the suspension is unquestionably arbitrable under the agreement. The governing statute provides that the "parties may include in any written agreement a grievance procedure culminating in final and binding arbitration to be invoked in the event of any dispute concerning the interpretation or application of such written agreement." The arbitrator's duty under the agreement is to determine whether there was just cause for disciplining the teacher. To achieve this end an evidentiary hearing is essential, though a narrower scope of the arbitrator's authority could be achieved through an agreement. [The statute] specifically provides for a full hearing with witnesses. Though a search of cases in the Commonwealth yields no jurisprudence on this issue, it seems that the result we reach is inherent in the very nature of the process. The only case material to this issue, which we have been able to discover, held that an arbitration panel was entitled to hold a de novo hearing in deciding whether a school committee had discharged an employee for just cause. *Fortney* v. *School Dist. of West Salem* 321 N.W. 2d 225 (Wisc. 1982).

In sum, we see nothing offensive to statutory construction or public policy in the more generous provisions for review in an arbitrator's hearing than those provided for a court. If the committee is disturbed by the breadth of this review, it can negotiate a narrower scope when an agreement is again collectively bargained.

Judgment reversed.

FOR DISCUSSION

1. The trial court overturned the arbitrator's decision on the grounds that it "is unfounded in reason and fact." Explain the court's reasoning. If Justice Nolan agrees that "the judge's criticism is well founded," why does he state that the trial court's "action in vacating the award is error?"

2. What other objections does the school committee have to the arbitration? Why does Justice Nolan reject them?

3. After reading *School Committee* v. *Waltham Educators Association* and *USPS* v. *National Association of Letter Carriers*, what do you think of Kaye's statement that "judicial review of arbitration awards has been highly circumscribed?" How strong is judicial deference to the decisions of arbitrators?

4. Justice Nolan tells the school committee that if it believes that the arbitrator was given too much authority, "it can negotiate a narrower scope when an agreement is again collectively bargained." If you were a negotiator for the committee, what changes would you ask for? What arguments could you use to gain support for your position?

5. How fair was the outcome of this case? Would the result have been better or worse had there been no arbitration provided for in the collective bargaining agreement?

LEGAL TERMS TO KNOW

Appellate court

Arbitration

Civil law

Diversity case

Domicile

In personam jurisdiction

Mediation

Per curiam opinion

Residence

Small claims court

Subject matter jurisdiction

Summons

Trial court

Writ of certiorari

ADDITIONAL QUESTIONS AND EXERCISES

1. Much of the picture of the courts that we have comes from the media. Compare what you have learned in this chapter with what is shown on television and written in newspapers. How accurate a picture do the media paint?

2. As the essays in this chapter indicate, growing court case loads have become a matter of concern. Select two proposals for reducing court overcrowding and evaluate the arguments for and against them.

3. Visit a trial court and evaluate the judge using the criteria suggested by Frankel.

4. The complexity of the American court system is confusing to most citizens. One way to simplify matters would be to require every state to have the same court structure, terminology, and rules of procedure. Write an essay arguing for or against such a proposal.

5. In *Justice in America*, Herbert Jacob argues that "The major criticism of the work of civil courts is that access to them is restricted by distrust, ignorance, and cost. The 'haves' know how to manipulate legal proceedings and have the resources to do so. The 'have nots' can rarely bring their cases to trial." Explain whether or not you agree. Do any of the cases in this chapter support your view?

FOR FURTHER READING

1. DRECHSEL, ROBERT E., *News Making in the Trial Courts*. New York: Longman, 1983.

2. JACOB, HERBERT, *Justice in America*, (4th ed.) Boston: Little Brown, 1984.

3. MINER, ROGER J., "Federal Courts at the Crossroads," *Constitutional Commentary*, 4 (Summer 1987), 251–58.

4. O'OBRIEN, DAVID M., *Storm Center: The Supreme Court in American Politics*. New York: W. W. Norton, 1986.

5. STUMPF, HARRY P., *American Judicial Politics*. San Diego: Harcourt Brace Jovanovich, 1988.

6. ZELERMAYER, WILLIAM, *The Legal System in Operation*. St. Paul, Minn.: West Publishing, 1977.

2

HOW COURTS
DIFFER
FROM LEGISLATURES

INTRODUCTION

When we first learned about the U. S. Constitution in grade school, one of the first lessons explained the separation of powers among the three branches. It was the job of Congress to make the laws, the president to execute them, and the courts to interpret them. Taken to its extreme, this view would give little power to the courts for they would merely use their legal knowledge to figure out what the legislature meant when it wrote a law then apply it to the case at hand. Several factors make the job of the courts both more important and more complicated than this, however. First, the separation of powers was deliberately made less than airtight. Fearing that one branch could become too powerful, the authors of the Constitution gave each of the three overlapping powers. As James Madison put it in *Federalist 51*, "The great security against a gradual concentration of the several powers in the same department, consists in giving to those who administer each department the necessary means and personal motives to resist encroachments of the others.... Ambition must be made to counteract ambition." One example of these overlapping powers is the method of selection of federal judges who are appointed by the President with the advice and consent of the Senate.

A second complicating factor is the power of judicial review, allowing courts to declare laws unconstitutional. As we shall see, this gives the courts considerable potential power over legislation. The Constitution does not specifically grant this power to the courts but in the case of *Marbury* v. *Madison*, 1 Cranch (5 U.S.) 137 (1803), the Supreme Court declared it implied by several provisions. This makes constitutional interpretation an important function of courts, especially the U. S. Supreme Court.

The third complicating factor is the frequent ambiguity of the law. Legislatures cannot foresee every possible contingency. Changes in society may leave the courts the problem of determining what the legislature intended the law to mean in a situation that the legislators had neither written into the law nor discussed during their debates. When the unforeseen occurs, the courts, although trying to act consistently with the legislature's intentions, are, in effect, making law. Sometimes, legislators, unable to agree on details, may even compromise by deliberately writing a law in broad strokes, leaving it to judges to fill in the details. These judicial interpretations, made on a case by case basis, are a major part of the case law that was introduced in the previous chapter and will be discussed in more detail in the chapter on precedent. In this chapter we will examine the major principles of statutory interpretation by looking at cases in which courts had to determine the meaning of specific laws.

How Powerful Should Judges Be?

The Constitution sets out the powers of the Congress in Article I, those of the president in Article II, and those of the federal courts in Article III. Article III, consisting of only six paragraphs (two of which define treason) is by far the least detailed, leaving it to historical practice to fill in the blanks. The authors of the Constitution feared the possibility of domination by the president or the Congress more than the judiciary for several reasons. Unlike the other two branches, the courts cannot initiate action but must wait for others to bring cases before them. Judges are also dependent on the other branches to enforce their decisions. For example, when southern states defied court orders to desegregate their public schools, the courts had to call on the executive branch to send the necessary troops or federal marshals to enforce their orders. Without such cooperation, the courts could not have enforced these decisions on their own. In other instances, money had to be appropriated by Congress to carry out court decisions.

In addition, if Congress disagrees with court interpretations of a statute, it can rewrite that law to overrule the court decision. Constitutional interpretations are more difficult to overrule, but the Constitution can be amended. Finally, it is the other two branches that choose federal judges. Despite these powers of the other two branches over the judiciary, there was considerable disagreement during the debate over the adoption of the Constitution about how powerful the courts should be. Those seeking a more limited role for the courts pointed out that federal judges are not elected and serve for life. Today we elect both houses of Congress and (even if indirectly) the president. If we do not like what they are doing, when their terms end, we can elect someone else. In this sense, the judicial branch is the least accountable to the public.

The question of how active judges should be has been debated ever since the adoption of the Constitution, especially when it comes to judicial review. If the courts declare a law unconstitutional, only a constitutional amendment can overrule them. Although this has been done on rare occasions such as the Sixteenth Amendment allowing Congress to enact an income tax, the amending process is too difficult to be used frequently. This makes the power of judicial review an awesome one, giving judges the final say over legislation. Advocates of judicial restraint argue that this power should be used rarely. Because legislatures are democratically elected, they are answerable to the public. Therefore judges should presume that laws are valid unless there is extremely strong evidence to the contrary. On the other side, judicial activists take a more expansive view of judicial power. As Judge Frank Johnson, Jr., has put it, "The role of the federal courts in deciding constitutional questions is and always has been an activist one. It is not a role which has been usurped by the judiciary, however, but is one which is inextricably intertwined with its duty to interpret the Constitution." [1] Judicial activists believe that courts can provide protection for unpopular minorities whose rights may be ignored or even trampled on by the other branches.

[1] Frank M. Johnson, Jr., "Judicial Activism Is a Duty—Not an Intrusion." *In Views from the Bench*, ed. Mark Cannon and David O'Brien (Chatham, N.J.:Chatham House, 1985), p. 279.

It is important not to overstate the distinction between the two categories. Although legislators can vote for or against bills because they dislike them, even the most fervent advocate of judicial activism does not advocate judges overturning laws simply because of personal preference. Judges must have a legal reason such as violation of a constitutional provision to invalidate a law. In addition, judges can only rule on the cases presented to them. Unlike legislators, who can consider passing laws on any subject within their power, judges must wait for others to bring cases into their courts. If a judge believes a law unconstitutional but no one challenges it in court, the law will remain in force. Furthermore, when cases are brought into court, judges must rely on the evidence presented by the contending parties; they cannot gather their own. As we pointed out earlier, they must also rely on others to enforce their decisions.

In the real world, judges practice both activism and self-restraint. All judges, including those who consider themselves activists, uphold most laws considered in their courtrooms. Even the strongest advocates of self-restraint will find laws they overturn as unconstitutional. This is true of liberals and conservatives, Democrats and Republicans, even former prosecutors and former defense attorneys. In the 1930s, conservative Supreme Court Justices overturned New Deal economic reforms; in the 1960s, a more liberal Court upheld challenges by racial minorities and criminal defendants.

Nevertheless, the debate between the two schools of interpretation continues and is worth our attention. In this chapter we will include a significant amount of material covering this debate from a variety of perspectives. Also included will be several cases showing how judges put these philosophies into action both at the federal and state levels.

Judicial Selection

Given these differing judicial philosophies, how should judges be chosen and what qualities should they possess? Because judges' terms are generally longer than those of legislators or chief executives, the selection process is extremely important. About half the states and the federal government allow the chief executive to select judges subject to legislative confirmation. In other states, the public elects judges just as they do governors, mayors, and legislators. Both methods have their critics. Appointment creates the danger that political connections will take precedence over merit. Judges may be selected more for who they know than for what they know and can do. Conversely, the voting public rarely knows much about judicial candidates who, unlike those running for other offices, cannot promise to take specific actions if elected. Imagine what would happen if a candidate promised to work to convict an unpopular defendant whose trial was scheduled after the election! As a result, elections for judge are dull affairs attracting little media attention, making it virtually impossible for the average voter to make an informed decision.

To meet these objections, several states have adopted the Missouri Plan. Under this system, the governor must choose someone from a list of names selected by a commission of distinguished and knowledgeable citizens. After serving a year or two, the judge must be confirmed by the voters in a referendum. Although this method has been gaining in popularity, it too has its weaknesses. In some states, the panels have given the governor lists of establishment types, avoiding those who might rock the boat by changing things too much. With only one candidate running in the referendum, defeats are rare events.

No judicial selection is more important than that of U.S. Supreme Court justices. Their life tenure allows them to influence the course of American law far longer than the presidents who choose them. Thus, it is not surprising that nominees for the Court receive considerable scrutiny. The process itself is easy to understand. The president nominates a candidate who must be approved by majority vote of the Senate. But just what qualities do we want in a Supreme Court justice? Article III of the Constitution requires no specific qualifications, not even that justices be lawyers. Stephen Wasby has suggested three types of qualification: representational, professional, and doctrinal.[2] There is little agreement on how important each of these categories should be, however. Do we want the Supreme Court to represent all groups? Justices have been selected because a particular region or religion was underrepresented on the Court. Most nominees have come from the same party as the president who chose them. Conversely, there have been only one woman and one black appointed. Is this a serious problem? Professional qualifications present a different problem. Which ones are important? For example, some of the greatest of Supreme Court justices such as Chief Justice John Marshall, had no previous judicial experience. Other possible indications of competence might be intellect, temperament, honesty, and professional respect. Think about which of these you find important and how you would measure them. Finally, what about judicial philosophy, which Wasby terms "doctrinal qualifications"? Should presidents nominate those who agree with their principles and policies? Should the Senate give consideration to these same issues? Can a nominee's views be so far out of the mainstream of legal thought that his or her candidacy should be rejected? In this chapter we will look at the recent controversy over the nomination of Robert Bork to the Supreme Court as a way of illustrating these issues.

Judicial Decision Making

To understand how courts operate, it is necessary to understand the differences between the methods judges use to make decisions and those used by legislators. Judges are far more limited in what they can decide than are those who serve in the legislature. The first limit is the case at hand. Judges must decide the issues in the cases brought before them even if they would prefer to deal with other subjects. A legislature is far freer in deciding on what issues it wishes to bring up and when. The judge's decision is aimed primarily at the litigants in the case although that decision may have significant policy implications for others. When Congress or a state legislature passes a law, conversely, it is written in universal terms so as to apply to everyone. A judge's decisions are based on the arguments brought up by the two adversaries in court while a legislature can seek information from any source it believes is significant. Courts, as we shall discuss in more detail, are bound by the specific language of the law and the Constitution as well as by precedents set in past cases. A legislature is free to change any laws it has made in the past in any way it sees fit as long as it does not exceed its constitutional powers. Members of Congress must maintain enough public support to gain reelection, a problem not faced by federal judges with life tenure and less important for state judges with longer terms than the two years of members of the U.S. House of Representatives or the six of Senators. Although the exact terms may differ, the situation is similar for state legislators and judges.

As with some of the other distinctions we have previously examined, however, we should not take these differences too far. As Jerome Corsi has written, "What has emerged from the writing of legal theorists in this century is at least an awareness that judges are not decision machines, that law is an adapting changing entity, and that judges through their individual views do exert an influence over which course law and its interpretation will take."[3]

[2]Stephen L. Wasby, *The Supreme Court in the Federal Judicial System,* 2 nd ed. (New York:Holt, Reinhart, and Winston, 1984), p. 86.

[3]Jerome R. Corsi, *Judicial Politics: An Introduction* (Englewood Cliffs, N.J.:Prentice Hall, 1984), p. 263.

JUDICIAL ACTIVISM VERSUS JUDICIAL SELF-RESTRAINT

After the Constitution was proposed, it had to be approved by the states. In New York, Alexander Hamilton, James Madison, and John Jay wrote a series of pamphlets, known as *The Federalist Papers*, arguing in favor of ratification. Because the Constitution is phrased in very general language these early interpretations have become influential in understanding its meaning. In *Federalist 78*, Hamilton claims that "the judiciary, from the nature of its functions, will always be the least dangerous to the political rights of the Constitution." Because of that, he argues for as strong and independent a judicial branch as possible.

READING   ## Federalist 78
                                       By Alexander Hamilton*

We proceed now to an examination of the judiciary department of the proposed government.

According to the plan of the convention, all judges who may be appointed by the United States are to hold their offices during good behavior. The standard of good behavior for the continuation in office of the judicial magistracy is certainly one of the most valuable of the modern improvements in the practice of government. In a monarchy it is an excellent barrier to the despotism of the prince; in a republic it is a no less excellent barrier to the encroachments and oppressions of the representative body. And it is the best expedient which can be devised in any government to secure a steady, upright, and impartial administration of the laws.

Whoever attentively considers the different departments of power must perceive that, in a government in which they are separated from each other, the judiciary, from the nature of its functions, will always be the least dangerous to the political rights of the Constitution; because it will be least in a capacity to annoy or injure them. The Executive not only dispenses the honors, but holds the sword of the community. The legislature not only commands the purse, but prescribes the rules by which the duties and rights of every citizen are to be regulated. The judiciary, on the contrary, has no influence over either the sword or the purse; no direction either of the strength or of the wealth of the society; and can take no active resolution whatever. It may truly be said to have neither FORCE nor WILL, but merely judgment; and must ultimately depend upon the aid of the executive arm even for the efficacy of its judgments.

This simple view of the matter suggests several important consequences. It proves incontestably that the judiciary is beyond comparison the weakest of the three departments; that it can never attack with success either of the other two; and that all possible care is requisite to enable it to defend itself against their attacks. It equally proves that though individual oppression may now and then proceed from the courts of justice, the general liberty of the people can never be endangered from that quarter; I mean so long as the judiciary remains truly distinct from both the legislature and the executive.

The complete independence of the courts of justice is peculiarly essential in a limited Constitution. By a limited Constitution, I understand one which contains certain specified exceptions to the legislative authority; for instance, as that it shall pass no bills of attainder, no *ex-post-facto* laws, and the like. Limitations of this kind can be preserved in practice no other way than through the medium of courts of justice, whose duty it must be to declare all acts contrary to the manifest tenor of the Constitution void. Without this, all the reservations of particular rights or privileges would amount to nothing.

Some perplexity respecting the rights of the courts to pronounce legislative acts void, because contrary to the Constitution, has arisen from an imagination that the doctrine would imply a superiority of the judiciary to the legislative power. As this doctrine is of great importance in all the American constitutions, a brief discussion of the ground on which it rests cannot be unacceptable.

There is no position which depends on clearer principles than that of every act of a delegated authority, contrary to the tenor of the commission under which it is exercised, is void. No legislative act, therefore, contrary to the Constitution, can be valid. The courts were designed to be an intermediate body between the people and the legislature, in order, among other things, to keep the latter within the limits assigned to their authority. The interpretation of the laws is the proper and peculiar province of the courts. A constitution is, in fact, and must be regarded by the judges, as a fundamental law. It therefore belongs to them to ascertain its meaning, as well as the meaning of any particular act proceeding from the legislative body. If there should happen to be an irreconcilable variance between the two, that which has the superior obligation and validity ought, of course, to be preferred; or, in other words, the Constitution ought to be preferred to the statute, the intention of the people to the intention of their agents.

Nor does this conclusion by any means suppose a superiority of the judicial to the legislative power. It only supposes that the power of the people is superior to both; and that where the will of the legislature, declared in its statutes, stands in opposition to that of the people, declared in the Constitution, the judges ought to be governed by the latter rather than the former. They ought to regulate their decisions by the fundamental laws, rather than by those which are not fundamental.

If, then, the courts of justice are to be considered as the bulwarks of a limited Constitution against legislative encroachments, this consideration will afford a strong argument for the permanent tenure of judicial offices, since nothing will contribute so much as this to that independent spirit in the judges which must be essential to the faithful performance of so arduous a duty.

This independence of the judges is equally requisite to guard the Constitution and the rights of individuals from the effects of those ill humors, which the arts of designing men or the influence of particular conjectures sometimes disseminate among the people themselves; and which, though they speedily give place to better information and more deliberate reflection, have a tendency, in the meantime, to occasion dangerous innovations in the government, and serious oppressions of the minor party in the community. It is not to be inferred that the representatives of the people, whenever a momentary inclination happens to lay hold of a majority of their constituents, incompatible with the provisions in the existing Constitution, would, on that account, be justifiable in a violation of those provisions; or that the courts would be under a greater obligation to connive at infractions in this shape, than when they had proceeded wholly from the cabals of the representative body. Until the people have by some authoritative act annulled or changed the established form, it is binding upon themselves collectively, as well as individually; and no presumption, or even knowledge, of their sentiments, can warrant their representatives in a departure from it, prior to such an act. But it is easy to see that it would require an uncommon portion of fortitude in the judges to do their duty as faithful guardians of the Constitution, where legislative invasions of it had been instigated by the major voice of the community.

But it is not with a view to infractions of the Constitution only that the independence of the judges may be an essential safeguard against the effects of occasional ill humors in the society. These sometimes extend no farther than to the injury of the private rights of particular classes of citizens by unjust and partial laws. Here also the firmness of the judicial magistracy is of vast importance in mitigating the severity and confining the operation of such laws.

That inflexible and uniform adherence to the rights of the Constitution and of individuals, which we perceive to be indispensable in the courts of justice, can certainly not be expected from judges who hold their offices by a temporary commission. Periodical appointments, however regulated or by whomsoever made, would, in some way or other, be fatal to their necessary independence. If the power of making them was committed either to the Executive or the legislature, there would be danger of an improper complaisance to the branch which possessed it; if to both, there would be an unwillingness to hazard the displeasure of either; if to the people or to persons chosen by them for the special purpose, there would be too great a disposition to consult popularity, to justify a reliance that nothing would be consulted but the Constitution and the laws.

There is yet a further and a weightier reason for the permanency of the judicial offices. It has been frequently remarked that a voluminous code of laws is one of the inconveniences necessarily connected with the advantages of a free government. To avoid an arbitrary discretion in the courts, it is indispensable that they should be bound down by strict rules and precedents; and it will readily be conceived from the variety of controversies which grow out of the folly and wickedness of mankind, that the records of those precedents must unavoidably swell to a very considerable bulk, and must demand long and laborious study to acquire a competent knowledge of them. Hence it is, that there can be but few men who will have sufficient skill in the laws to qualify them for the stations of judges. And making the proper deductions for the ordinary depravity of human nature, the number must be still smaller of those who unite the requisite integrity with the requisite knowledge. A temporary duration in office, which would naturally discourage such characters from quitting a lucrative line of practice to accept a seat on the bench, would have a tendency to throw the administration of justice into hands less able, and less well qualified, to conduct it with utility and dignity. In the present circumstances of this country and in those in which it is likely to be for a long time to come, the disadvantages on this score would be greater than they may at first sight appear; but it must be confessed that they are far inferior to those which present themselves under the other aspects of the subject.

Upon the whole, there can be no room to doubt that the convention acted wisely in copying from the models of those constitutions which have established *good behavior* as the tenure of their judicial offices, in point of duration. The experience of Great Britain affords an illustrious comment on the excellence of the institution.

NOTES

*From *Federalist 78*.

FOR DISCUSSION

1. According to Hamilton, of the three branches of government, the courts "will always be the least dangerous to the political rights of the Constitution." Explain why he thinks so. Has history proved him correct?

2. Why does Hamilton believe that the courts must have the power of judicial review? Can you point to any constitutional provisions supporting his view?

3. It has been argued that giving the Congress, whose members need public support to be reelected, the final say over the constitutionality of laws would be more democratic than entrusting it to unelected federal judges with life tenure. Explain whether you agree or disagree with this argument.

4. What does Hamilton think of electing judges? Explain whether you agree.

5. Explain and evaluate Hamilton's arguments in favor of life tenure for federal judges.

6. Federal judges' terms are contingent on "good behavior." What actions would constitute bad enough behavior to justify the removal of a federal judge? Would all convictions for violation of a criminal law be adequate grounds for removal? Are there any actions that are not violations of the law that would justify removal?

The next two essays show the two sides of the debate between advocates of judicial activism and self-restraint. In the first, written before President Reagan nominated him for the Supreme Court, Robert Bork argues that activist judges have exceeded their authority by substituting their own views for those of the authors of the Constitution. Instead, he argues for an approach that he calls "interpretivism", which means discovering the values that the Constitution's authors sought to enact and applying them to the case at hand. The courts should only declare laws unconstitutional if they clearly violate the intent of the framers as expressed in the text, structure, and history of the Constitution.

READING **Judicial Review and Democracy**
By Robert H. Bork*

The American ideal of democracy lives in constant tension with the American ideal of judicial review in the service of individual liberties. It is a tension that sometimes erupts in crisis. Franklin D. Roosevelt, frustrated by a court majority that repeatedly struck down New Deal economic measures, tried to pack the court with additional justices. That effort was defeated in Congress, though the attempt may have persuaded some justices to alter their behavior. In recent years there have been movements in Congress to deprive federal courts of jurisdiction over cases involving such matters as abortion, school busing, and school prayer—topics on which the Court's decisions have angered strong and articulate constituencies.

The problem is the resolution of what Robert Dahl called the Madisonian dilemma. The United States was founded as a Madisonian system, one that allows majorities to govern wide and important areas of life simply because they are majorities, but that also holds that individuals have some freedoms that must be exempt from majority control. The dilemma is that neither the majority nor the minority can be trusted to define the proper spheres of democratic authority and individual liberty.

It is not at all clear that the Founders envisaged a leading role for the judiciary in the resolution of this dilemma, for they thought of the third branch as relatively insignificant. Over time, however, Americans have come to assume that the definition of majority power and minority freedom is primarily the function of the judiciary, most particularly the function of the Supreme Court. This assumption places a great responsibility upon constitutional theory. America's basic method of policymaking is majoritarian. Thus, to justify exercise of a power to set at naught the considered decisions of elected representatives, judges must achieve, in Alexander Bickel's phrase, "a rigorous general accord between judicial supremacy and democratic theory, so that the boundaries of the one could be described with some precision in terms of the other." At one time, an accord was based on the understanding that judges followed the intentions of the Framers and ratifiers of the Constitution, a legal document enacted by majorities, though subject to alteration only by supermajorities. A conflict between democracy and judicial review did not arise because the respective areas of each were specified and intended to be inviolate. Although this obedience to original intent was occasionally more pretense than reality, the accord was achieved in theory, and that theory stated an ideal to which courts were expected to conform. That is no longer so. Many judges and scholars now believe that the courts' obligations to intent are so highly generalized and remote that judges are in fact free to create the Constitution they think appropriate to today's society. The result is that the accord no longer stands even theoretically. The increasing perception that this is so raises the question of what elected officials can do to reclaim authority they regard as wrongfully taken by the judiciary.

There appear to be two possible responses to a judiciary that has overstepped the limits of its legitimate authority. One is political, the other intellectual. It seems tolerably clear that political responses are of limited usefulness, at least in the short run. Impeachment and Court-packing, having failed in the past, are unlikely to be resorted to again. Amending the Constitution to correct judicial overreaching is such a difficult and laborious process that it is of little practical assistance. Democratic responses to judicial excesses probably must come through the replacement of judges who die or retire with new judges of different views. But this is a slow and uncertain process, the accidents of mortality being what they are and prediction of what new judges will do being so perilous.

There exist few, if any, usable and effective techniques by which federal courts can be kept within constitutional bounds. A Constitution that provides numerous checks and balances between president and Congress provides little to curb a judiciary that expands its powers beyond the allowable meaning of the Constitution. Nor is it clear that an institutional check—such as Senator Robert La Follette's proposal to amend the Constitution so that Congress could override a Supreme Court decision by a two-thirds majority—would be desirable. Congress is less likely than the Court to be versed in the Constitution. La Follette's proposal could conceivably wreak as much or more damage to the Court's legitimate powers as it might accomplish in restraining its excesses. That must be reckoned at least a possibility with any of the institutional checks just discussed and is probably one of the reasons they have rarely been used. In this sense, the Court's vulnerability is one of its most important protections.

In the beginning, there was no controversy over theory. Joseph Story, who was both an associate justice of the Supreme Court and Dane Professor of Law at Harvard, could write in his *Commentaries on the Constitution of the United States*, published in 1833, that "I have not the ambition to be the author of any new plan of interpreting the theory of the Constitution, or of enlarging or narrowing its powers by ingenious subtleties and learned doubts". He thought that the job of constitutional judges was to interpret:" The first and fundamental rule in the interpretation of all instruments is, to construe them according to the sense of the terms and the intention of the parties."

The performance of the courts has not always conformed to this interpretivist ideal. In the last decade or so of the nineteenth century and the first third of the twentieth the Supreme Court assiduously protected economic liberties from federal and state regulation, often in ways that could not be reconciled with the Constitution. The case that stands as the symbol of that era of judicial adventurism is *Lochner* v. *New York* in 1905, which struck down the state's law regulating maximum hours for bakers. That era ended when Franklin D. Roosevelt's appointments remade the Court, and *Lochner* is now generally regarded as discredited.

Nevertheless, if the Court stopped defending economic liberties without constitutional justification in the mid-1930s, it began in the mid-1950s to make other decisions for which it offered little or no constitutional argument. It had generally been assumed that constitutional questions were to be answered on grounds of historical intent, but the Court began to make decisions that could hardly be, and were not, justified on that basis. Existing constitutional protections were expanded and new ones created. The widespread perception that the judiciary was recreating the Constitution brought the tension between democracy and judicial review once more to a state of intellectual and political crisis.

Much of the new judicial power claimed cannot be derived from the text, structure, or history of the Constitution. Perhaps because of the increasing obviousness of this fact, legal scholars began to erect new theories of the judicial role. These constructs, which appear to be accepted by a majority of those who write about constitutional theory, go by the general name of noninterpretivism. They hold that mere interpretation of the Constitution may be impossible and is certainly inadequate. Judges are assigned not the task of defining the meanings and contours of values found in the historical Constitution but rather the function of creating new values and hence new rights for individuals against majorities. These new values are variously described as arising from "the evolving morality of our tradition," our "conventional morality" as discerned by "the method of philosophy," a "fusion of constitutional law and moral theory," or "higher law" of "unwritten natural rights." In all cases, these theories purport to empower judges to override majority will for extraconstitutional reasons.

Judges have articulated theories of their role no less removed from interpretation than those of the noninterpretivist academics. Writing for the Court in *Griswold* v. *Connecticut* in 1965, Justice William O. Douglas created a constitutional right of privacy that invalidated the state's law against the use of contraceptives. He observed that many provisions of the Bill of Rights could be viewed as protections of aspects of personal privacy. These provisions were said to add up to a zone of constitutionally secured privacy that did not fall within any particular provision. The scope of this new right was not defined but the Court has used the concept in a series of cases since, the most controversial being *Roe* v. *Wade* in 1973.

A similar strategy for the creation of new rights was outlined by Justice William Brennan in a 1985 address. He characterized the Constitution as being pervasively concerned with human dignity. From this, Brennan drew a more general judicial function of enhancing human dignity, one not confined by the clauses in question and, indeed, capable of nullifying what those clauses reveal of the Framers' intentions. Thus, Brennan stated that the judicial tolerance of capital punishment causes us to "fall short of the constitutional vision of human dignity." For that reason, Brennan continues to vote that capital punishment violates the Constitution. The potency of this method of generalizing from particular clauses, and then applying the generalization instead of the clauses, may be seen in the fact that it leads to a declaration of the unconstitutionality of a punishment explicitly assumed to be available three times in the Fifth Amendment and once again, some seventy-seven years later, in the Fourteenth Amendment. By conventional methods of interpretation, it would be impossible to use the Constitution to prohibit that which the Constitution explicitly assumed to be lawful.

Because noninterpretive philosophies have little hard intellectual structure, it is impossible to control them or to predict from any inner logic or principle what they may require. Though it is regularly denied that a return to the judicial function as exemplified in *Lochner* v. *New York* is underway or, which comes to the same thing, that decisions are rooted only in the judges' moral predilections, it is difficult to see what else can be involved once the function of searching for the Framers' intent is abandoned.

This mode of adjudication makes impossible any general accord between judicial supremacy and democratic theory. Instead, it brings the two into head-on conflict. The Constitution specifies certain liberties and allocates all else to democratic processes. Noninterpretivism gives the judge power to invade the province of democracy whenever majority morality conflicts with his own. That is impossible to square either with democratic theory or with the concept of law. By placing certain subjects in the legislative arena, the Constitution holds that the trade-off between principle and expediency we are entitled to is what the legislature provides. Courts have no mandate to impose a different result merely because they would arrive at a trade-off that weighted principle more heavily or that took an altogether different value into account.

A different reconciliation of democracy and noninterpretivist judicial review begins with the proposition that the Supreme Court is not really final because popular sentiment can in the long run cause it to be overturned. As we know from history, it may take decades to overturn a decision, so that it will be final for many people. Even then an overruling cannot be forced if a substantial minority ardently supports the result.

To the degree that the Constitution is not treated as law to be interpreted in conventional fashion, the clash between democracy and judicial review is real. It is also serious. When the judiciary imposes upon democracy limits not to be found in the Constitution, it deprives Americans of a right that is found there, the right to make the laws to govern themselves. As courts intervene more frequently to set aside majoritarian outcomes, they teach the lesson that democratic processes are suspect, essentially unprincipled and untrustworthy.

The main charge against a strictly interpretive approach to the Constitution is that the Framers' intentions cannot be known because they could not foresee the changed circumstances of our time. The argument proves too much. If it were true, the judge would be left without any law to apply, and there would be no basis for judicial review.

That is not what is involved. From the text, the structure, and the history of the Constitution we can usually learn at least the core values that the Framers intended to protect. Interpreting the Constitution means discerning the principle that the Framers wanted to enact and applying it to today's circumstances. As John Hart Ely put it, interpretivism holds that "the work of the political branches is to be invalidated only in accord with an inference whose starting point, whose underlying premise, is fairly discoverable in the Constitution."

This requires that constitutional doctrine evolve over time. Most doctrine is merely the judge-made superstructure that implements basic constitutional principles, and, because circumstances change, the evolution of doctrine is inevitable. The Fourth Amendment was framed by men who did not foresee electronic surveillance, but judges may properly apply the central value of that amendment to electronic invasions of personal privacy. The difference between this method and that endorsed by Justices Douglas and Brennan lies in the level of generality employed. Adapting the Fourth Amendment requires the judge merely to recognize a new method of governmental search of one's property. The justices, on the other hand, create a right so general that it effectively becomes a new clause of the Constitution, one that gives courts no guidance in its application. Modifying doctrine to preserve a value already embedded in the Constitution is an enterprise wholly different in nature from creating new values. The task of interpretation is often complex and difficult, but it remains the only model of the judicial role that achieves an accord between democracy and judicial review.

NOTES

*Reprinted with permission of Macmillan Publishing Co. from "Judicial Review and Democracy," by Robert Bork in *Encyclopedia of the American Constitution*, Leonard W. Levy, Kenneth L. Karst, and Dennis J. Mahoney, Editors. 1061–64. Copyright © 1986 by Macmillan Publishing Co., a Division of Macmillan, Inc.

FOR DISCUSSION

1. According to Bork, how can the courts "be kept within constitutional bounds?" Does he believe the courts have been using judicial review properly? Explain.

2. Discuss Bork's distinction between interpretivism and noninterpretivism. Evaluate his criticisms of the latter.

3. According to Bork, "The main charge against a strictly interpretive approach to the Constitution is that the Framers' intentions cannot be known because they could not foresee the changed circumstances of our time." How does he counter this criticism? Do you find his arguments convincing?

4. Would you classify Bork as an advocate of judicial self-restraint or judicial activism? A liberal or a conservative? Explain.

5. Would Bork agree with Hamilton that the courts are "The least dangerous" branch?

In the next essay, Supreme Court Justice William Brennan, one of those accused by Bork of "noninterpretivism," counters with the claim that "the genius of the Constitution rests not in any static meaning it might have had in a world that is dead and gone, but in the adaptability of its great principles to cope with current problems and current needs." For him the Constitution is a constantly evolving document, whose general language must be adapted to the modern world. Note that both Bork and Brennan believe that the Constitution can handle changes in society but that their approaches as to how, are in sharp conflict.

READING   **The Contemporary Constitution**
                        By William J. Brennan, Jr. *

The Constitution embodies the aspiration to social justice, brotherhood, and human dignity that brought this nation into being. The Declaration of Independence, the Constitution, and the Bill of Rights solemnly committed the United States to be a country where the dignity and rights of all persons were equal before all authority. In all candor we must concede that part of this egalitarianism in America has been more pretension than realized fact. But we are an aspiring people, a people with faith in progress. Our amended Constitution is the lodestar for our aspirations. Like every text worth reading, it is not crystalline. The phrasing is broad and the limitation of its provisions are not clearly marked. Its majestic generalities and ennobling pronouncements are both luminous and obscure. This ambiguity, of course, calls for interpretation, the interaction of reader and text. The encounter with the constitutional text has been, in many senses, my life's work.

The Constitution is fundamentally a public text—the monumental charter of a government and a people—and a Justice of the Supreme Court must apply it to resolve public controversies. For, from our beginnings, a most important consequence of the constitutionally created separation of powers has been the American habit, extraordinary to other democracies, of casting social, economic, philosophical, and political questions in the form of lawsuits, in an attempt to secure ultimate resolution by the Supreme Court. In this way, important aspects of the most fundamental issues confronting our democracy may finally arrive in the Supreme Court for judicial determination. Not infrequently, these are the issues upon which contemporary society is most deeply divided. They arouse our deepest emotions. The main burden of my 29 terms on the Supreme Court has thus been to wrestle with the Constitution in this heightened public context, to draw meaning from the text in order to resolve public controversies.

When Justices interpret the Constitution they speak for their community, not for themselves alone. The act of interpretation must be undertaken with full consciousness that it is, in a very real sense, the community's interpretation that is sought. Justices are not platonic guardians appointed to wield authority according to their personal moral predilections. Precisely because coercive force must attend any judicial decision to countermand the will of a contemporary majority, the Justices must render constitutional interpretations that are received as legitimate.

We current Justices read the Constitution in the only way that we can: as twentieth-century Americans. We look to the history of the time of framing and to the intervening history of interpretation. But the ultimate question must be, what do the words of the text mean in our time? For the genius of the Constitution rests not in any static meaning it might have had in a world that is dead and gone, but in the adaptability of its great principles to cope with current problems and current needs. What the constitutional fundamentals meant to the wisdom of other times cannot be their measure to the vision of our time. Similarly, what those fundamentals mean for us, our descendants will learn, cannot be the measure to the vision of their time. This realization is not, I assure you, a novel one of my own creation. Permit me to quote from one of the opinions of our Court, *Weems* v. *U.S.*, 217 U.S. 349, written nearly a century ago:

> Time works changes, brings into existence new conditions and purposes. Therefore, a principle to be vital must be capable of wider application than the mischief which gave it birth. This is peculiarly true of constitutions. They are not ephemeral enactments, designed to meet passing occasions. They are, to use the words of Chief Justice John Marshall, "designed to approach immortality as nearly as human institutions can approach it." The future is their care and provision for good and bad tendencies of which no prophesy can be made. In the application of a constitution, therefore, our contemplation cannot be only of what has been, but of what may be.

Interpretation must account for the transformative purpose of the text. Our Constitution was not intended to preserve a preexisting society but to make a new one, to put in place new principles that the prior political community had not sufficiently recognized. Thus, for example, when we interpret the Civil War Amendments to the charter—abolishing slavery, guaranteeing blacks equality under law, and guaranteeing blacks the right to vote—we must remember that those who put them in place had no desire to enshrine the status quo. Their goal was to make over their world, to eliminate all vestige of slave caste.

As augmented by the Bill of Rights and the Civil War Amendments, this text is a sparkling vision of the supremacy of the human dignity of every individual. The supreme value of a democracy is the presumed worth of each individual. And this vision manifests itself most dramatically in the specific prohibitions of the Bill of Rights, a term that I henceforth will apply to describe not only the original first eight amendments, but the Civil War Amendments as well. It is a vision that has guided us as a people throughout our history, although the precise rules by which we have protected fundamental human dignity have been transformed over time in response to both transformation of social condition and evolution of our concepts of human dignity.

Until the end of the nineteenth century, freedom and dignity in our country found meaningful protection in the institution of real property. In a society still largely agricultural, a piece of land provided men not just with sustenance but with the means of economic independence, a necessary precondition of political independence and expression.

But the days when common law property relationships dominated litigation and legal practice are past. To a growing extent, economic existence now depends on less certain relationships with government—licenses, employment contracts, subsidies, unemployment benefits, tax exemptions, welfare, and the like. Government participation in the economic existence of individuals is pervasive and deep. Now hundreds of thousands of Americans live entire lives without any real prospect of the dignity and autonomy that ownership of real property could confer. Protection of the human dignity of such citizens requires a much modified view of the proper relationship of individual and state.

In general, problems of the relationship of the citizen with government have multiplied and thus have engendered some of the most important constitutional issues of the day. As government acts ever more deeply upon those areas of our lives once marked "private," there is an even greater need to see that individual rights are not curtailed or cheapened in the interest of what may temporarily appear to be the "public good." And as government continues in its role of provider for so many of our disadvantaged citizens, there is an even greater need to ensure that government act with integrity and consistency in its dealings with these citizens. To put this another way, the possibilities for collision between government activity and individual rights will increase as the power and authority of government itself expands, and this growth, in turn, heightens the need for constant vigilance at the collision points. If our free society is to endure, those who govern must recognize human dignity and accept the enforcement of constitutional limitations on their power conceived by the Framers to be necessary to preserve that dignity and the air of freedom which is our proudest achievement. All the talk in the last half-decade about shrinking the government does not alter this reality or the challenge it imposes. The modern activist state is a concomitant of modern society; it is inevitably with us. We must meet the challenge rather than wish it were not before us.

If we are to be as a shining city upon a hill, it will be because of our ceaseless pursuit of the constitutional ideal of human dignity. For the political and legal ideals that form the foundation of much that is best in American institutions—ideals jealously preserved and guarded throughout our history—still form the vital force in creative political thought and activity within the nation today. As we adapt our institutions to the ever-changing conditions of national and international life, those ideals of human dignity—liberty and justice for all individuals—will continue to inspire and guide us because they are entrenched in our Constitution. The Constitution with its Bill of Rights thus has a bright future, as well as a glorious past, for its spirit is inherent in the aspiration of our people.

NOTES

*From *Kettering Review* (Fall 1987), 6–11.

FOR DISCUSSION

1. Bork classifies Justice Brennan as a leading noninterpretivist. After reading Brennan's essay, explain whether or not you agree.

2. Explain the importance of change in Brennan's philosophy of constitutional interpretation.

3. How do Bork and Brennan differ about the best way to protect individual rights?

4. Which of the two views do you think Hamilton would find preferable? Why?

5. Can a judge avoid bringing in personal values interpreting the Constitution? How has this been limited?

CONSTITUTIONAL INTERPRETATION

Because judges are called on to decide cases that involve the interpretation of the Constitution, the debate over judicial philosophy is not simply an abstract one. Justice Douglas's opinion in *Griswold* v. *Connecticut* is one of those criticized by Bork. Douglas argues that there is a constitutional right to privacy created not by any specific provision but by "penumbras, formed by emanations from those guarantees." Justice Goldberg locates the right to privacy in the Ninth Amendment, although it too makes no specific reference to such a right. This right to privacy is then used by the Supreme Court to overturn a Connecticut law against the use of birth control devices. The dissenters believe that the law may be "uncommonly silly" but that does not make it unconstitutional.

CASE

Griswold v. Connecticut
U. S. Supreme Court (1965)
381 U.S. 481, 85 S.Ct. 1678

Mr. Justice DOUGLAS delivered the opinion of the Court.   Appellant Griswold is executive Director of the Planned Parenthood League of Connecticut. Appellant Buxton is a licensed physician and a professor at the Yale Medical School who served as Medical Director for the League at its Center in New Haven. They gave information, instruction, and medical advice to *married persons* as to the means of preventing conception. They examined the wife and prescribed the best contraceptive device or material for her use. Fees were usually charged, although some couples were serviced free.

The statutes whose constitutionality is involved in this appeal are 53-32 and 54-196 of the General Statutes of Connecticut. The former provides:

> Any person who uses any drug, medicinal article or instrument for the purpose of preventing conception shall be fined not less than fifty dollars or imprisoned not less than sixty days nor more than one year or be both fined and imprisoned.

Section 54-196 provides:

> Any person who assists, abets, counsels, causes, hires or commands another to commit any offense may be prosecuted and punished as if he were the principal offender.

The appellants were found guilty as accessories and fined $100 each, against the claim that the accessory statute as so applied violated the Fourteenth Amendment.

We are met with a wide range of questions that implicate the Due Process Clause of the Fourteenth Amendment. Overtones of some arguments suggest that *Lochner* v. *New York*, 198 U.S. 45, should be our guide. But we decline that invitation. We do not sit as a super-legislature to determine the wisdom, need, and propriety of laws that touch economic problems, business affairs, or social conditions. This law, however, operates directly on an intimate relation of husband and wife and their physician's role in one aspect of that relation.

The association of people is not mentioned in the Constitution nor in the Bill of Rights. The right to educate a child in a school of the parents' choice—whether public or private or parochial—is also not mentioned. Nor is the right to study any particular subject or any foreign language. Yet the First Amendment has been construed to include certain of those rights. [Douglas then discusses a number of cases outlining these rights].

The foregoing cases suggest that specific guarantees in the Bill of Rights have penumbras, formed by emanations from those guarantees that help give them life and substance. Various guarantees create zones of privacy. The right of association contained in the penumbra of the First Amendment is one. The Third Amendment in its prohibition against the quartering of soldiers "in any house" in time of peace without the consent of the owner is another facet of that privacy. The Fourth Amendment explicitly affirms the "right of the people to be secure in their persons, houses, papers, and effects, against unreasonable searches and seizures." The Fifth Amendment in its Self-Incrimination Clause enables the citizen to create a zone of privacy which government may not force him to surrender to his detriment. The Ninth Amendment provides: "The enumeration in the Constitution, of certain rights, shall not be construed to deny or disparage others retained by the people."

The Fourth and Fifth Amendments were described in *Boyd* v. *U.S.*, 116 U.S. 616, as protection against all government invasions "of the sanctity of a man's home and the privacies of life." We recently referred in *Mapp* v. *Ohio*, 367 U.S. 643, to the Fourth Amendment as creating a "right to privacy, no less important than any other right carefully and particularly reserved to the people."

The present case, then, concerns a relationship lying within the zone of privacy created by several fundamental constitutional guarantees. And it concerns a law which, in forbidding the *use* of contraceptives rather than regulating their manufacture or sale, seeks to achieve its goals by means having a maximum destructive impact upon that relationship. Such a law cannot stand in light of the familiar principle, so often applied by this Court, that a "governmental purpose to control or prevent activities constitutionally subject to state regulation may not be achieved by means which sweep unnecessarily broadly and thereby invade the area of protected freedoms." *NAACP* v. *Alabama*, 377 U.S. 288. Would we allow the police to search the sacred precincts of marital bedrooms for telltale signs of the use of contraceptives? The very idea is repulsive to the notions of privacy surrounding the marriage relationship.

We deal with a right of privacy older than the Bill of Rights—older than our political parties, older than our school system. Marriage is a coming together for better or for worse, hopefully enduring, and intimate to the degree of being sacred. It is an association that promotes a way of life, not causes; a harmony in living, not political faiths; a bilateral loyalty, not commercial or social projects. Yet it is an association for as noble a purpose as any involved in our prior decisions.

Reversed.

Mr. Justice GOLDBERG, whom THE CHIEF JUSTICE and Mr. Justice BRENNAN join, concurring.

I agree with the Court that Connecticut's birth-control law unconstitutionally intrudes upon the right of marital privacy, and I join in its opinion and judgment. In reaching the conclusion that the right of marital privacy is protected, as being within the protected penumbra of specific guarantees of the Bill of Rights, the Court refers to the Ninth Amendment. I add these words to emphasize the relevance of that Amendment to the Court's holding. The language and history of the Ninth Amendment reveal that there are additional fundamental rights protected from governmental infringement, which exist alongside those fundamental rights specifically mentioned in the first eight constitutional amendments. The Amendment is almost entirely the work of James Madison. It was introduced in Congress by him and passed the House and Senate with little or no debate and virtually no change in language. It was proferred to quiet expressed fears that a bill of specifically enumerated rights could not be sufficiently broad to cover all essential rights and that the specific mention of certain rights would be interpreted as a denial that others were protected. [Justice Story] stated, referring to the Ninth Amendment:

This clause was manifestly introduced to prevent any perverse or ingenious misapplication of the well-known maxim, that an affirmation in particular cases implies a negation in all others.

These statements of Madison and Story make clear that the Framers did not intend that the first eight amendments be construed to exhaust the basic and fundamental rights which the Constitution guaranteed to the people

The Ninth Amendment to the Constitution may be regarded by some as a recent discovery and may be forgotten by others, but since 1791 it has been a basic part of the Constitution which we are sworn to uphold. To hold that a right so basic and fundamental and so deep rooted in our society as the right of privacy in marriage may be infringed because that right is not guaranteed in so many words by the first eight amendments to the Constitution is to ignore the Ninth Amendment and to give it no effect whatsoever.

In determining which rights are fundamental, judges are not left at large to decide cases in light of their personal and private notions. Rather they must look to the "traditions and [collective] conscience of our people" to determine whether a principle is "so rooted [there]…as to be ranked as fundamental." *Snyder* v. *Mass.*, 291 U.S. 97. The inquiry is whether a right involved "is of such a character that it cannot be denied without violating those 'fundamental principles of liberty and justice which lie at the base of all our civil and political institutions.'" *Powell* v. *Alabama*, 287 U.S. 45.

The entire fabric of the Constitution and the purposes that clearly underlie its specific guarantees demonstrate that the rights to marital privacy and to marry and raise a family are of similar order and magnitude as the fundamental rights specifically protected.

In sum, I believe that the right of privacy in the marital relation is fundamental and basic—a personal right "retained by the people" within the meaning of the Ninth Amendment. Connecticut cannot constitutionally abridge this fundamental right. I agree with the Court that petitioners' convictions must therefore be reversed.

Mr. Justice STEWART, whom Mr. Justice BLACK joins, dissenting.

Since 1879 Connecticut has had on its books a law which forbids the use of contraceptives by anyone. I think this is an uncommonly silly law. As a practical matter, the law is obviously unenforceable, except in the oblique context of the present case. As a philosophical matter, I believe the use of contraceptives in the relationship of marriage should be left to personal and private choice, based upon each individual's moral, ethical, and religious beliefs. As a matter of social policy, I think professional counsel about methods of birth control should be available to all, so that each individual's choice can be meaningfully made. But we are not asked in this case to say whether we think this law is unwise, or even asinine. We are asked to hold that it violates the United States Constitution. And that I cannot do.

In the course of its opinion the Court refers to no less than six Amendments to the Constitution: the First, the Third, the Fourth, the Fifth, the Ninth, and the Fourteenth. But the Court does not say which of these Amendments, if any, it thinks is infringed by this Connecticut law.

The Court also quotes the Ninth Amendment, and my brother GOLDBERG's concurring opinion relies heavily upon it. The Ninth Amendment was framed by James Madison and adopted by the States simply to make clear that the adoption of the Bill of Rights did not alter the plan that the *Federal* government was to be a government of express and limited powers and that all rights and powers not delegated to it were retained by the people and the individual states. Until today no member of this Court has ever suggested that the Ninth Amendment meant anything else, and the idea that a federal court could ever use the Ninth Amendment to annul a law passed by the elected representatives of the people of the State of Connecticut would have caused James Madison no little wonder.

What provision of the Constitution, then does make this state law invalid? The Court says it is the right of privacy "created by several fundamental constitutional guarantees." With all deference, I can find no such general right of privacy in the Bill of Rights, in any other part of the Constitution, or in any case ever decided by this Court.

At the oral argument in this case we were told that the Connecticut law does not "conform to current community standards." But it is not the function of this Court to decide cases on the basis of community standards. It is the essence of judicial duty to subordinate our own personal views, our own ideas of what legislation is wise and what is not. If, as I should surely hope, the law before us does not reflect the standards of the people of Connecticut, the people of Connecticut can freely exercise their true Ninth and Tenth Amendment rights to persuade their elected representatives to repeal it. That is the constitutional way to take this law off the books.

FOR DISCUSSION

1. Where in the Constitution does Justice Douglas find a right to privacy? What about Justice Goldberg? How convincing are their arguments?

2. Even though Justices Stewart and Black "think this is an uncommonly silly law," they vote to uphold it. Explain this apparent contradiction. Would they act differently if they were members of the Connecticut legislature?

3. Why does Bork criticize this decision? Do you agree with his criticisms?

4. Justice Brennan joins in both Douglas's and Goldberg's decisions. Explain how they reflect his philosophy of constitutional interpretation.

5. Eight years after this case, the Supreme Court ruled in *Roe* v. *Wade*, 410 U.S. 113, that the right to privacy included a woman's right to an abortion if the fetus was not yet viable. Was this a logical extension of *Griswold* or an example of overzealous judicial activism?

The following case deals with the interpretation of a state constitution. Most state constitutions are considerably longer and more detailed than the national constitution, giving the state's courts more provisions to interpret but less discretion in interpreting them. Because each state has its own constitution, its courts must interpret its meaning and determine whether state law conforms to the state constitution. Even if the wording of that constitution is the same as or similar to the federal constitution, state courts are free to interpret it differently. Because such interpretations are not federal questions, they are not subject to review by the U. S. Supreme Court unless they violate a federal law or provision of the United States Constitution.

CASE **State of Nebraska v. Public Employees Retirement Board**
Supreme Court of Nebraska (1987)
410 N.W. 2d 463.

PER CURIAM [A per curiam (for the court) opinion is one that represents the views of the court but is not signed by any single judge].   This is a declaratory judgment action, brought by the Attorney General of the State of Nebraska challenging the constitutionality of 1986 Neb. Laws, L.B. 1129. Respondents are public officers delegated duties to implement the law, including then Treasurer, now governor, Kay Orr.

L.B. 1129, which consists of 20 specific sections, attempts to create a pension program to provide retirement benefits to members of the Nebraska Legislature. Section 3 of the law establishes a retirement system to be known as the Legislators' Retirement System. Section 5 provides that the system is to be administered by the Public Employees Retirement Board and

9 creates a fund known as the Legislators' Retirement Fund. The act further provides that upon retirement eligible members shall receive a monthly allowance equal to $38 times the number of years of his or her creditable service, subject to certain other limitations set out in the act.

Each side cites to us a series of legal principles to be used when attempting to examine the constitutionality of a legislative act. We are reminded that statutes are presumed to be constitutional, and all reasonable doubt must be in favor of the statutes' constitutionality. The party challenging the constitutionality of a statute has the burden to show that it is unconstitutional. Courts must apply and must enforce the Constitution as it is written and constitutional provisions are not open to construction as a matter of course. Before construing a constitutional provision, it must be demonstrated that its meaning is not clear and that construction is necessary. If a constitutional provision is construed, its words and terms are to be interpreted in their most natural and obvious sense, although they should receive a more liberal construction than statutes and are not subject to rules of strict construction. The language of the Constitution is to be interpreted with reference to established laws, usages, and customs of the country at the time of its adoption, yet the terms and provisions of the Constitution "are constantly expanded and enlarged by construction to meet the advancing affairs of men." *State ex. rel. State Railway Commission* v. *Ramsey*, 37 N.W. 2d 502 (1949).

We turn first to the specific language of the Constitution which the Attorney General maintains invalidates L.B. 1129. The language in question is found in Art. III, Sec.7, and reads in relevant part as follows:

> Each member of the Legislature shall receive a salary of *not to exceed* four hundred dollars per month during the term of his office. In addition to his salary, each member shall receive an amount equal to his actual expenses in traveling by the most usual route once to and returning from each regular and special session of the Legislature. Members of the Legislature shall receive no pay nor perquisites other than said salary and expenses [Emphasis supplied by court.]

The question, simply stated, is: Does the granting of a retirement benefit to members of the Legislature constitute either "pay" or a "perquisite" otherwise prohibited by the provisions of Neb. Const. art. III, sec. 7?

While presented to us in a slightly different context, we did have an occasion to define the terms "pay" and "perquisite" in *State ex. rel. Douglas* v. *Beerman*, 347 N.W. 2d 297 (1984), where we said:

> Webster's third New International Dictionary, Unabridged (1968), tells us that "pay," as a noun, in an archaic sense, means, "something given in return by way of reward or retaliation"; that it is wages, salary, or remuneration. Black's Law Dictionary (5th ed. 1979) defines the noun "pay" as meaning compensation, wages, salary, commissions, or fees.
>
> "Perquisite" is defined in Webster's as casual income or profits; a privilege, gain or profit incidental to an employment in addition to regular salary or wages; a gratuity or tip; something held or claimed as an exclusive right or possession. Black's defines the word as meaning emoluments, fringe benefits, or other incidental profits or benefits attaching to an office or position.

We are unable to conceive how a retirement benefit awarded a former legislator for "creditable service" can be said not to be within one of the many meanings of either "pay" or "perquisites." Certainly the Legislature could not be making a gift of state money of its former members. The benefit can be nothing other than compensation for past services. Indeed, we have previously held that public employee retirement benefits or pensions constitute deferred compensation for services rendered. *Wilson* v. *Marsh*, 75 N.W. 2d 723 (1956).

Respondents point to decisions from other jurisdictions which they claim hold to the contrary. Relying on other decisions by other courts which in turn relied upon provisions of other constitutions serves little purpose in determining the meaning of our own specific Constitution.

Nonetheless, a careful analysis of the decisions upon which the respondents rely establishes that they differ from the situation presented by this case. *Knight* v. *Bd. etc. Employees' Retirement*, 196 P. 2d 547 (1948), reasoned that state legislators were state employees, and a constitutional provision specifically empowering the legislature to provide for the "payment of retirement salaries to employees of the State" modified the constitutional prohibition against legislators' receiving any "compensation for their services other than that fixed by the Constitution." Even if Nebraska's legislators are employees of the state, a question not before us and thus not decided, there is no Nebraska constitutional provision which modifies its prohibition against paying our legislators any "pay" or "perquisites" other than the specified salary and expenses.

The West Virginia Constitution prohibited paying legislators any "allowance or emolument" other than the salary and expenses specified in the Constitution. Yet *Campbell* v. *Kelly*, 202 S.E. 2d 369 (1974), held that the legislators' pension system constituted neither an "allowance" nor "emolument." In reaching that determination, the *Campbell* court noted it was dealing with language adopted in 1872, at which time 64 percent of the adult labor force was engaged in agriculture, there were no state pension plans in the country, and private pension plans were very rare. The *Campbell* court thus concluded that pension plans could not have been within the contemplation of the framers of the Constitution. The obvious distinction is that we are not dealing with 1872 language. The relevant date is 1934 and the record is silent as to the situation which then prevailed with respect to pension plans. More fundamentally, the rationale used by the *Campbell* court overlooks that, irrespective of whether the 1872 framers of the West Virginia Constitution contemplated pensions, they clearly stated that legislators were to receive nothing other than the sums specified in the Constitution. This jurisdiction is committed to the rule that the intent of the voters in adopting an initiative amendment to the Nebraska Constitution must be determined by the words of the initiative amendment itself, because there is no meaningful way to determine the motivations for submitting the initiative to the electorate or to determine the intent of those voting for its enactment.

Nor does the fact that the Legislature has chosen to declare the act constitutional in its preamble alter the true nature of the act. It is true that if the purpose of the act is unclear and the Legislature declares a public purpose which is not invalid on its face, a court will give strong consideration to the intent of the Legislature. Yet, if the act is clearly contrary to the Constitution, it is for the courts to make that decision, regardless of the proclaimed legislative intent. Such is the instant case.

Respondents have very properly and accurately described the great inequity our decision will bring about. Respondents specifically call our attention to the fact that under the current salary limitations members of the Nebraska Legislature are generally unable to save for old age security and, further, unable to earn credit in an alternate plan where they work because of their legislative duties. We are advised by respondents that, should we declare L.B. 1129 invalid, Nebraska's will be but one of only seven state legislatures which do not have pension programs for their members. While all of this is true and a fact which the people of the State of Nebraska should consider, it is not a basis upon which a court may ignore, nor amend, the provisions of the State's Constitution. Our function is to adhere to the Constitution, regardless of the inequities that may result.

L.B. 1129 is hereby declared to be invalid and unenforceable, and the respondents are hereby enjoined from performing any of the duties or obligations required thereunder.

FOR DISCUSSION

1. What principles does the Nebraska Supreme Court use in interpreting the State's constitution? Explain the logic behind these principles. Compare them to those articulated by Bork and by Brennan.
2. The key terms in this case are "pay" and "perquisites." How does the court determine their meaning?
3. Why does the court find rulings by courts of other states of no use?
4. In its preamble, the legislature declared the law constitutional. How significant is this? What does it tell you about the power of judicial review?
5. According to the legislators, overturning this law will bring about a "great inequity." Does the court agree or disagree? How does this affect their decision?
6. Would you classify this decision as interpretivist or noninterpretivist? How useful are these categories in understanding this case?

JUDICIAL SELECTION

One of the most controversial Supreme Court nominations in recent years was that of Robert Bork. Although Bork had served as a law professor, solicitor general, and U.S. Court of Appeals judge, his outspoken criticisms of many Supreme Court decisions led opponents to charge him with being outside the mainstream of constitutional interpretation and hostile to the claims of disadvantaged groups. The following two speeches are taken from the Senate debate. The Senate voted not to confirm him. Eventually, another conservative judge, Anthony Kennedy, was nominated by President Reagan and easily confirmed.

READING   **For Confirming Judge Bork**
By Senator Larry Pressler*

I rise in strong support of Judge Bork. I believe that he is a fine judge. When he was nominated to the U.S. Court of Appeals, he was unanimously approved. He was given the highest ratings by the American Bar Association. Basically, I think that our President deserves his choice for the Supreme Court, unless there is some overwhelming ethical or competence problem, or if the nominee is not in the mainstream of American judicial thinking.

Indeed, when President Carter was in office, I followed this philosophy and voted for many of his well qualified nominees even if I may have disagreed with some of their views. At that time, some urged me to vote against certain nominees for the court of appeals or elsewhere and it was my strongest conviction that under our Constitution a President is entitled to his nominee unless there is some overriding concern.

I think that the Supreme Court in the 1950's, 1960's, and 1970's has been a very liberal court, especially in the area of criminal law. I strongly believe that sometimes the victims of crime have fewer rights than the criminals. Because of the extensive Miranda warnings, many criminals can slip through loopholes, creating difficulties for prosecutors. The fact that the National Association of Sheriffs, the National Association of Prosecuting Attorneys, the National District Attorneys, the chiefs of police, and other law enforcement agencies have all endorsed Judge Bork indicates a desire for the Supreme Court not to have so many loopholes for criminals to use.The fact of the matter is that there is a feeling that it has become very difficult to prosecute criminals.

It has been my strongest feeling that the conservative side deserves an appointment. Ronald Reagan was elected and reelected. That is the way the system works. As a member of the U.S. Senate I am a believer in that system. I think it is the finest form of government devised by man.

I also happen to believe that Judge Bork is a fine man and a fair judge. He has written some provocative articles, and has taken some chances. He is a man, an academic man, who thinks and writes.

Are we to nominate only people to the Supreme Court who are so cautious in what they say and so careful in every word that they write that we get almost an intellectual eunuch on the Supreme Court? That is what is going to happen if we hold people to every sentence.

Let me say that I have been disturbed by some of the statements about Judge Bork. Some of the ads that have been run have been very misleading. It seems that the national media, which normally gets very upset when anything misleading is said, has been completely silent. It seems that Judge Bork has been fair game, so to speak.

There has been an effort to, somehow, portray Judge Bork as a person who is antiwoman and antiblack. I must say that the image that has been projected by the national media and by ads has been quite successful in that portrayal. But I have read his cases and a lot of his judicial record—not all of the record but a lot of it—and that is not true. Indeed, I would say he is prowoman and problack, in the sense of fairness.

So I shall vote with a great deal of pride and satisfaction for Judge Bork. I am disturbed by what has happened because I think we have politicized the nomination of a judge to the Supreme Court. I stand ready to evaluate the next nominee, if Judge Bork loses. However, I am saddened at making this speech because I believe very strongly that he deserves to be on the Supreme Court.

I also think that the country will miss out and future generations of law school will miss reading some great opinions. I think that the freedom that we enjoy and the role that the Supreme Court plays will not be as efficient, in terms of preserving freedom, dignity, and decency throughout our land.

But, worst of all, this sets a precedent, a very bad precedent, about the process of selecting a Supreme Court Justice. We are about to yield to a false national campaign and to Members becoming committed because of pressure groups. I am very, very saddened by this process.

READING   **Against Confirming Judge Bork**
*By Senator Alan Dixon**

Over the last several weeks we have heard a great deal about how the nomination of Judge Bork was treated by the Senate. I believe that Judge Bork received fair consideration by this body and will be rejected, not because of interest group campaigns, but based on problems with respect to his views on fundamental constitutional issues.

Both supporters and opponents of Judge Bork organized emotional, simplified appeals to mobilize public support and raise money for their position. In those appeals there have been excesses and exaggerations on both sides. That cannot be denied. However, it was not the efforts of grassroots citizens groups, or some media ads, that defeated the nomination; it was Judge Bork himself.

Public opinion polls clearly show that the advertising campaigns had no significant effect on how Judge Bork was viewed. The sharpest swing of public opinion against Judge Bork came as a direct result of his own 5-day testimony. The American people saw Judge Bork, considered his views on the Constitution, and rejected them.

When the President sent the nomination of Judge Bork to the Senate, my initial inclination was to favor the appointment. I had voted for Judge Bork's appointment to the D.C. Circuit Court of Appeals, and I remembered that the American Bar Association had rated him "exceptionally well qualified" for that position. Judge Bork was unanimously confirmed for the Circuit Court of Appeals.

However, after careful consideration, I decided to oppose the nomination of Judge Bork. My decision was not based on interest groups or media advertisements. Judge Bork's problems were caused by his own words in the Senate Judiciary Committee hearings, and in his writings.

I believe that the hearing process was very fair to Judge Bork. He testified before the committee for an unprecedented 5 days. He had an opportunity to fully present his views on fundamental constitutional issues and directly answer the charges of his critics. Judge Bork clearly had an ample time to make sure the Senate had a thorough and accurate record of his views. After hearing Judge Bork, I felt even more uncomfortable with his constitutional views regarding such important issues as civil rights, privacy, and equal protection.

During the Judiciary Committee hearings, it was not the public special interest groups that testified. Rather, the witnesses were a distinguished group of prominent lawyers, scholars, and government officials. The witnesses did not present simplified, emotional pleas, but instead provided detailed arguments regarding Judge Bork's record and writings. Sixty-two witnesses testified in support of Judge Bork's nomination, and 48 testified against. Clearly, there was more than a fair opportunity for Judge Bork's supporters to make their case before this body.

During these hearings it became clear to me and many of my colleagues that Judge Bork's judicial beliefs were not within the broad mainstream of American thought. It was not a question of conservative or liberal philosophy. Rather, it was a question of his fundamental views about our Constitution; how he sees the power of government and individual liberties; and the role he sees for the Court in protecting rights guaranteed by our Constitution.

President Reagan urged that the debate over Judge Bork not be politicized. Yet, in the next breath, he urges the public to call their Senators in support of Judge Bork. The President cannot have it both ways.

Furthermore, the debate on a Supreme Court nomination is inherently a political process—in the best sense of that phrase—and in a democratic society that is exactly what it should be. It is entirely appropriate for the Senate to examine Judge Bork's views on fundamental constitutional issues.

Let me say again that I do not object to the nomination of a judicial conservative to the Supreme Court. I think the President is entitled to nominees that share his philosophy. I have voted for judicial conservative nominees in the past, and I expect to support the nomination of judicial conservatives in the future.

The nominating process is working in the case of Judge Bork. He received fair and full consideration by the Senate. It was not the work of special interest groups distorting Judge Bork's views which caused Judge Bork problems. It was Judge Bork's views themselves, articulated by Judge Bork in the hearings and in his academic and legal opinions that have caused the majority in the Senate to reject his nomination.

NOTES

*Congressional Record, Vol. 133 (Oct.22), 1987.

FOR DISCUSSION

1. The Constitution gives the president the power to nominate "and by and with the Advice and Consent of the Senate" appoint Supreme Court justices. What factors should the Senate consider when voting on a nominee? Do you agree with Senator Pressler that "under our Constitution a President is entitled to his nominee unless there is some overriding concern"? Do you think Hamilton would agree?

2. How would Judge Bork's views expressed in "Judicial Review and Democracy" affect your opinion of whether he should have been confirmed? His critics pointed to his opposition to the Supreme Court's recognition of a constitutional right to privacy in *Griswold* as one reason they opposed him. Is this a valid reason?

3. Senators Pressler and Dixon both discuss public opinion. What role, if any, should it play in selecting Supreme Court justices?

4. The Senate had unanimously confirmed Bork as a judge of the Court of Appeals several years earlier. Then, in 1987, they voted to reject his nomination to the Supreme Court. Can you explain this?

5. According to Senator Dixon, "the debate on a Supreme Court nomination is inherently a political process." Explain what he means and whether you agree.

INHERENT COURT POWER

When it comes to court matters, judges are especially vigilant against encroachments from the other branches. In the next case, the Supreme Court of North Carolina uses its inherent power (one implied but not specifically stated by the constitution) to uphold one of its own orders against constitutional challenge. The Client Security Fund that the Court upholds is similar to many established by other states in recent years whose purpose is to compensate clients who have been victimized by unethical attorneys. Beard has no objections to such a fund but does not believe that the state's courts have the power under the North Carolina Constitution to require him to contribute to it.

CASE   **Beard v. North Carolina State Bar**
Supreme Court of North Carolina (1987)
357 S.E.2d 694

MARTIN, Justice.   The facts are undisputed. On 13 April 1984 defendant petitioned The Supreme Court of North Carolina to approve the establishment of the Client Security Fund. Thereupon an order of the Court was issued on 29 August 1984 which required each attorney admitted to practice in North Carolina to pay $50 each year into the fund, beginning with the year 1985. Plaintiff refused to make any payments pursuant to the Court order. For failing to make the 1985 payments, plaintiff's license to practice law in North Carolina was suspended by the North Carolina State Bar. Plaintiff does not challenge the validity of the structure and procedures of the fund.

Plaintiff's challenge is to the constitutionality of the Court's order requiring the annual payments. As plaintiff argues, if the order is valid, then the suspension of his license was lawful; otherwise not.

Plaintiff bases his challenge to the order requiring payments to the Client Security Fund solely on state constitutional grounds. No federal constitutional questions are at issue.

Plaintiff relies upon sections 6 and 8 of article I of the Constitution of North Carolina, the Declaration of Rights. Section 6 reads: "The legislative, executive, and supreme judicial powers of the State government shall be forever separate and distinct from each other." Section 8 reads: "The people of this State shall not be taxed or made subject to the payment of any impost or duty without the consent of themselves or their representatives in the General Assembly, freely given."

Simply put, plaintiff contends the payment is unconstitutional because under either provision only the General Assembly can impose such an obligation upon lawyers. We find no violation of either constitutional provision.

We recognize that our state constitution limits the plenary powers already existing in the government. Except as expressly limited by the constitution, the inherent power of the judicial branch of government continues.

The inherent power of the Court has not been limited by our constitution. To the contrary, the constitution protects such power. The General Assembly has no authority to deprive the judicial department "of any power or jurisdiction that rightfully pertains to it as a co-ordinate department of the government." N.C. Const. art.IV, sec. 1. Our courts have repeatedly made reference to and affirmed the existence and exercise of inherent judicial power. The existence of inherent judicial power is not dependent upon legislative action; however, we note that the General Assembly has recognized the existence of the inherent power of the court and that the General Assembly cannot abridge that power. N.C.G.S. 84-36 (1985).

Inherent power is that which the court necessarily possesses irrespective of constitutional provisions. Such power may not be abridged by the legislature. Inherent power is essential to the existence of the court and the orderly and efficient exercise of the administration of justice. Through its inherent power the court has authority to do all things that are reasonably necessary for the proper administration of justice.

We now turn to the issue of whether this Court's inherent power includes the authority to issue the order in question. We hold that it does. This Court has the inherent power to deal with its attorneys. As stated in *In re Burton*, 126 S.E.2d 581 (1962):

> The power is based upon the relationship of the attorney to the court and the authority which the court has over its own officers to prevent them from, or punish them for, committing acts of dishonesty or impropriety calculated to bring contempt upon the administration of justice.

The order by this Court requiring annual payments by attorneys to the Client Security Fund is an essential corollary to this function of the Court. This Court found in the order under consideration that attorneys by misuse of clients' property were bringing public disrespect upon the legal profession, the courts, and the administration of justice. It was necessary to establish the Client Security Fund to better protect the public and to promote public confidence in the courts and the administration of justice.

In ordering the assessment from attorneys for the support of the Client Security Fund, the Court was not imposing a tax, which is a legislative function. Rather, it was an act, found necessary by the Court, in aid of its own responsibility to see to the proper administration of justice. It is essential that the public have confidence in our system of justice in order for it to be effective. The public needed to know that it could safely entrust its property to members of the bar. Maintenance of the Client Security Fund through the assessment of attorneys was a major step in restoring that lost confidence.

The Court has the inherent authority to do what is reasonably necessary to effectuate its constitutional duty: the administration of justice. This Court has already manifested that inherent power. *In re Superior Court Order*, 338 S.E.2d 307 (1986) (requiring banks to disclose to district attorney bank records of customer); *State* v. *Davis*, 153 S.E.2d 749 (1967) (inherent power to appoint counsel for indigents). The order of this Court establishing the Client Security Fund was reasonably necessary to carry out the Court's constitutional duty to effectively administer justice.

We find three cases from our sister states to be persuasive. *In re Member of Bar*, 257 A.2d 382 (Del.1969), appeal dismissed, 396 U.S. 274 (1970), is on all fours with the case at bar. The Delaware Supreme Court by rule of court established a client security fund and required attorneys to contribute to it. That court held that the court rule was constitutional, not being a tax and being promulgated under the inherent power of the court to establish, control, and sustain the standards of the bar. [The Court then discussed similar cases from Maine and Massachusetts.]

We find the decisions of all three courts to be persuasive authority, and we adopt the reasoning of the Delaware court which is equally applicable to the instant case. Thus, we conclude that the payments required of plaintiff were not taxes but were funds required for the proper administration of justice. They were not for revenue but regulation. They were not levied generally, but only on a specific group involved with the administration of justice as officers of the court. Nor were the payments a general levy to support a public service.

An attorney, as an officer of the court, accepts his office subject to the burdens of the profession both in respect to the attorney's time and his purse. The order of this Court lawfully imposed such a burden upon the bar.

We hold the order of this Court of 29 August 1984 does not violate the Constitution of North Carolina.

FOR DISCUSSION

1. On what legal ground does Beard object to paying his fee into the Client Security Fund? Where does the North Carolina Supreme Court get the power to order him to pay?

2. What are inherent powers? Since they are not specifically listed in the constitution how do courts know what they are and what their limits are?

3. Why does the Court not agree with Beard that this fee is a tax? In his *Law Dictionary* (Barron's, 1975), Steven Gifis defines tax as "a rate or sum of money assessed on a citizen's person or property for the support of the government." Using this definition, explain whether you agree with the Court that this fee is not a tax.

4. Compare the use of cases from other states in *Beard* with that of the Nebraska Supreme Court in *State* v. *Public Employees Retirement Board*.

5. In this case, the Court is simultaneously refusing to uphold a constitutional challenge and upholding (and perhaps even expanding) its own power. Is this a case of judicial activism or of self-restraint?

6. If the state legislature passed a law eliminating the $50 fee do you think the Court would uphold it? Explain your reasoning.

STATUTORY INTERPRETATION

Interpreting the meaning of laws is one of the most basic functions of courts. We have therefore included three examples. In the first, when an Illinois court finds that the apparent meaning of a section of a law taxing alcoholic beverages conflicts with its overall goal, they use some creative interpretation to reconcile the two.

CASE   Federated Distributors, Inc. v. Johnson
                                      Appellate Court of Illinois (1987)
                                            516 N.E.2d 471

Justice LINN delivered the opinion of the court: Plaintiff Federated Distributors, Inc.
(Federated) brings this appeal seeking reversal of a trial court order which upheld the
constitutionality of an Illinois Department of Revenue (the Department) ruling imposing
a $2 per gallon tax on a product produced by Federated. The tax in question was imposed
pursuant to the Liquor Control Act (the Act). Under the Act, manufacturers of wine or
wine coolers containing less than 14% alcohol must pay a $.23 per gallon tax, while
manufacturers of "spirits" must pay a $2.00 per gallon tax. Federated manufactures "New
Products," a spirit-based fruit flavored drink similar to a "wine cooler." Although New
Products contains less than 14% alcohol, the Department determined that because the
alcohol in New Products was obtained from distillation rather than fermentation, the act
required Federated to pay the $2 per gallon tax.

   Important to the present dispute is the Act's distinction between "wine" and "spirits."
Under the Act, wine or wine coolers contain alcohol produced by fermentation, while spirits,
or "hard liquors," such as rum and whisky, contain alcohol derived from distillation. Wine
or wine coolers containing less than 14% alcohol are taxed at $.23 per gallon, while hard
liquor is taxed at $2 per gallon.

   In the instant case, New Products is an alcoholic drink which is produced from a
combination of water, flavoring, fruit juices, vegetable juices, sugar, corn syrup, artificial
carbonation and fortified by the addition of spirits. The alcohol in New Products is produced
by distillation rather than fermentation.

   The parties agree on the case law applicable to the issues raised in this appeal. It is well
settled that the legislature has broad powers in the area of establishing classifications to define
subjects of taxation. There is a general presumption favoring the validity of classifications created
by legislative bodies in taxing matters and the party who attacks the classification has the burden
of proving that the classification is unconstitutional. The legislature's authority is limited only
in that it cannot exercise its taxing power arbitrarily; the legislature must not, under the guise of
a "classification," discriminate against one and in favor of another where both are similarly
situated. Classifications created by the legislature must be based upon real and substantial
differences of condition or situation between those subject to the tax and those excluded and
must bear some reasonable relationship to the purpose of the legislation. Courts have found
classifications unconstitutional where the statute in question included within a class those in fact
not within it or have excluded from a class those properly belonging to it.

   In the case at bar, the parties' respective positions are fairly straightforward. The Department asserts that under the language of the Act, New Products falls within the definition of a
spirit. The Department points out, and Federated agrees, that the alcohol in New Products is
obtained from a distilling process rather than from fermentation. Therefore, New Products is a
"beverage which contains alcohol obtained by distillation and mixed with water or other
substances." (Ill. Rev. Stat. 1985, ch.43, par.95.02). That being the case, it is the Department's
contention that New Products is subject to the $2 per gallon tax, rather than the $.23 per gallon
tax, for New Products is, under the precise language of the Act, a spirit rather than a wine.

   Federated, on the other hand, argues that there is no real and substantial difference
between New Products and wine and wine coolers and that to tax New Products as a "spirit"
rather than a wine-based product is therefore unconstitutional. It is Federated's position that

New Products contains the same percentage of alcohol as wine and wine coolers, contains essentially the same ingredients, and is sold to the same consumer base. Federated further contends that the only distinction between New Products and wine and wine coolers is that the alcohol used in New Products is obtained through a different process from that used in wine and wine coolers. Finally, Federated asserts that classifying New Products with other "hard liquors" frustrates the Act's stated purpose; namely, fostering and promoting temperance in the consumption of alcoholic liquors.

Statutory construction demands that a court of law ascertain legislative intent not only from the language employed in a particular statute, but also from the law's purpose as gleamed from the overall spirit of the statute. In so doing, we should be mindful of the subject matter addressed by the statute and the legislature's apparent objective in enacting it.

In the present case we agree with Federated.

To begin, New Products and wine or wine coolers are virtually identical in every aspect except one; the method in which the alcohol in each product is obtained. Distillation and fermentation, however, are both simply processes. The purpose of each process, in the world of liquors, is to produce the same object: alcohol. It is the alcohol, not the process from which it is derived, that the Act is meant to regulate. New Products can only be classified differently from wine or wine coolers, therefore, if there exists a real and substantial difference between the ingredients and alcoholic content of New Products and the ingredients and alcoholic content of wine or wine coolers. However, since the ingredients in New Products are nearly identical to that of wine or wine coolers, and since the percentage of alcohol in both is precisely the same, there exists no real or substantial difference between the two types of beverages. To differentiate between two nearly identical alcoholic beverages based only on the process or method used to produce a single ingredient in those beverages constitutes an unreasonable and illogical interpretation of the Act.

The evil sought to be remedied by the Act is also not served by the Department's interpretation. The evil addressed by the Act is the abuse of alcohol. The Act seeks to alleviate that danger by making certain alcoholic beverages more expensive than others. The legislature determined that a greater danger of abuse is posed by these beverages, such as hard liquors which have a higher alcoholic content. As a means of discouraging their consumption, the Act places a higher tax on these beverages. Similarly, a lower tax is placed on beverages with a lower alcoholic content because they pose less danger of abuse when consumed.

Consequently, because New Products is, by its alcoholic content, in the same class as wine and wine coolers, taxing New Products at a higher rate bears no rational relationship to the evil sought to be remedied; a beverage of the least alcoholic content, and thus the least danger of abuse, is being taxed at the same rate as those posing the greatest danger of abuse. To be consistent with the overall theme of the Act, New Products should be taxed at the lowest rate as it poses the least danger of abuse.

In the same vein, placing a higher tax on New Products runs contrary to the Act's express purpose. The Act specifically states that "temperance in the consumption of alcoholic liquors shall be fostered and promoted...."

The Act's elevated taxation scheme reveals the legislature's attempt to promote temperance by making the price of certain beverages more expensive than the price of others. Running throughout the Act is a single consistent theme: the tax charged to a specific beverage is based on the danger of potential abuse which, in turn, is reflected in the percentage of alcohol which that beverage contains. Based on that legislative purpose, it is apparent that placing New Products in the same classification as hard liquors runs contrary to the legislature's intent.

In sum, we can find no real and substantial difference between the ingredients and alcoholic content contained in New Products and that contained in wine and wine coolers. Second, placing New Products in the same classification as hard liquors bears no rational relationship to the evil sought to be remedied by the act. And third, placing New Products in any classification other than that enjoyed by wine or wine coolers is contrary to the legislature's intent of promoting temperance through varying tax rates.

Accordingly, for the reasons set forth above, we reverse the trial court's ruling affirming the Department's decision and order that New Products be taxed at the same rate currently applicable to wine and wine coolers.

FOR DISCUSSION

1. How clearly does the Liquor Control Act distinguish between "wine" and "spirits"? In light of the law's wording, does the ruling of the Department of Revenue seem reasonable?

2. How does Justice Linn determine the purpose of the law? Why is its purpose important?

3. Would you classify this decision as interpretivist or noninterpretivist?

4. Was the outcome of this case a fair one? How logical is the Court's reasoning?

5. If you were a state legislator would you try to change this law? If so, how?

As in the previous case, *James* v. *Rowe* also requires a court to determine the intent of the legislature in enacting a series of laws. Be sure to compare the approaches of the two courts in both reading the words of the statutes and ascertaining the purposes of the legislatures in passing them.

CASE

James v. Rowe
U.S. District Court, Kansas (1987)
674 F. Supp. 332

SAFFELS, District Judge.   This case arises out of an accident that occurred at Tanglewood Lake on March 30, 1986. The plaintiff suffered a head injury, and defendants were called to the scene of the accident to provide emergency care and to transport him to a hospital capable of treating his injuries. Plaintiff claims defendants were negligent in treating him at the scene and in failing to transport him immediately to a facility capable of treating his injuries. Defendants now argue that the Kansas Good Samaritan Law, K.S.A. 65-2891 *et seq.* exempts them from all liability for ordinary negligence.

The Kansas Good Samaritan Law was passed in 1965 and has been amended several times since. It provides that:

> (a) Any health provider who in good faith renders emergency care or assistance at the scene of an emergency or accident...shall not be liable for any civil damages for acts or omissions other than damages occasioned by gross negligence or by willful or wanton acts or omissions by such person in rendering such emergency care.

To the casual reader, it might appear from the plain language of the statute that this statute abrogates defendants' liability in this case. Generally, when construing a statute a court must give words their ordinary meaning and construe the language in the context of the statute. However, we reject the notion that the Kansas Legislature intended to extinguish the law of common law negligence for all health care which might be given in an emergency. Such would be a far-sweeping move which would have consequences not only for ambulance services but for doctors, nurses, insurance carriers, and indeed the entire medical profession. We do not believe that other health care legislation or the legislative history of K.S.A. 65-2891 bears out defendants' misguided conclusion. In interpreting legislative acts, a court must give a statute that construction which is consistent with the intent and purpose of the statute, even if that construction is not within the literal meaning of the statute.

Plaintiff directs the court to two additional statutes that apply to ambulance attendants. K.S.A. 65-4307 abrogates the ambulance attendant's ordinary negligence when he or she is acting at the instruction of a doctor or nurse. K.S.A. 65-4337 exempts the ambulance attendant from liability for ordinary negligence when performing manual cardiac defibrillation. K.S.A. 4307 was passed in 1974, and K.S.A. 65-4337 was passed in 1985. If the Kansas Legislature intended the Good Samaritan Law to abrogate all ordinary negligence of the ambulance attendant acting in an emergency, then K.S.A. 65-4307 and 65-4337 would have been unnecessary and duplicative. There would have been no need to pass the additional statutes specifying certain instances when an ambulance attendant is exempt from liability, because the attendant would already be exempt in all emergency situations under K.S.A. 65-2891.

Certainly, then, the Kansas Legislature must have meant something else when it passed the Good Samaritan Law. Although we have no legislative history from the statute's original passage, records surrounding the passage of amendments since 1965 reveal the Legislature's true purpose behind the Good Samaritan Law.

In 1976, the Legislature added several professions to the list of health care providers covered by the statute, including pharmacists, optometrists, and mobile intensive care technicians. In its support of the bill, the Kansas Department of Health and Environment stated that the benefit of the amendment would be that it would "increase the chances of an accident victim receiving care." This comment indicates an underlying assumption that the bill sought to encourage anyone with medical training to assist a person in a medical emergency. There is certainly no indication that medical personnel in the ordinary course of their duties were refusing to treat patients in emergency situations for fear of later being sued. Such an assumption would border on absurdity. Instead, the Department of Health and Environment went on to state that the purpose of the bill was to reassure those "who now might not want to stop and help." Again, this language indicates a desire to encourage medically-trained personnel to "stop and help" anyone he or she might happen upon in an emergency situation.

This conclusion is in accord with the purpose behind the Good Samaritan laws now in effect in all fifty states. No Kansas court has before interpreted this state's law. However, those states which have interpreted similar laws have uniformly held that the law is not meant to exempt all medical personnel in every emergency situation, but only those personnel who happen across an emergency outside the normal course of their work and who otherwise have no duty to assist. See, e.g. *Colby* v. *Schwartz*, 78 Cal.App.3d 885 (1978) and *Lindsey* v. *Miami*, 689 S.W.2d 856 (Tenn.1985).

Finally, the court finds no merit in defendants' arguments that the 1987 Kansas Legislature's passage of the Certified First Responder Act supports their argument. They assert that by passing that Act, the Legislature meant to reinforce the fact that all health care providers' negligence is abrogated in an emergency situation. The simple purpose of the Certified First Responder Act was to create a new branch of medical care, by providing certification for firefighters, police officers, and others trained in first aid who are usually the first to arrive on the scene of an accident. The Legislature did not intend to "reinforce" the abrogation of negligence in all emergency situations because that was not the original intent behind the Good Samaritan Law.

IT IS BY THE COURT THEREFORE ORDERED that defendants Charles Rowe and Marjorie Rowe, d/b/a Linn County Ambulance Service, Inc.'s motion to dismiss for failure to state a claim is denied.

FOR DISCUSSION

1. Judge Saffels writes in his opinion, "To the casual reader, it might appear from the plain language of the statute that this statute abrogates defendants' liability in this case." What does he mean by this? Why does he disagree with such a "casual" reading?

2. How does Judge Saffels discover the intent of the state legislature? Compare his approach to that used in *Federated Distributors* v. *Johnson*.

3. What other law do the defendants cite in support of their arguments? How does Judge Saffels interpret that law?

4. Is this decision likely to have important consequences for any groups not involved in this case? If you were a member of the state legislature would this decision cause you to take any action? Explain your answer.

In this chapter's final case, a New York court is faced with two laws whose purposes appear to be inconsistent. The state's Insurance Law prohibits discrimination in the terms and conditions of life insurance on account of race or religion but not sex. However, the National Organization for Women argues that the state's Human Rights Law forbids such sex discrimination. The court seeks to reconcile the two by carving out separate spheres of action for each.

CASE   **National Organization for Women v. Metropolitan Life Insurance Co.**
Supreme Court, Appellate Division, First Department (1987)
516 N.Y.S.2d 934.

MEMORANDUM DECISION.   By summons and class action complaint dated October 9, 1985, the National Organization for Women and individual plaintiffs commenced this action for declaratory, compensatory, and injunctive relief against Metropolitan Life Insurance Company, arguing that defendant's refusal to sell, offer and advertise for sale to women life insurance and disability insurance policies on the same terms as for men is a discriminatory practice in violation of Executive Law 296(2)(a) (hereinafter the "Human Rights Law").

Defendant moved to dismiss the complaint for failure to state a cause of action on the grounds that certain provisions of the Insurance Law of New York State, enacted subsequent to the Human Rights Law, specifically sanctioned gender based risk classifications with respect to life and disability insurance policies. Special Term denied the motion. The court first determined that insurance companies fell within the ambit of Executive Law 296(2)(a) as providers of goods or services and therefore were subject to that statute's restrictions against denying anyone any advantages or privileges on the basis of gender. Then, relying on *Brooklyn Union Gas Company* v. *the New York State Human Rights Appeals Board*, 359 N.E.2d 393, the court concluded that the Human Rights Law, in imposing a greater obligation not to discriminate on the basis of gender, took precedence over the Insurance Law and created a cause of action herein.

A reading of *Brooklyn Union Gas Co.* and application of the basic rules of statutory construction, compel us to reverse the order appealed from, as there is no statutory cause of action under the Human Rights Law to challenge the alleged forms of gender discrimination raised herein.

To determine whether under these facts a cause of action for gender discrimination exists under the Human Rights Law, it is necessary to construe in conjunction with the Human Rights Law various provisions of the Insurance Law which sanction limited forms of gender classifications. In 1952 the Executive Law was amended to provide that it is unlawful for any "place of public accommodation, resort or amusement...to refuse, withhold from or deny to [any] person any of the accommodations, advantages, facilities or privileges thereof..." on the basis of, among other things, a person's sex. In 1960, the phrase "place of public accommodation, resort or amusement" was expressly defined to further clarify the jurisdiction of the State Commission Against Discrimination. Subsequent to this, the Insurance Law was also amended. As of 1961 Insurance Law 2606 expressly prohibited discrimination in the offering, renewal, or the establishment of the terms and conditions of life and disability insurance policies on the basis of an applicant's race, color, creed or national origin. Omitted from this section, however, is any ban on distinctions or discrimination based on sex. Section 2607 of the Insurance Law does specifically address sex discrimination, but provides only that:

> No individual or entity shall refuse to issue any policy of insurance or cancel or decline to renew such policy because of sex or marital status of the applicant or policy holder.

That the Insurance Law permits distinctions based on sex in the terms and conditions, but not the offering, of life and disability insurance policies is further demonstrated by Sections 4221(g)(6) and (h)(2) which permit certain "age set-back" gender-based adjustments in establishing the premiums and present values of life and other disability insurance policies.

To resolve the conflict between the general proscription against sex discrimination in the Human Rights Law and the limited proscription contained in the Insurance Law, we are to be guided by the canons of statutory construction. We are mindful, first of all, that in construing legislative enactments our role is not to determine the wisdom or propriety of any particular statute, or to correct supposed errors, omissions or defects, but simply and foremost to ascertain and give effect to the intent of the Legislature and to avoid construing any statute in such a way as to render it ineffective.

While it is the duty of courts, if at all possible and consistent with the canons of statutory interpretation, to construe two separate statutes in harmony, it is well recognized that a special statute in irreconcilable conflict with a general statute covering the same subject matter is controlling insofar as the special act applies. Furthermore, when two statutes utterly conflict with each other, the later constitutional enactment ordinarily prevails. Finally, we must presume that when the Legislature acts, it does so with full knowledge of its existing statutes.

In view of the foregoing, it is obvious that in amending the Insurance Law the Legislature intended that the Human Rights Law, which generally prohibits gender discrimination in the offering of services and privileges, would not override the later, more specific legislation in the Insurance Law expressly permitting use of some gender classifications with regard to the terms and conditions of life and disability insurance policies.

Notwithstanding repeated opportunities to do so, the Legislature has chosen not to amend Insurance Law 2606, so as to include a ban on gender-based discrimination in the terms and conditions of insurance policies. Instead, by an amendment to the Insurance Law which post-dates the Human Rights Law statute prohibiting sex discrimination, a widely publicized statute, the Legislature chose only to ban gender-based discrimination within the insurance industry with regard to the availability of insurance to women.

The Legislature's actions subsequent to passage of the Human Rights Law bespeak a clear intent to ban only limited forms of sex-based classifications in the insurance industry, and it is not our role to question the Legislature's wisdom in this regard. We have no choice but to determine that the Insurance Law provisions, being more specific and having been enacted subsequent to the Human Rights Law, are controlling with regard to establishing the terms and conditions of insurance policies. Accordingly, Executive Law 296(2)(a), the sole basis of plaintiffs' complaint, has no application to defendant's gender-based risk classification, rate-making policies which are expressly sanctioned by the Insurance Law.

Such a reading comports with our obligation to as far as possible not construe statutes so as to render one ineffective or a superfluous exercise in legislation. The Executive Law continues to apply generally to ban gender discrimination to providers of services or privileges, but within the context of the insurance industry, a legislative exception to the earlier rule of limited application, exists.

Special Term's reliance on *Brooklyn Union Gas Co.* was misplaced. In that case the court was obliged to resolve the incongruity between the Disability Benefits Law, which set minimum standards for disability benefits in the area of private employment, and the Executive Law 296(1)(a), banning sex discrimination in the compensation, terms, conditions or privileges of employment. Having been enacted subsequently to the Disability Benefits Law and applying a different command with respect to gender discrimination in employment, the court ruled that in those areas of employment within the reach of both statutes, the Human Rights Law rendered the Disability Benefits Law dormant. The court found that for those employers with three or fewer employees, those employees outside the commands of the Executive Law, the Disability Benefits Law was still operative. It is apparent then that the court in *Brooklyn Union Gas Co.* was merely applying general rules of statutory construction. In the present instance, however, it is the Human Rights Law which has been rendered dormant in the area of risk classification for life and disability insurance policies.

Because this action seeks a declaration of rights, in addition to compensatory and injunctive relief, we are obligated to declare that defendant has not violated the Human Rights Law, and we direct that the remainder of the complaint be dismissed for failure to state a cause of action.

FOR DISCUSSION

1. In this case the National Organization for Women is challenging the common insurance company practice of charging different rates to men and women. Why do insurance companies have such rates? If you were a New York state legislator would you support a bill to outlaw this practice?

2. What laws does the court find relevant? Is there a conflict between them?

3. How does the court interpret the intent of the legislature? What evidence do they cite to support their view? Is there any other evidence that they might have considered?

4. On what precedent did the lower court base its decision? How does the Appellate Division distinguish between the two cases?

5. Compare the approach to statutory interpretation used in this case to those used in the previous two. Are all three fairly similar or do you see significant differences?

6. What do you think Bork and Brennan would have to say about this decision?

LEGAL TERMS TO KNOW

Inherent power
Interpretivism
Judicial activism
Judicial review
Judicial self-restraint

Legislative intent
Missouri Plan
Per curiam opinion
Statutory interpretation

ADDITIONAL QUESTIONS AND EXERCISES

1. In *U.S.* v. *Butler*, 297 U.S. 1 (1936), Supreme Court Justice Owen Roberts wrote, "When an act of Congress is appropriately challenged in the courts as not conforming to the constitutional mandate, the judicial branch of the Government has only one duty—to lay the article of the Constitution which is invoked beside the statute which is challenged and to decide whether the latter squares with the former." Explain what you think of this approach, citing the materials in this chapter to support your opinion.

2. Hamilton claims that the American court system is a great improvement over that of Great Britain. Read some material on the British courts and compare the two systems, explaining which you prefer. A good place to start is Henry J. Abraham, *The Judicial Process: An Introductory Analysis of the Courts of the United States, England, and France*, (5th ed.). New York: Oxford University Press, 1986.

3. How are judges chosen in your state? Write an essay that either supports this method or proposes an alternative.

4. In interpreting a statute, judges often have to determine the intent of the legislature. Explain how much weight should be given to each of the following types of evidence of legislative intent—legislative debate, committee reports, statements by sponsors of the bill, interpretations of similar laws by courts of other states, other related state laws, other sections of the same law, and previous versions of the current law. Use the cases in this chapter to back up your arguments.

5. Explain whether you would prefer to serve in a state legislature or be an appellate judge.

FOR FURTHER READING

1. ABRAHAM, HENRY, *Justices and Presidents* (2nd ed.). New York: Oxford University Press, 1985.
2. BALL, HOWARD, *Courts and Politics*. Englewood Cliffs, N.J.: Prentice Hall, 1980.
3. CHOPER, JESSE, *Judicial Review and the National Political Process*. Chicago: University of Chicago Press, 1980.
4. HENSCHEN, BETH, "Statutory Interpretations of the Supreme Court: Congressional Response," *American Politics Quarterly*, 11 (October 1983), 441–58.
5. *The Judicial Power and the Constitution, Judicature*, 71 (August/September 1987).
6. WHITE, EDWARD G., *The American Judicial Tradition*. New York: Oxford University Press, 1976.

3

DUE PROCESS
OF LAW

INTRODUCTION

The Fifth Amendment prohibits the federal government from depriving anyone of life, liberty, or property without due process of law, a protection the Fourteenth Amendment extended to apply to the states. The familiarity of the phrase due process, however, can hide its complexity. As Justice Felix Frankfurter put it in the case of *Joint Anti-Fascist Refugee Committee* v. *McGrath*, 341 U.S. 123 (1951):

> "Due process," unlike some legal rules, is not a technical conception with a fixed content unrelated to time, place, and circumstances. ...Due process is not a mechanical instrument. It is not a yardstick. It is a delicate process of adjustment inescapably involving the exercise of judgment by those whom the Constitution entrusted with the unfolding of the process.

How can we understand a concept without a fixed meaning? Fortunately, that concept is so fundamental to our freedom and its history so rich with detail that we can set out standards for judgment even if exact definition is impossible.

The Limits of Due Process

Due process is basically a guarantee of government fairness. Government cannot take our lives, liberty, or property unless it provides us with the fair chance to protect our interests that is due process. In other words, the due process clauses protect us from arbitrary and unreasonable actions by government. This sets out the first limits of the concept. First, it applies to government actions, not private ones. When the Fifth Amendment was ratified, government played a relatively small role in the lives of most citizens so the distinction was clear. One of the major changes in our society has been the growth of government into virtually all areas of life. This has often created situations intertwining public and private action, making the boundary between the two more difficult to draw. Thus, the actions of a public college are covered by the due process guarantee but what about a private college that gets a substantial amount of government funding? In one of the cases presented in this chapter, a court will have to decide whether actions by a privately owned but state-regulated race track constitute state action for the purposes of due process. Such examples can be easily multiplied.

A second limit is that due process applies only to something—life, liberty, or property—that belongs to the person being deprived. If there is no such entitlement, there can be no deprivation, hence no requirement of due process. Thus, government cannot execute you, incarcerate you, or take something you own unless it acts within the guidelines of due process of law. However, a public hospital could ban smoking without violating the due process rights of smokers because there is no right to smoke. Even though smokers may be significantly inconvenienced, they are not being denied life, liberty, or property. The chapter on property will discuss what is or is not property subject to the protection of the due process guarantee.

Procedural and Substantive Due Process

Traditionally, due process has been divided into two areas: procedural and substantive. Originally, due process referred to the procedures by which laws were carried out. Procedural due process requires that before any deprivation, there must be notice and opportunity for a fair hearing before someone neutral and competent. The concept of due process was soon expanded to include substantive due process, which requires that laws be reasonable attempts to achieve legitimate government goals while putting the least burden on people's rights. It also requires laws to be clear enough so that citizens know what is allowed and what is not. Under the doctrine of substantive due process, the courts examine the content of laws to ensure that they do not violate traditional notions of fairness. This may require courts to protect rights that are not explicitly stated in the Constitution, giving judges significant discretion in determining what those rights are. Today, most legal scholars agree that the Supreme Court went overboard during the early twentieth century, using substantive due process to overturn economic reforms with which the justices disagreed. These decisions so discredited the concept that it nearly disappeared for a time. That is why Justice Douglas included language specifically refusing to base his decision in *Griswold* v. *Connecticut* (included in the previous chapter) on substantive due process.

This caution has not prevented courts from continuing to use substantive due process but the major change has been that it is now used more to protect civil rights than economic ones. During the first decades of the twentieth century, the Supreme Court used such "rights" as the right to enter into a contract to invalidate minimum wage, maximum hour, and child labor laws. Today society's values have changed so much that these decisions appear mistaken to most people. Courts are now more likely to use civil rights such as the right to privacy to limit what government can do. The concept of substantive due process is one of the clearest examples of how much changes in society result in changes in the meaning and application of legal doctrines.

Procedural due process is probably the more familiar of the two types. It requires fair procedures before government can deprive someone of life, liberty, or property; however, the Constitution makes little attempt to define these procedures except in criminal cases for which the Bill of Rights provides specific guarantees such as the right to counsel, to confront witnesses, and to avoid compelled self-incrimination. As indicated by the quote from Justice Frankfurter, the courts have held that the procedural requirements of due process vary with the situation. In general, the person being deprived must be given adequate notice and a fair hearing at which to present his or her side to a disinterested party. The greater the deprivation, the more formal the hearing, with criminal trials providing the greatest protection and minor deprivations the least. Conversely, emergency situations can justify more expedited procedures. There are many other factors that can affect the procedures necessary to meet the due process requirement. The materials in this chapter will help clarify this by looking at some of the specifics.

This introduction should provide a basic understanding of the main points of due process. Although it cannot be defined with precision, it is a basic guarantee requiring that when government deprives someone of life, liberty, or property, it must do so in a manner that both is and appears to be fair. This may give courts considerable discretion but it also provides the flexibility necessary to avoid injustice.

GOVERNMENT ACTION

In the following case, a Pennsylvania court has to decide whether actions by a state-regulated race track are government action necessary to trigger the due process clause. It also has to decide whether Staino was deprived of something he is entitled to—life, liberty, or property—when he was ejected from his seat by the racing association.

CASE **Staino v. Pennsylvania State Horse Racing Commission**
Commonwealth Court of Pennsylvania (1986)
512 A.2d 75.

BARBIERI, Senior Judge. Ralph Staino appeals here the adjudication of the Pennsylvania State Horse Racing Commission dismissing his appeal after being ejected from Keystone Race Track by the Eagle Downs Racing Association.

The Commission, after hearing, found that Mr. Staino was present at Keystone Race Track as a patron on September 29, 1982, when he was served with an ejection notice by a representative of the Eagle Downs Racing Association, a licensed corporation. The Commission concluded that, since under Section 215 of the Horse Race Industry Reform Act a licensed corporation's authority to eject patrons from the race track is limited only to the extent that the person may not be ejected because of his race, color, creed, sex, national origin or religion, and, since Mr. Staino had not established a prima facie case of ejectment for one or more of the prohibited reasons, his appeal must be dismissed.

Mr. Staino argues on appeal that a race track, because it raises revenue for the state through pari-mutuel betting and because it is closely regulated by the state, is a quasi-public facility whose actions are governed by the due process clause of the Fourteenth Amendment, that he was denied his constitutional right to attend the race track, and that the Commission's findings and conclusions are not supported by the substantial evidence of record.

We address Mr. Staino's argument that because the racing association operates a quasi-public facility that it is, therefore, bound by the Fourteenth Amendment to the Constitution. Mr. Staino refers to Eagle Downs and to the Commission interchangeably and without distinction provided by statute. Of course, ejection by the Commission is state action and thus, the statute provides certain procedural safeguards including a requirement that the ejection be for cause and that the person ejected be provided a hearing on the issue of cause.

The action of the private racing association, albeit a licensed corporation, in ejecting a patron is not state action. In *Jackson* v. *Metropolitan Edison Co.*, 419 U.S. 345 (1974), the United States Supreme Court set forth the following test for state action:

> ...the inquiry must be whether there is a sufficiently close nexus between the State and the challenged action of the regulated entity so that the action of the latter may be fairly treated as that of the State itself.

Mr. Staino would establish the nexus by pointing out that the racing association is closely regulated by the Commission, a state agency. Because a private corporation is licensed and pervasively regulated by the state does not make its actions "state action" meaning that those actions must comport with the requirements of the Fourteenth Amendment to the Constitution. In *Jackson*, the Supreme Court held that the action of a partial monopoly, a highly regulated utility company, in terminating service to a customer did not constitute state action.

Moreover, the fact that a private party follows a procedure outlined in a state statute does not convert the private action into state action. This contention was raised and disposed of in *Jackson* in which the plaintiff argued that the termination of utility service in a manner approved by the public utility commission constituted state action:

> Respondent's exercise of the choice allowed by state law where the initiative comes from it and not from the State does not make its action in doing so 'state action' for purposes of the Fourteenth Amendment.

Mr. Staino has not argued that Eagle Downs in conducting race meetings at Keystone Race Track is exercising a power traditionally reserved to the state nor that there is a symbiotic relationship between the state and the racing association as is present when a private corporation leases its facilities from the state. The only case cited by Staino in his brief in support of his argument that the ejection in the instant case constituted state action is *Jacobson* v. *New York Racing Association, Inc.*, 350 N.Y.S.2d 639, 305 N.E.2d 765 (1973). *Jacobson* is inapposite for several reasons. First, Jacobson was not a patron, but an owner and trainer of horses, i.e., a licensee. Also, the exclusion of Jacobson was by the New York Racing Association, a non-profit racing association which is incorporated under New York statute for the express purpose of owning and operating New York's racing facilities pursuant to a franchise granted by New York's racing commission. Thus, the relationship between the NYRA and the state of New York is symbiotic in nature. While the decisional law of the State of New York is not binding on this Court, we note that in *Presti* v. *New York Racing Association*, 363 N.Y.S.2d 24 (1975), citing *Jacobson*, the court reaffirmed the rule that the NYRA could eject an unlicensed person without cause.

We conclude that the Commonwealth of Pennsylvania is not sufficiently connected with Eagle Downs' action in ejecting Mr. Staino so as to make Eagle Downs' conduct in doing so attributable to the state for purposes of the Fourteenth Amendment.

In any event, contrary to Mr. Staino's argument, Mr. Staino has no constitutional right to a seat at the race track denial of which by state action would entitle him to the procedural protections of the Fourteenth Amendment. "The requirements of procedural due process apply only to the deprivation of interests encompassed by the Fourteenth Amendment's protection of liberty and property." *Board of Regents* v. *Roth*, 408 U.S. 564 (1972). Mr. Staino would assert he has a property right to a seat at the race track. The Supreme Court in *Roth* defined a property right as a security interest which a person has acquired in a specific benefit:

To have a property interest in a benefit, a person clearly must have more than an abstract need or desire for it. He must have more than a unilateral expectation of it. He must, instead, have a legitimate claim of entitlement to it.

The statutory law of Pennsylvania accords no property right to a seat at a race track to a patron. Mr. Staino's abstract desire or unilateral expectation of a right to be a patron cannot translate into a constitutionally protected right.

We now reach Mr. Staino's final contention that the Commission's findings and conclusions are not supported by substantial evidence of record. Initially, we would point out that Section 215 of the Act does not specifically require a hearing in the event of a patron ejection. Subsection (c), applicable to licensee ejections, however, does provide that "[t]he person refused admission or ejected shall receive a hearing before the appropriate commission, if requested, pursuant to rules and regulations adopted for that purpose by the appropriate commission and a decision rendered following that hearing." Licensees, unlike patrons, have more than an abstract desire for or a unilateral expectation of admission to the racetrack by virtue of the license given them to exercise their occupation at the race track. Denial of admission to or ejection of a licensee thus constitutes denial of the liberty to exercise his occupation which triggers the procedural protections of the Fourteenth Amendment.

Nevertheless, despite the fact that it was not statutorily obligated to do so, the Commission scheduled a hearing at Mr. Staino's request and heard testimony from Mr. Staino and from the Director of Security for Eagle Downs. Mr. Staino now argues that the ejection is not supported in the record by clear, unequivocal evidence of his misconduct at the race track or of the detrimental effect of his presence at the race track. As we have indicated, it was not necessary for Eagle Downs to establish that Mr. Staino's ejection was for cause. If Mr. Staino had alleged he had been ejected for one of the prohibited reasons, i.e., his race, color, creed, sex, religion, or national origin, Eagle Downs would of course then be required to rebut the evidence Mr. Staino would present in support of his position. In the absence of such an allegation, the Commission was not even required to question Eagle Downs'[s] motive in ejecting Mr. Staino. The Commission did not abuse its discretion in upholding Mr. Staino's ejection and dismissing his appeal. Accordingly we will affirm.

FOR DISCUSSION

1. What test does the Court use to determine when a private entity engages in state action? What result does it come to? Do you agree?
2. Can you give an example of the action of a private individual, group, or corporation engaging in state action?
3. Why is state action so important in this case?
4. According to the Court, Staino's ejection did not deprive him of a right protected by the Fourteenth Amendment. Why not? What if Staino had been a sports reporter? What if he earned his living as a tout (someone who sells tips and other information to bettors)?
5. If Staino did not have a property right to a seat at the race track what did he pay for when he bought a ticket?
6. After reading this case, we have no idea why Staino was ejected. Why does the Court not consider this to be important?

SUBSTANTIVE DUE PROCESS

In the following essay, Lawrence Friedman explains the origins and development of substantive due process, concentrating on the twentieth-century expansion of the concept.

READING   **The Flowering of Judicial Review**
*By Lawrence M. Friedman**

As late as the 1860s, the Supreme Court decided only four or five constitutional cases on average each year; by 1890, they were deciding about twenty-four. Under Chief Justice Fuller, the Court declared five federal acts unconstitutional in a single decade (1889–1899), together with thirty-four state laws and four municipal ordinances.

This great expansion of judicial review, in the late nineteenth century, pivoted on the "due process" clause. Doctrines sprang out of these few words like rabbits from a magician's hat. The draftsmen of the Fourteenth Amendment were almost certainly thinking only of procedure when they used the words due *process*. They were thinking of fair trials in courts of law. But by the turn of the century, the phrase had come to mean something quite different, and vastly greater. As the court saw it, an "unreasonable" or "arbitrary" law amounted to a deprivation of due process. Only the justices, of course, could say what was unreasonable. Too great an infringement of "liberty of contract," for example, violated the Constitution. Out of such bricks, the court built a structure which, in effect, made rugged free enterprise part of the constitutional scheme.

Not, of course, consistently; and not without loud voices from left and center crying out against the court's work. In some notorious instances, the Court used "substantive due process" to tear the guts out of popular laws—laws passed to give labor more power against capital. The high-water mark, perhaps, was *Lochner* v. *New York*, 198 U.S. 45, in 1905. The issue was a New York statute regulating bakeries. Among other things, it restricted the killing hours some bakers worked. Under the statute, no one could be "required or permitted" to work in a bakery more than sixty a week, or more than ten hours in a day.

The Supreme Court voided the law. Justice John Marshall Harlan, dissenting, pointed out that the majority had brushed aside evidence of subhuman work conditions: how bakers suffered from flour dust in their lungs; how "long hours of toil" produced "rheumatism, cramps, and swollen legs"; evidence that bakers were "palefaced," had delicate health, and "seldom" lived past fifty. Oliver Wendell Holmes, Jr., also dissented; to him, the majority rested its case "upon an economic theory which a large part of the country does not entertain." This was the theory of pure free enterprise. Holmes himself was sympathetic to this theory; but he did not wish to raise it to the level of constitutional principle. To the majority, however (speaking through Justice Rufus Peckham), none of this mattered. The health arguments were a sham. The statute was fatally flawed. It interfered with "the freedom of master and employee to contract with each other." A regulation of "hours of labor" of this kind violated the Fourteenth Amendment.

Some state courts were even more active, constitutionally, than the Supreme Court, along the same lines of doctrine. Labor and social laws seemed to fall like tenpins at the turn of the century. But it is hard to measure the actual impact of *Lochner* and its fellow travelers. Most statutes, in fact, survived constitutional challenge. Many were never tested at all. On the other hand, we can never know what statutes did not pass—or passed in weakened form—because legislators were afraid the courts would strike them down. Perhaps, too, the opposite sometimes happened: a legislature passed a "radical" law to please some constituents, hoping deep down that the court would kill it and take them off the hook.

One thing *is* clear: challenges to the validity of laws were common from the 1880s on, and had not been common before. They became, in effect, part of the life cycle of important laws. There was no turning back. Judicial review got stronger and stronger in the twentieth century. It did so, first of all, in terms of sheer volume: more statutes reviewed; more statutes struck down; new doctrines, some of them very bold, very sweeping. In a single year (1915), the Supreme Court voided twenty-two state statutes. The pace continued. An active, intrusive Supreme Court became a permanent part of the landscape.

What it is active *about* has also changed, and dramatically. In the Great Depression of the 1930s and during Franklin D. Roosevelt's New Deal, the country shifted to the left. Power flowed from the exhausted cities and states to Washington. The Supreme Court at first refused to get the message. In a series of cases, the Court nullified key New Deal statutes.

Once more there was great anger in the country—and in the White House, too. Roosevelt hit on a plan: he would "pack" the court (increase its size) by appointing new justices—men more to his liking, who would neutralize the "nine old men" who then sat on the court. Under the plan, the president was authorized to appoint one new justice for every sitting justice over seventy. There were six of these in 1937. But for once, his political sense had failed him; the court-packing plan was attacked from all sides as a threat to the independence of the justices and to the whole American system. The plan was hastily abandoned and soon died.

In the end, Roosevelt won his war against the Court. He was elected president four times, and the "nine old men" simply could not outlast him. He got his court without packing it; the Supreme Court after 1937 first rather meekly submitted to—then willingly and even eagerly embraced—the expansion of national power and the scope and methods of the regulatory state. Congress and state legislators could do as they liked with the economy; the Court would not say no.

This attitude was expressed in a line of cases whose climax, perhaps, was *Williamson* v. *Lee Optical*, 348 U.S. 483 (1955). William O. Douglas, one of Roosevelt's appointed judges, wrote the opinion. The facts turned on an Oklahoma law regulating the eyeglass business. No one was allowed to make eyeglasses or fit them except a licensed optometrist or ophthalmologist, or without having a prescription from one of these. The law was supposed to protect the public, and it had some vague connection with health; but these were rather skimpy grounds. The real motives seemed basically anticompetitive: opticians ("artisans qualified to grind lenses, fill prescriptions and fit frames") were the target of the law, and it hurt them badly in their business. The Supreme Court as it was in 1900 might have gone over the law with a fine comb and could well have struck it down. The Court of 1955, on the other hand, was not of a mind to interfere. Douglas brushed aside all objections to the act. Let Oklahoma do what it wants: "The day is gone," he said, when the Court made use of "due process" to "strike down...laws, regulatory of business...because they may be unwise."

Williamson is still the law of the land; and the Court, so far, has not gone back on it, spirit or letter. The Court takes a hands-off approach to laws that regulate business. But the energy saved, so to speak, simply flowed into other fields of action, into the so-called social issues: race relations (especially after *Brown* v. *Board of Education*, in 1954); the rights of criminal defendants; civil liberties in general; sex discrimination; and a motley collection of cases on what we can call, for want of a better term, personal life-style.

Here, the court has been active indeed. It has hacked away at dozens of old taboos. Laws against contraception and abortion were declared unconstitutional. All of these decisions have been in the highest degree controversial. Has the court gone too fast, too far? Many scholars—and citizens—think so. Others defend the Court. The noisy debate goes on.

NOTES

*Reprinted from *American Law: An Introduction* by Lawrence M. Friedman, New York: W. W. Norton, 1984, pp. 186–89, by permission of W. W. Norton & Company, Inc. Copyright © 1984 by Lawrence M. Friedman.

FOR DISCUSSION

1. Explain how the Supreme Court changed the notion of due process during the late nineteenth and early twentieth century.

2. What does Friedman criticize about the use of substantive due process in cases such as *Lochner* v. *N.Y.*?

3. How did the Supreme Court's use of substantive due process in reviewing government regulation of the economy change after 1937? Has the Court gone too far in the opposite direction? What other approach might it have taken?

4. How does the Supreme Court use substantive due process today? What does Friedman mean when he says, "The noisy debate goes on"?

5. Review *Griswold* v. *Conn.* in the previous chapter. Are any of the opinions based on substantive due process?

6. Was the Supreme Court more activist in the early twentieth century or today?

One of the commonest uses of substantive due process is to protect against vague laws. A law must define what conduct is required or prohibited clearly enough so that people know how to conform their conduct to it. Laws that fail to do so violate substantive due process. *Bell* v. *Arlington County* shows how courts evaluate claims that laws are unconstitutionally vague.

CASE

Bell v. Arlington County, Va.
United States District Court, E.D. Virginia, Alexandria Division (1987)
673 F.Supp. 767

CACHERIS, District Judge.   The issue in this case is the constitutionality of the Arlington County Code Sections which prohibit cross-sexual massages.

Both plaintiff and defendant moved for summary judgment on the constitutionality of Arlington County Code Chapter 49. The court finds that the statute is unconstitutionally vague and grants plaintiff's motion for Summary Judgment.

Plaintiff is a trained masseuse who has all the necessary business licenses and permits to provide massage services as a massage therapist. In May 1986, the defendants began an investigation of plaintiff's massage therapy practice. Despite her status as a licensed massage therapist, plaintiff was arrested under Chapter 49 and charged with violating the Code section which prohibits a massage technician from giving a massage to a member of the opposite sex.

On October 1, 1986, the Arlington County Commonwealth's Attorney dismissed the charge against the plaintiff. On November 14, 1986, the Arlington County Circuit Court expunged all police and court records relating to the criminal charge filed against Bell.

Plaintiff has moved for summary judgment on her claim for declaratory injunctive relief relative to Chapter 49, requesting the court to declare that the Code Section is unconstitutionally vague. The defendant Arlington County has opposed the motion and asked for summary judgment on the grounds that the statute is not unconstitutionally vague.

Summary judgment "should be granted only where it is perfectly clear that no issue of fact is involved and inquiry into the facts is not desirable to clarify the application of the law." The burden is on the moving party to "'show' that there 'is no genuine issue as to any material fact' and that he 'is entitled to judgment as a matter of law.'" *Charbonnages de France v. Smith*, 597 F.2d 406 (4th Cir.1979). In determining whether this showing has been made, we must assess the evidence as forecast in the documentary materials before the court in the light most favorable to the party opposing the motion. The movant need not negate his opponent's case; he need only to disclose the absence of evidence to support that case.

In Arlington County's Motion, the County argues that the ordinance sets up two distinct categories, massage therapist and massage technician. The former could perform a cross-sexual massage, while the latter was prohibited. However, prior to Bell's arrest, the Police Department operated on the understanding, given to them by Henry Hudson, Arlington County Commonwealth's Attorney, that neither massage therapists nor massage technicians could give cross-sexual massages.

As the basis for Bell's arrest, the police department had interpreted the ordinance to state that massage therapists were a subclass of massage technicians and, therefore, were prohibited from giving cross-sexual massages.

Police Chief Stover, who was charged with the responsibility of enforcing the ordinance, had several problems understanding the statute. Stover believed the ordinance was "too vague," could only be understood by a lawyer, "unfair" to Ms. Bell, unclear "to a reasonably ordinary intelligent person of what is and is not permissible," and that "it fails to give reasonable notice to a lay person as to what is lawful for a massage therapist."

Lt. John Karinshak, who was in charge of the Police's vice-control section, was under the belief that until last year all cross-sexual massages were illegal under the Arlington County Code. Karinshak thought that, based on his interpretation of law, the statute had problems and that it was vague. He felt it was not clear as to who could or could not give cross-sexual massages. As a result of problems with the Bell case, he found it necessary to draft a policy statement for the vice-squad in 1986 to prevent a repetition of an arrest similar to the one that occurred in this case. Karinshak's memorandum indicated that massage technicians could not engage in cross-sexual massages, however, massage therapists could. Nevertheless, even after the County clarified its policy, Detective Kozich was still unclear as to whether Bell was entitled to massage men under the current ordinance.

The standard for determining whether the ordinance is unconstitutionally vague is where "its prohibitions are not clearly defined" and where a "person of ordinary intelligence" is not given a "reasonable opportunity to know what is prohibited so that he may act accordingly." *Grayned v. City of Rockford*, 408 U.S. 104 (1972). The court continued in *Rockford* to state:

> [A] vague law impermissibly delegates basic policy matters to…[officials charged with enforcement] for resolution on an *ad hoc* and subjective basis, with attendant dangers of arbitrary and discriminatory applications.

It is quite obvious that the statute is unconstitutionally vague. The County's argument that the statute sets up one standard for massage technicians and another for massage therapists fails because the police officers who were charged with the responsibility of enforcing the ordinance have found that they themselves have difficulty in interpreting it. Reading 49-2's definition of massage technician ["Any person who administers a massage to another person for pay"] together with 49-7(2)'s prohibitions against cross-sexual massages, the statutes appear to say that any person who receives money from massages cannot give cross-sexual massages. This interpretation would include licensed massage therapists who receive money for massages. Yet, the Chapter appears to contemplate that massage therapists can give cross-sexual massages. Obviously the ordinance is confusing because the officers who were charged with the responsibility for enforcement are confused over its interpretation. If the officers are confused, it is too much to ask the citizenry to know what is prohibited. Therefore, the court finds that 49-7(2) is unconstitutionally vague. Plaintiff's Motion for Summary Judgment is GRANTED and defendants' Motion for Summary Judgment is DENIED.

FOR DISCUSSION

1. The Court never discusses the purpose of this law. What do you think it is?
2. Compare this case to *Williamson* v. *Lee Optical*, discussed by Friedman. Are the two decisions consistent?
3. Judge Cacheris gives a great deal of weight to the confusion of the police about the meaning of the law. If all of the police officers who testified in this case had agreed on the law's meaning, do you think it would change the result?
4. Can you articulate a standard for deciding when a law is too vague to meet the test of substantive due process?
5. Can you write a law that would accomplish the goals of Arlington County Code Chapter 49 and not be unconstitutionally vague? Would it help you to know that in a footnote, Judge Cacheris defined a massage therapist as "a massage technician with certain specified training"?
6. Could your law be challenged as discriminating on the basis of sex?

A law also violates substantive due process if it unduly burdens the exercise of a fundamental right, even if that right is not specifically mentioned in the Constitution. In the following case Julie Sokol argues that the right to bear children is such a fundamental right and that depriving her of unemployment compensation after she left her job due to her pregnancy is a violation of that right.

CASE   Sokol v. Smith
                  United States District Court, W.D. Missouri (1987)
                                    671 F.Supp. 1243

SCOTT O. WRIGHT, Chief Judge.   Plaintiff Julie Sokol was employed by William M. Mercer-Meidinger, Inc. from September 1, 1983, to June 29, 1984. During this time period, plaintiff became pregnant.

On her doctor's advice, plaintiff Julie Sokol took a maternity leave in order to alleviate the physical complications she was experiencing. At this time, Mrs. Sokol's employer granted her a leave of absence subject to the condition that she could return to work after the birth of her baby when the next position became available.

Mrs. Sokol gave notice that she was able to return to work six weeks after the baby was born. At that time, she was advised that no work was available.

Plaintiff then applied for unemployment compensation to assist her while she was seeking alternative employment. On November 13, 1984, Mrs. Sokol's application for unemployment compensation was denied by defendant Phillip Senger, Deputy of the Division of Employment Security of Missouri. The application was denied because defendants determined that plaintiff voluntarily quit her job without good cause attributable to the work or the employer and, therefore, was disqualified under Mo.Rev.Stat. 288.050.1(1).

This decision was appealed to the Appeals Tribunal which affirmed the Deputy's determination to deny Mrs. Sokol unemployment compensation. The plaintiff then filed a timely appeal with the Labor and Industrial Relations Commission of Missouri.

Summary judgment is appropriate when no genuine issue of material fact is present and judgment should be awarded to the movant as a matter of law. In making this determination, however, the Court must view the evidence in the light most favorable to the opposing party. In the case at bar, it is proper to grant the defendant's motion for summary judgment because the plaintiffs have failed to establish the existence of the essential elements of their claims. In particular, the plaintiffs have failed to establish that their right to unemployment compensation is a fundamental right protected by the Fourteenth Amendment.

The Due Process Clause of the Fourteenth Amendment is a means by which the courts can apply strict judicial scrutiny to any action of a state which limits the exercise of a fundamental Constitutional right. The "right to privacy" is an example of such a fundamental right.

The plaintiffs allege in their complaint that by denying unemployment compensation to plaintiffs and their class, the defendants are violating plaintiffs' substantive Due Process rights by placing an unconstitutional burden on the exercise of plaintiff's fundamental right to reproductive freedom. This Court remains unpersuaded that plaintiffs' Substantive Due Process rights have been violated because plaintiffs have failed to demonstrate a deprivation of life, liberty, or property as required by the Fourteenth Amendment. Rather, to support their Substantive Due Process claim, plaintiffs rely on a series of First Amendment cases dealing with freedom to exercise religion.

The plaintiffs have cited, for example, the case of *Hobbie v. Unemployment Appeals Commission of Florida,* 107 S.Ct. 1046 (1987), which deals with a Seventh-Day Adventist who was discharged for refusing to work on Saturdays. Hobbie, the former employee, then filed a claim for unemployment compensation with the Florida Department of Labor & Employment Security, which was denied. After Hobbie completed all proper procedures necessary to challenge her denial of benefits, the United States Supreme Court agreed to consider the issue and reversed the denial of benefits.

The United States Supreme Court held that Hobbie's disqualification from receipt of unemployment benefits violated the Free Exercise Clause of the First Amendment. The Court's reasoning was founded on the principle that the state's disqualification of Hobbie forced her to choose between following the precepts of her religion or abandoning her religion in order to accept work. "Governmental imposition of such a choice puts the same kind of burden upon the free exercise of religion as would a fine imposed against [her] for Saturday worship."

There are critical distinctions between the instant case and the First Amendment cases relied upon by the plaintiffs which make the First Amendment cases unpersuasive precedent. The plaintiffs' analogy to First Amendment cases is faulty in that the denial of unemployment compensation does not impinge upon the plaintiffs' right to bear children. Rather, the instant case is analogous to *Maher* v. *Roe,* 432 U.S. 464 (1977), where the United States Supreme Court identified a distinction between direct state interference with a fundamental right and a neutral policy consistent with legislative intent.[1]

---

[1]*Maher* upheld a ban on government funding for nontherapeutic abortions (editor's note).

The Missouri statute governing unemployment compensation represents a neutral policy toward the fundamental right to bear children. Neither the statute nor its application have any effect on a woman's right to bear children without state interference. The United States Supreme Court has found that the Missouri statute is a:

> neutral rule that incidentally disqualifies pregnant or formerly pregnant claimants as part of a larger group....To apply this law, it is not necessary to know that petitioner left because of pregnancy: all that is relevant is that she stopped work for a reason bearing no causal connection to her work or her employer. *Kimberly* v. *Labor and Industrial Relations Commission*, 107 S.Ct. 821 (1987).

The Supreme Court's finding that the Missouri unemployment compensation statute does not violate the Federal Unemployment Tax Act which provides that no state shall deny any compensation "solely on the basis of pregnancy or termination of pregnancy" supports the conclusion that the Missouri statute does not violate the Due Process Clause. In the instant case, the plaintiffs are not forced to choose between bearing children and accepting employment. The Missouri unemployment compensation statute does not impose such a choice on females in the workplace. All women in plaintiffs' position are free to choose to bear children without State interference. It is the legislature's intent to provide unemployment compensation only to employees who leave their employment with good cause attributable to the work or the employer. This neutral policy does not violate the plaintiffs' Due Process right to bear children.

This Court is sympathetic to the plaintiffs' position in losing their job and having no right to regain it after a reasonable maternity leave. The California legislature ameliorated this problem by amending its Fair Employment and Housing Act to prohibit employment discrimination on the basis of pregnancy. This statute requires employers to provide female employees an unpaid pregnancy disability leave of up to four months. It is the opinion of this Court that similar legislation should be enacted by the Missouri legislature. Until that time, it is beyond the scope of the judiciary to interfere with the function of the legislative branch.

Accordingly, it is hereby ORDERED that the defendants' motion for summary judgment is granted and plaintiffs' cross-motion for summary judgment is denied.

FOR DISCUSSION

1. What provision of state law is Sokol challenging in this case? How does she believe it hinders her right to due process?

2. What governmental interest does the law further? Is this a legitimate interest of government?

3. In support of her position, Sokol cites a series of cases in which Seventh-Day Adventists were fired for refusing to work on Saturday, their Sabbath. Since freedom of religion and the right to bear children are both fundamental rights, what difference does the Court see between the two situations?

4. Chief Judge Wright believes a more appropriate precedent is *Maher* v. *Roe*, in which the Supreme Court upheld a law denying Medicaid funds for women seeking abortions. What common principle does he find in the two cases?

5. The Court concludes that Sokol is "not forced to choose between bearing children and accepting employment" nor does the Missouri law "impose such a choice on females in the workplace." Explain whether or not you agree.

6. Since Judge Wright believes that Sokol is not being treated fairly, why does he not overturn the law? What does he suggest be done? Is it appropriate for a judge to make such a suggestion?

PROCEDURAL DUE PROCESS

A good way to understand the concept of procedural due process is to look at a specific area familiar to most readers, due process in schools. In the following essay, Albert S. Miles explains what rights students have when schools seek to punish them. Although his article concentrates on cases in the Eleventh Circuit and especially in Alabama, courts in other parts of the country have generally taken a similar approach. Some of the cases cited refer to the Fifth Circuit because they took place before that circuit was divided in two, creating a new (eleventh) circuit that currently includes Alabama.

READING   **The Due Process Rights of Students in Public School
or College Disciplinary Hearings**
By Albert S. Miles*

An attorney may be asked to represent a student or a public educational institution in a matter involving a possible student misconduct violation. The due process clause of the Fourteenth Amendment of the U.S. Constitution applies to public schools as well as public colleges because the requirement of state action is fulfilled in both instances, and both public school administrators and their college counterparts are state officers. The following is a review of the specific requirements of due process for a public school or college student in such a disciplinary situation.

Since the decision of *Dixon* v. *Alabama State Board of Education*, 294 F.2d 159 (11th Cir. 1961), public school and college students have been considered by the courts to have constitutional rights. The rudimentary rights of due process set forth in *Dixon* are that the student receive notice, a hearing, and an explanation before being suspended or expelled from a public school. In *Dixon*, students who had been expelled without notice or hearing from the Alabama state college claimed that they had a constitutional right to due process. The court ruled for the students. The recent decision in *Nash* v. *Auburn University*, 621 F.Supp. 948 (M.D.Ala. 1985), upholding the due process used by the University in a dismissal for cheating, supports *Dixon* and clarifies what specific due process rights are due students.

The terms *procedural due process* and *substantive due process* are used in this article. Procedural due process "contemplates the rudimentary requirements of fair play, which includes a fair and open hearing." *Almon* v. *Morgan County*, 16 So.2d 511 (1946). Substantive due process, or the substance of the school's decision being reasonable, is achieved if the decision is not "a substantial departure from academic norms." *Regents of the University of Michigan* v. *Ewing*, 106 S.Ct. 507 (1985).

The following 11 points address the circumstances in which due process is applicable in a public school or college student disciplinary hearing and, once it is determined that due process applies, the specifics of what kind of due process is owed to students.

1. The general rule is that only students in public schools and colleges have due process rights. The gateway to the due process clause in the 14th amendment of the U.S. Constitution is "state action." Since *Rendell-Baker* v. *Kohn*, 457 U.S. 830 (1982), "state action" has not been construed as a private school's receiving a great amount of government support, but "state action" usually applies only to students in public, not private schools. However, in *Van Look* v. *Curran*, 489 So.2d 525 (Ala.1986), the Alabama Supreme Court held that while only state action invokes the procedural due process clause, if a private school's contract with the parents or student includes terms that call for the use of due process, then the private school must grant the student due process. This is because the school included a right to due process in the terms of the contract, even though it did not have to.

2. Immediate temporary suspensions comport with due process where a student's presence "poses a continuing danger to persons or property or an ongoing threat of disrupting the academic process," and if the necessary notice and hearing "follow as soon as is practicable." *Goss* v. *Lopez*, 419 U.S. 565 (1975). The *Goss* decision agrees with the district court's guidelines in this case in that such a suspension, a hearing should be held within 72 hours of a student's removal.

3. Less stringent procedural due process is required when there is an academic dismissal, which results from academic evaluations, than when there is a dismissal for disciplinary reasons, where facts are questioned, such as for cheating or non-academic misconduct. The dismissal of a student for poor academic performance comports with the requirements of procedural due process if the student had prior notice of the faculty dissatisfaction with his performance and the possibility of dismissal, and the decision to dismiss was careful and deliberate. No formal hearing is required. *The Board of Curators of the University of Missouri* v. *Horowitz*, 435 U.S. 78 (1978).

Just as *Horowitz* spoke to the procedural due process required in an academic dismissal, *Regents of the University of Michigan* v. *Ewing* addressed substantive due process in academic expulsions. *Ewing* held that a student's substantive due process rights are not violated, if the academic dismissal was not "a substantial departure from academic norms."

4. In disciplinary dismissals, as well as in academic dismissals, both substantive and procedural due process are needed. Substantive due process in disciplinary dismissal was considered in *Krasnow* v. *Virginia Polytechnic Institute*, 551 F.2d 591 (4th Cir. 1977). The court held that the college's use of a rule allowing for disciplinary penalties for off-campus violations did not violate a student's substantive due process rights. *Dixon's* "rudiments" of notice, hearing, and explanation are a good guideline to procedural due process. Procedural due process refers to the implementation of the rule's being fair. Due process will adapt itself to the situation; it is not rigid. *Nash* at 955 makes the point that due process applies to public high school, undergraduate and graduate students, and allows for variation according to the type of student.

5. Some notice is required in procedural due process in a school or college disciplinary setting. *Nash* holds that as long as the charges and their implications are made known before the hearing, the list of witnesses and their expected testimony can be given to the accused student at the hearing itself in a case concerning cheating. Notice can be oral or written, and can be given immediately before the hearing. "The notice should contain a statement of the specific charges and grounds." *Dixon* at 158.

6. There usually is no absolute right to have an attorney present to present the student's case in procedural due process. Auburn University allowed plaintiffs to have counsel present during the hearing, but the counsel was allowed only to advise plaintiffs and was not permitted to actively participate in the hearing. The *Nash* court stated that Auburn, by allowing plaintiffs to have counsel present, afforded the plaintiffs more due process that the Constitution requires.

In *French* v. *Bashful*, 303 F.Supp. 1333 (E.D.La. 1969), the court held that a student had a right to have a retained (not appointed) counsel present at a disciplinary hearing for suspension or expulsion if the university was represented by a third-year law student or someone else with legal training.

Dixon is silent on the question of legal representation at student disciplinary hearings.

7. The rules of a student disciplinary hearing can be informal. Counsel often are allowed to students during disciplinary hearings, albeit with restrictions noted above, and often are reminded of this quote from *Board of Curators* v. *Horowitz*, at 88, "school is an academic institution, not a courtroom or administrative hearing room."

In *Boykins* v. *Fairfield Board of Education*, 492 F.2d 697 (5th Cir. 1974), the court noted that laymen in such a student disciplinary hearing are not bound by the common law rules of evidence. *Aaron* v. *Alabama State Tenure Commission*, 407 So.2d 136 (Ala.Civ.App. 1981), held "The [hearing] Board is allowed to admit and consider evidence of probative value, even though it might not be admissible in a court of law."

At the hearing, the student has the right to present his defense against the charges and "to produce other oral testimony or written affidavits of witnesses in his behalf." *Dixon* at 159.

8. The form and nature of the hearing can be before one administrator or a committee. The "timing and content of the notice and the nature of the hearing will depend on appropriate accommodation of the competing interests involved." *Goss* v. *Lopez*. The student has a right to an impartial tribunal, but *Nash* states that "the law in this circuit is settled that previous contact with the incident and even with the initial investigation does not automatically disqualify one from hearing and deciding a case in a college disciplinary proceeding."

9. No right to cross-examination exists in a student misconduct hearing. *Nash* states that the *Dixon* standards do not require the opportunity of cross-examination. *Nash* notes that the procedure Auburn University allowed, which was to allow the plaintiffs to ask the adverse witnesses questions by directing their questions through the chief hearing officer, was more procedural due process than called for in *Dixon*.

10. Students are entitled to an explanation of the results of the hearing and the implications of the decision. *Dixon* held, "If the hearing is not before the Board [of Education] directly, the results and findings of the hearing should be presented in a report open to the student's inspection." *Wright* v. *Texas Southern University*, 392 F.2d 728 (5th Cir. 1968), held that after the hearing, the findings should be presented to the student in a report.

11. No right to an appeal from the decision of a student hearing is called for, according to *Nash*. "All that due process requires is notice and an opportunity for hearing." Thus, *Nash* concludes regarding the plaintiff's complaint of no meaningful appeal, that "this court cannot find a violation of a non-existent right."

CONCLUSION

Nash v. *Auburn University* upholds *Dixon* as the law in this circuit concerning due process in student misconduct hearings. Once a public school or college student is given what is seen as fair notice, hearing, and explanation for a disciplinary dismissal, or notice and careful deliberation by faculty in an academic dismissal, no further appeal or other procedures are necessary in order for the administrator or school to afford due process to the student involved.

It is wise to realize that due process is not a rigid set of rules, and "fairness" is important. Thus, it is a good idea for a school or college to grant as much due process as it thinks is advisable, given a balance between the circumstances, the educational mission of the school and the rights of the student.

NOTES

*From "Disciplinary Hearings" by Albert S. Miles, in *The Alabama Lawyer*, 48 (May 1987), 144–46. Reprinted by permission of the author and publisher.

FOR DISCUSSION

1. According to Miles, due process can differ for high school, undergraduate, and graduate students. What differences in procedures would you think appropriate for each type of student?

2. The Courts have provided different standards of due process for academic and disciplinary dismissals. Can you explain the reasoning behind this?

3. One of the decisions quoted by Miles says that schools can meet the requirements of substantive due process if their decisions are not "a substantial departure from academic norms." Compare this to the standards used in *Bell* v. *Arlington County* and *Sokol* v. *Smith*. Do you find it a clear enough standard for schools and students to understand?

4. What rights have the courts found absolutely necessary for disciplinary hearings to meet the requirements of procedural due process? What makes these rights so important?

5. List the rights the courts have not required for hearings to be acceptable. Explain whether you agree or disagree.

6. Miles concludes that "due process is not a rigid set of rules." Why isn't it? How would you reply to someone who said that it should be?

The next case presents an example of what happens when a university disciplinary hearing is challenged in court as violating procedural due process. Note the standards the court uses to determine whether the school's actions met the minimum requirements of due process.

CASE
Rosenfeld v. Ketter
United States Court of Appeals, Second Circuit (1987)
820 F.2d 38

WINTER, Circuit Judge.   Alan Rosenfeld appeals from a grant of summary judgment dismissing his complaint against three officials of the State University of New York at Buffalo ("SUNYAB" or "University"). We affirm.

The facts are essentially undisputed. In February 1982, Rosenfeld was a third-year law student at SUNYAB. Students had scheduled a rally for the evening of February 26 to protest the University's plan to convert the student union, known as Squire Hall, into a facility for the dental school. The students planned to remain in Squire Hall past its 2:00 A.M. closing time. Rosenfeld and other students intended to be present at the rally as "legal observers" to witness any arrests and prevent violence.

On the afternoon of February 26, Rosenfeld described his plans to Ronald Stein, assistant to University President Robert Ketter. Stein informed him that the building would be closed at 2:00 A.M. the next morning and that anyone who remained after being told to leave would be arrested pursuant to President Ketter's instructions. Stein stated that no exceptions would be made for "legal observers." Stein relayed Rosenfeld's plans to Ketter, who reiterated his instructions to arrest anyone who did not leave the building. Stein then conveyed Rosenfeld's plans and Ketter's instructions to Lee Griffin, director of public safety at SUNYAB, and Griffin's assistant, John Grela.

That evening, Rosenfeld attended the Squire Hall rally. At approximately 2:00 A.M. on February 27, Griffin announced to those in the building that they no longer had permission to remain and that they had ten minutes to leave. He further stated that those who did not leave would be arrested and that if they were students, they would also be suspended. Rosenfeld concedes that Griffin's general announcement was repeated several times and that Griffin and Grela personally told him that he too would be arrested if he remained in the building. At some point thereafter, Rosenfeld attempted "once again" (in his words) to explain to Griffin that he was present not as a participant in the rally, but only as a witness to the arrests and would voluntarily leave the building after the arrests were completed. Griffin told Rosenfeld that he would not be allowed to observe because he would be arrested if he did not leave the building.

At about 2:40 A.M., Rosenfeld, then the sole "legal observer" remaining in the building, was arrested and charged with third-degree criminal trespass. Following his arrest, he was served with a notice indicating that he had been "temporarily suspended immediately as a student," which meant that all of his "rights and privileges as a University student [we]re suspended" and that he was "barred from participating in any University activity or entering onto or being in any property owned or operated by [SUNYAB]." The notice did not state the duration of the temporary suspension, but the attached summons did indicate that a formal hearing before the Hearing Committee for the Maintenance of Public Order was scheduled for March 20.

Rosenfeld was released from custody sometime before 4:00 A.M. on February 27. Later that day, he requested and received an informal hearing before President Ketter concerning his suspension. At the hearing, Ketter concluded that Rosenfeld might continue to disrupt the orderly operations of SUNYAB and therefore declined to remove the temporary suspension. Two days later, on March 1, Rosenfeld received a second informal hearing before Steven Sample, who had replaced Ketter as president earlier that day. Sample lifted Rosenfeld's temporary suspension on March 3.

The formal hearing, originally scheduled for March 20, was held on March 13. The Hearing Board found that Rosenfeld had violated University Rule 535.3g, which prohibits persons from refusing to leave a building after being told to do so by an authorized administrative officer. Rosenfeld was therefore placed on disciplinary probation for the remainder of the spring 1982 semester.

On July 1, 1982, Rosenfeld commenced this action seeking declaratory relief and damages. On December 10, 1986, Judge Elfvin granted summary judgment against him. On his appeal, Rosenfeld limits his arguments to two claims: first that his suspension on the morning of February 27 without a predeprivation hearing violated his right to due process; and, second, that the provisions of the suspension order prohibiting him from entering SUNYAB property violated his first amendment rights. Finding these claims to be without merit, we affirm.

Relying on *Goss* v. *Lopez*, 419 U.S. 565 (1975), Rosenfeld argues that he was denied due process because he was not afforded a hearing before he was suspended from February 27 to March 3. In *Goss*, The Supreme Court held that a high school student facing temporary suspension "of 10 days or less" must "be given oral or written notice of the charges against him and, if he denies them, an explanation of the evidence the authorities have and an opportunity to present his side of the story." A formal hearing is unnecessary. "In the great majority of cases the disciplinarian may informally discuss the alleged misconduct with the student minutes after it has occurred." While this requirement "add[s] little to the fact-finding function where the disciplinarian himself has witnessed the conduct forming the basis for the charge...things are not always as they seem to be, and the student will at least have the opportunity to characterize his conduct and put it in what he deems the proper context."

The conceded facts plainly reveal that Rosenfeld was afforded all of the process required by *Goss*. Rosenfeld remained in Squire Hall after being asked to leave, and there was thus no doubt as to the relevant facts. His conversation with Stein on the afternoon before the demonstration afforded him an opportunity to air his claim of immunity as a "legal observer" with a university. Moreover, just before Rosenfeld's arrest and suspension, Griffin warned him to leave, Rosenfeld "once again" argued his claim of immunity, and he was told that it would not be accepted. These discussions afforded Rosenfeld the opportunity required by *Goss* to characterize his conduct, put it in the proper context and urge that University rules not be enforced against him. An additional or more formal hearing would have been wholly redundant.

Rosenfeld argues that the terms of the suspension order, which prohibited him from participating in any University activity or entering any University property, violated his first amendment rights. He contends that those restrictions deprived him of the opportunity to participate in the cultural and political activities at the University that are open to students and to the general public. We find this claim to be entirely without merit.

The suspension order did not prevent Rosenfeld from participating in any political activity, speaking on any subject or assembling with any group. The order merely barred him from doing those things, or anything at all, *at the University*. Rosenfeld has not argued that this restriction was not reasonably related to the University's interests in punishing him and preventing further disruption—interests that are unrelated to the suppression of speech. The Supreme Court has held that in circumstances such as these, "an incidental burden on speech is no greater than is essential, and therefore is permissible..., so long as the neutral regulation promotes a substantial government interest that would be achieved less effectively absent the regulation." *U.S.* v. *Albertini*, 472 U.S. 675 (1985). We will not second-guess the University's view that excluding Rosenfeld from campus was the most appropriate method of promoting the University's interests in this case. Given the virtually unlimited opportunities for free expression that remained available to Rosenfeld, he simply has not stated a valid claim under the first amendment.

The decision of the district court is therefore affirmed.

FOR DISCUSSION

1. If Rosenfeld had been a student at a private rather than a public law school would this case have been different in any way?

2. According to one of the cases quoted by Miles, immediate temporary suspensions are permitted when a student's presence "poses a continuing danger to persons or property or an ongoing threat of disrupting the academic process." Judge Winter also relies heavily on this precedent, *Goss* v. *Lopez*. Explain whether you agree that, based on this standard, Rosenfeld's temporary suspension was justified.

3. Judge Winter concludes that Rosenfeld's discussions with university officials prior to and during the demonstration constituted an informal hearing giving him a chance to make his case and that "an additional or more formal hearing would have been wholly redundant." Explain whether or not you agree.

4. After the imposition of the temporary suspension, Rosenfeld was granted a hearing before President Ketter. Was this the "impartial tribunal" discussed by Miles in the eighth of his eleven points?

5. According to Miles, due process is flexible enough to provide "for variations according to the type of student." Did the fact that Rosenfeld was a law student permit the university to treat him differently from the way it would some other student? If so, what differences in treatment would be justified?

6. Using Miles's eleven points as a guide, explain whether the university's actions did or did not violate Rosenfeld's procedural due process rights? How fair was the university's treatment of Rosenfeld?

Of course, student disciplinary hearings are not the only situations in which procedural due process must be followed. Any time the state seeks to take away someone's life, liberty, or property, it can only do so in accord with due process. Taking custody of a child from a parent is a deprivation that requires due process. In the next case, the Court of Appeals of Kentucky rules that when a court orders a significant change in child custody arrangements, the appearance of fairness can be as important as the correctness of the decision.

CASE

Lynch v. Lynch
Court of Appeals of Kentucky (1987)
737 S.W.2d 184

REYNOLDS, Judge.   This appeal arises from an order of the Fayette Circuit Court which changed appellant's sole custody of the parties' two minor children into a "joint reciprocal custody" arrangement in favor of both parents. Appellant maintains she was denied due process of law and a fair trial. We reverse as the record reflects, at a minimum, the appearance of a denial of due process.

Sherryl Frey Lynch (appellant) and Boyd Lee Lynch (appellee) were married on August 4, 1973. Two children were born of the marriage, John (approximately 13 years old), and Leanne (approximately 8 years old). On October 13, 1982, appellee filed a petition for divorce. A decree of dissolution was entered by the Fayette Circuit Court on May 13, 1983. This decree, pursuant to a separation agreement, gave custody of the two children to appellant and provided appellee with open visitation.

However, this policy of open visitation was not successful and, within four months, appellee made his first motion for specific visitation. The parties' inability to reach any sort of understanding on visitation is amply illustrated in the over 400 pages of record which accompanied this action. The current dispute began on April 21, 1986, when appellee filed a motion for a change of custody.

A hearing on this motion began on September 2, 1986, and continued into the next day. During these two days, appellee presented most of his case-in-chief. By agreement, one of appellant's witnesses, a licensed psychologist, testified out of order. The hearing was then continued to October 3, 1986.

Appellee concluded his case-in-chief on that day. Appellant then began her argument and completed all of her evidence, except for one witness who the trial court deemed unnecessary. It was at this point that the court presented each party with a 16-page document explaining:

> I have heard all of this testimony and I strongly believe that the decision should be immediately in this case. I have undertaken to draw up Findings of Fact and Conclusions of Law and an Order in anticipation of not learning anything new today. I will give you copies of it, copies so that you and your clients may read it.

Over appellant's objection, this order was subsequently entered.

The order, citing the inability of the parties to work out their visitation disagreement set up a system known as "joint reciprocal alternative custody." Briefly, this procedure divides the year into four three-month periods. During the first three months, one party (in this situation, appellant) would have custody for three weeks, followed by one week in which the other party (appellee) would have custody, followed by three weeks for appellant, followed by one week for appellee, and so on. At the end of the first three-month period the times switch, giving appellee custody for three weeks, followed by appellant for one week, and so on. The sequence continues to reverse with each quarter.

It is not necessary for this Court to decide the appropriateness of such a system at this time. Appellant's primary argument is concerned with the manner in which this order was entered.

It is clear from the record that the trial court prepared its findings, conclusions, and order prior to the final day of testimony. Except for one witness, taken out of order, appellant had not presented any evidence until after the document had been prepared. Due process requires, at the minimum, that each party be given an opportunity to be heard. Hearings should be conducted in a manner which leaves no question to their regularity. Although the trial court retained the option of not releasing its previously prepared order, its action in this situation creates the appearance that it had made up its mind before it had all of the evidence.

The record does contain information which might explain the trial court's desire for a quick solution. The two children had been in a state of uncertainty, because of their parent's inability to work together, since the divorce. We understandingly sympathize with the trial court's attempt to bring this matter to an equitable solution as soon as possible, but due process cannot be ignored.

Appellant has directed us to a recent criminal case which somewhat parallels our situation. In that action, the trial court had prepared the final judgment prior to a sentencing hearing. The Kentucky Supreme Court held that this was an abuse of discretion, even though the trial court retained the option of changing the judgment if the defendant produced some compelling evidence. *Edmonson v. Commonwealth, Ky.*, 725 S.W.2d 595 (1987). The trial court's discretion "must be exercised only after the defendant has had a fair opportunity to present evidence at a meaningful hearing...."

In *Edmonson*, the Kentucky Supreme Court vacated the judgment, and returned the case for action by a different circuit judge. We conclude that this would also be the correct procedure in this situation. There is a complete record, including video transcripts of the hearing, making additional testimony unnecessary.

For the foregoing reasons, the order of the Fayette Circuit Court is vacated and this action is remanded with directions that it be assigned to a different circuit judge for new findings and conclusions, based on the present record.

FOR DISCUSSION

1. Does the Court of Appeals conclude that there is anything wrong with the order of the trial court?

2. Is there any evidence that the trial court judge was concerned with anything other than the welfare of the Lynch's children? If not, why does Judge Reynolds conclude that Sherryl Frey Lynch's due process rights were violated?

3. According to Judge Reynolds, procedural due process requires "that each party be given a meaningful opportunity to be heard." Since Ms. Lynch presented her case before the trial court how were her rights violated?

4. The trial judge could have changed his opinion if Ms. Lynch had presented strong arguments. Does this repair any due process violations?

5. If the trial judge had waited a day or two before releasing his decision would there have been any violation of Ms. Lynch's procedural due process rights?

6. When a court order is vacated the case is often returned to the original trial judge who is likely to be the most familiar with the case. Why does the Court of Appeals direct that this case be assigned to a different judge who will have to rely on a video taped transcript of the original hearing?

LEGAL TERMS TO KNOW

Procedural due process   Substantive due process
State action   Summary judgment

ADDITIONAL QUESTIONS AND EXERCISES

1. Get a copy of your school's disciplinary rules and write an essay either defending them as meeting the requirements of due process or criticizing them for not meeting those requirements. If you attend a private school, explain whether these rules would have to be changed if your school's actions were considered state action.

2. Now that you have read the cases and essays in this chapter, explain whether you agree or disagree with the quote from Justice Frankfurter at the beginning of the chapter.

3. If a foreign exchange student asked you to explain what due process meant, how would you answer?

4. Originally, due process only meant procedural due process. Would we be better or worse off if we eliminated substantive due process and returned to that view? What do you think Friedman would say about that?

5. According to Friedman, the Supreme Court does not use substantive due process any less today than it did during the 1920s and 1930s; it has merely changed the subject matter. Examine the Supreme Court's rulings during the past year and write an essay explaining whether you agree or disagree with Friedman. You do not have to read all the cases since many periodicals publish articles reviewing them after the end of the Court's term, which usually runs from October to July.

6. In essence, due process is a guarantee of fairness. Examine the cases in this chapter and explain whether their outcomes were basically fair.

FOR FURTHER READING

1. EBERLE, EDWARD J., "Procedural Due Process: The Original Understanding," 4 Constitutional Commentary (Summer 1987), 339–62.
2. MCCARTHY, KEVIN, "Some Kind of Hearing," New York State Bar Journal 59 (May 1987), 44–48.
3. MONOGHAN, HENRY, "Of 'Liberty' and 'Property,'" 62 Cornell Law Review (1977), 405.
4. PENNOCK, J. ROLAND, and J. CHAPMAN, eds., Due Process: Nomos XVIII (New York: New York University Press, 1977).
5. RATNER, LEONARD, "The Function of the Due Process Clause," 116 University of Pennsylvania Law Review (1968), 1048.

4

PRECEDENT

INTRODUCTION

When most of us first learned about American government, we were told that legislatures made the law that courts then interpreted. As we have already seen, this is a misleading simplification. There are many ambiguities in the law as well as the constant occurrence of situations unforeseen by its authors. When they fill these gaps, courts are, in effect, making law. Such judge-made law is termed case law. To keep the case law consistent and predictable, judges generally try to follow past decisions of equal or higher courts within their jurisdiction. This following of precedent is called *stare decisis,* which is Latin for "let the decision stand." Although no law or constitutional provision requires it, the custom is so well established that there is a strong presumption in favor of following precedent. Judicial decisions are published and their meaning is debated by lawyers, legal scholars, government officials, and even students and ordinary citizens. Only these reported decisions are considered precedents.

In this chapter we will examine why judges try to follow precedent and when they sometimes, although rarely, overrule past decisions. In our changing society, judges must balance the values of consistency and predictability against the need to adapt to technological and social change. Given this tension, it is not surprising that there is considerable disagreement not only over how stare decisis should be used but even over whether it is a wise policy. Radical critics argue that it frequently serves to hide protection of the interests of those with wealth and power behind a facade of judicial neutrality. In other words, these critics claim that precedent is generally followed when it serves these interests, ignored when it does not. Of course, most lawyers and judges do not agree with this view.

Because stare decisis is a custom rather than a formal requirement, it is up to each court to decide what is or is not a binding precedent and whether to follow it. Despite this, the rule of binding precedent, even if not compulsory, is more than a legal game. It may be flexible, but it does limit the freedom of action of judges. Training and experience have ingrained stare decisis in judicial thinking. Failure to follow precedent increases the possibility of an embarrassing reversal by a higher court. Furthermore, if judges appear to ignore precedents too often, the displeasure of the public and other governmental officials might be expressed in changes in the law, in court structure, or in the election or appointment of new judges promising stricter adherence to the rule of precedent. Judges do try, when possible, to follow past decisions or, at least, to write opinions appearing to do so.

MEANING OF STARE DECISIS

In the following essay, Sol Wachtler, chief judge of New York State's highest court, explains why judges follow precedents even if they disagree with them. He also points out that courts can and do overrule some past decisions and tries to show just what factors may lead to this result.

READING   **Stare Decisis and a Changing New York Court of Appeals**
*By Sol Wachtler**

The judicial complement of the New York Court of Appeals has undergone dramatically greater changes in the recent past than at any other time in its 115-year history, and the next two years promise even more change. In addition to the appointment of a new Chief Judge, the Court has seen three of its members retire and be replaced since April 1983; within the next two years, two more of the sitting associate judges will retire. At present, for the first time, all members of the Court are serving by virtue of gubernatorial appointment rather than by election. This dramatic change in the Court's composition has led to speculation that the Court's position on legal issues may be subject to similarly dramatic change. The purpose of this article is to allay that fear by explaining the importance of the doctrine of stare decisis, which assures an element of stability in the court, while providing a process by which orderly change may occur.

I must confess that when I first came to the Court, after five years as a trial judge, I thought it would be both easy and desirable to bring my enlightened perspective to the law and clear out the dust bin of archaic legal thinking, thus bringing a renaissance to New York jurisprudence. After a few months, however, I came to appreciate the need to adhere to precedent in our common-law process. My notions regarding the significance of stare decisis changed drastically.

Although Blackstone stated that it was subject to exception, until recently stare decisis has been a doctrine rigidly adhered to in the [British] House of Lords. In contrast a more moderate view has always prevailed in our country, particularly in the New York Court of Appeals. This moderate approach serves two competing goals. On the one hand is a recognition that following precedent provides the necessary stability in the law, thereby serving the goals of efficiency, predictability, and uniformity. On the other hand, however, this stability aspect is tempered by a recognition that change is, in some cases, necessary. As Lord Chamberlain aptly stated:

> A deliberate or solemn decision of a court or judge made after argument on a question of law fairly arising in a case, and necessary to its determination, is an authority, or binding precedent, in the same court or in other courts of equal or lower rank, in subsequent cases, where "the very point" is again in controversy; but the degree of authority belonging to such a precedent depends, of necessity, on its agreement with the spirit of the times or the judgment of subsequent tribunals

upon its correctness as a statement of the existing or actual law, and the compulsion or exigency of the doctrine is, in the last analysis, moral and intellectual, rather than inflexible.[1]

The approach to stare decisis employed by the Court of Appeals in recent years recognizes as already suggested, the "conservative" goals of efficiency, predictability, and uniformity. Without a general policy of reliance on precedent, said Cardozo, "the labor of judges would be increased almost to the breaking point if every past decision could be reopened in every case, and one could not lay one's own course of bricks on the secure foundation of the courses laid by others who had gone before him."[2]

If courts are not obliged to follow precedent, the everyday business affairs of men and women would be impossible to conduct. Acknowledging the element of continuity is essential to protecting the interests of the diverse groups that make up society. Indeed, it is common knowledge that every attorney who drafts a contract or will, or renders business advice of any kind relies on the notion that, if litigation becomes necessary, the court will give the document or act the same effect it has given similar documents or acts in the past.

A predisposition to follow precedent assures that like cases will be treated similarly, a precept that is the cornerstone of our judicial system of laws. Of equal importance, stare decisis guarantees uniformity by assuring similar cases will be treated similarly, even if before different judges. This uniformity of treatment of different litigants is one of special concern in this time of rapidly changing personnel on our Court of Appeals.

Bearing in mind these "conservative" goals and principles, the question becomes in which types of cases does a relatively strict adherence to precedent outweigh a need for change? First, and perhaps foremost, are those cases in which the rule is one necessarily relied upon when structuring the transfer of property, such as cases involving wills, title to land, commercial transactions, and contracts. Second are those cases involving the construction of a statute, especially when the rule involved is long-standing, since the legislature is in a better position to change the statute if the court's interpretation is inconsistent with the legislative intent. Other cases in which it has been said that adherence to precedent should be closely followed are those in which, as Cardozo observed, "the commitment to an outworn policy is too firm to be broken by the tools of the judicial process."[3]

There are, of course, cases in which the doctrine of stare decisis should not be adhered to so rigidly. In any of these types of cases, the basic prerequisite to be satisfied before abandoning stare decisis is that the necessity for change in a particular area of the law outweighs the conservative policies that underly the promotion of adherence to the doctrine. This approach to the application of stare decisis in New York indicates that the doctrine is "moral and intellectual, rather than arbitrary and inflexible."[4] Chief Judge Cardozo similarly stated:

> that when a rule, after it has been duly tested by experience, has been found to be inconsistent with the sense of justice or with the social welfare, there should be less hesitation in frank avowal and full abandonment. …There should be greater readiness to abandon an untenable position when the rule to be discarded may not reasonably be supposed to have determined the conduct

[1] L. Chamberlain, *Stare Decisis* 19.

[2] B. Cardozo, *The Nature of the Judicial Process* 149 (1921).

[3] *Ibid.*, at 63.

[4] L. Chamberlain, sup. n.2, at 150–51.

of the litigants, and particularly when in its origin it was the product of institutions or conditions which have gained a new significance or development with the progress of the years.[5]

In which types of cases should the doctrine of stare decisis be adhered to less rigidly? Courts more readily reexamine rules they themselves have promulgated, for example, common-law rules of tort liability. Interpretations of constitutional, as opposed to statutory, provisions are also more properly changed by the judiciary, in light of the far greater difficulty of securing a corrective amendment of a constitution. In the realm of procedural, as opposed to substantive law, the courts have overruled precedent with perhaps the least reservation, for the policies that compel strict adherence to stare decisis are simply not as strong when substantive rights are not involved. In criminal cases, any change in rule or statutory interpretation that would be detrimental to a defendant should be avoided, and may indeed violate due process, but changes favorable to a defendant should be, and frequently are, made.

Chief Judge Breitel issued a particularly apt warning, sure to be followed by the present bench:

> No particular court as it is then constituted possesses a wisdom surpassing that of its predecessors. Without this assumption there is jurisprudential anarchy. There are standards for the application or withholding of stare decisis, the ignoring of which may produce just that anarchy. ...The ultimate principle is that a court is an institution and not merely a collection of individuals; just as a higher court commands superiority over a lower not because it is wiser or better but because it is institutionally higher. That is what is meant, in part, as the rule of law and not of men.[6]

Judiciously applied in a proper case, the doctrine of stare decisis will allay the fears of those who look with apprehension upon the ongoing personnel changes in the Court of Appeals. Perhaps more importantly, however, the prudent withholding of application of the doctrine, in accordance with the principles recounted above, will quiet the concerns of those who see the same changes as an excuse for the Court to forego its role as one of the leading courts of last resort in the nation. The New York Court of Appeals has had the courage to reflect in its judgments not inherited institutions, but its principles, its morality, and its own informed sense of justice. I am confident that my colleagues can strike the necessary balance between stability and innovation, and I look forward to working with them to meet that challenge.

NOTES

[*]Reprinted by permission: Wachtler, *Stare Decisis* and a Changing New York Court of Appeals, 59 *St. John's Law Review*, 445–56 (1985).

FOR DISCUSSION

1. Every writer has an audience in mind while writing. To what sort of audience does Judge Wachtler address his essay? Use examples from the text to support your reasoning.

2. How does Wachtler define stare decisis? What other term does he use almost interchangeably?

[5] B. Cardozo, sup. n.2, at 150–51.

[6] *People* v. *Hobson*, 39 N.Y.2d 479, 348 N.E.2d. 894, 384 N.Y.S.2d. 419 (1976).

3. Based on this essay, is the New York Court of Appeals by tradition a conservative court or a more innovative one? How does Wachtler feel about this?

4. What, according to Wachtler, are the two competing goals of the "moderate" approach to stare decisis?

5. What are the benefits of the "conservative" approach to stare decisis?

6. In what instances does the need for stability outweigh the need for change? Why? Do you agree?

7. In what types of cases is a more flexible approach to stare decisis justified?

8. Wachtler's remarks suggest that courts should generally defer to the legislature. Can you find support for this in the text? Does Wachtler indicate when deference to the legislature might not be advisable?

9. It has been said that courts are essentially conservative institutions. Compare the views of Lord Chamberlain, Judge Cardozo, and Judge Breitel on the doctrine of star₂ decisis. Which is the most conservative? The most liberal? Which do you find the most satisfactory?

STARE DECISIS IN PRACTICE

The following case shows that even the decision to uphold a well-established precedent can present problems. In 1922 the U.S. Supreme Court held that professional baseball was more of a game than a business, thereby exempting it from the antitrust laws. Whether or not this was accurate in 1922, only the most naïve would not consider professional baseball a business today. In his lawsuit, which was brought before the collective bargaining agreement allowed free agency, Curt Flood asked the Court to reconsider the original precedent and declare baseball's "reserve clause," binding him to a single team for as long as it wanted him, invalid.

CASE

Flood v. Kuhn
U.S. Supreme Court (1972)
92 S.Ct. 2099, 407 U.S. 258

Mr. Justice BLACKMUN delivered the opinion of the Court: The petitioner, Curtis Charles Flood, began his major league career in 1956. In October 1969, Flood was traded to the Philadelphia Phillies. He was not consulted about the trade. In December he complained to the Commissioner of Baseball [Bowie Kuhn] and asked to be made a free agent and be placed at liberty to strike his own bargain with any other major league team. His request was denied.

Flood then instituted this antitrust suit in January 1970 in federal court. The complaint charged violation of the federal antitrust laws and civil rights statutes. Petitioner sought declaratory and injunctive relief and treble damages.

[The trial judge] held that *Federal Baseball Club* v. *National League*, 259 U.S. 200, 42 S.Ct. 465 (1922) and *Toolson* v. *New York Yankees*, 346 U.S. 356, 74 S.Ct. 78 (1953) were controlling. On appeal, the Second Circuit felt "compelled to affirm."

The Legal Background

Federal Baseball Club was a suit initiated by a member of the Federal League against the National and American Leagues and others. Mr. Justice Holmes in speaking succinctly for a unanimous court said:

The business is giving exhibitions of baseball, which are purely state affairs.... But the fact that in order to give the exhibitions the Leagues must induce free persons to cross state lines and pay for their doing so is not enough to change the character of the business.... [T]he transport is a mere incident, not the essential thing. That to which it is incident, the exhibition, although made for money would not be called trade or commerce in the commonly accepted sense of those words.

In the years that followed, baseball continued to be subject to intermittent antitrust attack. The courts, however, rejected these challenges on the authority of *Federal Baseball*. In some cases stress was laid, although unsuccessfully, on new factors such as the development of radio and television with their substantial additional revenues to baseball.

[In *Toolson*] *Federal Baseball* was cited as holding "that the business of providing baseball games for profit between clubs of professional baseball players was not within the scope of the federal antitrust laws." [There are] four reasons for the Court's affirmance of *Toolson* and its companion cases: (a) Congressional awareness for three decades of the Court's ruling in *Federal Baseball* coupled with congressional inaction. (b) The fact that baseball was left alone to develop for that period upon the understanding that the reserve system was not subject to existing federal antitrust laws. (c) A reluctance to overrule *Federal Baseball* with consequent retroactive effect. (d) A professed desire that any needed remedy be provided by legislation rather than by court decree. The emphasis in Toolson was on the determination, attributed even to *Federal Baseball*, that Congress had no intention to include baseball within the reach of federal antitrust laws.

In view of all this, it seems appropriate now to say that:

1. Professional baseball is a business and it is engaged in interstate commerce.

2. With its reserve system enjoying exemption from the federal antitrust laws, baseball is, in a very distinct sense, an exception and an anomaly. *Federal Baseball* and *Toolson* have become an aberration confined to baseball.

3. It is an aberration that has been with us now for half a century, one heretofore deemed fully entitled to the benefit of stare decisis, and one that has survived the Court's expanding concept of interstate commerce. It rests on a recognition and an acceptance of baseball's unique characteristics and needs.

4. Other professional sports operating interstate—football, boxing, basketball, and, presumably, hockey and golf—are not so exempt.

5. The advent of radio and television, with their consequent increased coverage and additional revenues, has not occasioned an overruling.

6. The Court has emphasized that since 1922 baseball, with full and continuing congressional awareness, has been allowed to develop and expand unhindered by federal legislative action. Remedial legislation has been introduced repeatedly in Congress but none has ever been enacted.

7. The Court has expressed concern about the confusion and the retroactivity problems that inevitably would result with a judicial overturning of *Federal Baseball*. It has voiced a preference that if any change is to be made, it come by legislation that, by its nature, is only prospective in operation.

Accordingly, we adhere once again to *Federal Baseball* and *Toolson*. If there is any inconsistency or illogic in all this, it is an inconsistency and illogic of long standing that is to be remedied by Congress and not by this Court. Under these circumstances, there is merit in consistency even though some might claim that beneath that consistency is a layer of inconsistency.

Judgment affirmed.

Mr. Justice DOUGLAS, with whom Mr. Justice BRENNAN concurs, dissenting.

This Court's decision in *Federal Baseball* is a derelict in the stream of the law that we, its creator, should remove. Only a romantic view[*] of a rather dismal business account over the last 50 years would keep that derelict in midstream.

An industry so dependent on radio and television as is baseball and gleaning vast interstate revenues would be hard put to say with the Court in the *Federal Baseball* case that baseball was only a local exhibition, not trade or commerce.

Baseball is today big business that is packaged with beer, with broadcasting, and with other industries. The beneficiaries of the *Federal Baseball* decision are not the Babe Ruths, Ty Cobbs, and Lou Gehrigs.

The owners whose records many say reveal a proclivity for predatory practices do not come to us with equities. The equities are with the victims of the reserve clause.

If congressional inaction is our guide, we should rely upon the fact that Congress has refused to enact bills broadly exempting professional sports from antitrust regulation. The only statutory exemption granted by Congress to professional sports concerns broadcasting rights. I would not ascribe a broader exemption through inaction than Congress has seen fit to grant explicitly. The unbroken silence of Congress should not prevent us from correcting our own mistakes.

NOTES

*While I joined the Court's opinion in *Toolson*, I have lived to regret it; and I would now correct what I believe to be its fundamental error.

FOR DISCUSSION

1. In the previous essay, Judge Wachtler said that adherence to precedent should be closely followed in cases "in which, as Cardozo observed, 'the commitment to an outworn policy is too firm to be broken by the tools of the judicial process.'" Is this such a case? If "the tools of the judicial process" cannot prevail in such a case, what alternative is available?

2. One argument against overturning the *Federal Baseball* and *Toolson* cases is that for fifty years the baseball owners have been permitted to rely on those rulings in ordering their business affairs. Give arguments for and against this position.

3. People expect the law to be fair, reasonable, evenhanded, and consistent. Given this, do you think that the majority promotes respect for the law?

4. The majority states that baseball's "unique characteristics and needs" justify its exemption from federal antitrust laws. What unique characteristics and needs distinguish baseball from other professional sports such as football, basketball, and boxing, which are not exempt?

5. The decision in *Flood* rests heavily upon deference to the legislature as the preferred agent of change in this situation. Why might Congress be better suited than the Supreme Court to decide whether baseball should be exempt from the antitrust laws? *Hint*: Review some of the debate over judicial activism in Chapter 2.

6. In the decision, much is made of congressional inaction with respect to the status of baseball. Do you think legislative inaction should have the same force and influence as legislative action in a case of this kind?

7. Judge Wachtler also believes that courts should defer to the legislature in many instances, but one type of case that he identifies as particularly suitable for a flexible approach to stare decisis is when a court considers overturning its own prior judicial rule. How is that relevant to *Flood* v. *Kuhn*?

HOW USEFUL IS STARE DECISIS?

In the following essay, David Kairys takes the position that, despite the ideals expressed by judges and scholars, in reality stare decisis is used to protect the legitimacy and power of the courts, that "law is simply politics by other means." Judges, like other public officials, resolve policy conflicts not by following a set of objective rules but by weighing conflicting values and selecting the one they prefer. They then rationalize their decisions by referring back to past cases. In essence, the following of precedent is often a mask hiding judicial protection of the status quo against social change.

READING   **Legal Reasoning**
                          *By David Kairys**

The idealized model of the legal process is based on the notion that there is a distinctly legal mode of reasoning and analysis that leads to and determines "correct" rules, facts, and results in particular cases. The concept of legal reasoning is essential to the fundamental legitimizing claim of government by law, not people; it purports to distinguish legal analysis and expertise from the variety of social, political, and economic considerations and modes of analysis that, in a democratic society, would be more appropriately debated and determined by the people, not judges.

This [article] focuses on one of the basic elements or mechanisms of legal reasoning, stare decisis, which embodies the notion of judicial subservience to prior decisions or precedents. The notion is that judges are bound by and defer to precedents, thereby restricting their domain to law rather than politics.

If legal reasoning has any real meaning, stare decisis, applied by a skilled and fair legal mind, should lead to and require particular results in specific cases. But anyone familiar with the legal system knows that some precedents are followed and some are not; thus, not all precedents are treated similarly or equally. Moreover, the meaning of a precedent and its significance to a new case are frequently unclear. The important questions, largely ignored by judges, law teachers, and commentators, are: How do courts decide which precedents to follow? How do they determine the significance of ambiguous precedents? Do precedents really matter at all? Why do lawyers spend so much time talking about them?

The Supreme Court's recent decisions concerning exercise of free-speech rights in privately owned shopping centers provide a good illustration. In *Amalgamated Food Employees Union Local 590* v. *Logan Valley Plaza*, 391 U.S. 308 (1968), the Court upheld the constitutional right of union members to picket a store involved in a labor dispute in the shopping center where it was located. The Court recognized that shopping centers have to a large extent replaced inner-city business districts. The best, and perhaps only, place to communicate with suburbanites is in shopping centers. Citing *Marsh* v. *Alabama*, 326 U.S. 501 (1946), in which First Amendment freedoms were held applicable to a "company town," the Court ruled that the interest in free speech outweighed the private-property interests of shopping-center owners.

However, only four years later, in *Lloyd* v. *Tanner*, 407 U.S. 551 (1972), the Court held that an antiwar activist had no right to distribute leaflets in a shopping center, even though this center regularly attracted political candidates by avowing that it provided the largest audience in the state. The majority opinion justified the decision by claiming to differentiate the facts involved from those in *Logan Valley* primarily on the ground that speech concerning a labor dispute relates more closely to the activities of a shopping center than does antiwar speech. (In legal parlance, this is called distinguishing a precedent).

Then, in *Hudgens* v. *NLRB*, 424 U.S. 507 (1976), the Court announced that, contrary to explicit language in *Lloyd*, the Court had actually overruled *Logan Valley* in the *Lloyd* case. The Court said that to treat labor speech differently from antiwar speech would violate the norm that First Amendment freedoms do not depend on the content of the speech, a result that surely was not intended in *Lloyd*. Having rewritten *Lloyd*, the *Hudgens* court went on to say that it was bound by *Lloyd* (as rewritten) and to hold that union members involved in a labor dispute with a store located in a shopping center do not have a constitutional right to picket in that shopping center. The stated rationale for this complete turnaround, within only eight years, was stare decisis: "Our institutional duty is to follow until changed the law as it now is, not as some members of the Court might wish it to be (at 518)."

The Court offered no explanation of what happened to this "institutional duty" in *Lloyd*, since the *Lloyd* court would seem to have been bound by *Logan Valley* (which the *Hudgens* court held had decided the same issue decided in *Lloyd*). Nor did the Court explain how its duty to "follow until changed the law as it now is" binds it in any real sense, since even within the system of stare decisis it is understood that the Court can change the law or overrule, ignore, or rewrite prior decisions. The Supreme Court is never really *bound* by a precedent. Finally, the majority opinion in *Hudgens* castigated the dissenting justices for deciding cases on the basis of what they "might wish [the law] to be," but there is no indication of how the majority's decision-making process is different. The majority simply outnumbered the minority.

There were ample precedents supporting each of the conflicting policies in *Hudgens*. Freedom of speech was favored over property in *Marsh* (from an earlier period when First Amendment rights were being expanded) and in *Logan Valley* itself. Private property and the interests of suburbanites in isolation were favored in earlier cases and recently in *Lloyd*. This policy conflict clearly was not—and could not be—resolved by some objective or required application of stare decisis or any other legal principle.

Unstated and lost in the mire of contradictory precedents and justifications was the central point that none of these cases was or could be decided without ultimate reference to values and choices of a *political* nature. The various justifications and precedents emphasized in the opinions serve to mask these little discussed but unavoidable social and political judgments. In 1968, a majority of the members of the Court resolved the conflict in favor of freedom of speech; in 1972, a majority retreated from that judgment; in 1976, a majority decided that property interests would prevail.

In short, these cases demonstrate a central deception of traditional jurisprudence: the majority claims for its social and political judgment not only the status of law (in the sense of binding authority), which it surely has, but also that its judgment is the product of distinctly legal reasoning, of a neutral, objective application of legal expertise. This latter claim, essential to the legitimacy and mystique of the courts, is false.

Stare decisis is so integral to legal thinking and education that it becomes internalized by people trained in the law, and its social role and ideological content become blurred and invisible. To see those aspects of and to understand stare decisis, it is helpful to separate the social role from the functional impact on the decision-making process.

Our legal norms are broadly and vaguely stated. They do not logically lead to particular results or rationales concerning most important or difficult issues. A wide variety of interpretations, distinctions, and justifications are available; and judges have the authority and power to choose the issues they will address and to ignore constitutional provisions, statutes, precedents, evidence, and the best legal arguments.

Moreover, there are prior decisions similar or related by analogy to both sides of almost any difficult or important issue. This should not be surprising, since issues are difficult or important largely because there are significant policies, rooted in social reality and/or legal doctrine, supporting both sides. Each such policy, or a closely related policy, will have been favored or given high priority in some context and/or during some period. Usually the various relevant precedents will provide some support for both sides rather than lead to a particular rule or result.

Indeed, often the same precedent will provide support for both sides. For example, suppose after *Hudgens* an antinuclear activist claimed the right to distribute leaflets and picket in a privately owned railroad terminal. The terminal's counsel would argue that *Hudgens* should be broadly construed as definitively resolving the issue of speech on private property that is open to the public. He or she would emphasize the physical and functional similarities of shopping centers and train terminals. On the other hand, the activist's counsel would urge that *Hudgens* be narrowly construed as applicable only to the particular problem of labor picketing and only to the shopping center involved in that case or, at most, to shopping centers generally. He or she would emphasize the differences between train terminals and shopping centers. Much of legal education consists of training students to make arguments and distinctions of this kind. Both sides would argue that *Hudgens,* properly construed (a phrase likely to be found in both briefs), supports each of them. The judge would then decide the case, citing *Hudgens* as support for his or her decision regardless of which side won. There is no *legal* explanation in any of this; the law has provided a falsely legitimizing justification for a decision that is ultimately social and political.

Judicial decisions ultimately depend on judgments based on values and priorities that vary with particular judges (and even with the same judge, depending on the context) and are the result of a composite of social, political, institutional, experiential, and personal factors. The socially and legally important focus of judicial decision making— hidden by stare decisis and the notion of legal reasoning, and largely ignored in law schools, opinions, and law review articles—should be on the content, origins, and development of these values and priorities.

This does not mean that judicial values and priorities, or the results in particular cases, are random or wholly unpredictable. The shared backgrounds, socialization, and experience of our judges, which include law school and usually law practice, yield definite patterns in the ways they categorize, approach, and resolve social and political conflicts. Moreover, some rules and results are relatively uncontroversial and predictable in a particular historical context, not based on stare decisis or any other legal principle but because of widely shared social and political assumptions characteristic of that context.

While seeming to limit discretion and to require objective and rational analysis, stare decisis in fact provides and serves to disguise enormous discretion. This discretion is somewhat broader in the higher courts, but it exists at all levels. Lower courts have an added institutional concern, since their decisions can be reviewed, but they also have added discretion stemming from their relatively larger control over the facts and the credibility of witnesses.

Functionally, stare decisis is not a process of decision making or a mechanism that ensures continuity, predictability, rationality, or objectivity. Precedents are largely reduced to rationalizations, not factors meaningfully contributing to the result; they support rather than determine the principles and outcomes adopted by judges.

Stare decisis is integral to the popular conception of the judicial process and an important component of the ideology with which judicial power is justified and legitimized. This ideological role is perhaps easiest to see if one looks at the historical development of stare decisis. Viewing stare decisis as a component of a neutral, objective, or quasi-scientific discipline, one would expect a progressive development and a general tendency toward reliance on precedent, or at least toward concrete, rational standards for determining when precedent will not be followed. However, it is clear that stare decisis has not developed this way. The meaning and importance of stare decisis are not fixed by or independent of social and historical circumstances, and there has been no long-term tendency toward refinement. Rather, stare decisis has conveniently fallen by the wayside in periods when the legitimacy and power of the courts stood to be enhanced by openly rejecting continuity in favor of politically popular change.

In sum, stare decisis, while integral to the language of legal discourse and the mystique of legal reasoning, serves a primarily ideological rather than functional role. Nor is there any more validity to the notion of legal reasoning when the source of law is a statutory or constitutional provision or the language of an agreement. Courts determine the meaning and applicability of the pertinent language; similar arguments and distinctions are available; and the ultimate basis is a social and political judgment. Law is simply politics by other means.

NOTES

*From *The Politics of Law: A Progressive Critique* edited by David Kairys. "Legal Reasoning." Copyright © 1982 by David Kairys. Reprinted by permission of Pantheon Books, A Division of Random House, Inc.

FOR DISCUSSION

1. At the end of his essay, Kairys states, "Law is simply politics by other means." What political and social interests are served by the decision in *Flood* v. *Kuhn*? What interests suffer as a result of the decision?

2. In dissenting in *Flood*, Justice Douglas reversed the position he took in *Toolson*. Does this support Kairys's argument about the nature of stare decisis? Explain.

3. Compare Kairys's definition of stare decisis with Judge Wachtler's. How do they differ?

4. According to Kairys, what is a central deception of traditional jurisprudence and why does it persist?

5. Does it matter to us if law is ideologically influenced instead of objective and neutral? Why? Is it possible for law to be objective and neutral?

6. In *The Nature of the Judicial Process*, Justice Cardozo commented: "Back of precedents are the basic juridicial conceptions which are the postulates of judicial reasoning and farther back are the habits of life, the institutions of society, in which those conceptions had their origins, and which, by a process of interaction, they have modified in turn." How would Kairys interpret this statement? Would he be likely to agree with it?

In contrast to Kairys's argument that the ambiguity in law that courts must deal with gives judges so much discretion that it makes stare decisis little more than rationalization, Lief Carter argues that such ambiguity may actually be desirable. Rather than retarding legal change as Kairys maintains, the discretion that stare decisis gives to judges facilitates changes in legal rules. After reading Carter's essay you may wish to examine the cases in this and previous chapters to see if you can find support for either of these opposing viewpoints.

READING   **Unpredictability in Law**
                                   By Lief Carter*

REASONING FROM WORDS

Cases often go to courts because the law does not determine the outcome. Both sides believe they have a chance to win. The legal process is in these cases *unpredictable*. Legal rules are made with words, and we can begin to understand why law is unpredictable by examining the unpredictability of words. Sometimes our language fails to give us precise definitions. More often, words and statements that seem clear enough in the abstract may, nevertheless, have different meanings to each of us because we have all had different experiences with the objects or events in the world that the word has come to represent. The experiences of each of us are unique in many respects, so no one word or set of words necessarily means the same thing to all of us. How many parents must reject some names for a new child because, while the mother associates a given name with a friend or hero from the past, the father once knew a villain of the same name?

Words, furthermore, are malleable: people can shape them to suit their own interests. To illustrate, in 1962, Congress, to encourage new business investment, allowed business people up to a 10 percent tax credit for investing in new personal property for their business. Investments like new machinery would qualify, but new buildings and permanent building fixtures would not. In 1982 the Justice Department sued the accounting firm of Ernst and Whinney for using words to disguise real property as personal property. What the accountants called "movable partitions," "equipment accesses," and "decorative fixtures" were in reality doors, manholes, and windows—all real property unqualified for the tax deduction. A "freezer" was in reality an entire refrigerated warehouse, "cedar decoration" was a wood-paneled wall, and "movable partitions—privacy" described toilet stalls.

The disorderly conduct of words affects legal reasoning most immediately when a judge faces the task of interpreting a statute for the first time, when no judicial precedent interpreting the statute helps the judge to find its meaning.

The previous paragraph suggests that precedents help narrow the range of legal choices judges face when they resolve a case. Indeed, precedents do just that, but they never provide complete certainty. Reasoning by example also perpetuates a degree of unpredictability in law. To see why, we must proceed through six analytical stages.

Stage One: Reasoning by Example in General

Reasoning by example, in its simplest form, means accepting one choice and rejecting another because the past provides an example that the accepted choice somehow "worked." Robert, for example, wants to climb a tree but wonders if its branches will hold. He chooses to attempt the climb because his older sister has just climbed the tree without mishap. Robert reasons by example. His reasoning hardly guarantees success: His older sister may still be skinnier and lighter. Robert may regret a choice based on a bad example, but he still reasons that way. If he falls and survives, he will possess a much better example from which to reason in the future.

The most important characteristic of reasoning by example in any area of life is that no rules tell the decider *how* to select the facts that are similar or different. Let us therefore see how this indeterminacy occurs in legal reasoning.

Stage Two: Examples in Law

In law, precedents provide the examples for legal reasoning. For starters, a precedent contains the analysis and the conclusion reached in an earlier case in which the facts and legal question(s) resemble the current conflict a judge has to resolve. Even where a statute or constitutional rule is involved, a judge will look at what other judges have said about the meaning of that rule when they applied it to similar facts and answered similar legal questions. How does a judge know what the conclusion of a prior case was, or whether its facts do resemble those in the case before him?

Trials themselves do *not*, as a rule, produce precedents. Trials seek primarily to discover who is lying, whose memory has failed, and who can reliably speak the truth of the matter. When the jury hears the case, the judge acts as an umpire, making sure the lawyers present the evidence properly to the jury so that it decides the "right" question. Often judges do the jury's job altogether. The law does not allow jury trials in some kinds of cases. When the law does allow jury trials, the parties may elect to go before a judge anyway, perhaps because they feel the issues are too complex for laypeople, perhaps because "bench trials" take less time. In law, time is money, a lot of money.

Of course, a trial judge must decide all the issues of law that the lawyers raise. The conscientious trial judge will explain to the parties orally for the record why and how he resolves the key legal issues in their case. In some instances he will give them a written opinion explaining his legal choices and some of these find their way into the reported opinions. But since at a trial the judge pays most attention to the historical part of the case, deciding what happened, he usually keeps his explanations at the relatively informal oral level. As a result other judges will not find these opinions reported anywhere; they cannot discover them even if they try. Hence, few trial judges create precedents even though they resolve legal issues.

If one party feels the outcome of the trial was erroneous because the judge applied the wrong law to the facts, he will, if he can afford it, appeal the case to a court of appeals. Judges who hear appeals from trials concern themselves primarily with the legal issues in the case. They learn the facts in the case by reading the trial transcript, the written record of facts and conclusions produced in the oral give and take of the trial. But appellate judges then usually *assume* facts to exist as the jury or the judge found them and ask whether the trial judge applied the proper law to them. Judges who review these legal questions routinely write opinions explaining their conclusions.

Thus, the masses of legal precedents that fill the shelves of law libraries mostly emerge from the appellate process. You should not, however, lose sight of the fact that lawyers use many of the same legal reasoning techniques when they base their recommendations to their clients on appellate precedents and when they manipulate precedents to their advantage in litigation.

Stage Three: The Three-Step Process of Reasoning by Example

Legal reasoning often involves reasoning from the examples of precedents. Powerful legal traditions impel judges to solve problems by using solutions to similar problems reached by judges in the past. Thus, a judge seeks to resolve conflicts by discovering a statement about the law in a prior case—his example—and then applying this statement or conclusion to the case before him. Lawyers who seek to anticipate problems and prevent conflicts follow much the same procedure. Professor Edward Levi calls this a three-step process in which the judge sees a factual similarity between the current case and one or more prior cases, announces the rule of law on which the earlier case or cases rested, and applies the rule to the case before him.

Stage Four: How Reasoning by Example Perpetuates Unpredictability in Law

To understand this stage we must return to the first step in the three-step description of the legal reasoning process, the step in which the judge decides which precedent governs. The judge must *choose* the facts in the case before him that resemble or differ from the facts in the case, or line of cases, in which prior judicial decisions first announced the rule. The judge no doubt accepts his obligation, made powerful by legal tradition, to "follow precedent," but he is under no obligation to follow any particular precedent. He completes step one *by deciding for himself* which of the many precedents are similar to the facts of the case before him and *by deciding for himself* what they mean.

No judicial opinion in a prior case can require that a judge sift the facts of his present case one way or another. He is always free to do this himself. A judge writing his opinion can influence a future user of the precedent he creates by refusing to report or consider some potentially important facts revealed in the trial transcript. But once he reports them, precedent users can use the facts in their own way. They can call a fact critical that a prior judge reported but deemed irrelevant; they can make a legal molehill out of what a prior judge called a mountain. Thus, the present judge, the precedent user, retains the freedom to choose the legal example from which the legal conclusion follows.

I call this judicial freedom to choose the governing precedent by selectively sifting the facts "fact freedom." Our inability to predict with total accuracy how a judge will use his fact freedom is the major source of uncertainty in law. Legal reasoning explores the ways judges use and abuse this freedom. Thus, we cannot say that "the law" applies known or given rules to diverse factual situations because we don't know the applicable rules until after the judge uses his fact freedom to choose the precedent.

Stage Five: An Illustration of Unpredictability in Law

Consider the following example from the rather notorious history of enforcing the Mann Act. The Mann Act, passed by Congress in 1910, provides in part that: "Any person who shall knowingly transport or cause to be transported...in interstate or foreign commerce...any woman or girl for the purpose of prostitution or debauchery, or for any other immoral purpose...shall be deemed guilty of a felony." Think about these words for a minute. Do they say that if I take my wife to Tennessee for the purpose of drinking illegal moonshine whiskey with her I shall be deemed guilty of a felony? What if I take her to Tennessee to rob a bank? Certainly robbing a bank is an "immoral purpose." Is it "interstate commerce?" For the moment you should see only that the Congress has chosen some rather ambiguous words and then move to the main problem: choosing the "right" example to decide the following case.

Mr. and Mrs. Mortensen, owners and operators of a house of prostitution in Grand Island, Nebraska, decided to take some of the employees for a well-earned vacation at Yellowstone and Salt Lake City. The girls did lay off their occupation completely during the entire duration of the trip. Upon their return they resumed their calling. Over a year later federal agents arrested the Mortensens and, on the basis of the vacation trip, charged them with violation of the Mann Act. The jury convicted the Mortensens. Their lawyer has appealed the case to you, an appellate court judge.

Unpredictability in law arises when the judge cannot automatically say that a given precedent is or isn't factually similar. To simplify matters here, let us now assume that you examine only one precedent, the decision of the U.S. Supreme Court in *Caminetti*

v. *U.S.*, 242 U.S. 470 (1917). You must choose whether this example does or does not determine the result in *Mortensen*. Assume that in *Caminetti* a man from Wichita met but did not linger with a woman during a brief visit to Oklahoma City. After his return home, he sent this "mistress" a train ticket, which she used to travel to Wichita. There she did spend several nights with her friend, but not as a commercial prostitute. Assume that on these facts the Supreme Court in *Caminetti* upheld the conviction under the Mann Act. Does this precedent bind you? To answer these questions you must decide whether this case is factually similar to *Mortensen*. Is it?

In one sense, of course it is. In each case the defendants transported women across state lines, after which sex out of wedlock occurred. In another sense it isn't. Without her ticket and transportation the Oklahoma woman could not have slept with the defendant. But if the Mortensens had not sponsored the vacation, the women would have continued their work. The Mortensens' transportation *reduced* the frequency of prostitution. The rancher maintained or increased "illicit sex." Should this difference matter? You the judge are free to select one interpretation of the facts or the other in order to answer this question. Either way you decide you will create a new legal precedent. It is precisely this freedom to decide either way that increases unpredictability in law.

Stage Six: Reasoning by Example Facilitates Legal Change

Why does judicial fact freedom make law change constantly? Legal rules change every time they are applied because no two cases ever have exactly the same facts. Although judges treat cases as if they were legally the same whenever they lift the rule out of one case and drop it into another, deciding the case in terms of the rule adds to the list of cases a new and unique factual situation. To rule in the Mortensens' favor, as the Supreme Court did in 1944 (*Mortensen* v. *U.S.*, 322 U.S. 369), gave judges new ways of looking at the Mann Act. With those facts, judges after 1944 could, if they wished, read the Mann Act more narrowly than *Caminetti* did. *Mortensen* thus potentially changed the meaning of the Mann Act, thereby changing the law.

But as the situation turned out, the change did not endure. In 1946 the Court upheld the conviction, under the Mann Act, of certain Mormons, members of a branch known as Fundamentalists, who took multiple wives across state lines to Utah. No prostitution at all was involved here, and traveling to Utah did not cause them to marry bigamously. Fact freedom worked its way again (*Cleveland* v. *U.S.*, 329 U.S. 14). The Court extended *Caminetti* and by implication isolated *Mortensen*. The content of the Mann Act, then, has changed with each new decision and each new set of facts.

Is law always as confusing and unclear as these examples make it seem? In one sense certainly not. To the practicing lawyer, most legal questions the client asks possess clear and predictable answers. But in such cases the problems probably do not get to court at all. Uncertainty helps convert a human problem into a legal conflict. We focus on uncertainty in law because that is where reason in law takes over.

In another sense, however, law never entirely frees itself from uncertainty. Lawyers always cope with uncertainties about what happened, uncertainties that arise in the historical part of law. If they go to trial on the facts, even if they think the law is clear, the introduction of new evidence or the unexpected testimony of a witness may raise new and uncertain legal issues the lawyers didn't consider before the trial. Lawyers know they can never fully predict the outcome of a client's case, even though much of the law is clear to them most of the time.

IS UNPREDICTABILITY IN LAW DESIRABLE?

Is it desirable that legal rules do not always produce clear and unambiguous answers to legal conflicts? Should the legal system strive to reach the point where legal rules solve problems in the way, for example, that the formula for finding square roots or numbers provides automatic answers to all square root problems?

Despite the human animal's natural discomfort in the presence of uncertainty, some unpredictability in law is desirable. Indeed, if a rule had to provide an automatic and completely predictable outcome before courts could resolve conflicts, society would become intolerably repressive, if not altogether impossible. There are two reasons why.

First, since no two cases ever raise entirely identical facts, society must have some way of treating cases *as if they were the same* in a way litigants accept as fair. Of course, judicial impartiality is an important element of fairness. But you should also think about this fact: If the legal system resolved all conflicts automatically, people would have little incentive to *participate* in the process that resolves their disputes. If the loser knew in advance he would surely lose, he would not waste time and money on litigation. He would not have the opportunity to try to persuade the judge that his case, always somewhat factually unique, *ought* to be treated by a different rule. Citizens who lose will perceive a system that allows them to "make their best case" as fairer than a system that tells them they lose while they sit helplessly.

Only in unpredictable circumstances will each side have an incentive to present its best case. Because the law is ambiguous, each side thinks it might win. This produces an even more important consequence for society as a whole, not just for the losers. The needs of society change over time. The words of common law, statutes, and constitutions must take on new meanings. The participation that ambiguity encourages constantly bombards judges with new ideas. The ambiguity inherent in reasoning by example gives the attorney the opportunity to persuade the judge that the law ought to say one thing rather than another. Lawyers thus keep pushing judges to make their interpretations of "the law" fit newer shared beliefs about right and wrong.

I am not encouraging legislators and judges to create or applaud legal uncertainty. Rather, I am arguing that uncertainty in law is unavoidable. This uncertainty is, however, more a blessing than a curse. The participation that uncertainty in law encourages gives the legal process and society itself a vital capacity to change its formal rules with the less formal changes in human needs and values.

NOTES

*From *Reason in Law*, 3/e by Lief H. Carter 26–35, Copyright © 1988 by Lief H. Carter. Reprinted by permission of Harper Collins Publishers.

FOR DISCUSSION

1. In his essay, Carter ascribes unpredictability in law at least in part to what he calls "the disorderly conduct of words"—different meanings for a word based on different experiences and interests. Can Kairys's ideologically based view of stare decisis be hidden in "the disorderly conduct of words?" How might Carter respond to this?

2. Both Carter and Kairys acknowledge that following precedent is not a straightforward, automatic task, yet the theses of these two essays are very different. What major differences do you see between their approaches?

3. Carter states: "Citizens who lose will perceive a system that allows them to 'make their best case' as fairer than a system that tells them they lose while they sit helplessly." After reading Flood v. Kuhn, do you think the loser in that case would have walked away with a feeling that the legal system was fair?

4. How would Kairys respond to the Carter statement in question 3?

5. Compare Carter's analysis of the use of precedent in the Mann Act cases to Kairys's analysis of the Shopping Center/Free Speech cases. What differences do you see? Which viewpoint do you find more persuasive?

WHEN NOT TO FOLLOW PRECEDENT

Because overturning a precedent is relatively unusual, courts that do so take great pains to explain why. In the following case the New York State Court of Appeals reconsiders and overturns a precedent not just by simply pointing to changed circumstances or flaws in the reasoning of the original decision but by showing that other subsequent precedents have weakened the force of the original. In reading this case, compare the court's reasoning to the arguments put forth in the preceding essays.

CASE

Buckley v. City of New York
New York State Court of Appeals (1982)
452 N.Y.S.2d 331, 437 N.E.2d 1088

Opinion of the Court, GABRIELLI, Judge.   Each of the cases involved in these appeals presents the question of whether the fellow-servant rule continues to apply in New York. In each case an employee of the City of New York, who was injured through the negligence of a coemployee, brought an action against the municipality. In *Buckley* v. *City of New York* a police officer was accidentally shot in the leg when a gun being loaded by a fellow officer discharged in the station house locker room and in *Lawrence* v. *City of New York* a fire fighter was seriously injured when a fellow fire fighter threw a smoldering couch from the second story window of a fire-damaged building and struck the plaintiff while he was standing in the yard. In each case the plaintiff secured a jury verdict against the city on a theory of vicarious liability and the city's motion to dismiss the complaint on the basis of the fellow-servant rule was denied. The Appellate Division has affirmed the judgments in both instances and leave has been granted to appeal to this court. We now affirm the orders below.

   Under the rule of respondeat superior, an employer will be liable to third parties for torts of an employee committed within the scope of his employment. By virtue of the fellow servant rule, however, if an employee is injured by a fellow employee in the workplace he will have no recourse against the employer in respondeat superior. Succinctly stated, the rule provides that "where a servant is injured through the negligence or fault of a fellow servant, engaged in a common business and employment, ...and the master is himself free from fault, the master is not responsible for the injury" (36 N.Y.Jur., Master and Servant, 130).

   The fellow-servant rule had its origin in England in 1837 and was adopted in the United States shortly afterward. The rationales attributed to the rule are varied; the most convincing is that the rule promotes the safety of the public and the workers by encouraging each employee to be watchful of the conduct of others for his own protection. It has also been suggested that the rule was based upon the notion that an employee assumes the risk of negligence on the part of his fellow servants or, more fundamentally, that the rule simply reflected a 19th century bias by the courts in favor of business (see Prosser, Torts, 4th ed., pp. 528–529). The theoretical underpinnings of this rule have, to a large extent, been discredited in recent years (see *Poniatowski* v. *City of N.Y.*, 248 N.Y.S.2d 849, 198 N.E.2d 237). Logically there appears to be little reason for denying an employee the right which a third party possesses to recover from the employer in respondeat superior, since for one thing, in both instances the employer might have avoided the injury by selection of more careful employees. Moreover, the class of persons most frequently endangered by the negligence of an employee—his fellow workers—should not, without compelling reason, be denied a remedy accorded the general public.

The overall effect of the fellow-servant rule was drastically curtailed by the advent of workers' compensation legislation, for the rule, involving injuries sustained in the course of one's employment provides no defense to a demand for this remedy. Nevertheless, the rule has not yet been completely obliterated since there are some areas of employment, such as those involved in the present appeal where the Workers' Compensation Law does not apply.

In *Poniatowski* v. *City of N.Y.* our court signaled the beginning of the end of the fellow-servant rule in New York. There, a police officer was injured in a motor vehicle accident through the negligence of a fellow officer. Although the plaintiff's cause was sustained in our court on the basis of a statute which obviated the necessity of directly confronting the fellow servant rule, we referred to this rule in passing by stating that "[t]he inherent injustice of a rule which denies a person, free of fault, the right to recover for injuries sustained through the negligence of another over whose conduct he has no control merely because of the fortuitous circumstances that the other is a fellow officer is manifest. ...This may well suggest the desirability of abolishing the rule but we leave decision of that question to the future." Today we are squarely presented with the question left open in *Poniatowski*—whether the fellow-servant rule is to survive in New York. The rule had its birth in the 19th century, was severely crippled with the advent of workers' compensation, and was dealt an almost fatal blow in *Poniatowski*. Today, in rejecting this rule entirely, we inter its remains.

In constructing its argument for retention of the fellow-servant rule, the defendant city has largely abandoned the rationales originally underpinning the rule and, instead, asserts that the rule should be retained primarily because it has enjoyed a lengthy tenure in our jurisprudence. While the longevity of a rule requires that its re-examination be given careful scrutiny, it does not demand that its effect be given permanence. The continued vitality of a rule of law should depend heavily upon its continuing practicality and the demands of justice, rather than upon its mere tradition. Although the policy of stare decisis is not to be lightly cast aside, this court has previously noted that "[i]t was intended not to effect a 'petrifying rigidity,' but to assure the justice that flows from certainty and stability. If, instead, adherence to precedent offers not justice but unfairness, not certainty but doubt and confusion, it loses its right to survive, and no principle constrains us to follow it." *Bing* v. *Thunig*, 163 N.Y.S.2d 3, 143 N.E.2d 3.

Furthermore, we make it abundantly clear that we do not subscribe to the view that the abolition of the fellow-servant rule is strictly a matter for legislative attention. The fellow-servant rule originated as a matter of decisional law, and it remains subject to judicial re-examination.

The fellow-servant rule serves no continuing valid purpose in New York, but instead works an unjustifiable hardship upon individuals injured in the workplace, and we must thus conclude that the fellow-servant rule is no longer to be followed in New York.

Accordingly, the orders of the Appellate Division should be affirmed, with costs.

FOR DISCUSSION

1. What changes have weakened the original reasons behind the fellow-servant rule? How strong were those reasons in the first place?

2. Suppose the reasoning of the *Buckley* court about whether to honor a precedent purely because it is old had been applied to *Flood* v. *Kuhn*. Would the outcome in that case have been different? Why?

3. How would Kairys explain the outcome in *Buckley*?

4. *Buckley* is a decision of the New York Court of Appeals. How does this decision compare to Judge Wachtler's observations about the operation of that court?

5. Apply Carter's description of legal reasoning by example to the discussion of precedents in *Buckley*.

Because no cases involve exactly the same facts and circumstances as a previous precedent setting decision, both sides cite similar (or even the same!) cases which support their arguments. Our next case shows one method of deciding which of two precedents with different outcomes should be applied. Courts are required only to follow those parts of past cases that were essential to the decision, termed "the rule of the case." Any other statements in the decision are merely incidental comments, known legally as *obiter dicta* (frequently abbreviated to dicta or its singular, dictum), which future courts are not bound to follow if they disagree. The reasoning behind this is similar to the rule against advisory opinions. Lacking the concrete details of a specific case, judges' answers to hypothetical questions are likely to be based on less information and be less well thought out than when the adversaries will gain or lose something specific as a result of the court's reasoning. In the case below, the Supreme Court of Florida uses this doctrine in interpreting the meaning of a statute.

CASE

Continental Assurance Co. v. Carroll
Supreme Court of Florida (1986)
485 So.2d 406

MCDONALD, Justice.   The Fourth District Court of Appeal has certified the following question as one of great public importance: Does the special concurrence in *National Standard Life Insurance Co.* v. *Permenter* modify the strict rule set forth in *Life Insurance Co. of Virginia* v. *Shifflet* that all misrepresentations material to the acceptance of risk will invalidate an insurance policy, even if made in good faith?

This case began as an action to recover the proceeds of a twenty-thousand dollar life insurance policy which the Continental Life Assurance Company issued upon the life of the Carroll's infant son Brian. Soon after Brian's birth on May 4, 1982, the Carrolls began making inquiries concerning a life insurance policy for the baby. On June 14th Brian's mother took him to Dr. Kamal Taslimi for a checkup. Although Dr. Taslimi apparently assured Mrs. Carroll that her baby was generally healthy, he also informed her that Brian had developed a heart murmur and needed both an EKG and x-rays.

One week later, the Carrolls filled out a life insurance application with Continental. Continental issued the policy on July 2 and Brian died of congenital heart disease nine days later. When the Carrolls filed a claim under the policy, Continental denied coverage and returned the premium payment. The insurance company grounded its claim for recision of the insurance contract on the following questions and answers from the application:

Q. Is child, to the best of your knowledge and belief, in good health and free from deformity and defect?

A. Yes.

Q. Who is the child's doctor?

A. Kamal Taslimi.

Q. When and why was he last consulted?

A. 6-14-82.

Q. What did doctor say about his findings?

A. Normal.

Q. What treatment and drugs did he prescribe?

A. None.

Q. Is child still under treatment?

A. No.

Q. Any other consultations with him? If yes, give details.

A. No.

The company claimed it would never have taken the policy had the Carrolls related the true facts on the application.

At the close of the Carroll's case at trial, Continental moved for a directed verdict based on section 627.409, Florida Statutes (1981) and *Life Insurance Co.* v. *Shifflet*, 201 So.2d 715 (Fla. 1967). In *Shifflet* this Court held that any misrepresentation materially affecting risk would invalidate an insurance policy, even if made in good faith. Nevertheless the trial court denied Continental's motion. The jury awarded the Carrolls the full amount of the policy plus costs, attorney's fees, and interest.

The district court affirmed on appeal, ruling that a concurring opinion in *National Standard Life Insurance Co.* v. *Permenter*, 204 So.2d 206 (Fla. 1967) modified *Shifflet*. According to the district court, where insurance applicants in good faith make erroneous expressions of opinion or judgment, or where a question is couched in language beyond the applicant's understanding, the applicant's error does not void the policy. The district certified the instant question, however, because this Court has never directly declared that *Permenter* modified the *Shifflet* rule.

Section 627.409(1), Florida Statutes (1981), provides that misrepresentations, omissions, concealment of facts, and incorrect statements on an insurance application shall not prevent a recovery unless they are either: (1) fraudulent; (2) material to the risk being assumed; or (3) the insurer in good faith either would not have issued the policy or would have done so only on different terms had the insurer known the true facts.

In *Shifflet* this court construed section 627.01081 of the Florida Statutes, the predecessor to section 627.409. Section 627.01081 read identically to the statute before us today. In *Shifflet* we answered the stipulated question of "whether clearly incorrect and untrue statements to questions on an insurance application, material to the acceptance of the risk of the contract, must be given with the knowledge of the incorrectness and untruth to vitiate the policy under section 627.01081." In answering this question we noted that the statute was unambiguous and we therefore accorded the statute its plain and obvious meaning. We held that the statute precluded recovery under an insurance policy where either the misrepresentation materially affects the acceptance of risk or the insurer would not have issued the policy under the same terms had it known the true facts. In short, *Shifflet* stands for the proposition that misrepresentations need not be knowingly made in order to void the policy.

Less than seven months after this Court decided *Shifflet*, we decided *Permenter*. *Permenter* consisted of a one sentence per curiam statement discharging our writ of certiorari for lack of jurisdiction. Justice Ervin, however, concurred specifically in *Permenter* and a majority of the Court joined in his concurrence. Justice Ervin departed from the matter at hand in *Permenter* and commented upon *Shifflet*, noting his concern with potential applications of the *Shifflet* rule and expressing his belief that *Shifflet's* sweeping rule could work injustice under certain circumstances. Justice Ervin then attempted to draw a distinction between statements of opinion or judgment and statements of pure fact. He also suggested exceptions to the *Shifflet* rule where the applicant either honestly misunderstands or has insufficient knowledge to answer the questions on the insurance application.

The sole holding in *Permenter* was a finding that this court lacked jurisdiction. We do not know its facts and any statements beyond the simple finding of no jurisdiction were obiter dicta. Such dicta is at most persuasive and cannot function as groundbreaking precedent. *Shifflet*, therefore, remains as the binding precedent in this state.

Although the district court may have agreed with Justice Ervin's concerns, no district court can legitimately circumvent a decision of this court. If indeed the district court believed Justice Ervin's approach constituted "the better rule," the proper course would have been to rule in accordance with *Shifflet* and then certify the question to this Court.

The language of section 627.409 remains as unambiguous today as the wording of its predecessor examined in *Shifflet*. The plain meaning of the statute indicates that, where either an insurer would have altered the policy's terms had it known the true facts or the misstatement materially affects risk, a nonintentional misstatement in an application will prevent recovery under an insurance policy. The statute recognizes the principle of law that a contract issued on a mutual mistake of fact is subject to being voided and defines the circumstances for the application of this principle. This Court cannot grant an exception to a statute nor can we construe an unambiguous statute different from its plain meaning.

In the instant case the application asked what Doctor Taslimi said about the child's health. Mr. Carroll responded to that question with one word, "normal." The statute allowed the insurance company to rely on this response. To permit the jury to draw a questionable distinction as to whether this response was fact or opinion and then base the outcome of this case on that distinction was error. The trial judge should have directed a verdict in favor of Continental.

Accordingly, we answer the certified question in the negative, quash the opinion of the district court, and remand for proceedings consistent with this opinion.

BOYD, C.J., and OVERTON, EHRLICH, and SHAW, JJ. concur.

ADKINS, J., dissents.

FOR DISCUSSION

1. Compare the Court's remarks about statutory interpretation and precedent in this case with those of Judge Wachtler. Explain whether you think he would have reached the same result as the Florida Supreme Court in this case.

2. The different interpretations of "misrepresentation" illustrate Carter's "disorderly conduct of words." Explain the different interpretation in *Shifflet* and *Permenter*. Why does the *Continental Assurance* court agree with *Shifflet's* interpretation? How does it justify ignoring Justice Ervin's opinion in *Permenter*?

3. What conflicting interests would Kairys see in *Continental Assurance*? How would he interpret the result?

4. In *Buckley* v. *City of New York* the court overturned a precedent but the *Continental Assurance* court stated that it did not. What differences do you see between the two cases? Do these differences justify the opposing results?

LEGAL TERMS TO KNOW

Case law	Respondeat superior
Fact freedom	Rule of the case
Obiter dicta	Stare decisis

ADDITIONAL QUESTIONS AND EXERCISES

1. Look up the shopping center/free speech cases discussed by Kairys. Read them and explain whether you agree with Kairys's analysis. Then compare *Pruneyard Shopping Center* v. *Robins*, 447 U.S. 74 (1980), explaining whether it confirms or contradicts your view and his.

2. Using the readings in this chapter, write an essay defining stare decisis. Write your essay from the viewpoint that your definition is better than those given in the various readings and explain why.

3. Based on the readings in the chapter, describe the *process* by which judges decide whether or not to follow a precedent. What is the value of this process to the people who use it?

4. Judge Wachtler says that the "conservative" concern with stability, predictability, and uniformity requires adherence to precedent, particularly in matters concerning wills and property, yet the New York Court of Appeals has not always followed that view. Read *Riggs* v. *Palmer,* 115 N.Y. 506 (1889), and write an essay summarizing the opposing viewpoints in that case, which decides whether a murderer should be permitted to inherit property under his victim's will. Consider how both Wachtler and Kairys might explain the *Riggs* decision.

5. For additional analysis of *Riggs*, read Benjamin Cardozo, *The Nature of the Judicial Process* (New Haven: Yale University Press, 1921), pp. 40–43, and Ronald Dworkin, *Taking Rights Seriously* (Cambridge, Mass: Harvard University Press, 1977), pp. 22–31.

6. Using the cases and readings in this chapter for support, write an essay defining "fairness" as an important concern of the legal system.

FOR FURTHER READING

1. CARDOZO, BENJAMIN, *The Nature of the Judicial Process. New Haven: Yale University Press, 1921.*

2. FRANK, JEROME, *Courts on Trial: Myth and Reality in American Justice.* New York: Atheneum, 1967.

3. GOLDING, MARTIN, *Legal Reasoning.* New York: Knopf, 1984.

4. LEVI, EDWARD, *An Introduction to Legal Reasoning*, Chicago: University of Chicago Press, 1948.

5. SCHAEFFER, WALTER, "Precedent and Policy: Judicial Opinions and Decision Making," in *Views From the Bench*, eds. Mark Cannon and David O'Brien. Chatham, N.J.: Chatham House, 1985, pp. 91–99.

6. UNGER, ROBERTO MANGABEIRA, *The Critical Legal Studies Movement.* Cambridge, Mass.: Harvard University Press, 1986.

5

LIMITS
ON COURTS

INTRODUCTION

One of the main reasons that Alexander Hamilton termed the judiciary the least dangerous branch was the constitutional limitation of its power to "cases" and "controversies." Since most Americans consider any lawsuit to be a case, this seems merely a restatement of the obvious but, as with so many of the terms we have examined, the words "case" and "controversy" have a much more specific meaning in law than in everyday language.

The courts will not hear a lawsuit unless it meets the specific requirements that make it a case or controversy. Although these requirements vary slightly from state to state and between state and federal courts, the basic concepts are widely accepted. To be heard the suit must be a genuine dispute between two parties who stand to gain or lose something as a result of the court's decision. It must also arise from a specific factual situation. When the two sides are not truly adversaries, the suit will be dismissed as collusive. With the exception of a few states (Massachusetts and Alabama are two examples), courts will not issue advisory opinions, preferring to wait for the concreteness of a specific factual situation. The requirement of standing ensures that both sides have a stake in the outcome of the decision. If events beyond the control of the courts have resolved the question before the court has made its decision, rather than making a ruling without effect, a court will declare the case moot. If another branch should more appropriately resolve a problem, a court can declare it a political question.

These limitations on courts serve an important purpose. Because courts do not gather their own information, they need to ensure that the two adversaries, who provide that information, will exercise maximum efforts in arguing their cases. If the two sides are in collusion, this may not happen. If one side does not stand to lose anything but an argument should the court rule against it, that party has less of an incentive to make the best possible arguments. The specifics of a particular situation help a judge see how a law works out in practice.

In addition, as discussed in Chapter 2, courts depend on voluntary compliance to enforce most decisions. When that compliance does not come, another branch's help may be necessary to compel adherence. The doctrine of political questions, by preventing courts from stepping on the toes of the other branches too often, helps to ensure that they will supply enforcement power when asked.

In this chapter we will examine these limits on courts, as well as such other limits as statutes of limitations and governmental immunity. The introduction and first essay will give us an overview after which we will see how these limits are applied in practice.

Standing

The doctrine of standing requires that a plaintiff challenging a law show evidence of harm. A person cannot simply read about a statute that appears unconstitutional then ask a court to annul it. A plaintiff must show specific damage from that law, not merely that it is bad policy or harms the public as a whole. This threat of direct harm both eliminates frivolous suits that could further clog an already crowded court system and provides an incentive for every plaintiff and defendant to make the strongest possible arguments to prevent that threat from becoming reality. The most common threats are financial or physical harm or the loss of liberty, but, in recent years, standing has been liberalized to include less obvious threats such as danger to the environment.

Courts will also refuse to hear a case that is moot. When external factors have resolved a case, thus rendering any judicial decision a mere opinion without force, the case will generally be declared moot and dismissed. For example, if a parent sues to try to get his or her child into a specific high school but the case does not get to court until the student has graduated from another high school and entered college, the case would be declared moot. However, there are two exceptions to the mootness rule. If the defendant tries to avoid an adverse decision by stopping the activity being challenged, the court can continue the case. Questions that are likely to be repeated can also be heard even if the case is otherwise moot. This second exception explains how the Supreme Court heard challenges to antiabortion laws. Because pregnancy terminates in far less than the two or three years it takes a case to work its way up to the Supreme Court, it would hardly be fair for that tribunal to eliminate all such claims from review. Therefore, the Supreme Court has decided cases challenging state restrictions on abortion that would otherwise appear moot.

Political Questions

All plaintiffs, even members of Congress, must have standing to sue in order for courts to hear their cases. Because of the doctrine of separation of powers, however, courts are reluctant to get involved in disputes between the other branches even when plaintiffs in such suits have standing. The doctrine of political questions provides a way of keeping out, but courts have had a difficult time defining exactly what constitutes a political question. As one scholar has put it, "Like other jurisdictional doctrines, the political-question doctrine means what the justices say it means."[1] Even its name is misleading as the Supreme Court often rules on questions that most would consider political such as abortion and affirmative action. Because of this, one leading text states that "it should more properly be called the doctrine of nonjusticiability, that is that the subject matter is inappropriate for judicial

[1] David M. O'Brien, Storm Center: *The Supreme Court in American Politics* (New York: W. W. Norton, 1986), p. 172.

consideration."[2] A court will declare a lawsuit a nonjusticiable political question if it should be decided by one of the other branches of government either because the Constitution says so or because judicial standards are lacking.

The lack of precision in defining the political question doctrine has resulted in many changes in its application, another of our continuing series of illustrations of how the law continually changes. One of the most prominent examples is the series of legislative apportionment cases decided by the U. S. Supreme Court. In a 1946 case, *Colegrove* v. *Green* (328 U.S. 549), the Court held that the apportionment of state legislatures was a political question not appropriate for courts to get involved in unless there was racial discrimination. During the next fifteen years America became more urbanized and industrialized, but a number of states refused to change their legislative districts to reflect these changes. This gave rural areas a disproportionate influence in their legislatures. In *Baker* v. *Carr*, 369 U.S. 186, the Supreme Court reconsidered its earlier view, deciding that unequally populated districts could be challenged as violating the Fourteenth Amendment's guarantee of equal protection of the laws. This decision opened the courts to a series of challenges to state and federal legislative districts that has continued to this day. *Baker* v. *Carr* is also important because it represents the court's most thorough attempt to define the meaning of the political question doctrine.

Statute of Limitations

With the exception of murder, the law sets a limit on how much time a plaintiff or prosecutor has to bring a case. The purpose of such statutes of limitation is to prevent cases from coming to court so long after the original events that memories have faded and witnesses and evidence have become difficult to produce. Each legislature determines the appropriate amount of time. In general, the more serious the injury, the longer the statute of limitations. The legislature can also stop the clock (the legal term is *toll*) for events such as wartime military service or injuries occurring before the victim has reached the age of majority.

Modern technology has added a complicating factor—illnesses caused by the exposure to toxic chemicals. Because such diseases often occur years after the original exposure, statutes of limitation which start the clock at the time of the injury may expire by the time the disease is diagnosed. Some states have addressed this problem by starting the period from the date the disease is or should have been diagnosed. Whether this solves the problem is open to debate. If someone contracts cancer twenty years after the alleged exposure, intervening events may have been a major or partial cause. In addition, finding witnesses after so many years may be so difficult that it prevents a fair trial. This explains why there has been no consensus among states about what to do. You may wish to examine how your state has handled this problem.

Governmental Immunity

The final limit on the courts we will consider is governmental immunity. Neither federal nor state government can be sued without its permission. This immunity does not extend to municipal governments, however. The doctrine of governmental immunity originated from the English view that "the King can do no wrong." Today such immunity is justified by the danger of bankrupting the government if it must defend too many such suits. After all, it will be the taxpayers rather than any wrongdoer who will pay the costs.

---

[2] John Nowak, Ronald Rotunda, and J. Nelson Young, *Handbook on Constitutional Law* (St. Paul, Minn.: West Publishing, 1978), p. 100.

As government has expanded, the doctrine of governmental immunity has lost some of its force. The government can be sued when its actions are proprietary rather than governmental; in other words, when it is acting more as a business (Amtrak, for example) than as a government. Legislation such as the Federal Tort Claims Act and judicial decisions have also expanded the rights of injured persons to seek damages from the government. Nevertheless, immunity remains a significant barrier to suits against government.

Governmental immunity can also extend to officials in the performance of their duty. Thus, a police officer who believes he or she has probable cause to make an arrest, cannot be sued for false arrest even if the charges are dismissed in court. However, this immunity only extends to actions within the scope of the officer's duty. Should the arrest be made simply out of personal dislike or racial prejudice or should excessive force be used, the victim would not be barred from suing.

Without such immunity, government officials could be so afraid of being sued that they would do as little as possible. Our hypothetical police officer might make very few arrests, limiting them to cases of 100 percent certainty. As government has grown, the problem of who should be given such immunity has come up more frequently. Much as courts had to decide when state action was involved in due process cases (see Chapter 3), they also need to decide whether employees of private companies acting under government mandated rules or in government-regulated businesses or under government contracts are entitled to governmental immunity.

In general, the greater the discretion given to a public official and the higher his or her office, the greater the immunity. Judges have virtually complete immunity from suit for their judicial actions, although, of course, they can be removed from office for serious misconduct. Similarly, Article I, Section 6, of the Constitution states that "for any speech or debate," members of Congress "shall not be questioned in any other place," meaning that they cannot be sued or arrested for their official acts. Of course, both judges and representatives, like the rest of us, can be brought to court for their private acts. In other words, a judge cannot be sued for a bad decision, even if it has absolutely no basis in law. If, however, he or she committed murder, prosecution would be appropriate as would a civil suit by the victim's family.

Conclusion

As the preceding discussion indicates, not every legal dispute will be decided by a court. The rules defining a case or controversy serve several purposes. They reduce case loads. They also help ensure that the cases that do come to court will provide fair vehicles for judicial decision making—they will be genuine disputes between well-motivated adversaries with specific factual situations that have occurred recently enough for evidence to be reliable. Questions best decided by other governmental bodies will be kept out of court. These rules also have a cost, however. Many people with legitimate grievances will never be given their day in court. The changes in many of these doctrines are a result of the efforts of courts and legislatures to improve the balance between these costs and benefits.

THE CASE OR CONTROVERSY RULES

Jonathan Varat's essay provides an overview of the origins and development of the requirements for deciding whether the issue before a court is a case or controversy.

READING   **Cases and Controversies**
                                By Jonathan D. Varat*

Article III of the Constitution vests the judicial power of the United States in one constitutionally mandated Supreme Court and such subordinate federal courts as Congress may choose to establish. Federal judges are appointed for life with salaries that cannot be diminished, but they may exercise their independent and politically unaccountable power only to resolve "cases" and "controversies" of the kinds designated by Article III, the most important of which are cases arising under the Constitution and other federal law. The scope of the federal judicial power thus depends in large measure on the Supreme Court's interpretations of the "case" and "controversy" limitation applicable to the Court itself and to other Article III tribunals.

That limitation not only inhibits Article III courts from arrogating too much power unto themselves; it also prevents Congress from compelling or authorizing decisions by federal courts in nonjudicial proceedings and precludes Supreme Court review of state court decisions in proceedings that are not considered "cases" or "controversies" under Article III. The limitation thus simultaneously confines federal judges and reinforces their ability to resist nonjudicial tasks pressed on them by others.

The linkage between independence and circumscribed power is a continuously important theme in "case" or "controversy" jurisprudence and the power of judicial review of government acts for constitutionality—a power that *Marbury* v. *Madison* (1803) justified primarily by the need to apply the Constitution as relevant law to decide a "case." During the Constitutional Convention of 1787, Edmund Randolph proposed that the President and members of the federal judiciary be joined in a council of revision to veto legislative excesses. The presidential veto power was adopted instead, partly to keep the judiciary out of the legislative process and partly to insure that the judges would decide cases independently, without bias in favor of legislation they had helped to formulate. Similar concerns led the convention to reject Charles Pinckney's proposal to have the Supreme Court provide advisory opinions at the request of Congress or the President. Finally, in response to James Madison's doubts about extending the federal judicial power to expound the Constitution too broadly, the Convention made explicit its understanding that the power extended only to "cases of a Judiciary nature." The framers understood that the judicial power of constitutional governance would expand if the concept of "case" or "controversy" did.

What constitutes an Article III "case," of a "judiciary nature," is hardly self-evident. No definition was articulated when the language was adopted, but only an apparent intent to circumscribe the federal judicial function, and to insure that it be performed independently of the other branches. In this century, Justice Felix Frankfurter suggested that Article III precluded federal courts from deciding legal questions except in the kinds of proceedings entertained by the English and colonial courts at the time of the Constitution's adoption. But the willingness of English courts to give advisory opinions then—a practice clearly inconsistent with convention history and the Court's steadfast policy since 1793—refutes the suggestion. Moreover, from the outset the separation of powers aspect of the "case" or "controversy" limitation has differentiated constitutional courts (courts constituted under Article III) from others. Most fundamentally, however, the indeterminate historical contours of "cases" or "controversies" inevitably had to accommodate changes in the forms of litigation authorized by Congress, in the legal and social environment that accompanied the nation's industrial growth and the rise of the regulatory and welfare state, and in the place of the federal judiciary in our national life.

After two centuries of elaboration, the essential characteristics of Article III controversies remain imprecise and subject to change. Yet underlying the various manifestations of "case" or "controversy" doctrine are three core requirements: affected parties standing in an adverse relationship to each other, actual or threatened events that provoke a live legal dispute, and the courts' ability to render final and meaningful judgments. These criteria—concerning, respectively, the litigants, the facts, and judicial efficacy—have both independent and interrelated significance.

As to litigants, only parties injured by a defendant's behavior have standing to sue. Collusive suits are barred because the parties' interests are not adverse.

As to extant factual circumstances, advisory opinions are banned. This limitation not only bars direct requests for legal rulings on hypothetical facts but also requires dismissal of unripe or moot cases, because, respectively, they are not yet live, or they once were but have ceased to be by virtue of subsequent events. The parties' future or past adversariness cannot substitute for actual, current adversariness. Disputes that have not yet begun or have already ended are treated as having no more present need for decision than purely hypothetical disputes.

The desire to preserve federal judicial power as an independent, effective, and binding force of legal obligation is reflected both in the finality rule, which bars decision if the judgment rendered would be subject to revision by another branch of government, and in the rule denying standing unless a judgment would likely redress the plaintiff's injury. These two rules are the clearest instances of judicial self-limitation to insure that when the federal courts do act, their judgments will be potent. To exercise judicial power ineffectively or as merely a preliminary gesture would risk undermining compliance with court decrees generally or lessening official and public acceptance of the binding nature of judicial decisions, especially unpopular constitutional judgments. Here the link between the limitations on judicial power and the power's independence and effectiveness is at its strongest.

Historically, congressional attempts to expand the use of Article III judicial power have caused the greatest difficulty, largely because the federal courts are charged simultaneously with enforcing valid federal law as an arm of the national government and with restraining unconstitutional behavior of the coequal branches of that government. The enforcement role induces judicial receptivity to extensive congressional use of the federal courts, especially in a time of expansion of both the federal government's functions and the use of litigation to resolve public disputes. The courts' checking function, however, cautions judicial resistance to congressional efforts to enlarge the scope of "cases" or "controversies" for fear of losing the strength, independence, or finality needed to resist unconstitutional action by the political branches.

The early emphasis of "case" or "controversy" jurisprudence was on consolidating the judiciary's independence and effective power. The Supreme Court's refusal in 1793 to give President George Washington legal advice on the interpretation of treaties with France—the founding precedent for the ban on advisory opinions—rested largely on the desire to preserve the federal judiciary as a check on Congress and the executive when actual disputes arose. Similarly, *Hayburn's Case* (1792) established that federal courts would not determine which Revolutionary War veterans were entitled to disability pensions so long as the secretary of war had the final say on their entitlement: Congress could employ the federal judiciary power only if the decisions of federal courts had binding effect.

Preserving judicial authority remains an important desideratum in the twentieth century, but the growing pervasiveness of federal law as a means of government regulation—often accompanied by litigant and congressional pressure to increase access to the federal courts—inevitably has accentuated the law-declaring enforcement role of the federal judiciary and tended to expand the "case" or "controversy" realm. *Muskrat* v. *United States* (1911) cited the courts' inability to execute a judgment as a reason to reject Congress'[s] authorization of a test case to secure a ruling on the constitutionality of specific statutes it had passed. Similarly, the Court initially doubted the federal courts' power to give declaratory judgments. Yet, by the late 1930s, the Supreme Court had upheld both its own power to review state declaratory judgments and the federal Declaratory Judgment Act of 1934. The declaratory judgment remedy authorizes federal courts to decide controversies before legal rights are actually violated. The judge normally enters no coercive order, but confines the remedy to a binding declaration of rights. So long as the controversy is a live one, between adverse parties, and the decision to afford a binding remedy rests wholly with the judiciary, the advisory opinion and finality objections pose no obstacles. A controversy brought to court too early may fail Article III ripeness criteria, but the declaratory remedy itself does not preclude the existence of a "case" or "controversy."

Congress has succeeded in expanding the reach of federal judicial power not only by creating new remedies for the federal judicial courts to administer but also by creating new substantive rights for them to enforce. The Supreme Court maintains as a fundamental "case" or "controversy" requirement that a suing party, to have standing, must have suffered some distinctive "injury in fact." The injury must be particularized, not diffuse; citizen or taxpayer frustration with alleged government illegality is insufficient by itself. In theory, Congress cannot dispense with this requirement and authorize suits by individuals who are not injured. Congress may, however, increase the potential for an injury that will satisfy Article III, simply by legislating protection of new rights, the violation of which amounts to a constitutional "injury in fact." For example, *Trafficante* v. *Metropolitan Life Insurance Company* (1972) held that a federal civil rights ban on housing discrimination could be enforced not only by persons refused housing but also by current tenants claiming loss of desired interracial associations; the Court interpreted the statute to create a legally protected interest in integrated housing. To a point, then, Article III "cases" or "controversies" expand correspondingly with the need to enforce new federal legislation. Yet, the scope of congressional power to transform diffuse harm into cognizable Article III injury remains uncertain and apparently stops short of providing everyone a judicially enforceable generalized right to be free of illegal governmental behavior, without regard to more individualized effects.

The historically approved image is that federal judges decide politically significant public law issues only to resolve controversies taking the form of private litigation. Over the years, however, this picture has had to accommodate not only congressional creation of enforceable rights and remedies but also the modern realities of public forms of litigation such as the class action, the participation of organized public interest lawyers, and lawsuits aimed at reforming government structures and practices. Public law adjudication, especially constitutional adjudication, is certainly the most important function of the federal courts. The inclination to stretch the boundaries of "cases" or "controversies" to provide desired legal guidance on important social problems, although it has varied among federal judges and courts of different eras, increases in response to congressional authorization and the perception of social need. Offsetting that impulse, however, are two countervailing considerations. First, the judges realize that the more public the issues raised, the more democratically appropriate is a political rather than a judicial resolution. Second, they understand the importance of a litigation context that does not threaten judicial credibility, finality, or independence; that presents a realistic need for decision; and that provides adequate information and legal standards for confident, well-advised decision making. These competing considerations will continue to shape the meaning of "cases" and "controversies," setting the limits of the federal judicial function in ways that preserve the courts' checking and enforcement roles in the face of changes in the forms and objectives of litigation, in the dimensions of federal law, and in the expectations of government officials and members of the public.

NOTES

*Reprinted with permission of Macmillan Publishing Company from "Cases and Controversies" by Jonathan D. Varat in *Encyclopedia of the American Constitution*, Leonard W. Levy, Kenneth L. Karst, and Dennis J. Mahoney, Editors. Copyright © 1986 by Macmillan Publishing Company, a Division of Macmillan, Inc.

FOR DISCUSSION

1. For what reasons does the Constitution limit the powers of the federal courts to cases or controversies? Are those reasons still valid today?
2. As Varat points out, courts have often resisted attempts to expand the definition of cases or controversies even though this would give them more power. Can you explain why?
3. How has the definition of cases and controversies changed since the writing of the Constitution?
4. According to Varat, "The historically approved image is that federal courts decide politically significant public law issues only to resolve controversies taking the form of private litigation." Does he agree with the accuracy of this image? Do you believe that this image is the way federal courts ought to operate?

STANDING

No matter how important a plaintiff, he or she must still demonstrate standing before a court will hear any arguments on the merits of the suit. The next case presents a suit by sixteen members of Congress seeking a court order declaring that the Congress itself was unconstitutionally stopping President Reagan from carrying out his policy of aiding the antigovernment rebels (contras) in Nicaragua. Before ruling on the constitutional issues, the Federal District Court must determine whether the plaintiffs are harmed enough by the law to have standing to sue.

CASE

Dornan v. Secretary of Defense
U.S. District Court, District of Columbia (1987)
676 F. Supp. 6

GESELL, District Judge.   This is a sincere but misdirected declaratory judgment suit seeking a constitutional decision relating to the role of Congress and President in a current foreign policy dispute. Sixteen congressmen, a Senator and fifteen Members of the House of Representatives have sued President Reagan and key members of his Cabinet, in their official capacities, requesting the Court to declare that Congress is unconstitutionally constraining the President from carrying out his announced policy to support the contras in Nicaragua. This complaint recites the authority of the President to guide American foreign policy and points to his duty to implement that policy, as well as treaties and laws deemed consistent with his decision to aid the contras. Actions of the Congress that reflect rejection or disagreement with aspects of the President's contra initiative are alleged to be unconstitutional in that they frustrate foreign policy powers of the President in disregard of Article II of the Constitution which specifies the President shall faithfully execute the laws and conduct foreign affairs.

The President and members of his Cabinet who have been sued oppose this action by a Motion to Dismiss. The motion must be granted and the complaint dismissed because the complaint completely fails to allege a justiciable controversy.

Plaintiffs contend they have the right as individual congressmen to seek an order from the Court that would declare the President in violation of the Constitution because he allegedly has abdicated his foreign affairs responsibilities by submitting to unconstitutional laws and because he has failed to keep his official and political promise to lend this country's full support to the anti-Sandinista resistance fighters.

Federal courts cannot pronounce upon the constitutionality of every government action someone desires to question. They may adjudicate only the legal rights of litigants in actual controversies. The "Case" and "Controversy" language of Article III presents a threshold, jurisdictional issue the Court must decide before the merits of any questioned action can be reached. Whether the relief requested in a complaint is equitable or monetary, the Supreme Court has repeatedly noted that Article III requires that a plaintiff bringing suit must first establish a genuine "personal stake" in the outcome of a controversy before a federal court may consider exercising its judicial power. There are two essential elements of this concept of a "personal stake," or so-called standing requirement: the plaintiff must have suffered or be threatened with some "distinct and palpable injury," *Warth* v. *Seldin*, 422 U.S. 490 (1975), and there must be some causal connection between the plaintiff's asserted injury and the defendant's challenged action. In addition, the "palpable injury" alleged by a plaintiff must be "likely to be redressed if the requested relief is granted." *Gladstone, Realtors* v. *Village of Bellwood*, 441 U.S. 91 (1979).

In the present case the congressmen suing the President and cabinet officers mistakenly contend that they are unlike ordinary citizens and appear to assume they have the right to sue whenever they object to how the government is being run. Conscious of established precedent, they attempt to assert two distinct and "palpable injuries" to legal rights which they claim are guaranteed them as members of Congress under Article I: first, they claim they are being deprived of their "rights to be consulted and to vote on compliance with treaty obligations" as well as "their ability to participate in the internal processes of Congress and to advance legislative proposals for their constituents affecting the nation's commitment to the Nicaraguan democratic resistance forces"; and, secondly, they claim that "the effectiveness" of their votes and the use of their votes "to support the national commitment to the democratic resistance" have been nullified.

Much as they protest, these are not "palpable injuries" to the legal interests of any of the sixteen members of Congress which by even the greatest stretch of imagination are protected by the Constitution. The Constitution protects only certain specific legal interests of congressmen as legislators. Plaintiffs have not and cannot allege in an identifiable manner any actual nullification of a specific right to act as a congressman or any deprivation of an opportunity to vote as an individual legislator on any issues arising in the Congress which have been caused by Executive action. The congressional injury recognized in *Kennedy* v. *Sampson*, 511 F.2d 430 (D.C.Cir. 1974), as constituting "palpable injury" was wholly different for in that instance the will of the Congress as a whole was being opposed by the President. Nor have they pointed to a specific legal interest protected by any provision of the Constitution or vested in them either as members of Congress which has been violated by the President.

The congressmen merely plead a diminution in their individual effectiveness as legislators based on their own subjective views as to what should be done. Laws have been duly enacted to restrain the President's announced contra policy. Given these circumstances, the Constitution does not protect the interest of those legislators who favor a foreign policy, inconsistent with congressional legislation, which they personally find attractive. The wishes of the majority of their colleagues must control. Nor does the Constitution extend judicial power by enabling courts to review the President's actions in responding, albeit grudgingly, to congressional action simply because legislators such as plaintiff profess to have doubts that the President is making the proper accommodation to congressional action.

Plaintiffs' claim, therefore, amounts to no more than a generalized grievance such as that shared by some other citizens who feel President Reagan should be allowed more fully to commit our Nation to paramilitary support of the contras. As members of congress they remain free to debate the President's conduct, to voice their support of the contras on the floors of the House or Senate and to propose and vote on legislation committing this Nation's resources in the contra cause—all of which they have done and continue to do. Plaintiffs have simply failed to persuade their colleagues to their point of view and under our system of government, they must live with the result.

Beyond this lack of "palpable injury," the lack of a justiciable controversy is even more apparent when the underlying circumstances of this particular litigation are examined. Plaintiffs are volunteers meddling in a dispute between two branches of government, neither of which desires court intervention. The President and his co-defendant Cabinet members, who are the parties plaintiffs seek to help, ask the Court not to interfere.

Conversely, while plaintiffs also purport to sue on behalf of Congress as a whole, there is not the slightest indication the congress presently desires to alter its restraints on the President's freedom to carry out some aspects of his policy in Nicaragua. Congress is not a party to this action and has taken no position authorizing plaintiffs to speak for it. Since Congress has not authorized plaintiffs to speak for it nor indicated that it concurs with plaintiffs' position, plaintiffs may not substitute their personal beliefs for the will of Congress.

The Court lacks the expertise or authority to resolve policy differences regarding the contras which exist between Congress and the White House. There are no guiding standards. Resolution of such differences, which shift and vary, must be left to the traditional government process or the ballot box.

Such prudential considerations cause federal courts to stay their hands where they lack a clear constitutional role and their inability to enforce any order emanating from a decision is apparent. In the present situation the Court could not define the precise limitations on congressional authority, nor could it implement any directive designed to free the President from undue congressional restraint were limitations deemed appropriate. Our tradition is one of conflict and cooperation between Congress and the Chief Executive. The interplay between these two branches has stood the country well, unaided by judicial intervention. The federal courts neither make nor carry out foreign policy and their involvement in this area should be rare indeed.

This Court is not authorized under Article III to accept jurisdiction in this case. There is no ripe case or controversy. Plaintiffs lack standing, having failed to demonstrate an injury to them individually or as a group, and the issues are, for prudential reasons, wholly inappropriate for Article III consideration.

Accordingly, defendants' motion to dismiss is granted and plaintiffs' Amended Complaint is dismissed with prejudice.

FOR DISCUSSION

1. What injury do Dornan and the other members of Congress claim to have incurred? Why does Judge Gesell believe this is not adequate to give them standing to sue?

2. Had the plaintiffs won the case, the District Court would have issued a declaratory judgment stating "that Congress is unconstitutionally constraining the President from carrying out his announced policy to support the contras in Nicaragua." Assuming that the judgment was not reversed on appeal, what do you think Congress and the President would then have done? Should the court take the probable consequences of such a decision into account in deciding whether there is a case or controversy?

3. According to Judge Gesell, the involvement of the courts in foreign policy "should be rare indeed." Why do you think he says this? Do you agree?

4. Varat argues that there is an important connection "between the limitations on judicial power and that power's independence and effectiveness." Does this case provide evidence for or against his view?

5. What are the main purposes of the standing rule? Is Judge Gesell's opinion consistent with these purposes?

POLITICAL QUESTIONS

In the following essay, Lawrence Tribe begins by stating that "The political question doctrine is in a state of some confusion." He tries to clear up some of that confusion by explaining the major theories of political questions and the extent to which they are or are not consistent with Supreme Court decisions, concluding with his own view of the current state of the doctrine.

READING   **The Political Question Doctrine**
                        By Laurence H. Tribe*

The political question doctrine is in a state of some confusion. A *classical* view would impose the requirement of deciding all cases and issues before it unless the Court finds, purely as a matter of constitutional interpretation, that the Constitution itself has committed the determination of the issue to the autonomous decision of another agency of government. A *prudential* view would treat the political question doctrine as a means to avoid passing on the merits of a question when reaching the merits would force the Court to compromise an important principle or would undermine the Court's authority. Unlike the classical or prudential views, a *functional* approach to the role of the Court would have it consider such factors as the difficulties in gaining judicial access to relevant information, the need for uniformity of decision, and the wider responsibilities of the other branches of government, when determining whether or not to decide a certain issue or case.

One conventional view of the doctrine grounds it in the assumption that there are certain constitutional questions which are *inherently* nonjusticiable. These "political questions," it is said, concern matters as to which departments of government other than the courts, or perhaps the electorate as a whole, must have the final say. With respect to these matters, the judiciary does not define constitutional limits. Professor Louis Henkin, however, has forcefully criticized the idea that there are parts of the Constitution to which the judiciary must be blind. The political question cases, he argues, do not support such a proposition. In these cases, the Supreme Court concluded or could have concluded that a particular legislative or executive action fell within a constitutional grant of authority and without the scope of any constitutional limitation, and thus that the action at issue, because constitutionally proper, was open only to political challenge. Alternatively, Henkin urges, the Court ruled or could have ruled that a particular constitutional restriction was unenforceable because it did not confer standing to sue upon the parties who sought to invoke it or because it required for its enforcement remedies which were judicially unmanageable or equitably unwise.

Professor Henkin is clearly right that one should not accept lightly the proposition that there are provisions of the Constitution which the courts may not independently interpret, since it is plainly inconsistent with *Marbury* v. *Madison's* [5 U.S. (1 Cranch) 137 (1803)] basic assumption that the Constitution is judicially declarable law. In order to account for the political question doctrine, however, it is not necessary to postulate that there are parts of the Constitution to which the judiciary is blind. The Supreme Court does not surrender its power of judicial review by holding that, while a particular provision may grant Congress or the Executive authority to act, it is not susceptible of an interpretation which would yield judicially enforceable rights, rights whose enforcement would either constrain congressional or executive action or alternatively provide the basis for an exercise of judicial power parallel to the actions of the political branches. Such a holding does not deprive the Court of all power to interpret a Constitutional provision; the Court retains the power to determine whether a particular congressional or executive action comes within the terms of the constitutional grant of authority. The ultimate issue is whether it is possible to translate the principles underlying the constitutional provision at issue into restrictions on government or affirmative definitions of individual liberty which courts can articulate and apply.

The political question cases themselves suggest that it is this inquiry—the inquiry into whether particular constitutional provisions yield judicially enforceable rights—which has concerned the Supreme Court. Because this inquiry ultimately focuses on the limits of judicial competency, the political question doctrine is plainly a part of justiciability doctrine as a whole.

The central line of political question cases runs from *Luther* v. *Borden* [48 U.S. (7 How.) 1 (1849)] to *Baker* v. *Carr* [369 U.S. 186 (1962)]. *Luther* arose out of Dorr's Rebellion: an ultimately successful attempt by Rhode Island citizens who were disenfranchised under the original colonial charter to force the adoption of a new and more democratic constitution despite the opposition of the government established under the charter. The specific issue *Luther* raised was whether soldiers of the charter government committed a trespass by breaking into plaintiff's home at a point in the rebellion when the rebels had prematurely proclaimed the adoption of a new constitution notwithstanding the charter government's continued insistence on the governing power of the charter. In resolving this issue, the Supreme Court had to consider two questions: whether a federal court could independently determine which of the two competing governments was the "true" government of Rhode Island; and even if the charter government was in power, whether that government, by proclaiming martial law, had acted unlawfully by departing from principles of republican government in contravention of the guaranty clause of article IV.

The Court concluded that a federal court could not independently decide which state government was in power. The question was not one which fell within the judicial competence: the evidentiary problems would be staggering. Congress, moreover, did possess such a power under the guaranty clause, which in this case it had delegated to the President, who had exercised it. The fact that Congress possessed the power confirmed that the power was lacking in the judiciary: this was not the sort of question which would admit of conflicting answers, a possibility if more than one branch of government could pass on it. With respect to the question of whether, even if it were the lawful government, the charter government had acted unlawfully in adopting martial law, the Court took a more activist approach: it assumed that a federal court could decide whether a state government had violated the guaranty clause, but held that in this case, since the period of martial law was of only temporary duration, Rhode Island had not acted unconstitutionally.

A number of nineteenth century cases in which litigants invoked the protection of the guaranty clause follow the pattern of *Luther* v. *Borden*: the Supreme Court did not doubt that the guaranty clause could be applied to protect individual rights, but held that, on the facts of the particular case, the challenged state action did not constitute a departure from principles of republican government.

An issue is political not because it is one of particular concern to the political branches of government but because the constitutional provisions which litigants would invoke as guides to resolution of the issue do not lend themselves to judicial application. A plurality of the Supreme Court departed from this approach in *Colegrove* v. *Green* [328 U.S. 549 (1946)]. There, litigants challenged the constitutionality of a state's malapportioned congressional districts. Justice Frankfurter, joined by three other Justices, wrote the principal opinion, holding that "appellants ask of this Court what is beyond its competence to grant": "due regard for the effective working of our Government reveal[s] this issue to be of a peculiarly political nature and therefore not meet for judicial determination." Justice Frankfurter noted his view that a court was without remedial power to reapportion voting districts by itself, and further observed that the Constitution plainly granted authority to Congress to deal with the problem. Frankfurter, however, never identified the "various provisions of the United States Constitution" which the litigants invoked, and accordingly did not ground his analysis in any conclusion that the particular provisions which the litigants would have the Court enforce did not suggest criteria which courts could apply to protect individual rights. Instead, the Justice treated the issue itself as beyond judicial competence: "Courts ought not to enter this political thicket."

The Supreme Court, however, decisively repudiated Justice Frankfurter's analysis in *Baker* v. *Carr* [369 U.S. 186 (1962)]. This was another apportionment case, involving a constitutional challenge to a state's districting of its state legislature. Justice Brennan's majority opinion unequivocally rejected the *Colegrove* formulation of the political question doctrine: "The doctrine of which we treat is one of 'political questions,' not one of political 'cases.' The courts cannot reject as 'no lawsuit' a bona fide controversy as to whether some action denominated 'political' exceeds constitutional authority." Instead, Justice Brennan returned to the traditional approach, asking whether the constitutional provision which the litigants invoked could be successfully translated into judicially enforceable rights. Plaintiffs had argued that because the populations of the various legislative districts differed, the votes of the residents of the more populous districts were "debased" relative to the votes of residents of less populous districts. This inequality of treatment, plaintiffs claimed, violated the Fourteenth Amendment equal protection clause. The Court had little difficulty in finding the equal protection clause to be judicially enforceable: "Judicial standards under the Equal Protection Clause are well developed and familiar...."

The Supreme Court's decisions since *Baker* v. *Carr* reflect the approach to the political question doctrine which *Baker* exemplifies. In *United States* v. *Nixon* [418 U.S. 683 (1974)], for example, the Supreme Court held that the intra-executive nature of the dispute between President Nixon and Special Prosecutor Jaworski did not give rise to a political question: because the President had himself restricted his discretion to deal with Jaworski, the President, until he repealed the regulations limiting his discretion, could refuse Jaworski's demands only by asserting a valid claim of privilege; the issue of privilege, of course, was " 'of a type which [is] traditionally justiciable.' "

Gilligan v. *Morgan* [413 U.S. 1 (1973)] is the only case since *Baker* v. *Carr* in which the Supreme Court has invoked the political question doctrine to hold an issue nonjusticiable. Plaintiffs had asked the federal courts to evaluate the training of the Ohio National Guard under the Fourteenth Amendment due process clause; if that training was found constitutionally deficient, they sought appropriate injunctive relief. The Supreme Court's decision that the issue was nonjusticiable turned on a number of factors. Chief among them, however, were the facts that article I, Sec. 8, authorized Congress to engage in just such supervision, and that judicial review in this area would be essentially standardless: "[I]t is difficult to conceive of an area of government activity in which the courts have less competence. The complex, subtle, and professional decisions as to the composition, training, equipping, and control of a military force are essentially professional military judgments, subject *always* to civilian control of the Legislative and Executive Branches."

There is, thus, a political question doctrine. It does not mark certain provisions of the Constitution as off-limits to judicial interpretation. But it does require federal courts to determine whether constitutional provisions which litigants would have judges enforce do in fact lend themselves to interpretation as guarantees of enforceable rights. To make such a determination, a court must first of all construe the relevant constitutional text, and seek to identify the purposes the particular provision serves within the constitutional scheme as a whole. At this stage of the analysis, the court would find particularly relevant the fact that the constitutional provision by its terms grants authority to another branch of government; if the provision recognizes such authority, the court will have to consider the possibility of conflicting conclusions, and the actual necessity for parallel judicial and political remedies. But, ultimately, the political question inquiry turns as much on the court's conception of judicial competence as on the constitutional text. Thus, the political question, like other justiciability doctrines, at bottom reflects the mixture of constitutional interpretation and judicial discretion which is an inevitable by-product of the efforts of federal courts to define their own limitations.

NOTES

*From "The Political Question Doctrine" by Laurence Tribe in *American Constitutional Law*, 2/e, © 1978 by The Foundation Press, Mineola, N.Y. Reprinted by permission.

FOR DISCUSSION

1. At the beginning of his essay, Professor Tribe discusses three theories of judicial review—the classical, prudential, and functional. Which of these does Tribe seem to agree with most?

2. How would Tribe define a political question?

3. If Judge Gesell had relied on the doctrine of political questions instead of standing, could he have dismissed *Dornan* v. *Secretary of Defense* as a nonjusticiable political question? Answer this question using Tribe's definition, the approach he terms "one conventional view," and the one he attributes to Professor Henkin. Do the three definitions yield the same or different results?

4. What does Tribe object to in Justice Frankfurter's approach to the political question doctrine in *Colegrove* v. *Green*?

5. Would Varat agree with the last sentence in Tribe's essay?

6. Formulate your own working definition of when a case presents a nonjusticiable political question.

In the following case, a former government official brings suit against a variety of people, claiming that there is a conspiracy against him. He argues his own case rather than having an attorney act in his behalf. The term *pro se*, for himself, is the legal term for actions brought without benefit of legal representation.

CASE   Eveland v. Director of C.I.A.
                     U.S. Court of Appeals, First Circuit (1988)
                                43 F.2d 46

PER CURIAM.   On November 12, 1986, appellant, Wilbur Crane Eveland, III, commenced a *pro se* action in the District Court for the District of Massachusetts. The
complaint, in its caption, names William J. Casey and the Central Intelligence Agency
(CIA) as defendants. Additional individuals and government agencies are named in the
body of the complaint and in an accompanying document entitled "Charges and Petition."
We will refer to both items as the "complaint."

Eveland bases jurisdiction on the Racketeer Influenced and Corrupt Organizations
Act (RICO). Although the complaint is complex and confusing, his substantive allegations appear to fall within two general categories. The first concerns United States
foreign policy in the Middle East. Eveland, who apparently has had extensive experience
in government service in the Middle East, offered to assist the Reagan administration in
its efforts to resolve certain crises, such as the hostage situation in Lebanon, in that region
of the world. He claims that various officials, including [Secretary of State] Schultz,
obstructed his efforts and refused to accept his guidance. Eveland goes on to allege
generally that [former Secretary of State] Kissinger has assumed the powers of the
President and has enabled the government of Israel to dominate the conduct of United
States foreign policy. He recites detailed and convoluted historical data concerning
events from 1940 through the present to support this claim.

The second category involves allegations that government officials engaged in tortious
conduct against Eveland. Such activity includes libel, slander, character assassination, the
publication of false charges, and attempted murder and other life-threatening actions.
Specifically, Eveland alleges that Kissinger acted to discredit Eveland as a national security
risk, did away with Eveland's "business interests and professional position," caused Eveland
to live below the poverty level and engaged in measures to eliminate Eveland. Some of these
allegations concern events that took place in 1975 and involve a lawsuit in England. Eveland
also alleges that in 1951 [James] Angleton, acting with Israel's Mossad, falsified documents
which indicated that Eveland had passed classified information to British double agent, Kim
Philby. He finally alleges that his mail was intercepted.

Eveland seeks various forms of relief. He asks for compensatory and punitive damages.
He requests that the CIA, the Department of State, the National Security Council and other federal
entities produce all documents relating to him. He seeks an order requiring the CIA, Federal
Bureau of Investigation, United States Postal Service, Secret Service and other United States
law enforcement agencies to expunge from their files and alert lists all "unwarranted" information concerning him. Finally, Eveland asks that letters of apology be issued and that he be awarded
any medals, citations and commendations for which he was recommended.

The government defendants moved to dismiss Eveland's complaint. On May 1, 1987,
the district court granted their motion. It held that there is no case or controversy concerning
the foreign policy allegations because Eveland was not in "danger of any immediate and
direct injury as a result of the defendants' conduct." In addition, it pointed out that the
administration of foreign policy and national security raised "purely political questions" for
which there is no judicial remedy. The court further noted that Eveland had not established
that the court had personal jurisdiction over the individual defendants. Finally, the court held
that the conduct of foreign policy and national security did not state a claim under RICO.

Because Eveland is appearing *pro se*, his complaint is held to "less stringent standards" than pleadings drafted by attorneys. *Haines* v. *Kerner*, 404 U.S. 519 (1972). Even reading Eveland's papers liberally, however, we conclude that the district court was correct in dismissing the complaint. We base our conclusion on three grounds: failure to state a justiciable cause of action, lack of personal jurisdiction over the individual defendants and principles of sovereign immunity.

The allegations concerning the conduct of the United States in the Middle East clearly reflect Eveland's attempt to litigate his disagreement with how this country's foreign policy is managed. The United States Supreme Court has held that:

> the very nature of executive decisions as to foreign policy is political not judicial. Such decisions are wholly confided by our Constitution to the political departments of the government, Executive and Legislative. They are delicate, complex, and involve large elements of prophecy. They are and should be undertaken only by those directly responsible to the people whose welfare they advance or imperil. They are decisions of a kind for which the Judiciary has neither aptitude, facilities, nor responsibility and which has long been held to belong in the domain of political power not subject to judicial intrusion or inquiry.

Chicago & Southern Air Lines, Inc. v. *Waterman Steamship Corp.*, 333 U.S. 103 (1948). Although courts will address some areas of foreign relations, Eveland's dispute with Middle Eastern policy does not fall within any of these narrow exceptions. As a result, Eveland has no judicial remedy for his claims involving foreign relations and his place in the conduct of such relations.

Eveland's RICO claims also were properly dismissed under the political question doctrine. The only intelligible mention of RICO in the complaint is a statement that "Henry Kissinger, and those who have worked with him, and still are, have sold America to a RICO-controlled organization: the present government of Israel." It is clear that such an allegation concerns foreign policy and again reflects Eveland's attempt to air his differences with the government's conduct of Middle Eastern foreign policy. Eveland cannot use RICO to seek judicial redress for such a political question.

The remaining claims concern Eveland's allegations of tortious conduct. We begin our consideration of these claims with the well-settled principle that the United States may not be sued without its consent. As for Eveland's claims for money damages, the United States has consented to suit for certain torts in the Federal Tort Claims Act. However, even if Eveland had based his tort claims on the Tort Claims Act, the district court would not have been able to consider them.

Section 2675 applies to procedure under the Tort Claims Act:

> An action shall not be instituted upon a claim against the United States for money damages for injury or loss of property or personal injury or death caused by the negligent or wrongful act or omission of any employee of the Government while acting within the scope of his office or employment, unless the claimant shall have first presented the claim to the appropriate Federal agency and his claim shall have been finally denied by the agency in writing and sent by certified or registered mail.

28 U.S.C 2675 (a). There is no evidence that Eveland has followed this administrative process. Such failure deprives the district court of jurisdiction over his tort claims against the government agencies.

To bring an action against the individual defendants in their personal capacities, Eveland must establish that the individual defendants, both present and former officials, are subject to the personal jurisdiction of the district court. It appears that all of the defendants were served with process outside of Massachusetts. We assume, therefore, that none of the defendants resided in Massachusetts at the time suit was commenced. Because Eveland's claims against defendants in their personal capacities would appear to be based on state tort law, we look to the long-arm statute of Massachusetts.

Without discussing whether the requirements of the long-arm statute have been met, we find that defendants lack the constitutionally required "minimum contacts" with Massachusetts to support an assertion of jurisdiction over them by the district court. From even a liberal reading of the complaint, it appears that defendants have absolutely no contacts with Massachusetts. There are no indications that they have done business here or have engaged in any other activity within this jurisdiction. Certainly none of the conduct about which Eveland complains took place in Massachusetts. Rather, it appears that defendants' actions occurred in California, Washington, D.C., the Middle East, and parts of Europe. As a result, defendants have not purposefully availed themselves "of the privilege of conducting activities within the forum State, thus invoking the benefits and protections of its laws." *Hanson* v. *Denckla*, 357 U.S. 235 (1958). Because defendants have no reason to anticipate being haled into court in Massachusetts, due process forbids the maintenance of this suit against them.

In summary, we find that Eveland's suit is barred by the political question doctrine in so far as it concerns foreign policy in the Middle East. His claims for money damages are barred by principles of sovereign immunity and the lack of personal jurisdiction over the individual defendants. The judgment of the district court is therefore *Affirmed.*

FOR DISCUSSION

1. According to the Court, Eveland's suit presents a political question. On what basis did it make this decision?

2. In his essay, Tribe wrote that, "ultimately, the political question inquiry turns as much on the court's conception of judicial competence as on the constitutional text." Does the ruling in this case support or contradict his argument?

3. According to the Court, most issues of foreign policy present nonjusticiable political questions although there are a few "narrow exceptions." Can you think of any of these "narrow exceptions?" Do you agree with the Court's view?

4. Do you think the outcome of this case would have changed in any way had Eveland hired an attorney to argue his case instead of acting *pro se*?

5. Eveland's allegations of a large governmental conspiracy would appear far-fetched to most people. If true, however, they would be serious indeed. Assuming that an appeal to the Supreme Court is unsuccessful, does he have any recourse?

MOOTNESS

In the next case, a group of minority fire fighters are challenging fiscal layoffs that would result in the firing of those most recently hired, a group that had a relatively high percentage of minorities because of the settlement of a previous civil rights suit. Because these layoffs would be based on seniority, they argue, the result would be to return to the low percentage of minorities that existed due to previous discrimination. While the lower court decision was being appealed, Massachusetts passed a law reinstating all those who had been laid off. The U.S. Supreme Court remanded the case to the Court of Appeals to determine whether or not that made it moot.

CASE
Boston Chapter, NAACP v. Beecher
United States Court of Appeals, First Circuit (1983)
716 F.2d 931

PER CURIAM.   This case is before the court on remand from the Supreme Court, 461 U.S. 477 for consideration of mootness. Since 1975, the Boston police and fire departments have been subject to consent decrees requiring preferential hiring of minorities to relieve the effects of prior discrimination. In 1981, facing proposed fiscal layoffs which would substantially vitiate any progress made under the decrees, plaintiffs sought and obtained modification of the original decrees. *Castro* v. *Beecher*, 522 F.Supp. 873 (D.Mass. 1981). The modifying order prohibited both Boston departments from reducing minority percentages in their workforces, with the practical result that non-minority firemen and police officers would have to be laid off before junior minority firemen and police officers notwithstanding the state's last-hire, first-fired statute.

The modification was affirmed on appeal to this court in the above-cited case, and defendants obtained certiorari from the Supreme Court. Meanwhile, however, Massachusetts enacted the so-called Tregor Act mandating reinstatement of all police and firefighters laid off during the reduction in force. The Supreme Court therefore vacated the court's judgment and remanded for consideration of mootness.

"The usual rule in federal cases is that an actual controversy must exist at stages of appellate or certiorari review...." *Roe* v. *Wade*, 410 U.S. 113 (1973). When, as here, intervening acts destroy the interest of a party to the adjudication, the case is mooted. The Tregor Act's mandatory reinstatement of the laid off police and firefighters and its requirement of minimum staffing levels through June 30, 1983, removed plaintiffs' stake in the proceeding which they had instituted in 1981 at a time when layoffs were taking place.

This is not an example of the "voluntary cessation of allegedly illegal conduct" which does not render a case moot. *U.S.* v. *W. T. Grant Co.*, 345 U.S. 629 (1953). Rather the city of Boston has acted pursuant to a supervening state statute. Furthermore, the case does not present a question "capable of repetition, yet evading review." *Southern Pacific Terminal Co.* v. *ICC*, 219 U.S. 498 (1911). Future layoffs might occur, but there is no reason to assume that a similar state enactment would once again render the case moot before resolution by the Supreme Court.[1]

Appellants' contention that the case remains alive because the modifying order prohibits the adjudication of state Civil Service Commission claims for back pay is not persuasive. According to the established practice of the federal courts, when a case is found moot, the district court's judgment will be vacated. Thus, even assuming, which we do not decide, that the district court's order directly inhibits the state Civil Service Commission respecting the back pay claims, it will no longer do so. To be sure, a definitive ruling on the

---

[1] The Supreme Court has granted cetiorari on a case presenting the same issue as the case before us. *Stotts* v. *Memphis Fire Department*, 679 F.2nd. 541 (6th Cir. 1982), cert. granted, 462 U.S. 1105.

constitutionality of the district court's past order might facilitate the Civil Service Commission's resolution of the back pay claims. But such a ruling now—rendered in the absence of a present case or controversy in this proceeding—would amount to no more than an advisory opinion. The federal courts are forbidden by Article III of the Constitution from giving advisory opinions. Plaintiffs now lack the "personal stake" necessary to keep alive the controversy which engendered this proceeding. The Civil Service Commission must therefore be left to decide the back pay claims under the governing state law without an advisory resolution of the constitutional issue by the federal courts.

Accordingly, we vacate the district court's order of August 7, 1981, and remand to the district court to dismiss as moot the motion for modification, without prejudice to further actions under the district court's continuing jurisdiction to monitor the original consent decrees.

FOR DISCUSSION

1. This lawsuit met all the requirements for a case or controversy when it was heard in both District Court and the Court of Appeals. Why did the Supreme Court remand it to determine whether it was a case or controversy?

2. There are two exceptions to the mootness rule. What are they? Why does the Court of Appeals believe that neither of them applies to this case? Explain whether you agree.

3. The appellants argue that the suit still presents a live controversy because of their claims for back pay. What is the Court's view of this argument?

4. As the Court points out in a footnote, the Supreme Court accepted another case "presenting the same issue as the case before us" for review. If so, why did the Supreme Court not simply rule on the issue the first time it was presented to them and save the time and work of hearing the same issue for a second time?

5. The case mentioned in the footnote and in question 4 was decided in *Firefighters* v. *Stotts*, 467 U.S. 561 (1984). Read that case and explain whether the two decisions are consistent with one another.

Matthews v. *Marsh* shows how much discretion the case or controversy rules give to judges. Diane Matthews had been discharged from the Army Reserve Officers Training Corps because of her statement that she was a lesbian but a Federal District Court held that this violated her right to free speech and ordered her reinstated. The Court of Appeals avoids ruling on this political hot potato by noting that new evidence not in the trial record may have shown that Matthews had actually engaged in homosexual conduct rather than merely speaking about it. Although courts rarely take information not heard at trial into account, in this case, the appellate court is able to use it to remand the case to the trial court to determine whether it had become moot.

CASE

Matthews v. Marsh
United States Court of Appeals, First Circuit (1985)
755 F.2d 182

TORRUELLA, Circuit Judge.   This appeal arises from a suit brought by Diane L. Matthews to challenge her disenrollment from the Reserve Officers Training Corps which followed her voluntary admission that she was a homosexual. For the reasons set out below, we vacate the district court's decision and remand the case for further proceedings.

Commencing in 1976 Appellee Matthews served in the United States Army for four years as a field communications equipment mechanic, during the course of which service she received numerous awards and high performance ratings, and rose to the level of sergeant. Upon completion of her tour of duty she was honorably discharged in September 1980. Two months after her discharge, Matthews enlisted as a sergeant in an United States Army Reserve unit in Scarborough, Maine. The following September she enrolled in college at the University of Maine at Orono, and thereafter she also joined the ROTC program.

On November 3, 1981, Matthews asked her ROTC lab instructor, Captain Alexander Miller, to excuse her from a lab session so that she might attend a student senate meeting at the university. Upon further inquiry by Captain Miller, Matthews stated that the meeting involved discussing the budget allocation for the "Wilde-Stein Club." Upon inquiry by Captain Miller regarding the nature of that club, Matthews informed him that it was a campus homosexual organization of which she was a member. In further explaining her relationship to the club, Matthews also stated "I am a lesbian." Captain Miller then told Matthews that he would have to report that fact to his superiors, which he promptly did. He did not interfere in any way however with her attendance or participation in the club or the mentioned meeting. Later that day Matthews was informed by Captain Edwards that an investigation would be conducted to determine whether her homosexuality was cause for separation.

Army regulations and Department of Defense directives define a homosexual as one "who engages in, desires to engage in, or intends to engage in homosexual acts." They further provide that a finding of homosexuality in any service member requires his immediate separation from military service.

At the Army's request, Matthews underwent psychiatric consultation. In his report the psychiatrist concluded that "disclosure of Matthews' homosexual identification was necessary for her as a matter of principal" [*sic*].

On completion of the Army's investigation, Captain Edwards issued a report concluding that Matthews came within the Regulation's definitions and that this was cause for her separation.

Matthews appealed the decision, exhausting her administrative remedies. Obtaining no relief through those channels, she then filed suit in the United States District Court. The parties consented to a non-jury trial before a federal magistrate without a jury.

At trial, the Army neither alleged nor proved that Matthews had participated in homosexual conduct. Rather it contended, as it still contends on this appeal, that Matthews was properly disenrolled on the basis of her "intent or desire" for homosexual activity, as stated in the regulations.

The district court held that Matthews'[s] statement about her sexual preferences and her status as a homosexual both fall within the general ambit of First Amendment rights, and that the Army's regulations were an unconstitutional infringement of those rights. The court ordered her reenrolled, and this appeal followed.

During the course of the briefing for the appeal, this court was made aware of additional evidence that may affect the disposition of this case on grounds other than those considered below. While this appeal was pending, Matthews had reapplied for entry into the ROTC, pursuant to the district court order. On her application, reproduced in the appellant's brief, she apparently signed a statement that described her as having "engaged in homosexual acts numerous times, last one being recently." Since Matthews has not challenged the Army's right to disenroll her for her homosexual *conduct*, but only for her status, her statement might supply alternate grounds for disenrollment.

It is not ordinarily proper for an appellate court to take notice of new evidence not in the record. Nonetheless, it would be preferable to resolve this case on the grounds of actual conduct rather than to undertake a review of the serious constitutional issues presented in the district court opinion.

In addition, a constitutional ruling in plaintiff's favor may be an exercise in futility. Plaintiff seeks reinstatement. If reinstatement were ordered, it is quite possible that the Army would again find plaintiff unfit for duty. This time, however, it might base its opinion on evidence related to grounds of actual conduct, which grounds plaintiff does not challenge on a constitutional basis.

In view of the new evidence of apparent homosexual conduct, we think that the parties are in effect requesting an advisory opinion, which, of course, is impermissible.

Therefore, we remand the case to the district court for further proceedings not inconsistent with this opinion.

Judge Breyer believes that this court should not remand but should decide the merits of the appeal.

FOR DISCUSSION

1. Even though the Court of Appeals sees nothing in the trial record indicating that this case is moot, they return it to that court to see if it is in fact moot. Can you explain why?

2. As Judge Torruella states, "It is ordinarily not proper for an appellate court to take notice of new evidence not in the record." Why does he ignore this warning and consider new evidence?

3. In *Oran's Dictionary of the Law* (St. Paul, Minn.: West Publishing, 1983), p. 275, Daniel Oran defines moot as "no longer important or no longer needing a decision because *already decided*." Applying this definition do you find *Matthews* v. *Marsh* moot? What about *Boston Chapter, NAACP* v. *Beecher*?

4. In *Boston Chapter, NAACP* v. *Beecher*, two exceptions to the mootness rule were discussed. Are either of them applicable to this case?

5. Why do you think the court went so far out of its way to declare this case moot instead of deciding it on the merits?

6. Judge Breyer wanted the case decided on the merits but did not write an opinion explaining why. Write a short essay explaining what his reasons might be. Do you agree with this reasoning or was the majority's decision correct?

STATUTE OF LIMITATIONS

The next case illustrates the problem discussed in the chapter introduction, illnesses caused by exposure to chemicals in the workplace. Berkley argues that he sued after Texas's two-year statute of limitations had expired only because his employer deceived him. The court has to decide whether the alleged fraud tolled the statute of limitations.

CASE
Berkley v. American Cyanamid Co.
United States Court of Appeals, Fifth Circuit (1986)
799 F.2d 995

GARWOOD, Circuit Judge.   Berkley, forty-two years of age at the time he filed this suit, had worked for American Cyanamid since 1955. He was forced to leave his job at American Cyanamid in 1975 because of his worsening medical condition due to chemical exposure. He was permanently disabled. After leaving, Berkley continued to seek medical attention and in 1977 several doctors at John Sealy Hospital in Galveston, Texas, treated him. The doctors advised Berkley that his medical problems were due to exposure to vanadium pentoxide, one of the chemicals used at American Cyanamid. Berkley stated in his deposition that before this diagnosis had been made his supervisors at American Cyanamid had told him that vanadium pentoxide was not harmful or at worst could cause a nosebleed or throat irritation. Berkley testified that when he told his doctors that his employer had advised him that none of the chemicals was harmful, one doctor stated that American Cyanamid had lied to him. After this diagnosis, Berkley requested and obtained in 1977 a list of all the chemicals to which he was exposed while he was employed at American Cyanamid. In March 1979, after the start of the instant litigation against other parties, Berkley deposed his former supervisor regarding the toxicity of the chemicals to which Berkley was exposed. This supervisor stated that he had no knowledge of any danger caused by these chemicals. However, Berkley claims that in early 1982 he received, through discovery in the litigation against other parties, certain documents establishing that, despite American Cyanamid's assertions to the contrary, it had been informed that certain chemicals it used were dangerous.

On November 3, 1975, Berkley filed a claim for worker's compensation benefits with the Texas Industrial Accident Board. In 1977, disagreeing with the Board's award of worker's compensation benefits, Berkley appealed it by filing a worker's compensation suit against American Cyanamid's worker's compensation carrier in a Texas state court to determine the amount of benefits to which he was entitled. Berkley and the carrier subsequently settled that suit in 1980 or 1981, and Berkley received a lump sum settlement of $70,000, with the carrier also being required to make payment of his future medical expenses. In 1979, Berkley filed the present suit against Union Carbide and numerous other manufacturers who supplied chemicals to American Cyanamid, alleging that the chemicals they manufactured caused his injuries. A settlement agreement was reached with these manufacturers and entered in the district court on November 8, 1982, in which Berkley received a total of $17,500.

Also on November 8, 1982, Berkley filed an amended complaint in the present action which for the first time named American Cyanamid as an additional defendant, alleging that its actions constituted intentional or reckless injury and fraud. After the settlement against the chemical manufacturers was approved, only the claim against American Cyanamid remained. Berkley alleged that American Cyanamid committed intentional or reckless injury and fraud by knowingly and willfully exposing him to toxic chemicals despite its knowledge of the dangers of these substances. He also alleged that American Cyanamid concealed these dangers from him, and that this caused him to receive improper medical treatment during and after his employment. American Cyanamid moved for summary judgment, claiming that the two-year statute of limitations barred the claim. In response to American Cyanamid's motion, Berkley alleged that since he did not actually discover American Cyanamid's fraud until 1982 when he received the documents which allegedly proved that American Cyanamid was lying, the statute of limitations did not begin running until that time. However, the district court ruled that the statute of limitations began running in 1977 when Berkley's doctors told him that vanadium pentoxide had caused his injuries and Berkley learned that American Cyanamid used that chemical at its plant.

Texas law concededly governs this diversity action. The sole issue we address on this appeal is whether the district court correctly granted summary judgment against Berkley on the ground that the Texas two-year statute of limitations barred the suit.

Berkley alleges that American Cyanamid committed intentional or reckless injury and common-law fraud. Article 5526, Tex. Rev. Civ. Stat. Ann., which provides for a two-year statute of limitations period, governs actions for personal injury and common-law fraud. Moreover:

[t]he statute of limitations on a cause of action based on fraud does not begin to run until the fraud is discovered, or until the plaintiff acquires such knowledge as would lead to its discovery if reasonable diligence was exercised. *Whatley* v. *National Bank of Commerce*, 555 S.W.2d 500 (Tex.Civ.App., Dallas 1977, no writ).

In this connection, we have noted that "[t]he Texas courts have held that knowledge of facts which would lead to discovery of the fraud if diligently pursued by a reasonably prudent person is equivalent to knowledge of the fraud as a matter of law." *Westchester Corp.* v. *Peat, Marwick, Mitchell & Co.*, 626 F.2d 1212 (5th Cir. 1980). Here, the undisputed facts establish as a matter of law that Berkley's action against American Cyanamid was filed more than two years after he had knowledge of facts that should have led him to uncover the fraud claim, and we accordingly hold that the district court's summary judgment dismissal of Berkley's suit on statute of limitation grounds was proper.

In Berkley's deposition, he testified that he was told by doctors at the University of Texas at Galveston in 1977 that he was suffering from exposure to vanadium pentoxide. When Berkley commented to these doctors that American Cyanamid had told him that none of the chemicals used at the plant were harmful, one doctor stated to him that American Cyanamid was lying. Following this diagnosis and commencing in 1977, Berkley was treated, and he then knew he was being treated, for exposure to vanadium pentoxide. Moreover, in July 1977, Berkley received from American Cyanamid a list of all the chemicals with which he could have come into contact while he was working there, and this list included vanadium pentoxide. The material accuracy of this list is not questioned. Further, in 1975, Berkley filed a worker's compensation claim for injuries due to chemical exposure at the American Cyanamid facility where he worked, and although he did not know which chemical had harmed him at this time, he knew that some chemical had caused his injuries. The record also contains evidence that American Cyanamid had told Berkley before the doctors diagnosed vanadium pentoxide as the root of his injuries in 1977 that the chemicals with which he worked were not harmful and could cause, at most, a nosebleed or a throat irritation. These uncontroverted facts establish that by 1977 Berkley had discovered his injury (chemical poisoning); the cause of his injury (vanadium pentoxide poisoning from American Cyanamid and any delay in treatment caused by American Cyanamid's misrepresentations); and the fact that American Cyanamid had misrepresented to him the facts in this respect, including those concerning the toxicity of vanadium pentoxide and its relation to his injury. We have recently held that knowledge of an injury and its cause triggers the running of the statute of limitations. See *Timberlake* v. *A. H. Robins Co.*, 727 F.2d 1363 (5th Cir. 1984). We find that all these facts taken together were sufficient to give Berkley actual knowledge of the possible fraud by his employer.

Berkley claims that the statute of limitations should not have begun running until 1982, when he allegedly uncovered a document which revealed that American Cyanamid had been informed all along that the chemicals to which its workers were exposed were hazardous. Thus, Berkley asserts, he was not put on notice of any alleged wrongdoing by American Cyanamid until 1982, and therefore his complaint joining American Cyanamid as a party in November 1982 was timely. We faced this issue in a related context in *Timberlake*. There the plaintiff suffered acute pelvic inflammation and had to undergo a hysterectomy in 1978. Her doctor informed her that an IUD caused her problems. Three years later the plaintiff saw a television program concerning the Dalkon Shield IUD and became aware that her IUD manufacturer may have been negligent in the manufacture and sale of the IUD that she had purchased. She filed suit over two years after her doctor told her that the IUD caused her medical problems, but only four months after she learned that she might have a cause of action. On appeal, the plaintiff argued that the statute of limitations did not begin running until she had knowledge of the manufacturer's wrongdoing. We rejected this argument, stating that, "Timberlake knew of her injury and its cause in March 1978. At that point, the statute of limitations was triggered and she had two years to investigate any possible wrongdoing by Robins."

As we noted above, the discovery rule is applicable in a common-law action for fraud under Texas law. However, in *Timberlake*, we stated with respect to the discovery rule and the requisite knowledge required to begin the running of the statute of limitations that "[n]one [of the Texas discovery rule cases] implies that the statutory period should be tolled until the plaintiff learns that the defendant's conduct may have been wrongful." With respect to fraud, this certainly does not require more than knowledge on the plaintiff's part of the falsity of defendant's statements and their relationship to the claimed injury.

Having determined that Berkley knew the actual cause of his injury more than two years from the date on which he filed suit against American Cyanamid, and thus outside the applicable statute of limitations, we affirm the judgment of the district court.

FOR DISCUSSION

1. Explain the arguments for and against statutes of limitations.

2. American Cyanamid argues that Berkley's suit is barred by the two-year statute of limitations. How does he counter this argument? When does he claim the statute should have begun to run? Why?

3. When does the Court of Appeals rule that the statutory time limit began? Why? What result does that lead to in this case?

4. Judge Garwood relies on *Timberlake* v. *A. H. Robins Co.* as a precedent. What standard did it set out to determine when fraud tolls a statute of limitations? Do you agree with this standard?

GOVERNMENTAL IMMUNITY

Should someone whose package is lost by the U.S. Postal Service be permitted to sue to recover the full value of its contents or is the suit prevented by sovereign immunity? Originally, the Post Office was a cabinet department in the executive branch but was changed during the Nixon administration into what the Court terms "an independent establishment of the executive branch of the government of the United States," in the hope of improving its efficiency. Did this reorganization cause it to lose its governmental immunity? Is Express Mail a governmental function or is it more a business, similar to the growing number of private overnight express companies? The Federal District Court must determine whether these changes affect the immunity of the Postal Service.

CASE   **Allied Coin Investment, Inc. v. U.S. Postal Service**
United States District Court, D. Minnesota (1987)
673 F.Supp. 982

ROSENBAUM, District Judge.   A package containing coins, valued in excess of $17,000, was lost in the "Express Mail," a service of the United States Postal Service (USPS). The package belonged to the plaintiff who now sues seeking the recovery of the value of its coins. The USPS denies liability based upon its claim of sovereign immunity. For the purposes of this motion, these facts are not in dispute.

Defendant USPS has moved for summary judgment, contending the action is barred by the Federal Tort Claims Act [FTCA]. For its side, plaintiff Allied Coin Investments, Inc. (Allied Coin), moves for summary judgment asserting that "Express Mail" is a commercial entity in the marketplace, a non-governmental function, and therefore, the USPS cannot shield itself behind the FTCA.

Plaintiff Allied Coin is a Minnesota corporation with its principal place of business in Richfield, Minnesota. Allied Coin is in the business of buying and selling rare coins. Defendant USPS is an independent establishment of the executive branch of the government of the United States.

On or about August 14, 1985, Paul Del Grosso, acting as agent for the plaintiff, purchased rare coins in the State of Michigan. Pursuant to plaintiff's instructions, Del Grosso delivered a package, which plaintiff asserts contained rare coins worth $17,698.25 to a post office in Madison Heights, Michigan, for delivery to plaintiff, at Richfield, Minnesota, via USPS "Express Mail."

The package was never delivered. It was apparently lost in the mail. Plaintiff was reimbursed $500 for its loss, the maximum amount allowable for lost "Express Mail," pursuant to the Domestic Mail Manual (DMM), Section 294. Plaintiff brought this action, alleging a claim for money damages against the USPS in the amount of $17,198.25, which the plaintiff contends is the balance due and owing after defendant's $500 payment.

The question presented is whether the USPS is immune from liability under the doctrine of sovereign immunity for the loss of a package sent through its "Express Mail" service. As seen below, the question devolves into the ultimate issue—is "Express Mail" postal matter?

The Court notes at the outset that plaintiff's claim against the USPS is a suit against the government of the United States. The United States, as sovereign, is "immune from suit save as it consents to be sued…and the terms of its consent to be sued in any court define that court's jurisdiction to entertain the suit." *Lehman* v. *Nakshian*, 453 U.S. 156 (1981). Thus, if Congress waives the government's sovereign immunity from suit, a plaintiff's rights are limited to the terms of the government's consent to be sued. Limitations and conditions which the government places on its consent to be sued must be strictly observed and exceptions are not to be implied.

By enacting the FTCA, Congress provided a waiver of sovereign immunity in certain cases. However, the FTCA specifically retains sovereign immunity for tort claims against the United States for "loss, miscarriage, or negligent transmission" of the mails or postal matter.

Notwithstanding this postal restriction of the waiver of sovereign immunity, plaintiff argues that this immunity no longer exists in view of the Postal Reorganization Act of 1970. The Postal Reorganization Act includes a provision that "[t]he Postal Service shall have [the power] (1)to sue and be sued in its official name.…" Plaintiff contends the Supreme Court's decision in *Franchise Tax Bd. of Cal.* v. *U.S. Postal Service*, 467 S.S. 512 (1984) establish[es] the proposition that not all services provided by the USPS are protected by the FTCA and that the "sue and be sued" clause should be construed so as to find an exception.

The *Franchise Tax Bd.* case involved the question of whether the USPS was required to honor a garnishment order against a USPS employee resulting from an unpaid state administrative tax. The Franchise Tax Board of California served a garnishment on the USPS ordering the withholding of delinquent amounts from the employees' checks. In that lawsuit, no sum of money was claimed against the United States. The Supreme Court held the USPS was required to honor the garnishment. Thus, the "sue and be sued" clause now permits actions against the USPS which were prohibited against its predecessor such as a suit requiring the Postal Service to honor a garnishment order resulting from a state administrative tax levy. But this is not a limitation of the FTCA.

The present case, ultimately, asserts that the United States owes and must pay money. This is the core of the issue of sovereign immunity. As to this the FTCA defines the limits of the United States' willingness to assume this legal obligation.

Plaintiff, here, argues that Congress has launched the USPS into the commercial world, and, therefore, this Court must construe the "sue and be sued" clause in a fashion whereby the USPS may be held liable for lost packages in the same manner a private commercial business enterprise would be. The Court is not persuaded by this argument. While Congress did provide a general waiver of immunity for the USPS in the Postal Reorganization Act of 1970, it specifically retained sovereign immunity as to lost postal matter. Congress may have launched the USPS into the commercial world but it did not send it off to fly alone. Congress maintained the Postal Service under the protective wing of Section 2680(b) of the FTCA [which] states that the bar of sovereign immunity is not waived with respect to "loss, miscarriage or negligent transmission of the mails."

Plaintiff asserts "Express Mail" is a commercial venture and those items it carries are not "postal matter." The Court holds to the contrary. "Express Mail" is a mail classification under DMM, Section 221.1. Therefore, any mailable matter sent via USPS "Express Mail" is mail or postal matter.

The DMM defines the limit of the postal service's liability: "Parcels will be insured against loss, damage or rifling: coverage is limited to $500.00." Therefore, under the applicable postal service regulation, plaintiff's potential recovery is limited to $500. It is acknowledged by counsel for both parties that the USPS has already tendered a check to plaintiff in the amount of $500 for his contract claim.

Based on the foregoing, and upon review of the files, records, and proceedings herein, IT IS ORDERED that:

1. Defendant's motion for summary judgment is granted.
2. Plaintiff's motion for summary judgment is denied.
3. The cause may be, and hereby is, dismissed.

FOR DISCUSSION

1. In this case everyone agrees that the Postal Service lost a package worth about $17,000. Why do they only have to pay $500? If they had to pay the full amount, where would the money ultimately come from? How would this differ if the defendant had been a private corporation?

2. According to Allied Coin, the "sue and be sued" provision of the Postal Reorganization Act allows them to sue the USPS. Explain how their interpretation differs from that of Judge Rosenbaum. Which do you find most convincing?

3. Allied Coin argues that "Express Mail" is more like a private business such as Federal Express than a government agency. Explain what the Court thinks of this argument.

4. Would it be a reasonable argument to claim that a business that frequently used the mail as Allied Coin did should have been aware of the Postal Service's regulations limiting liability and therefore was treated fairly?

5. If you were the president of Allied Coin and decided to write to your representative in Congress based on your experience in this lawsuit, what changes in the law would you suggest and why?

Governmental immunity extends to many acts performed by government employees. One important recent trend has been the contracting out of government services to private companies. Some states have even gone so far as to hire private companies not only to build but to operate prisons. Should the employees of these companies receive the same immunity as would government employees performing comparable duties? In the case that follows, the Supreme Court of New Jersey has to decide whether a company hired to provide security at a government-owned sports complex has immunity from being sued by someone injured while attending a football game.

CASE   **Vanchieri v. New Jersey Sports and Exposition Authority**
Supreme Court of New Jersey (1986)
514 A.2d 1323

CLIFFORD, J.   The New Jersey Tort Claims Act provides public entities and public employees with broad immunity from suit in tort. In this case we must decide whether that immunity extends to an independent contractor, and, if it does, under what circumstances.

Plaintiffs sued to recover on account of personal injuries sustained by plaintiff Jean Vanchieri at the Meadowlands Sports Complex. The trial court granted summary judgment in favor of defendants, New Jersey Sports and Exposition Authority (NJSEA), the public operator of the Meadowlands Sports Complex, and Wackenhut Company, an independent contractor engaged by NJSEA to provide security services. The Appellate Division affirmed. We granted certification limited to the issue of Wackenhut Company's right to summary judgment. We now reverse the judgment below as to that defendant.

Plaintiffs Jean and Michael Vanchieri, accompanied by their friends Shirley and Robert Sassi, attended a pre-season football game at Giants Stadium in the Meadowlands Sports Complex on September 4, 1982. The two couples waited in their seats for approximately fifteen minutes after the game, then started to leave the stadium. While crossing a hallway or turning to cross a hallway, Jean Vanchieri was knocked down by one of three young men who were roughhousing in or near the exit area. Ms. Vanchieri received emergency treatment at the Stadium and thereafter at two hospitals. Her injury, a subcapital displaced fracture of the left hip, eventually required insertion of a prosthetic replacement.

Plaintiffs brought suit against NJSEA, Wackenhut Company, and various fictional defendants. As to Wackenhut, plaintiffs' complaint charged defendant with "the responsibility for maintaining security at Giants Stadium and providing uniformed guards on the premises to accomplish security and control of those on the premises," and alleged that "as a result of Wackenhut's negligence in failing to provide proper security and/or supervision," plaintiff Jean Vanchieri was injured. Although Wackenhut's answer did not plead immunity under the Tort Claims Act, Wackenhut followed NJSEA in moving for summary judgment, contending that it was "entitled to the same immunity [as that] afforded to the Authority."

The trial court granted summary judgment to both defendants, relying principally on *Rodriguez* v. *New Jersey Sports and Exposition Auth.*, 472 A.2d 146 (App.Div. 1983). In that case, Crispin Rodriguez was injured in the parking lot outside the Meadowlands Race Track. The Appellate Division affirmed the trial court's dismissal of Rodriguez's complaint against NJSEA and Pinkerton's, Inc., an independent contractor that provided security services. The trial court in this case found no basis for distinguishing *Rodriguez*, and therefore granted defendant's motions. The Appellate Division held that,

"Wackenhut, as a private security agency under contract with the Authority, is within the immunity provisions of the New Jersey Tort Claims Act." This opinion addresses that holding of the court below.

The Tort Claims Act was enacted in response to a perception that although the common-law doctrine of complete sovereign immunity was inherently unfair, at the same time some immunity was necessary.

> The legislature recognizes the inherently unfair and inequitable results which occur in the strict application of the traditional doctrine of sovereign immunity. On the other hand the Legislature recognizes that while a private entrepreneur may readily be held liable for negligence within the chosen ambit of his activity, the area within which government has the power to act for the public good is almost without limit and therefore government should not have the duty to do everything that might be done. [N.J.S.A. 59:1-2.]

NJSEA is a public entity within the meaning of the Tort Claims Act. A public employee, also entitled to statutory immunity, is an employee of a public entity. Although the term "employee" is defined broadly, independent contractors are expressly excluded from its scope. Wackenhut is not entitled, under the language of the Act, to immunity from tort claims. Nonetheless, independent contractors in general, and Wackenhut Company in particular, do, under well-recognized principles, share to a limited extent the immunity of public entities with whom they contract.

When a public entity provides plans and specifications to an independent contractor, the public contractor will not be held liable for work performed in accordance with those plans and specifications. This rule rests on two important principles. First, the immunity of the entity itself would become meaningless if contractors complying with its design were liable in tort for defects in that design. If contractors never shared government immunity, their costs of doing business would be passed on to the government entities hiring the contractors. In respect of costs, therefore, the effect would be nearly the same as if the public entity were liable itself.

The second principle underlying public contractor immunity concerns notions of fairness. An independent contractor bound to specifications that are provided by a public entity and over which it has no control is not responsible for defects in those specifications. It would be fundamentally unfair to hold a contractor liable in that instance for injury caused by defective plans, at least in the absence of a blatant, obvious danger that the contractor should have brought to the attention of the public entity.

Balanced against the policies favoring immunity for contractors is a legitimate concern that injured plaintiffs not be unduly denied compensation for their injuries. This concern requires careful scrutiny of contractors' claims to immunity, lest immunity be granted too freely and in the absence of circumstances giving rise to its justification. Wackenhut should not be immune from suit by the mere fortuity that it contracted with NJSEA rather than with a private entity. Moreover, public contractors' derivative immunity under the Tort Claims Act is an affirmative defense. A party seeking this immunity bears not only the burden of pleading it but also the burden of persuasion.

In this case defendant Wackenhut Company has not established that the NJSEA provided plans and specifications for the deployment of security personnel for the pre-season game at which Jean Vanchieri was injured. Wackenhut did submit its contract with the Authority. The contract shows that Authority had the power to specify how security functions were to be carried out. The record is barren of any proof, however, that NJSEA exercised that power for the game on September 4, 1982. And of course, absent evidence of those plans and specifications, Wackenhut could not have shown that it complied with them. It was not for plaintiffs to prove these essential elements of Wackenhut's affirmative defense, but for Wackenhut to do so. In the absence of those proofs, the trial court erred in granting summary judgment for Wackenhut.

Whether NJSEA's immunity is viewed as stemming from its general immunity for the exercise of discretion or its more specific immunity for failure to provide sufficient police services, the elements of Wackenhut's defense are identical. If it can show that NJSEA exercised its contractual right to make necessary, discretionary decisions concerning the September 4, 1982, game, including specifying the number of guards to be employed for the game, their posts, and the type and amount of equipment to be used, and if Wackenhut further establishes that it did not deviate from those specifications, then Wackenhut will have proven its right to share any statutory immunity from liability to which NJSEA is entitled in this suit. On the other hand, if Wackenhut cannot prove these elements, the defense of derivative sovereign immunity will not apply, and Wackenhut will be amenable to suit under ordinary negligence principles. In that event, plaintiffs may proceed in their attempt to establish that Wackenhut was negligent and that its negligence proximately caused Jean Vanchieri's injuries.

The judgment below is reversed as to defendant Wackenhut Company and the cause is remanded for further proceedings consistent with this opinion.

FOR DISCUSSION

1. The trial court granted summary judgment for both Wackenhut and the NJSEA, but the Supreme Court of New Jersey only reviewed the judgment for Wackenhut. Explain why it did not review the judgment for NJSEA.

2. On what basis did the lower courts rule for Wackenhut?

3. In this case, the New Jersey Supreme Court has to weigh the arguments for and against extending government immunity to private companies under government contract. Explain the arguments on both sides and how the Court balances them in this case. Do you agree with their result?

4. The Court remands the case to the trial court "for further proceedings consistent with this opinion." What will each side try to prove in these proceedings? What standard of proof will the trial court use in making its decision?

5. If, in *Allied Coin Investment Co.* v. *U.S. Postal Service*, the Postal Service had hired a private company to deliver "Express Mail" would the outcome have been different? Explain your reasoning.

LEGAL TERMS TO KNOW

Advisory opinion	Nonjusticiable
Class action	Political question
Collusive case	Pro se
Declaratory judgment	Standing
Immunity	Statute of Limitations
Mootness	Toll

ADDITIONAL QUESTIONS AND EXERCISES

1. Writing about standing and mootness, in *Judicial Policies: Implementation and Impact*, (Washington, DC: CQ Press, 1984, p. 41) by Charles A. Johnson and Bradley C. Canon claim that they can sometimes give lower court judges "sufficient discretion to dismiss a suit that otherwise might force him or her to apply an unacceptable policy." Review the appropriate cases in this chapter and write an essay explaining whether you agree or disagree. If you agree, do you think this is good or bad?

2. Explain the original reasons behind the case or controversy rule. To what extent are they still valid?

3. A city announces it will close a small park for fiscal reasons. Upon hearing this, a citizen who has occasionally visited the park sues to block its closing. Write two briefs, one arguing in favor of giving the citizen standing, the other against.

4. In recent years, there has been a trend to limit the extent of sovereign immunity. Some observers have suggested that it should be completely abolished. Explain whether you agree or not.

5. Although most states do not allow advisory opinions, a few permit a governor to request the opinion of the state's highest court on the constitutionality of pending legislation. Explain whether you believe this is a good idea.

6. Should taxpayers have standing to challenge any government spending? For contrasting views, see *Flast* v. *Cohen*, 392 U.S. 83 (1968) and *Valley Forge Christian College* v. *Americans United for Separation of Church and State*, 454 U.S. 464 (1982).

FOR FURTHER READING

1. BRILMAYER, LEA, "The Jurisprudence of Article III: Perspectives on the 'Case or Controversy' Requirement," 93 *Harvard Law Review* (1979), 297–321.

2. CURRIE, DAVID, "Misunderstanding Standing," *The Supreme Court Review* (1981), 41–47.

3. HENKIN, LOUIS, "Is There a 'Political Question' Doctrine?" 85 *Yale Law Journal* (1976), 597.

4. MORRISON, HARRY JR., "Sovereign Immunity," 60 *Florida Bar Journal*, (April 1986), 1–46.

5. RADCLIFFE, JAMES E., *The Case-or-Controversy Provision*. University Park: Pennsylvania State University Press, 1978.

6. STRUM, PHILIPPA, *The Supreme Court and "Political Questions."* University: University of Alabama Press, 1974.

6

PROPERTY

INTRODUCTION

Property is the oldest of the substantive subjects in common law, and one of the most important and respected. The right to own property, together with freedom of contract, builds the foundation for capitalist society and is specifically protected by the U. S. Constitution. It is not really a joke or an exaggeration when law school students are told that all law is about property—how to get it, how to keep it, and how to pass it on.

This chapter examines what property is and what it means to own something. These are ideas that have changed somewhat over time, even though property, more than most legal subjects, appears to represent what we might call "well-settled law"— concepts and rules that were firmly established centuries ago and are remarkably resistant to change. Nevertheless, our ideas about property have both expanded and contracted over the years, and it is likely that William Blackstone, who surveyed the English law of property in the middle of the eighteenth century, or Oliver Wendell Holmes, Jr., who commented on principles of property law in late nineteenth-century America, would be surprised by some features of the modern law of property.

Definitions of Property

Generally, when lay persons use the word "property," they are referring to specific tangible objects and, most often, to land. Although land and material objects are frequently the subjects of property, property encompasses a great deal more than material things. In modern legal terms, property is not things at all, but rather a collection of rights and entitlements people have in relation to things and, perhaps even more important, in relation to other people. The right of property includes the right to acquire, possess, use, enjoy, and

145

dispose of that which is owned. This legal right predates the Constitution, but is affirmed and guaranteed by it in the Fifth and Fourteenth Amendments, which state that the federal and state government may not deprive a person of property without due process of law.

Just how seriously this fundamental, "inalienable," right of property has been taken, and how central a role given to it, may be determined from the following statement:

> The ancient and established maxims of Anglo-Saxon law which protect the fundamental rights in the use, enjoyment, and disposal of private property are but the outgrowth of the long and arduous experience of mankind. They embody a painful, tragic history—the record of the struggle against tyranny, the overseership of prefects, and the overlordship of kings and nobles, when nothing so well bespoke the serfdom of the subject as his inability to own property. They proclaim the freedom of men from those odious despotisms, their liberty to earn and possess their own, to deal with it, to use and dispose of it, not at the behest of a master, but in the manner that benefits all men. *Spann* v. *Dallas*, 111 Tex 350, 235 SW 513, 19 ALR 1387.

Property exists as a subject of both common law and legislation. It has been guaranteed and protected by the U.S. Constitution, not only through traditional due process but also through other provisions, such as the contract clause. In the late nineteenth and early twentieth centuries, a concept of "substantive due process" was virtually invented to protect private property against interference by the government through social welfare legislation![1]

Although the Constitution protects the right of property, it does not define the term, and the meaning of "property" varies from state to state, and even from statute to statute within a state, depending on the statute's purpose. "Property," for the purposes of constitutional guarantees, is construed broadly, but nevertheless the property right to be protected must have been recognized or created by a court or legislature.

Traditionally, there are constituent elements, or incidents, that characterize property, and that include the unrestricted rights of **use, enjoyment**, and **disposal**. Although **possession** is an important incident of ownership, possession alone does not guarantee title to property, and it is quite possible to be an owner without having possession of the property that is owned.

Ownership implies rights of **possession, dominion**, and **control** over the property at issue, and ownership further implies the **right to exclude other people** from that which is owned. Ownership of property also involves the **right to the benefits of the property**, such as its products (in the case of land), or its increase (such as when money deposited in a bank earns interest, or shares of stock increase in price and, therefore, in value to the owner).

Although we may think of property and ownership principally in terms of rights and benefits, there are also legally imposed limitations to the right of property. Ownership is not absolute: The property owner is bound, for example, by the limitation of the maxim "sic utere tuo ut non alienum laedas" (so use your property as not to injure that of another), as well as by the rule that ownership of property may subject that property to the claims of the owner's creditors. The old saying, "You can't have your cake and eat it, too," applies to property law in the sense that a person who owns a thing is equally vulnerable to having that thing seized to satisfy his debts.

There are also governmental powers that limit the right of property including: the right of **eminent domain** (the power to take private property for public use by the state, on payment of compensation); the right of **taxation**; and the right of the **police power** (the right to place restraints especially on the use of property for the protection of public safety, health, welfare, and morals).

---

[1]This doctrine, which found its classic expression in *Lochner* v. *New York*, 198 U.S. 45 (1905), did not enjoy a long life and met its final end in 1937 in *West Coast Hotel Co.* v. *Parrish*, 300 U.S. 379.

Types of Property

In its most general sense, property encompasses every type of thing, right, or interest that one person can own and transfer to another person, and that is capable of being given a monetary value. Property is traditionally divided into two basic types: **tangible (corporeal) property** and **intangible (incorporeal) property**.

Tangible property consists of things that have physical, material substance. It includes **real property** (land) and **tangible personal property** (all material objects that can be owned except land). Tangible personal property includes goods, money, and movable chattels. **Chattels** are movable things; material objects of personal property not connected to real estate, such as vehicles, furniture, equipment, and so forth.

Not all personal property is tangible. There are many types of **intangible personal property**: rights and interests that are not directly related to material things. Here, the "property" consists essentially of relationships between people that have exchangeable value and that can be legally recognized and enforced. Stocks, bonds, debts, patents, copyrights, good will, trademarks and trade names, franchises, and trade secrets are examples of intangible personal property. Another type of intangible personal property is a **right of action**. Rights of action involve things that one does not presently possess, but that are obtainable through a legal action (lawsuit). Rights of action can arise from both contract and tort, and involve rights to recover money or chattels by means of a lawsuit. These include payments due under contracts, debts, unpaid accounts receivable, and mortgages, among many others. A right to bring an action for actual (compensatory) damages is property, has monetary value, and may be sold or otherwise transferred.

In American law, all persons have the legal right to acquire and hold property. Ownership involves a collection of rights to use and enjoy property including the rights to sell it, give it away, or even destroy it. Although ownership may encompass all the traditional incidents of property simultaneously (use, benefit, disposal), some types of ownership do not. Sometimes one may own a thing and not possess it, as when one owns stock in a corporation. Or one may own a thing and not be able to sell it, as a license to practice law or medicine. One may also own a thing only during his or her lifetime (a **life interest** in property) —he or she may possess it and use it, yet not be able to sell it, bequeath it, or give it away, because another "owner" (the **remainderman**) already has a right to the property when the life owner dies. A **trustee** is an "owner" who is obligated to administer property for the benefit of another, the **beneficiary**. And even the classic owner of real property in "fee simple absolute," the most complete form of ownership, does not have unlimited rights to do what he or she wants with the property. Zoning, nuisance, police powers, and property rights of other individuals limit the powers of an owner with respect to his or her property. Nevertheless, we traditionally think of property much more in terms of our rights over it than of the limitations to those rights. The right to acquire property, to amass wealth, to increase one's estate, is fundamental to our legal system and to the ideology that underlies it.

NATURE AND ORIGIN OF PROPERTY

Our legal system traditionally devotes much time and energy to determining who owns what, and the absorbing task of figuring out who owns a thing has led to a great concentration on **acquisition** of property. Today, it is considered a basic tenet of property law that people have a right to acquire property in any lawful or legitimate way, which may include buying it, inheriting it, receiving it as a gift, or even by occupying it at the expense of another owner, within certain limitations. (We will talk about acquisition of property by **adverse possession** later in this chapter.) In the seventeenth century, many thinkers, including John Locke,[2] considered and debated the question of the origin of private property. In Locke's conception, acquisition of title to property originates in the **labor** a person expends to appropriate or improve some natural thing that, through the labor expended, acquires a greater **value** and becomes the property of that person who expended his or her labor on it.

READING   Of Property
John Locke *

27. Though the Earth, and all inferior Creatures be common to all Men, yet every Man has a *Property* in his own *Person*. This no Body has any Right to but himself. The *Labour* of his Body, and the *Work* of his Hands, we may say, are properly his. Whatsoever then he removes out of the State that Nature hath provided, and left it in, he hath mixed his *Labour* with, and joyned it to something that is his own, and thereby makes it his *Property*. It being by him removed from the common state Nature placed it in, hath by this *labour* something annexed to it, that excludes the common right of other Men. For this *Labour* being the unquestionable Property of the Labourer, no Man but he can have a right to what that is once joyned to, at least where there is enough, and as good left in common for others.

28. He that is nourished by the Acorns he pickt up under an Oak, or the Apples he gathered from the Trees in the Wood, has certainly appropriated them to himself. No Body can deny but the nourishment is his. I ask then, When did they begin to be his? When he digested? Or when he eat? Or when he boiled? Or when he brought them home? Or when he pickt them up? And 'tis plain, if the first gathering made them not his, nothing else could. That *labour* put a distinction between them and common. That added something to them more than Nature, the common Mother of all, had done; and so they became his private right. And will any one say he had no right to those Acorns or Apples he thus appropriated, because he had not the consent of all Mankind to make them his? Was it a Robbery thus to assume to himself what belonged to all in Common? If such a consent as that was necessary, Man had starved, notwithstanding the Plenty God had given him. We see in *Commons*, which remain so by Compact, that 'tis the taking any part of what is common, and removing it out of the state Nature leaves it in, which *begins the Property*; without which the Common is of no use. And the taking of this or that part, does not depend on the express consent of all the Commoners. Thus the Grass my Horse has bit; the Turfs my Servant has cut; and the Ore I have digg'd in any place where I have a right to them in common with others, become my *Property*, without the assignation or consent of any body. The *labour* that was mine, removing them out of that common state they were in, hath *fixed* my *Property* in them....

31. It will perhaps be objected to this, That if gathering the Acorns, or other Fruits of the Earth, &c. makes a right to them, then any one may *ingross* as much as he will. To which I Answer, Not so. The same Law of Nature, that does by this means give us Property, does also *bound* that *Property* too. *God has given us all things richly*, 1 Tim. vi. 17, is the Voice of Reason confirmed by Inspiration. But how far has he given it us? *To enjoy*. As much as

---

[2]John Locke (1632–1704) was an English political philosopher whose ideas about natural rights, liberty, and limited governmental power exercised a powerful influence on the men who shaped American government and law. Locke's *Second Treatise on Government*, for example, was a model for the Declaration of Independence, and Jefferson borrowed several significant phrases directly from Locke's essay.

any one can make use of to any advantage of life before it spoils; so much he may by his labour fix a Property in. Whatever is beyond this, is more than his share, and belongs to others. Nothing was made by God for Man to spoil or destroy. And thus considering the plenty of natural Provisions there was a long time in the World, and the few spenders, and to how small a part of that provision the industry of one Man could extend itself, and ingross it to the prejudice of others; especially keeping within the *bounds*, set by reason of what might serve for his *use*; there could be then little room for Quarrels or Contentions about Property so establish'd.

32. But the *chief matter of Property* being now not the Fruits of the Earth, and the Beasts that subsist on it, but the *Earth itself*, as that which takes in and carries with it all the rest; I think it is plain, that *Property* in that too is acquired as the former. As much Land as a Man Tills, Plants, Improves, Cultivates, and can use the Product of, so much is his *Property*. Nor will it invalidate his right to say, Every body else has an equal Title to it; and therefore he cannot appropriate, he cannot inclose, without the Consent of all his Fellow-Commoners, all Mankind. God, when he gave the World in common to all Mankind, commanded Man also to labour, and the penury of his Condition required it of him. God and his Reason commanded him to subdue the Earth, i.e. improve it for the benefit of Life, and therein lay out something upon it that was his own, his labour. He that in Obedience to this Command of God, subdued, tilled and sowed any part of it, thereby annexed to it something that was his Property, which another had no Title to, nor could without injury take from him....

45. Thus *Labour*, in the Beginning, *gave a right of Property*, where-ever anyone was pleased to imploy it, upon what was common, which remained, a long while, the far greater part, and is yet more than Mankind makes use of. Men, at first, for the most part, contented themselves with what un-assisted Nature Offered to their Necessities; and though afterwards, in some parts of the World (where the Increase of People and Stock, with the *Use of Money*) had made Land scarce, and so of some Value, the several *Communities* settled the Bounds of their distinct Territories, and by Laws within themselves, regulated the Properties of the private Men of their Society, and so, *by Compact* and Agreement, *settled the Property* which Labour and Industry began; and the Leagues that have been made between several States and Kingdoms, either expressly or tacitly disowning all Claim and Right to the Land in the others Possession, have, by Common Consent, given up their pretences to their natural common Right, which originally they had to those Countries, and so have, by *positive agreement, settled a Property* amongst themselves, in distinct Parts and parcels of the Earth; yet there are still *great Tracts of Ground* to be found, which (the Inhabitants thereof not having joyned with the rest of Mankind, in the consent of the Use of their common Money) *lie waste*, and are more than the People, who dwell on it, do, or can make use of, and so still lie in common. Tho' this can scarce happen amongst that part of Mankind, that have consented to the use of Money.

46. The greatest part of *things really useful* to the Life of Man, and such as the necessity of subsisting made the first Commoners of the World look after, as it doth the *Americans* now, *are* generally things *of short duration*; such as, if they are not consumed by use, will decay and perish of themselves: Gold, Silver, and Diamonds, are things, that Fancy or Agreement hath put a Value on, more then real Use, and the necessary Support of Life. Now of those good things which Nature hath provided in common, every one had a Right (as hath been said) to as much as he could use, and had a Property in all that he could affect with his Labour: all that his Industry could extend to, to alter from the State Nature had put it in, was his. He that *gathered* a Hundred Bushels of Acorns or Apples, had thereby a *Property* in them: they were his Goods as soon as gathered. He was only to look that he used them before

they spoiled; else he took more than his share, and robb'd others. And indeed it was a foolish thing, as well as dishonest, to hoard up more than he could make use of. If he gave away a part to any body else, so that it perished not uselessly in his Possession, these he also made use of. And if he bartered away Plumbs that would have rotted in a Week, for Nuts that would last good for his eating a whole Year, he did no injury; he wasted not the common Stock; destroyed no part of the portion of Goods that belonged to others, so long as nothing perished uselessly in his hands. Again, if he would give us Nuts for a piece of Metal, pleased with its colour; or exchanged his Sheep for Shells, or Wool for a sparkling Pebble or a Diamond, and keep those by him all his Life, he invaded not the Right of others, he might heap up as much of these durable things as he pleased; the *exceeding of the bounds of his* just *Property* not lying in the largeness of his Possession, but the perishing of any thing uselessly in it.

47. And thus came in the use of Money, some lasting thing that Men might keep without spoiling, and that by mutual consent Men would take in exchange for the truly useful, but perishable Supports of Life.

48. And as different degrees of Industry were apt to give Men Possessions in different Proportions, so this *Invention of Money* gave them the opportunity to continue to enlarge them. For supposing an Island, separated from all possible Commerce with the rest of the World, wherein there were but a hundred Families, but there were Sheep, Horses, and Cows, with other useful Animals, wholsome Fruits, and Land enough for Corn for a hundred thousand times as many, but nothing in the Island, either because of its Commonness, or Perishableness, fit to supply the place of *Money*: What reason could any one have there to enlarge his Possessions beyond the use of his Family and a plentiful supply to its Consumption, either in what their own Industry produced, or they could barter for like perishable, useful Commodities, with others? Where there is not something both lasting and scarce, and so valuable to be hoarded up, there Men will not be so apt to enlarge their *Possessions of Land*, were it never so rich, never so free for them to take. For I ask, What would a Man value Ten Thousand, or a Hundred Thousand Acres of excellent *Land*, ready cultivated, and well stocked too with Cattle, in the middle of the in-land Parts of *America*, where he had no hopes of Commerce with other Parts of the World, to draw *Money* to him by the Sale of the Product? It would not be worth the inclosing, and we should see him give up again to the wild Common of Nature, whatever was more than would supply the Conveniences of Life to be had there for him and his Family.

49. Thus in the beginning all the World was *America*, and more so than that is now; for no such thing as *Money* was any where known. Find out something that hath the *Use and Value of Money* amongst his Neighbours, you shall see the same Man will begin presently to *enlarge* his *Possessions*.

50. But since Gold and Silver, being little useful to the Life of Man in proportion to Food, Rayment, and Carriage, has its *value* only from the consent of Men, whereof Labour yet makes, in great part, *the measure*, it is plain, that Men have agreed to disproportionate and unequal Possession of the Earth, they having by a tacit and voluntary consent found out a way, how a man may fairly possess more land than he himself can use the product of, by receiving in exchange for the overplus, Gold and Silver, which may be hoarded up without injury to any one, these metals not spoiling or decaying in the hands of the possessor. This partage of things, in an inequality of private possessions, men have made practicable out of the bounds of Societie, and without compact, only by putting a value on gold and silver and tacitly agreeing in the use of Money. For in Governments the Laws regulate the right of property, and the possession of land is determined by positive constitutions.

51. And thus, I think, it is very easy to conceive without any difficulty, *how Labour could at first begin a title of Property* in the common things of Nature, and how the spending it upon our uses bounded it. So that there could then be no reason of quarreling about Title, nor any doubt about the largeness of Possession it gave. Right and conveniency went together; for as a Man had a Right to all he could imploy his Labour upon, so he had no temptation to labour for more than he could make use of. This left no room for Controversie about the Title, nor for Incroachment on the Right of others; what Portion a Man carved to himself, was easily seen; and it was useless and dishonest to carve himself too much, or take more than he needed.

NOTES

*From *The Second Treatise of Government*, 1689/90.

FOR DISCUSSION

1. According to Locke, what factors initially give value to things?
2. What limitations does Locke set upon the legitimate acquisition of property?
3. What kinds of property are affected by these limitations and why?
4. What happens to Locke's original limited property when people become interested in owning things beyond that which is needed for subsistence?
5. According to Locke, how do attitudes toward property change when there is no longer enough for people to just take what they can use?
6. As there are more people in the world and societies become more advanced, how are rights in property secured?
7. According to Locke, why is the introduction of money necessary for progress?
8. Locke acknowledges that the introduction of money leads to inequality in the ownership of property. What justifications does he give for this?
9. Locke says, "In the beginning all the World was *America*," meaning that the whole world was primeval, uncultivated Nature, open and available for appropriation by industrious, enterprising people. Today there are no more "Americas" on the continents of the earth, but what about acquiring property on the floor of the ocean or in outer space? Do you think Locke's ideas should apply there?
10. What considerations might lead nations in the modern world *not* to allow the Lockean process of acquisition of private property on the seabed or in space?

What Can Be Classified as Property

In his discussion of the nature and origin of property, Locke states that "every man has a property in his own person," yet there has always been a general agreement in our legal system that the human body itself, alive or dead, ought not be a subject of property. (One way of rationalizing the legally recognized practice of slavery with this notion was to argue that blacks were not human beings.) That does not mean, however, that disputes do not arise over custody or possession of the human body that may sometimes be expressed in terms of property rights. The most basic of these involves the right and obligation of the next of kin to take custody of the corpse of a deceased person and see to its burial. This so-called right of sepulchre is not a property right, and today violations result in actions for damages in tort for mental anguish and distress, not actions to enforce a right of property. Nevertheless many states have called this right "quasi property," apparently in an effort to express its exclusive and protected nature. This has caused considerable confusion, and has reinforced the tendency to claim a property right in the corpse as a means of gaining the protection of the Fifth or Fourteenth Amendments, which require due process before a property right can be interfered with, as in cases involving autopsies done without consent of the relatives or other situations in which a coroner or other governmental official has temporarily retained custody of the body of the deceased.

As medical technology has become more advanced, however, questions regarding property rights in the human body have multiplied and become more complex, as the following case illustrates.

CASE

Georgia Lions Eye Bank, Inc., et al. v. Lavant
Supreme Court of Georgia (1985)
255 Ga. 60, 335 S.E.2d 127, 54 A.L.R.4th 1209
OPINION OF THE COURT

WELTNER, Justice.   This appeal is from an order of the State Court of Chatham County holding unconstitutional OCGA § 31-23-6(b)(1), which authorizes, under specified circumstance, removal for transplant of the corneal tissue of decedents if no objection is made by decedent in his life or by his next-of-kin after death.

This law was enacted by a virtually unanimous General Assembly in 1978. The record indicates that before its passage, approximately 25 corneal transplants were performed each year. In 1984, however, more than 1000 persons regained their sight through transplants.

Pursuant to this Code section, officials of the Georgia Lions Eye Bank removed during autopsy the corneal tissue of an infant, who had died of sudden infant death syndrome. While the parents of the infant did not object, there was no notice of the intended removal, nor any realistic opportunity to object. Sometime later, the mother discovered for the first time that the corneal tissue had been removed. She brought suit against St. Joseph's Hospital and the Georgia Lions Eye Bank for the wrongful removal of the tissue.

The court held the statute violative of due process in that it deprives a person of a property right in the corpse of his next-of-kin, and fails to provide notice and an opportunity to object.

1. In the earlier days of the common law, so Blackstone avers, no property right existed relative to a dead body, and matters concerning corpses were left to the ecclesiastical courts. "But though the heir has a property in the monuments and escutcheons of his ancestors, yet he has none in their bodies or ashes; nor can he bring any civil action against such as indecently, at least, if not impiously, violate and disturb their remains, when dead and buried." 2 W. Blackstone, Commentaries 429 (T. Cooley, ed. 1899).

Because there were no ecclesiastical courts in this country to resolve matters relating to corpses, the courts conceived the notion of "quasi-property right," when referring to the interest of relatives in the bodies of their next of kin. Dean Prosser noted: "It seems reasonably obvious that such "property" is something evolved out of thin air to meet the occasion, and that in reality the personal feelings of the survivors are being protected under a fiction likely to deceive no one but a lawyer." W. L. Prosser and W. P. Keeton, *Prosser and Keeton on Torts*, p. 63 (5th ed. 1984).

In Georgia, an early case concerning this interest of next of kin is *Louisville Railroad Co.* v. *Wilson*, 123 Ga. 62, 51 S.E. 24 (1905). The precise nature of the interest was never defined, although we held that some type of claim was stated. However, in *Pollard* v. *Phelps*, 56 Ga.App. 408, 415, 193 S.E. 102, 107 (1937), the court held that "[a]t common law no property right was held to exist in a dead body; and though this view is still maintained in a strict sense, the courts of civilized and Christian countries regard respect for the dead as not only a virtue but a duty, and hold that, in the absence of testamentary disposition, a quasi property right belongs to the husband or wife, and, if neither, to the next of kin." See also *Rivers* v. *Greenwood Cemetery*, Inc., 194 Ga. 524, 525, 22 S.E.2d 134 (1942), wherein we held, "that a dead body is quasi property over which the relatives of the deceased have rights which the courts will protect."

Thus it can be seen that in Georgia, there is no *constitutionally* protected right in a decedent's body. Rather, the courts have evolved the concept of quasi property in recognition of the interests of surviving relatives in the possession and control of decedent's bodies. We do not find this common law concept to be of constitutional dimension.

2. A right of action existing at common law may be modified or abrogated by the legislature. *Teasley* v. *Mathis*, 243 Ga. 561, 255 S.E.2d 57 (1979).

"A person has no property, no vested interest, in any rule of the common law. That is only one of the forms of municipal law, and is no more sacred than any other. Rights of property which have been created by the common law itself cannot be taken away without due process; but the law itself, as a rule of conduct, may be changed at the will, or even at the whim, of the legislature, unless prevented by constitutional limitations. Indeed, the great office of statutes is to remedy defects in the common law as they developed, and to adapt it to the changes of time and circumstances." *Munn* v. *Illinois*, 4 Otto 113, 94 U.S. 113, 134, 24 L.E. 77 (1876).

3. "'The preservation of the public health is one of the duties devolving upon the State as a sovereign power. In fact, among all the objects sought to be secured by governmental laws, none is more important than the preservation of the public health'; ... 'Health regulations are of the utmost consequence to the general welfare; and if they are reasonable, impartial, and not against the general policy of the State, they must be submitted to by individuals for the good of the public, irrespective of pecuniary loss." *Abel* v. *State*. 64 Ga.App. 448, 452-453, 13 S.E.2d 507 (1941).

Certainly, the General Assembly has it within its power, in the interest of the public welfare, to authorize this procedure, which yearly benefits hundreds of Georgians.

The motions for summary judgment of the hospital and the eye bank should have been granted.

Judgment reversed.

FOR DISCUSSION

1. Why are the parents in this case arguing that they were deprived of property without due process of law? What purpose does their claim serve?

2. Does human corneal tissue have a monetary value? Is there a market for it? How would it fit into Locke's discussion of private property and its acquisition?

3. What reasons, if any, are given by the decision to explain why human body parts should *not* be regarded as property? Are there any reasons why they should?

4. Given the reasoning in this case, should human embryos be classified as property? Human sperm and eggs? Aborted fetuses? If not, who should control the disposition of such things?

5. Sir Henry Maine described a legal fiction as a device that "conceals ...the fact that a rule of law has undergone alteration, its letter remaining unchanged, its operation being modified."[3] Does the term "quasi property" to describe the right involved in this situation fit Maine's definition? Explain your answer.

When in the *Second Treatise of Government*, John Locke stated: "Though the Earth, and all inferior Creatures be common to all Men, yet every Man has a *Property* in his own *Person*," the rest of the cited passage makes clear that he was referring to the tangible products of a person's labor: "The *Labour* of his Body, and the *Work* of his Hands, we may say, are properly his." While the preceding case established the principle that the human body itself may not be regarded as property, the following case deals with the common law property right in the publicity value of one's own person. We are not talking about the more common situation in which the person claims an intangible property right in the products of his intellect and creativity, because all the effort has been concentrated on promoting the person (or personality) as a valuable commodity. Here, in a sense, the person *becomes* the property.

CASE

Muhammad Ali v. Playgirl, Inc.
Tony Yamada, and Independent News Company
United States District Court, S.D. New York (1978)
447 F.Supp. 723

GAGLIARDI, District Judge.   Plaintiff Muhammad Ali, a citizen of Illinois and until recently the heavyweight boxing champion of the world, has brought this diversity action for injunctive relief and damages against defendants for their alleged unauthorized printing, publication and distribution of an objectionable portrait of Ali in the February 1978 issue of Playgirl Magazine, a monthly magazine published by Playgirl, Inc. and distributed in New York by Independent. The portrait complained of depicts a nude black man seated in the corner of a boxing ring and is claimed to be unmistakably recognizable as plaintiff Ali. Alleging that the publication of this picture constitutes, inter alia, a violation of his rights under Section 51 of the New York Civil Rights Law and of his related common law "right of publicity," Ali now moves for a preliminary injunction pursuant to Rule 65, Fed.R.Civ.P., directing defendants Playgirl, Inc. and Independent to cease distribution and dissemination of the February 1978 issue of Playgirl Magazine, to withdraw that issue from circulation and recover possession of all copies presently offered for sale, and to surrender to plaintiff any printing plates or devices used to reproduce the portrait complained of. For the reasons which follow and to the extent indicated below, plaintiff's motion for a preliminary injunction is granted.

Discussion

This court concludes that plaintiff has satisfied the standard established in this Circuit for determining whether a preliminary injunction should issue. *Sonesta International Hotels* v. *Wellington Associates*, 483 F.2d 247 (2d Cir. 1973). The familiar alternative test formula is that

---

[3]Ancient Law (London: J. Murray, 1861), p. 26.

a preliminary injunction should issue only upon a clear showing of either (1) probable success on the merits *and* possible irreparable injury, *or* (2) sufficiently serious questions going to the merits to make them a fair ground for litigation *and* a balance of hardships tipping decidedly toward the party requesting preliminary relief.

Id. at 250 (emphasis in original). As set forth below, this court is satisfied that under either branch of the *Sonesta* test Ali is entitled to the preliminary relief he seeks.

Liability on the merits In determining the issues of probable success on the merits or sufficiently serious questions going to the merits of this action, it is agreed that this court must look to the substantive law of New York. To be considered are plaintiff's claims that his statutory "right of privacy" under §51 of the New York Civil Rights Law and his common law "right of publicity" have been violated.

Section 51 of the New York Civil Rights Law provides in pertinent part:

> Any person whose name, portrait, or picture is used within this state ... for the purposes of trade without the written consent [of that person] may maintain an equitable action ... against the person, firm or corporation so using his name, portrait or picture, to prevent and restrain the use thereof; and may also sue and recover damages for any injury sustained by reason of such use....

Defendants do not, and indeed cannot, seriously dispute the assertion that the offensive drawing is in fact Ali's "portrait or picture." This phrase, as used in §51, is not restricted to photographs, but generally comprises those representations which are recognizable as likenesses of the complaining individual. Even a cursory inspection of the picture which is the subject of this action strongly suggests that the facial characteristics of the black male portrayed are those of Muhammad Ali. The cheekbones, broad nose and wideset brown eyes, together with the distinctive smile and close cropped black hair are recognizable as the features of the plaintiff, one of the most widely known athletes of our time. In addition, the figure depicted is seated on a stool in the corner of a boxing ring with both hands taped and outstretched resting on the ropes on either side. Although the picture is captioned "Mystery Man," the identification of the individual as Ali is further implied by an accompanying verse which refers to the figure as "the Greatest." This court may take judicial notice that plaintiff Ali has regularly claimed that appellation for himself and that his efforts to identify himself in the public mind as "the Greatest" have been so successful that he is regularly identified as such in the news media.

It is also clear that the picture has been used for the "purpose of trade" within the meaning of §51. In this regard it is the established law of New York that the unauthorized use of an individual's picture is not for a "trade purpose," and thus not violative of §51, if it is "in connection with an item of news or one that is newsworthy." *Gautier* v. *Pro-Football, Inc.*, 304 N.Y. 354, 359, 107 N.E.2d 485, 488 (1952). In the instant case there is no such informational or newsworthy dimension to defendants' unauthorized use of Ali's likeness. Instead, the picture is a dramatization, an illustration falling somewhere between representational art and a cartoon, and is accompanied by a plainly fictional and allegedly libelous bit of doggerel. Defendants cannot be said to have presented "the unembroidered dissemination of facts" or "the unvarnished, unfictionalized truth," *Sidis* v. *F-R Pub. Corporation*, 113 F.2d 806, 810 (2d Cir.). The nude portrait was clearly included in the magazine solely "for purposes of trade— *e.g.* merely to attract attention." *Grant* v. *Esquire, Inc.*, 367 F.Supp. 876, 881 (S.D.N.Y. 1973).

Finally, defendants concede that Ali did not consent to the inclusion of his likeness in the February 1978 Playgirl Magazine. Defendants contend, however, that even if their use of Ali's likeness is determined to be unauthorized and for trade purposes within the meaning of §51, the statutory right of privacy does not extend to protect "someone such as an athlete ... who chooses to bring himself to public notice, who chooses, indeed, as clearly the plaintiff here does to rather stridently seek out publicity." Defendants are plainly in error in disputing liability on the basis of Ali's status as a public personality. Such a contention

> confuses the fact that projection into the public arena may make for newsworthiness of one's activities, and all the hazards of publicity thus entailed, with the quite different and independent right to have one's personality, even if newsworthy, free from commercial exploitation at the hands of another....
>
> That [plaintiff] may have voluntarily on occasion surrendered [his] privacy, for a price or gratuitously, does not forever forfeit for anyone's commercial profit so much of [his] privacy as [he] has not relinquished. [Citations omitted.]

Booth v. *Curtis Publishing Co.*, 15 A.D.2d 343, 351-52, 223 N.Y.S.2d 737, 745, (1st Dept.), *aff'd*, 11 N.Y.2d 907, 228 N.Y.S.2d 468, 183 N.E.2d 812 (1962). Accordingly, this court is satisfied that plaintiff Ali has established probable success on the merits of his claimed violation of privacy under §51 of the New York Civil Rights Law.

The foregoing discussion also establishes the likelihood that plaintiff will prevail on his claim that his right of publicity has been violated by the publication of the offensive portrait. This Circuit has long held that New York recognizes the common law property right of publicity in addition to, and distinct from, the statutory right under §51. *Haelan Laboratories, Inc.* v. *Topps Chewing Gum, Inc.*, 202 F.2d 866, 868 (2d Cir.) *cert. denied*, 346 U.S. 816, 74 S.Ct. 26, 98 L.Ed. 343 (1953).

It must be noted, however, that the courts of New York do not regularly distinguish between the proprietary right of publicity, discussed *infra*, and the §51 right of privacy. The latter has been characterized as establishing and limiting the right of a person "to be left alone" and protecting "the sentiments, thoughts and feelings of an individual ... from [unwanted] commercial exploitation," *Flores* v. *Mosler Safe Co.*, 7 N.Y.2d 276, 280, 196 N.Y.S.2d 975, 977-8, 164 N.E.2d 853, 855 (1959), but numerous cases blend the concepts together and expressly recognize a right of recovery under §51 for violations of an individual's property interest in his likeness or reputation.

The distinctive aspect of the common law right of publicity is that it recognizes the commercial value of the picture or representation of a prominent person or performer, and protects his interest in the profitability of his public reputation or "persona." As held by this Circuit, New York State recognizes that, independent of his §51 rights, "a man has a right in the publicity value of his photograph, i.e., the right to grant the exclusive privilege of publishing his picture." *Haelan Laboratories* v. *Topps Chewing Gum, supra*, 202 F.2d at 868. This common law publicity right is analogous to a commercial entity's right to profit from the "goodwill" it has built up in its name and the interest which underlies protecting the right of publicity "'is the straightforward one of preventing unjust enrichment by the theft of good will.'" Kalven, *Privacy in Tort Law —Were Warren and Brandeis Wrong?*, 31 Law and Contemporary Problems, 326, 331 (1966), quoted in *Zacchini* v. *Scripps-Howard Broadcasting Co.*, 433 U.S. at 576, 97 S.Ct. 2849.

Accordingly, this right of publicity is usually asserted only if the plaintiff has "achieved in some degree a celebrated status." *Price* v. *Hal Roach Studios, Inc.*, 400 F.Supp. 836, at 847, quoting Gordon, *Right of Property in Name, Likeness, Personality and History*,

55 Nw.U.L.Rev. 553, 607 (1960). In the instant case, it is undisputed that plaintiff Ali has achieved such a "celebrated status" and it is clear to this court that he has established a valuable interest in his name and likeness. As in *Grant* v. *Esquire, Inc., supra*, this court "can take judicial notice that there is a fairly active market for exploitation of the faces, names and reputations of celebrities." 367 F.Supp. at 881. There can be little question that defendants' unauthorized publication of the portrait of Ali amounted to a wrongful appropriation of the market value of plaintiff's likeness.

Irreparable Injury   It is established that plaintiff must make a showing of irreparable injury under either branch of the *Sonesta* test, and under the circumstances outlined *supra*, this court is persuaded that plaintiff has met this burden.

As has been noted, in the course of his public career plaintiff has established a commercially valuable proprietary interest in his likeness and reputation, analogous to the good will accumulated in the name of a successful business entity. To the extent that defendants are unlawfully appropriating this valuable commodity for themselves, proof of damages or unjust enrichment may be extremely difficult. In virtually identical circumstances it has been observed that "a celebrity's property interest in his name and likeness is unique, and therefore there is no serious question as to the propriety of injunctive relief." *Uhlaender* v. *Henrickson*, 316 F.Supp. 1277, 1238 (D.Minn. 1970). Furthermore, defendants appear not only to be usurping plaintiff's valuable right of publicity for themselves but may well be inflicting damage upon this marketable reputation. As described previously, the "likeness" of Ali which has been published is a full frontal nude drawing, not merely a sketch or photograph of him as he appears in public. Damages from such evident abuse of plaintiff's property right in his public reputation are plainly difficult to measure by monetary standards. As this Circuit has noted in the preliminary injunction context, "difficulty [in computing damages] is especially common when damage to reputation, credibility or good will is present." *Dino DeLaurentis Cinematographica* v. *D-150, Inc.*, 366 F.2d 373, 376 (2d Cir. 1966) (citing cases). Such difficulty in determining monetary damages leaves plaintiff without an adequate remedy at law and satisfactorily establishes irreparable injury for purposes for preliminary equitable relief.

This court also notes that, although it appears that routinely scheduled newsstand circulation of the contested issue of Playgirl Magazine has ceased, it is established that voluntary cessation of illegal conduct does not deprive the court of the power to grant injunctive relief. Under all the circumstances, plaintiff has satisfied the court that preliminary relief is needed. The market for publications in New York is not limited to newsstand sales, plaintiff's counsel indicated that there may be such demand for copies of the magazine that premium prices are offered, and the disputed issues are within the jurisdiction of the court. Consequently, the effectiveness of the discontinuance of violations is not guaranteed, and this court concludes that preliminary relief is in order.

FOR DISCUSSION

1. According to the court, what is the difference between the statutory "right of privacy" and the common-law "right of publicity"?

2. In connection with his right of publicity, what does Muhammad Ali actually *own*?

3. Can Ali sell his right of publicity in his own person, even though we would not permit him to sell his person itself? What is the distinction?

4. How is it that such a widely known public figure as Muhammad Ali can still control some aspects of his public persona and exclude others from using them without his permission? What rights has he given up, and what does he still retain?

5. What kinds of things did Ali do to create the right of publicity he is now seeking to protect?

6. What damages to the value of his property may Ali sustain through such unauthorized use of his likeness? How does this compare to the possible damages that were of concern in the previous case?

Blackstone's *Commentaries on the Laws of England* is one of the most influential legal treatises ever published. Indeed, the *Commentaries* were probably more influential in America than in England, because early America sorely lacked the trained judges and lawyers needed to make a common-law legal system operate effectively. Next to the Bible and common sense, Blackstone's *Commentaries* became a legal bible of early American common law. In the *Commentaries* Blackstone proclaimed that property was one of the three absolute rights inherent in every [English]man, the other two being life and liberty. Blackstone devoted one entire volume of his *Commentaries* to the law of property. Unlike Locke, Blackstone's considerations of property were very practical and pragmatic, as befits a legal treatise writer rather than a philosopher. Blackstone moves beyond considerations of how a person acquires property to examine the rules by which one keeps the property one has acquired and may pass it on.

READING   **Of the Rights of Things**
                                   William Blackstone*

There is nothing which so generally strikes the imagination and engages the affections of mankind, as the right of property, or that sole and despotic dominion which one man claims and exercises over the external things of the world, in total exclusion of the right of any other individual in the universe. And yet there are very few, that will give themselves the trouble to consider the original and foundation of this right. Pleased as we are with the possession, we seem afraid to look back to the means by which it was acquired, as if fearful of some defect in our title; or at the best we rest satisfied with the decision of the laws in our favour, without examining the reason or authority upon which those laws have been built. We think it enough that our title is derived by the grant of the former proprietor, by descent from our ancestors, or by the last will and testament of the dying owner; not caring to reflect that (accurately and strictly speaking) there is no foundation in nature or natural law, why a set of words upon parchment should convey the dominion of land; why the son should have a right to exclude his fellow creatures from a determinate spot of ground, because his father had done so before him; or why the occupier of a particular field or of a jewel, when lying on his death-bed and no longer able to maintain possession, should be entitled to tell the rest of the world which of them should enjoy it after him. These enquiries, it must be owned, would be useless and even troublesome in common life. It is well if the mass of mankind will obey the laws when made without scrutinizing too nicely into the reasons of making them. But, when law is to be considered not only as a matter of practice, but also as a rational science, it cannot be improper or useless to examine more deeply the rudiments and grounds of these positive constitutions of society....

Property, both in lands and moveables, being thus originally acquired by the first taker, which taking amounts to a declaration that he intends to appropriate the thing to his own use, it remains in him, by the principles of universal law, till such time as he does some other act which shews an intention to abandon it: for it then becomes, naturally speaking, *publici juris* once more, and is liable to be again appropriated by the next occupant. So if one is possessed of a jewel, and casts it into the sea or a public highway, this is such an express dereliction, that a property will be vested in the first fortunate finder that will seise it to his own use.

But this method, of one man's abandoning his property, and another's seising the vacant possession, however well founded in theory, could not long subsist in fact. It was calculated merely for the rudiments of civil society, and necessarily ceased among the complicated interests and artificial refinements of polite and established governments. In these it was found, that what became inconvenient or useless to one man was highly convenient and useful to another; who was ready to give in exchange for it some equivalent, that was equally desirable to the former proprietor. This mutual convenience introduced commercial traffic, and the reciprocal transfer of property by sale, grant, or conveyance: which may be considered either as a continuance of the original possession which the first occupant had; or as an abandoning of the thing by the present owner, and an immediate successive occupancy of the same by the new proprietor. The voluntary dereliction of the owner, and delivering the possession to another individual, amount to a transfer of the property; the proprietor declaring his intention no longer to occupy the thing himself, but that his own right of occupancy shall be vested in the new acquirer. Or, taken in the other light, if I agree to part with an acre of my land to Titius, the deed of conveyance is an evidence of my having abandoned the property, and Titius, being the only or first man acquainted with such my intention, immediately steps in and seises the vacant possession: thus the consent expressed by the conveyance gives Titius a good right against me; and possession, or occupancy, confirms that right against all the world besides.

The most universal and effectual way, of abandoning property, is by the death of the occupant; when, both the actual possession and intention of keeping possession ceasing, the property, which is founded upon such possession and intention, ought also to cease of course. For, naturally speaking, the instant a man ceases to be, he ceases to have any dominion: else, if he had a right to dispose of his acquisitions one moment beyond his life, he would also have a right to direct their disposal for a million of ages after him; which would be highly absurd and inconvenient. All property must therefore cease upon death, considering men as absolute individuals, and unconnected with civil society: for then, by the principles before established, the next immediate occupant would acquire a right in all that the deceased possessed. But as, under civilized governments which are calculated for the peace of mankind, such a constitution would be productive of endless disturbances, the universal law of almost every nation (which is a kind of secondary law of nature) has either given the dying person a power of continuing his property, by disposing of his possessions by will; or, in case he neglects to dispose of it, or is not permitted to make any disposition at all, the municipal law of the country then steps in, and declares who shall be the successor, representative, or heir of the deceased; that is, who alone shall have a right to enter upon this vacant possession, in order to avoid that confusion, which its becoming again common would occasion. And farther, in case no testament be permitted by the law, or none be made, and no heir can be found so qualified as the law requires, still, to prevent the robust title of occupancy from again taking place, the doctrine of escheats is adopted in almost every country; whereby the sovereign of the state, and those who claim under his authority, are the ultimate heirs, and succeed to those inheritances, to which no other title can be formed.

While property continued only for life, testaments were useless and unknown; and, when it became inheritable, the inheritance was long indefeasible, and the children or heirs at law were incapable of exclusion by will. Till at length it was found, that so strict a rule of inheritance made heirs disobedient and head-strong, defrauded creditors of their just debts, and prevented many provident fathers from dividing or charging their estates as the exigence of their families required. This introduced pretty generally the right of disposing one's property, or a part of it, by *testament*; that is, by written or oral instructions properly *witnessed* and authenticated, according to the *pleasure* of the deceased; which we therefore emphatically style his *will*. This was established in some countries much later than in others. With us in England, till modern times, a man could only dispose of one third of his moveables from his wife and children: and, in general, no will was permitted of lands till the reign of Henry the eighth; and then only of a certain portion: for it was not till after the restoration that the power of devising real property became so universal as at present.

Wills therefore and testaments, rights of inheritance and successions, are all of them creatures of the civil or municipal laws, and accordingly are in all respects regulated by them; every distinct country having different ceremonies and requisites to make a testament completely valid: neither does any thing vary more than the right of inheritance under different national establishments. In England, particularly, this diversity is carried to such length, as if it had been meant to point out the power of the laws in regulating the succession to property, and how futile every claim must be that has not its foundation in the positive rules of the state. In personal estates the father may succeed to his children; in landed property he never can be heir, by any the remotest possibility: in general only the eldest son, in some places only the youngest, in others all the sons together, have a right to succeed to the inheritance: in real estates males are preferred to females, and the eldest male will usually exclude the rest; in the division of personal estates, the females of equal degree are admitted together with the males, and no right of primogeniture is allowed.

This one consideration may help to remove the scruples of many well-meaning persons, who set up a mistaken conscience in opposition to the rules of law. If a man disinherits his son, by a will duly executed, and leaves his estate to a stranger, there are many who consider this proceeding as contrary to natural justice: while others so scrupulously adhere to the supposed intention of the dead, that if a will of lands be attested by only *two* witnesses instead of *three*, which the law requires, they are apt to imagine that the heir is bound in conscience to relinquish his title to the devisee. But both of them certainly proceed upon very erroneous principles: as if, on the one hand, the son had by nature a right to succeed to his father's lands; or as if, on the other hand, the owner was by nature entitled to direct the succession of his property after his own decease. Whereas the law of nature suggests, that on the death of the possessor the estate should again become common, and be open to the next occupant, unless otherwise ordered for the sake of the civil peace by the positive law of society. The positive law of society, which is with us the municipal law of England, directs it to vest in such person as the last proprietor shall by will, attended with certain requisites, appoint; and, in defect of such appointment, to go to some particular person, who, from the result of certain local constitutions, appears to be the heir at law. Hence it follows that, where the appointment is regularly made, there cannot be a shadow of right in any one but the person appointed: and where the necessary requisites are omitted, the right of the heir is equally strong and built upon as a solid a foundation, as the right of the devisee would have been, supposing such requisites were observed.

But, after all, there are some few things, which notwithstanding the general introduction and continuance of property, must still unavoidably remain in common; being such wherein nothing but an usufructuary property is capable of being had; and therefore they still belong to the first occupant, during the time he holds possession of them, and no longer. Such (among others) are the elements of light, air, and water; which a man may occupy by means of his windows, his gardens, his mills, and other conveniences: such also are the generality of those animals which are said to be *ferae naturae*, or of a wild and untameable disposition; which any man may seise upon and keep for his own use or pleasure. All these things, so long as they remain in his possession, every man has a right to enjoy without disturbance; but if once they escape from his custody, or he voluntarily abandons the use of them, they return to the common stock, and any man else has an equal right to seise and enjoy them afterwards.

Again; there are other things, in which a permanent property *may* subsist, not only as to the temporary use, but also the solid substance; and which yet would be frequently found with-out a proprietor, had not the wisdom of the law provided a remedy to obviate this inconvenience. Such are forests and other waste grounds, which were omitted to be appropriated in the general distribution of lands: such also are wrecks, estrays, and the species of wild animals, which the arbitrary constitutions of positive law have distinguished from the rest by the well-known appellation of game. With regard to these and some others, as disturbances and quarrels would frequently arise among individuals, contending about the acquisition of this species of property by first occupancy, the law has therefore wisely cut up the root of dissension, by vesting the things themselves in the sovereign of the state; or else in his representatives, appointed and authorized by him, being usually the lords of manors. And thus the legislature of England has universally promoted the grand ends of civil society, the peace and security of individuals, by steadily pursuing that wise and orderly maxim, of assigning to every thing capable of ownership a legal and determinate owner.

NOTES

*From "Of Property in General," in *Commentaries on the Laws of England*, Vol. 2 Ch. 1, 1765, I.

FOR DISCUSSION

1. How do people in an advanced society acquire property *after* it has been appropriated by the first taker? What is the reason underlying these rules?

2. Why shouldn't a person be able to control the disposition of possessions "for a million of ages after him"? Blackstone says that would be "highly absurd and inconvenient," but why?

3. What is the rationale for permitting transfer of property by will or by inheritance, despite the reluctance to give people the unlimited right to dispose of property after death?

4. How do Blackstone's justifications for the necessity of the right of property compare with Locke's? What view of humanity do they express? Do you find them convincing?

5. Why, according to Blackstone, is it a good idea to permit an ancestor to disinherit his or her children? Are there disadvantages as well?

6. What sorts of things may a person possess and use, but not own? Does this make sense?

Blackstone's conception of property, as Locke's, restricted it to tangible things, and, as was accepted at the time, treated property principally from the standpoint of real property, which was, even in the eighteenth century, the principal source of wealth and power. Today, conversely, personal property, much of it intangible, is the principal source of wealth and figures in more than 90 percent of all property disputes. Nevertheless, Blackstone's views of property still color many of our conceptions today. The following case deals with a thing that is definitely tangible, but which still poses some unlikely problems as to classification. Is it real property or personal property?

Vidal Gomez et al. v. D. A. Dykes et al.
Supreme Court of Arizona (1961)
89 Ariz 171, 359 P.2d 760, 82 A.L.R.2d 1093

JENNINGS, J.   This appeal involves the incidents arising out of contracts for the sale of real and personal property wherein appellants Vidal Gomez and Jessie Gomez, husband and wife (hereinafter called plaintiffs), are the buyers, and appellees D. A. Dykes and Florence E. Dykes, husband and wife (hereinafter called defendants), are the sellers.

Prior to October 7 through 10, 1952, the parties hereto negotiated for the sale and purchase of a ranch located in south Phoenix, Arizona, composed of real and personal property owned by the defendants. On or about October 10 the parties concluded their negotiations by signing and executing a contract and an agreement of sale which specifically described certain real and personal property to be transferred to plaintiffs for an agreed consideration.

Pertinent, but not in contention was an agreement that the defendants could feed and keep their cattle in various cattle pens on the premises until February 1, 1953. Thereafter dispute arose between the parties and after negotiation, it was stipulated that defendants might remain in possession of the cattle feeding pens from February 1, 1953, to and including May 31, 1953, as tenants from month to month on payment of an agreed rental. During the same period following February 1, 1953, further dispute arose whereby plaintiffs claimed they were entitled under the agreement of sale to a clodbuster which they claimed had been removed from the premises. Plaintiffs also contended that they were entitled to a trailer house which had been on the premises.

A third dispute concerned manure in the cattle feeding pens. On or about May 31, 1953, defendants removed some 1,645 tons of manure from pens 1 through 8. Thereafter defendants sought to remove the manure from the remaining pens 9 through 11 but were prevented by the plaintiffs from so doing. The facts also disclose that the plaintiffs did thereafter remove some 660 tons of manure from pens 9 through 11.

On these matters of dispute the trial court ruled for the defendants and based its decision on ten specific findings of fact from which it laid down its six conclusions of law…

…, As relates to the trailer house the question arises, was the trailer house a fixture and therefore realty to pass under the realty agreement or, was it not a fixture so that it retained its character of personalty? The rule is set forth in *Fish* v. *Valley Nat. Bank of Phoenix*, 64 Ariz 164, 170, 167 P.2d 107, 111:

> The mere affixing of personal property to real estate may or may not cause it to lose its personal characteristics. It may retain its identity as a chattel personal and not become a chattel real. The rule is that for a chattel to become a fixture and be considered as real estate, three requisites must unite: There must be an annexation to the realty or something appurtenant thereto; the chattel must have adaptability or application as affixed to the use for which the real estate is appropriated; and there must be an *intention* of the party to make the chattel a permanent accession to the freehold. 36 C.J.S., Fixtures, § 1, p. 892. The testimony in this case is wholly barren of these requisites. (Emphasis ours.)

This rule applies in the absence of an agreement between the parties which would otherwise determine the character of the item.

As this Court stated in *Voight* v. *Ott*, 86 Ariz 128, 134, 341 P.2d 923, 927: "The modern tendency is to place less emphasis on the method or mode of annexation of the chattel and to give greater consideration to the intention of the parties as respects the use and adaptability thereof.…"

Based on this law we find that the evidence supports the trial court's findings and conclusions of law No. II. The trailer house belonged not to defendants but to an employee named Vale who brought it to defendants' premises when he came to work there. It was parked near the permanent employee house, temporarily attached thereto merely by a piece of tin held in place by a temporary placement of cement blocks. With no evidence of electrical, water or gas connections of any kind having been made to the trailer house, the evidence discloses that there was no permanent annexation to the realty.

The second requisite to the rule could have been met. However, there is no evidence of the third requisite, intent, which as above mentioned, is the most important element of proof. Defendant Dykes could have no such intent. The trailer house did not belong to him but to his employee. Further, the rule provides that all three elements must unite. Since this did not happen the trailer house retains its character of personalty. As such, it did not pass to plaintiffs under the personalty agreement because it was not listed therein.

This jurisdiction is faced with a dearth of law to resolve the question whether the manure on the premises at the time of the sale, and whether that which accumulated after the sale, is realty or personalty.

The great weight of authority in other jurisdictions holds that manure produced by animals fed upon the products of the farm is part of the realty, since such manure was used to supply the drain made upon the soil in the production of said crops. Whereas, considered to be personalty is that manure which was not made in the ordinary course of husbandry but which is manure from animals fed on products grown elsewhere than on the farm where the manure is dropped.

Collier v. *Jenks*, 19 RI 137, 32 A 208, 61 Am St Rep 741, states: "Manure made in livery stables, or in barns *not connected* with farms, or otherwise than in the usual course of husbandry, forms no part of the realty on which it may be piled, but is regarded as personal estate...." (Emphasis ours.)

This sentence carries with it the connotation that manure is personal estate when it is produced by transient owners' animals situated in temporary quarters or when the manure is made otherwise than in the usual course of husbandry. The reason for this rule is the strong public policy to keep that which has never become a true part and parcel of the land freely alienated from same. By the same token, if the animals have not been fed with the products of the land, the land has not been impoverished, and consequently, the animals' owner owes no duty to leave the manure to replenish the land.

Taylor v. *Newcomb*, 123 Mich 637, 82 NW 519, which dealt with a landlord and tenant relationship, sustains this proposition, namely: "The great weight of authority in this country sustains the rule that, as between landlord and tenant,... if the manure were not produced directly or indirectly from the land, and were in no sense the product of agritural [*sic*] demised premises,—such as accumulates in livery stables and the like,—it is no part of the realty, and may be removed by the tenant at the close of his term."

We adopt this rule.

Should the result be different, where animals owned by the fee simple owners of farmland are permanently located on land connected with the farm, and where manure from such animals accumulates over a period of time? We think not. The test still remains, were the animals fed from products of the land or were the animals fed from products grown elsewhere. The good husbandman has a duty to protect the quality of his land; to replace and replenish when the soil or products of the soil have been taken. But there is no corresponding duty to add to the quantity of the land.

For the above-mentioned reasons, the trial court properly held that the manure dropped by the defendant's cattle rightfully belonged to defendants.

The evidence is undisputed, both by witnesses for the plaintiffs and the admissions of the defendant Dykes, that the manure deposited in the feeding corrals by both plaintiffs' and defendants' cattle was mixed with and churned into the native soil of the corrals, which was sandy in character. It is also readily apparent that an added complication, difficult of extraction, entered this case when the manure of defendants' cattle mixed with the manure of the new fee simple owner. Therefore, calculating the proper quantity of manure belonging to each litigant and affixing the value thereof is no easy chore. Though difficult, this matter was purely within the discretion of the trial court and we do not find that the court abused its discretion wherein it awarded 660 tons of manure at the rate of $2.50 per ton to defendants....

Accordingly, the judgment of the trial court is affirmed.

FOR DISCUSSION

1. What is a "fixture" or "chattel real," and what are its characteristics?
2. If the disputed trailer was personalty, why didn't it pass to the plaintiffs under the agreement to convey the personalty belonging to the defendants? Is the real issue that the trailer wasn't *listed* in the agreement?
3. Admittedly manure is a tangible thing, but does it have the traditional characteristics of property?
4. In the absence of any law on the subject, do you think manure would ordinarily be classified as real property or personal property?
5. Do the legal distinctions that the court cites regarding the classification of manure as realty or personalty make any sense? Even if they once did, do they make sense today, in the era of chemical fertilizers?
6. Should it really matter whether manure is classified as real or personal property? Why?

Acquisition of Property

Blackstone suggests that the law is designed to keep property from reverting to its original state, in which title by occupancy could again be asserted over it. The principal reason for this is the eminently practical one of keeping the peace. Nevertheless, the law does continue to recognize a form of acquisition of property by occupancy, at the expense of an already existing owner. Not surprisingly, this process, called **adverse possession**, is held to very strict rules, as the following case illustrates.

CASE

Georgia Simos Raftopolous v. Ben Monger
Supreme Court of Colorado (1983)
656 P.2d 1308, 39 A.L.R.4th 1141

LEE, JUSTICE.   We granted certiorari to review the decision of the court of appeals in *Monger* v. *Raftopoulos*, No. 79CA0073 (Colo. App. 1980). The case involves the adverse possession claim of plaintiffs-respondents Ben and Lois Monger to 120 acres of rangeland in Routt County. The record owners of the property, and the petitioners here, are Georgia Simos Raftopoulos and Constantina S. Simos (Raftopoulos).

After trial to the court judgment was entered for the plaintiffs. The court held that the Mongers had clearly established their claim of adverse possession, and quieted title to the property in them. The court of appeals affirmed. We reverse.

The record establishes that the disputed tract is bordered on the west and north by the ranch owned by Raftopoulos, and on the east and south by the ranch owned by Monger. The petitioners Raftopoulos hold legal title to the tract in question and have paid taxes thereon since 1933. The Mongers claim the land by adverse possession asserting that they have used the land continuously from 1934 to the present to graze cattle and horses. The Raftopoulos family disputes that claim based upon their annual usage of the land for sheep grazing.

The following evidence was presented in support of the Mongers' claim of adverse possession. Ben Monger testified that he fenced the north and west boundary of the disputed property, although the fence was not "sheep-tight" around the disputed area. He admitted that he had seen Raftopoulos sheep on this property at least twice, but he acknowledged that he could not see the disputed area from his house, and that he visited that area infrequently. He testified that he chased the sheep off the property each time he saw them. He testified that he had used the property for grazing cattle and horses from 1934 until he and his family moved off the ranch in the late 1950s, when he leased his ranch to others.

After reviewing the evidence, the trial court found that Raftopoulos sheep had grazed on the disputed property from time to time over the years. The court concluded, however, that Raftopoulos had failed to meet the burden of refuting Monger's adverse possession claim because the precise dates the sheep had grazed on the property were not sufficiently established to demonstrate that Monger's use for grazing livestock had been interrupted. The court then determined that the Mongers had established that their possession was "actual, adverse, open and hostile and under claim of right and that it had been exclusive and uninterrupted for the statutory period." *Bushey* v. *Seven Lakes Reservoir Co.*, 37 Colo.App. 106, 545 P.2s 158 (1975). We reverse.

One claiming title by adverse possession has the burden of proving his claim by clear and convincing evidence. He must prove not only that his possession was actual, adverse, hostile, and under claim of right, but also that it was exclusive and uninterrupted for the statutory period. Moreover, "the possession of the adverse claimant must be such that the true owner is wholly excluded therefrom. Any sort of joint or common possession by the adverse claimant and the record owner prevents the possession of the one claiming adversely from [attaining] the requisite quality of exclusiveness." *Dzuris* v. *Kucharik*, 164 Colo. at 282, 434 P.2d at 416; *Vider* v. *Zavislan*, 146 Colo. 519, 362 P.2d 163 (1961).

Our view of the evidence considered in the light most favorable to the Mongers convinces us that the requisite element of exclusive possession was not established by clear and convincing evidence. Thus, the court was in error in concluding that the Mongers had acquired title by adverse possession.

The Mongers testified that they maintained a partial fence around the property during the statutory period; however, the evidence also showed that there were gates in the fences adjoining the disputed property, by which the Raftopoulos shepherds gained access to the property. It was admitted that the fence bordering the property was not sheep-tight, and that the sheep were able to and did easily go under and through the fence, and onto the disputed tract for grazing. The corroborated testimony of two shepherds demonstrated that the property was grazed on a regular annual basis by the Raftopoulos sheep. Moreover, the trial court specifically found that the Raftopoulos sheep had indeed grazed on the disputed property from time to time. Although the evidence established that the sheep grazed the disputed land for only a small number of days each year, the use to which the land was put was consistent with its arid character and the speed with which a sizeable flock of sheep could deplete its vegetation. Other portions of the Raftopoulos property were used in the same manner. We believe the evidence presented to the trial court establishes that the possession of the property was joint, and the use by the Mongers was permissive rather than adverse.

In our view, the reliance by the trial court and the court of appeals on *Bushey* v. *Seven Lakes Reservoir Company*, 37 Colo. App. 106, 545 P.2d 158 (1975), is misplaced. In some circumstances a mere casual entry for a limited purpose by the record owner may be insufficient to prove that the use of the property was joint. *McElvey* v. *Cooper*, 165 Colo. 102, 437 P.2d 346 (1968). The evidence in the present case indicates that the Raftopoulos'[s] entry into the disputed tract was not casual or for a limited purpose, but rather was a part of their usual customary ranch operation, the seasonal grazing of sheep on the disputed tract.

Colorado cases have recognized that a presumption of adversity arises after the claimant has demonstrated that he has been in actual and exclusive possession of the property for the statutory period. However, proof of adverse possession must extend beyond mere actual possession and establish that the record owner has been effectively excluded, and further, that the possession relied upon is not joint.

As we have noted above, the record before the court does not sustain the conclusion that the Mongers proved the requisite exclusive, uninterrupted possession to support their claim of adverse possession. Therefore:

> We are persuaded that these circumstances, coupled with the fact that [Raftopoulos] held legal title to the property, bring into operation the rule that in case of mixed or common possession of land by both parties to a suit, the law adjudges the rightful possession to him who holds legal title, and no length of time of possession can give title by adverse possession as against the legal title. [Citations omitted.] *Vider* v. *Zavislan*, 146 Colo. 519, 524, 362 P.2d 163, 166 (1961).

Accordingly, the judgment of the court of appeals is reversed. The case is returned to the court of appeals with directions to remand the cause to the trial court with instructions to enter a judgment and decree quieting the title to the disputed property in the record owners Raftopoulos.

FOR DISCUSSION

1. It has been said that legal title carries with it the presumption that the record owner has been possessed of the premises and that the occupation by another is *subordinate, not hostile*, to legal title. Which party is favored by this presumption, the record owner or the adverse claimant?

2. What does it take to shift the burden of proof to the record owner to prove his title against the claim of the adverse possessor?

3. Why were the Mongers unsuccessful in this case? What facts seemed to work most against them?

4. As far as you can determine from this case, are the rules regarding adverse possession strictly or liberally construed? Explain your answer.

5. Why might it be a good thing to sometimes permit an adverse possessor to take title to property away from an existing owner?

It has been said that a person has the right to acquire property by any lawful or legitimate means. One means of acquiring property that might seem obviously impermissible is to kill someone to inherit from that person. Nevertheless, the first American cases that dealt with this problem nearly all found in favor of the murderer and permitted him or her to inherit. The courts, in their somewhat exaggerated deference to legislative arrangements regarding the transfer of property by will or inheritance, refused to interfere with the state's statutory plan, even if a murderer benefited from it. In 1889, however, the New York Court of Appeals, in the landmark case of *Riggs* v. *Palmer*, 115 N.Y. 506, 22 N.E. 188, held that a murderer could not inherit from his victim, notwithstanding the statutory rules of descent and distribution: "…All laws as well as all contracts may be controlled in their operation and effect by general, fundamental maxims of the common law. No one shall be permitted to profit by his own fraud, or to take advantage of his own wrong, or to found any claim upon his own iniquity. These maxims are dictated by public policy, have their foundation in universal law administered in all civilized countries, and have nowhere been superseded by statutes." This case was not followed by courts in most states, however, and it was generally left to legislatures to deal with the problem. In contrast, New York has continued to refine and extend its judicial rule for nearly a century, dealing case by case with the problems involved in such a judicially formulated "slayer rule."

The following case illustrates that almost one hundred years after *Riggs* there are still difficulties to be addressed in the administration of this rule. One of the most serious, which has been at issue from the beginning, involves adhering to the narrow line of preventing a wrongdoer from profiting by a crime without compelling the wrongdoer to forfeit property he or she already possesses. In *Matter of Nicpon* this is particularly difficult and delicate because the form of ownership involved is a **tenancy by the entirety**, a form of joint ownership of real property by a husband and wife in which, according to the law, the two owners become as one person. This leaves the court with the task of determining how to keep the killer-spouse from benefiting from the victim-spouse without taking away the property that the wrongdoer-spouse already has.

CASE

In Re Nicpon's Estate
New York Surrogate's Court (1980)
102 Misc.2d 619, 424 N.Y.S.2d 100

WILLIAM J. REGAN, Surrogate.   The Public Administrator in and for the Country of Erie has filed a petition seeking judicial settlement of his accounts as voluntary administrator in the Estate of Irene Nicpon. The petition requests a judicial determination be made with respect to determining the interest of the respondents, to wit: Adam Nicpon, the husband of the decedent who is presently incarcerated in the New York State Department of Correction at Attica; Lucy Nicpon, John Nicpon, and Ann Nicpon, all children of the decedent and the respondent, Adam Nicpon.

It appears that the respondent, Adam Nicpon, was indicted on October 24, 1975, and charged with second-degree murder of his wife Irene Nicpon, the decedent herein. On December 13, 1976, the respondent, Adam Nicpon, pled guilty to manslaughter in the First Degree and was sentenced to an indeterminate term of imprisonment and is presently incarcerated at the Attica Correctional Facility.

The only issue to be resolved in this proceeding concerns the rights of the parties in and to the real property commonly known and referred to as 110 St. Louis Street, Buffalo, New York. The title in said property was in the name of the decedent and the respondent, Adam Nicpon, as tenants by the entirety.

It is well settled and established that one may not inherit or succeed to property as a result of his own wrongful act. *Riggs* v. *Palmer,* 115 N.Y. 506, 511, 512, 22 N.E. 188, 190. Likewise, a wrongdoer's estate may not benefit from the wrongful act. *Bierbrauer* v. *Moran,* 244 A.D. 87, 279 N.Y.S. 176; *Matter of Pinnock,* 83 Misc.2d 233, 371 N.Y.S.2d 797.

A similar question was addressed by my learned colleague, Bertram R. Gelfand. Surrogate. *In the Matter of Pinnock,* 83 Misc.2d 233, 371 N.Y.S.2d 797. In that case, Surrogate Gelfand held that the estate of the decedent wife was the sole owner of the premises owned by both decedents as tenants by the entirety. The Court stated that "When both tenants by the entirety were alive, each had no more than a life interest in an undivided one half of the property, with the possibility that if one survived the other tenant, upon such survival, the survivor would own the entire property outright in fee simple absolute." To convert the husband's life tenancy with the possibility of ownership to a tenancy in common would improperly elevate his ownership, wrongful misconduct contrary, and therefore benefit from his wrongful act.

The factual circumstances in the instant matter are distinguishable from that in the *Matter of Pinnock* in that in *Pinnock* there was a murder-suicide and, thus, the Court did not, after equating the husband's interest to "no more than a life interest in an undivided one half of the property," address itself to whether he would have had a life estate in the property had he not committed suicide.

Although the law is well established that one may not benefit by his act, it also is well settled that the interest of the wrongful party cannot be diminished. Inasmuch as the respondent, Adam Nicpon, possessed an undivided one half life interest in the premises, this interest cannot be extinguished. Likewise, the interest of the respondent, Adam Nicpon, cannot be increased as was very ably decided in the *Pinnock* case.

It is, therefore, the determination of this Court that the fee absolute title in the real property held by the decedent and the respondent, Adam Nicpon, as tenants by the entirety, by virtue of the wrongful act of Adam Nicpon, passes through the estate of Irene Nicpon and the Public Administrator is hereby authorized and directed to execute a deed conveying the title to said premises to the children of the parties, subject, however, to a life estate in the respondent, Adam Nicpon.

FOR DISCUSSION

1. According to Surrogate Gelfand, what is the legal effect of a tenancy by the entirety? What do the parties actually own?

2. If a husband and wife are divorced, their real estate held as tenants by the entirety is automatically converted to a **tenancy in common;** that is, each party owns one half of the property and is free to sell it or to leave it to someone other than the co-tenant. Why is it unsatisfactory to let the killing of one spouse by the other convert the tenancy by the entirety into a tenancy in common?

3. One way to handle such cases is for the court to treat the couple's property as if the killer had died before the victim. Why can't the Court in *Nicpon* do that?

4. What disposition of the couple's property does the court finally make? Do you consider the disposition to be a fair one?

5. Why might one argue that a "slayer rule" such as that applied in *Matter of Nicpon* interferes with established property rights?

6. Why might one argue that a "slayer rule" protects and promotes established property rights?

EXERCISING RIGHTS IN PROPERTY

William Blackstone stated that the permanent right to property was a civil right rather than a natural right. Indeed, one can legitimately say that Blackstone's approach to the law of property was essentially **positivistic**; it relied on the law as written or declared by the sovereign government, rather than upon some "higher" or "natural" law. Nevertheless, Blackstone does not state his positivism so explicitly as it is expressed in the following passage by Jeremy Bentham, who makes no pretense about the nature of the foundation of any right of property.

READING **Of Property**
Jeremy Bentham*

The better to understand the advantages of law, let us endeavour to form a clear idea of *property*. We shall see that there is no such thing as natural property, and that it is entirely the work of law.

Property is nothing but a basis of expectation; the expectation of deriving certain advantages from a thing which we are said to possess, in consequence of the relation in which we stand to it.

There is no image, no painting, no visible trait, which can express the relation that constitutes property. It is not material, it is metaphysical; it is a mere conception of the mind.

To have a thing in our hands, to keep it, to make it, to sell it, to work it up into something else; to use it—none of these physical circumstances, nor all united, convey the idea of property. A piece of stuff which is actually in the Indies may belong to me, while the dress I wear may not. The aliment which is incorporated into my very body may belong to another, to whom I am bound to account for it.

The idea of property consists in an established expectation: in the persuasion of being able to draw such or such an advantage from the thing possessed, according to the nature of the case. Now this expectation, this persuasion, can only be the work of law. I cannot count upon the enjoyment of that which guarantees it to me. It is law alone which permits me to forget my natural weakness. It is only through the protection of law that I am able to inclose a field, and to give myself up to its cultivation with the sure though distant hope of harvest.

But it may be asked, What is it that serves as a basis to law, upon which to begin operations, when it adopts objects which, under the name of property, it promises to protect? Have not men, in the primitive state, a *natural* expectation of enjoying certain things,—and expectation drawn from sources anterior to law?

Yes. There have been from the beginning, and there always will be, circumstances in which a man may secure himself, by his own means, in the enjoyment of certain things. But the catalogue of these cases is very limited. The savage who has killed a deer may hope to keep it for himself, so long as his cave is undiscovered; so long as he watches to defend it, and is stronger than his rivals; but that is all. How miserable and precarious is such a possession! If we suppose the least agreement among savages to respect the acquisitions of each other, we see the introduction of a principle to which no name can be given but that of law. A feeble and momentary expectation may result from time to time from circumstances purely physical; but a strong and permanent expectation can result only from law. That which, in the natural state, was an almost invisible thread, in the social state becomes a cable.

Property and law are born together, and die together. Before laws were made there was no property; take away laws, and property ceases.

As regards property, security consists in receiving no check, no shock, no derangement to the expectation founded on the laws, of enjoying such and such a portion of good. The legislator owes the greatest respect to this expectation which he has himself produced. When he does not contradict it, he does what is essential to the happiness of society; when he disturbs it, he always produces a proportionate sum of evil.

NOTES

*From *Theory of Legislation*, Ch. viii, 111–113, 1896 ed.

FOR DISCUSSION

1. According to Bentham, what is property?
2. How does Bentham's conception of property differ from that of Locke or Blackstone?
3. Is Bentham's conception of property irreconcilable with the views of Locke and Blackstone?
4. What does the legislator owe society with respect to the security of property?
5. If the right of property depends solely on positive rules of law rather than on some higher or more basic law, is there anything to prevent the law of property from being changed?
6. Considering Locke and Blackstone, as well as Bentham, what limitations will there be to the legislator's power to change the law of property?

Incidents of Ownership

Ownership of property is characterized by a number of rights. Ownership implies the right to possession and control of that which is owned. Such ownership implies the right to exclude others, including, within limits, the right to expel others from invasion or occupation of the property. In addition, ownership involves the rights to use the property, enjoy the benefits or increase of that which is owned, and dispose of the property by sale, gift, will, inheritance, or even by destruction.

Possession   Possession is the state of having dominion and control over property. It may be actual, when the owner has direct physical control of the property, or constructive, when the owner does not have direct physical control, but retains the right to direct the use and disposition of the property. Possession is not the same as mere custody of the property: Possession implies not only having the thing but being able to exercise other rights of ownership over it.

Superficially, possession seems to be the most obvious demonstration of ownership of property, yet in a complex society, it is probably the least reliable indicator of ownership. As Bentham noted in his essay, one may not own a garment he is wearing (and so clearly possesses), yet own others that are hundreds of miles away and not in his possession. Nevertheless, possession is an important incident of ownership and a right that may be legally protected from interference, as the following case demonstrates.

CASE

Jean Loretto, on Behalf of Herself and all Others Similarly Situated
v. Teleprompter Manhattan CATV Corp. et al.
United States Supreme Court (1982)
458 U.S. 419, 102 S.Ct. 3164, 73 L.Ed.2d 868

Justice MARSHALL delivered the opinion of the Court.   This case presents the question whether a minor but permanent physical occupation of an owner's property authorized by government constitutes a "taking" of property for which just compensation is due under the Fifth and Fourteenth Amendments of the Constitution. New York law provides that a landlord must permit a cable television company to install its cable facilities upon his property. In this case, the cable installation occupied portions of appellant's roof and the side of her building. The New York Court of Appeals ruled that this appropriation does not amount to a taking. Because we conclude that such a physical occupation of property is a taking, we reverse.

Appellant Jean Loretto purchased a five-story apartment building located at 303 West 105th Street, New York City, in 1971. The previous owner had granted appellees Teleprompter Corp. and Teleprompter Manhattan CATV permission to install a cable on the building and the exclusive privilege of furnishing cable television services to the tenants.

Prior to 1973, Teleprompter routinely obtained authorization for its installations from property owners along the cable's route, compensating the owners at the standard rate of 5% of the gross revenues that Teleprompter realized from the particular property. To facilitate tenant access to CATV, the State of New York enacted §828 of the Executive Law, effective January 1, 1973. Section 828 provides that a landlord may not "interfere with the installation of cable television facilities upon his property or premises," and may not demand payment from any tenant for permitting CATV, or demand payment from any CATV company "in excess of any amount which the [State Commission on Cable Television] shall, by regulation, determine to be reasonable. The landlord may, however, require the CATV company or the tenant to bear the cost of installation and to indemnify for any damage caused by the installation. Pursuant to §828(1)(b), the State Commission has ruled that a one-time $1 payment is the normal fee to which a landlord is entitled.

Appellant did not discover the existence of the cable until after she had purchased the building. She brought a class action against Teleprompter in 1976 on behalf of all owners of real property in the State on which Teleprompter has placed CATV components, alleging that Teleprompter's installation was a trespass and, insofar as it relied on §828, a taking without just compensation. She requested damages and injunctive relief. Appellee City of New York, which has granted Teleprompter an exclusive franchise to provide CATV to certain areas of Manhattan, intervened. The Supreme Court, Special Term,[4] granted summary judgment to Teleprompter and the city, upholding the constitutionality of §828 in both crossover and noncrossover situations.

On appeal, the Court of Appeals, over dissent, upheld the statute. The Court concluded that the law requires the landlord to allow both crossover and noncrossover installations but permits him to request payment from a CATV company under §828(1)(b), at a level determined by the State Cable Commission, only for noncrossovers. The court then ruled that the law serves a legitimate police power purpose—eliminating landlord fees and

---

[4]In the State of New York, Supreme Court is the state-level trial court, not an appellate court. The highest appellate court in New York is the Court of Appeals.

conditions that inhibit the development of CATV, which has important educational and community benefits. Rejecting the argument that a physical occupation authorized by government is necessarily a taking, the court stated that the regulation does not have an excessive economic impact upon appellant when measured against her aggregate property rights, and that it does not interfere with any reasonable investment-backed expectations. Accordingly, the court held that §828 does not work a taking of appellant's property. Chief Justice Cooke dissented, reasoning that the physical appropriation of a portion of appellant's property is a taking without regard to the balancing analysis courts ordinarily employ in evaluating whether a regulation is a taking.

The Court of Appeals determined that §828 serves the legitimate public purpose of "rapid development of and maximum penetration by a means of communication which has important educational and community aspects," 53 N.Y.2d at 143-44, 440 N.Y.S.2d, at 852, 423 N.E.2d, at 329, and thus is within the State's police power. We have no reason to question that determination. It is a separate question, however, whether an otherwise valid regulation so frustrates property rights that compensation must be paid. We conclude that a permanent physical occupation authorized by government is a taking without regard to the public interests it may serve. Our constitutional history confirms the rule, recent cases do not question it, and the purposes of the Takings Clause compel its retention.

In *Penn Central Transportation Co.* v. *New York City*, 438 U.S. 104, 98 S.Ct. 2646, 57 L.Ed.2d 631 (1978), the Court surveyed some of the general principles governing the Takings Clause. The Court noted that no "set formula" existed to determine, in all cases, whether compensation is constitutionally due for a government restriction of property. Ordinarily, the Court must engage in "essentially ad hoc, factual inquiries." *Id.*, at 124, 98 S.Ct., at 2659. But the inquiry is not standardless. The economic impact of the regulation, especially the degree of interference with investment-backed expectations, is of particular significance. "So, too, is the character of the governmental action. A 'taking' may be more readily found when the interference with property can be characterized as a physical invasion by government, than when interference arises from some public program adjusting the benefits and burdens of economic life to promote the common good." *Ibid.*

As *Penn Central* affirms, the Court has often upheld substantial regulation of an owner's use of his own property where deemed necessary to promote the public interest. At the same time, we have long considered a physical intrusion by government to be a property restriction of an unusually serious character for purposes of the Takings Clause. Our cases further establish that when the physical intrusion reaches the extreme form of a permanent physical occupation, a taking has occurred. In such a case, "the character of the government action" not only is an important factor in resolving whether the action works a taking but also is determinative.

The historical rule that a permanent physical occupation of another's property is a taking has more than tradition to commend it. Such an appropriation is perhaps the most serious form of invasion of an owner's property interests. To borrow a metaphor, *cf. Andrus* v. *Allard*, 444 U.S. 51, 65-66, 100 S.Ct. 318, 326-327, 62 L.Ed.2d 210 (1979), the government does not simply take a single "strand" from the "bundle" of property rights: it chops through the bundle, taking a slice of every strand.

Property rights in a physical thing have been described as the rights "to possess, use and dispose of it." *United States* v. *General Motors Corp.*, 323 U.S. 373, 378, 65 S.Ct. 357, 359, 89 L.Ed. 311 (1945). To the extent that the government permanently occupies physical property, it effectively destroys *each* of these rights. First, the owner has no right to possess the occupied space himself, and also has no power to exclude the occupier from possession and use of the space. The power to exclude has traditionally been considered one of the most treasured strands in an owner's bundle of property rights. Second, the permanent physical occupation of property forever denies the owner any power to control the use of the property; he not only cannot exclude others, but can make no nonpossessary use of the property. Although deprivation of the right to use and obtain a profit from property is not, in every case, independently sufficient to establish a taking, it is clearly relevant. Finally, even though the owner may retain the bare legal right to dispose of the occupied space by a transfer or sale, the permanent occupation of that space by a stranger will ordinarily empty the right of any value, since the purchaser will also be unable to make any use of the property.

Moreover, an owner suffers a special kind of injury when a *stranger* directly invades and occupies the owner's property. As Part II-A, supra, indicates, property law has long protected an owner's expectation that he will be relatively undisturbed at least in the possession of his property. To require, as well, that the owner permit another to exercise complete dominion literally adds insult to injury. Furthermore, such an occupation is qualitatively more severe than a regulation of the *use* of property, even a regulation that imposes affirmative duties on the owner, since the owner may have no control over the timing, extent or nature of the invasion.

The traditional rule also avoids otherwise difficult line-drawing problems. Few would disagree if the State required landlords to permit third parties to install swimming pools on the landlords' rooftops for the convenience of the tenants, the requirement would be a taking. If the cable installation here occupied as much space, again, few would disagree that the occupation would be a taking. But constitutional protection for the rights of private property cannot be made to depend on the size of the area that is permanently occupied. Indeed, it is possible that in the future, additional cable installations that more significantly restrict a landlord's use of the roof of his building will be made. Section 828 requires the landlord to permit such multiple installations.

Finally, whether a permanent physical occupation has occurred presents relatively few problems of proof. The placement of a fixed structure on land or real property is an obvious fact that will rarely be subject to dispute. Once the fact of occupation is shown, of course, a court should consider the *extent* of the occupation as one relevant factor in determining the compensation due. For that reason, moreover, there is less need to consider the extent of the occupation in determining whether there is a taking in the first instance.

Teleprompter's cable installation on appellant's building constitutes a taking under the traditional test. The installation involved a direct physical attachment of plates, boxes, wires, bolts, and screws to the building, completely occupying space immediately above and upon the roof and along the building's exterior wall.

In light of our analysis, we find no constitutional difference between a crossover installation and a noncrossover installation. The portions of the installation necessary for both crossovers and noncrossovers permanently appropriate appellant's property. Accordingly, each type of installation is a taking.

Our holding today is very narrow. We affirm the traditional rule that a permanent physical occupation of property is a taking. In such a case, the property owner entertains a historically rooted expectation of compensation, and the character of the invasion is qualitatively more intrusive than perhaps any other category of property regulation. We do not, however, question the equally substantial authority upholding a State's broad power to impose appropriate restrictions upon an owner's *use* of his property.

The judgment of the New York Court of Appeals is reversed, and the case is remanded for further proceedings not inconsistent with this opinion.

FOR DISCUSSION

1. The Supreme Court describes ownership of property as a "bundle of rights." According to the opinion, what are some of the rights involved?

2. Why, according to the decision, does a physical occupation of property effectively destroy the owner's rights in her property?

3. Will this interference with the owner's possession of property adversely affect the market value of the property in question? Will this be so even if every property owner in New York City is subject to the same interference?

4. The State argued in this case that the public purpose of its law was more important than the minor interference with the owner's property rights. Did the Supreme Court agree with that argument? Explain your answer.

5. Does this decision mean that Mrs. Loretto can refuse to permit Teleprompter to install crossover and noncrossover lines on the roof of her building? If not, what has she gained?

6. If it turns out to be true that Mrs. Loretto has, in fact, suffered relatively little adverse economic impact from the occupation of a portion of her property, her actual monetary compensation will be low. What legal principle is upheld by the decision, irrespective of the financial impact of the ruling?

Right of Alienation   Among the most fundamental incidents of ownership is the right to freely dispose of property. In the following case, we see a limitation placed upon the **right of alienation** (the right to sell or otherwise dispose of property) by a statute regulating the activities of pawnbrokers. The plaintiffs claim that the statute takes their property without compensation by restricting their right to sell immediately goods that they had acquired.

CASE   **Frank Peterman and Bruce Horne v. Gerry Coleman,**
as Sheriff of Pinellas County, FL. and Pinellas County, Florida
U.S. Court of Appeals, Eleventh Circuit (1985)
764 F.2d 1416

R. LANIER ANDERSON, III, Circuit Judge.   Pinellas County, Florida, enacted Ordinance No. 84-17 on May 22, 1984, to regulate businesses that deal in second-hand goods. Appellant Horne is the owner and operator of such a business. Ordinance No. 84-17 requires appellant to maintain records relating to his purchases of used goods, describing the goods in detail and identifying the person from whom any particular item is bought. Appellant must make these records available for inspection by law enforcement officers. The ordinance further requires that dealers in second-hand goods hold items they acquire for five days before reselling them.

Appellant and two other dealers in second-hand goods filed a complaint in federal district court seeking an injunction against enforcement of Ordinance No. 84-17. The sheriff of Pinellas County and Pinellas County, by and through its commissioners, were named as defendants in the action. The parties submitted memoranda of law on the appropriateness of injunctive relief, and plaintiffs filed their affidavits in which they asserted that the ordinance would impinge upon their business by increasing their costs and by making potential buyers and sellers less willing to conduct business with them. Plaintiffs also submitted the affidavits of three Pinellas County residents who said that they were unwilling to comply with the identification requirements of the ordinance and that they would choose to sell their goods in adjoining counties if the ordinance were enforced.

The district court denied injunctive relief, rejecting the various constitutional challenges to the ordinance. Only plaintiff Horne appealed from the district court's order. On appeal, Horne challenges the ordinance on several constitutional grounds. We have considered each of these challenges and find none to have merit. Accordingly, we affirm the district court's order denying injunctive relief.

Deprivation of Property Without Due Process

Appellant argues that since the ordinance's five-day holding period deprives him of his right to transfer possession of goods he has bought, his property is taken without compensation in violation of the Fifth and Fourteenth Amendments to the United States Constitution. Appellant further argues that the holding period deprives him of his property without procedural due process of law in violation of the Fourteenth Amendment.

Incidental impediments on the use of property are distinguished from more substantial effects that require compensation. "[A]cts done in the proper exercise of governmental powers, and not directly encroaching upon private property, though their consequences may impair its use, are universally held not to be a taking within the meaning of the constitutional provision." *Northern Transportation Co.*, v. *City of Chicago*, 99 U.S. 635, 642, 9 Otto 635, 25 L.Ed. 336 (1879). Under Ordinance No. 84-17, appellant is free to transfer title to his property at any time. The ordinance only requires that he retain possession until the five-day holding period has expired. Although the right to transfer possession of property is an important attribute of ownership, we cannot say that by briefly suspending this right the County has "taken" appellant's property. If indeed there is any diminution in value by virtue of a dealer's temporary inability to transfer possession, such an effect is too incidental to amount to a taking for which compensation is required under the Constitution.

Appellant's procedural due process argument is likewise without merit. Appellant relies principally on *Fuentes* v. *Shevin*, 407 U.S. 67, 92 S.Ct. 1983, 32 L.Ed.2d 556 (1972), which invalidated state statutes that allowed creditors to be awarded possession of debtors' property without notice and a hearing and prior to any judgment determining the parties' rights. The Court in *Fuentes* v. *Shevin* observed that "it is now well settled that a temporary, nonfinal deprivation of property is nonetheless a 'deprivation' in the terms of the Fourteenth Amendment." *Id.* at 84-85, 92 S.Ct. at 1996-97. The Court noted that "the Fourteenth Amendment draws no bright lines around three-day, 10-day, or 50-day deprivations of property. Any significant taking of property by the State is within the purview of the due process clause." *Id.* at 86, 92 S.Ct. at 1997.

The Court in *Fuentes* v. *Shevin* confirmed that when a fundamental right in property, such as the right of possession, is taken under color of state law, the temporary nature of the deprivation does not remove it from Fourteenth Amendment protection. In the present case, however, the ordinance does not deprive appellant of his right to possession of his property, but only requires that possession not be transferred for five days. This temporary curtailment of one possessary interest is clearly distinguishable from the complete deprivation of possession at issue in *Fuentes* v. *Shevin*.

Even if the ordinance's holding period were considered to be a deprivation in the constitutional sense, however, we can readily conclude that appellant has received all the process that is due under the circumstances. The Supreme Court has recognized that determinations that are legislative in character may satisfy due process without the requirement of individualized notice and hearing for each instance in which a deprivation occurs. *See Bi-Metallic Investment Co.* v. *State Board of Equalization*, 239 U.S. 441, 36 S.Ct. 141, 60 L.Ed. 372 (1915).

> General statutes within the state power are passed that affect the person or property of individuals, sometimes to the point of ruin, without giving them a chance to be heard. Their rights are protected in the only way that they can be in a complex society, by their power, immediate or remote, over those who make the rule.

Id. at 445, 36 S.Ct. at 142.

In summary, we conclude that the five-day holding period in Ordinance No. 84-17 does not result in a "taking" of appellant's property so as to require compensation under the Fifth and Fourteenth Amendments. Furthermore, while the holding period may have some effect on one of appellant's interests in the property, we do not think this slight attenuation is a deprivation of property in the constitutional sense. To the extent that the holding period might amount to some slight deprivation, we conclude that the Pinellas County Commission in reaching its considered decision to impose the requirement furnished appellant all the process required under the Fourteenth Amendment.

Affirmed.

FOR DISCUSSION

1. Because one of the main attributes of property is the right to freely dispose of it, does the Pinellas County ordinance adversely affect the plaintiff's ownership of his property?

2. How might the value of property be affected if a person may not sell a thing that he or she owns?

3. The Court of Appeals makes a distinction between temporarily depriving a person of possession of a thing that is owned and requiring a person to temporarily retain possession of a thing that is owned. Does that distinction make sense? Does the one act constitute more of a deprivation than the other?

4. Although the Court of Appeals concedes that there may be a deprivation in this case, it decides that the deprivation is too minimal to require constitutional protection. Might the Court have decided differently if the statute had forbidden the dealer to *sell* his secondhand goods for five days?

5. What appears to be the purpose of this statute? Does the State have an interest here that may be more important than the small interference with plaintiff's right to dispose of his property? Explain your answer.

Limitations on Rights of Property

Despite Blackstone's proclamation of the right of property as "that sole and despotic dominion which one man claims and exercises over the external things of the world, in total exclusion of the right of any other individual in the universe," the right of property has never been quite that absolute. Property as a creature of positive law, as Bentham saw it, has always contained or allowed for restrictions on what a person can do with property, even though these restrictions were traditionally kept as limited as possible. The law allows for two principal ways to place limits on uses of land that cause harm or inconvenience to others. One is "private," the action for nuisance, by which private individuals seek to limit another party's uses of land that interfere with their use and enjoyment of their own land. The other is "public," when the government enacts legislation imposing general restrictions on the use of land, such as zoning, environmental regulation, landmark preservation, rent control, and similar measures.

Nuisance The maxim "sic utere tuo ut non alienum laedas" (so use your property as not to injure that of another) underlies the concept of nuisance. **Nuisance**, a tort law concept, is a wrong arising from unreasonable or unlawful use of property to the discomfort, annoyance, inconvenience, or damage of another. Nuisance generally involves continuous or recurrent acts that annoy or disturb the free use of another's property. Although nuisance often involves actual physical damage or substantial interference with actual use and enjoyment of property, in modern society complaints of nuisance frequently rest on less tangible injuries, as the following case illustrates.

CASE

Joel Rose et ux. et al. v. Joseph Chaikin et ux.
New Jersey Superior Court, Chancery Division (1982)
187 N.J. Super 210, 453 A2d 1378, 36 A.L.R. 4th 1148

GIBSON, J. S. C. This action seeks to enjoin the operation of a privately owned windmill. Plaintiffs occupy neighboring properties and allege that the unit constitutes both a private nuisance and a violation of local zoning laws. Defendants deny the allegations and have counterclaimed. Based on the evidence presented at trial, factual findings may be made.

All of the parties are residents and/or owners of single-family homes located in a contiguous residential neighborhood in Brigantine, New Jersey. On or about June 18, 1981, defendants, in an effort to save on electric bills and conserve energy, obtained a building permit for the construction of a windmill. Pursuant to that permit they erected a 60'-high tower on top of which was housed a windmill and motor. The unit is located ten feet from the property line of one of plaintiffs. Shortly after the windmill became operational it began to produce offensive noise levels, as a result of which plaintiffs experienced various forms of stress-related symptoms, together with a general inability to enjoy the peace of their homes.

Although the evidence was in sharp dispute concerning the impact of the noise levels when the windmill is operational, this court is satisfied that those levels are of such a nature that they would be offensive to people of normal sensibilities and, in fact, have unreasonably interfered with plaintiffs' use and enjoyment of their properties. Measurements at the site reveal that the sound levels produced by the windmill vary, depending on the location, but generally show a range of 56 to 61 decibels (dBA). In all instances those levels exceed the 50 dBA permissible under the controlling city ordinance. Ordinance 11-1981, §906.6.3, City of Brigantine. Although there are other sources of sounds in the area, for the most part they are natural to the site.

The impact on plaintiffs is significant. Both the lay and expert testimony support the conclusion that, in varying degrees, all of them experienced tension and stress-related symptoms when the windmill was operational. Those symptoms included nervousness, dizziness, loss of sleep and fatigue. The sounds disturbed many of the activities associated with the normal enjoyment of one's home, including reading, eating, watching television and general relaxation.

The basic standards for determining what constitutes a private nuisance were set forth by our Supreme Court in *Sans* v. *Ramsey Golf & Country Club*, 29 N.J. 438, 149 A.2d 599 (1959). The court made clear that a case-by-case inquiry, balancing competing interests in property, is required.

The essence of a private nuisance is an unreasonable interference with the use and enjoyment of land. The elements are myriad.... The utility of the defendant's conduct must be weighed against the *quantum* of harm to the plaintiff. The question is not simply whether a person is annoyed or disturbed, but whether the annoyance or disturbance arises from an unreasonable use of the neighbor's land.... [At 448-49, 149 A.2d 599.]

Unreasonableness is judged

"...'not according to exceptionally refined, uncommon or luxurious habits of living, but according to the simple tastes and unaffected notions generally prevailing among plain people.'" 50 N.J. Super 127, at page 134, 141 A.2d 335, citing *Stevens* v. *Rockport Granite Co.*, 216 Mass. 486, 104 N.E. 371 (Sup.Jud.Ct. 1914). [At 449, 149 A.2d 599.]

Defendants resist plaintiffs' claim by advancing three basic arguments: first, that noise, standing alone, cannot constitute a private nuisance; second, that even if noise can amount to a nuisance, the noise from their windmill does not exceed the applicable threshold; and third, that in any event the circumstances of this case do not warrant the "extraordinary relief" of an injunction.

The first argument is without merit. New Jersey case law makes it clear that noise may, under the principles of unreasonable use, constitute an actionable private nuisance. Noise is an actionable private nuisance if two elements are present: (1) injury to the health and comfort of ordinary people in the vicinity, and (2) unreasonableness of that injury under all the circumstances. The "circumstances" may be multiple and must be proven by "clear and convincing" evidence.

Broadly stated, the noises which a court of equity normally enjoins are those which affect injuriously the health and comfort of ordinary people in the vicinity to an unreasonable extent.... *Thus, the character, volume, frequency, duration, time, and locality are relevant factors in determining whether the annoyance materially interferes with the ordinary comfort of human existence. [Lieberman* v. *Saddle River Tp.*, 37 N.J. Super at 67, 116 A.2d 809; emphasis supplied]

To the factors listed in *Lieberman* may be added several others gleaned from New Jersey cases and cases in other jurisdictions applying a "reasonableness under the circumstances" test. For example, the availability of alternative means of achieving the defendant's objective has been found to be relevant. So, also, might the social utility of defendant's conduct, judged in light of prevailing notions of progress and the demands of modern life, be relevant. Whether a given use complies with controlling government regulations, while not dispositive on the question of private nuisance, does impact on its reasonableness.

An application of these factors to the present case supports the conclusion that defendants' windmill constitutes an actionable nuisance. As indicated, the noise produced is offensive because of its character, volume and duration. It is a sound which is not only distinctive, but one which is louder than others and is more or less constant. Its intrusive quality is heightened because of the locality. The neighborhood is quiet and residential. It is well separated, not only from commercial sounds, but from the heavier residential traffic as well. Plaintiffs specifically chose the area because of these qualities and the proximity to the ocean. Sounds which are natural to this area—the sea, the shore birds, the ocean breeze—are soothing and welcome. The noise of the windmill, which would be unwelcome in most neighborhoods, is particularly alien here.

The duration of the windmill noise is also significant. Since the prevailing winds keep the unit operating more or less constantly, the noise continues night and day. Interfering, as they do, with the normal quiet required for sleep, nighttime noises are considered particularly intrusive. Since ambient sounds are usually reduced at night, an alien sound is even more offensive then. The sound levels are well documented and clearly exceed permissible levels under the zoning ordinance. Independent of the ordinance, the evidence supports the conclusion that the noise is disturbing to persons of ordinary sensibilities. It can and does affect injuriously the health and comfort of ordinary people in the vicinity to an unreasonable extent.

When consideration is given to the social utility of the windmill and the availability of reasonable alternatives, the conclusion supporting an injunction is the same. Defendants' purpose in installing the windmill was to conserve energy and save on electric bills. Speaking to the latter goal first, clearly the court can take judicial notice that alternative devices are available which are significantly less intrusive. As to its social utility, a more careful analysis is required. Defendants argue that the windmill furthers the national need to conserve energy by the use of an alternate renewable source of power. The social utility of alternate energy sources cannot be denied; nor should the court ignore the proposition that scientific and social progress sometimes reasonably require a reduction in personal comfort. On the other hand, the fact that a device represents a scientific advance and has social utility does not mean that it is permissible at any cost. Such factors must be weighed against the quantum of harm the device brings to others.

In this case the activity in question substantially interferes with the health and comfort of plaintiffs. In addition to the negative effect on their health, their ability to enjoy the sanctity of their homes has been significantly reduced. The ability to look to one's home as a refuge from the noise and stress associated with the outside world is a right to be jealously guarded. Before that right can be eroded in the name of social progress, the benefit to society must be clear and the intrusion must be warranted under all of the circumstances. Here, the benefits are relatively small and the irritation is substantial. On balance, therefore, the social utility of this windmill is outweighed by the quantum of harm that it creates.

In conclusion, it is the view of this court that, for a variety of reasons, the defendants' windmill constitutes an actionable nuisance. An alternative basis for granting relief is defendants' violation of the municipal zoning ordinance. An order should be entered accordingly.

FOR DISCUSSION

1. According to the court, what is necessary for noise to constitute an actionable private nuisance?
2. In applying its "reasonableness under the circumstances" test, what factors does the court consider?
3. Operating a windmill to conserve energy is, as the court admits, a socially useful activity. Why doesn't the social utility of this activity prevent it from being characterized as a nuisance?
4. It has been said that "quiet enjoyment" of property does not guarantee enjoyment of quiet. What concrete uses of plaintiffs' property have been impaired? Does the fact that these are residential properties make a difference in the court's analysis?
5. Given the analysis in this case, do you think the outcome would have been the same if the windmill had been operating on the site *before* plaintiffs moved into the neighborhood? Explain.
6. Suppose the city government had erected the windmill to supply electricity for the entire neighborhood. Do you think that would change the outcome of this case? Should it? Explain.

Government Regulation of Land Use   Although nuisance provides a means for individuals to place limits on their neighbors' use of property that interferes with reasonable use and enjoyment of their own, governments use a variety of statutory means of regulating and limiting the use of property. The number of such regulations has grown over the years. As the number of social and economic problems addressed by government has grown, the rights of ownership of land, once thought of as "absolute," have correspondingly been restrained.

In "The New Property" (see below) Charles Reich writes: "Property is not a natural right but a deliberate construction by society. If such an institution did not exist, it would be necessary to create it, in order to have the kind of society we wish. The majority cannot be expected, on specific issues, to yield its power to the minority. Only if the minority's will is established as a general principle can it keep the majority at bay in a given instance. Like the Bill of Rights, property represents a general, long range protection of individual and private interests, created by the majority for the good of all." Zoning,[5] however, seems to be a prime example of an area in which a minority of property owners has been singularly unsuccessful at keeping the majority at bay. Under a comprehensive zoning plan, the opportunities for "whim, caprice, irrationality and antisocial activities" become exceedingly limited. Other land-use regulations operate in much the same way, compelling some property owners to act in ways repugnant or inconvenient to them, for the greater good of the community as a whole. The following case illustrates a challenge to such a regulation.

CASE   **Jerome J. Nash v. City of Santa Monica**
                         Supreme Court of California (1984)
                         37 Cal.3d 97, 207 Cal.Rptr. 285 688 P.2d 894

GRODIN, Justice.   In this case we are called upon to determine the validity of Santa Monica City Charter section 1803, subdivision (t)—which prohibits removal of rental units from the housing market by conversion or demolition absent a removal permit from the Santa Monica Rent Control Board—as it applies to prevent the owner of an apartment building from evicting his tenants and tearing the building down. The trial court held that the ordinance, as so applied, constitutes a deprivation of property without due process of law in violation of the Fourteenth Amendment of the United States Constitution and article I, section 7, subdivision (a) of the California Constitution.

     As is so often the case in constitutional litigation, the issues appear different depending upon one's perspective. For Santa Monica, the challenged provision is nothing more than a land use regulation designed to effectuate the purposes of the city's rent control ordinance of which it is a part, while Nash views it as a means of forcing him to remain a landlord despite his wish to "go out of business"—an interest which he asserts is among the "basic values" implicit in the concept of "ordered liberty." *City of Carmel-By-The Sea* v. *Young* (1970) 2 Cal.3d 259, 266, 85 Cal.Rptr. 1, 466 P.2d 225. There is a degree of merit in both perspectives, but neither is adequate to resolve the issue presented. Rather, as we shall explain, what is required is a realistic appraisal of the impact of the challenged provision upon Nash and the alternatives available to him, on one hand, and of the relationship of that provision to the objectives of the rent control ordinance, on the other. On the basis of that

---

[5]Zoning is legislative action, usually on the municipal level, which separates or divides a municipality into districts for the purpose of regulating use of the property and the type of buildings or other structures that can be erected within the districts established by the zoning law.

appraisal, we will conclude that while the challenged provision may be said to implicate interests which are entitled to a high degree of constitutional protection—including one's choice whether to remain in a particular business or occupation—the actual limitation upon those interests posed by the challenged provision is minimal and not significantly different from other, constitutionally permissible, limitations upon the use of private property imposed by government regulation. At the same time, the provision, by protecting existing tenants against eviction and the scarce supply of rental housing in Santa Monica against further erosion, clearly serves important public objectives. Consistent with the settled precedent of this court, and the United States Supreme Court, we shall hold that section 1803, subdivision (t), is not constitutionally infirm.

I. The vacancy rate for rental housing in Santa Monica was, at the time of trial, approximately 1.7 percent. In the late 1970's, the city was confronted with a severe shortage of its traditionally scarce housing stock, precipitated by what came to be known as the "Demolition Derby." This term was coined to describe a 15-month period during which Santa Monica landlords razed over 1,300 rental units and converted hundreds of other such units into condominiums. Rental housing units were removed from the market at 10 times the rate of removals (relative to population) of neighboring Los Angeles.

In 1979, the citizens of Santa Monica by initiative added article XVIII to the city's charter. This new article provided for a rent control board with the authority to set and adjust maximum rents and to control the removal of rental units from the housing market. The rent control law also regulates tenant evictions. Section 1803, subdivision (t) of the rent control law requires a landlord to obtain a permit before demolishing a building. Where the landlord both owns habitable property and does not wish to rebuild, a demolition permit will be granted only upon a finding that (1) the building is not occupied by persons of low or moderate income, (2) cannot be afforded by persons of low or moderate income, (3) removal will not adversely affect the housing supply, and (4) the owner cannot make a reasonable return on his investment.

Respondent Nash was a 17-year-old student when, approximately a year before the rent and demolition controls were enacted, his mother obtained on his behalf a $260,000 apartment building in Santa Monica. He soon became disenchanted, however, with operating rental housing. "There is only one thing I want to do, and that is to evict the group of ingrates inhabiting my units, tear down the building, and hold on to the land until I can sell it at a price which will not mean a ruinous loss on my investment."

Nash began the process of filing for a removal permit, so that he might indeed destroy the building and allow the land to appreciate in value. Because he could concededly earn a fair return on his investment, however, it soon became clear to him that he would not be issued the permit. Thus, rather than complete the statutorily mandated, but probably, for him, futile removal permit application process, Nash sought to circumvent the regulations by filing a petition for writ of mandate in Los Angeles Superior Court.

At trial, Nash admitted that if the apartment were left standing and remained occupied, he could earn a fair return on his investment in the property. He further conceded that demolition of his building would adversely affect the supply of housing in Santa Monica. The court found the units in Nash's building were occupied by persons of very low, low, or moderate income, and that the rents charged were affordable by them. Thus, the trial court found the prerequisites to the acquisition of a demolition permit had not been satisfied.

Based on these findings, the trial court accepted Nash's argument that the challenged provision operated to deprive Nash of property without due process of law. It also declared, *sua sponte*, that the provision resulted in a taking of his property without just compensation. It ordered a writ of mandate commanding the City of Santa Monica and the Santa Monica Rent Control Board to grant Nash a removal permit for his property.

II. We begin by examining the nature of Nash's claim. Notwithstanding the trial court's alternative ruling, Nash expressly disclaims any contention that the city's ordinance effects a "taking" of his property in violation of federal or state constitutions. Nor, in the light of applicable authority, would such a claim appear to have merit. In *Penn Central Transp. Co. v. New York City* (1978) 438 U.S. 104, 98 S.Ct. 2646, 57 L.Ed.2d 631, the United States Supreme Court considered a constitutional challenge to New York City's Landmark Preservation Law, which authorizes a city commission to prohibit the demolition of designated historic structures. The court held that no taking was involved in application of the ordinance to plaintiff, which desired to modify its railroad terminal by construction of an office building in its place, since the regulation did not interfere with the owner's "primary, investment-backed expectations," and did not render the owner unable to receive a reasonable return on his investment. It is undisputed that both prongs of the *Penn Central* test are met here. We are aware of no authority which would impose different requirements under the California Constitution.

Nash asserts that he is "not seeking compensation from the City of Santa Monica for being forced to stay in the apartment-rental business, but only the right to go out of that business." Conceding that there are no decisions precisely on point, and without identifying any particular constitutional provision, Nash contends that there must be limitations upon the power of the state to compel a person to pursue a particular business or occupation against his will.

We agree. The Thirteenth Amendment to the United States Constitution prohibits involuntary servitude. This court has spoken of the basic liberty to pursue and obtain happiness by engaging in the common occupations of the community. The exercise of state power to force upon an individual a career chosen by the state would surely raise substantial questions of constitutional dimension.

The City of Santa Monica has not done that to Nash, however. Rather, it has told him that so long as tenants remain in his apartment units, and so long as he continues to receive a fair rate of return on his investment, he may not evict them and demolish the building. Nash remains free to minimize his personal involvement by delegating responsibility for rent collection and maintenance to a property manager. He remains free under the ordinance to withhold rental units from the market as they become vacant. And, he remains free to sell his property and invest the proceeds elsewhere. The problem arises from the fact that Nash prefers to do none of these things, but to demolish the building and keep the land beneath as an investment. This he claims an absolute right to do, as owner of the property.

The state Constitution protects the rights of "acquiring, possessing, and protecting property...." Cal.Const., art.I, §1. Both federal and state constitutions protect against deprivation of property without due process of law. Yet, "[i]t is thoroughly established in this country that the rights preserved to the individual by these constitutional provisions are held in subordination to the rights of society. Although one owns property, he may not do with it as he pleases any more than he may act in accordance with his personal desires." *Miller* v. *Board of Public Works* (1925) 195 Cal. 477, 488, 234 P. 381. Thus, an ordinance restrictive of property use will be upheld, against due process attack, unless its provisions "are clearly arbitrary and unreasonable, having no substantial relation to the public health, safety, morals, or general welfare." *Village of Euclid* v. *Ambler Realty Co.* (1926) 272 U.S. 365, 395, 47 S.Ct. 114, 121, 71 L.Ed. 303.

Nash seeks to elevate the standard of constitutional review from the "rational relationship" test normally used in appraising the validity of property regulation to a more restrictive "strict scrutiny" test, on the ground that the Santa Monica ordinance implicates his "fundamental right" to cease doing business as a landlord. His argument is that the city has conditioned the exercise of that "fundamental right" upon the relinquishment of his right not to sell his property, and that this is constitutionally impermissible, absent a compelling governmental interest which, he asserts, does not exist.

Even were we to accept Nash's theory we would be hard pressed to say that there is no compelling governmental interest in the preservation of scarce rental housing against destruction.

We find it unnecessary to reach that level of analysis, however, since in our view the indirect and minimal burden imposed upon Nash's asserted liberty interest by the demolition control provisions of the Santa Monica ordinance does not warrant departure from the traditional tests used to determine the validity of economic regulation. All regulation of property entails some limitation upon the liberty of the owner; and, to the extent that the regulation limits the uses to which the property may be put, it entails limitation upon the owner's liberty to pursue his chosen occupation or business at that location. If the owner wishes to pursue his preference, he may be constrained to sell his property and move elsewhere. If the value of his property has decreased as a result of the regulation, he may perceive that to be an undesirable alternative, and to that extent feel economically constrained to continue in his present field of endeavor. Yet, the existence of these legal and de facto limitations upon his freedom of choice do not operate to subject the property regulation to a strict scrutiny test under modern legal principles.

The strict scrutiny standard which Nash invokes would call into question a variety of land use regulations which have thus far withstood constitutional attack. Ordinances which prohibit demolition of historic monuments, such as the one upheld in *Penn Central Transp. Co.* v. *New York City*, supra, 438 U.S. 104, 98 S.Ct. 2646, 57 L.Ed.2d 631, not only limit the freedom of choice of the owner as to the use of his property, and as to the type of business or occupation he may engage in upon the premises, but also impose upon the owner, as a minimal duty which he cannot legally escape without sale, the obligation to maintain the premises in a state of repair.

In the arena of landlord-tenant law, demolition controls may be viewed as an adjunct to limitations upon eviction which have generally been upheld by the courts. Such limitations, depending upon the context, may similarly inhibit an owner's desire to curtail his function as a landlord.

Nash is not being called upon to operate a business or engage in a profession unrelated to the property; his landlordly obligations are those which arise out of the ownership of the sort of property which he acquired. As Justice Holmes said, in rejecting a Thirteenth Amendment attack by a landlord upon an ordinance which made it a misdemeanor to fail to furnish certain services to tenants: "It is true that the traditions of our law are opposed to compelling a man to perform strictly personal services against his will even when he has contracted to render them. But the services in question ['water, heat, light, elevator, telephone, or other services as may be required by the terms of the lease and necessary to the proper or customary use of the building'] although involving some activities are so far from personal that they constitute the universal and necessary incidents of modern apartment houses. They are analogous to the services that in the old law might issue out of or be attached to the land." (*Marcus Brown Holding Co., Inc.* v. *Feldman* (1921) 256 U.S. 170, 199, 41 S.Ct. 465, 466, 65 L.Ed. 877.)

Finally, insofar as Nash feels constrained by the ordinance to sell his property rather than undertake other alternatives available to him, he is in no worse position than if the City of Santa Monica were to exercise its power of eminent domain to compel a sale to private parties—a procedure recently upheld in a unanimous decision of the United States Supreme Court. Indeed, he is in a better position, since he retains the option of continuing to own the property and to operate it at what he considers to be a fair rate of return. Thus, Nash's argument that the ordinance unconstitutionally impinges upon his right to retain property rather than sell it simply does not hold water.

We conclude the questioned provision, as applied to respondent Nash, is valid. Accordingly, we reverse the judgment below.

FOR DISCUSSION

1. How does the ordinance in question limit plaintiff's use of his land? Is this a serious limitation?
2. What is the purpose of the ordinance? Does the ordinance seem appropriate to achieve its purpose?
3. Has the value of plaintiff's land been adversely affected by the ordinance? Explain your answer.
4. Is plaintiff complaining because the value of his land has been diminished? If not, what is the basis of his complaint?
5. What standards must a land-use regulation of this type meet in order to be valid?
6. How does this case compare with the previous case concerning nuisance? In your opinion, which landowner has suffered the greater limitation to his ability to use his property as he pleases? Explain your answer.

REDEFINING RIGHTS IN PROPERTY

Blackstone wrote, "There is nothing which so generally strikes the imagination and engages the affections of mankind as the right of property...." The property Blackstone had in mind was tangible property, first and foremost land, and he proclaimed that people should have as close to absolute dominion over their property as possible. As we have seen in this chapter, the meaning of the term property has changed a great deal over several centuries, and today when we think of property we think more of personal property and intangible property, and much less of land, which no longer constitutes the principal source of wealth. Even where real property is concerned, intangible rights seem to have overtaken the more tangible ones. People sell the airspace over their existing buildings for further development or sell the exploration and development rights of the various strata beneath their land to oil and gas companies. Not only have our ideas about property changed with respect to classification but also with respect to absolute dominion. It seems almost commonplace today that everyone owns "subject" to governmental limitations or the rights of other owners or the public: taxation, easements, rights-of-way, zoning, landmark and historical preservation, environmental conservation—these are but a few of the interests that may limit ownership.

When Charles A. Reich published "The New Property" in 1964, he could not have known in advance how influential it would be. Some of Reich's vision affected the law directly, as when it influenced the decision of the U.S. Supreme Court in *Goldberg* v. *Kelly*, 397 U.S. 254 (1970), the case that established due process protection of a "property interest" in welfare benefits, or indirectly as a teaching tool in the law schools of America. There is scarcely a case book on property in existence that does not contain an excerpt of Reich's article. Reich offered a new conception of property, which he defined as wealth in the form of government largess and/or entitlements, as a bulwark of individualism against dependence upon the government and the corresponding tyranny of the "public interest state." Not a particularly "liberal" notion in the modern sense of the term, the Reich ideal nevertheless flourished during liberal administrations and has languished during the succeeding conservative ones. Despite some advances, Reich's conception of the "new property" is still far from being realized. Nevertheless, his ideas continue to be considered and debated.

READING   **The New Property**
                                                    Charles A. Reich*

The institution called property guards the troubled boundary between individual man and the state. It is not only the guardian; many other institutions, laws, and practices serve as well. But in a society that chiefly values material well-being, the power to control a particular portion of that well-being is the very foundation of individuality.

One of the most important developments in the United States during the past decade has been the emergence of government as a major source of wealth. Government is a gigantic syphon. It draws in revenue and power, and pours forth wealth: money, benefits, services, contracts, franchises, and licenses. Government has always had this function. But while in early times it was minor, today's distribution of largess is on a vast, imperial scale.

The valuables dispensed by government take on many forms, but they all share one characteristic. They are steadily taking the place of traditional forms of wealth—forms which are held as private property. Social insurance substitutes for savings; a government contract replaces a businessman's customers and goodwill. The wealth of more and more Americans depends upon a relationship to government. Increasingly, Americans live on government largess—allocated by the government on its own terms, and held by recipients subject to conditions which express "the public interest."

The growth of government largess, accompanied by a distinctive system of law, is having profound consequences. It affects the underpinnings of individualism and independence. It influences the workings of the Bill of Rights. It has an impact on the power of private interests, in their relation to each other and to government. It is helping to create a new society....

C. *Largess and the Changing Forms of Wealth*

The significance of government largess is increased by certain underlying changes in the forms of private wealth in the United States. Changes in the forms of wealth are not remarkable in themselves; the forms are constantly changing and differ in every culture. But today more and more of our wealth takes the form of rights or status rather than of tangible goods. An individual's profession or occupation is a prime example. To many others, a job with a particular employer is the principal form of wealth. A profession or a job is frequently far more valuable than a house or a bank account, for a new house can be bought, and a new bank account created, once a profession or job is secure. For the jobless, their status as governmentally assisted or insured persons may be the main source of subsistence.

The automobile dealer's chief wealth is his franchise from the manufacturer which gives him exclusive sales rights within a certain territory, for it is his guarantee of income. His building, his stock of cars, his organization, and his goodwill may all be less valuable than his franchise. Franchises represent the principal asset of many businesses: the gasoline station, chain restaurant, motel or drug store, and many other retail suppliers. To the large manufacturer, contracts, business arrangements, and organization may be the most valuable assets. The steel company's relationships with coal and iron producers and automobile manufacturers and construction companies may be worth more than all its plant and equipment.

The kinds of wealth dispensed by government consist almost entirely of those forms which are in the ascendancy today. To the individual, these new forms, such as profession, job, or right to receive income, are the basis of his various statuses in society, and may therefore be the most meaningful and distinctive wealth he possesses.

II. THE EMERGING SYSTEM OF LAW

Wealth or value is created by culture and by society; it is culture that makes a diamond valuable and a pebble worthless. Property, on the other hand, is the creation of law. A man who has property has certain legal rights with respect to an item of wealth; property represents a relationship between wealth and its "owner." Government largess is plainly "wealth," but it is not necessarily property.

Government largess has given rise to a distinctive system of law. This system can be viewed from at least three perspectives; the rights of holders of largess, the powers of government over largess, and the procedure by which holders' rights and governmental power are adjusted. At this point, analysis will not be aided by attempting to apply or reject the label "property." What is important is to survey—without the use of labels—the unique legal system that is emerging.

A. *Individual Rights in Largess*

As government largess has grown in importance, quite naturally there has been pressure for the protection of individual interests in it. The holder of a broadcast license or a motor carrier permit or a grazing permit for the public lands tends to consider this wealth his "own," and to seek legal protection against interference with his enjoyment. The development of individual interests has been substantial, but it has not come easily.

From the beginning, individual rights in largess have been greatly affected by several traditional legal concepts, each of which has had lasting significance:

Right v. Privilege. The early law is marked by courts' attempts to distinguish which forms of largess were "rights" and which were "privileges." Legal protection of the former was by far the greater. If the holder of a license had a "right," he might be entitled to a hearing before the license could be revoked; a mere "privilege" might be revoked without notice or hearing.

The gratuity principle. Government largess has often been considered a "gratuity" furnished by the state. Hence it is said that the state can withhold, grant, or revoke the largess at its pleasure. Under this theory, government is considered to be somewhat in the position of a private giver.

The whole and the parts. Related to the gratuity theory is the idea that, since government may completely withhold a benefit, it may grant it subject to any terms or conditions whatever. This theory is essentially an exercise in logic: the whole power must include all of its parts.

Internal management. Particularly in relation to its own contracts, government has been permitted extensive power on the theory that it should have control over its own housekeeping or internal management functions. Under this theory, government is treated like a private business. In its dealings with outsiders it is permitted much of the freedom to grant contracts and licenses that a private business would have.

Quite often these four theories are blurred in a single statement of judicial attitude. One court put the idea in somewhat more pithy form: "...in accepting charity, the appellant has consented to the provisions of the law under which the charity is bestowed." *Wilkie* v. *O'Connor*, 261 App. Div. 373, 25 N.Y.S.2d 617, 620 (Sup. Ct. 1941).

These sentiments are often voiced in the law of government largess, but individual interests have grown up nevertheless. The most common forms of protection are procedural, coupled with an insistence that government action be based on standards that are not "arbitrary" or unauthorized. The courts have most readily granted protection to those types which are intimately bound up with the individual's freedom to earn a living. They have been reluctant to grant individual rights in those types of largess which seem to be exercises of the managerial functions of government, such as subsidies and government contracts....

IV. PROPERTY AND THE PUBLIC INTEREST: AN OLD DEBATE REVISITED

The public interest state...represents in one sense the triumph of society over private property. This triumph is the end point of a great and necessary movement for reform. But somehow the end result is different from what the reformers wanted. Somehow the idealistic concept of the public interest has summoned up a doctrine monstrous and oppressive. It is time to take another look at private property, and at the "public interest" philosophy that dominates its modern substitute, the largess of government.

A. *Property and Liberty*

Property is a legal institution the essence of which is the creation and protection of certain private rights in wealth of any kind. The institution performs many different functions. One of these functions is to draw a boundary between public and private power. Property draws a circle around the activities of each private individual or organization. Within that circle, the owner has a greater degree of freedom than without. Outside, he must justify or explain his actions, and show his authority. Within, he is master, and the state must explain and justify any interference. It is as if property shifted the burden of proof; outside, the individual has the burden; inside, the burden is on the government to demonstrate that something the owner wishes to do should not be done.

Thus, property performs the function of maintaining independence, dignity and pluralism in society by creating zones within which the majority has to yield to the owner. Whim, caprice, irrationality and "antisocial" activities are given the protection of law; the owner may do what all or most of his neighbors decry. The Bill of Rights also serves this function, but while the Bill of Rights comes into play only at extraordinary moments of conflict or crisis, property affords day-to-day protection in the ordinary affairs of life. Indeed, in the final analysis the Bill of Rights depends upon the existence of private property. Political rights presuppose that individuals and private groups have the will and the means to act independently. But so long as individuals are motivated largely by self-interest, their well-being must first be independent. Civil liberties must have a basis in property, or bills of rights will not preserve them.

Property is not a natural right but a deliberate construction by society. If such an institution did not exist, it would be necessary to create it, in order to have the kind of society we wish. The majority cannot be expected, on specific issues, to yield its power to a minority. Only if the minority's will is established as a general principle can it keep the majority at bay in a given instance. Like the Bill of Rights, property represents a general, long range protection of individual and private interests, created by the majority for the ultimate good of all.

Today, however, it is widely thought that property and liberty are separable things; that there may, in fact, be conflicts between "property rights" and "personal rights." Why has this view been accepted? The explanation is found at least partly in the transformations which have taken place in property.

During the industrial revolution, when property was liberated from feudal restraints, philosophers hailed property as the basis of liberty, and argued that it must be free from the demands of government or society. But as private property grew, so did abuses resulting from its use. In a crowded world, a man's use of his property increasingly affected his neighbor, and one man's exercise of a right might seriously impair the rights of others. Property became power over others; the farm landowner, the city landlord, and the working man's boss were able to oppress their tenants or employees. Great aggregations of property resulted in private control of entire industries and basic services capable of affecting a whole area or even a nation. At the same time, much private property lost its individuality and in effect became socialized. Multiple ownership of corporations helped to separate personality from property, and property from power. When the corporations began to stop competing, to merge, agree, and make mutual plans, they became private governments. Finally they sought the aid and partnership of the state, and thus by their own volition became part of public government.

These changes led to a movement for reform, which sought to limit arbitrary private power and protect the common man. Property rights were considered more the enemy than the friend of liberty. The reformers argued that property must be separated from personality.

During the first half of the twentieth century, the reformers enacted into law their conviction that private power was a chief enemy of society and of individual liberty. Property was subjected to "reasonable" limitations in the interests of society. The regulatory agencies, federal and state, were born of the reform. In sustaining these major inroads on private property, the Supreme Court rejected the older idea that property and liberty were one, and wrote a series of classic opinions upholding the power of the people to regulate and limit private rights.

The struggle between abuse and reform made it easy to forget the basic importance of individual private property. The defense of private property was almost entirely a defense of its abuses—an attempt to defend not individual property but arbitrary power over human beings. Since this defense was cloaked in a defense of private property, it was natural for the reformers to attack too broadly.

The reform took away some of the power of the corporations and transferred it to government. In this transfer there was much good, for power was made responsive to the majority rather than to the arbitrary and selfish few. But the reform did not restore the individual to his domain. What the corporation had taken from him, the reform simply handed on to the government. And government carried further the powers formerly exercised by the corporation. Government as an employer, or as a dispenser of wealth, has used the theory that it was handing out gratuities to claim a managerial power as great as that which the capitalists claimed. Moreover, the corporations allied themselves with, or actually took over, part of government's system of power. Today it is the combined power of government and the corporations that presses against the individual.

From the individual's point of view, it is not any particular kind of power, but all kinds of power, that are to be feared. This is the lesson of the public interest state. The mere fact that power is derived from the majority does not necessarily make it less oppressive. Liberty is more than the right to do what the majority wants, or to do what is "reasonable." Liberty is the right to defy the majority, and to do what is unreasonable. The great error of the public interest state is that it assumes an identity between the public interest and the interest of the majority.

The reform, then, has not done away with the importance of private property. More than ever the individual needs to possess, in whatever form, a small but sovereign island of his own.

V. TOWARD INDIVIDUAL STAKES IN THE COMMONWEALTH

There can be no retreat from the public interest state. It is the inevitable outgrowth of an interdependent world. An effort to return to an earlier economic order would merely transfer power to giant private governments which would rule not in the public interest, but in their own interest. If individualism and pluralism are to be preserved, this must be done not by marching backwards, but by building these values into today's society. If public and private are now blurred, it will be necessary to draw a new zone of privacy. If private property can no longer perform its protective functions, it will be necessary to establish institutions to carry on the work that private property once did but can no longer do.

In these efforts government largess must play a major role. As we move toward a welfare state, largess will be an ever more important form of wealth. And largess is a vital link in the relationship between the government and private sides of society. It is necessary, then, that largess begin to do the work of property.

The chief obstacle to the creation of private rights in largess has been the fact that it is originally public property, comes from the state, and may be withheld completely. But this need not be an obstacle. Traditional property also comes from the state, and in much the same way. Land, for example, traces back to grants from the sovereign. In the United States, some was the gift of the King of England, some that of the King of Spain. The sovereign extinguished Indian title by conquest, became the new owner, and then granted title to a private individual or group. Some land was the gift of the sovereign under laws such as the Homestead and Preemption Acts. Many other natural resources—water, minerals and timber, passed into private ownership under similar grants. In America, land and resources all were originally government largess. In a less obvious sense, personal property also stems from government. Personal property is created by law; it owes its origin and continuance to laws supported by the people as a whole. These laws "give" the property to one who performs certain actions. Even the man who catches a wild animal "owns" the animal only as a gift from the sovereign, having fulfilled the terms of an offer to transfer ownership.

If all property is government largess, why is it not regulated to the same degree as present-day largess? Regulation of property has been limited, not because society had no interest in property, but because it was in the interest of society that property be free. Once property is seen not as a natural right but as a construction designed to serve certain functions, then its origin ceases to be decisive in determining how much regulation should be imposed. The conditions that can be attached to receipt, ownership, and use depend not on where property came from, but on what job it should be expected to perform. Thus in the case of government largess, nothing turns on the fact that it originated in government. The real issue is how it functions and how it should function....

D. *From Largess to Right*

The proposals discussed above, however salutary, are by themselves far from adequate to assure the status of individual man with respect to largess. The problems go deeper. First, the growth of government power based on the dispensing of wealth must be kept within bounds. Second, there must be a zone of privacy for each individual beyond which neither government nor private power can push—a hiding place from the all-pervasive system of regulation and control. Finally, it must be recognized that we are becoming a society based on relationship and status—status deriving primarily from source of livelihood. Status is so closely linked to personality that destruction of one may well destroy the other. Status must therefore be surrounded with the kind of safeguards once reserved for personality.

Eventually those forms of largess which are closely linked to status must be deemed to be held as of right. Like property, such largess could be governed by a system of regulation plus civil or criminal sanctions, rather than a system based upon denial, suspension and revocation. As things now stand, violations lead to forfeitures—outright confiscation of wealth and status. But there is surely no need for these drastic results. Confiscation, if used at all, should be the ultimate, not the most common and convenient penalty. The presumption should be that the professional man will keep his license, and the welfare recipient his pension. These interests should be "vested." If revocation is necessary, not by reason of the fault of the individual holder, but by reason of overriding demands of public policy, perhaps payment of just compensation would be appropriate. The individual should not bear the entire loss for a remedy primarily intended to benefit the community.

The concept of right is most urgently needed with respect to benefits like unemployment compensation, public assistance, and old age insurance. These benefits are based upon a recognition that misfortune and deprivation are often caused by forces far beyond the control of the individual, such as technological change, variations in demand for goods, depressions, or wars. The aim of these benefits is to preserve the self-sufficiency of the individual, to rehabilitate him where necessary, and to allow him to be a valuable member of a family and a community; in theory they represent part of the individual's rightful share in the commonwealth. Only by making such benefits into rights can the welfare state achieve its goal of providing a secure minimum basis for individual well-being and dignity in a society where each man cannot wholly be the master of his own destiny.

NOTES

*From 73 *Yale Law Journal* 733–86 (1964). Reprinted by permission of *The Yale Law Journal Company* and Fred B. Rothman & Company from *The Yale Law Journal Company*.

FOR DISCUSSION

1. Do you recognize features of the "new society" that Reich describes? What forms of largess have you or your family experienced?

2. According to Reich, how has our society's conception of the forms of private wealth changed?

3. What does Reich mean when he says, "Wealth or value is created by culture and by society; it is culture that makes a diamond valuable and a pebble worthless. Property, on the other hand, is the creation of law."

4. Would Locke, Blackstone, and Bentham have agreed with the statement in question 3?

5. Bentham suggested that property, as the creation of the positive law, could be changed, but he was also concerned about the "security of expectations" in relation to property. How do Reich's ideas affect the security of expectations a modern person has in regard to property?

6. One recent writer has suggested that whether a thing is called a "right," "privilege," "gratuity," etc. is not as important in establishing it as valuable property as is the thing's relationship to the "personhood" of the holder. Do you think Reich would agree with that view?

7. Reich says that, "the public interest state... represents in one sense the triumph of society over private property." Since private property clearly brings with it inequality (see Locke), shouldn't the public interest state be a good thing? What are Reich's reservations?

8. Reich says that, "property draws a circle around the activities of each private individual or organization." What does he mean by this? Can you give examples from some of the cases you have read?

9. What is Reich's solution to the "public interest state" dilemma?

10. Do you agree with Reich's proposals? Explain your answer.

The following case involves a dispute over the disposition of a piece of the "new property," in Reich's sense of the term, a license to practice medicine. Here, however, the conflict is not directly between the individual trying to earn a living, and maintain his status, and the tyranny of the confiscatory public interest state. Rather, it is the state that must intervene on behalf of another individual who also claims an interest in this admittedly valuable property.

CASE

Michael O'Brien v. Loretta O'Brien
New York Court of Appeals (1985)
66 N.Y.2d 576.498 N.Y.S.2d 743. 489 N.E.2d 712

SIMONS, Judge.   In this divorce action, the parties' only asset of any consequence is the husband's newly acquired license to practice medicine. The principal issue presented is whether that license, acquired during their marriage, is marital property subject to equitable distribution under Domestic Relations Law §236(B)(5). Supreme Court held that it was and accordingly made a distributive award in defendant's favor. It also granted defendant maintenance and arrears, expert witness fees and attorneys' fees. On appeal to the Appellate Division, a majority of that court held that plaintiff's medical license is not marital property and that the defendant was not entitled to an award for the expert witness fees. It modified the judgment and remitted the case to Supreme Court for further proceedings, specifically for a determination of maintenance and a rehabilitative award. The matter is now before us by leave of the Appellate Division.

We now hold that plaintiff's medical license constitutes "marital property" within the meaning of Domestic Relations Law §236(B)(1)(c) and that it is therefore subject to equitable distribution pursuant to subdivision 5 of that part. That being so, the Appellate Division erred in denying a fee, as a matter of law, to defendant's expert witness who evaluated the license.

I. Plaintiff and defendant married on April 3, 1971. At the time both were employed as teachers at the same private school. Defendant had a bachelor's degree and a temporary teaching certificate but required 18 months of postgraduate classes at an approximate cost of $3,000, excluding living expenses, to obtain permanent certification in New York. She claimed, and the trial court found, that she had relinquished the opportunity to obtain permanent certification while the plaintiff pursued his education. At the time of the marriage, plaintiff had completed only three and one-half years of college but shortly afterward he returned to school at night to complete sufficient premedical courses to enter medical school. In September 1973 the parties moved to Guadalajara, Mexico, where plaintiff became a full-time medical student. While he pursued his studies defendant held several teaching and tutorial positions and contributed her earnings to their joint expenses. The parties returned to New York in December 1976 so that plaintiff could complete the last two semesters of medical school and internship training here. After they returned, defendant resumed her former teaching position and she remained in it at the time this action commenced. Plaintiff was licensed to practice medicine in October 1980. He commenced this action for divorce two months later. At the time of trial, he was a resident in general surgery.

During the marriage both parties contributed to paying the living and educational expenses and they received additional help from both their families. They disagreed on the amounts of their respective contributions but it is undisputed that in addition to performing household work and managing the family finances defendant was gainfully employed throughout the marriage, that she contributed all of her earnings to their living and educational expenses and that her financial contributions exceeded those of plaintiff. The trial court found that she had contributed 76% of the parties' income exclusive of a $10,000 student loan obtained by defendant. Finding that plaintiff's medical degree and license are marital property, the court received evidence of its value and ordered a distributive award to defendant.

Defendant presented expert testimony that the present value of plaintiff's medical license was $472,000. Her expert testified that he arrived at this figure by comparing the average income of a college graduate and that of a general surgeon between 1985, when plaintiff's residency would end, and 2012, when he would reach age 65. After considering Federal income taxes, an inflation rate of 10% and a real interest rate of 3% he capitalized the difference in average earnings and reduced the amount to present value. He also gave his opinion that the present value of defendant's contribution to plaintiff's medical license was $103,390. Plaintiff offered no expert testimony on the subject.

The court, after considering the life-style that plaintiff would enjoy from the enhanced earning potential his medical license would bring and defendant's contributions and efforts toward attainment of it, made a distributive award to her of $188,800, representing 40% of the value of the license, and ordered it paid in 11 annual installments of various amounts beginning November 1, 1982, and ending November 1, 1992. The court also directed plaintiff to maintain a life insurance policy on his life for defendant's benefit for the unpaid balance of the award and it ordered plaintiff to pay defendant's counsel fees of $7000 and her expert witness fee of $1000. It did not award defendant maintenance.

A divided Appellate Division, relying on its prior decision in *Connor* v. *Connor*, 97 A.D.2d 88, 468 N.Y.S.2d 482, and the decision of the Fourth department in *Lesman* v. *Lesman*, 88 A.D.2d 153, 452 N.Y.S.2d 935, *appeal dismissed* 57 N.Y.2d 956, concluded that a professional license acquired during marriage is not marital property subject to distribution. It therefore modified the judgment by striking the trial court's determination that it is and by striking the provision ordering payment of the expert witness for evaluating the license and remitted the case for further proceedings.

On these cross appeals, defendant seeks reinstatement of the judgment of the trial court. Plaintiff contends that the Appellate Division correctly held that a professional license is not marital property but he also urges that the trial court failed to adequately explain what factors it relied on in making its decision, that it erroneously excluded evidence of defendant's marital fault and that the trial court's awards for attorneys and expert witness fees were improper.

II. The Equitable Distribution Law contemplates only two classes of property: marital property and separate property. Domestic Relations Law §236(B)(1)(c)(d). The former, which is subject to equitable distribution, is defined broadly as "*all* property acquired by either or both spouses during the marriage and before the execution of a separation agreement or the commencement of a matrimonial action, *regardless of the form in which title is held*." Plaintiff does not contend that his license is excluded from distribution because it is separate property; rather, he claims that it is not property at all but represents a personal attainment in acquiring knowledge. He rests his argument on decisions in similar cases from other jurisdictions and on his view that a license does not satisfy common-law concepts of property. Neither contention is controlling because decisions in other States rely principally on their own statutes, and the legislative history underlying them, and because the New York Legislature deliberately went beyond traditional property concepts when it formulated the Equitable Distribution Law. Instead, our statute recognizes that spouses have an equitable claim to things of value arising out of the marital relationship and classifies them as subject to distribution by focusing on the marital status of the parties at the time of acquisition. Those things acquired during marriage and subject to distribution have been classified as "marital property" although, as one commentator has observed, they hardly fall within the traditional property concepts because there is no common-law property interest remotely resembling marital property. "It is a statutory creature, is of no meaning whatsoever during the normal course of a marriage, and arises full-grown, like Athena, upon the signing of a separation agreement or the commencement of a matrimonial action. [Thus] [i]t is hardly surprising, and not at all relevant, that traditional common law property concepts do not fit in parsing the meaning of 'marital property.'" Florescue, "Market Value," *Professional Licenses and Marital Property: A Dilemma in Search of a Horn*, 1982 N.Y.St.Bar Assn. Fam.L.Rev. 13(Dec.). Having classified the "property" subject to distribution, the Legislature did not attempt to go further and define it but left it to the courts to determine what interests come within the terms of section 236(B)(1)(c).

We made such a determination in *Majauskas* v. *Majauskas*, 61 N.Y.2d 481, 474 N.Y.S.2d 699, 463 N.E.2d 15, holding there that vested but unmatured pension rights were marital property subject to equitable distribution. Because pension benefits are not specifically identified as marital property in the statute, we looked to the express reference to pension rights contained in section 236(B)(5)(d)(4), which deals with equitable distribution of marital property, to other provisions of the equitable distribution statute and to the legislative intent behind its enactment to determine whether pension rights are marital property or separate property. A similar analysis is appropriate here and leads to the conclusion that marital property encompasses a license to practice medicine to the extent that the license is acquired during the marriage.

Section 236 provides that in making an equitable distribution of marital property, "the court shall consider:... (6) any equitable claim to, interest in, or direct or indirect contribution made to the acquisition of such marital property by the party not having title, including joint efforts or expenditures and contributions and services as a spouse, parent, wage earner and homemaker, and *to the career or career potential* of the other party [and]... (9) the impossibility or difficulty of evaluating any component asset or any interest in a business, corporation or *profession*." Domestic Relations Law §236(B)(5)(d)(6)(9) [emphasis added]. Where equitable distribution of marital property is appropriate but "the distribution of an interest in a business, corporation or *profession* would be contrary to law" the court shall make a distributive award in lieu of an actual distribution of the property. The words mean exactly what they say: that an interest in a profession or professional career potential is marital property which may be represented by direct or indirect contributions of the non-title-holding spouse, including financial contributions and nonfinancial contributions made by caring for the home and family.

The history which preceded enactment of the statute confirms this interpretation. Reform of section 236 was advocated because experience had proven that application of the traditional common-law title theory of property had caused inequities upon dissolution of a marriage. The Legislature replaced the existing system with equitable distribution of marital property, an entirely new theory which considered all the circumstances of the case and of the respective parties to the marriage. Equitable distribution was based on the premise that a marriage is, among other things, an economic partnership to which both parties contribute as spouse, parent, wage earner or homemaker. Consistent with this purpose and implicit in the statutory scheme as a whole, is the view that upon dissolution of the marriage there should be a winding up of the parties' economic affairs and a severance of their economic ties by an equitable distribution of the marital assets. Thus, the concept of alimony, which often served as a means of lifetime support and dependence for one spouse upon the other long after the marriage was over, was replaced by the concept of maintenance which seeks to allow "the recipient spouse an opportunity to achieve [economic] independence." Assembly Memorandum, 1980 Legis.Ann., at 130.

The determination that a professional license is marital property is also consistent with the conceptual base upon which the statute rests. As this case demonstrates, few undertakings during a marriage better qualify as the type of joint effort that the statute's economic partnership theory is intended to address than contributions toward one spouse's acquisition of a professional license. Working spouses are often required to contribute substantial income as wage earners, sacrifice their own educational or career goals and opportunities for child rearing, perform the bulk of household duties and responsibilities and forego the acquisition of marital assets that could have been accumulated if the professional spouse had been employed rather than occupied with the study and training necessary to acquire a professional license. In this case, nearly all of the parties' nine-year marriage was devoted to the acquisition of plaintiff's medical license and defendant played a major role in that project. She worked continuously during the marriage and contributed all of her earnings to their joint effort, she sacrificed her own educational and career opportunities, and she traveled with plaintiff to Mexico for three and one-half years while he attended medical school there. The Legislature has decided, by its explicit reference in the statute to the contributions of one spouse to the other's profession or career that these contributions represent investments in the economic partnership of the marriage and that the product of the parties' joint efforts, the professional license, should be considered marital property.

The majority at the Appellate Division held that the cited statutory provisions do not refer to the license held by a professional who has yet to establish a practice but only to a going professional practice. There is no reason in law or logic to restrict the plain language of the statute to existing practices, however, for it is of little consequence in making an award of marital property, except for the purpose of evaluation, whether the professional spouse has already established a practice or whether he or she has yet to do so. An established practice merely represents the exercise of the privileges conferred upon the professional spouse by the license and the income flowing from that practice represents the receipt of the enhanced earning capacity that licensure allows. That being so, it would be unfair not to consider the license a marital asset.

Plaintiff's principal argument, adopted by the majority below, is that a professional license is not marital property because it does not fit within the traditional view of property as something which has an exchange value on the open market and is capable of sale, assignment or transfer. The position does not withstand analysis for at least two reasons. First, as we have observed, it ignores the fact that whether a professional license constitutes marital property is to be judged by the language of the statute which created this new species of property previously unknown at common law or under prior statutes. Thus, whether the license fits within traditional property concepts is of no consequence. Second, it is an overstatement to assert that a professional license could not be considered property even outside the context of section 236(B). A professional license is a valuable property right, reflected in the money, effort and lost opportunity for employment expended in its acquisition, and also in the enhanced earning capacity it affords its holder, which may not be revoked without due process of law. That a professional license has no market value is irrelevant. Obviously, a license may not be alienated as may other property and for that reason the working spouse's interest in it is limited. The Legislature has recognized that limitation, however, and has provided for an award in lieu of its actual distribution.

Accordingly, in view of our holding that plaintiff's license to practice medicine is marital property, the order of the Appellate Division should be modified, with costs to the defendant, by reinstating the judgment and the case remitted to the Appellate Division for determination of the facts, including the exercise of that court's discretion, and, as so modified, affirmed. Question certified answered in the negative.

FOR DISCUSSION

1. What is the statutory definition of "marital property" in this case? What was plaintiff's argument against his medical license being classified as marital property?
2. Given the definitions of property you have encountered in other cases, would you consider a license to practice medicine to be property?
3. Why, according to the court, is the New York Equitable Distribution Law an unusual and progressive treatment of the concept of property in marriage?
4. On what conception of the marital relationship did the New York Legislature base the Equitable Distribution Law? Does it make sense?
5. What kinds of inequities is the Equitable Distribution Law supposed to redress? Do you think Reich would approve of this statute?
6. Does the fact that a medical license cannot be sold or transferred, and therefore has no exchange value, adversely affect its value or its status as property? What would Reich say to this?
7. In effect, according to the Court of Appeals, what is "property"?
8. Do you think the outcome in this case is fair? Explain.

Although people feel instinctively that the Constitution ought to protect them generally from arbitrary and unreasonable government action, the Due Process Clause does not work that way. As one writer has stated, "Procedures are important, not for themselves and not as symbols of the perfect society, but only as a means of protecting *matters of value*. These matters of value are not the procedures themselves, but the *interests* they protect." Simon, "Liberty and Property in the Supreme Court: A Defense of *Roth* and *Perry*," 71 *California Law Review* 146, 186 (1983) [Emphasis supplied.]. Although the Supreme Court has recognized several property interests in what Reich would call government largess, beginning with welfare benefits in *Goldberg* v. *Kelly*, 397 U.S. 254 (1970), not every economic interest of vital concern to citizens has received legal protection. One obstacle to legal recognition of such interests is the traditional property distinction between vested rights and expectancies. A **vested right** is fixed and absolute, a right that is no longer contingent on the fulfillment of any conditions, whereas an **expectancy** is a hope or expectation that is contingent on the fulfillment of conditions or is contingent on the will or benevolence of an individual (or the government). If an uncle makes a bequest to you in his will, you have nothing but an expectancy as long as your uncle remains alive; he could change his will or dispose of all his property, thus defeating your expectation of receiving his property. Conversely, if your employer promises to pay you a retirement benefit on your completion of twenty years of continuous employment, your right to the retirement benefit becomes vested after the completion of twenty years of service. That benefit is your property, even if you do not choose to retire immediately. If, however, you leave the company before completing twenty years of service, you have no property right because the right had not vested at the time of your termination from employment. The retirement benefits remain an expectancy until the required conditions are fulfilled.

In the following case, the plaintiffs, retirees, argue that their right to a cost-of-living adjustment is an **entitlement,** a right to benefits that may not be abridged without due process, or a vested property right that may not be taken without just compensation. The court, however, must determine whether that benefit is an entitlement or a mere expectancy.

CASE

Harry H. Zucker et al. v. The United States et al.
United States Court of Appeals
Federal Circuit (1985)
758 F.2d 637

BISSELL, Circuit Judge.   This is an appeal from a decision of the United States District Court for the Southern District of New York, 578 F.Supp. 1239, granting the appellees' motion for summary judgment. The appellants challenged the constitutionality of a statute that modified the cost-of-living adjustment (COLA) for civil service annuitants. We affirm.

Background

The appellant retirees receive benefits under the Civil Service Retirement Act, now codified in 5 U.S.C. §§8331-8348. In 1962 Congress amended the Civil Service retirement Act to provide an automatic COLA based on the change in the price index. In 1969, section 8340(b) was amended by Pub.L. No. 91-93, 83 Stat. 139 (1969) to provide for 1% to be added on top of the COLA ("1% add-on"). In October 1976, Congress amended section 8340(b) by rescinding the 1% add-on and by decreasing the frequency of the COLA calculation.

After exhausting their administrative remedies, the retirees filed suit in the district court. Appellants Zucker and Sapienza, who retired prior to the 1976 amendment, claimed that that amendment retroactively and unconstitutionally diminished their vested property right in retirement benefits. The other two appellants, Acker and Corcoran, who retired after the 1976 amendment, joined the first two in challenging the constitutionality of the 1976 amendment on the grounds that it violated their property rights without due process of law.

The district court determined that the retirees did not have a constitutionally protected property interest in future COLA benefits. The court also determined they had no contractual right to the benefits.

On appeal, the retirees continue to press their constitutional claims.

Opinion

Although appellants and appellees have briefed their arguments in terms of the retirees' degree of entitlement to retirement benefits in gross, the issue before us is much narrower. The question is whether a retiree has a constitutionally protected right to receive a COLA in successive years after retirement based on the COLA formula in effect on the date he retired.

I. The retirees argue that their right to future annuity benefits calculated under the 1969 COLA formula is constitutionally protected and that any change to the COLA formula which results in a decrease in their rate of increase is violative of the due process clause.

It is well settled that potential retirees have no protected property interest in any particular level of retirement benefits as they have no legitimate claim of entitlement to benefits which are subject to lawful change.

To have a property interest in a benefit protected by procedural due process, a person must have a legitimate claim of entitlement to the benefit. *Board of Regents* v. *Roth*, 408 U.S. 564, 577, 92 S.Ct. 2701, 2709, 33 L.Ed.2d 548 (1972). "Property interests, of course, are not created by the Constitution. Rather, they are created and their dimensions are defined by existing rules or understandings that stem from an independent source...." *Id.*

The key words are "claim of entitlement." Although the retirees may have a protected property interest when they are entitled to immediate payment under preexisting law *i.e.*, the payment of an annuity upon retirement, their entitlement to any post-retirement increases in that annuity stems from the independent source that creates and defines their property interest in same, *i.e.*, the COLA provision of the Civil Service Retirement Act, 5 U.S.C. § 8340. Until a retiree becomes eligible to receive a particular COLA, his or her right to that adjustment is subject to any lawful changes made to the section from which the claim to entitlement arises.

Further, legislative acts adjusting the burdens and benefits of economic life have "a presumption of constitutionality, and... the burden is on one complaining of a due process violation to establish that the legislature has acted in an arbitrary and irrational way." *Usery* v. *Turner Elkorn Mining Co.*, 428 U.S. 1, 15, 96 S.Ct. 2882, 2892, 49 L.Ed.2d 752 (1976). These retirees have not carried their burden since they have not demonstrated that the Act was arbitrary or irrational.

II. The employees who retired before the COLA formula changed also assert a vested property right to the 1% add-on provision protected by the takings clause. They maintain that the COLA is a form of deferred compensation and, alternatively, that they have a contractual interest which amounts to a compensable property interest. While the government concedes that the retirees have an economic interest in future COLA benefit levels, it argues that their interest does not rise to the level of property protected by the takings clause.

A. The retirees argue that their property right derives from their statutory entitlement to retirement benefits, a form of deferred compensation. They assert Congress is without power to diminish their retirement benefits because the Civil Service Retirement Act contains no clause reserving such power. Thus, they conclude that since the COLA is part of their entitled retirement benefits Congress cannot diminish their COLA.

The legislative history lends some support to the view that the basic annuity was intended as deferred compensation. Similarly, there is case law that can be construed to support a concept of deferred compensation.

This court does not reach the question of the compensatory nature of the basic annuity to which the retiree becomes entitled upon retirement. Our ruling is strictly limited to post-retirement COLA benefits.

The retirees cite *United States* v. *Larionoff*, 431 U.S. 864, 97 S.Ct. 2150, 53 L.Ed.2d 48 (1977), as authority for a protected property interest in compensation due "for services already performed, but still owing." *Id.* at 879, 97 S.Ct. at 2159. Although the government in *Larionoff* was required to pay the special reenlistment bonus to service members who had become entitled to it before the statute authorizing it was repealed, the government was not required to provide that benefit prospectively. Likewise, the government here is not required to continue to provide a particular COLA benefit. To hold otherwise would fly in the face of well-established doctrines of federal employment. Generally, as in this case, federal workers serve by appointment, and their rights are therefore a matter of "legal status" even where compacts are made. In other words, their entitlement to retirement benefits must be determined by reference to the statute and regulations governing these benefits, rather than to ordinary contract principles. "Applying th[is] doctrine[], courts have consistently refused to give effect to government-fostered expectations that, had they arisen in the private sector, might well have formed the basis for a contract or estoppel." *Kizas* v. *Webster,* 707 F.2d 524, 535. Even if we had held that the retirement benefits (including COLA formulas) are an incident of employee compensation to which the employees have an indefeasible right, *Kizas* v. *Webster*, 707 F.2d at 536, the COLA portion until received by way of an increased annuity is nothing more than a "government-fostered expectation" that retirees will be provided retirement annuities which will not be ravaged by inflation. Such an "expectation" does not rise to the level of "property" protected by the takings clause.

B. The retirees assert that because 5 U.S.C. §8334 required payments of their own money into the Civil Service Retirement and Disability Fund, which payments they say were tantamount to premiums in an insurance program, a contract implied in fact arose. They argue that a contract is private property for purposes of the takings clause, and that a unilateral change in their entitlement under the alleged contract is a taking of that property.

There may be some language in the cases to support the claim of a contract with respect to the basic annuity. As indicated above, however, we deal here only with post-retirement COLA benefits, not with whether the retirees have a right, contractual or otherwise, to their basic annuity.

The retirees have cited no case law holding and no legislative history declaring that retired federal civil servants such as themselves have a contractual right to COLA increases after they retire. In short, the retirees have not persuaded us that the government is contractually bound to continue to provide COLA increases subsequent to retirement.

III. We have carefully reviewed the record and have considered the retirees' other arguments which we conclude are not persuasive. Accordingly, we affirm the decision of the district court granting summary judgment in favor of the appellees.

Affirmed.

FOR DISCUSSION

1. According to the court, what is the source of property interests?

2. Does the court seriously question whether the retirees have a protected property right in their basic retirement annuity? If not, what is the focus of their concern?

3. In the decision, the court concedes that the legislation establishing the COLA and the 1% add-on created an expectation in retired federal employees that their retirement annuities would not be greatly diminished by inflation. Why does this expectation not rise to the level of a property right?

4. The court accepts the premise that the affected employees have an economic interest in future COLA benefits but is not willing to give that interest legal protection by calling it property. Would Charles Reich agree with this decision? Support your answer.

5. The discussion in this case draws a clear distinction between "vested rights" and "expectancies" or "contingent benefits." Who benefits by such a distinction? If the overriding purpose of bestowing the benefit were to provide "a secure minimum basis for individual well-being in a society where each man cannot be the master of his own destiny" (Reich), would this distinction be necessary?

LEGAL TERMS TO KNOW

adverse possession	personal property
chattels	police power
eminent domain	quiet enjoyment
entitlement	real property
escheat	tangible property
expectancy	title
intangible property	vested right
interest	zoning
nuisance	

ADDITIONAL QUESTIONS AND EXERCISES

1. How have your views of property changed after reading the materials in this chapter? How do you think property has changed over time? Use the readings and the cases as examples.

2. Write an essay in which you describe the relationship between property and liberty. Is your view of the matter closer to Locke or to Reich?

3. Based on your understanding of the cases and readings in this chapter, write an essay in which you explain what gives a thing or an interest **value**. Does the law always protect things according to the value they have for the person who owns them? Use cases you have read as an example.

4. As the concept of "property" has changed and expanded over time, people have been confronted with the possibility that any valuable interest could be called property, which would make the term "property" meaningless, as well as make it impossible to protect all species of property equally. The response to this problem has been to say that property is whatever the law (mainly legislative) says it is and to let the determination of what is or is not property rest on the demands of public policy. How does this solution correspond to your ideas of what the law is and what role it should play in society? How do you think Bentham would respond to this? How would Reich respond?

5. Reich discusses the distinction between "rights" and "privileges." Explain how you would classify each of the following: a college education, social security benefits, a tenured civil service job, affordable health care. After having read both Reich's essay and the cases in this chapter, how do you think the present legal classification of these items differs from your classification?

FOR FURTHER READING

1. HOLMES, JR., OLIVER WENDELL, "The Bailee at Common Law" and "Possession" in *The Common Law*, Mark DeWolfe Howe, ed., Boston: Little, Brown, 1963, pp. 130–194.

2. RADIN, MARGARET J., Property and Personhood, *Stan. L.Rev.* 34 (1982), pp. 957–1015.

3. SCOTT, WILLIAM B, *In Pursuit of Happiness: American Conceptions of Property from the Seventeenth to the Twentieth Century*, Bloomington: University Press, Indiana 1977.

4. VAN ALSTYNE, WILLIAM W., "Cracks in the 'New Property': Adjudicative Due Process in the Administrative State," *Cornell L.Rev.* 62 (1977), pp. 445–493.

5. VANDEVELDE, KENNETH J. "The New Property of the Nineteenth Century: The Development of the Modern Concept of Property," *Buffalo L. Rev.* 29 (1980), pp. 325–367.

7

CONTRACTS

INTRODUCTION

A contract is a promissory agreement between two or more parties that creates a legally enforceable obligation to do or not do a particular thing. Traditionally, its essentials include competent parties, subject matter, a legal consideration, mutuality of agreement, and mutuality of consideration.

If that definition seems a bit complicated and intimidating at first, you can be assured that you are not alone in that feeling. Contracts is not considered a "user–friendly" subject by most people. In fact, classical contract law is an extensive, complex, highly abstract body of doctrine in which, it sometimes seems, the odds of anyone doing it all correctly and successfully seem very small indeed. And yet, ordinary people make and perform contracts successfully nearly every day of their lives without even thinking about it very much. They buy goods, obtain insurance policies, have their house painted or their lawn mowed, go to the doctor—all these routine activities involve contracts and, like everyone else, we only become aware of the underlying body of doctrine and rules when things go wrong.

Most people are likely to say that contracts are not only necessary but a good thing. Contracts have come to have an almost mystical significance in our legal system. Just as private property promises to ensure our liberty and provides the means of acting as we please with a minimum of interference from others, contract embodies similar guarantees: the freedom to make the agreements that seem good to us, individual liberty, the right to acquire, maintain, and transfer wealth. In the nineteenth century Sir Henry Maine, in his treatise *Ancient Law*, declared that the hallmark of civilized, progressive society is the transition from relationships based on status to those based on contract. That reflects a great expansion of opportunity. It is no longer who you are (or who your family is) that counts; rather, it is what you can do, in collaboration with others, that determines your ability to be successful.

Contracts create wealth and maximize efficient use of resources, encourage both cooperation and competition, and give people the opportunity to act in their own best interest—take risks, make gains, exercise their freedom.

Conversely, all this freedom and opportunity brings with it certain dangers. The parties with whom we contract may be smarter than we are, or more powerful, or more farsighted. Some of the agreements we make may not turn out to benefit us after all. If I agree to deliver goods to you six months from now at what seems a very favorable price at the time, I may find that in the meantime the market has changed and that my contract price is too low to be profitable at the time I have to deliver. At that point I may deeply regret my bargain and wish to get out of it. You, conversely, will have every reason to want to hold me to it. The law of contracts provides a system of rules, and intervention by the state to both make and enforce them, that will give us possibilities and also impose limits on how we may deal with our situation.

People who make contracts that are unsatisfactory or unsuccessful often discover that the world of contracts is a tough and uncompromising one. Classical contract law is an arena where people play "hardball" according to a complicated set of rules that generally favors the strong and the experienced. It is probably no coincidence that the formulations of classical contract law doctrine in England and the United States occurred in societies that had just encountered Darwin and his idea of the "survival of the fittest," and that were intensively engaged in expansion of industry and commerce, exploration, conquest, and exploitation of new territories, and acquisition and accumulation of enormous material wealth. The people engaged in these activities believed firmly in freedom of contract. They wanted no limitation on their capacity to act in pursuit of their goals, and they believed as well that freedom of contract benefited society as a whole. Today we are less willing to accept many of the harsh results classical contract law mandates in support of freedom of contract and recognize more general, socially imposed duties that temper the harsh results: We are more concerned about the relative bargaining power of the parties to contracts, about third parties who are affected by contracts yet have no recourse, about people who make voluntary agreements that do not fit the rigid formal requirements of contract law. Indeed, it has been said that contract law is in the process of being swallowed up by the law of tort and that it will not be missed. Several of the readings in this chapter debate the question of whether contract law is dead, and whether, if it is still alive, it can be looked on in the same way as it was in the past.

The requirements for the formation of a legally valid contract are: (1) an **offer**; (2) an **acceptance**; (3) **competent parties** who have the legal capacity to make a contract; (4) lawful **subject matter**; (5) **mutuality of agreement**; (6) **consideration**; and (7) **mutuality of obligation**. In addition there may be a requirement that the contract be in writing if that is required by statute. All of these elements are illustrated to some extent in the cases and readings that follow.

The contracting process goes through several distinct stages: **formation** (which may be preceded by **negotiation**); **performance** (which will be the end of the process if both parties perform as agreed); **breach** (when one or more parties do not perform as agreed); and **remedy** (which will be a judicial remedy in the event that one or more of the parties turns to the legal system for relief). We must remember that not all contracts that are breached end up being the basis of lawsuits. In a great many cases the parties work matters out for themselves and salvage the transaction as best they can. This is particularly the case when contracting parties have an interest in a long-term relationship with one another. After all, the adversarial proceedings in a lawsuit are not conducive to continued good relations between the parties.

Despite the prevalence of contracts in our lives, most people know little about them. For example, most people assume that contracts must be written, although in actual fact only certain contracts must be written to be enforceable. There are several types of contracts with which you need to be familiar to get the most out of the readings and cases in this chapter. Contracts may be either **express** or **implied**. They may be **bilateral** or **unilateral**. They may be **executory** or **executed**.

An **express contract** is one whose existence and terms are clearly manifested by the parties. Express contracts may be oral or written. **Implied contracts** are those whose existence and terms are not clearly manifested but which are implied by the actions of the parties. The parties to an express contract create the legal obligations involved by their agreement; conversely, the legal obligations of an implied contract are imposed externally by operation of law.

A **bilateral contract** is a two-sided contract, because each party to the contract makes a promise to the other. It is the exchange of mutual, reciprocal promises. In the case of a **unilateral contract**, only one party makes a promise, which the other party can accept by performing a requested action.

An **executory contract** is one that is not yet completed because some act or other promise has yet to be performed. An **executed contract** is one that is completed; there is nothing left to be done to accomplish the agreement.

An underlying assumption of contract is that agreements are mutual and voluntary. In reality, however, there are several factors that may adversely affect a party's ability to consent freely to a contract. Several of these factors, such as lack of capacity, mistake, fraud, or duress, are discussed in the following materials. Another factor that affects the reality of consent to an agreement has to do with the relative bargaining power of the parties. If one party has a great deal more power than the other, the result may be an extremely one-sided contract that unfairly favors the more powerful party. Such exploitative contracts may be unenforceable because they are **unconscionable**, that is, so unfair and one-sided that no informed person would ever freely agree to them. (Unconscionability is discussed in more detail in Chapter 9.)

Breach-of-contract lawsuits involve a great range of disputes that may focus on flaws in any of the elements of contract or any of the stages of the contracting process. Sometimes the very existence of a contract is disputed. In other cases, there may be disputes about the meaning of the terms of the contract or whether the parties have performed as agreed. The nature of these disputes may determine what sort of **remedy** the injured party is seeking. The commonest remedy in contract law remains **damages**, and the traditional measure of damages seeks to compensate the injured party by putting him in as good a position as he would have been had the contract been performed. Other possible remedies include specific performance, reformation, and restitution. (These will be dealt with in more detail in Chapter 10.)

FORMATION OF CONTRACT

At the heart of classical contract law is the idea of contract as an exchange of promises. This central notion of contract as promise has been under attack in recent years. In the following excerpt Charles Fried, Carter Professor of General Jurisprudence at Harvard, and solicitor general of the United States during the Reagan administration, defends the idea of contract as promise against its modern attackers. You should pay particular attention to the author's underlying assumptions: Why is it important to Fried that the notion of promise remain central to the law of contract? What makes the idea of promise so special and worthy of protection?

READING   **The Life of Contract**
                                        *Charles Fried**

The promise principle, which in this book I argue is the moral basis of contract law, is that principle by which persons may impose upon themselves obligations where none existed before.

Security of the person, stability of property, and the obligation of contract were for David Hume the bases of a civilized society. Hume expressed the liberal, individualistic temper of his time and place in treating respect for person, property, and contract as the self-evident foundations of law and justice. Through the greater part of our history, our constitutional law and politics have proceeded on these same premises. In private law particularly these premises have taken root and ramified in the countless particulars necessary to give them substance. The law of property defines the boundaries of our rightful possessions, while the law of torts seeks to make us whole against violations of those boundaries, as well as against violations of the natural boundaries of our physical person. Contract law ratifies and enforces our joint ventures beyond those boundaries. Thus the law of torts and the law of property recognize our rights as individuals in our persons, in our labor, and in some definite portion of the external world, while the law of contracts facilitates our disposing of these rights on terms that seem best to us. The regime of contract law, which respects the dispositions individuals make of their rights, carries to its natural conclusion the liberal premise that individuals have rights. And the will theory of contract, which sees contractual obligations as essentially self-imposed, is a fair implication of liberal individualism.

This conception of contractual obligation as essentially self-imposed has been under increasing pressure over the last fifty years. One essentially historicist line of attack points out that until the eighteenth century communal controls, whether of families, guilds, local communities, or of the general government, hardly conceded enough discretion to individuals over their labor or property to give the liberal conception much to work on. And beginning in the last century and proceeding apace since, the state, unions, corporations, and other intermediate institutions have again withdrawn large areas of concern from individual control and thus from the scope of purely contractual arrangements. That there has been such an ebb and flow of collective control seems fairly clear. But from the fact that contract emerged only in modern times as a principal form of social organization, it does not follow that therefore the concept of contract as promise (which is indeed a centerpiece of nineteenth century economic liberalism) was itself the invention of the industrial revolution; whatever the accepted scope for contract, the principle of fidelity to one's word is an ancient one. Still less does it follow that the validity, the rightness of the promise principle, of self-imposed obligation, depended on its acceptance in that earlier period, or that now, as the acceptance is in doubt, the validity of the principle is under a cloud. The validity of a moral, like that of a mathematical truth, does not depend on fashion or favor.

A more insidious set of criticisms denies the coherence or the independent viability of the promise principle. Legal obligation can be imposed only by the community, and so in imposing it the community must be pursuing its goals and imposing its standards, rather than neutrally endorsing those of the contracting parties. These lines of attack—found recently in the writings of legal scholars such as Patrick Atiyah, Lawrence Friedman, Grant Gilmore, Morton Horwitz, Duncan Kennedy, Anthony Kronman, and Ian Macneil, as well as in philosophical writings—will provide the foil for much of my affirmative argument. Here I shall just set out their main thrust so that my readers may be clear what I am reacting against.

Not all promises are legally enforced, and of those which are, different categories receive differing degrees of legal recognition: some only if in writing, others between certain kinds of parties, still others only to the extent that they have been relied on and that reliance has caused measurable injury. And some arrangements that are not promissory at all—preliminary negotiations, words mistakenly understood as promises, schemes of cooperation—are assimilated to the contractual regime. Finally, even among legally binding arrangements that are initiated by agreement, certain ones are singled out and made subject to a set of rules that often have little to do with that agreement. Marriage is the most obvious example, but contracts of employment, insurance, or carriage exhibit these features as well. Thus the conception of the will binding itself—the conception at the heart of the promise principle—is neither necessary nor sufficient to contractual obligation. Indeed it is a point of some of these critics (for example, Friedman, Gilmore, Macneil) that the search for a central or unifying principle of contract is a will-o'-the-wisp, an illusion typical of the ill-defined but much excoriated vice of conceptualism. These critics hold that the law fashions contractual obligation as a way to do justice between, and impose social policy through, parties who have come into a variety of relations with each other. Only some of these relations start in an explicit agreement, and even if they do, the governing considerations of justice and policy are not bound by the terms or implications of that agreement.

Though the bases of contract law on this view are as many and as shifting as the politics of the judicial and legislative process, two quite general considerations of justice have figured prominently in the attack on the conception of contract as promise: benefit and reliance. The benefit principle holds that where a person has received a benefit at another's expense and that other has acted reasonably and with no intention of making a gift, fairness requires that the benefit be returned or paid for. I discuss this idea in detail in subsequent chapters. Here I shall make my point by the more pervasive notion of reliance. Proceeding from a theme established in Lon Fuller and William Perdue's influential 1936 article, a number of writers have argued that often what is taken as enforcement of a promise is in reality the compensation of an injury sustained by the plaintiff because he relied on the defendant's promise. At first glance the distinction between promissory obligation and obligation based on reliance may seem too thin to notice, but indeed large theoretical and practical matters turn on that distinction. To enforce a promise as such is to make the defendant render a performance (or its money equivalent) just because he has promised that very thing. The reliance view, by contrast, focuses on an injury suffered by the plaintiff and asks if the defendant is somehow sufficiently responsible for that injury that he should be made to pay compensation.

The latter basis of liability, the compensation of injury suffered through reliance, is a special case of tort liability. For the law of torts is concerned with just the question of compensation for harm caused by another: physical harm caused by willful or negligent conduct, pecuniary harm caused by careless or deceitful representations, injury to reputation caused by untrue statements. Now tort law typically deals with involuntary transactions—if a punch in the nose, a traffic accident, or a malicious piece of gossip may be called a transaction—so that the role of the community in adjudicating the conflict is particularly prominent: What is a safe speed on a rainy evening, what may a former employer say in response to a request for a reference? In contrast, so long as we see contractual obligation as based on promise, on obligations that the parties have themselves assumed, the focus of the inquiry is on the will of the parties. If we assimilate contractual obligation to the law of torts, our focus shifts to the injury suffered by the plaintiff and to the fairness of saddling the defendant with some or all of it. So, for instance, if there has been no palpable injury because the promisee has not yet relied on the promise there seems to be nothing to compensate, while at other times a generalized standard of fair compensation may move us to go beyond anything that the parties have agreed. The promise and its sequelae are seen as a kind of encounter, like a traffic accident or a street altercation or a journalistic exchange, giving rise to losses to be apportioned by the community's sense of fairness. This assimilation of contract to tort is (and for writers like Gilmore, Horwitz, and Atiyah is intended to be) the subordination of a quintessentially individualist ground for obligation and form of social control, one that refers to the will of the parties, to a set of standards that are ineluctactably collective in origin and thus readily turned to collective ends.

Another line of attack on contract as promise denies the coherence of the central idea of self-imposed obligation. Some writers argue that obligation must always be imposed from outside. Others work from within: For promissory obligations to be truly self-imposed, the promise must have been freely given. If this means no more than that the promisor acted intentionally, then even an undertaking in response to a gunman's threat is binding. If, as we must, we insist that there be a *fair* choice to promise or not, we have imported external standards of fairness into the very heart of the obligation after all. Having said, for instance, that a promise to pay an exorbitant price for a vital medicine is not freely undertaken, while a promise to pay a reasonable price is, why not dispense with the element of promise altogether and just hold that there is an obligation to supply the medicine at an externally fixed price to all who need it? This and more subtle related suggestions have been put forward by writers who are particularly concerned about the connection between contract as promise and the market as a form of economic organization. Some like Robert Hale, Duncan Kennedy and Anthony Kronman see in the concepts of duress and unconscionability the undoing of the arguments for the free market and for the autonomy of contract law. Others, most particularly Richard Posner, also denying any independent force to promissory obligation, derive such force as the law gives to contracts from social policies such as wealth maximization and efficiency, which are usually associated with the operation of the market.

I begin with a statement of the central conception of contract as promise. This is my version of the classical view of contract proposed by the will theory and implicit in the assertion that contract offers a distinct and compelling ground of obligation. In subsequent chapters I show how this conception generates the structure and accounts for the complexities of contract doctrine. Contract law is complex, and it is easy to lose sight of its essential unity. The adherents of the "Death of Contract" school have been left too free rein to exploit these complexities. But exponents of the view I embrace have often adopted a far more rigid approach than the theory of contract as promise requires. For instance, they have typically tended to view contractual liability as an exclusive principle of fairness, as if relief had to be either based on a promise or denied altogether. These rigidities and excesses have also been exploited as if they proved the whole conception of contract as promise false. In developing my affirmative thesis I show why classical theory may have betrayed itself into such errors, and I propose to perennial conundrums solutions that accord with the idea of contract as promise and with decency and common sense as well.

NOTES

*From *Contract as Promise: A Theory of Contractual Obligation* (Cambridge, Mass.: Harvard University Press, 1981), pp. 1–6. Reprinted with permission, © 1981 by The President and Fellows of Harvard College.

FOR DISCUSSION

1. After reading this essay, how would you define Fried's conception of a "promissory obligation"?
2. Describe the "historicist" position against the conception of self-imposed contractual obligation.
3. Explain the social- or community-oriented position against voluntarily assumed contractual obligations.
4. How have the ideas of benefit and reliance worked against the notion of contract as promise?
5. According to Fried, what makes contract essentially different from tort?
6. Fried is concerned to preserve the idea of contract as a free expression of the will of the individual. Why might this seem problematic in the contemporary world? Can you think of any forces that seem to be opposing this conception?
7. Based on your own experience, do you consider most contractual obligations to be freely assumed? Can you give examples?
8. Given the contemporary meaning of these terms, would you describe Fried's position as a liberal or a conservative one? Explain.

Preliminary Negotiations, and Agreements to Make a Contract or Agree on Terms

Before a contract can be made, the prospective parties have to communicate with one another about the subject matter and possible terms of their agreement. The parties have to be able to ascertain whether the other is interested, whether the goods or services are available, whether the price is acceptable, whether delivery can be made at an acceptable time, and many other things. During this stage of preliminary negotiations, it is possible that one of the parties may conclude that agreement has been reached, whereas the other does not. If negotiations break off at that stage, the one party may sue the second party to enforce the contract that has allegedly been made.

The traditional position has always been that no contract exists until both parties fully agree—until there has been what is called "a meeting of the minds." Conversely, some people argue that when it looks to an outsider as if a contract has been reached, then it exists irrespective of what the parties believe. Contemporary contract law tries to find a middle ground between a subjective, "will"-oriented view and a totally objective one. There is concern to know what the parties thought and meant, but there is an equal need to examine what they have actually said and done, and measure that against some external standard of reasonableness and ordinary behavior.

The central issue, therefore, in determining whether the negotiation process has led to the formation of a legally binding contract is whether the parties have, in some objectively discernible way, manifested their intent to be bound. If they have, there is a contract. If not, there is no contract. For a decision maker called on to determine whether parties have legally bound themselves on the basis of their negotiations, two basic questions need to be answered: (1) Have the parties, through their words and actions, manifested an intent to be legally bound? (2) If the parties have manifested an intent to be bound, to what have they bound themselves? If the judge cannot answer yes to the first question and give a clear and definite answer to the second, then no contract has yet been formed.

Offer and Acceptance

When people communicate with one another in the course of negotiating a contract, they often may not fully understand one another. This is true in face to face negotiations, and is even more true when the parties communicate back and forth in writing. The language and behavior they use constitute a series of symbols that have to be interpreted. In the law of contract, a set of rules has grown up over time to define what legal meaning certain behavioral and linguistic symbols will have. If a contract is to be concluded, eventually preliminary negotiations will lead to one party making an **offer**, which the other party may **accept**. If the offer communicated is accepted, then the terms of the offer will constitute the terms of the contract.

But what is an offer? And how does one know if an offer has been accepted? In the following essay, the author attempts to explain and illustrate the problems that underlie this type of communication and the legal solutions that have developed in response to those problems.

READING   **The Language of Offer and Acceptance:**
Speech Acts and the Question of Intent.
Peter M. Tiersma*

Language and law interact in a number of ways, the most obvious of which is that laws are expressed in language. Lawyers often look at language to determine the meaning of specific statutes. In such a relatively artificial context, words are chosen and interpreted with unusual care. But elsewhere, the law must interpret utterances of a more spontaneous sort, where the actual meaning of a word or phrase is not always found in a standard dictionary or a grammar text. This especially holds true when the law must give legal effect to the utterances of private individuals. The interpretation of private utterances is an important part of contract law, particularly in the area of offer and acceptance. Courts attempt to discover whether the parties have assented to an agreement by examining their words and deeds. There is no standard verbal formula or prescribed conduct which invariably signifies assent. On the contrary, the case law suggests a great variety of ways to reach agreement.

This Comment makes two main points. The first is that offer and acceptance are not matters of *expression* or *manifestation* of intent. Rather, they are *acts* that commit the speaker to a particular course of conduct. The second major point is that although the intent of the speaker does not create the obligation, it is nonetheless necessary that the act be accompanied by a certain state of mind. Loosely stated, the speaker must intend to create in the hearer the perception that in saying the words, the speaker is committing himself to a particular proposal....

I. THE NATURE OF THE PROBLEM

The difficulty pervading the concepts of offer and acceptance is that there is no simple relationship between the use of the words "offer" or "accept" and legal obligation. This is not necessarily so in all areas of legal commitment. In some situations a speaker may be legally bound only if he utters a predetermined formula. During the wedding ceremony, for example, the bride and groom can commit themselves to one another by saying "I do," "with this ring I thee wed," or perhaps, merely "yes."

While at one time the common law demanded specific formulas to achieve particular legal effects, today an offer does not require any particular incantation. In fact, there are cases in which use of the word "offer" does not result in a legally binding offer. For example, in *Moulton* v. *Kershaw* (59 Wis. 316, 18 N.W. 172 [1884]) the seller wrote: "We are authorized to offer Michigan fine salt, in full car-load lots of eighty to ninety-five [barrels], delivered at your city, at 85 [cents] per [barrel].... Shall be pleased to receive your order." Despite the presence of the word "offer," the Supreme Court of Wisconsin held that this letter was not a legally binding commitment, in large part because the seller had not indicated how much salt was available. Similarly, the use of the word "offer" in "We offer the lowest prices on stereo equipment in town" would probably not bind the advertiser to sell at a specific price.

On the other hand, there are numerous cases in which the word "offer" was not used, but courts nonetheless found a binding commitment. *Embry* v. *Hargadine, McKittrick Dry Goods Co.* (127 Mo. App. 383, 105 S.W. 777 [1907]) involved a worker whose employment contract expired at the end of the year. On December 23, he went to his boss to ask for a renewal of the contract. His employer replied, "Go ahead, you're all right; get your men out and don't let that worry you." The court held that the employer had assented to the terms of a bargain.

The crucial element is not simply the words used, but the context or circumstances in which the utterance is made. For example, a proposal or a price quotation does not usually constitute a legally binding offer. Nonetheless, some courts have found that words such as "proposal" or "quotation" are not dispositive. In *Parker* v. *Meneley* (106 Cal. App. 2d 391, 235 P.2d 101 [1951]), the court found that a form contract constituted an offer notwithstanding its use of the words "estimate" and "we propose." Similarly, the words "We quote you Mason fruit jars...Pints $4.50, quarts $5.00...for immediate acceptance," made in response to an inquiry, were deemed an offer despite the use of the word "quote."

The relationship between the word "accept" and the legal concept of acceptance is even more tenuous. The most unequivocal acceptance occurs when the offeree states "I hereby accept your offer." Yet once again, no single formula is necessary to effectuate acceptance. For instance, the words "will exercise our option to buy ... Mail deed with draft" have been held to constitute acceptance. When a definite offer has been made, responses such as "it's a deal" or "you're on" generally will suffice.

Moreover, it is now well established that the conduct of an offeree may constitute acceptance. For example, in *Gomez* v. *Federal Stevedoring Co.* (5 N.J. Super. 100, 68 A.2d 482 [1949]) a hatch boss told several men, including plaintiff Gomez, that they had a job in Brooklyn and that they should meet him there at a specific time and place. The court held that by appearing at the appointed time, Gomez had accepted the offer. The court emphasized that both words and conduct must be given the meaning that a reasonable person would attribute to them under the circumstances.

An offer may further be accepted by "silence." Since conduct is often silent as well, it is better to speak of this as acceptance by *inaction*. A well-known case illustrating this principle is *Hobbs* v. *Massasoit Whip Co.* (158 Mass. 194, 33 N.E. 495 [1893]). The plaintiff at times shipped eel skins to the defendant, who regularly paid for them. After the defendant had kept one particular shipment for a while, its warehouse burned and the skins were destroyed. The defendant claimed that it had never accepted the skins. Since the parties' previous conduct indicated that the defendant should have responded immediately if it had wished to reject the shipment, the court interpreted the defendant's inaction as acceptance.

The relationship between a legally binding offer or acceptance and the words or deeds used to express such offer or acceptance may be indirect at best. The ambiguity inherent in words and deeds has in some cases led to the notion that when such "manifestations of assent" are unclear, the intent of the party becomes relevant....

IV. INTERPRETATION

D.2. *Implication in the Bargaining Context*

There are many ways in which particular words can imply offer or acceptance in a commercial setting. *A* might offer *B* a certain sum of money to work in *A*'s office, and *B* might simply reply, "I look forward to working with you" or "When do I start?" Neither of these utterances has the direct illocutionary force[1] of acceptance, but they imply in these circumstances the equivalent of "I hereby accept your offer."

Fairmount Glass Works v. *Crunden-Martin Wooden Ware Co* (106 Ky. 659, 51 S.W. 196 [1899]) is a case involving implied assent. The buyer wrote the seller asking for the lowest price on ten carloads of Mason green jars. The seller wrote back, "Replying to your favor of April 20th, we quote you Mason fruit jars ... Pints, $4.50; quarts, $5.00 ... for immediate acceptance." The buyer ordered ten carloads, which the seller refused to provide. Even though price quotations usually do not constitute offers, the court decided that the seller's reply was indeed a definite offer to sell.

Superficially, the seller did nothing more than respond to a request for information, the literal meaning of the language gave no indication that there was a bargain between two parties. In a commercial context, however, a request for a price presupposes some interest in buying. This implication was even stronger in *Fairmount* because the buyer specifically asked for the lowest price on a specific number of jars. The request was roughly equivalent to: (1) "We wish to buy ten carloads of Mason fruit jars"; (2) "What is your lowest price?" A relevant answer would speak to both issues. A seller who did not wish to sell would have answered, "No Mason fruit jars for sale," rebuffing the buyer's attempt to buy and rendering the question of price irrelevant. The seller, however, did not respond directly to the buyer's implicit request to purchase ten carloads of jars. Therefore, the buyer was justified in interpreting the seller's price quotation as relevant to the implicit request and could infer that the seller was making an offer.

In the English case *Harvey* v. *Facey* (1893 A.C. 552), the buyer telegraphed the seller, asking, "Will you sell us Bumper Hall Pen? Telegraph lowest cash price." The seller responded, "Lowest price for Bumper Hall Pen £900." The buyer then accepted what it considered to be an offer to sell. These facts parallel *Fairmount*, except that the purchaser's desire to buy was explicit, rather than implied. The court nevertheless concluded that the seller's response was not an offer because the seller had failed to answer the question regarding whether it would sell Bumper Hall Pen. It is perhaps dangerous to impose an anachronistic interpretation upon facts which occurred almost a century ago and which may have turned upon particular trade conventions. But if such an interchange took place today, the seller's response would probably be viewed as an offer.

It is useful to consider the proper response had the seller not intended to make an offer. The seller should then have made clear that its response addressed only the question of price, and that it was preserving its options regarding a possible sale. If the seller did not wish to sell under any circumstances, it should have said so explicitly or have not answered at all. There are two logical interpretations of the seller's silence on the question of whether it

---

[1]In an earlier section of this article the author explained that in John Searle's philosophy of language, speech acts consist of two types: propositional acts and illocutionary acts. Illocutionary acts have to do with expressing the intent of a speaker with respect to the proposition he/she makes in a statement. Illocutionary acts include asking, asserting and commanding. The illocutionary force of a statement is significant in determining whether a speaker is committing him/herself to something, such as: "I promise to fix your fence tomorrow."

wished to sell: (1) the seller did not answer the question; or (2) the seller's quotation of a lowest acceptable price implied an offer to sell. Grice's cooperative principle states that if one bothers to reply at all, the response must be relevant to the question posed. The seller's communication is relevant only if the price quotation is an actual offer.

Compare these cases to *Owen* v. *Tunison* (131 Me. 42, 158 A. 926 [1932]), in which the buyer asked whether the seller would be willing to sell its store property for $6000. The seller responded, "[I]t would not be possible for me to sell it unless I was to receive $16,000.00 cash." As in *Harvey*, the seller quoted a minimum price which one assumes was higher than what he actually expected to receive. Yet in answer to the question regarding whether he would sell, he used the conditional phrases "it would" and "unless I was." This answer is ambiguous; the [seller] either could have been implying that he would sell if he received $16,000, or that he was uncertain that he would sell even at that price. Either response would be relevant to the question. The court's decision that this response was not an unequivocal offer was therefore justified, since it is not clear that by these words the potential [seller] was committing himself to the proposed bargain.

Some courts have explicitly refused to acknowledge that indirect acts can have the force of offer or acceptance. The seller in *Nebraska Seed Co.* v. *Harsh* (98 Neb. 89, 152 N.W. 310 [1915]) sent a seed sample to the buyer with the words "I want $2.25 per cwt. for this seed." Holding that this communication amounted to preliminary negotiations rather than an offer, the court explained that the seller "[did] not say I offer to sell it to you." However, the lack of the formula "I offer to sell it to you" is not the problem in this case. The real problem is the lack of the formula or *equivalent language* committing the seller to the proposed bargain. One indication that the seller's communication does not have the force of an offer is the incomplete propositional content—there is no indication of how much seed is available. A businessman probably would not commit himself to so nebulous a bargain. In addition, the supposed offer does not contain or imply the presence of a "you." Even if it were clear that the seller wanted to sell, it is not evident that the seller was committing himself to a specific bargain with this particular buyer.

These considerations are not definitive, but they do serve to make explicit some of the ways in which native speakers reach conclusions as to whether parties have committed themselves to a proposed bargain. What is important is to realize that these indirect ways of expressing offer and acceptance may communicate the same message as the more explicit "I hereby offer you that *p*" formula.[2] The crucial question is whether the parties, by their words or deeds, have in fact committed themselves. To the extent that the law is concerned with enforcing actual commitments of the parties, it will have to interpret the language and the actions of the parties in the same manner that the parties themselves interpret them.

NOTES

*From "The Language of Offer and Acceptance: Speech Acts and the Question of Intent," 74 *California Law Review* 189 (1986). From the article originally published in *California Law Review*, Vol. 74, No. 1, January 1986, pp. 189–232. © by *California Law Review, Inc.* Used with permission.

[2]Earlier in this article the author stated: "The most unambiguous way to indicate the force of an utterance is by means of a formula which is in the first person, present tense, and contains the word *hereby*. The force of an offer, for example, is rendered most explicit in the formula "I hereby offer you that *p*," where *p* represents the terms of the offer. Although many words, phrases, and acts may constitute offers, this Comment will argue that an utterance or act can commit the speaker only if it is the equivalent of, or expressible as, "I hereby offer you that *p*" (p. 190).

FOR DISCUSSION

1. According to the author, words alone will not tell you whether the person uttering them is making or accepting an offer. What more is needed?
2. Is it possible to accept an offer without using any words at all? How might this be done?
3. What appears to be the best way to reject an offer? Give examples from the essay of successful and not so successful rejections.
4. If someone sends you a sample of a product and says he wants a certain price for the merchandise, why isn't that an offer?
5. Do you think it would be better if the law required the "I hereby offer you that *p*" formula for a valid offer? Can you see any problems with such a requirement?
6. In the case of a dispute, who ultimately determines whether an offer or acceptance has been made? Do you think that an analysis like the one in this article would help in making that kind of decision?

Offer and **acceptance** in contract are governed by an extremely technical set of rules. These rules have a practical purpose, however, which is to create a climate in which people engaged in business can plan ahead, and predict what others will do and what the consequences of their own behavior will be. The goals of certainty, predictability, and uniformity are necessary to facilitate that process of planning and reliance.

An offer is a definite proposal to enter into a contract. An offer involves a promise by one party in exchange for a promise, act, or forbearance given by another party, who thereby accepts the offer. A legally valid offer must meet certain criteria. First, an offer must be a definite proposal. Second, that proposal must be made with the intention of committing oneself to a contract. And third, the offer must be communicated to another party in order to be effective. Since the terms of the offer will constitute the terms of the contract, the offer must be definite and certain, as well as specific enough so that the offeree can know what he or she is accepting and, in the event the offer is accepted, so that both parties will know what they have agreed to and what the nature of their obligation is.

Usually an offer needs to be directed at a specific person in order to be effective. A proposal directed at the public at large, through an advertisement, for example, is generally not considered to be a binding offer, but rather is looked upon as an invitation to negotiate or discuss terms.

A person accepts an offer when he or she expresses assent to its terms. Although there is no set formula for accepting an offer, any more than there is for making one, acceptance has to be expressed in a way that the offeror expects and can understand as acceptance. The acceptance must agree exactly with all the terms of the offer and be communicated to the offeror. A person can only accept an offer that is open: If the offer has been revoked, withdrawn, or otherwise terminated, then it cannot be accepted. Acceptance of an offer can sometimes be inferred from the offeree's action, inaction, or silence, but generally silence or inaction will not constitute acceptance of an offer unless there is a prior course of dealing that indicates that silence or inaction is, in fact, an established mode of acceptance between these contracting parties. Otherwise, silence or inaction constitutes rejection of an offer.

Other ways of rejecting an offer are by express rejection or by making a **counter-offer**. If the offeree responds to an offer by proposing changes in its terms, that is not acceptance. Rather, it is a counter-offer, which rejects the original offer and substitutes in its place. The counter-offer can then be accepted or rejected in the same way as the original offer. A person who makes an offer can put a definite time limit on the life of the offer and may also specify the exact manner in which the offer must be accepted. If those conditions are not complied with, then there is no contract.

The purpose of all these rules is to establish some external standards for ascertaining whether the parties agree and what they are agreeing to. Since no one can read another person's mind, there must be some objective manifestation of the intent to contract, and the rules of offer and acceptance are designed to accomplish that. Some of the traditional rules of offer and acceptance are regarded as too strict and have been modified by statute in various jurisdictions. The Uniform Commercial Code, for example, tolerates a greater degree of ambiguity in offer and acceptance than traditional contract law ever did, especially with respect to the definiteness of the terms of an offer.

Making a Definite Offer

The following case deals with the difference between a definite offer and a mere proposal or invitation to negotiate. In general an advertisement in a newspaper is considered to be an invitation to make an offer rather than an offer itself. If a newspaper advertisement is to be more than an invitation to make an offer, then it must specifically set out all the terms upon which the contract will be based. One way to see this distinction is to compare the average automobile dealer's advertisement with the lengthy, detailed advertisements of airline "supersaver" fares, for example.

CASE
James L. O'Keefe v. Lee Calan Imports, Inc.
Illinois Appellate Court (1970)
128 Ill. App. 2d 410, 262 N.E.2d 758, 43 A.L.R.3d 1097

McNAMARA, J.   Christopher D. O'Brien brought suit against defendant for an alleged breach of contract. O'Brien died subsequent to the filing of the lawsuit, and the administrator of his estate substituted in his stead. Field Enterprises, Inc. was joined as a third party defendant, but was dismissed from the suit, and that order of dismissal is not involved in this appeal. Plaintiff and defendant filed cross-motions for summary judgment. The court denied plaintiff's motion for summary judgment and granted defendant's motion. This appeal follows. The facts as set forth in the pleadings and cross-motions for summary judgment are not in dispute.

On July 31, 1966, defendant advertised a 1964 Volvo Station Wagon for sale in the Chicago Sun-Times. Defendant had instructed the newspaper to advertise the price of the automobile at $1,795. However, through an error of the newspaper and without fault of the part of the defendant, the newspaper inserted a price of $1,095 for said automobile in the advertisement. O'Brien visited defendant's place of business, examined the automobile and stated that he wished to purchase it for $1,095. One of defendant's salesmen at first agreed, but then refused to sell the car for the erroneous price listed in the advertisement.

Plaintiff appeals, contending that the advertisement constituted an offer on the part of defendant, which O'Brien duly accepted and thus the parties formed a binding contract. Plaintiff further contends that the advertisement constituted a memorandum in writing which satisfied the requirements of the Statute of Frauds.[3]

---

[3]The Statute of Frauds requires certain types of contracts to be in writing in order to be enforceable. Each state has its own Statute of Frauds. This rule will be dealt with in more detail later in the Chapter.

It is elementary that in order to form a contract there must be an offer and an acceptance. A contract requires the mutual assent of the parties. *Calo, Inc.* v. *AMF Pinspotters, Inc.*, 31 Ill. App. 2d 2, 176 N.E. 2d 1 (1961).

The precise issue of whether a newspaper advertisement constitutes an offer which can be accepted to form a contract or whether such an advertisement is merely an invitation to make an offer, has not yet been determined by the Illinois courts. Most jurisdictions which have dealt with the issue have considered such an advertisement as a mere invitation to make an offer, unless the circumstances indicate otherwise. As was stated in *Corbin on Contracts* §25 (1963):

> It is quite possible to make a definite and operative offer to buy or sell goods by advertisement, in a newspaper, by a handbill, or on a placard in a store window. It is not customary to do this, however; and the presumption is the other way. Neither the advertiser nor the reader of his notice understands that the latter is empowered to close the deal without further expression by the former. Such advertisements are understood to be mere requests to consider and examine and negotiate; and no one can reasonably regard them as otherwise unless the circumstances are exceptional and the words used are very plain and clear.

In *Craft* v. *Elder & Johnston Co.*, 38 N.E.2d 416 (Ohio App. 1941), defendant advertised in a local newspaper that a sewing machine was for sale at a stated price. Plaintiff visited the store, attempted to purchase the sewing machine at that price, but defendant refused. In holding that the newspaper advertisement did not constitute a binding offer, the court held that an ordinary newspaper advertisement was merely an offer to negotiate. In *Ehrlich* v. *Willis Music Co.*, 93 Ohio App. 246, 113 N.E.2d 252 (1952), defendant advertised in a newspaper that a television set was for sale at a mistaken price. The actual price was ten times the advertised price. The court found that no offer had been made, but rather an invitation to patronize defendant's store. In *Lovett* v. *Frederick Loeser & Co.*, 124 Misc. 81, 207 N.Y.S. 753 (1924), a newspaper advertisement offering radios for sale at 25% to 50% reductions was held to be an invitation to make an offer.

We find that in the absence of special circumstances, a newspaper advertisement which contains an erroneous purchase price through no fault of the defendant advertiser and which contains no other terms, is not an offer which can be accepted so as to form a contract. We hold that such an advertisement amounts only to an invitation to make an offer. It seems apparent to us in the instant case, that there was no meeting of the minds nor the required mutual assent by the two parties to a precise proposition. There was no reference to several material matters relating to the purchase of the automobile, such as equipment to be furnished or warranties to be offered by defendant. Indeed the terms were so incomplete and so indefinite that they could not be regarded as a valid offer.

In *Lefkowitz* v. *Great Minneapolis Surplus Store*, 251 Minn. 188, 86 N.W.2d 689 (1957) defendant advertised a fur stole worth $139.50 for sale at a price of $1.00, but refused to sell it to plaintiff. In affirming the judgment for plaintiff, the court found that the advertisement constituted a valid offer and, upon acceptance by plaintiff, a binding contract. However, in that case, unlike in the instant case, there was no error in the advertisement, but rather, defendant deliberately used misleading advertising. And in *Lefkowitz*, the court held that whether an advertisement was an offer or an invitation to make an offer depended upon the intention of the parties and the surrounding circumstances.

In *Johnson* v. *Capital City Ford Company*, 85 So.2d 75 (La. App. 1955), defendant advertised that anyone who purchased a 1954 automobile could exchange it for a 1955 model at no additional cost. Plaintiff purchased a 1954 automobile and subsequently attempted to exchange it for a 1955 model, but was refused by defendant. The court held that the advertisement was an offer, the acceptance of which created a contract. However, in that case, the advertisement required the performance of an act by plaintiff, and in purchasing the 1954 automobile, plaintiff performed that act. In the case at bar, the advertisement did not call for any performance by plaintiff, and we conclude that it did not amount to an offer.

Because of our view of these proceedings, it is unnecessary to consider the issue of whether the newspaper advertisement constituted a memorandum in writing satisfying the requirements of the Statute of Frauds.

Judgment affirmed.

FOR DISCUSSION

1. Suppose the advertisement in question had stated: "1964 Volvo Station Wagon. One previous owner. $1,095." Are there missing terms in this "offer"? What other matters would the prospective buyer be likely to discuss with the car dealer?

2. Given that the general rule seems to be that the seller is not bound by an inadvertent error in selling price in an advertisement, why was the *Lefkowitz* case decided differently? Do you think the outcome in that case was fair?

3. Given the facts of this case (*O'Keefe*), what exactly does the court mean when it says there was no "meeting of the minds" with respect to this transaction?

4. How is the *Johnson* case different from the situation at issue here? Do you think the defendant in that case ought to have been held to his bargain? Why?

5. Would the problem in this case have been avoided if Tiersma's "I hereby offer you that *p*" formula had been in effect? Explain.

Accepting an Offer

Generally speaking, acceptance of an offer requires express assent to its terms by the party to which the offer was directed. Silence or inaction is rarely an acceptable method of accepting an offer, but that does not prevent parties from trying to establish silence or inaction as the mode of acceptance, as the following case illustrates:

CASE   **Sandra J. Sorg v. Fred Weisz & Associates**
                            California Court of Appeal (1970)
                            14 Cal.App.3d 78, 91 Cal.Rptr. 918

FILES, Presiding Justice.   Defendant appeals from a judgment awarding plaintiff an amount which the court concluded was due under a contract. The facts are stipulated and are set forth below.

G. M. Russell and Catherine S. Russell are the owners of a 40-acre parcel of land in Los Angeles, California, 1 acre of which is leased to Paul R. McClintock. On December 26 and 27, 1967, pursuant to a purported authorization obtained from McClintock, defendant dumped approximately 15 truckloads of asphalt, concrete, and other waste material on the Russell property. The authorization in fact related only to the McClintock leasehold, 200 feet distant from the closest portion of the deposited material.

Between December 26, 1967, and February 9, 1968, the Russells informed defendant that this dumping was improper and requested removal of the waste material. On February 12 defendant received the following letter from the Russells' attorneys:

February 9, 1968

Gentlemen:

On or about December 26-27, 1967 you and your company unlawfully dumped an estimated 200-300 tons of waste and rubbish on our client's land near 135th Street and South Broadway, Los Angeles, California.

Repeated demands made on you to remove this waste and rubbish from said land have been ignored. Demand is again made on you to immediately remove this waste and rubbish from said land.

Your conduct constitutes an unlawful trespass and conversion and our client will look to you for all damages flowing therefrom. Compensation for such trespass at the rate of $150.00 per day is demanded by return remittance.

Our client is willing to grant you a revocable license to continue your storing this waste and rubbish and use of the land to the extent the same is presently being used. This revocable license is contingent upon the payment to our client of the sum of $150.00 per day for each day such use continues. Said sums are to be payable daily and any unpaid sums are to bear interest at full legal rate plus reasonable attorneys fees and all costs of collection whether or not an action that proceeds to judgment is brought.

Your continued use of the property for storing this waste and rubbish will constitute your acceptance of this revocable license.

Yours very truly,

of ROEMER AND HAMWI

Defendant did not reply to this letter until two weeks later, when in a letter dated February 26, 1968, an attorney representing defendant asserted that the dumping had been done with the permission of P. R. McClintock who (the letter stated) was then "the person in lawful possession of the premises." The letter further asserted that McClintock intended to use the asphalt and concrete as fill on his property. On March 14, 1968, however, 32 days after the receipt of the "offer" letter, defendant caused the waste material to be removed from the property in question.

It was further stipulated that the cause of action upon which the suit was brought was duly assigned to plaintiff by the Russells, that the defendant acknowledged that it did not have the right to dump the waste material on the Russell property, and that the sole issue to be determined at trial was whether plaintiff was "entitled to be compensated pursuant to the terms and conditions set forth in said letter of February 9, 1968" for the 32-day period during which the waste material was located there.

After a nonjury trial the court concluded that the February 9 letter constituted an offer of a revocable license for continued use of the Russell property, and that defendant, by its failure to remove the waste material within a reasonable time after receipt of the letter (which the court found to be four days), was "deemed to have accepted said offer," forming a contract in accordance with the terms contained therein. Judgment was entered for plaintiff under the contract, whereupon defendant prosecuted this appeal.

The tactic of attempting to create a contract by a letter stating a price, on the theory that silence and inaction would constitute an acceptance, has been consistently rejected by the courts. See *Leslie* v. *Brown Bros., Inc.* (1929) 208 Cal. 606, 621, 283 P. 936; *Russell* v. *Union Oil Co* (1970) 7 Cal.App.3d 110, 86 Cal.Rptr. 424; *Sherman* v. *Associated Telephone Co.* (1950) 100 Cal.App.2d 806, 224 P.2d 846; *Pacific States Corporation* v. *Arnold* (1914) 23 Cal.App. 672, 675, 139 P. 239. See also *Wright* v. *County of Sonoma* (1909) 156 Cal. 475, 477, 105 P. 409. The *Russell* case, *supra*, involves the same property owners as in this case, attempting to create an obligation to pay $150 per day for a telephone line placed across the Russell property.

"Silence in the face of an offer is not an acceptance, unless there is a relationship between the parties or a previous course of dealing pursuant to which silence would be understood as an acceptance." *Southern Cal. Acoustics Co.* v. *C. V. Holder, Inc* (1969) 71 Cal.2d 719, 722, 79 Cal.Rptr. 319, 322, 456 P.2d 975, 978. See also Rest., Contracts, §72.

In the case at bench there is no showing of any prior dealings or communication or any other relationship between the Russells and defendant. There is certainly no basis upon which the Russells could reasonably have concluded that defendant intended to accept the obligation to pay $150 per day. The trial court made no finding that defendant did so intend, and there was no basis for an implied finding to that effect. Rather the decision rests upon the supposed legal effect of the Russells' letter and the defendant's silence and inaction for a period in excess of four days.

The Russells attempted to construct a bilateral agreement by the fictional grant of a license "for storing waste and rubbish." Even if it could be said that defendant was using the Russell property, its silence and inaction did not constitute acceptance of the price named by the owners. In the *Russell* and *Sherman* cases, *supra*, the plaintiffs were offering to grant licenses for telephone lines already on the property; in *Pacific States*, *supra*, the plaintiff was trying to fix rent to be paid by a party already in possession; and in *Wright*, *supra*, the plaintiff was trying to fix a price for taking water. Yet in each of those cases the plaintiff's letter was held not to establish a contract price.

The case at bench is even stronger for defendant. In the cited cases the defendants were obtaining continuing benefits from the trespasses. Here the defendant dumped rubbish on the Russell land. It is a misuse of the English language to assert that defendant was "storing" this pile of broken asphalt and concrete. The plain truth was that defendant had abandoned it. Defendant's conduct was a trespass, for which reasonable damages might have been assessed upon proof of damage, but not on any pretense that a license had been sought or accepted.

The judgment is reversed.

FOR DISCUSSION

1. Does the "offer" made by the Russells conform to the "I hereby offer you that *p*" formula for a valid offer?

2. According to the court, what is the major flaw in the language of this offer? Does it conform to what defendant had actually done?

3. How might defendant have made a binding acceptance of this offer? Does the Tiersma article offer any possibilities?

4. According to the court, may silence or inaction ever constitute a binding acceptance of a valid offer? Why doesn't the *Russell* case qualify?

5. This case indicates that it is not unusual for persons to try to construct situations in which silence or inaction would constitute acceptance of an offer to contract. These cases might be regarded as "private" attempts to alter the existing law of contract. Why do you think these attempts have not been successful?

Formal Requisites of a Contract

Contracts need not be written in order to be enforceable, unless they are required by statute to be written. The **Statute of Frauds**, which requires certain contracts to be in writing in order to be valid, is discussed in detail later in this chapter. Oral contracts, although generally valid, do have certain disadvantages. It is more difficult to prove that such contracts exist at all, let alone determine their terms.

We usually think of formal validity of contracts mainly in terms of those contracts that are written, but clearly there are certain formal requirements for *all* contracts, as the law concerning offer and acceptance has demonstrated. Those formal requirements go to certainty, definiteness, and uniformity, as well as to demonstrating that there has been a true "meeting of the minds" of the contracting parties.

Although there is generally no special form that contracts must comply with, there are certain formal requisites for written contracts in particular. They are generally expected to be dated, signed, and delivered to both parties. ("Signed, sealed and delivered" is a saying that goes back to the time when certain contracts were required to bear a **seal** to be formally valid. Today the presence of a seal on a contract has no significance, but even so many printed form contracts still have a printed seal at the signature lines.)

A totally written contract is called an **integrated contract**; that is, all the preliminary negotiations and communications between the parties, whether written or oral, are said to be "merged" into the final written document, which then constitutes the entire and only agreement between the parties. Proof of such a contract is governed by the **Parol Evidence Rule**, which does not permit evidence of prior or contemporaneous oral or written communications to be offered to vary, alter, or contradict a written contract. For example, suppose you enter into a contract to deliver a ton of cabbage to a market at no later than 8 A.M. on a certain day, and the written contract contains a provision that you will forfeit a certain amount of your fee if you deliver late. As you sign the agreement you say to the other party, "Of course, I won't lose anything if I am only fifteen minutes late," and the other party agrees. The parol evidence rule would not allow your statement to be used to vary what the written agreement actually says. Whether or not the written contract actually reflects what the parties intended, the parol evidence rule generally prevents them from using their prior statements to contradict what the written agreement says. When the language of the agreement is ambiguous, however, prior statements may be permitted to aid in interpreting what the language of the contract actually means.

In the following reading, Oliver Wendell Holmes, Jr., one of the greatest theorists of American contract law, examines the nature of contractual promises and their legal effect. For Holmes, a major concern is the promisor's liability: What are the consequences if he does not do what he has undertaken to do by his promise?

READING   **Contract**
                                        Oliver Wendell Holmes, Jr. *

An assurance that it shall rain tomorrow, or that a third person shall paint a picture, may as well be a promise as one that the promisee shall receive from some source one hundred bales of cotton, or that the promisor will pay the promisee one hundred dollars. What is the difference in the cases? It is only in the degree of power possessed by the promisor over the event. He has none in the first case. He has equally little authority to make a man paint a picture, although he may have larger means of persuasion. He probably will be able to make sure that the promisee has the cotton. Being a rich man, he is certain to be able to pay the one hundred dollars, except in the event of some most improbable accident.

But the law does not inquire, as a general thing, how far the accomplishment of an assurance touching the future is within the power of the promisor. In the moral world it may be that the obligation of a promise is confined to what lies within the reach of the will of the promisor (except so far as the limit is unknown on one side, and misrepresented on the other). But unless some consideration of public policy intervenes, I take it that a man may bind himself at law that any future event shall happen. He can therefore promise it in a legal sense. It may be said that when a man covenants that it shall rain tomorrow, or that *A* shall paint a picture, he only says, in a short form, I will pay if it does not rain, or if *A* does not paint a picture. But that is not necessarily so. A promise could easily be framed which would be broken by the happening of fair weather, or by *A* not painting. A promise then, is simply an accepted assurance that a certain event or state of things shall come to pass.

But if this be true, it has more important bearings than simply to enlarge the definition of the word *promise*. It concerns the theory of contract. The consequences of a binding promise at common law are not affected by the degree of power which the promisor possesses over the promised event. If the promised event does not come to pass, the plaintiff's property is sold to satisfy the damages, within certain limits, which the promisee has suffered by the failure. The consequences are the same in kind whether the promise is that it shall rain, or that another man shall paint a picture, or that the promisor will deliver a bale of cotton.

If the legal consequence is the same in all cases, it seems proper that all contracts should be considered from the same legal point of view. In the case of a binding promise that it shall rain tomorrow, the immediate legal effect of what the promisor does is, that he takes the risk of the event, within certain defined limits, as between himself and the promisee. He does no more when he promises to deliver a bale of cotton.

If it be proper to state the common-law meaning of promise and contract in this way, it has the advantage of freeing the subject from the superfluous theory that contract is a qualified subjection of one will to another, a kind of limited slavery. It might be so regarded if the law compelled men to perform their contracts, or if it allowed promises to exercise such compulsion. If, when a man promised to labor for another, the law made him do it, his relation to his promisee might be called a servitude *ad hoc* with some truth. But that is what the law never does. It never interferes until a promise has been broken, and therefore cannot possibly be performed according to its tenor. It is true that in some instances equity does what is called compelling specific performance.[4] But, in the first place, I am speaking of the common law, and in the next, this only means that equity compels the performance of certain elements of the total promise which are still capable of performance. For instance, take a promise to convey land within a certain time, a court of equity is not in the habit of interfering until the time has gone by, so that the promise cannot be performed as made. But if the conveyance is more important than the time, and the promisee prefers to have it late rather than never, the law may compel the performance of that. Not literally compel even in that case, however, but put the promisor in prison unless he will convey. This remedy is an exceptional one. The only universal consequence of a legally binding promise is, that the law makes the promisor pay damages if the promised event does not come to pass. In every case it leaves him free from interference until the time for fulfillment has gone by, and therefore free to break his contract if he chooses.

A more practical advantage in looking at a contract as the taking of a risk is to be found in the light which it throws upon the measure of damages. If a breach of contract were regarded in the same light as a tort, it would seem that if, in the course of performance of the contract the promisor should be notified of any particular consequence which would result from its not being performed, he should be held liable for that consequence in the event of non-performance. Such a suggestion has been made. But it has not been accepted as the law. On the contrary, according to the opinion of a very able judge, which seems to be generally followed, notice, even at the time of making the contract, of special circumstances out of which special damages would arise in case of breach, is not sufficient unless the assumption of that risk is to be taken as having fairly entered into the contract. If a carrier should undertake to carry the machinery of a sawmill from Liverpool to Vancouver's Island, and should fail to do so, he probably would not be held liable for the rate of hire of such machinery during the necessary delay, although he might know that it could not be replaced without sending to England, unless he was fairly understood to accept "the contract with the special condition attached to it." *British Columbia Saw-Mill Co.* v. *Nettleship*, L.R. 3 C.P. 499, 509.

It is true that, when people make contracts, they usually contemplate the performance rather than the breach. The express language used does not generally go further than to define what will happen if the contract is fulfilled. A statutory requirement of a memorandum in writing would be satisfied by a written statement of the promise as made, because to require more would be to run counter to the ordinary habits of mankind, as well as because the statement that the effect of a contract is the assumption of risk of a future event does not mean that there is a second subsidiary promise to assume that risk but that the assumption follows as a consequence directly enforced by the law, without the promisor's cooperation. So parol evidence would be admissible, no doubt to enlarge or diminish the extent of the liability assumed for non-performance, where it would be inadmissible to affect the scope of the promise.

But these concessions do not affect the view here taken. As the relation of contractor and contractee is voluntary, the consequences attaching to the relation must be voluntary. What the event contemplated by the promise is, or in other words what will amount to a breach of contract, is a matter of interpretation and construction. What consequences of the breach are assumed is more remotely, in like manner, a matter of construction having regard

---

[4]**Specific performance** is an equitable remedy that requires a person who has breached a contract to actually perform as agreed under the contract rather than pay damages. Specific performance is discussed in more detail in Chapter 10.

to the circumstances under which the contract is made. Knowledge of what is dependent upon performance is one of those circumstances. It is not necessarily conclusive, but it may have the effect of enlarging the risk assumed.

The very office of construction is to work out, from what is expressedly said and done, what would have been said with regard to events not definitely before the minds of the parties, if those events had been considered. The price paid in mercantile contracts generally excludes the construction that exceptional risks were intended to be assumed. The foregoing analysis is believed to show that the result which has been reached by courts on grounds of practical good sense falls in with the true theory of contract under the common law.

NOTES

From *The Common Law* , Ch. viii, "The Elements of Contract, " 1881.

FOR DISCUSSION

1. According to Holmes, what are the legal consequences of a binding promise at common law?

2. Even today, courts are reluctant to require a person to specifically perform a contract of employment. How would Holmes explain that reluctance? Does his explanation make sense?

3. Why should a promisor be free to break his contract if he chooses? Do you think that Fried would agree with Holmes that this is a good thing?

4. Could it be to a promisor's advantage to break a contract and pay damages rather than to perform as agreed? Should the law allow that?

5. Can one ever bind the other party to a contract to pay special damages in the event of breach? How, according to Holmes, must one do that?

6. In Holmes's view, the voluntary nature of the relationship between contracting parties limits their liability under the contract. Why is this so? Would Fried agree with this?

7. How can the price paid in a commercial contract indicate whether exceptional risks were intended to be assumed? Do you think this would be a good indication of the parties' intentions?

8. What factors are likely to be considered by a person who must construe (interpret) the meaning of a contract? Is this likely to be an easy task?

One of the time-honored formal requirements of a valid contract is that it must be signed by all the parties thereto. As the following case shows, however, that formal requirement may be waived in certain circumstances.

CASE   **Sandra Skinner and Alex Easton v. William K. Haugseth**
Florida Court of Appeals 2 Dist. (1983)
426 So.2d 1127

GRIMES, Acting Chief Judge.   This appeal is taken from an order dismissing with prejudice an amended complaint for specific performance.

The complaint was filed by William and Sandra Skinner, his wife, and Alex Easton against William Haugseth. After the court granted Haugseth's motion to dismiss, an amended complaint was filed only in the names of Sandra Skinner and Alex Easton, thereby dropping William Skinner from the suit. They alleged that on November 23, 1981, they offered to purchase from Haugseth a certain parcel of real estate and that, as indicated on the contract attached to the complaint, Haugseth accepted the offer on November 27, 1981. They further alleged that on or before January 15, 1982, they were ready, willing and able to perform pursuant to the terms of the contract but that Haugseth declined to consummate the sale.

The sales contract was written on a printed form and dated November 23, 1981. It first recited that "William and Sandra Skinner, Alex Easton et al.—hereinafter called the purchaser" had deposited $100 "as earnest money and in part payment on account of the purchase price" of the real estate thereafter described. The total purchase price of $15,000 was payable as follows: $100 down, $1400 additional earnest money within seven days, $7500 cash at closing and the assumption of a $6000 mortgage. The broker acknowledged receipt of the deposit subject to certain conditions customary in real estate sales contracts. The closing date was specified as January 15, 1982.

Beneath the signature of the real estate broker there appeared the following words. "I/we hereby agree to purchase the above described property at the price and upon the terms and conditions above set forth. I/we understand that this is a legally binding contract." The attested signatures of Alex K. Easton and Sandra Skinner, as purchasers, followed this language. The next section of the contract stated that "I/we hereby accept the offer and agree to deliver the above described property at the price and upon the terms and conditions above stated." William Haugseth's attested signature then followed with the notation that he had signed as seller on November 27, 1981.

The record establishes that the amended complaint was dismissed because William Skinner failed to sign the contract. On appeal, Sandra Skinner and Alex Easton argue that the contract was enforceable because their signatures gave it mutuality and Haugseth's signature satisfied the statute of frauds. Haugseth argues that the contract was not binding until all of the parties signed it. Anticipating the possible argument that William Skinner had ratified the contract by joining in the lawsuit, Haugseth also points out that he repudiated the contract long before this occurred.

The only Florida case reasonably relevant to the subject is *Hughes* v. *Russell*, 391 So.2d 256 (Fla. 4thDCA 1980). Mr. Russell, a New York resident on a business trip to West Palm Beach, inspected a home owned by Mr. and Mrs. Hughes. Mr. Russell decided that he and his wife would purchase it for the agreed price of $185,000. He instructed his wife who was in New York and who had never seen the home to execute and return the deposit receipt contract prepared by the Hughes'. While the contract referred to Mr. and Mrs. Russell as the purchaser, only Mrs. Russell signed it. Mrs. Russell deposited the 10% deposit in trust with the broker and returned the contract to Florida where the sellers then executed it. Later, the Russells decided not to close the transaction.

Mrs. Russell filed suit to terminate the contract and obtain the return of the $18,500 deposit. The complaint alleged that the contract was subject to termite and plumbing inspections and that the reports of these inspections were unsatisfactory. The defendants admitted the existence of the contract but asserted that the plaintiffs had breached it. They sought to retain the deposit as liquidated damages under the contract. At the conclusion of the trial, the court announced that the contract was void because it had not been signed by Mr. Russell. Since the contract was unenforceable, the court ordered the return of the deposit.

On appeal, our sister court reasoned that when Mrs. Russell made the deposit and signed the contract and the Hughes' accepted and signed it, a binding contract resulted. However, the court remanded for a new trial to consider whether the Russells could properly terminate the contract and obtain the return of the deposit based upon the termite and plumbing inspections. The *Hughes* case differs from the case at hand only by virtue of the fact that only one of them had signed the contract; whereas, here the seller seeks to sustain his position because less than all the purchasers signed the contract.

The evolution toward a principle of law predicated upon intent is well illustrated in *Angell* v. *Rowlands*, 85 Cal.App.3d 536, 149 Cal.Rptr. 574 (1978). Originally, California followed the rule, first announced in *Tewksbury* v. *O'Connell*, 21 Cal. 60 (1862), that a contract is invalid until it is signed by all of the parties who are purportedly bound by it. Subsequently, there developed a somewhat contrary line of authority first represented by *Cavanaugh* v. *Casselman*, 88 Cal. 543, 26 P. 515 (1891). In *Angell* a husband seller and a husband buyer both signed a real estate contract. The wives did not sign despite spaces for their signatures. In a suit for damages brought by the seller for failure to purchase the property, the buyer defended on the ground that neither wife had signed the contract. The court affirmed a judgment upholding the contract and awarding damages to the seller. After analyzing the conflicting lines of authority, the court said:

> We therefore decline to follow the *Tewksbury* line of cases insofar as they hold that an agreement is invariably incomplete until signed by all parties purportedly bound. Instead, we adopt the *Cavanaugh* line of cases, i.e., that a contract is invalid if not signed by all parties purportedly bound *only when it is shown*, either by parol or express condition, that the contract was not intended to be complete until all parties had signed. Conversely, in the absence of a showing that the contract is not intended to be complete until signed by all parties, the parties who did sign it will be bound.
>
> 85 Cal. App. 3d at 542, 149 Cal.Rptr. at 578.

In *Curtis* v. *Hannah*, 414 N.E.2d 962 (Ind.App. 1981), the plaintiffs sued for specific performance of a contract signed by only two of three tenants in common even though the contract contemplated that the third tenant would also sign. The trial court entered summary judgment for the defendants. On appeal, the court reversed for a trial on the merits, holding that there was an issue of fact over the intent of the parties with respect to whether the signing tenants would be bound individually. The court observed that it could not as a matter of law say that the document displayed an intent that all of the parties needed to sign before any were bound, or that the owners signed only in partial consideration for the third tenant signing.

The Utah Supreme Court in *Cox* v. *Berry*, 19 Utah 2d 352, 431 P.2d 575 (1967), made the following pertinent observation:

> Even where it appears that it was intended that others sign an agreement, it is not necessarily invariably true that all must sign before any are bound. This depends upon the agreement and whether it appears that part of the consideration for signing was that other would also sign and be bound jointly with them. It is usually to be assumed that the parties signing an agreement are bound thereby unless it appears that they did not so intend unless others also signed.
>
> 19 Utah 2d at 357, 431 P.2d at 579 (footnotes omitted).

In *Schlosberg* v. *Shannon & Luchs Co.*, 53 A.2d 722 (D.C.Mun.App. 1947), Jack Schlosberg and Jack Coopersmith signed a contract for the purchase and sale of real estate. Schlosberg gave the real estate broker a $2,000 check as a deposit on the purchase price. Thereafter, Schlosberg announced that he would not complete the purchase and stopped payment on his check. The real estate broker sued Schlosberg for the amount of the deposit.

As a defense, Schlosberg asserted that he signed the agreement on the condition, made known to the seller, that it would not be binding unless his wife also signed. He pointed out that the contract recited a receipt of the deposit from "Jack and Dorothy Schlosberg" and that there were two spaces for the signatures of the purchasers. In affirming a judgment for the brokers on disputed facts, the court stated:

> Of course, one may sign an agreement on condition that he shall not be bound thereby until another also signs, and until the other does sign the first is not bound. But unless it clearly appears from the face of the instrument that it is the understanding of the parties that the agreement is not to be effective without the signatures of all, resort must be had to parol testimony to determine the intent of the parties. Mere expectation that another will sign does not necessarily prevent those signing from being bound even though the expected party does not sign.
>
> 53 A.2d at 723 (footnotes omitted).

The court in *Palman* v. *Reynolds*, 310 Mich. 35, 16 N.W.2d 657 (1944), noted that a party signatory to a contract has the burden of showing he did not intend to be bound unless the contract was fully executed by all of the other parties. The court quoted with approval from an early case which held that if a party does not intend to be bound he has to declare his intentions at that time rather than simply testifying to this effect at a later date.

Accordingly, we hold that a contract not signed by all of the parties, but otherwise valid, may be upheld against a signing party, unless the nature or the wording of the contract indicates that his signature was conditioned upon all other parties signing the contract, or he can prove by parol evidence that when he signed the contract he made it known to the other parties who now seek to sustain the contract that he only intended to be bound if all parties signed it.

Measured by the foregoing standard, it is evident that the order of dismissal must be reversed. Patently, there was no issue concerning indemnity because Haugseth had no co-parties against whom he could make such a claim. At the time Haugseth signed the contract, Sandra Skinner and Alex Easton had already signed it. Therefore, he knew that William Skinner had not signed the contract. Yet, there is nothing in the contract specifying Haugseth's intent not to go through with the sale if William Skinner did not sign. The provision for the assumption of the mortgage suggests that Haugseth could have been concerned with who bought his property, but it was not enough to make the contract unenforceable as a matter of law if signed by less than all the parties. The complaint clearly states a cause of action.

FOR DISCUSSION

1. Why might Haugseth have been unwilling to complete the sale of his land if one of the purchasers failed to sign the contract?

2. How could Haugseth have indicated his unwillingness to be bound by the contract until all the other parties had signed it? Did he have an opportunity to make his intent known?

3. Given the facts recited in the case, does it appear that all the signatories intended to be bound by the contract?

4. Historically, one reason for the insistence on strict rules of formal validity of contracts was to avoid confusion about how and when parties intended to be bound by an agreement. This case seems to indicate less concern with formality and more with the manifestation of the parties' intent. Do you think Holmes would agree with that view? Explain your answer.

Definiteness and Certainty

As we have said earlier, for there to be mutuality of assent, a true "meeting of the minds," then the offer must be clear and definite enough for both parties to know what they are agreeing to.

In the following case, the omission of a material element of a contract is held to affect its definiteness and certainty to the extent that no contract existed.

CASE

Kenneth J. Neiss et al. v. Joseph Franze et al.
New York Supreme Court (1979)
101 Misc.2d 871, 422 N.Y.S.2d 345

HAROLD J. HUGHES, JR., Justice. The defendants move for summary judgment dismissing the plaintiffs' complaint and granting judgment in their favor upon their counterclaim. Plaintiffs have requested that the court grant summary judgment against defendants.

The action is by vendors of real property for specific performance of a contract, and the counterclaim is for return of the vendees' $1,000 deposit. The contract was executed by the defendants on October 17, 1978, and contained a clause stating "This agreement is contingent upon purchaser obtaining approval of a conventional mortgage loan of $29,000. Purchaser agrees to use diligent efforts to obtain said approval." The clause goes on to provide that the contingency shall be waived unless the purchasers notified the vendors within 30 days of their inability to obtain such a mortgage. The deposit of $1,000 was given upon the signing of the agreement. Defendants sought a mortgage loan from the Chase Manhattan Bank and were denied same. Thereafter, they sought a mortgage from the Union National Bank and were advised that such bank was not at that time accepting applications for mortgages at 8 1/2 per cent interest for a term of 20 years. Defendants advised plaintiffs, pursuant to the contract, that they could not obtain a mortgage and requested the return of the $1,000 deposit which was not forthcoming.

The position of plaintiffs on this motion is that they were at all times ready, willing and able to complete the sale and that the defendants did not use diligent efforts to obtain a mortgage. More particularly, plaintiffs take the position that the term "conventional mortgage" envisioned a mortgage for a term unspecified by the plaintiffs at any interest rate that was allowed to be charged by a federally-chartered bank, even though that interest rate might be in excess of New York State's usury laws. The defendants take the position that the term "conventional mortgage" is so ambiguous as to render the contract a nullity since there was no meeting of the minds. In the alternative, defendants argue that the term "conventional mortgage" means a mortgage for a term of 20 years at the maximum rate of interest permitted by New York State's usury laws. Defendants allege that they requested such a mortgage from two different banks and were refused, and that this constituted diligent effort.

The omission of a material element from a contract renders the contract unenforceable since there has been no meeting of the minds. *Willmott* v. *Giarraputo*, 5 N.Y.2d 250, 253, 184 N.Y.S.2d 97, 157 N.E.2d 282. When the term "conventional mortgage" is used in a clause such as the instant one, there should also be set forth the term of the mortgage and at what interest rate the mortgage shall be. *Donato* v. *Baltrusaitis*, 56 Misc.2d 935, 936, 290 N.Y.S.2d 659. Omitting the terms of the mortgage renders a contract unenforceable. The court concludes that the term "conventional mortgage" standing alone, without a designation of the interest rate or length of term of the mortgage, is so ambiguous that there was never any meeting of the minds between the buyer and the seller as to this essential part of the transaction. This term could mean, as argued by plaintiffs, any mortgage given by a bank at any interest rate, for any term, that is not guaranteed by a governmental entity (such as FHA or VA mortgages). Alternatively the phrase could mean, as urged by defendants, a mortgage for a 20-year term at the interest rate allowed by New York State law. For that matter, it could refer to a 25-year or a 30-year term at the interest rate allowed by law. Under the circumstances of this case, the seller has no enforceable contract and the defendants are entitled to the return of their deposit.

The motion of the defendants for an order granting summary judgment dismissing the plaintiffs' complaint and awarding summary judgment upon their counterclaim shall be granted, without motion costs. The cross motion of the plaintiffs for summary judgment shall be denied, without costs.

FOR DISCUSSION

1. Which of the defendants' alternative defenses does the court base its decision on?
2. Would the defendants have won if the case had been determined on the basis of whether they had used "diligent efforts" to obtain a mortgage?
3. What problems would the court have to address in responding to question 2?
4. Was there a meeting of minds in this case? Explain.

Consideration

Contract is founded on the idea of exchange, and consideration, an exchange of value between the contracting parties, is required to support a valid contract. Promises alone, without consideration, do not make a legally binding contract. Consideration takes many forms, but it always involves a token of commitment to the contractual relationship, a concrete manifestation of the intent to be bound. A more general meaning of "consideration" is money or a money substitute, and often money does constitute the consideration offered by one party in exchange for goods, services, or some other valuable thing rendered by the other. Consideration may be a promise, or some action other than a promise, or forbearance (refraining from doing something one is legally entitled to do), or a promise to forbear. The hallmarks of consideration are benefit to the promisor and detriment to the promisee—the notion that one party gives something up to induce the other party to do or give something in return: such as money in exchange for goods, land, or services; performance of an act in exchange for a promise to pay money; forbearance in exchange for a promise to act.

The benefits and detriments need not be of enormous value, but they must be real. For example, if someone promises to do something that they are already legally required to do, or promises not to do something they have no legal right to do anyway, that would not be consideration. If there is no legally sufficient consideration, there is no contract. But where there is legally sufficient consideration, it is not necessary that there be an even exchange in value. Courts generally do not inquire into the adequacy or fairness of the exchange; people are free to make the bargains that seem good to them, whether they are "fair" or not, as long as they are voluntary.

In the following excerpt, Lon Fuller considers some reasons for the requirement of consideration. Although some of the reasons given are quite simple and practical, Fuller's primary concern is the role that contract plays in determining the form of social relationships, a task that is so important that it cannot be left to mere moral obligation to honor the promises made.

READING   ## Consideration and Form
Lon Fuller*

That consideration may have both a "formal" and a "substantive" aspect is apparent when we reflect on the reasons which have been advanced why promises without consideration are not enforced. It has been said that consideration is "for the sake of evidence" and is intended to remove the hazards of mistaken or perjured testimony which would attend the enforcement of promises for which nothing is given in exchange. Again, it is said that enforcement is denied gratuitous promises because such promises are often made impulsively and without proper deliberation. In both these cases the object relates, not to the content and effect of the promise, but to the manner in which it is made. Objections of this sort, which touch the form rather than the content of the agreement, will be removed if the making of the promise is attended by some formality or ceremony, as by being under seal. On the other hand, it has been said that the enforcement of gratuitous promises is not an object of sufficient importance to our social and economic order to justify the expenditure of the time and energy necessary to accomplish it. Here the objection is one of "substance" since it touches the significance of the promise made and not merely the circumstances surrounding the making of it....

...Among the basic conceptions of contract law the most pervasive and indispensable is the principle of private autonomy. This principle simply means that the law views private individuals as possessing a power to effect, within certain limits, changes in their legal relations. The man who conveys property to another is exercising this power; so is the man who enters a contract. When a court enforces a promise it is merely arming with legal sanction a rule or lex[5] previously established by the party himself. This power of the individual to effect changes in his legal relations with others is comparable to the power of a legislature. It is, in fact, only a kind of political prejudice which causes us to use the word "law" in one case and not in the other, a prejudice which did not deter the Romans from applying the word lex to the norms created by private agreement....

...Form has an obvious relationship to the principle of private autonomy. Where men make laws for themselves it is desirable that they should do so under conditions guaranteeing the desiderata described in our analysis of the functions of form. Furthermore, the greater the assurance that these desiderata are satisfied, the larger the scope we may be willing to ascribe to private autonomy.

NOTES

*From 41 *Columbia Law Review* 799 (1941). Reprinted with permission. Copyright ©1941 by the Directors of the Columbia Law Review Association, Inc. All rights reserved. This article originally appeared at 41 Col.L.Rev. 799 (1941).

[5]**Lex** is the Latin word for "law". It also means "compact" or "agreement."

FOR DISCUSSION

1. Who is responsible for determining the proper form and substance of private agreements?
2. According to Fuller, what exactly are people doing when they enter into a contract?
3. If the real issue is using state power to require people to do or not do certain things, why use contract for that purpose? In other words, what does contract symbolize for Fuller?
4. Do you think that Fried would agree with Fuller's position?

Sufficiency of consideration is a key issue for the court to consider in determining whether a valid contract exists. In the following case, the issue is not whether there was a fair exchange between the parties in terms of value, but whether there was any exchange at all.

CASE

C. Verne Hale, Jr. v. Jerry Dean Brewster
New Mexico Supreme Court (1970)
81 N.M. 342, 467 P.2d 8, 43 A.L.R.3d 1420

MOISE, Ch. J. Appellant, Jerry Dean Brewster, appeals from an order refusing to vacate a default judgment entered against appellant and Mrs. W. E. Brewster, appellant's mother.

The record discloses a complaint filed by appellee against appellant and Mrs. W. E. Brewster, seeking judgment for $900.53, being the unpaid balance on a promissory note for $1,000.00 plus interest and attorney's fees. Summons issued in the case was returned July 31, 1968, and recites that service was made on both defendants by delivery of a copy of the summons and complaint on July 24, 1968, to one Judy Brewster, "a person over fifteen years of age, residing at the usual place of abode of defendants Mrs. W. E. Brewster and Jerry Brewster, who at the time of such service was [*sic*] absent therefrom." On August 28, 1968, judgment as prayed in the complaint was entered by default, with a recital in the judgment that the defendants had been "duly served with process more than thirty days heretofore, all of which appears more fully by returns of service on file herein...."

On October 11, 1968, appellant filed a motion under Rule 60(b) seeking to have the default judgment against him vacated, and claiming that the default occurred because of his mistake, inadvertence, surprise or excusable neglect in that the summons in the cause had been served on appellant's mother in his absence, and he had no knowledge of the fact until after the judgment was entered. Further, in the motion appellant asserts a defense because of the claimed fraud of appellee in taking a note from appellant to cover an attorney fee when appellee had been appointed by the court to represent appellant on a criminal charge and, thereafter, had been paid and had accepted an $85.00 fee from the court for such representation, which appellant had assumed satisfied his obligation to appellee. Thereafter, the order appealed from herein was entered denying the motion to vacate, but reducing the judgment previously entered by the amount of $85.00, being the payment from the court fund.

Appellant, for his second point, asserts a defense to the complaint in that the note sued on was lacking in consideration. The question presented concerns the right and propriety of an attorney taking compensation for representation of an indigent charged with a crime when he has been appointed by the court to represent the indigent and has been paid by the court for the services rendered.

Our Constitution, in Art. II, §14, guarantees to an accused in a criminal prosecution "the right to appear and defend himself in person, and by counsel." At the time appellee was appointed to represent appellant. §§41-11-2 and 41-11-3, NMSA 1953, were in effect. These sections read:

> 41-11-2. The court before whom any person shall be indicted, or informed against, for any offense which is capital, or punishable by imprisonment in the penitentiary, is hereby authorized and required to assign to such person counsel not exceeding two [2], if the prisoner has not the financial means to procure counsel, and such counsel shall have full access to the prisoner at all reasonable hours.

> 41-11-3. The court, assigning such counsel, shall authorize the payment of the attorney fees of such counsel out of the court fund and in such amount as the court shall fix, not less than twenty-five dollars [$25.00] and not exceeding the sum of one hundred dollars [$100] in any case other than homicide.

These sections have since been repealed.

Aside from the constitutional provision and the statute requiring that counsel be appointed for indigents charged with crime, and paid for the services rendered, it has always been considered that attorneys admitted to practice at the bar are officers of the court and have a duty and obligation to accept such appointments and to serve their clients to the best of the attorneys' abilities. *Powell* v. *Alabama*, 287 U.S. 45, 53 S.Ct. 55, 77 L.Ed. 158 (1932).

The right of the courts to impose the duty on lawyers to defend indigent persons accused of crime without compensation has been upheld in all jurisdictions but four—Indiana, Iowa, New Jersey and Wisconsin. Be this as it may, we have a statute, quoted above, providing for pay, and appellant asserted in his motion that appellee had in fact been paid a fee of $85.00 by the State. Although the motion was overruled, it appears that appellant was given credit for this amount on the judgment previously entered.

However, this does not resolve the question raised by this appeal. We must decide if payment of a fee by the State makes the note executed by appellant invalid because lacking consideration. We have found only one case directly in point. It is *Commonwealth* v. *Wormsley*, 294 Pa. 495, 144 A. 428 (1928), where the court said:

> ...Petitioners, having been appointed by the court to represent defendant, had a duty to appeal, if they considered that course essential to protect his rights, and the fee paid them by the county must be their exclusive compensation. Under the circumstances, they had no right to contract with others for fees and expenses.

That this rule is correct would seem to follow from the duty of appellee to represent to the best of his ability plus the payment and receipt of a fee from the state. Where can the consideration be found for appellant's promise to pay an additional amount? We do not see how appellant received anything that he was not entitled to receive without payment of any amount, and accordingly there is no consideration. Compare *In re Quantius' Will*, 58 N.M. 807, 277 P.2d 306 (1954), where we held that "the promise to do what a person is already obligated by law or contract to do is not sufficient consideration for a promise made in return." This rule is one of almost universal general application. It follows from what has been said that if the note was given to appellee as a fee for services, which he was already bound to perform by virtue of his appointment by the court, the appellant had a good and valid defense which he could have presented if the default judgment had been vacated.

The cause must be reversed and remanded with instructions to proceed in a manner consistent herewith. It is so ordered.

FOR DISCUSSION

1. What exactly was Hale proposing to give Brewster in exchange for the $1,000 fee?
2. Is it possible that the court appointment of counsel, that is, Hale agreeing to defend Brewster in exchange for a fee paid by the state, could be characterized as a contract? Does Brewster qualify as a contracting party in this arrangement?
3. Even if Hale did not have a contract with the state, would a promise to defend Brewster constitute consideration in this situation?
4. Assuming that $1,000 was an appropriate fee to charge Brewster under the circumstances, is Hale being treated unfairly by being forced to accept only $85? What is the court's reasoning with respect to Hale's obligation?

Factors Affecting Formation of a Contract (Mistake, Ignorance, Fraud, Duress and Undue Influence)

Because the parties must mutually assent to the terms of a contract for it to be enforceable, the voluntary character of the agreement and the reality of consent are important issues in the law of contracts. Freedom of contract assumes that people are agreeing freely to enter into contracts, and a "meeting of the minds" presupposes that people know what they are doing and what they are getting themselves into. As we said in the case of consideration, when people freely and knowingly agree to do something, then the fairness of their bargain may not be an issue for outside scrutiny, but there must be assurances that the contract really was made voluntarily by informed parties.

Mistake, ignorance, and fraud (or misrepresentation, deliberate or innocent) prevent people from fully knowing what they are agreeing to. Duress and undue influence prevent people from freely agreeing. In any of these cases, the contract may be nonexistent or unenforceable.

Mistake In most cases, a **unilateral mistake** (an error by one party) will not render a contract unenforceable. Similarly, when one or both parties are fully aware of the facts relating to their transaction but are mistaken about the legal effect of what they are attempting to do, the contract remains valid and enforceable. Conversely, when there has been a **mutual mistake** about the facts underlying an agreement, there has been no real meeting of the minds, and the contract is invalid.

Sometimes, however, a unilateral mistake is so serious and material that enforcing the resulting "bargain" would permit one party to take unfair advantage of the other. The following case illustrates such a situation.

CASE   City of Syracuse v. Sarkisian Brothers, Inc.
               New York Supreme Court, Appellate Division, 4th Department (1982)
                                 87 A.D.2d 984, 451 N.Y.S.2d 945

MEMORANDUM   In response to plaintiff's advertisement for bids in connection with the construction of a junior high school, defendant Sarkisian Brothers, Inc. prepared a preliminary bid proposal in accordance with the plans and specifications of plaintiff. Before the bid was submitted, Sarkisian determined that it would be able to reduce its bid by $21,300.00. In transposing this reduction from its work sheet to the bid proposal, however, the sum of $213,000.00 was inadvertently deducted instead of $21,300.00, resulting in a bid on the job of $3,547,000.00, whereas its intended bid was $3,738,700.00. On the same day the bids were submitted and opened, Sarkisian discovered its error and notified plaintiff and requested that its bid be withdrawn. Plaintiff thereupon requested the bidder's work sheets which were promptly forwarded. Almost three weeks after the bid submission and notification of the error, plaintiff awarded the contract to Sarkisian Brothers, Inc. based upon its erroneous bid. The contractor declined to perform and the plaintiff readvertised the job and awarded a contract in an amount closely approximating the bid which Sarkisian had intended to submit. This action seeking money damages and bond forfeiture ensued. Defendants moved for summary judgment rescinding the contract, which motion was denied by Special Term. We reverse.

The clerical mistake made by defendant contractor was excusable and material and of such an amount as to make enforcement of the contract unconscionable. The error was subject to objective determination by comparing the work sheets with the bid proposal.

The criteria for rescission of a contract as is herein involved has been stated in *Balaban-Gordon Co.* v. *Brighton Sewer District No. 2*, 41 A.D.2d 246, 247, 342 N.Y.S 2d 435. "A bid is a binding offer to make a contract. It may be withdrawn in the case of unilateral mistake by the bidder where the mistake is known to the other party to the transaction and (1) the bid is of such consequence that enforcement would be unconscionable, (2) the mistake is material, (3) the mistake occurred despite the exercise of ordinary care by the bidder and (4) it is possible to place the other party in *status quo*." 13 Williston, Contracts (3d ed.), §1573; Ann.52 A.L.R.2d 793-794. These tests have been met and plaintiff should not be permitted to enforce the bargain. Plaintiff's position has not been damaged since it received prompt actual notice of the error and could have awarded that contract to the second bidder. The election to rebid was its own and not required by any act of Sarkisian Brothers. There was never a meeting of minds of the parties which could give rise to a contract since the bidder never submitted its real bid but instead, an erroneous one not at all expressing its intent.

Since the bid is rescinded, the bid bond must be cancelled for the contractor has no legal obligation to fulfill its bond.

Order unanimously reversed with costs, defendant's motion granted and complaint dismissed.

FOR DISCUSSION

1. According to the court, what are the criteria for determining whether to permit a bidder who makes a mistake in his proposal to withdraw the bid?

2. When Sarkisian notified plaintiff of its error in the bid proposal, plaintiff requested that Sarkisian submit its work sheets. How does the evidence of the work sheets support defendant Sarkisian's position?

3. What actions of the plaintiff aggravated this situation? Should Sarkisian be held responsible for the consequences of those actions?

4. Was there ever a genuine "meeting of minds" in this case? Explain.

5. The court concludes that enforcement of this contract would be unconscionable. Based on the facts of this case, how would you define the term "unconscionable"? Explain your answer.

Duress

Usually duress involves physical force or the threat of physical force to the person, or a threat to property, while undue influence either involves putting some psychological pressure on the other party or abusing a relationship of trust in order to take advantage of someone. A specialized type of duress is economic or business duress, which occurs when one party takes unfair advantage of the other party's bad economic situation, or an imminent threat of financial ruin, to coerce the person into making a contract that he otherwise would not have made.

In either case, the issue is voluntariness. Was one party so coerced or influenced by the other that he or she could not freely choose to enter into the contract? The following case examines such a situation.

CASE

City of Miami et al. v. Delores Kory
Florida D.C.A.3 Dist. (1981)
394 So.2d 494

SCHWARTZ, Judge.   This is an appeal by the City of Miami from a declaratory judgment rendered after a non-jury trial, which determined that Delores Kory's resignation as a probationary city employee was void because it was executed under duress. We reverse.

The facts are almost entirely undisputed. Under the civil service rules, an employee may be discharged without cause or explanation at any time during the first six months of employment, after which he attains permanent civil service status. On October 1, 1978, the appellee began work for the city in the Department of Management and Budget. At 1:00 P.M. on March 30, 1979, the last working day of Ms. Kory's probation, her supervisor, Manohar S. Surana, the Assistant Director of the Department, handed her a memorandum signed by him, which stated that she would be terminated "effective 2:00 P.M. today, Friday March 30, 1979." After reading the memo, and without prompting from Surana, Ms. Kory told him she was seeking another position with the city. She asked if, in order to avoid being fired, which would have precluded her securing another city job, it would be possible for her to resign instead. Surana replied that he had no objection to a resignation but that the decision was entirely up to her. After going out to lunch to "give this some thought," Ms. Kory returned at 1:50 P.M. with a handwritten resignation, which bore the time "1:55 P.M.," intended specifically to become effective prior to her discharge. The note stated:

> As I can no longer comply with the requirements of the position I occupy, I am tendering my resignation, effective immediately.

Surana accepted the resignation.

During April Ms. Kory made several attempts to obtain other employment from the city and to extend her probationary status with the Department of Management and Budget. After all such efforts proved unsuccessful, she sought the advice of counsel on April 26, 1979. It was then that she first learned the fact which the trial court found to be decisive in granting her relief; although, he testified at the trial, he (like Ms. Kory) did not know it at the time, Surana, as the *assistant* director of his department did not have the authority to discharge a probationer. Under the city code, only the director of a department, with the approval of the City Manager, possesses the power to do so. Thus, if Surana's letter had been the cause of Ms. Kory's termination, it would have been ineffective as contrary to the requirements of the city's own regulations.

This was the basis of Ms. Kory's action below, which was to set aside the instrument which *did* end her employment with the city, her own resignation of March 30. She contended essentially that the resignation was the product of duress created by the invalid notice of dismissal. The trial judge agreed, set aside the resignation, and ordered the plaintiff restored to the position she would have occupied had it not been tendered—that is, as a non-probationary civil service employee—with full back pay and emoluments. We are unable to approve this conclusion.

An early and often-cited definition of duress is contained in *Herald* v. *Hardin*, 95 Fla. 889, 116 So. 863, 864 (1928):

> Duress is a condition of mind produced by an improper external pressure or influence that practically destroys the free agency of a party and causes him to do an act or make a contract not of his own volition.

As this formulation of the rule and all the equivalent ones indicate, there are in essence two factors which must coexist in order to establish duress—one which deals with the party allegedly under duress; the other, with the party allegedly imposing it. It must be shown (a) that the act sought to be set aside was effected involuntarily and thus not as an exercise of free choice or will and (b) that this condition of mind was caused by some improper and coercive conduct of the other side. "[U]nderlying all definitions of 'duress' is the dual concept of external pressure and internal surrender or loss of volition in response to outside compulsion." 17 C.J.S. Contracts, §168 at 943 (1963). Although both elements of this duality are indispensable to a finding of duress, we think that neither existed in the present circumstances.

Resignation Voluntary Act of Plaintiff

As was said in *Azalea Drive-In Theatre* v. *Sargoy*, 394 F.Supp. 568, 574 (E.D.Va. 1975), rev'd on other grounds, 540 F.2d 713 (4th Cir. 1976):

> The authorities are in agreement that the ultimate fact to be determined whenever the question of duress is raised is whether the purported victim's will was so overcome as to deprive him of free choice. See generally 25 Am.Jur.2d [Duress and Undue Influence], §3, at 353 and 355-7; 17 C.J.S. [Contracts §168], at 948.

On the facts of this case it is clear that Ms. Kory's resignation was to the contrary of this requirement, entirely the product of her own choice. The idea of her resigning was initiated entirely by her, and was not suggested, much less forced upon her by Surana. The case is thus completely different from those cited by the appellee, in which the resignation was affirmatively requested, indeed required by the employer as the only alternative to a similarly unlawful discharge. In a word, Surana did not tell Ms. Kory to "quit or be fired"; he said, "you're going to be fired," and Ms. Kory asked, "may I quit first?" Furthermore, after she herself first raised the possibility of resignation, the plaintiff made a conscious decision to take that course for reasons which seemed to render it in her own best interests to do so. When, as here, a particular course of action is raised on one's own volition, and is finally decided upon in a deliberate and considered choice between alternatives, no finding of involuntariness, and thus no conclusion of duress may be sustained.

Resignation Not Product of Improper Conduct of City

Turning to the other side of the coin, the conduct of the city, we find the plaintiff's case equally inadequate. As has been demonstrated, the act supposedly coerced must be caused by some improper or illegal conduct of the defendant. In this regard, it is not improper and therefore not duress to threaten what one has a legal right to do. To the extent that any action of the city brought about Ms. Kory's resignation, it was obviously and only her proposed discharge. But it is undisputed that the city had the perfect right to do just that, fire Ms. Kory as a then-probationer without cause. The only aspect of that anticipated action which was arguably improper was the means by which it was about to be effected, that is, by Mr. Surana, rather than the head of the department. It was demonstrated, however, that this irregularity had absolutely nothing to do with Ms. Kory's decision to resign. To carry the burden of establishing the required causal connection between the unlawful conduct of the defendant and a resulting coerced action of the plaintiff, Ms. Kory would have had to show that she would not have resigned if the memo had been executed by the proper official, and thus that she was forced into resigning by the fact that it was signed by the wrong one. The record shows the exact opposite. Ms. Kory was not aware of the procedural deficiency and her actions were completely unrelated to its existence. A voluntary action cannot be deemed the result of duress because the surrounding transaction involves a technical impropriety which is discovered long afterwards and which has no direct influence on the result.

Even if, as it did not, the "improper" feature of the discharge had something to do with the resignation, the actions of Surana could not be deemed coercive. As the trial judge found, he was totally unaware of the contrary rule, and believed in good faith that he had the authority himself to fire the plaintiff. Thus, the principle stated as follows in 13 Williston on Contracts, §1606, at 672-73 (3d ed. Jaeger rev. 1970) is directly applicable:

> [A] threat to bring a civil action or to resort to remedies available under a contract is not such duress as will justify rescission of a transaction induced thereby. This is true even though it is subsequently determined that there is no legal right to enforce the claim, provided the threat is made in good faith, i.e., in the reasonable belief that a possible cause of action exists.

In submitting a memo he sincerely believed was effective to terminate her, Surana simply did nothing wrongful toward the plaintiff, which could vitiate her subsequent decision to resign.

Approaching the issue from a somewhat different point of view, the plaintiff's position is really that the anticipated discharge was in breach of the civil service rules. If that were so, she had a perfectly satisfactory remedy for reinstatement in the courts, just as did the plaintiff in the case upon which she so heavily relies. *City of Hialeah* v. *Stola*, 330 So.2d

825 (Fla. 3d DCA 1976). The rule is, however, that threatened action cannot constitute duress, when there are adequate legal remedies available with which to challenge it. This principle is particularly applicable to employment situations such as this "because a suit will effectively supply damages or other reparation." 13 Williston, supra, §1621, and cases collected at 764.n. 4. Had the plaintiff wished to challenge the discharge, she should and could have done so; her choice not to take that course cannot be deemed the result of duress.

In the last analysis, what Ms. Kory did was take a voluntary action which seemed like a good idea at the time. In hindsight, it turned out to have been a mistake; what she should have done was let herself be improperly fired and then inevitably win the subsequent lawsuit. But "[i]t cannot [therefore] be held that [s]he acted under duress, for, if so, every settlement of a disputed matter made under a mistake of law could be overturned." *Mills* v. *Forest Preserve Dist. of Cook County*, 345 Ill. 503, 178 N.E. at 131.

For the reasons stated, the judgment below is reversed and the cause remanded with direction to dismiss the complaint.

FOR DISCUSSION

1. How does this court define "duress"? Does the definition differ from common notions about what duress is?

2. According to this opinion, why does duress invalidate a contract?

3. The court says that the plaintiff did what seemed like a good idea at the time but which turned out to be the wrong thing to do. Nevertheless, according to the court, no duress was involved. Is there anything about this situation—an individual confronting her municipal employer with her job at stake—that may have impeded plaintiff's ability to determine what the right thing to do was? Why doesn't that constitute duress? Should it?

4. After reading this opinion, can you think of examples of situations in which duress would occur? Explain.

ENFORCEMENT OF CONTRACTS

An unjustified failure to perform a contractual obligation is a breach of contract. When a breach occurs, the injured party must decide whether to seek judicial enforcement of the contract. Enforcement does not generally mean compelling the nonperforming party to actually perform his or her obligation as agreed (specific performance), although that may sometimes be the case. Instead, enforcement usually involves being compensated for the losses sustained as a result of the breach. This means that one hotly contested issue in enforcement of contracts is what remedy is appropriate and to what extent the injured party should properly be compensated. There are, however, many other technical obstacles to enforcement, which are illustrated in the following cases.

In the following excerpt, Melvin Eisenberg considers how and why traditional contract law favors a particular measure of damages for breach of contract, when other measures are available. To some extent, this consideration must deal with how the abstractions of classical contract law deviate from reality as people generally experience it in their everyday transactions.

READING ### The Bargain Principle and Its Limits.
*Melvin Aron Eisenberg**

The institution of contract is central to our social and legal systems, both as reality and as metaphor. At the present time, however, the institution is in conceptual disarray. In the late nineteenth and early twentieth centuries, scholars and courts constructed a philosophical system of contract law characterized in substantial part by logical deduction from received axioms. This system fell into inevitable decline because it failed to recognize that deduction is a means, not an end, and that the purpose of contract law is not simply to create conditions of liability, but also to respond to the social process of promising. As part of this decline, in the last thirty to forty years there has been a wholesome reaction against logical deduction as a dominant mode of contract reasoning. Unfortunately, that reaction has often been accompanied by a wholesale retreat from any conceptualization of contract law—a retreat represented in its extreme forms by suggestions that contract is being absorbed into tort or that there is no institution of contract as such, but only particular transaction-types. These approaches neglect the possibility of reconceptualizing contract law through the development of principles that are intellectually coherent, yet sufficiently open-textured to account for human reality and to unfold over time....

The subject of this Article is the bargain principle and its limits. By bargain, I mean an exchange in which each party views the performance that he undertakes as the price of the performance undertaken by the other. Although parties may barter bargained-for performances without making any promises, contract law is concerned with those bargains that involve a present promise to render a future performance—that is, that involve an exchange over time. By bargain principle, I mean the common law rule that, in the absence of a traditional defense relating to the quality of consent (such as duress, incapacity, misrepresentation, or mutual mistake), the courts will enforce a bargain according to its terms, with the object of putting a bargain promisee in as good a position as if the bargain had been performed....

I. THE BARGAIN PRINCIPLE

Since the law does not enforce promises as such, a legal analysis of bargain promises must start with the question whether such promises should be enforceable at all. In considering this question, it is easiest to begin with those bargains in which one party's performance is both due and rendered before the other's, so that the bargain has become a half-completed or credit transaction. For convenience, I shall generally call the unperformed promise a half-completed bargain promise; the party who has already rendered performance the plaintiff; and the party who has bargained for that performance the defendant.

Whether any given type of promise should be legally enforceable turns on both substantive and administrative considerations. As a substantive matter, the state (speaking through the courts) may fairly take the position that its compulsory processes will not be made available to redress every hurt caused by broken promises, but only to remedy substantial injuries, to prevent unjust enrichment, or to further some independent social policy, such as promotion of the economy. As an administrative matter, the state may fairly take into account the extent to which enforcement of a certain type of promise would involve difficult problems of proof. Cutting across both substantive and administrative categories is the question whether the type of promise at issue is normally made in a deliberative manner, so that it fairly reflects the promisor's wants and resources.

Given these considerations, the half-completed bargain promise presents the strongest possible appeal for legal enforcement. The interests of the plaintiff are typically substantial, because he has incurred the cost of performance and, normally, has seen the defendant enriched to the extent of that performance. The state has independent interests in enforcing such promises. The very strength of the plaintiff's injury may implicate the state's interest in keeping the peace, because a party who has rendered a bargained-but-unpaid-for performance might resort to self-help if the state refused to act on his behalf. Perhaps more important, the nature of the transaction implicates the state's interest in the smooth functioning of its economy. A modern free enterprise system depends heavily on exchanges over time and on private planning. The extent to which actors will be ready to engage in such exchanges, and are able to make reliable plans, depends partly on the probability that promises to render a bargained-for performance will be kept. Other criteria for enforceability point in the same direction. The fact that a valuable performance has been rendered to an unrelated party helps satisfy the criterion of evidentiary security. The fact that a bargain promise is rooted in self-interest rather than altruism tends to ensure that it will be finely calculated and deliberatively made.

The hard question, therefore, is not *whether* half-completed-bargain promises should be legally enforced, but the *extent* to which such promises should be enforced. Three broad possibilities serve as starting points. Such a promise may be enforced: (1) to the extent of the plaintiff's cost, including his opportunity cost (the reliance measure); (2) to the extent of the value conferred upon the defendant (the restitution measure); or (3) to the extent of the value to the plaintiff of the promised performance—that is, the amount required to put the plaintiff in as good a position as if the contract had been performed (the expectation measure). Often these three measures coincide. But what if they do not? Suppose, in particular, that the defendant resists all but restitutionary damages, on the ground that the terms of the bargain were unfair, in the sense that the value of the performance he promised to render exceeded the value he was to receive in exchange.

Generally speaking, the answer of the common law has been to invoke what I have called the bargain principle, which is commonly expressed by such catchphrases as "courts do not inquire into the adequacy of consideration" or "mere inadequacy of consideration will not void a contract." When stated in this way, the principle appears to be substantive, but in large part it is a rule about remedies. What it means is that damages for unexcused breach of a bargain promise should invariably be measured by the value the promised performance would have had to the plaintiff, rather than, and regardless of, the cost or value of the performance for which the defendant's promise was exchanged—a formulation that can be expressed by the concept that a bargain promise should be enforced to its full extent.

If this principle were to be rigorously applied, bargain promises could never be reviewed for fairness of terms. A number of arguments can be made on the bases of fairness and economic efficiency, that the principle should be so applied, at least in the context of a half-completed bargain.

First. The idea of reviewing a bargain for fairness of terms implies that an objective value can be placed upon a bargained-for performance. It can be argued, however, that objective value of a bargained-for performance is not a meaningful concept, because the value of such a performance is that which the parties assign to it. A related argument is that a party who has received a bargained-for performance cannot legitimately object to paying a price that reflects its value to him, and his agreement shows that he valued the performance at least as high as the promised price.

Second.   If *A* has rendered a bargained-for performance to *B*, we know that *A* was willing to render that performance to *B* for the agreed-upon price. We cannot know whether *A* would have rendered that performance to *B* for any lesser price. It can therefore be argued that, having rendered the performance *A* cannot legitimately be required to accept any lesser price. Such a requirement would unfairly convert *A* from a voluntary to an involuntary actor, because had he known in advance that the price would be reduced, he might not have contracted and performed.

Third.   The extent to which private actors are willing to engage in credit transactions (that is, bargains involving exchanges over time) and make plans on the basis of those transactions depends partly on the probability that bargain promises will be kept. It can therefore be argued that failure to enforce bargain promises to their full extent would subvert efficiency by diminishing the willingness of private actors to enter into and plan upon the basis of credit transactions.

Fourth.   The contract price is normally the most efficient price, in the economist's sense of that term, because permitting the price of a commodity to be determined by the interaction of buyers and sellers will normally move the commodity to its highest-valued uses, as expressed by the amounts competing buyers are willing to pay, and will best allocate the factors necessary for the commodity's production.

These arguments find their fullest justification in what might be called the exemplary case for application of the bargain principle—that is, a half-completed bargain in a perfectly competitive market. Such a market involves four elements: a homogeneous commodity (which may consist of either goods or services); a marketplace at which perfect cost-free information concerning price is readily available (hereinafter referred to as a homogeneous marketplace); productive resources that are sufficiently mobile that pricing decisions readily influence their allocation; and participants whose market share is so small that none can affect the commodity's price, so that each takes the market price as given by outside forces.

Now assume such a market, and let the parties to a bargain be the plaintiff-seller, *S*, and a defendant buyer, *B*. Given a homogeneous commodity and a homogeneous market-place, the contract price will be the market price. A number of reasons support the proposition that this price is fair: (1) The mechanism by which the price is generated, a perfectly competitive market, is generally regarded as a fair mechanism. (2) By normal measures of value, the contract price will be equal to the benefit *S* has conferred upon *B*. (3) *S* would not voluntarily have transferred the commodity to *B* at any lower price, because if *B* had not agreed to pay the market price, *S* could have sold it to another buyer at that price. (4) A party who has performed under a half-completed bargain should usually be entitled at a minimum to enforce the other's promise to the extent of his cost. Because *S* probably could have sold the commodity to another buyer at the market price if *B* had not acquired it, the contract price is likely to equal *S*'s opportunity cost. Given perfect competition, the contract price will also normally approximate *S*'s marginal cost.

The price in a perfectly competitive market is also efficient. If the price does exceed marginal cost, then given that pricing decisions readily influence the allocation of productive resources, the prospect of above-normal profits will provide an incentive to increase supply, leading to an increase in capacity and a new (and lower) equilibrium price that yields only normal profits. In contrast, to the extent the price is kept from rising to the equilibrium or market price, there is an incentive to decrease capacity by reallocating resources to other uses and not replacing depleted capital stock. Moreover, because perfect competition prevails, demand for the commodity would exceed the supply at any price less than the market price. Some mechanism other than price would therefore be required for rationing the supply among competing buyers, and the supply would not be allocated to its highest valued uses, as measured by the amounts competing buyers are willing to pay—assuming, at least, that income is either distributed optimally or can best be redistributed by techniques other than price, such as taxation and subsidy.

In short, in the exemplary case the bargain principle is supported by considerations of both fairness and efficiency. Indeed, the bargain principle may well have been formulated on the premise that real cases did not materially differ from the exemplary case. In practice, however, such differences frequently arise, and the balance of this Article considers the strength of the bargain principle when the assumptions of the exemplary case are relaxed.

NOTES

*From 95 *Harvard Law Review* 741 (February 1982). Reprinted with permission. Copyright © 1982 by the Harvard Law Review Association.

FOR DISCUSSION

1. According to Eisenberg, what is a "bargain"? What is the "bargain principle"?
2. What factors may the state consider in determining whether a certain type of promise is to be legally enforceable? How does Eisenberg's view compare with Lon Fuller's?
3. What does the common-law "bargain principle" say about the proper measure of damages a person should be expected to pay in the event of a breach of contract? How does Eisenberg's formulation compare with Holmes's statements about contract liability?
4. Why is the "expectation measure" of damages considered to be the most fair and reasonable one?
5. Eisenberg explains how the expectation measure of damages (bargain principle) operates in the perfectly competitive market situation. Can you think of any objections or reservations with respect to this explanation?

Void and Voidable Contracts

Contracts may be either **void** or **voidable.** Contracts are called void when there is some flaw in the formation of the contract that results in a situation in which no valid contract exists. In that situation, neither party is bound to the contract, and the courts will not enforce it.

A voidable contract, conversely, is one that is otherwise valid and enforceable, but that does not bind one party because he or she was not legally competent to make the contract or was induced to do so through fraud. Such a contract is merely voidable, because the party on whom it is not binding may, nevertheless, choose to honor the agreement, which is called ratification. In any case, the other party to the contract may not use the voidable nature of the agreement as an excuse not to perform it. For example, an adult enters into a contract with a minor for the sale and purchase of stereo equipment. For the minor, the contract is voidable. He may choose to perform it or refuse and offer his lack of capacity as a justification for not performing. The adult, however, is bound to perform the contract as agreed and may not use the other party's lack of competence to make the contract in the first place as an excuse not to perform.

In the following case the court distinguishes between "fraud in the factum," which renders a contract void, and "fraud in the inducement," which renders a contract voidable.

CASE

Robert Mix v. Edgar L. Neff, Jr.
New York Supreme Court, Appellate Division (1984)
99 A.D.2d 180, 473 N.Y.S.2d 31

WEISS, Justice Plaintiff commenced this action for specific performance of an oral contract for the sale of his garage and towing service (which included equipment) or, alternatively, for money damages. It appears that defendant took possession of the equipment, refinanced the same at a bank, paid the cash agreed upon to plaintiff, but refused to execute a promissory note or pay the balance of $18,000. Defendant alleged that plaintiff made fraudulent representations and warranties as to the condition of the equipment and as to certain written contracts for towing with three customers. The answer, which contains an affirmative defense and counterclaim, seeks rescission of the contract and money damages based upon the false and fraudulent representations. On this appeal, defendant contends that the trial court erred by denying its motion, made at the end of plaintiff's case, to dismiss on the ground that plaintiff had failed to prove a prima facie case, and by instructing the jury that defendant had the burden of proof on the issue of fraud in the inducement or false representation.

Defendant first contends that its motion to dismiss at the close of plaintiff's proof should have been granted because plaintiff failed to prove performance on his part. Although the complaint alleged that the sale included "ongoing business relationships and contracts with Cornell University, the Ithaca Police Department, and the United States Post Office," plaintiff testified that he had no contracts with these entities other than a position upon a rotating list of those called when towing services were required. Other proof showed that this position on the lists was assignable and that defendant, had he so desired, could have replaced or succeeded plaintiff on the lists. In the absence of a written agreement of sale, plaintiff's proof of what performance was required of him constituted the only evidence on this issue before the trial court when defendant's motion to dismiss was considered. The court, in denying the motion, held that the term "contract," as used by the parties, was ambiguous and left to the jury the determination of whether plaintiff had "conveyed to defendant what he agreed to give him and whether or not the contract had been breached." We agree. The rule of law on this subject may be found in the case of *Lipsius* v. *White*, 91 A.D.2d 271, 276, 458 N.Y.S.2d 928, where the court said:

> In reviewing [a motion for] the dismissal of plaintiff's complaint this court is required (as was the trial court) to view the evidence in the light most favorable to the plaintiff, and all questions as to witnesses' credibility must be resolved in plaintiff's favor.

In order to have granted defendant's motion, the trial court would have had to find that by no rational process could the jury have found in plaintiff's favor upon the evidence presented. Our review of the record shows the existence of sufficient evidence to support the jury's determination.

Defendant next urges that the trial court erroneously charged the jury that defendant had the burden of proving fraud in the inducement or false representation. This argument underscores a complex dichotomy in the case law which makes a distinction between fraud in the *factum* (or quantum) (*Gilbert* v. *Rothschild*, 280 N.Y. 66, 72, 19 N.E.2d 785) and fraud in the *inducement*. The burden of proof differs in each of these instances. Fraud in the factum generally connotes an attack upon the very existence of a contract from its beginning, in effect alleging that there was no legal contract and that the instrument never had a valid inception. The attack is upon certain facts which occurred at the time of the alleged execution of the agreement, upon which facts the validity of the agreement depends. For example, the claim could be that the signatory signed an instrument different from that which he understood it to be. In such case, the instrument would be void *ab initio* (*id.* at 71, 19 N.E.2d 785). In essence, this defense is "in substance negative" (*Murray* v. *Narwood*, 192 N.Y. 172, 177, 84 N.E. 958) and results in the requirement that a "plaintiff, in undertaking to prove the contract upon which his action is based, [has] cast upon him the burden of establishing by a preponderance of evidence, that it was a good and valid contract having a legal inception which was binding upon the defendant" (*Fleming* v. *Ponziani*, 24 N.Y.2d 105, 110, 299 N.Y.S.2d 134, 247 N.E.2d 114). In such cases, rescission is unnecessary.

To be distinguished is the claim where an opponent of a contract asserts the defense of fraud in the inducement, which, if proven, renders the contract voidable (see *Adams* v. *Gillig*, 199 N.Y. 314, 317, 92 N.E. 670). This form of fraud is usually based on facts occurring prior or subsequent to the execution of the contract which tend to demonstrate that an agreement, valid on its face and properly executed, is to be limited or avoided. When an opponent of a contract alleges fraud in the inducement, whether as an affirmative defense or by way of a counterclaim seeking rescission, he must sustain the burden of persuasion. That burden of proving fraud in the inducement or a cause of action seeking rescission on that ground, requires that the proof be "by most satisfactory evidence" (*Adams* v. *Gillig*, *supra*, 199 N.Y. at p. 323, 92 N.E. 670), which we interpret to be clear and convincing evidence rather than only a fair preponderance of the credible evidence. We have also accepted the principle that innocent misrepresentations are sufficient to make a contract voidable.

These principles in mind, an examination of this record shows that the charge to the jury was correct with respect to the imposition upon defendant of the burden of proving the claims of fraud in the inducement and misrepresentation made in his affirmative defense and counterclaim. Since defendant conceded a valid *oral* contract, plaintiff was relieved of the burden of proving the absence of fraud in the factum attendant execution. Since defendant instead argued that the fraud and misrepresentation centered upon the condition of the equipment sold and the presence or absence of written contracts for towing services with Cornell University, the Ithaca Police Department, and the United States Post Office and sought rescission and money damages in his counterclaim, the burden of persuasion rested upon defendant as to those allegations. The trial court did, however, err in that portion of its jury instructions dealing with the quantum of proof required to fulfill that burden when it described the burden as "a fair preponderance of the credible evidence." Although the burden of proof actually requires "the most satisfactory evidence," the error here favored defendant by imposition of a lesser standard of proof, and it, therefore, does not require reversal.

The judgment should be affirmed, with costs.

FOR DISCUSSION

1. What is the definition of "fraud in the factum"? Who has the burden of proof when fraud in the factum is alleged?

2. What is "fraud in the inducement"? Who has the burden of proof in this situation?

3. What was the disadvantage to defendant of having an oral agreement?

4. What is the difference between proof "by most satisfactory evidence" and "by a fair preponderance of the evidence"? Why might a claim of fraud in the inducement require a different standard of proof?

5. Suppose a party to a contract realizes subsequently that he has made an unwise bargain. Based on this case, does it seem likely that he can avoid having to perform it?

Statute of Frauds

The Statute of Frauds requires certain contracts to be in writing to be enforceable. Each state has its own statute of frauds, and the types of contracts covered vary from one jurisdiction to another. Most statutes of frauds, however, require the following types of contracts to be written: (1) contracts for the sale of an interest in real property; (2) contracts that cannot be performed in one year; (3) contracts made by an executor or administrator in respect of debts made by the decedent; (4) contracts made in consideration of marriage; and (5) contracts in which one person agrees to answer for the debts of another.

In the following case, the respondents offer the Statute of Frauds as a defense to a claim involving an oral contract. In New York State, the Statute of Frauds (General Obligations Law §5-701) contains a provision that a contract that cannot be performed during the promisee's lifetime must be in writing to be enforceable.

CASE

In the Matter of Sol Kittay, deceased.
Susan Schleger, Appellant v. Arlene J. Imberman et al.
New York Supreme Court, Appellate Division (1986)
118 A.D.2d 647, 500 N.Y.S.2d 6

MEMORANDUM BY THE COURT. In a proceeding to compel an accounting, the petitioner appeals from an order of the Surrogate's Court, Westchester County (Brewster, S.), dated July 18, 1984, which granted the respondents' motion for summary judgment and dismissed her petition.

Order affirmed, with costs payable by the appellant personally.

The petitioner alleged that she and the decedent entered into an express oral agreement wherein she was to serve as the decedent's social and traveling companion and confidante in return for which he was to "take care of" and "support" her for the rest of her life. There were no witnesses to this oral agreement.

Upon decedent's death, the petitioner filed a claim against his estate seeking the sum of $3,200,000. The executors moved for summary judgment dismissing the claim. The Surrogate granted the executors' motion and we affirm.

On this motion for summary judgment, the evidence must be viewed in the light most favorable to the petitioner. When so viewed, it is apparent that the alleged agreement, by its terms, was not capable of performance before the end of the petitioner's lifetime. Therefore, her claim was barred by the Statute of Frauds (see General Obligations Law §5-701[a][1]; *Meltzer* v. *Koenigsberg*, 302 N.Y. 523, 99 N.E.2d 679).

Further, in the context of this record, the alleged agreement, which contained no specifics as to the form, frequency and amount of payment, was too vague to spell out a meaningful promise (see *Dombrowski* v. *Somers*, 41 N.Y.2d 858, 393 N.Y.S.2d 706, 362 N.E.2d 257).

FOR DISCUSSION

1. Why can't the contract alleged in this case be performed within the petitioner's lifetime? Does this seem reasonable?

2. Suppose the Statute of Frauds did not apply to this case, how would petitioner have proven the terms of the agreement?

3. Are contracts such as the one alleged by petitioner in this case favored by society? Do you think that may have some influence on the outcome of the case?

Contracts in Violation of Law

One of the fundamental elements of a contract is that it must have a legal subject matter. The court will not enforce a contract that involves a violation of the law. (Similarly, a promise to do something illegal is not sufficient consideration for a contract.) If parties agree to do something illegal, they are left to themselves in the event the contract is breached. In the following case, the contract at issue obviously exists within the context of illegal conduct, and so the court must scrutinize the parties' agreement very carefully to determine whether it should be judicially enforced.

CASE   **Frohlich & Newell Foods, Inc. v. New Sans Souci Nursing Home**
Civil Court of the City of New York (1981)
109 Misc.2d 974, 441 N.Y.S.2d 335

MARA T. THORPE, Judge.   In this action, the plaintiff, a wholesale supplier of food to more than twenty nursing homes, seeks to recover $2211.55, an amount representing the value of some food sold and delivered to the nursing home owned by the defendants between March 1974 and March 1977, for which the defendants never paid. The defendants concede that they owe the plaintiff the sum sought, but counterclaim for $6475.00 which the plaintiff overbilled the defendants during the same period. The case was submitted on stipulated facts.

The law and public policy of New York are clear on the subject of contracts involving commercial bribery, kickbacks, and other forms of corruption. In *Stone* v. *Freeman*, 298 N.Y. 268, 271, 82 N.E.2d 571, the Court stated that it is well settled that "a party to an illegal contract cannot ask a court of law to help him to carry out his illegal object...." This principle was reaffirmed in *McConnell* v. *Commonwealth Pictures Corporation*, 7 N.Y.2d 465, 199 N.Y.S.2d 483, 166 N.E.2d 494, where the court held that recovery could be barred even under a contract which in itself was entirely legal, but where the course of performance of the contract by the plaintiff took an illegal form and the illegality was central to or a dominant part thereof.

Here, the agreement in March 1974, that the plaintiff continue to sell food to the nursing home, was predicated upon Frohlich's agreement to submit false bills to the nursing home for food delivered (in essence overbilling it) and to "kick back" in cash to the home's operators that part of the payment which did not reflect food actually delivered. According to the stipulated facts, both parts of the agreement were carried out from 1974 to March 1977.

Although there may be nothing illegal per se about such an agreement between a vendor and the owner of a business, which Frohlich though Konstam (the general manager of the nursing home) to be, or about the implementation of the agreement, as stated in *People* v. *Lerner*, 90 Misc.2d 513, 394 N.Y.S.2d 514, 516 "without a doubt a man of ordinary intelligence would realize, in these circumstances, that this is not conduct within the normal business practices." Indeed, it was obviously so singular a business procedure as to put Frohlich on notice that the phoney bills probably, and in fact, were being utilized by the nursing home operators for a fraudulent purpose. A businessman of ordinary intelligence in Frohlich's situation would infer that, at the least, there was a substantial chance that the false billings would be put to an illegal use. He cannot both fail to govern his conduct as if such fact existed, until he could ascertain its existence or non-existence, and thereafter invoke the aid of the courts in recovering fruits of the arrangement when it turned out in fact to be tainted with illegality.

Thus, by willingly supplying false bills to the nursing home operators and being on notice that the bills he supplied might well be used for an illegal purpose, Frohlich's conduct was tantamount to the crime of criminal facilitation (Penal Law §115.00), since reimbursement in the amount of $3459.60 was in fact feloniously[6] obtained from the State on the basis of the false bills.

For the foregoing reasons, the court has concluded that the agreement upon which the plaintiff seeks to recover was sufficiently permeated with fraud and illegality to bring this case within the spirit of *Stone* v. *Freeman, supra,* and *McConnell* v. *Commonwealth Pictures Corporation, supra,* if not their four corners. Accordingly, the Court holds that the State's public policy bars the plaintiff from recovery here.

The complaint is dismissed and judgment shall be for the plaintiff on the counterclaim.

FOR DISCUSSION

1. What were the terms of the agreement between Frohlich and the operators of the nursing home? Was this contract in itself illegal?

2. What should Frohlich have known or suspected about the ultimate objective of his contract with the nursing home? Could he reasonably expect the courts to sanction such an agreement?

3. According to the court, of what crime was Frohlich probably guilty? Of what crimes were the nursing home operators guilty?

4. According to this case, what is New York law governing enforcement of illegal contracts, and why did this court refuse to enforce a contract about which it said there was "nothing illegal per se"?

Contracts against Public Policy

As we have said previously, contracts that provide for the commission of a crime or any illegal objective, or that are in violation of the law, are void and unenforceable. Another category of unenforceable contracts is contracts against public policy. Contracts that promote or encourage immoral behavior, for example, may be void as against public policy even if a direct violation of law (such as statutes making producing an obscene film a crime) is not involved.

---

[6]Obtaining reimbursement for false bills is conduct amounting to grand larceny, second degree (Penal Law §155.35), and the offering of a false instrument for filing, first degree (Penal Law §175.35), both felonies.

One lawsuit that has attracted national attention recently is the *Baby M.* case, in which the New Jersey Supreme Court held that a surrogate mother contract in which a woman was paid $10,000 to bear a child for a man and his infertile wife, and who was then expected to renounce her rights to her child so that the father's wife could adopt the child, was unenforceable both as illegal and as against public policy. According to the court, the contract was illegal because it violated the New Jersey adoption law, which prohibited payment in exchange for adopting a child. The contract was also found to be against public policy by its modification of the rights of parents to a child without a hearing to determine the child's best interests and by its establishment of exclusive rights to the child in favor of the father by extinguishing the rights of the mother. Although this decision had direct application only in New Jersey, it has indirectly affected surrogate mother contracts all over the country, either by discouraging people from entering into such agreements, encouraging parties to such contracts to refuse to perform them, or by encouraging state legislatures to address the issue of surrogacy through legislation.

Another category of contracts that has frequently been found to violate public policy is that involving agreements between unmarried cohabitants to divide or distribute their jointly owned property. In 1976, in *Marvin* v. *Marvin*, 557 P.2d 106, the famous "palimony" case involving actor Lee Marvin, the California Supreme Court held that such agreements were not against public policy in California, as long as the explicit consideration for the contract was not sexual services. Not every court in the United States has followed that ruling, however, and many such contracts are declared void as against public policy.

In the following case, the plaintiff seeks to enforce a contract of employment associated with his participation in a fraudulent activity of his employer. To a great extent the court seems to identify illegal subject matter of a contract and violation of public policy; however, you should examine carefully the standards the court sets forth to determine whether a contract can be said to violate public policy.

CASE　　　　　　　　**Greg Sacks v. Dallas Gold & Silver Exchange, Inc.**
Texas Court of Appeals-Dallas (1986)
720 S.W.2d 177

MCCRAW, Justice.　Greg Sacks filed suit against Dallas Gold & Silver Exchange, Inc. (DGSE) and G. Michael Oyster, seeking enforcement of an agreement to pay accrued compensation allegedly due to him at the time his DGSE employment ended. The jury found that DGSE breached its agreement to pay Sacks and that DGSE forced Sacks to resign due to his refusal to carry out a fraudulent rent reduction scheme. The trial court, however, sustained DGSE's motion for judgment notwithstanding the verdict and ordered that Sacks take nothing. Sacks now appeals from this judgment in three points of error asserting that the trial court erred. We disagree with Sacks' assertions and, accordingly, affirm the trial court's judgment.

Sacks was employed by DGSE as an "assistant controller-credit manager" in October 1982. There was no written employment contract. In April 1983, Sacks received a promotion to "controller"; his oral employment agreement with DGSE allowed over-time compensation. Sacks, as controller, was to prepare quarterly statements for DGSE's landlord, to determine proper rental payments. The rent was based upon a percentage of DGSE's sales.

Upon assuming his role as controller, Sacks found that the previously submitted statements were falsified to show lesser rental amounts owing. Sacks wrote a memo to several DGSE officers about the enormous amount of the rent obligation. The memo presented four options for resolving the problem: (1) pay the additional $114,396 as required by the lease; (2) renegotiate the lease immediately; (3) terminate the lease; or (4) keep two sets of books. In response, Sacks was told to take care of the matter and to submit the report to show DGSE only owing $3,000.00.

Sacks states he expressed his concern over submission of fraudulent reports and the eventual inspection of the books by the landlord's auditors. In July 1983, Sacks received $11,000 as partial payment for his 100 hours accrued overtime, leaving $29,918 unpaid. Later, on February 9, 1984, the matter of the impending audit resurfaced. Sacks was embarrassed and did not want to be involved in this audit since he had been preparing incorrect monthly statements. Sacks attempted to resign, but changed his mind when he was told that his overtime would not be paid unless he stayed. As an incentive to stay with DGSE, Sacks was offered a $25,000 bonus for helping them through the audit. Sacks received this bonus. On February 28, 1984, Sacks' last day of employment, an agreement was drafted by DGSE agreeing to pay Sacks for overtime, wages, and accrued vacation. This is the agreement upon which Sacks bases his cause of action.

In his first point of error, Sacks claims that the trial court erred in entering a judgment notwithstanding the verdict as there was sufficient evidence to support the jury verdict: (1) awarding exemplary damages for wrongful discharge, and (2) awarding damages for breach of the February 28, 1984, agreement. We disagree. In reviewing the entry of a judgment notwithstanding the verdict, we must consider the evidence in the light most favorable to the party against whom the judgment was rendered, and every reasonable inference must be indulged in that party's favor. It must be determined that there is no evidence of probative force upon which the jury could have made the findings relied upon.

Sacks claims that there is adequate evidence to support the jury's finding that he was wrongfully discharged. We disagree. The statement of facts before us shows that Sacks was the only witness to testify. We do not find any evidence supporting the proposition that Sacks was wrongfully discharged. The words "resigned" and "quit" are the words Sacks himself uses to describe his attempted termination and actual termination.

The statement of facts in no way indicates that Sacks was fired or ousted as controller for DGSE. To the contrary, all the evidence indicates Sacks' superiors wanted him to stay. We hold there is no evidence of probative force to support the jury finding that Sacks was wrongfully discharged and, therefore, sustain the trial court's judgment notwithstanding the verdict on this finding.

Sacks also complains that there is sufficient evidence to support the jury's verdict for damages due to the breach of the February 28, 1984, agreement to pay him for his accrued wages and benefits. These amounts were from Sacks' work, which admittedly consisted of aiding and assisting DGSE in the perpetration of a fraud. Sacks acknowledges his complicity in the illegal activities in his first amended petition for relief:

> After aiding and assisting Defendants and virtually all other employees of Dallas Gold and Silver Exchange in the "Folsom Project" (*the sceme* [*sic*] *to defraud* [*the Landlord*]) during the period of 14 February through 28 February 1984, Plaintiff on 28 February met the individual defendants and Terry Hanlon, the general manager of Dallas Gold & Silver Exchange, and announced his refusal to *continue in the illegal activities.* At that time Defendants delivered [the agreement sued upon]. [Emphasis added.]

Clearly, Sacks was aware and joined in DGSE's fraudulent activities shortly after he assumed the position of controller in April 1983. Thereafter, he continued in that activity until he resigned in February 1984. The evidence indicates that these activities covered approximately a ten-month period and not, as Sacks contends, merely a period of time in February 1984 during which the audit took place.

The courts will not enforce a contract whose provisions are against public policy. *Baron* v. *Mullinax, Wells, Mauzy & Baab, Inc.*, 623 S.W.2d 457, 461 (Tex.-App.—Texarkana 1981, writ ref'd n.r.e.). In examining an agreement to determine if it is contrary to public policy the court must look for a tendency to be injurious to the public good. *Hazelwood* v. *Mandrell Industries Co.*, 596 S.W.2d 204, 206 (Tex.Civ.App.—Houston [1st Dist.] 1980, writ ref'd n.r.e.). The DGSE-Sacks agreement to pay accrued compensation on its face is not contrary to public policy. But, when the agreement's underlying facts were examined by the trial court, it was clear that the fraudulent rent reduction scheme was injurious to the public good and contrary to public policy. We hold that the trial court correctly refused to enforce Sacks'[s] agreement.

Sacks has argued that the monies due him were not earned as the result of illegal activity and, therefore, he should be compensated. Upon review of the record, we find that the time Sacks worked in legal activity is so commingled with his illegal activity that no differentiation can be made. In this situation, where illegal provisions in a contract are not severable from the legal provisions, the entire agreement will be invalid. *Redgrave* v. *Wilkinson*, 208 S.W.2d 150, 152 (Tex.Civ.App.—Waco 1948, writ ref'd n.r.e.). Therefore, the trial court correctly disregarded the jury's finding that there was a breach of contract between the parties. Sacks' point of error one is overruled.

In his third point of error, appellant contends that the trial court erred in failing to enter a judgment on the jury verdict based solely on Sacks' refusal to commit a fraud, since the *in pari delicto* defense is not available as a matter of law. We disagree with this final point of error.

A party may assert the defense of illegality to prevent the enforcement of an illegal contract against him even though he was himself equally guilty with the other party. *Emco,. Inc.* v *Healy*, 602 S.W.2d 309, 313 (Tex.Civ.App—Texarkana 1980, no writ). When parties are in equal fault the courts generally will not aid in the enforcement of the illegal contract, nor provide relief to a party who has executed the contract, but will leave the parties as they find them. Accordingly, this Court will not intervene to enforce the illegal agreement between the parties, but will leave the parties as they are. Sacks'[s] third point of error is overruled. The judgment of the trial court is affirmed.

FOR DISCUSSION

1. According to this opinion, how does a court determine whether a contract is against public policy?

2. What public policy does the contract in this case appear to violate?

3. The court states that the contract in this case is not against public policy "on its face." Given the court's discussion of the matter, what do you think that means?

4. In this case, the court frequently describes the contract at issue as illegal. What makes this contract illegal? Is it possible that a contract could be against public policy even if it is not illegal? Support your answer.

5. By refusing to enforce the contract between DGSE and Sacks, isn't the court rewarding DGSE for the same conduct for which it is punishing Sacks? Does this seem fair? Do you see any way out of this dilemma?

Unconscionable Contracts

Unconscionability is an increasingly frequent reason offered to justify not performing a contract. According to *American Jurisprudence*, "An unconscionable agreement is one such as no individual in his senses and not under a delusion would make on one hand, and as no honest or fair person would accept, on the other, the inequality being so strong and manifest as to shock the conscience and confound the judgment of any person of common sense. As a general proposition, unconscionability requires some showing of an absence of meaningful choice on the part of one of the parties together with contract terms which are unreasonably favorable to the other party."[7] The elements of unconscionable agreements include inflated prices, unfair disclaimers of warranty, termination clauses, high pressure sales tactics, misrepresentation, and unfair bargaining.

In the case of an unconscionable contract, one party is claiming that the terms of the bargain, or the conditions under which it was agreed to, were so unfair and one-sided as to deprive the other party of any meaningful choice in the matter. This argument has been made most successfully in cases involving consumer agreements where a seller is in the position to dictate terms to a vulnerable and often ill-informed consumer-buyer. As the following case indicates, claims of unconscionability in a commercial context are much less likely to be successful.

CASE

Seymour Gillman etc. v. Chase Manhattan Bank
New York Supreme Court, Appellate Division (1987)
135 A.D.2d 488, 521 N.Y.S.2d 729

MEMORANDUM BY THE COURT. Jamaica Tobacco & Sales Corp. (hereinafter Jamaica Tobacco), located in Queens, New York, was a business engaged in the wholesale trade of tobacco and related items. As such it was required to purchase cigarette tax stamps from the City and State of New York and attach them to each package sold. Jamaica Tobacco generally purchased these stamps on a credit basis, collateralized by a surety bond from Aetna Casualty and Surety Company (hereinafter Aetna). Aetna required security for its bond in the form of a bank letter of credit.

On July 28, 1981, Stephen Frohlich, the president of Jamaica Tobacco applied to the defendant Chase Manhattan Bank, N.A. (hereinafter Chase) for a $400,000 letter of credit. Immediately above the signature line, the application form provided in bold print and capital letters that "The Security Agreement on the reverse hereof is hereby accepted and made applicable to this Application and the Credit." On the reverse thereof, and in pertinent part, the form contained provisions which essentially gave Chase the right to set off any of its obligations under the letter of credit against any account maintained by Jamaica Tobacco, and to apply the proceeds or balance to any potential obligation in the event it felt insecure. Frohlich testified that he never read this security agreement and that no one at Chase had brought it to his attention. On August 10, 1981, Chase issued the irrevocable letter of credit for the benefit of Aetna. In conjunction therewith, Chase required Frohlich to sign a subordination agreement, a negative pledge agreement and personal guarantees. Jamaica also opened and maintained a checking account with Chase.

[7]21 Am Jur.2d, Contracts, §141, p. 547.

In October 1982 Frohlich met with the officers of the bank and his accountant. At the outset of the meeting, Chase assured him that the letter of credit had been reissued in August 1982. However, upon reviewing Jamaica Tobacco's financial statement of October 1982 covering the year 1981, Chase's officers became concerned with the financial state of the corporation and they asked Frohlich for collateral. Frohlich refused to provide collateral because he claimed he did not have any further assets. He explained that the corporation had experienced difficulty when he had left control thereof with his son-in-law and his son-in-law's brother: he had fired them and retaken control. In addition Chase's officers accused him of violating the subordination agreement because the financial statement showed that debts to the officers had decreased. Frohlich denied that Jamaica Tobacco has paid off any of its debts to its officers.

A few days later, Chase deemed itself insecure and segregated $372,921 from Jamaica Tobacco's checking account into a separate account. Chase had discovered that, shortly after their officers' meeting with him, Frohlich had allowed his parents to file UCC perfecting statements against the corporation to secure their loans upon its accounts receivables and inventory.

Aetna did not make a demand under the letter of credit until June 2, 1983. Chase paid out under its obligation on June 22, 1983. However, by this time, Jamaica Tobacco had been put out of business and one month after the segregation, Jamaica Tobacco executed an assignment for the benefit of its creditors. The instant action brought by the assignee of Jamaica Tobacco ensued.

Chase essentially denied the allegations of the complaint, and asserted that it had lawfully segregated the funds from Jamaica Tobacco's checking account under its rights pursuant to the security agreement on the reverse of the application for the letter of credit. In addition, Chase asserted that it had acted in good faith in so doing, and that, since it had paid out the funds to Aetna pursuant to its demand on June 22, 1983, it had no funds owing to Jamaica Tobacco and in fact it had a deficiency with Jamaica Tobacco in the amount of $27,079. Finally, it claimed that the plaintiff had waived any claim he had and that he was estopped from maintaining the action.

After a trial of the action in which, by motion to conform the pleadings to the proof, Jamaica Tobacco asserted an additional claim premised upon the allegedly unconscionable terms of the security agreement, the trial court determined that the terms of the security agreement were unconscionable. The court determined that, since the application for the letter of credit was labeled as such, it was reasonable for Frohlich to have considered it in its limited function and to have assumed that any conditions upon the granting of credit would have been imposed at the time the letter of credit was actually approved, and not in the application. The court also found that the clauses granting the right to segregate funds from the account were unreasonably favorable to Chase because they provided it with the opportunity to seize and deplete Jamaica Tobacco's account and to completely destroy its credit and its business without giving it the opportunity to alleviate any insecurity. The court further found that the terms of this security agreement were so unfair and manifesting of a lack of good faith and common business decency that those terms shocked the conscience and good judgment of the court. It was noted that the terms were in fine print and were inconspicuous to the point of being unreadable and that there was never any proof offered to show that such an agreement was being commonly used in the industry. Finally, the court found that the actions of Chase were so immoral and egregious that it awarded the plaintiff punitive damages in the amount of $500,000.

The general rule is that if the signer of an agreement could have read it in its entirety, to not have read it was gross negligence. If he could not read it, then he should procure someone to read it for him and to fail to do so is equally negligent. In either case, the agreement is binding upon him. Therefore, it is incumbent upon the signer of a contract to read it and his claim that he failed to do so will not generally serve to invalidate the contract.

Moreover, the doctrine of unconscionability has little applicability in the commercial setting because it is presumed that businessmen deal at arm's length with relative equality of bargaining power. Apparently, the doctrine is primarily a means with which to protect the "commercially illiterate consumer beguiled into a grossly unfair bargain by a deceptive vendor or finance company." *Equitable Lbr. Corp.* v. *IPA Land Development Corp.*, 38 N.Y.2d 516, 523, 381 N.Y.S.2d 459, 344 N.E.2d 391.

There is no possible explanation for Frohlich's failure to have read the security agreement on the reverse of the application or to have procured counsel to read it for him. According to the testimony of Frohlich himself, he had received the completed but unsigned application from Chase in his office. At that time, and before signing it, he could have read it at his leisure. Furthermore, although the print is fine and the lines are close together, the actual language is entirely readable. Moreover, there is a "conspicuous" legend (see Uniform Commercial Code §1-201[10]) immediately above the signature line which is in capital letters and bold print and which clearly directed his attention to the security agreement on the reverse side. Furthermore, it is noted that this letter of credit was not the first one that Frohlich had applied for or received. He had been in the business of selling tobacco products for 15 years, and he was well aware that Chase was assuming a great risk by giving such credit. Moreover, there is nothing inherently wrong with the attempt by Chase to decrease its exposure under the letter of credit by giving it some means to secure payment from Jamaica Tobacco inasmuch as the letter of credit was irrevocable and had established an obligation that was independent from the ability of Jamaica Tobacco to reimburse.

In addition, other factors militate against a finding of unconscionability. Firstly, there is no evidence that it was necessary for Frohlich to have dealt with Chase in seeking the letter of credit such that he would have had no meaningful choice in accepting the terms of the security agreement. He could have gone to any other bank to apply for a letter of credit. Moreover, the size of the transaction alone should have alerted Frohlich to the necessity of reading all of the papers provided by Chase and it was unreasonable for him not to have considered that Chase would be seeking additional security for its substantial risk.

Reversed.

FOR DISCUSSION

1. What factors did the trial court use to support its finding that the security agreement was unconscionable?

2. What factors did the appellate court use to decide that the agreement was *not* unconscionable?

3. How could the two courts have such diametrically opposed views of this transaction? What seems to be the decisive factor in the case?

4. In this opinion, the court cites a "general rule" that if people fail to read the contracts they sign they are grossly negligent. Is the rule fairly applied in the *Gillman* case you have just read?

5. Why does it make a difference that Frohlich could have gone to another bank for his letter of credit?

6. Given the situation described in this case, what does it mean when the court says that businessmen deal with one another "at arm's length"? Does it make sense that consumers should not be treated in the same fashion? Explain your answer.

PERFORMANCE OR NONPERFORMANCE

The casebooks and the law reports are filled with examples of failed or flawed contracts. Despite this, most contracts are successful. Not surprisingly, it is the unsuccessful ones that get most of the attention. In the previous sections of this chapter, we have examined problems in the formation of contracts, as well as problems with enforceability. The cases in this section deal with possible remedies for breach of contract and defenses against such actions. (The subject of contract remedies will be dealt with again in Chapter 10, which discusses judicial remedies.

In the following excerpt, Grant Gilmore discusses the classical conception of contractual liability and expresses his skepticism about the ability of traditional contract law to deal with the problems of real people in the modern world.

READING

The Death of Contract
Grant Gilmore *

It appears that, before addressing ourselves to the mystery of the death of contract, we must spend some time on what may be even the greater mystery of its birth.

In a remarkable recent book, Professor Lawrence Friedman has contributed some novel insights into the nature of what he calls the "pure" or "classical" theory of contract, by which he refers to the theory as it developed in the nineteenth century.... Although we shall depart from his analysis at some points, we may retain as central ideas the concept of the general law of contract as a residual category—what is left over after all the "specialized" bodies of law have been added up—highly abstract, in close historical relationship with the free market of classical economic theory, a theoretical construct which, having little or nothing to do with the real world, would not—or could not—change as the real world changed. Professor Friedman goes on to comment on another significant aspect of the contract construct—which is that it resisted, and continues to resist, codification long after most, if not all, of the fields of law most closely related to it had passed under the statutory yoke. We must indeed provide ourselves at some point with an explanation of why it was that, instead of a Uniform Contracts Act, we got a *Restatement of Contracts*.

I have credited Dean Langdell with the almost inadvertent discovery of the general theory of Contract. The reference was to his pioneering casebook on Contracts which appeared just a hundred years ago and, even more, to the "Summary of the Law of Contracts" which he added as an appendix to the second edition of the casebook in 1880....

...To judge by the casebook and the Summary, Langdell was an industrious researcher of no distinction whatever of mind or...of style. But it is with Langdell that, for the first time, we see Contracts as, in Professor Friedman's term, an "abstraction"—a remote, impersonal, bloodless abstraction. The three principal chapters into which the casebook is divided are entitled: Mutual Assent, Consideration and Conditional Contracts: we are evidently at a far remove from Story's list of "commercial contracts." The casebook according to Langdell, was to contain—and presumably did contain—all the important contract cases that had ever been decided. "All the cases" turned out to be mostly English cases, arranged in historical sequence from the seventeenth century down to the date of publication; the English cases were occasionally supplemented by comparable sequences of cases from New York and Massachusetts—no other American jurisdictions being represented. The Summary, which runs to a hundred and fifty pages or so, is devoted almost entirely to explaining which of the cases in the main part of the casebook are "right" and which are "wrong." The explanation, typically, is dogmatic rather than reasoned; Langdell knew right from wrong, no doubt by divine revelation, and that should suffice for the student. This aspect of the Summary of the Law of Contracts throws an entertaining light on the origins of case-method teaching. At least in Langdell's version, it had nothing whatever to do with getting students to think for themselves: it was, on the contrary, a method of indoctrination through brainwashing.

Langdell, then, did little more than launch the idea that there was—or should be—such a thing as a general theory of contract. The theory itself was pieced together by his successors—notably Holmes, in broad philosophical outline, and Williston, in meticulous, although not always accurate, scholarly detail. At this point it is necessary to give some idea of the content of what we may call the Holmes-Williston construct— which I shall attempt to do impressionistically rather than scientifically. Having accomplished that chore, we can return to the far more interesting business of speculating on why Langdell's idea, brilliantly reformulated by Holmes, had the fabulous success it did instead of going down the drain into oblivion as a hundred better ideas than Langdell's do every day of the week.

The theory seems to have been dedicated to the proposition that, ideally, no one should be liable to anyone for anything. Since the ideal was not attainable, the compromise solution was to restrict liability within the narrowest possible limits. Within those limits, however, liability was to be absolute: as Holmes put it, "The only universal consequence of a legally binding promise is, that the law makes the promisor pay damages if the promised event does not come to pass." Liability, although absolute—at least in theory—was nevertheless, to be strictly limited. The equitable remedy of specific performance was to be avoided as far as possible—no doubt we would all be better off if Lord Coke's views had prevailed in the seventeenth century and the equitable remedy had never developed at all. Money damages for breach of contract were to be "compensatory," never punitive; the contract-breaker's motivation, Holmes explained, makes no legal difference whatever and indeed every man has a right "to break his contract if he chooses"—that is a right to elect to pay damages instead of performing his contractual obligation. Therefore the wicked contract-breaker should pay no more in damages than the innocent and the pure in heart. The "compensatory" damages, which were theoretically recoverable, turned out to be a good deal less than enough to compensate the victim for the losses which in fact he might have suffered. Damages in contract, it was pointed out, were one thing and damages in tort another; the contract-breaker was not to be held responsible, as the tortfeasor was, for all the consequences of his actions. Another aspect of the theory was that the courts should operate as detached umpires or referees, doing no more than to see that the rules of the game were observed and refusing to intervene affirmatively to see that justice or anything of that sort was done. Courts do not, it was said, make contracts for the parties. The parties themselves must see that the last "i" is properly dotted, the last "t" properly crossed; the courts will not do it for them. And if A, without the protection of a binding contract, improvidently relies, to his detriment, on B's promises and assurances, that may be unfortunate for A but is no fit matter for legal concern. Contract liability, furthermore, was to be sharply differentiated from tort liability and there was to be no softening or blurring of the harsh limitations of contract theory by the recognition of an intermediate no-man's-land between contract and tort; the idea which later flourished as "quasi-contract" was no part of the Holmesian theory....

Where did the idea for this curious— one is tempted to say, monstrous—machine come from? It is fair to say that the theory of contract did not come as the natural result of a continuing case-law development; in fact, it represented a sharp break with the past, even the recent past. The inventors of the theory did not make it all up out of their own heads. Indeed they made industrious use of whatever bits and pieces of case law, old and new, could be made to fit the theory....

...The balance wheel of the great machine was the theory of consideration, newly reformulated and put to some hitherto unsuspected uses. The word "consideration" has been around for a long time, so it is tempting to think that we have had a theory of consideration for a long time. In fact until the nineteenth century the word never acquired any particular meaning or stood for any theory....

...The new day dawned with Holmes....

It seems perfectly clear that Holmes was, quite consciously, proposing revolutionary doctrine and was not in the least interested in stating or restating the common law as it was. He was, at the time he wrote the lectures which make up *The Common Law*, as learned in the history of the law—including the law of contracts—as any lawyer in the English-speaking world. Yet his analysis of the true meaning of "consideration" comes forth almost naked of citation of authority or precedent. He starts with an off-hand reference to what is commonly "said" and commonly "thought." However, what is clear to Holmes "has not always been sufficiently borne in mind" by others. Whereupon, we are off to the races at a startling clip....

...With the Holmesian formulation, consideration became a tool for narrowing contractual liability. "The whole doctrine of contract," he noted in this connection, "is formal and external." Unless the formalities were accomplished, there could be no contract and, consequently, no liability. The austerity of doctrine would not be tempered for the shorn lambs who might shiver in its blast.

The theoretical basis having thus been provided, the next step was the extension of the newly minted theory of consideration to the entire life-history of a contract, from birth to death. Consideration theory was used to explain why offers, even if they are expressed to be irrevocable, are in their nature necessarily revocable at any time before acceptance—why modifications of going contracts under which A promises to pay B more than the originally agreed contract price for doing the work are not binding on A—why agreements by creditors to discharge their debtors on payment of less than the amount due are not binding on the creditors. For the result in each of these situations there was indeed some case law precedent, past or current, but accommodation of the cases to the newfangled theory required something like major surgery on the cases themselves....

Let us assume, arguendo, that it is the fate of contract to be swallowed up by tort (or for both of them to be swallowed up in a generalized theory of civil obligation). We must still provide ourselves with an explanation of what contract—the classical or general theory of contract, as we have called it—was about in the first place and, if it is now dead or dying, what caused the fatal disease.

We started with Professor Friedman's suggestion that the "model" of classical contract theory bore a close resemblance to the "model" of what he calls "liberal"—or, I suppose, laissez-faire— economic theory. In both models, as he put it, "parties could be treated as individual economic units which, in theory, enjoyed complete mobility and freedom of decision." I suppose that laissez-faire economic theory comes down to something like this: If we all do exactly as we please, no doubt everything will work out for the best. Which does seem to be about the same thing that the contract theory comes down to, with liability reduced to a minimum and sanctions for breach cut back to the vanishing point. I do not mean to suggest—nor, I am sure, did Professor Friedman—that the lawyers and economists who constructed the two "models" were influenced by, or were even conversant with each other's work. Holmes, for one, remained blissfully ignorant of economic theory throughout his life. It is rather that the lawyers and economists, both responding to the same stimuli, produced theoretical systems which were harmonious with each other and which, in both cases, evidently responded to the felt needs of the time.

It seems apparent to the twentieth century mind, as perhaps it did not to the nineteenth century mind, that a system in which everybody is invited to do his own thing, at whatever cost to his neighbor, must work ultimately to the benefit of the rich and powerful, who are in a position to look after themselves and to act, so to say, as their own self-insurers. As we look back on the nineteenth century theories, we are struck most of all, I think, by the narrow scope of social duty which they implicitly assumed. No man is his brother's keeper; the race is to the swift; let the devil take the hindmost. For good or for ill, we have changed all that. We are now all cogs in a machine, each dependent on the other. The decline and fall of the general theory of contract and, in most quarters, of laissez-faire economics may be taken as remote reflections of the transition from nineteenth century individualism to the welfare state and beyond.

NOTES

FOR DISCUSSION

1. What are Gilmore's criticisms of classical contract law?
2. Is Gilmore saying that Oliver Wendell Holmes essentially invented "classical" contract law? Explain your answer.
3. What are the advantages of having no one be liable to anyone for anything? What are the disadvantages?
4. How does the doctrine of consideration further Holmes's aims with respect to liability?
5. According to Gilmore, how does Holmes's theory of contract make it more abstract and impersonal? What does Holmes leave out of his considerations?
6. Do you see any points of comparison between Eisenberg's illustration of the "bargain principle" in a perfectly competitive market and Gilmore's description of Holmes's contract theory?
7. According to Gilmore, what is the relationship between classical contract theory and laissez-faire economics?
8. Given what Gilmore says, do you think classical contract law is appropriate for modern society? Explain.

Substantial Performance/ Partial Performance

Sometimes a contract's terms have not been followed to the letter and yet the objectives of the contract have essentially been accomplished. In such cases, if one party claims that the contract has been breached, the other party may offer the defense of substantial performance. The doctrine enables courts to avoid injustice by not holding liable for breach of contract when the deviation from the terms of the agreement is not a material one. Nevertheless, the party who did not perform fully may be required to pay damages for any injury suffered by the other party as a result of the contract not being fully performed.

In other cases, a contract may only be partially performed, and the injured party may sue for damages to cover the cost to him of getting whatever work completed that the nonperforming party failed to finish. Similarly, a party who has partially performed a contract may be able to recover compensation for the work done on the theory that the other party would otherwise be unjustly enriched.

In the following case, the plaintiff refused to pay because the defendant had not performed all the agreed-on services. The impact of substantial performance in a particular situation is considered by the court in determining the proper outcome.

CASE

Ira M. Weiss v. Nurse Midwifery Associates
Civil Court of the City of New York (1984)
124 Misc.2d 141, 476 N.Y.S.2d 984

JOHN R. CANNIZZARO, Judge.   In this action plaintiff seeks recovery for a $750 fee paid to defendant Nurse Midwifery Associates, and further compensatory damages relating to the defendant's alleged dereliction of duties.

Plaintiff's principal allegation is that defendant failed to render adequate services to wit: by dispensing improper and/or incomplete pre-natal advice to plaintiff's wife and by neglecting to provide services during the birth of plaintiff's son.

For reasons stated below, this Court holds that plaintiff's cause of action is not based in substantive law and, consequently, shall be dismissed.

Testimony adduced at trial indicates that a contractual arrangement was created between the plaintiff and the defendant for certain midwifery services. It appears that, for various administrative reasons, no fee was to be charged by defendant for services rendered during childbirth, but that the agreed upon fee was for pre-natal and post-natal care. Nevertheless, this court believes that the promise of defendant to be present during the childbirth was a material factor for plaintiff to retain the services of defendant and was therefore an important part of the contract. Even so, it does not appear that defendant's presence at childbirth was unconditionally guaranteed or that, even if it was guaranteed, defendant was a fault in not attending that event.

Plaintiff argues, and this court agrees, that defendant promised to perform delivery services during the childbirth. However, it is apparent to this Court that such service was an integral part of a *package* of services—preliminary to, during and subsequent to the childbirth. Since defendant was obligated to perform a total package of services, the failure to perform only one facet, the attendance at the childbirth, did not necessarily constitute a material breach of the contract.

The facts indicate that plaintiff received a substantial benefit of the bargain by requesting and accepting the rendition of defendant's pre-natal and post-natal services on approximately one dozen occasions. Although the failure of defendant to attend the child-birth was indeed unfortunate, defendant did expend a significant amount of time, energy and expertise. As a result, it is the Court's opinion that defendant performed a substantial portion of the obligations which arose upon the formation of the contractual relationship and therefore did not materially breach the contract.

Notwithstanding the finding that the alleged failure to act was not a material breach, this Court also holds that defendant's conduct could not, even in a non-material manner be considered a breach of the contract.

We recognize, at the outset, an implicit understanding between the parties that defendant would make "best efforts" to attend to the delivery of the child. Such interpretation is based upon the fact that the parties were in frequent contact, as per defendant's promise to render services to plaintiff's wife "as needed." Attendance at the childbirth would be an expected part of these services, but would necessarily be dependent upon plaintiff first notifying defendant that the childbirth was imminent.

In *Aron v. Gillman*, 309 N.Y. 157, 163, 128 N.Y.S.2d 284 (1955), the Court of Appeals stated that, "In construing the provisions of a contract, we should give due consideration to the circumstances surrounding its execution ... and, if possible, we should give to the agreement a fair and reasonable interpretation." Under the circumstances existing at the time that *this* contract was created, this court believes that, according to *Gillman*, defendant would be obligated to make "best efforts" to attend to the delivery, and that such obligation would arise only after proper notification of this event was relayed to defendant.

The facts indicate that plaintiff's wife contacted the defendant several hours prior to the childbirth and complained of various pains in her stomach and head. However, plaintiff admits that defendant questioned plaintiff's wife extensively and *then*, based upon the answers given, concluded that plaintiff's wife was not experiencing labor pains. Indeed, plaintiff further admits that the pains suffered by his wife immediately prior to the childbirth *were* of a substantially qualitative difference and *were* obviously labor pains. Since the labor pains did not begin until just a few minutes before the childbirth, proper notification of plaintiff's wife's condition could not be conveyed to defendant. As a result, defendant was not provided an opportunity to exert the best efforts to attend this childbirth.

Stated in a more "legalistic" fashion, defendant should not be liable for breach of contract because the purported breach was directly caused by plaintiff's breach of *his* contractual condition, *i.e.*, the timely notification to defendant of the forthcoming birth. It is not necessary that plaintiff's breach be intentional—a mere failure to perform the condition would be enough to vindicate the defendant. Thus, even if defendant had "guaranteed" to attend the childbirth, plaintiff's inability and resultant failure to notify defendant of the forthcoming birth, relieved defendant of its "guaranteed" obligation.

In the case of *Kooleraire Serv. v. Board of Educ.*, 28 N.Y. 101, 320 N.Y.S.2d 46, 268 N.E.2d 782 (1971), the court outlined the general rule that a party to a contract cannot rely on the failure of another to perform where the original party has *frustrated* or *prevented* the occurrence of the condition. Similarly, in *U.S. v. Bedford Associates*, 548 F.Supp. 732 (DCNY 1982), the District Court, applying New York law, stated that (p. 737) "... where one of the parties to a contract makes performance by the other materially more difficult or expensive, the latter will be discharged."

The above cited cases indicate that plaintiff's failure to satisfy the condition precedent—notification of defendant of the impending birth—should relieve this defendant of the obligation to attend that event. Justice dictates that this rule apply even though plaintiff's failure to notify defendant in a timely manner was unintentional and unavoidable. This holding seems clearly to be the most equitable disposition of the instant action, especially in light of the degree of services rendered by defendant, even without attendance at the childbirth.

Based upon the finding that defendant's failure to attend the childbirth did not constitute a breach of its contractual obligations, and that defendant performed in a significant and substantial manner, this Court holds that plaintiff's action to recover payments made to defendant should be dismissed in its entirety.

FOR DISCUSSION

1. The court characterizes the contract in this case as an agreement to provide "a package of services." How does that characterization affect the court's interpretation of the contract and its performance?

2. According to the court, did defendant "guarantee" to attend the childbirth? What did defendant obligate itself to do with respect to attendance at the childbirth?

3. What failure of plaintiff's changed defendant's obligations under the contract? How did those obligations change?

4. Here, plaintiff's failure to perform his part of the bargain was clearly unintentional and unavoidable. Is it fair under those circumstances to relieve defendant of its obligation under the contract? How does the court justify this?

5. In this case, the court uses the terms "material," "significant," and "substantial" to describe defendant's performance. What do those terms mean within the context of this particular contract? Do you agree with the court's assessment?

Affirmative Defenses to a Contract Action

There are several affirmative defenses that can be made in response to an action for breach of contract. Some common affirmative defenses are failure of consideration, breach of warranty, and usury.

Failure of consideration refers to a situation in which bargained-for consideration has either ceased to exist, become worthless, or has not been performed as promised. **Breach of warranty** claims that a guarantee as to the quality or condition of a thing contracted for has not been lived up to. **Usury** refers to the charging of an exorbitant or unconscionable rate of interest. Usury is illegal, and most states have usury laws that establish the legal rates of interest that can be charged.

Affirmative defenses are not mere denials of the plaintiff's allegations. Since they allege new facts, they must be pleaded and proven. The defendant has the burden of proof with respect to an affirmative defense.

Impossibility of Performance

Another defense to breach of contract is **impossibility of performance.** One form of impossibility of performance is when the promisor is physically unable to perform his obligation, due to death or illness. Another form of impossibility of performance involves external circumstances that make it impossible for the promisor to perform his obligation, such as the destruction of the subject matter of the agreement, the frustration of its purpose, or some intervening factor that makes it impossible for anyone to perform as was agreed. For example, if I agree to sell you a particular house, and the house is destroyed by fire before the transaction can be completed, it is now objectively impossible for me to perform as I have promised.

In the following case, the defendant itself made it impossible for the plaintiff to perform a necessary condition to the agreement and, through its conduct, effectively put plaintiff out of business.

CASE

Babe, Inc., a Florida Corporation
v. Baby's Formula Service, Inc., a Florida Corporation
Florida District Court of Appeal (1964)
165 So.2d 795, 6 A.L.R.3d 320

HENDRY, J.   Plaintiff-appellant appeals and defendant-appellant cross-appeals from a final judgment entered pursuant to a jury verdict of $21,215.00 in favor of the plaintiff and $2,092.72 in favor of the defendant, on its counter-claim, leaving a balance of $19,122.28 in favor of the plaintiff.

Plaintiff entered into a contract with defendant whereby plaintiff would be the sole distributor, in a five county area on the west coast of Florida, for defendant's prepared baby formula. The mechanics of the operation consisted of the defendant preparing and delivering the formula to the plaintiff in St. Petersburg from its plant in Miami. The defendant was to deliver the formula in sealed containers which the plaintiff never disturbed, thereupon, the plaintiff delivered the formula in the same containers to its customers.

The contract was entered into on October 15, 1959, and provided for the payment by the plaintiff of $10,000.00 to the defendant for the exclusive franchise to the plaintiff. The plaintiff paid $5,000.00 to the defendant at the execution of the agreement, and was obligated to pay the balance six months later on April 14, 1960.

As a result of the execution of this agreement, the plaintiff invested sums of money in establishing a place of business in St. Petersburg, and solicited business from various hospitals and other users of the formula for infants. Things proceeded smoothly for several months until problems developed, and of course, at this point the facts become contested and the versions of what occurred varied.

The plaintiff began complaining that the formula which it was receiving was spoiled and could not be used. As a result of continued receipt by the plaintiff of spoiled formula monthly billing was not paid and credits were not given for returned formula. During this same period of time, the $5,000.00 became due and was not paid. The parties agreed to having the payments made at a later date and in a different manner. The plaintiff also failed to make payments for a certain amount of merchandise that had been shipped and used by the plaintiff.

The plaintiff continued to receive spoiled formula from defendant, even after much complaining, and this finally resulted in plaintiff losing all of its customers and going out of business. The instant action was instituted to recover damages suffered by the plaintiff for breach of the contract by the defendant. The defendant counter-claimed for the recovery of the merchandise used but not paid for by the plaintiff, and for the unpaid $5,000.00.

After a trial by jury, plaintiff was awarded $21,215.00 as damages on its complaint, and defendant was awarded $2,092.72 on its counter-claim as a set-off leaving a balance in plaintiff's favor of $19,122.28.

Plaintiff appeals seeking a new trial based on the refusal of the trial court to charge the jury that plaintiff was entitled as part of its damage, loss of future profits.

Defendant cross-appealed raising seven points, all of which have been considered and those that are not specifically dealt with in this opinion have been deemed to be without merit.

The plaintiff's assignment of error is found to be without merit and the trial court is affirmed. Plaintiff correctly contends that prospective profits are a permissible element of a breach of contract action, but fails to realize that prior to its consideration by the jury there must be sufficient proof thereof.

The Supreme Court in the *Utility Battery* case (*New Amsterdam Casualty Co.* v. *Utility Battery Mfg. Co.*, 122 Fla. 718, 166 So. 856), considered this point and explained

> The general rule is that the anticipated profits of a commercial business are too speculative and dependent upon changing circumstances to warrant a judgment for their loss. There is an exception to this rule, however, to the effect that the loss of profit from the interruption of an established business may be recovered where the plaintiff makes it reasonably certain by competent proof what the amount of his actual loss was.

The trial judge correctly ruled that plaintiff had failed to produce sufficient proof to entitle it to go to the jury on this issue, and correctly instructed the jury in regard to the measure of damages.

Defendant, first raises as error the failure of the trial court to direct a verdict or in the alternative to dismiss the complaint. The basis alleged in support of this relief is the failure of plaintiff to make the $5,000.00 payment of April 1960 pursuant to the contract thereby failing to perform a condition precedent[8] to defendant's contractual obligation. Defendant correctly argues that in order for plaintiff to maintain its contract action, it must first establish performance on its part of the contractual obligations thereby imposed. However, defendant fails to recognize the similarly well established exception to this principle that, one who makes impossible a happening of the condition precedent may not take advantage of it, and avoid his liability on the contract.

In the present litigation, it was vigorously contended by defendant that plaintiff first breached the contract by failing to make the $5,000.00 payment, and on the other hand plaintiff just as energetically protested that defendant first breached the contract by supplying plaintiff with spoiled formula, thereby excusing plaintiff's further performance under the contract. The question of who first breached the contract was clearly one for the jury, and they evidently decided that question in plaintiff's favor. It was therefore not error for the court to so rule.

Defendant next objects to the trial court permitting the plaintiff's witness to testify to statements made by the defendant's officer, as to events which occurred prior to the execution of the contract. Again, as a general rule, such testimony would be inadmissible, but here it comes within an exception to the rule where such testimony is permitted to explain and make clear an ambiguous portion of the contract. We agree with the trial court that the phrase in the contract, "the home office hereby warrants that the quality of its product will at all times remain at the present high level," is ambiguous, and required testimony to determine the meaning and import of that term.

The defendant next contends that the agreement between the parties extending the time within which the plaintiff would pay the second $5,000.00 was a novation[9] thereby extinguishing the original contract and substituting a new one. A very careful scrutiny of the record which was submitted to this court reveals that the first mention of the word novation was made in the defendant's motion for a judgment non obstante veredicto. A novation is in the nature of an affirmative defense, and must therefore be pleaded and proved. Having failed to comply with this requirement, this issue is not properly before us. An appellate court may not consider what has not been raised below.

---

[8] A **condition precedent** is a fact, act, or event that must occur or exist before a promise is required to be performed.

[9] A **novation** is the substitution of a third party for one of the original parties to a contract, with the agreement of all three parties. This discharges the old contract and substitutes a new one with the same terms, but at least one new party.

As noted previously those errors raised by defendant and not discussed herein were considered and deemed to be without merit. Accordingly, the judgments appealed from are affirmed.

Affirmed.

FOR DISCUSSION

1. According to the court, why wasn't plaintiff entitled to damages to compensate for loss of future profits? How would such damages be calculated?
2. Both plaintiff and defendant failed to perform as promised under their original agreement. Why did the jury find that plaintiff's further performance under the contract had been excused?
3. Plaintiff argued, among other things, that defendant had breached its express warranty as to the quality and condition of the baby formula. Why was testimony about conversations and events that occurred prior to the execution of the written contract not barred by the parol evidence rule?
4. Why was defendant's contention that the agreement to extend the time for paying the $5,000 was a novation rejected by the court? In your opinion was there a novation?

Capacity to Contract

A valid contract requires competent parties. Some people, however, are deemed to lack the capacity to contract. Infants, the mentally incapable, and intoxicated persons are not competent parties. Generally, contracts made by parties lacking the capacity to contract are voidable, although a contract made by a person who has been adjudicated insane is void. The rules regarding capacity to contract are intended to protect those who are vulnerable through lack of experience or lack of comprehension from being taken advantage of.

The following case deals with an exception to the rule that contracts made by a minor are voidable. This exception holds that contracts made by a minor that involve the provision to the minor of items considered to be necessaries are not voidable. Traditionally, "necessaries" refers to food, clothing, shelter, and medical care, but the category of necessaries has expanded over time and may include such things as legal services, for example. In this case, the Supreme Court of Wisconsin expresses its uneasiness with the whole concept of voidable contracts involving minors, which appears to be reflected in its ruling involving the provision of a so-called necessary:

CASE   **Madison General Hospital v. Bruce A. Haack and Debra Hughes Haack**
Supreme Court of Wisconsin (1985)
124 Wis.2d 398, 369 N.W.2d 663, 53 A.L.R. 4th 1235

ABRAHAMSON, Justice.   Madison General Hospital, the plaintiff, sued Debra Haack (nee Debra Hughes), Bruce Haack (Debra Haack's husband), and Donald J. Hughes (Debra Haack's father) for $2,319.08, the unpaid balance of a hospital bill totaling $4,613.91. This unpaid balance was for medical services rendered to Debra Haack in connection with the birth of her infant. Medicaid had paid the portion of the bill directly related to the care of the infant.

The facts giving rise to this appeal are undisputed. When Debra Hughes, accompanied by her mother, was admitted to the hospital on February 3, 1976, she was 16 years old, apparently was living with her parents, and had no financial assets of her own. She was 34 weeks pregnant and suffering from severe labor convulsions. She delivered the infant by caesarian section on February 16, 1976, and, after post-operative treatment was released on February 22, 1976.

On April 12, 1976, Bruce Haack and Debra Hughes (hereafter referred to as Debra Haack) were married. Pursuant to sec. 245.25, Stats. 1975, the child "thereby became legitimated and enjoy[ed] all the rights and privileges of legitimacy" as if the child had been born during the marriage of the parents.

The hospital attempted to collect from Medicaid the cost of delivery and the cost of the care of Debra Haack, but Medicaid covered only the costs associated with the care of the infant. The hospital then attempted to collect the remainder of its bill from Donald J. Hughes'[s] health insurer. The insurer did not pay. The hospital then commenced this action to collect payment from Debra Haack, Bruce Haack, and Donald J. Hughes. The hospital did not commence action against Dorothy Hughes, Debra Haack's mother. The hospital never served Donald J. Hughes, and the suit against him was dismissed.[10]

The hospital urges several theories under which Debra Haack may be held liable for payment of the medical expenses. First, the hospital asserts that Debra Haack is liable under the common law doctrine that when a minor contracts for necessaries the minor cannot disaffirm the contract. Emergency medical services are generally considered necessaries, and this point is not in dispute in this case.

For Debra Haack to be liable under this "doctrine of necessaries," she had to have entered into a contract, express or implied in fact, to pay for the medical services. Neither party cites Wisconsin case law, and we could find none, declaring a minor liable for emergency health care service provided the minor in the absence of the minor's contracting for the service. The common law rule appears to be that a minor is not liable if necessaries were furnished to the minor on someone else's credit.

The circuit court found that Debra Haack did not enter a contract with the hospital for her medical care. The circuit court characterized Debra Haack's testimony as follows: "At the trial Debra testified without contradiction that she herself was indigent, that she was very ill when she entered the hospital, and in no condition to agree to anything. In other words, she states that she *in no way ever impliedly agreed to pay the medical bill.* In light of the circuit court's finding that the minor did not enter into an express or implied in fact contract, we conclude that the common law doctrine that a minor may be liable for necessaries furnished on the credit of the minor is not applicable here.

The essence of the hospital's argument is that Debra Haack is liable for the medical expenses under a theory of unjust enrichment, that is, a quasi-contractual obligation imposed by law. Express contracts and contracts implied in fact rest on the assent of the parties; a quasi-contractual obligation does not. A quasi-contractual obligation is imposed by law on grounds of justice and equity to prevent unjust enrichment. *In the Matter of the Estate of Stromsted*, 99 Wis.2d 136, 139, n.1, 142, n.5, 299 N.W.2d 226 (1980). The law may require a person enriched by a benefit to compensate the person furnishing the benefit when it would be inequitable to allow retention of the benefit without payment.

---

[10]The circuit court also dismissed the claims against Debra Haack and Bruce Haack. The Supreme Court of Wisconsin, in this opinion, affirmed the judgment involving Debra Haack and reversed the judgment involving Bruce Haack.

The hospital asserts that Debra Haack received medical care necessary to save her life and the life of her infant, that she knew and appreciated that such care was necessary, that she accepted the care which the hospital was required to render, and that she refused to pay for these benefits. These facts, argues the hospital, satisfy the elements of a cause of action in equity for unjust enrichment.

The hospital's theory of Debra Haack's liability under the doctrine of unjust enrichment, however, overlooks the fact that when a minor has not contracted for necessaries, the law has traditionally imposed a quasi-contractual liability on a minor's father, not on the minor, under the doctrine of necessaries. In *Monk* v. *Hurlburt*, 151 Wis. 41, 45, 138 N.W. 59 (1912), this court stated that "the law implies a promise [that a parent will pay] where a parent, with full knowledge of the facts and without objection, allows and approves of his child being furnished with necessaries." A parent's quasi-contractual obligation, under the doctrine of necessaries, arises because a third party has fulfilled the legal obligation of the parent to support the minor. Traditionally the law imposed the duty of support for the minor on the male parent. Today the wife shares with the husband the legal duty of support for the family.

In this case Mr. and Mrs. Hughes were under a duty to provide their daughter with medical services. Mrs. Hughes knew that Debra Haack needed medical attention, accompanied her to the hospital, consented to the medical procedures by signing a form authorizing treatment, and knew that the hospital would expect payment for services. Aside from this authorization of treatment, no express agreement exists between the hospital and Mrs. Hughes, Mr. Hughes, or Debra Haack. Under the common law doctrine of necessaries, the party or parties unjustly enriched by the medical care provided Debra Haack and liable for payment of the medical expenses appear to be one or both of Debra Haack's parents. Dorothy Hughes (and perhaps Donald J. Hughes), not Debra Haack, may thus be liable on a quasi-contractual, unjust enrichment theory under the doctrine of necessaries.

The hospital, however, asserts that Debra Haack is liable for payment of medical services because her parents defaulted in paying for the medical services. Several cases cited as authority for this proposition of law are collected in Annot., *Liability of Infant for Medical, Dental or Hospital Services to Him*, 71 A.L.R. 226 (1931), and Annot., *Liability of Infant for Necessaries Where He Lives With His Parents*, 70 A.L.R. 572 (1931), and supplements thereto. The cases, however, are not clear in their statement of this rule or its application.

A key case placing liability on the minor when the father defaults is *Cole* v. *Wagner*, 197 N.C. 692, 150 S.E. 339 (1929). In *Cole* the court said that "[t]he father did not provide this attention necessary to save his life and usefulness; the hospital did. The infant now has an estate and it is unthinkable that the guardian of the infant should not pay the reasonable expense for saving the child's life and usefulness." 150 S.E. at 341. In *Cole* the child had recovered a judgment for $4,500, in which it was alleged that "the hospital, medical, and surgical treatment rendered... was a material and substantial consideration.... *Id*. As a result of this aspect of the *Cole* case, courts may view the *Cole* rule as applicable only to situations in which the child's estate consists of damages which include recovery for medical and hospital expenses.

Although courts suggest that a minor may be liable for necessaries if a parent defaults in payment these courts frequently refuse to hold the minor liable, determining that the proof of the parent's neglect, failure, refusal, or inability to pay is insufficient.

Even if we were to conclude that a minor should be liable for medical expenses when a parent neglects, fails, refuses, or is unable to pay, we would conclude that the record in this case is insufficient to establish the parents' neglect, failure, refusal, or inability to pay. There is no evidence that the hospital ever sought payment from Mrs. Hughes. With regard to Mr. Hughes we know only that he apparently resided at the same address as Debra Haack at the time the medical services were rendered, that the hospital was unsuccessful in collecting payment from his health insurer, that the hospital may have mailed some bills to him, that he apparently left Wisconsin after the infant's birth, and that the hospital filed suit more than four years after the medical services had been rendered and failed to obtain service on him.

On the basis of this record, we conclude that Debra Haack is not liable to the hospital for the medical services furnished to her. She was not a party to an express contract or to one implied in fact and therefore any rules regarding a minor's liability under a contract for necessaries are inapplicable. Her parents, not she, would be liable under the common law doctrine of necessaries or unjust enrichment. Although some jurisdictions may impose liability on a minor when a parent does not meet the obligations imposed upon them by law under the doctrine of necessaries, the record in this case does not justify allowing recovery from Debra Haack under this theory.

There is a sense of uneasiness attached to following traditional common law and concluding that Debra Haack need not pay for the medical services she received. She appears to be profiting at the expense of the hospital, which did its best for her welfare. We expressed a similar uneasiness in a prior holding that a minor who disaffirms a contract for the purchase of an item which is not a necessary may recover the purchase price without liability for use, depreciation, damage or other diminution in value. *Halbman* v. *Lemke*, 99 Wis.2d 241, 251, 298 N.W.2d 562 (1980). We recognize that the laws relating to the capacity of infants to contract balance society's interests in protecting the minor and the family against interests in protecting innocent creditors. Similarly the doctrine of necessaries and the various exceptions thereto make this balance. We have been unwilling to modify the traditional rules governing infants' contractual liability, saying modification is best left to the legislature. We similarly conclude in this case that the balance made in the common law rules regarding the immunity and quasi-contractual liability of a minor for necessaries should not be modified at this time.

FOR DISCUSSION

1. According to this opinion, who should be responsible for payment of medical services rendered to a minor, and why? Do you agree with the court's reasoning in this case?

2. In another section of this opinion, the court found that Debra's husband (an adult at the time of the birth of the child) should be liable for the medical expenses based on "[t]he public policy ...that the father of the infant should bear the responsibility for expenses incurred as a result of a pregnancy in which he participated." Suppose Mr. Haack had been a minor at the time of the birth, would he still be liable to pay?

3. What competing societal interests are in conflict in this case? Does the court attempt to clearly resolve the conflict?

4. Why might the legislature be better suited to determine minors' liability for the debts they incur?

5. If a vendor who sells an item to a minor on credit cannot rely on being able to recover payment for the item, does it seem likely that vendors will be willing to sell to minors? What safeguards might the vendor employ to assure payment?

Modification of a Contract

Sometimes the parties to a contract agree to change the terms of their agreement before it is fully performed. Such a change is called a **modification**. The traditional rule is that a modification of a contract is in itself a contract and must be supported by consideration. Two important issues are whether one party to the modification had authority to make the new agreement and whether there was, in fact, an exchange of legally sufficient consideration. As we have said previously, a promise to do what one is already legally required to do is not consideration.

LEGAL TERMS TO KNOW

acceptance	modification
breach of contract	offer
capacity	parole evidence rule
consideration	statute of frauds
contract	substantial performance
duress	unconscionable contract
illegal contract	void contract
impossibility	voidable contract

ADDITIONAL QUESTIONS AND EXERCISES

1. Do you think contract has "died"? Use the readings and cases in this chapter to support your opinion.

2. After having read the materials in this chapter, what do you think "freedom of contract" means? Do you agree more with Holmes and Fried, or do you agree more with Gilmore's views?

3. Gradually, statutes are replacing much of classical contract law and, in some instances, modifying it. What rule of contract that you have studied would you like to see changed by statute, and how would you change it? Explain your answer thoroughly.

4. As in many other areas of the law, ordinary people are compelled to use rules of contract law that have been created in response to commercial situations involving parties with considerable power and resources. Do you think there should be a separate law of contract for ordinary routine transactions involving noncommercial parties? What aspects of contract may be too strict for ordinary situations?

5. What are some of the dangers that may be associated with relaxing certain rules of contract law? Choose a rule that you believe protects people who make contracts, and explain why it should be retained.

FOR FURTHER READING

1. ATIYAH, PATRICK S., *The Rise and Fall of Freedom of Contract*, Oxford: Oxford University Press, 1979.

2. EISENBERG, MELVIN A., "Donative Promises," *U. Chi. L. Rev.* 47 (1979) pp. 1–33.

3. FRIEDMAN, LAWRENCE M., *Contract Law in America*, Madison: University of Wisconsin Press, 1965.

4. GOETZ, CHARLES J. and SCOTT, ROBERT E., "Enforcing Promises: An Examination of the Basis of Contract," *Yale L. J.* 89 (1980). pp.1261–1322.

5. KENNEDY, DUNCAN, "Form and Substance in Private Law Adjudication," *Harv. L Rev.* 89 (1976), pp. 1685–1778.

8

TORTS

INTRODUCTION

Tort law is the broadest and easily the most volatile area of substantive law that we have yet considered. It is difficult even to define tort adequately, because so many different types of actions are encompassed by this concept. Generally, a tort is a civil wrong, other than a breach of contract, for which the offender must pay damages. Tort includes both deliberate wrongs (intentional torts) and inadvertent or accidental wrongs (negligent torts), as well as wrongs for which the offender is held liable regardless of his motivation or ability to prevent the injury (strict liability).

Tort law is available to redress a great variety of wrongs and compensate for a wide range of injuries to the person and to property. Torts involving injury to the person range from actual physical injury to emotional harm to injury to a person's reputation, while torts involving injury to property go beyond actual damage to property to an ever-expanding range of economic harms.

It is said that in the early history of the common law, people were absolutely liable for all the harm they created, no matter what their intent might have been. Even assuming that to have been the case, the recent history of tort (from the nineteenth century to the present) has been based on the concept of **fault**—that is, that people were entitled to compensation for at least some of the consequences of another person's blameworthy behavior. In the nineteenth century, in particular, tort law came to be articulated in terms of *limitations* on the liability of the actor for the harm he caused. This is consonant with those views that underlay property and contract law of the same period: ideas of liberty and individualism, concern with acquisition of wealth, a desire to conquer and exploit new resources and markets. A prevailing belief in progress and survival of the fittest, even if not always expressed in Darwinian terms, left little room for concern for the victims of progress.

It is not surprising that people with such views were unwilling to accept the constraints that would necessarily be imposed upon their activities if they were made to pay for all the damages and harm that they caused. The tort law of the nineteenth century, therefore, confined liability to certain specific types of situations, largely by means of the concepts of fault and causation that were employed. You will recall that in Chapter 7 Grant Gilmore commented that the extreme view of contract and tort in the nineteenth century, as expressed by Oliver Wendell Holmes, Jr., was that no one should be liable to anyone for anything. Although that is something of an exaggeration, the nineteenth century tort theorists would be amazed by the enormous expansion of tort liability that has occurred in the twentieth century. This expansion of tort liability, as we shall see, is not without its opponents and critics. While it is unacceptable today that no one should be liable to anyone for anything, some modern commentators find it equally unacceptable that everyone should be liable to everyone else for everything. They argue that the trend toward compensation of every possible harm or injury will bring about economic destruction.

What is tort, and what is its purpose? The principal objectives of tort are to compensate people for harm they have suffered as a result of other people's wrongful conduct and to place the burden of the cost of injuries on the wrongdoer rather than on the victim, at least in part with a view to discouraging such conduct in the future or compelling the wrongdoer to be more careful. In the case of deliberate harm the goal is to make the wrongdoer accountable and to discourage repetition of the harmful conduct in future, whereas the goals in the case of negligent and strict liability harm are more complex. Many of the activities that bring about compensable harm are favored activities—that is, activities that we find necessary and desirable, such as manufacturing goods, transporting people and products, or carrying on a business. In such cases, tort law forces the person carrying on the activity to find ways of doing so with a minimum of harm to others or to bear the costs of the harm he does cause. Tort becomes a kind of risk and cost allocation system that lifts the burden of the expense of harm from the individual victim and eventually redistributes it throughout society as a whole. This occurs because the costs of minimizing the risk of harm and compensating for injury are passed on to the general public in the form of higher costs for goods and services. If compensating victims for harm suffered as a result of another's wrongful conduct is a social goal, then it is one that comes with a certain social cost—changes in the relationships people have with one another, higher prices for goods and services, higher costs of insurance, and occasional lack of availability of certain high-risk but necessary activities.

In a sense, we can have as much tort law protection as we are willing to pay for, and, so far, we have not reached the limit. That does not mean that we are not forced to accept certain inconveniences as the price of legal protection: Everyone is familiar, for example, with cities that are forced to close their parks or suspend their youth sports leagues, for example, because the cost of liability insurance has become too high, and the likelihood of lawsuits is too great to carry on the activity without insurance. You may have seen advertisements that claim that jury awards for damages in tort actions are disproportionately high, and that "the tort system is out of control." As you read the materials in this chapter, you may ask yourself whether such claims are true and whether society can truly afford to expand tort liability at the current pace.

The character of the tort obligation is determined by its social dimensions. Obligations concerning property arise from an interest in, or possession of, property, and obligations in contract arise from the voluntary agreement of the parties to the contract, whereas obligations in tort are involuntary and arise "by operation of law" rather than by agreement. That is, tort duties are socially imposed duties—obligations imposed on individuals to achieve the social goals discussed earlier.

In this chapter we will examine the dimensions of tort duties and obligations in some detail, considering their origin, the nature and extent of the duties, and the role of causation in determining liability. We will see that, despite the expansion of the scope of liability in recent years, there are still harms that the law does not compensate. You will have the opportunity to consider arguments both for and against the expansion of liability and gain an appreciation of the central role that tort law plays in protecting the individual in our changing society.

NEGLIGENCE

Society imposes a duty on individuals to act carefully so as not to subject others to unreasonable risks of harm. Negligence is conduct that falls below the legally established standards of careful behavior and thereby causes injury to others. Negligence requires: (1) the existence of a duty of care owed by the defendant to the plaintiff, and (2) a breach of that duty of care by defendant that proximately results in injury to the plaintiff. The defendant's subjective intent is generally not a consideration in negligence. Behavior is deemed negligent if it deviates from an objective standard of reasonably careful conduct, no matter what the defendant intended. In negligence, the question is: How would a reasonably prudent person in similar circumstances have acted? Also, there is no liability unless the conduct results in harm to someone else. Recklessly dangerous conduct that does not injure anyone may be undesirable, but it is not actionable.

Foundations of Legal Liability

In the following reading, Judge Richard A. Posner, a leading theorist in the area of law and economics, considers the origins of tort liability in negligence. The question of how much tort protection we can reasonably afford is a prominent consideration in Posner's analysis.

READING **A Theory of Negligence**
Richard A. Posner*

I. There is an orthodox view of the negligence concept to which I believe most legal scholars and historians would subscribe that runs as follows: Until the nineteenth century a man was liable for harm caused by his accidents whether or not he was at fault; he acted at his peril. The no-fault standard of liability was relaxed in the nineteenth century under the pressure of industrial expansion and an individualistic philosophy that could conceive of no justification for shifting losses from the victim of an accident unless the injurer was blameworthy (negligent) and the victim blameless (not contributorily negligent). The result, however, was that accident costs were "externalized" from the enterprises that caused them to workers and other individuals injured as a byproduct of their activities. Justification for the shift, in the orthodox view, can perhaps be found in a desire to subsidize the infant industries of the period but any occasion for subsidization has long passed, laying bare the inadequacy of the negligence standard as a system for compensating accident victims. The need for compensation is unaffected by whether the participants in the accident were careless or careful and we have outgrown a morality that would condition the right to compensation upon a showing that the plaintiff was blameless and the defendant blameworthy.

There are three essential points here. The first, that the adoption of the negligence standard was a subsidy to the expanding industries of the nineteenth century, is highly ambiguous. It is true that if you move from a regime where (say) railroads are strictly liable for injuries inflicted in crossing accidents to one where they are liable only if negligent, the costs to the railroads of crossing accidents will be lower, and the output of railroad services probably greater as a consequence. But it does not follow that any subsidy is involved—unless it is proper usage to say that an industry is being subsidized whenever a tax levied upon it is reduced or removed. As we shall see, a negligence standard of liability, properly administered, is broadly consistent with an optimum investment in accident prevention by the enterprises subject to the standard. Since it does not connote, as the orthodox view implies, an underinvestment in safety, its adoption cannot be equated with subsidization in any useful sense of that term. We shall also see that many accident cases do not involve strangers to the enterprise (such as a traveler at a crossing), but rather customers, employees, or other contracting parties, and that a change in the formal law governing accidents is unlikely to have more than a transient effect on the number of their accidents. Finally, whether the period before the advent of the negligence standard is properly characterized as one of liability without fault remains, so far as I am aware, an unresolved historical puzzle.

The second major point implicit in the orthodox view is that the dominant purpose of civil liability for accidents is to compensate the victim for the medical expenses, loss of earnings, suffering, and other costs of the accident. Hence, if it is a bad compensation system, it is a bad system. Yet Holmes, in his authoritative essay on the fault system, had rejected a compensation rationale as alien to the system. People, he reasoned, could insure themselves against uncompensated accidents, and there was accordingly no occasion for a state accident-compensation scheme. Holmes left unclear what he conceived the dominant purpose of the fault system to be, if it was not to compensate. The successful plaintiff does recover damages from the defendant. Why? Suppose a major function of the negligence system is to regulate safety. We are apt to think of regulation as the action of executive and administrative agencies. But the creation of private rights of action can also be a means of regulation. The rules are made by the judges aided by the parties. The burdens of investigation and of presenting evidence are also shouldered by the parties. The direct governmental role is thus minimized—a result highly congenial to the thinking of the nineteenth century. Such a system cannot function unless the damages assessed against the defendant are paid over to the plaintiff. That is the necessary inducement for the plaintiff to play his regulatory role of identifying violations of the applicable judge-made rule, proving them, and when appropriate pressing for changes in the rule.

The third essential point in the orthodox view is that negligence is a moral concept—and in the setting of today, a moralistic one. The orthodox view does not explore the moral roots of fault, but contents itself with asserting that such moral judgments as can be made in the usual accident case are an anachronistic, even frivolous, basis for determining whether to grant or withhold redress. The rejection of moral criteria as a basis for liability follows easily from the conception of the fault system as a compensation scheme and nothing more; it would be odd to deny welfare benefits on the ground that the recipient's misfortune was not the product of someone's wrongful conduct.

Characterization of the negligence standard as moral or moralistic does not advance analysis. The morality of the fault system is very different from that of everyday life.

Negligence is an objective standard. A man may be adjudged negligent though he did his best to avoid an accident and just happens to be clumsier than average. In addition, a number of the established rules of negligence liability are hard to square with a moral approach. Insane people are liable for negligent conduct though incapable of behaving carefully. Employers are broadly responsible for the negligence of their employees. The latter example illustrates an immensely important principle. In less than four per cent of the cases in our sample was the defendant accused of actually being negligent.[1] In all other cases the defendant was sued on the basis of the alleged negligence of employees or (in a few cases) children. The moral element in such cases is attenuated.

Moreover, to characterize the negligence concept as a moral one is only to push inquiry back a step. It is true that injury inflicted by carelessness arouses a different reaction from injury inflicted as the result of an unavoidable accident. We are indignant in the first case but not the second. The interesting question is why. What causes us to give the opprobrious label of careless to some human conduct but not other and to be indignant when we are hurt by it? The orthodox view gives no answer.

II. It is time to take a fresh look at the social function of liability for negligent acts. The essential clue, I believe, is provided by Judge Learned Hand's famous formulation of the negligence standard—one of the few attempts to give content to the deceptively simple concept of ordinary care. Although the formulation postdates the period of our primary interest, it never purported to be original but was an attempt to make explicit the standard that the courts had long applied. In a negligence case, Hand said, the judge (or jury) should attempt to measure three things: the magnitude of the loss if an accident occurs; the probability of the accident's occurring; and the burden of taking precautions that would avert it.[2] If the product of the first two terms exceeds the burden of precautions, the failure to take those precautions is negligence. Hand was adumbrating, perhaps unwittingly, an economic meaning of negligence. Discounting (multiplying) the cost of an accident if it occurs by the probability of occurrence yields a measure of the economic benefit to be anticipated from incurring the costs necessary to prevent the accident. The cost of prevention is what Hand meant by the burden of taking precautions against the accident. It may be the cost of installing safety equipment or otherwise making the activity safer, or the benefit foregone by curtailing or eliminating the activity. If the cost of safety measures or of curtailment—whichever cost is lower—exceeds the benefit in accident avoidance to be gained by incurring that cost, society would be better off, in economic terms, to forgo accident prevention. A rule making the enterprise liable for the accidents that occur in such cases cannot be justified on the ground that it will induce the enterprise to increase the safety of its operations. When the cost of accidents is less than the cost of prevention, a rational profit-maximizing enterprise will pay tort judgments to the accident victims rather than incur the larger cost of avoiding liability. Furthermore, overall economic value or welfare would be diminished rather than increased by incurring a higher accident-prevention cost in order to avoid a lower accident cost. If, on the other hand, the benefits in accident avoidance exceed the costs of prevention, society is better off if those costs are incurred and the accident averted, and so in this case the enterprise is made liable, in the expectation that self-interest will lead it to adopt the precautions in order to avoid a greater cost in tort judgments.

[1]The author is basing much of his argument on information gained from reviewing 1528 American appellate court decisions in accident cases from 1875 to 1905.

[2]*United States* v. *Carroll Towing Co.*, 159 F.2d 169 (2d Cir. 1947); *Conway* v. *O'Brien*, 111 F.2d 611 (2d Cir. 1940).

One misses any reference to accident avoidance by the victim. If the accident could be prevented by the installation of safety equipment or the curtailment or discontinuance of the underlying activity of the victim at lower cost than any measure taken by the injurer would involve, it would be uneconomical to adopt a rule of liability that placed the burden of accident prevention on the injurer. Although not an explicit part of the Hand formula this qualification, as we shall see, is implicit in the administration of the negligence standard.

Perhaps, then, the dominant function of the fault system is to generate rules of liability that if followed will bring about, at least approximately, the efficient—the cost-justified—level of accidents and safety. Under this view, damages are assessed against the defendant as a way of measuring the costs of accidents, and the damages so assessed are paid over to the plaintiff (to be divided with his lawyer) as the price of enlisting their participation in the operation of the system. Because we do not like to see resources squandered, a judgment of negligence has inescapable overtones of moral disapproval, for it implies that there was a cheaper alternative to the accident. Conversely, there is no moral indignation in the case in which the cost of prevention would have exceeded the cost of the accident. Where the measures necessary to avert the accident would have consumed excessive resources, there is no occasion to condemn the defendant for not having taken them.

If indignation has its roots in inefficiency, we do not have to decide whether regulation, or compensation, or retribution, or some mixture of these best describes the dominant purpose of negligence law. In any case, the judgment of liability depends ultimately on a weighing of costs and benefits....

NOTES

*From *Journal of Legal Studies* 29 (1972). Reprinted with permission. Copyright © 1972 by The University of Chicago. All rights reserved.

FOR DISCUSSION

1. According to Posner, how does a properly administered negligence standard of liability promote optimum investment in accident prevention by the enterprises subject to the standard?

2. What does Posner see as the major function of the negligence system? How does his view differ from what he calls the "orthodox view"?

3. What does the Learned Hand formula of negligence contribute to Posner's theory of the negligence standard as accident prevention?

4. Posner sees negligence as a way of assuring an efficient level of accident prevention without unduly involving the government in such regulation. What role does the award of damages to the plaintiff play in this scheme?

5. How does a judgment of "inefficiency" play a comparable role to moral blameworthiness in Posner's economic view of negligence?

Not everyone sees economic efficiency as an acceptable rationale for the negligence standard of liability. In the following reading, Richard L. Abel condemns Posner's economic view and, indeed, all capitalist or "bourgeois" tort theory, as exploitative and destructive.

READING   **Torts**
                              *Richard L. Abel**

CRITIQUE OF CAPITALIST TORT LAW

Producing Illness and Injury

Capitalist tort law systematically encourages unsafety. The dynamic of capitalism—competitive pursuit of profit—impels the enterprise to endanger the workers it employs, the consumers of its products and services, and those who inhabit the environment it pollutes. The cost of safety almost always diminishes profits. The capitalist, therefore, *must* be as unsafe as he can get away with being.

Tort law purports to curb these destructive consequences of capitalism. The legal-economic rationale that presently dominates and shapes tort principles is market deterrence, which argues that the most efficient way to promote an optimum level of safety is to internalize accident costs by making those who negligently cause accidents legally liable for their consequences. But there are fundamental theoretical and empirical reasons why market deterrence does not and cannot work. First, the very name is deceptive: there cannot be market deterrence because there is no market for injury and illness. The determination of what an accident costs can only be decided collectively, whether by a judge, a jury, or a legislature. Furthermore, the decision necessarily introduces a large margin of error, since it must not only value intangibles but also make predictions about an *individual* future: lost earnings, career, change in number of dependents, life expectancy, prognosis for recovery, possible medical discoveries, etc.

Second, a court is required to decide whether a particular injury was negligently inflicted; but the economic conceptualization of negligence as suboptimal safety (epitomized in Learned Hand's formula weighing the cost of accident avoidance against the cost of injury discounted by its probability) can be meaningfully applied only to an ongoing activity. Thus the inevitable errors in determining negligence will result in inadequate safety.

Third, a court is required to determine whether or not a particular actor caused a given injury or illness. But we know that causation is probabilistic and that for any event there are a multiplicity of contributing causes. The imposition of liability on one party (or even several) necessarily fails to internalize the accident costs in other causal activities.

Fourth, there is an inescapable tension between promoting safety through accident-cost internalization and spreading these costs—another goal of tort law. The most important mechanism for spreading costs is liability insurance, which has become so widespread and which discriminates so crudely among the insured in setting premiums that it alone virtually destroys the capacity of tort liability to optimize safety.

Fifth, in order for liability costs to alter the behavior of entrepreneurs, the latter must be unable to pass these costs on to consumers; but this condition will not be satisfied if liability costs are an insignificant percentage of the good or service, if demand is relatively price inelastic (the good or service is a necessity), or if the market is highly oligopolistic.

Sixth, market deterrence assumes that all actors who "cause" accidents are economic maximizers; consequently it argues that victims must be *denied* compensation, in whole or in part, in order to be motivated to protect themselves. This can only diminish the concern of capitalists for the safety of others.

Seventh, and most important, market deterrence assumes that the legal system fully internalizes *all* the costs of negligent accidents. Yet we have just seen in the previous section that capitalist tort law systematically denies compensation for injury and illness and does so in an extremely discriminatory manner. Therefore, the theory of market deterrence logically compels the conclusion that capitalist tort law encourages unsafety and subjects the most oppressed sectors of the population to the greatest danger. It motivates the entrepreneur to reduce liability costs, not accident costs, and to seek to evade the consequences of carelessness, not to enhance safety. Thus, we have Ford producing a Pinto with a gasoline tank it knows to be explosive, Johns-Manville continuing to subject its workers to asbestos for decades after it learns they will suffer lung damage and cancer, McDonnell-Douglas producing and American Airlines flying the DC-10 that crashed in Chicago when both knew of the faulty pylon and other design defects. The capitalist response to the threat of tort liability is to strive to externalize accident costs by concealing information (denying workers access to their medical records), threatening retaliation against those who seek compensation, and using the enormous resources of the enterprise (and of its liability insurer) to coerce victims into accepting inadequate settlements, to overwhelm them in litigation, and to pass legislation that immunizes the enterprise from liability costs (as the nuclear-energy industry has done with the Price-Anderson Act). We know from studies of the deterrent effect of criminal sanctions that certainty is more important than severity; because it is so unlikely that damages will ever be paid, tort liability is often an empty threat, incapable of promoting safety.

If market deterrence worked the way it claims it does, state regulation of danger would be wholly unnecessary. The capitalist enterprise would balance the cost of safety against the cost of accidents; and whatever level of danger it chose would, by definition, be optimally efficient. Indeed, the mythical efficiency of the market is often invoked to oppose all regulation, or at least to require agencies to conform to the fictitious criteria of cost-benefit analysis, as in the attacks on the Occupational Safety and Health Administration (OSHA) by capitalists, the Supreme Court, and now the Reagan administration. Yet surely the failure of tort as a means of control is visible in the proliferation of regulation in such areas as food and drugs; environmental pollution; toxic wastes; pesticides; air, rail, and road transportation; nuclear energy; consumer products; professional services; and the workplace. Virtually everyone concedes the need for rules in at least some of these areas, e.g., traffic laws or the testing of medicines. Indeed, capitalists often welcome regulation as a protection against the competitive market. But we also know that these agencies fail to achieve acceptable levels of safety because, when compared to the capitalist enterprises they seek to regulate, they are inadequately funded, more restrained by legal formalism, denied effective sanctions, and readily captured by the industries they purport to control.

The most insidious consequence of dependence upon market deterrence and state regulation has been the undermining of collective efforts by those endangered to protect their own safety. Critics have often noted that the regulatory agency can lull citizens into a false sense of security, and hence into passivity, by appearing vigorously to champion public interests. The politics of safety are transformed into the administration of safety, thereby obscuring the political interests the administrative apparatus continues to serve. But if the bankruptcy of government regulation is a familiar tale, the effect of dependence on market deterrence is less widely recognized, and yet such dependence is even more dangerously seductive. Market deterrence, by mandating the payment of money damages to the injured persons, subverts collective efforts to exert control over safety. Damages are paid only to individuals (not collectivities) because the injury, like the individual, is viewed as unique; group reparations and class actions are unavailable to those who share the experience of having been injured by the same polluter, manufacturer of a defective product, or employer.

Damages are paid only for an injury caused by the defendant's act. This means both that unsafe conduct causing no injury is not deterred and that legal attention is focused on the temporally delimited act of an individual rather than on the ongoing activity of a collectivity. Capitalist tort law, like capitalist medicine, is obsessed with individual cure at the expense of collective prevention because (among other reasons) capitalism creates a market only for the former. Money damages undermine the sense of a collective interest in safety both by conveying the false impression that they adequately compensate for the injury, so that greater safety is unnecessary, and by arousing jealousy of the victim, thereby dividing those who might be injured in the future from the unfortunate victim who has suffered already.

At the same time that the class of victims, actual and potential, is individualized, those responsible for creating the danger and potentially liable for damages are collectivized—by the corporate form, the doctrine of *respondeat superior*, an expansive interpretation of proximate cause, and the spread of liability insurance. This aggregation is necessary because tort damages have grown too large to be paid by the individual (again the subversion of control in the name of spreading costs). But the inequality between the individual victim and collective tortfeasor is also constructed by the legal system: although the collective liability insurer can aggressively badger the victim for a release, the personal injury lawyer cannot solicit the victim for authority to represent him in suing the insurer; group legal service plans, originally created by automobile owners to provide lawyers for accident victims, were long illegal; corporations often refuse to bargain with unions over safety practices, claiming these as "management prerogatives"; and of course most workers, consumers, and citizens are not organized collectively. Thus, the legal structure of the struggle over safety pits the individual victim—or potential victim—against a collectivity in the legislature, the regulatory agency, the court, and at the negotiating table.

NOTES

*From *The Politics of Law: A Progressive Critique*, ed. David Kairys, (New York: Pantheon Books, 1982), pp. 190–193. Reprinted with permission. Copyright © 1982 by Richard Abel.

FOR DISCUSSION

1. Can Learned Hand's formula for liability, as elucidated by Posner, possibly give rise to the abuses described by Abel? Defend your answer.

2. According to Abel, why does so-called market deterrence fail to promote safety?

3. How does Abel's critique of the capitalist negligence system compare with what you know about the tobacco companies and their fight to avoid liability for injuries arising from smoking?

4. How does dependence on market deterrence undermine the public's collective efforts to protect itself from injury caused by enterprises? What role does the award of damages to plaintiffs play in Abel's theory?

5. Which view of negligence corresponds more closely to your experience, Posner's or Abel's? Explain.

In our present negligence system, fault is the foundation of legal liability. That requires that there be a duty owed by defendant to plaintiff, the breach of which is considered the proximate result of the harm suffered by the injured party. The following case deals with a problem that has not yet found legal recognition by the courts, the suit for "wrongful life," and the question of the existence of a duty owed by defendant to plaintiff, which underlies any finding of fault, is at the heart of the debate over this action. The plaintiffs are two sets of parents who claim that, had they been properly advised of the defects their children would have, they never would have conceived the children at all. The question considered by the court is who, if anyone, has suffered compensable injuries?

CASE

Dolores E. Becker et al. v. Eugene D. Schwartz et al.
N.Y. Court of Appeals (1978)
46 N.Y.2d 401, 413 N.Y.S.2d 895, 386 N.E.2d 807
OPINION OF THE COURT

JASEN, Judge.   From its earliest days, the common law steadfastly clung to the notion that "in civil court the death of a human being could not be complained of as an injury." *Baker* v. *Bolton*, 1 Camp. 493, 170 Eng.Rep. 1033 KB, 1808. Judicial hesitance to chart a novel course beyond the safe harbors afforded by prevailing legal theory, particularly the principle that a tort died with its victim, spurred legislative recognition of the cause of action since known as "wrongful death." Ironically, in the relatively brief period since the enactment of the first wrongful death statute, evolving legal theory has come full cycle. Although no longer shackled by the conceptual difficulties formerly posed by a "wrongful death" action, courts have again been drawn toward the murky waters at the periphery of existing legal theory to test the validity of a cause of action for what has been generically termed "wrongful life."

In *Becker* v. *Schwartz*, Dolores Becker, then 37 years of age, conceived a child in September 1974. After Dolores and her husband, Arnold Becker, learned of the pregnancy in October, they engaged the services of defendants, specialists in the field of obstetrics and gynecology. Thereafter, from approximately the tenth week of pregnancy until the birth of their child, Dolores Becker remained under the defendants' exclusive care. Tragically, on May 10, 1975, Dolores Becker gave birth to a retarded and brain-damaged infant who suffers, and will continue to suffer for the remainder of her life, from Down's Syndrome, commonly known as mongolism.

It is plaintiffs' contention that throughout the period during which Dolores Becker was under the care of defendants plaintiffs were never advised by defendants of the increased risk of Down's Syndrome in children born to women over 35 years of age. Nor were they advised, allege plaintiffs, of the availability of an amniocentisis test to determine whether the fetus carried by Dolores Becker would be born afflicted with Down's Syndrome.

Plaintiffs commenced this action seeking damages on behalf of the infant for "wrongful life," and, in their own right, for the various sums of money they will be forced to expend for the long-term institutional care of their retarded child. Plaintiffs' complaint also seeks damages for the emotional and physical injury suffered by Dolores Becker as a result of the birth of her child, as well as damages for the injury suffered by Arnold Becker occasioned by the loss of his wife's services and the medical expenses stemming from her treatment.

Upon motion by defendants, Special Term dismissed plaintiffs' complaint in its entirety as failing to state a cause of action. The Appellate Division modified the order of Special Term, however, sustaining plaintiffs' complaint except to the extent that it seeks recovery of damages "for psychiatric injuries or emotional distress of plaintiff Dolores E. Becker and to the extent that plaintiff Arnold Becker's claim for loss of services and medical expenses is based upon such psychiatric injuries." Defendants now appeal to this court on a certified question.

At the outset, emphasis must necessarily be placed upon the posture in which these cases are now before this court. The question presented for review is not whether plaintiffs should ultimately prevail in this litigation, but rather, more narrowly, whether their complaints state cognizable causes of action. For the purposes of our review, limited as it is to an evaluation of the sufficiency of plaintiffs' complaints, their allegations must be assumed to be true. Accordingly we accept, without expressing any opinion as to defendants' liability, each of plaintiffs' allegations: to wit, that defendants failed to inform plaintiffs accurately of the risks of their pregnancies, and, in *Becker*, of the availability of an amniocentisis test; and, that had they been accurately informed, plaintiffs would have, in *Park*,[3] chosen not to conceive a second child, and, in *Becker*, undergone an amniocentisis test, the results of which would have precipitated a decision on their part to terminate the pregnancy.

Even as a pure question of law, unencumbered by unresolved issues of fact, the weighing of the validity of a cause of action for the wrongful causation of life itself casts an almost Orwellian shadow, premised as it is upon concepts of genetic predictability once foreign to the evolutionary process. It borders on the absurdly obvious to observe that the resolution of this question transcends the mechanical application of legal principles. Any such resolution, whatever it may be, must invariably be colored by notions of public policy, the validity of which remains, as always, a matter upon which reasonable men may disagree.

Thoughtful analysis of the validity of "wrongful life" as an emerging legal concept requires, in the first instance, a clear understanding of the alleged wrong upon which the cause of action is predicated. Not surprisingly, the term "wrongful life" has functioned as a broad umbrella under which plaintiffs alleging factually divergent wrongs have sought judicial recognition of their claims. To be distinguished from the cases before us are those in which recovery is sought for what might perhaps be most appropriately labeled "wrongful conception," wherein parents, one of whom has undergone an unsuccessful birth control procedure, have sought damages for the birth of an unplanned child. There, damages have not been sought on behalf of the child—a healthy and normal infant—but by the parents for expenses attributable to the birth, including the pecuniary expense of rearing the child. Judicial reaction to the "wrongful conception" cause of action has been mixed. In a somewhat similar vein, recovery has been sought for damages incurred upon the birth of a child attributable to a "wrongful diagnosis" of an existing pregnancy, resulting in the deprivation of the mother's choice to terminate the pregnancy within the permissible time period.

While courts have struggled with the concepts of "wrongful conception" or "wrongful diagnosis" as cognizable causes of action, they have had little difficulty in rejecting a cause of action which may be distinguished by use of the term "wrongful birth." In the latter cause of action an illegitimate, but otherwise healthy child, seeks recovery in his or her own behalf for the injury suffered as a consequence of his or her birth into this world as a stigmatized child. To this point, courts have refused to sustain this cause of action.

Standing distinctly apart from claims based upon a wrongful conception, a failure to diagnose a pregnancy, or an illegitimate birth, in which the essence of the wrong for which compensation is sought is the birth of a healthy and normal—albeit, unplanned—child, plaintiffs' claims are premised upon the birth of a fully intended but abnormal child for whom extraordinary care and treatment is required. It is not contended that the defendant physicians' treatment of Dolores Becker and Hetty Park caused the abnormalities in their

[3]*Park* v. *Chessin*, a companion case in which parents claimed that, through the negligence of their physicians, they gave birth to a second child with polycystic kidney disease. The child died in infancy, as had their first child.

infants, but only that had plaintiffs been properly advised by defendants of the risks of abnormality, their infants would never have been born.

Irrespective of the label coined, plaintiffs' complaints sound essentially in negligence or medical malpractice. As in any cause of action founded upon negligence, a successful plaintiff must demonstrate the existence of a duty, the breach of which may be considered the proximate cause of the damages suffered by the injured party.

An examination of plaintiffs' complaints leads to the conclusion that, insofar as plaintiffs allege claims on behalf of their infants, whether denominated as claims for wrongful life or otherwise, they have failed to state legally cognizable causes of action. If it be assumed that under the facts at bar defendants, as physicians, owed a duty to the infants *in utero* as well as to their parents, defendants' breach of that duty may be viewed as the proximate cause for the infants' birth. Had Hetty and Steven Park been accurately advised by their physicians of the chances that a future child of theirs would suffer from polycystic kidney disease, they allege that they would not have chosen to conceive a second child. Similarly, had Dolores and Arnold Becker been accurately advised of the chances that their already conceived child would be born afflicted with Down's Syndrome, and of the availability of an amniocentisis test, they allege that they would have undergone that test, and had it indicated the presence of Down's Syndrome in their child, that they would have terminated the pregnancy within the permissible time period.

However, there are two flaws in plaintiffs' claims on behalf of their infants for wrongful life. The first, in a sense the more fundamental, is that it does not appear that the infants suffered any legally cognizable injury. There is no precedent for recognition at the Appellate Division of "the fundamental right of a child to be born as a whole, functional human being." Surely the use of somewhat similar words in another context affords no such basis. Whether it is better never to have been born at all than to have been born with even gross deficiencies is a mystery more properly left to the philosophers and the theologians. Surely the law can assert no competence to resolve the issue, particularly in view of the very nearly uniform high value which the law and mankind has placed on human life, rather than its absence. Not only is there to be found no predicate at common law or in statutory enactment for judicial recognition of the birth of a defective child as an injury to the child; the implications of any such proposition are staggering. Would claims be honored, assuming the breach of an identifiable duty, for less than a perfect birth? And by what standard or by whom would perfection be defined?

There is also a second flaw. The remedy afforded to an injured party in negligence is designed to place that party in the position he would have occupied but for the negligence of the defendant. Thus, the damages recoverable on behalf of an infant for wrongful life are limited to that which is necessary to restore the infant to the position he or she would have occupied were it not for the failure of the defendant to render advice to the infant's parents in a non-negligent manner. The theoretical hurdle to an assertion of damages on behalf of an infant accruing from a defendant's negligence in such a case becomes at once apparent. The very allegations of the complaint state that had the defendant not been negligent, the infant's parents would have chosen not to conceive, or having conceived, to have terminated rather than to carry the pregnancy to term, thereby depriving the infant plaintiff of his or her very existence. Simply put, a cause of action brought on behalf of an infant seeking recovery for wrongful life demands a calculation of damages dependent upon a comparison between the Hobson's choice of life in an impaired state and non-existence. This comparison the law is not equipped to make. Recognition of so novel a cause of action requiring, as it must, creation of a hypothetical formula for the measurement of an infant's damages is best reserved for legislative, rather than judicial, attention. Accordingly, plaintiffs' complaints insofar as they seek damages on behalf of their infants for wrongful life should be dismissed for failure to state legally cognizable causes of action.

There remains for consideration, however, the validity of plaintiffs' causes of action brought in their own right for damages accruing as a consequence of the birth of their infants. There can be no dispute at this stage of the pleadings that plaintiffs have alleged the existence of a duty flowing from defendants to themselves and that the breach of that duty was the proximate cause of the birth of their infants. That they have been damaged by the alleged negligence of defendants has also been pleaded. Unlike the causes of action brought on behalf of their infants for wrongful life, plaintiffs' causes of action, founded essentially upon a theory of negligence or medical malpractice, do allege ascertainable damages: the pecuniary expense which they have born, and in *Becker* must continue to bear, for the care and treatment of their infants. Certainly, assuming the validity of plaintiffs' allegations, it can be said in traditional tort language that but for the defendants' breach of their duty to advise plaintiffs, the latter would not have been required to assume these obligations. Calculation of damages necessary to make plaintiffs whole in relation to these expenditures requires nothing extraordinary. The fact that plaintiffs' wrongful life claims brought on behalf of their infants do not state legally cognizable causes of action inasmuch as they fail to allege ascertainable damages in no way affects the validity of plaintiffs' claims for pecuniary loss. Plaintiffs state causes of action in their own right predicated upon a breach of a duty flowing from defendants to themselves, as prospective parents, resulting in damage to plaintiffs for which compensation may be readily fixed. There is now no occasion, in passing on the sufficiency of the complaints to state a cause of action, to determine with particularity what items of expense or loss may properly be taken into account in computation of the damages recoverable. Such questions properly await consideration and resolution presumably on trial, after liability has been proved, if it can be....

Accordingly, in *Becker* v. *Schwartz* the question certified is answered in the negative. The order of the Appellate Division should be modified, with costs, by dismissing plaintiffs' complaint except to the extent that it seeks recovery of the sums expended for the long-term institutional care of their retarded child.

In *Park* v. *Chessin*, the question certified is answered in the negative. The order of the Appellate Division should be modified, with costs, by dismissing plaintiffs' complaint except to the extent that it seeks recovery for the sums expended for the care and treatment of their child until her death.

FOR DISCUSSION

1. Did the physicians in the two cases covered by this opinion actually cause the defects suffered by the infants?

2. What duty, if any, do physicians in these circumstances owe to as-yet unborn infants and their parents?

3. Why, according to the court, did neither infant in this case suffer a legally cognizable injury?

4. Do the parents in these cases have valid causes of action in negligence against their physicians? Explain.

5. Assuming the physicians in these cases were negligent, describe the duty they had, to whom it was owed, how it was breached, and what damages were suffered.

6. Do you agree with the outcome of this case? Justify your answer.

Elements of Actionable Negligence

The elements of actionable negligence may be summarized as follows: (1) a duty to exercise reasonable care; (2) breach of the duty to exercise reasonable care (negligence); (3) proximate (or legal) cause; and (4) actual harm. Cases in negligence frequently involve disputes over the existence of a duty of care, as well as whether such a duty, if it exists, was breached.

In determining whether the defendant has a duty to exercise reasonable care with respect to the plaintiff, the law starts with a basic rule that an individual has a duty to all persons to act in a way so as not to subject others to an unreasonable risk of harm. Despite this general rule, persons may not be held liable for harm they cause in every instance. The defendant is expected to act as a reasonably prudent person would in the particular circumstances of that case. Sources for standards of conduct in specific situations may be found in statutes, or in the customary practice and usage in a particular trade or profession. In cases involving either a statutorily imposed duty or what we may call a common-law duty of care, consideration will focus on whether the defendant's conduct would create a foreseeable risk of harm to another in that situation. In many cases, the common-law duty of care arises out of some relationship between the plaintiff and the defendant that obligates the defendant not to harm the plaintiff. Often these relationships are very specific, but sometimes a defendant is held to have a duty to the public at large that would encompass many potential plaintiffs.

In our legal system, people generally do not have an affirmative duty to assist another person who is in danger. (This is not the case in Western Europe and in many other parts of the world.) Conversely, if a person does voluntarily undertake to assist another, then he or she is responsible not to make the other person's situation worse or prevent others from assisting.

The following case examines the question of what duty a vendor of intoxicating beverages owes to members of the public with respect to sale of liquor to minors. The case deals, therefore, with what can be called third-party liability: the issue is not what duty the vendor owes to the minor, but whether the vendor has a duty to third parties to protect them from the consequences of conduct by a minor to whom he has sold liquor. Third-party liability cases are not uncommon; several of the other cases in this chapter are also third-party liability cases. Third-party liability with respect to vendors of alcohol, in particular, is not a new concept, but third-party liability with respect to social providers of alcohol, called "social host liability," has only been established very recently. A leading case in this area is *Kelly* v. *Gwinnell*, 96 N.J. 538, 476 A.2d 1219 (1984), in which the Supreme Court of New Jersey held that social hosts were liable for the torts of their guests whom they had allowed to consume intoxicating beverages to excess. The central issue in *Kelly* v. *Gwinnell* was to determine whether a social host had a duty to protect third parties from harm caused by his intoxicated guest. The court found that there was such a duty, founded in social considerations, such as fairness, safety, and the reduction of drunken driving. The court stated: "Whatever the motive behind making alcohol available to those who will subsequently drive, the provider has a duty to the public not to create foreseeable, unreasonable risks by this activity." 476 A.2d at p. 1224. In the following opinion, establishing a duty to protect third parties in the case of a vendor of alcoholic beverages is somewhat easier. You should carefully consider the source of that duty as you read the case.

CASE

Ellena B. Michnik-Zilberman, Individually and as Administratrix
v. Gordon's Liquor, Inc.
Supreme Judicial Court of Massachusetts (1983)
390 Mass. 6, 453 N.E.2d 430

ABRAMS, Justice.   On July 25, 1977, Thomas A. Thoele, a minor, operated an automobile after consuming alcoholic beverages purchased from the defendant, Gordon's Liquor, Inc. (store) and struck David Zilberman. Zilberman sustained injuries and died as a result of the accident. The plaintiff, Ellena B. Michnik-Zilberman, brought this action in Superior Court against the store to recover compensation for her husband's injuries and death. The jury found for the plaintiff. The Appeals Court affirmed, determining that there was evidence supporting the store's liability under the theory that the "injuries inflicted by Thoele were a foreseeable consequence of the negligent sale of alcoholic beverages to him." The case came here on the store's motion for further appellate review. We affirm.

We summarize the evidence. Late in the afternoon of July 25, 1977, Thomas Thoele, who had recently turned seventeen years of age, drove to the store and parked in its parking lot. He entered the store, took a six-pack of twelve ounce containers of beer from the cooler, and paid the cashier. The store had a policy of requiring identification from youthful-looking customers to avoid sales to minors. Although he had a young appearance at the time and had not yet begun to shave, Thoele was not asked for identification.

Thoele drove home from the store, showered, ate dinner, and then left for the evening with the beer he had just purchased. He drank three or four beers between 8:30 P.M. and 10 P.M., and consumed some of it while in his automobile. At approximately 10 P.M., Thoele drove down Crescent Street, Waltham, where Zilberman was riding his bicycle. Zilberman was an experienced cyclist, who bicycled to and from his job once or twice a day. Thoele saw the bicycle's rear reflector about 100 feet ahead of him on the right side of the road. As he pulled forward, he hit the bicycle with the right side of his car. Zilberman died as a result of the injuries he sustained in the accident.

There was evidence that the portion of the street on which the accident occurred was straight and well-lighted. There was no sign of braking on the road, but there was evidence that Thoele's automobile hit a wooden utility pole after hitting the bicycle. Approximately eighty feet before the automobile came to the light pole, it passed an engine block resting on the edge of the road, protruding approximately fifteen to eighteen inches from the curb. Scattered around the engine block were bicycle reflector pieces, indicating that the deceased had collided with the side of the engine block.

The store asserts that there was insufficient evidence that the sale was the proximate cause of the accident....

2. *Liability of a vendor for damages caused by a minor to whom it negligently sold alcoholic beverages when the minor was not intoxicated.* The store asserts that liability extends to vendors of alcoholic beverages for injuries caused by their customers only when the sale of those beverages is to an intoxicated customer. We do not agree. It is the rule of this Commonwealth that negligence on the part of a seller or supplier of alcoholic beverages to a minor, as well as to an inebriated person, as each is proscribed by statute. See G.L.c. 138, §§34, 69. See also *Rappaport* v. *Nichols*, 31 N.J. 188, 202, 156 A.2d 1 (1959). Thus, the sale of alcoholic beverages to a minor is evidence of negligence even if the minor is not intoxicated at the time of the transaction. It is the sale or furnishing of alcohol itself which is critical.

The Legislature has in explicit terms prohibited sales to minors as a class because it recognizes their very special susceptibilities and the intensification of the otherwise inherent dangers when persons lacking in maturity and responsibility partake of alcoholic beverages.... It seems clear...that [the statutes'] broadly expressed restrictions were not narrowly intended to benefit the minors and intoxicated persons alone but were wisely intended for the protection of members of the general public as well.

Id. at 201-202, 156 A.2d 1. Once a vendor places liquor in the hands of a minor, it may set in motion the very harm which the Legislature has attempted to prevent.

The Legislature has placed on every vendor who holds a license to furnish alcoholic beverages and a concomitant right to profit from its sale the responsibility to refrain from supplying those beverages to minors or to intoxicated persons. The Legislature has approved two cards, a liquor identification card, and a driver's license, on which vendors of alcoholic beverages may reasonably rely to ascertain the age of youthful customers. A vendor may protect itself by maintaining a record of the identification card numbers, as well as the name, address, and age of any youthful person to whom it sells liquor.

In order to comply with the Legislature's objective to protect the public and minors through its prohibition of sales to underage buyers, vendors must exercise the care of a reasonably prudent person. "When a statute provides that under certain circumstances particular acts shall or shall not be done, it may be interpreted as fixing a standard for all members of the community from which it is negligence to deviate." Prosser, Torts §36, at 190 (4th ed. 1971). Thus, if a vendor fails to exercise due care and sells liquor to a minor, it is responsible for all proximately caused injuries. "The legislative policy, being clear, is not to be rendered futile of practical accomplishment," *Adamian* v. *Three Sons, Inc.*, 353 Mass. 498, 500, 233 N.E.2d 18 (1968), by absolving vendors of alcoholic beverages from all liability but rather will be enforced so as to encourage adherence to the law.

Further, the vendor need not foresee the particular kind of harm which might occur from its negligent sales. Of course, the act and the harm must be reasonably foreseeable. One of the more foreseeable risks is that the minor may drive and cause harm to third persons while intoxicated. In the case before us, the jury found that the minor caused serious injuries and death to a third person only hours after he had purchased the liquor. "[Q]uestions of proximate and intervening cause are left to the jury for its factual determination." *Rappaport* v. *Nichols*, 31 N.J. 188, 203, 156 A.2d 1 (1959).

Other jurisdictions have also recognized that the sale of liquor to a minor by a vendor may be the proximate cause of injuries to a third party caused by the minor after he becomes intoxicated.

3. Existence of evidence supporting the verdict for the plaintiff. The store asserts that there was no evidence that it knew or it should have known that Thoele was a minor, that he would use an automobile while intoxicated, and that Thoele's intoxication was the actual cause of the accident. We treat each of these contentions in turn, to determine whether the verdict was "inconsistent with substantial justice." Mass.R.Civ.P. 61.

The plaintiff introduced evidence to show that at the time of the sale Thoele was in fact a minor, that he had a youthful appearance, that he did not shave, and that he was not asked for any identification. At trial, Thoele stated that he shaved only once or twice a week, although he was twenty-one years of age. The jury had the opportunity to judge from Thoele's appearance, as well as from other evidence, whether Thoele appeared young enough to have been a minor at the time the liquor was sold to him.

Even if there were a question whether Thoele was a minor, the store could easily have complied with its policy to request identification, such as a liquor identification card or a driver's license. Had such a request been made, this might well be a different case. The Legislature has facilitated a store's ability to determine the age of a buyer, and the store's failure to do this is probative on the issue whether it should have known that Thoele was a minor.

The store also contends there was no evidence that it had knowledge that Thoele would use an automobile while intoxicated. Although such evidence may have been before the jury, it was not essential to a determination of liability. Since the accident occurred within the scope of the risk of the negligent sale, the plaintiff need not prove the store's ability to foresee the actual manner in which the harm would occur.

There was also evidence before the jury that Thoele's intoxication while driving was an actual cause of the accident. The store contests this point, arguing that the existence of the engine block in the road, and the lack of eyewitness testimony demonstrates that there was no evidence on causation before the jury. However, we conclude that the jury had some evidence before it to determine that Thoele's intoxication was a "substantial legal factor in bringing about the harm to the plaintiff." *Tritsch* v. *Boston Edison Co.*, 363 Mass. 179, 182, 293 N.E.2d 264 (1974). The plaintiff need not establish that Thoele's intoxicated driving was the sole cause of the accident. *Id.*

To prove its case, the plaintiff offered evidence that Thoele was intoxicated at the time of the accident by Thoele's own admission and by the testimony of two police officers at the scene. In addition, Zilberman was visible to Thoele from a distance of 100 feet. There was no evidence that Thoele was confronted with oncoming traffic or unusual traffic conditions. Rather, Crescent Street was well-lighted and thirty-five feet wide, so that a careful driver could easily have avoided striking a bicyclist. Instead, Thoele struck the bicycle along the length of his automobile. There was evidence that Thoele did not apply his brakes and that he ran into a utility pole before stopping. Finally, the engine block protruded only fifteen to eighteen inches from the curb. Even if Zilberman had hit the engine block, it was a question for the jury whether Thoele was negligent in being so close to Zilberman that he could not avoid striking him.

Thus, there was evidence from which the jury could infer that Thoele was at least a partial cause of the accident. While "[t]he occurrence of an accident, standing alone, is not always evidence of negligence," *Wardwell* v. *George H. Taylor Co.*, 333 Mass. 302, 305, 130 N.E.2d 586 (1955), in this case there was evidence to show that Zilberman's death was a "likely consequence of the defendant's negligence." *Dolan* v. *Suffolk Franklin Sav. Bank*, 355 Mass. 665, 670, 246 N.E.2d 798 (1969). Because there was a close causal connection between the sale of liquor and the accident, *Reeves* v. *Margey*, 321 Mass. 752, 76 N.E.2d 314 (1947), is distinguishable. We conclude that there was no error in submitting the case to the jury, nor was the verdict "inconsistent with substantial justice...."

Judgment affirmed.

FOR DISCUSSION

1. What was the source of the store's duty not to provide liquor to minors?
2. According to the court, what was the legislature's objective in passing the statutes referred to in this case?
3. What means were available to prevent a minor from purchasing liquor?

4. Is a vendor of alcoholic beverages being held to a higher standard of care than an ordinary person would be?

5. How does the vendor's failure to comply with its duty not to sell liquor to minors translate into negligence toward plaintiff's decedent?

6. What type of harm might a vendor reasonably foresee in connection with providing intoxicating beverages to underage persons?

Although it is not unusual for a statute to provide some or all of the justification for imposing a duty of care upon a defendant, the following case demonstrates that the existence of a statute may not in and of itself create a duty of care that must be followed. This is a case in which the foreseeability of harm to persons in the decedent's position is very great, but that, too, is not enough of itself to create a duty. This case uses a form of analysis which is very similar to the Learned Hand formula discussed by Posner earlier in the chapter. You should keep Posner's arguments in mind as you read the court's opinion.

CASE   **Gloria Jean Hosein v. Checker Taxi Company, Inc.**
Appellate Court of Illinois (1981)
95 Ill.App.3d 150, 50 Ill.Dec. 460, 419 N.E.2d 568

HARTMANN, Presiding Justice.   Plaintiff, administrator of the estate of Kadir Hosein, brought a wrongful death action sounding in negligence against Checker Taxi Company (hereinafter "Checker"), alleging that Hosein had leased a taxicab from Checker and was killed during the operation of that cab on April 21, 1978, when one or two passengers shot him. The complaint alleged that Checker owed a duty of due care, arising either from common law principles or section 12-605 of the Illinois Vehicle Code, to provide a shield or other protective partition between the driver's seat and the back seat, and that the failure to install such a shield was the proximate cause of Hosein's death. Checker's motion to dismiss the complaint for failure to state a cause of action was denied and we allowed Checker's interlocutory appeal therefrom under Supreme Court Rule 308. For the reasons set forth below, we reverse the trial court's denial of the motion to dismiss.

We first address the applicability of section 12-605 to this action. Plaintiff asserted below that the complaint stated a cause of action for negligence based on Checker's alleged violation of section 12-605 because this penal statute, while not specifically providing for a civil remedy, was intended to protect the class, of which Hosein was a member, from the type of injury which Hosein received, and the injury [had] a direct and proximate connection with the violation. Checker responds that section 12-605, having been declared unconstitutionally vague in *Meyerson* v. *Carter* (1974), 22 Ill.App.3d 73, 316 N.E.2d 240, cannot be employed here to establish a statutorily defined duty and standard of conduct. The following summary of the legislative amendments and judicial interpretations of section 12-605 is a necessary prelude to an analysis of the issues and arguments raised herein.

Section 12-605 was derived from sections 441 and 442 enacted by Public Act 76-1054 (1969 Ill.Laws), effective August 28, 1969, which took the following form:

> In municipalities with 1,000,000 or more population, any taxicab manufactured, owned or operated after September 1, 1970, and regularly operated in such a municipality must have a bullet-proof shield completely separating the driver's seat from the back seat.

> Any person owning a taxicab which is in violation of this Act shall be fined not to exceed $500.

Effective January 1, 1972, sections 441 and 442 were repealed by Public Act 77-37 (1971 Ill.Laws) and section 12-605 of the Illinois Vehicle Code was enacted in their place. Public Act 77-2720 substituted the words "guilty of a petty offense" for the words "fined not to exceed $500." This amendment to the penalty provision was necessary to conform section 12-605 to the Uniform Code of Corrections.

In August of 1974, this court held in *Meyerson* that section 12-605 was unconstitutionally vague because the term "bullet-proof shield" was too indefinite and therefore capable of inconsistent interpretations. The term had not been defined in the statute and the expert testimony elicited at the trial indicated that no special or technical definition of the term existed for application in this context. Thus neither the statute nor a commonly understood meaning of the term prescribed a norm of conduct as a guide to those who would be imposed with the duty to follow it.

After *Meyerson* was decided, in September of 1977 the Illinois Legislature enacted Public Act 80-911 (1977 Ill.Laws) which, effective October 1, 1977, deleted from section 12-605 the language "any person owning a taxicab which is in violation of this section shall be guilty of a petty offense," and, at the same time, amended section 16-104 so that it provided that "Every person convicted of a violation of any provision of this Act for which another penalty is not provided shall for a first or second conviction thereof be guilty of a petty offense; and for a third or subsequent conviction within one year of the first conviction, such person shall be guilty of a Class C misdemeanor." Section 16-101 makes section 16-104 applicable to section 12-605. A transcript of the House and Senate debates on Public Act 80-911, included in the record on appeal by Checker, indicates that the sole purpose behind the 1977 amendment to section 12-605 was to change the penalty previously set forth therein by deleting it and deferring to the graduated penalty scheme of section 16-104. A reading of Public Act 80-911 indicates that the penalty provisions of numerous other sections of the vehicle code were also eliminated in deference to the scheme of section 16-104. Noticeably absent from the debate's transcript is any mention of the *Meyerson* decision rendered three years previously.

In response to Checker's assertion that *Meyerson* precludes use of section 12-605 in the instant case, plaintiff claims, first, that even if a penal statute has been declared invalid so that its criminal sanction is inoperative, the statute may still be employed to establish duty and standard of conduct in a negligence case citing *Clinkscales* v. *Carver* (1943), 22 Cal.2d 72, 136 P.2d 777; *West Texas Coaches, Inc.* v. *Madi* (Tex.Civ.App. 1930), 26 S.W.2d 199; and *Ponca City* v. *Reed* (1925), 115 Okl. 166, 242 P.2d 164. These cases did hold that the statute or ordinance was properly used in establishing the relevant standard of conduct in a negligence case despite an infirmity which prevented enforcement of the statute for its intended purpose; however, none of these cases involved the situation present in the principal case where the infirmity preventing enforcement of the statute also necessarily precludes its use in a negligence case. Unlike the cases cited, *Meyerson* found section 12-605 to be unconstitutionally vague as to the meaning of bulletproof shield and that the penal provision specifically included therein could not be enforced. Yet, plaintiff seeks to employ this same indeterminate term to impose a duty of compliance on Checker in a civil case. This position is untenable. Where a statute is so vague and indeterminate that persons of common intelligence must necessarily guess at its meaning and differ as to its application, neither civil nor criminal liability can arise therefrom. Therefore, *Meyerson* having determined that the statute was too vague to permit enforcement of its penal provision, also effectively terminated the use of this section as a legislatively prescribed duty and standard of care in a negligence case otherwise allowed by *First National Bank* v. *City of Aurora* (1978), 71 Ill.App.2d 1, 15 Ill.Dec. 642, 373 N.E.2d 1326.

The plaintiff next asserts that the Legislature's intent in amending section 12-605 in 1977 was to eliminate all penal liability and instead impose only civil liability, and, that in any event, the amendment should result in a hearing below, as was conducted in *Meyerson*, to determine whether the term has acquired a generally understood and technical definition since *Meyerson*, which would cure the defect found to exist in that case. We find neither argument persuasive. First, in enacting the October 31, 1977, amendment to section 12-605, the Legislature simply altered the previously existing criminal sanction of that section by deferring to the graduated penalty scheme of section 16-104. There is no indication from this change of any legislative intent to transform section 12-605 from a criminal liability section to a civil liability section. As to the need for a new hearing on the meaning of "bullet-proof," we note that the Legislature made no effort to alter the language which was the source of the infirmity. It cannot be held, therefore, that the intention of the Legislature was to cure the constitutional defect by enacting the amendment. Under these circumstances, the amendment does not operate as a new enactment, but is deemed to be a continuation of the unchanged portion, and is not ripe for another constitutional test.

The second issue presented for review is whether Checker was under a common law duty to protect decedent taxicab-lessee from the criminal acts of third parties while using the taxicab. The existence of a duty is a question of law to be determined by the court. Whether the law imposes a duty does not depend on foreseeability alone but is also a function of the likelihood of the injury, the magnitude of the burden of guarding against it and the desirability of imposing that duty on the defendant. At common law, in the absence of a special relationship between the defendant and the injured person, there is no duty imposed upon a defendant to protect an injured party against the criminal acts of third parties. The courts in Illinois have adopted those special relationships enumerated in section 34A of the Second Restatement of Torts which include common carrier-passenger, innkeeper-guest, business invitor-invitee, and custodian-ward. The complaint in the instant case, having failed to set forth any of these special relationships, should have been dismissed....

Reversed.

FOR DISCUSSION

1. According to the plaintiff, what was the legislative purpose of section 12-605 of the Illinois Vehicle Code?

2. Why does the court refuse to accept this statute as establishing a duty of care owed by defendant to the decedent?

3. According to the court, what are the elements to be considered in imposing a common-law duty of care on the defendant?

4. What types of "special relationships" might impose a duty on defendant to exercise due care with respect to the decedent?

5. If the statute at issue in this case had not been fatally flawed, do you think it ought to have imposed a duty of care on defendant? Explain.

The following case demonstrates that issues of public policy may influence whether a defendant is held to have a duty to exercise due care with respect to the plaintiff. You should compare this case closely with the *Michnik-Zilberman* case to determine why this situation is treated so differently. It is clear that someone who provides residential treatment for convicted criminals can reasonably foresee that such an occupation might cause harm to others, and it would not be unreasonable to argue that persons engaged in this type of activity owe a duty to the public to protect them from harm, but those arguments do not prevail here. Why should a vendor of alcoholic beverages have a duty to protect the public and the operator of a private facility to rehabilitate dangerous offenders not have a similar duty?

CASE

Donald Beauchene v. Synanon Foundation, Inc.
Court of Appeal of California (1979)
(1979) 88 Cal.App.3d 342, 151 Cal.Rptr. 796

CHRISTIAN, Associate Justice.   Donald Beauchene appeals from a judgment of dismissal which was rendered after the court sustained a demurrer[4] to his complaint in which he had alleged that Synanon Foundation, Inc. was liable for the intentional criminal behavior of Lynn Bentley, who injured appellant after eloping from a Synanon home.

On appeal after a sustained demurrer, the court must assume the truth of the factual allegations of the complaint. The function of a demurrer is to test the legal sufficiency of the challenged pleading.

Appellant in his complaint as modified by admissions in his briefs, alleges that Synanon Foundation, Inc. is a voluntary private rehabilitation institution that provides a structured or controlled environment for its residents. Its primary purpose is the rehabilitation of drug addicts, alcoholics, and other people with character disorders. With the prior approval of Synanon, California courts have sometimes sent convicted persons to Synanon rather than to a county jail or state prison. Before respondent accepts a convicted person, the person alleged is screened and interviewed to determine whether his involvement in the program will be dangerous to himself, to Synanon, or to society generally. If respondent were to determine the candidate's involvement would be dangerous, respondent would not accept the person, even if a court were willing to send him to the program.

Lynn Bentley was convicted of first degree burglary on May 2, 1975. The superior court admitted Bentley to probation on condition that he enter the "Synanon program and not leave said program without prior approval of the Probation Officer and the staff of Synanon."

Prior to accepting Bentley, respondent allegedly had rejected several dangerous individuals who had been referred by the courts. When respondent accepted Bentley, respondent knew or should have known that he had a long history of behavioral difficulties, arrests, convictions, criminal confinement, and escape attempts. One superior court had ordered that Bentley, after serving time in jail for one conviction, enter the Delancey Street drug program and not leave there without approval of the program staff. The Probation Department later recommended that Bentley's probation to Delancey Street be revoked, because of his inability to cooperate and comply with the rules of probation. Probation was revoked.

Respondent admitted Bentley on May 10; five days later Bentley, in violation of the court's order and without the permission of the Synanon staff, "escaped" from the program. Bentley went on a "crime spree" that included the harming or killing of several people. On May 23, 13 days after leaving the program, Bentley shot appellant in the arm.

---

[4]A **demurrer** is the equivalent to a motion to dismiss in modern practice. It challenges the legal sufficiency of plaintiff's complaint, arguing that even if all facts alleged are true, they do not make out a cause of action. If the demurrer is sustained, the action is over. In modern practice, if the demurrer is overruled, the case continues. (In prior times if the demurrer had been overruled, the plaintiff would have won the case.)

Appellant argues that respondent had a duty to exercise due care in accepting convicted persons into the Synanon program. Alternatively, appellant argues that respondent had an affirmative duty to prevent Bentley from leaving the program.

Actionable negligence generally involves five elements:

(a) a defendant's duty to exercise due care;

(b) defendant's breach of that duty;

(c) the breach was the actual ("but for") cause of plaintiff's injury;

(d) the breach as the proximate or legal cause of plaintiff's injury; and

(e) damages to plaintiff.

See Prosser, Torts (4th ed. 1971), p. 143; 4 Witkin, Summary of Cal. Law (8th ed. 1974), pp. 2749–2750. Elements (b), (c), (d), and (e) are ordinarily questions of fact for a jury. The existence of a legal duty is primarily a question of law. See 4 Witkin *supra*, pp. 2755–59).

Appellant argues respondent is liable for Bentley's criminal behavior under either of two theories. First, appellant argues respondent was under a duty (1) to refuse admittance to applicants whose record and history show that they constitute an unreasonably high risk, or (2) to reject all candidates who are unlikely to be rehabilitated, present a clear and immediate danger to the community, and would otherwise be jailed or imprisoned, or (3) to establish a blanket policy of refusing admittance to any felony probationer. Respondent allegedly breached the claimed duty by admitting Bentley to the program. Respondent's officials knew or should have known that admitting Bentley, in light of his history of criminal and antisocial behavior, presented an unreasonably dangerous risk to society. Respondent's breach was the actual cause of appellant's injury: but for respondent's accepting Bentley, Bentley would have been sent to prison, where he could not have harmed appellant. Respondent's breach was the proximate cause of appellant's injuries: Bentley's criminal behavior was allegedly not a superseding cause. Respondent was negligent precisely because of the reasonably foreseeable likelihood that Bentley would commit criminal or antisocial acts. "If the likelihood that a third person may act in a particular manner is the hazard or one of the hazards which makes the actor negligent, such an act, whether innocent, negligent, intentionally tortious, or criminal does not prevent the actor from being liable for harm caused thereby." Rest. 2d Torts, §449. See also *Hoyem* v. *Manhattan Beach City Sch. Dist.*, 22 Cal.3d 508, 521-22, 150 Cal.Rptr. 1, 585 P. 2d 851, 4 Witkin, Summary of Cal. Law, *supra*, at pp. 2922–2923.

Under a second theory of liability, appellant argues that because of the special relationship that respondent undertook by admitting Bentley into its program, respondent had a duty to control Bentley's behavior so as to prevent Bentley from "escaping" or leaving the program without authorization. Because admitting Bentley presented a risk to society, argues appellant, respondent breached its duty to control Bentley by not constructing "improvements to some of their physical plants so as to render them secure enough to prevent their dangerous probation inmates from escaping."

Both theories of liability fail because of the faulty premise that respondent owed a duty of care to appellant. Generally, a person owes no duty to control the conduct of another. Exceptions are recognized in limited situations where a special relationship exists between the defendant and the injured party, or between the defendant and the active wrongdoer. *Tarasoff* v. *Regents of University of California* (1976) 17 Cal.3d 425, 435, 131 Cal.Rptr. 14, 551 P.2d 334. Appellant does not contend the first exception is applicable. The issue is whether respondent owed appellant a duty under the second exception.

"Duty" is "an expression of the sum total of those considerations of policy which lead the law to say that the particular plaintiff is entitled to protection" against the defendant's conduct. Prosser, Torts, *supra*, pp. 325–326.) The questions of duty and proximate cause are sometimes the same. Principal policy considerations in deciding whether a duty exists include

> the foreseeability of harm to the plaintiff, the degree of certainty that the plaintiff suffered injury, the closeness of the connection between the defendant's conduct and the injury suffered, the moral blame attached to the defendant's conduct, the policy of preventing future harm, the extent of the burden to the defendant and consequences to the community of imposing a duty to exercise care with resulting liability for breach, and the availability, cost, and prevalence of insurance for the risk involved.
>
> *Rowland* v. *Christian* (1968) 69 Cal.2d 108, 113, 70 Cal.Rptr. 97, 100, 443 P.2d 561, 564.

Here, the court must balance "the public interest in safety from violent assault" (*Tarasoff* v. *Regents, supra,* 17 Cal.3d 425, 440, 131 Cal.Rptr. 14, 26, 551 P.2d 334, 336) against the public policy favoring innovative criminal offender release and rehabilitation programs. Although appellant's injuries may be grievous, "[o]f paramount concern is the detrimental effect a finding of liability would have on prisoner release and rehabilitation programs. Were we to find a cause of action stated we would in effect be encouraging detention of prisoners in disregard of their rights and society's needs." *Whitcombe* v. *County of Yolo* (1977) 73 Cal.App.3d 698, 716, 141 Cal.Rptr. 189, 199. Each member of the general public who chances to come into contact with a parolee or probationer must risk that the rehabilitative effort will fail.

The above cited cases applied Government Code section 845.8 to establish that a public entity or employee enjoys absolute immunity from liability for:

(a) Any injury resulting from determining whether to parole or release a prisoner or from determining the terms and conditions of his parole or release or from determining whether to revoke his parole or release.

(b) Any injury caused by:

(1) An escaping or escaped prisoner;

(2) An escaping or escaped arrested person; or

(3) A person resisting arrest.

Respondent concededly is not a "public entity or employee" within the meaning of section 845.8. But the same public policy that moved the Legislature to immunize *public* release and rehabilitation programs from liability—to encourage such innovations in the interests of criminal justice—compels the conclusion that respondent's *private* release and rehabilitation program owed no legal duty to this appellant. In light of the purpose behind the governmental immunity, it would be incongruous to hold that, while the state is immune from liability for its decision to assign Bentley to, and his unauthorized departure from, the Synanon program, the program itself owed appellant a duty not to accept Bentley or to prevent his unauthorized departure. To hold respondent civilly liable would deter the development of innovative criminal offender release and rehabilitation programs, in contravention of public policy.

Because respondent owed no duty of due care to appellant, the complaint failed to state a cause of action.

The judgment is affirmed.

FOR DISCUSSION

1. Why doesn't Synanon's acceptance of clients only after subjecting them to a screening process to determine their suitability (including lack of dangerousness) constitute a voluntary assumption of a duty of care toward the public?

2. Suppose the alternative to Synanon accepting Bentley were that he remain in jail. Would that impose a duty of care on Synanon? Suppose the alternative were that Bentley be released into the community. Would that make a difference?

3. Was it foreseeable that Bentley might commit criminal acts if released to Synanon? Does that impose a duty of care on Synanon?

4. Why does the court conclude that defendant owed no duty of care to plaintiff? What "public policy" considerations support that conclusion?

5. Do you agree with the court's decision? Explain your answer.

There was a time when owners of real property owed virtually no duty to exercise care toward others on their premises, with certain well-established exceptions. That lack of a duty of care on the part of premises owners has been overcome in most jurisdictions, principally in recognition of a greater social interest in protecting people from harm and a declining concern with absolute rights of property. Nevertheless, the growing trend to make premises owners liable for the safety of tenants from criminal attack strains the limits of the recently established duty of care owed by premises owners to persons on their property. The following article describes this trend and its origin.

READING   **Growing Liability for Premises Owners**
Janet L. Brown and Delia A. Doyle*

The age of consumerism and of individual rights has brought a new liability trend. Premises owners are increasingly being held liable for injuries intentionally inflicted by third parties unrelated to the victim or the premises owner.

Assume a student is assaulted as she returns to her dorm from a night at the campus library. Did the university have a duty to protect her from such harm? Witness the newspaper articles describing campus escort services, computer card access to dormitories and better lighting. Governmental bodies, private entities and individuals are making greater efforts to protect visitors from harm by third parties—and to protect themselves from liability.

FAILURE TO REMEDY

The plaintiffs' theories may vary, depending on the circumstances. The most common claim charges the premises owner with a negligent failure to remedy a situation that is conducive to the commission of a tortious act. Liability is still predicated upon fault; the preliminary issue is whether the premises owner owed the victim a duty to protect him or her from harm. If so, the courts must then determine the scope of that duty and whether the injury that occurred is the direct result of the defendant's failure to carry out his duty.

There are several special relationships between victims and premises owners that can result in the imposition of a duty upon premises owners. The common element is that the premises owner controls places of public usage. The principle that a landowner has a duty to take reasonable precautions to protect an invitee from the foreseeable acts of third parties has rapidly developed in the context of landlords, business owners, innkeepers and governmental bodies.

PROTECTION FROM INTRUDERS

At common law, the landlord-tenant relationship did not impose upon landlords a duty to protect tenants from intruders. Although the common law view has not been abrogated, an increasing number of courts have held that the landlord must take reasonable precautions to protect tenants from a foreseeable risk of crime. See *Pippin* v. *Chicago Housing Authority*, 399 N.E.2d 596 (Ill. 1979), and *Feld v. Merriam*, 483 A.2d 742 (Pa. 1984).

In the landmark landlord liability case of *Kline* v. *1500 Massachusetts Avenue*, 439 F.2d 477 (D.C. Cir. 1970) the plaintiff was assaulted in the hallway of her apartment building. She sued her landlord, claiming he failed to provide reasonable security to prevent intruders from gaining access to the building.

The court held that landlords have a duty to take reasonable precautions to protect their tenants from foreseeable assaults and that this duty had been breached. The court's rationale was that landlords who retain control over common areas of apartment buildings are able to take precautions that tenants cannot take and that it is fair to place a duty on the landlord to take these precautions. Subsequent cases involved allegations that landlords should install locks on entrances to apartment buildings. See *Scott* v. *Watson*, 359 A.2d 548 (Md. 1976) and *Johnson* v. *Harris*, 198 N.W.2d 409 (Mich. 1972).

A landlord's duty to provide safe common areas, however, has been extended even further. For example: in *Holley* v. *Mt. Zion Terrace Apartments, Inc.*, 382 So.2d 98 (Fla. 1980), the court held that a landlord may have a duty to provide security personnel. In *Holley*, a tenant was raped and murdered by an intruder who entered her apartment through a second floor window, which opened onto a common area of her apartment complex. The plaintiff alleged that the landlord was negligent in failing to provide a reasonable security in the common area.

The appellate court reversed a summary judgment and concluded that a jury could find that the landlord's duty to keep the common areas reasonably safe required him to provide a guard or other security measures.

Innkeepers have also been faced with a growing number of suits for damages caused by the intentional acts of third parties. As with landlords, the liability of innkeepers depends upon the control exercised over the premises and the foreseeability of criminal acts. Courts generally find that an innkeeper's duty requires the exercise of reasonable care. See, for example, *Nixon* v. *Royal Coach Inn*, 464 S.W.2d 900, 902 (Tex. 1971) and *Rosier* v. *Gainesville Inns Associations, Ltd.*, 347 So.2d 1100, 1102 (Fla, 1977). In one of the most renowned cases, singer Connie Francis was awarded $2.5 million in damages on the basis that the motel she was staying in when she was raped did not provide adequate security. *Garzilli* v. *Howard Johnson's*, 419 F.Supp. 1210 (E.D. New York 1976).

Most cases involve actions taken by a third person whose presence was unknown to the innkeeper. The issue is generally what security precautions innkeepers can reasonably be expected to provide. The courts seem to agree that the failure to take obvious precautions—such as installing good locks or safeguarding room keys—constitutes a breach of the duty to exercise reasonable care. *Kiefel* v. *Las Vegas Hacienda, Inc.*, 404 F.2d 1163 (7th Cir.), cert. den. 395 U.S. 908 (1968).

CRIME RATE

Some courts have attempted to identify the elements of a landlord's duty. In *Peters* v. *Holiday Inns, Inc.*, 278 N.W.2d 208 (Wisc. 1979), the court stated that these factors include industry standards, the community's crime rate, the extent of criminal activity in the area, the presence of suspicious persons and the particular security problems created by the hotel's design.

Businesses also are being found liable for the actions of third parties. For example, in *Winn-Dixie Stores, Inc.*, v. *Johnstoneaux*, 395 So.2d 599 (Fla. 1981), the court affirmed a jury's finding that a supermarket had breached its duty of reasonable care to its invitees by failing to take security measures to protect them from assaults in the parking lot. The court found the history of similar crimes on the premises to be particularly noteworthy. The court states that an owner of a business does not have a duty to protect its patrons from all crimes, but that it does have a duty to protect them from those that can be shown to have been reasonably foreseeable.

COLLEGES AND UNIVERSITIES

Governmental bodies are also finding themselves defendants in suits that are based on the acts of third parties. Some of the most common defendants are universities and colleges. Plaintiffs frequently allege that these institutions have a duty to provide a safe campus or to guard against unreasonably dangerous conditions. *Hayes* v. *State*, 521 P.2d 855 (Calif. 1974).

Sometimes, however, harmful third party conduct will not be characterized as a dangerous condition without some concurrent contributing defect in the property itself. In *Relyea* v. *State*, 385 So.2d 1378 (Fla. 1980), for example, the plaintiffs' decedents returned to their automobile after an evening class and were murdered.

The plaintiffs asserted that the defendant educational institution has a duty to exercise reasonable care to provide security for its students and that it had breached that duty by failing to provide sufficient security patrols, failing to post security guards at campus entrances and parking lots and failing to provide adequate lighting.

The court refused to recognize a duty to safeguard university property and stated that a property owner has no duty to protect one from criminal attack by a third person because that act is an independent, intervening and unforeseeable cause of injury.

In *School Board of Palm Beach County* v. *Anderson*, 411 So.2d 940 (Fla. 1982), the court also recognized that a landowner's responsibility is to keep the premises in a reasonably safe condition and to guard against dangerous conditions of which it is aware or might reasonably foresee. In light of a history of serious crimes on campus, the *Anderson* court found there was sufficient evidence to raise a jury question as to whether the previous criminal attacks imposed a duty upon the defendant to protect students from similar attacks by third persons.

To date, most cases against institutions have met with mixed success. Although many states have abrogated the doctrine of sovereign immunity, the doctrine may preclude recovery in those that have not. Additionally, plaintiffs bear a difficult burden of proof in such negligence actions. See Hauserman, "Rape on Campus: Post Secondary Institutions as a Third Party Defendant," 8 *Journal of College and University Law* 182 (1981).

Thus, the liability of premises owners for the intentional acts of third parties is created when the owner places the plaintiff in a situation where the injury is foreseeable, or when the premises owner has failed to exercise due care in the face of a foreseeable danger.

This duty is not generally imposed on homeowners. Perhaps this is attributable to the fact that homeowners, unlike entities that hold their property open to others, do not impliedly warrant that their premises are in a reasonably safe condition. To hold a homeowner liable for the acts of third parties might require them to acquire private security forces for their property when they are the victims of criminal activity. Notably, though, one judge recently observed that this may be where the law is heading. *Palumbo* v. *Lily General Stores Corporation*, 453 So.2d 1170 (Fla. 1984).

How far the courts will go in extending the liability of premises owners is open to speculation, but recent suits indicate an increased recognition and approval of such liability by courts throughout the nation.

NOTES

*From 72 *American Bar Association Journal* 64 (March 1, 1986). Reprinted with permission.

FOR DISCUSSION

1. The *Beauchene* case stated that generally persons have no duty to control the conduct of others. Should that rule not apply to premises owners as well?

2. What is the source of a duty of care owed by premises owners to tenants or visitors?

3. How does the owner's control of all or part of the premises affect liability?

4. What are the elements of a landlord or innkeeper's duty of care?

5. Is it unreasonable for students at a college to expect the college to have adequate locks on the doors and adequate lighting in parking lots and on walkways?

6. Why are homeowners generally exempted from the duty of care imposed on landlords, innkeepers, and businesses?

Proximate Cause

One of the central elements in a cause of action in negligence is proximate cause—that is, that defendant's negligent conduct proximately caused the harm to plaintiff. The term **proximate cause** is often used interchangeably with the terms **direct cause** or **legal cause**. Causation is one of the most frequently disputed aspects of negligence cases, and a precise definition of proximate cause is not easy to give. Proximate cause is generally employed to place limits on a defendant's liability for the consequences of his conduct. That means that certain consequences of his actions may lie beyond what can be fairly or reasonably attributed to his conduct. Generally, a defendant can only be held responsible for consequences that could be reasonably foreseen in that set of circumstances, even though the exact manner in which the injury occurs does not need to be foreseeable.

In establishing proximate cause, the plaintiff must begin by establishing actual cause or "cause in fact." Often the "but for" test is employed to establish actual cause: "but for" defendant's conduct, the injury would not have occurred. Beyond that, however, lies proximate cause and the doctrine of foreseeability. This doctrine was elucidated by Justice Cardozo in the well-known case of *Palsgraf* v. *Long Island Railroad*, 248 N.Y. 339 (1928). That case both limited and expanded the consequences for which a defendant could be held liable. It limited liability to consequences that could reasonably be foreseen by the defendant (so that the Long Island Railroad could not be held liable for a distant object falling on Mrs. Palsgraf in connection with an accident involving fireworks that occurred some distance down the platform in a train station), but it expanded liability to cover all consequences that could, in fact, be reasonably foreseen by the defendant (which attacked the doctrine of "objective causation" that had protected defendants by limiting their liability to a single direct and immediate cause).[5] Both the consequences of an act and the person to whom the harm occurs can be unforeseeable. In addition to foreseeability, there is the question of intervening or superseding cause. An intervening cause may cut off the defendant's liability if it acts to substitute for the defendant's conduct in causing the harm to plaintiff. Otherwise, an intervening cause may not cut off defendant's liability if the intervening cause was reasonably foreseeable within the scope of the risk caused by the defendant.

All this may serve to reinforce the notion that proximate cause is a mysterious and confusing concept. In dealing with the following materials, you should think of proximate cause as an act or conduct that sets in motion a train of events that leads directly to the harm caused to plaintiff, without the intervention of any superseding cause. For example, suppose an architect designs a building that contains a serious structural flaw that will cause it to fall if too much weight is placed on a certain part of the building. Subsequently, some other party unknowingly places too much weight on the weak structure and causes it to fall. The architect's negligent design may nevertheless be a proximate cause of the harm, because it was his negligent act that set into motion the train of events that led to the injury.

The following case illustrates the basic principles of proximate cause within the context of a personal injury accident in an apartment.

CASE

Adam Pagan et al. v. Sandor Goldberger
New York Supreme Court, Appellate Division (1976)
51 A.D.2d 508, 382 N.Y.S.2d 549

HOPKINS, Acting Presiding Justice.   The infant plaintiff, three years old, and his mother, bring this action to recover damages for an injury suffered by the infant and claimed to have been caused by the defendant's negligence. The defendant was the mother's landlord; she and her husband and seven children had occupied an apartment for three years. One of the employees of the landlord, acting under a complaint, removed the adjuster or knob from the radiator, thus exposing a sharp metal top on which the adjuster had been located. Though the mother drew the attention of the landlord and his superintendent to the condition of the radiator, the condition was not remedied. Some five months later the mother, while in the kitchen, heard the infant scream and she found the infant lying on the floor with his face on the exposed sharp edge of the stem.

Trial Term dismissed the complaint at the end of the plaintiffs' case, on the ground that the plaintiffs had failed to prove both proximate cause and foreseeability as elements of the claim of negligence on the part of the defendant. We reverse and grant a new trial. The proof of proximate cause and foreseeability sufficiently raised issues for the determination of the jury.

Negligence as a legal concept traditionally includes both proximate cause and foreseeability as tests of liability. The common law recognizes fault as the primary ground of responsibility to another for injury; and proximate cause and foreseeability represent attempts to measure fault. In most cases the focus is directed on the kind of conduct which is claimed to have been injurious, and the jury is called upon to determine, upon varying

---

[5]For more information on this subject, see Horwitz, Morton J., "The Doctrine of Objective Causation," in *The Politics of Law*, ed. David Kairys (New York: Pantheon Books, 1982), pp. 201–13.

evidence, what the nature of the conduct really was, and whether the injury really was sustained as a result of the conduct.

Nevertheless, unusual or freakish accidents occur, in which the defendant's conduct is not directly related in the continuum of time or space or personal status to the plaintiff's injury. In these instances, the use of the tests of proximate cause and foreseeability serves to place reasonable limits on liability as a matter of public policy. As Holmes said (The Common Law, pp. 93–96), an intolerable burden would be cast on human activity if every voluntary act was committed at one's peril.

The definition of proximate cause has been elusive, probably because the public policy underlying the concept cannot be described other than in general terms. Courts have attempted to find rational formulations for the rule of limitation of liability by resort to distinction between cause and condition, the "but for" test, or the relationship between principal and intervening causes (see Prosser, Law of Torts [4th ed.], §42, pp. 244–249). All of these attempts have not been completely satisfactory and Prosser, in the end, agrees with the observation of Street that proximate cause must "be determined on the facts of each case upon mixed considerations of logic, common sense, justice, policy and precedent" (Prosser, *id.*, at p. 249, quoting from 1 Street, Foundations of Legal Liability, 110).

The defendant draws our attention to the opinion of Mr. Justice Jenks in *Trapp* v. *McClellan*, 68 App.Div. 362, 74 N.Y.S. 130 as a source for a reliable test of proximate cause. In that case the plaintiff was injured when his leg was caught in a mooring line attached to a cleat on a fireboat while he was trying to remove the line from the cleat. The defendant had fastened the line from its coal barge to the cleat. Mr. Justice Jenks held that the defendant's negligence in fastening the line had not been the proximate cause of the plaintiff's injury, because the starting of the fireboat was an intervening cause. In his view, the placing of the rope from the barge to the fireboat was the *causa sine qua non*,[6] but the starting of the fireboat was the *causa causans*.[7]

These terms, as the footnotes indicate, are so general that they merely describe a result reached by the court.

Nor are we aided substantially by the test which Mr. Justice Jenks culled from *Insurance Co.* v. *Boon*, 95 U.S. 117, 130, 24 L.Ed. 395: "'It is only when the causes are independent of each other that the nearest is, of course, to be charged with the disaster'" (*Trapp* v. *McClellan*, 68 App.Div. 362, 367, 74 N.Y.S. 130, 133, *supra*). The defect in this test is readily apparent, since it does not obtain in all cases of several causes of an accident. "Although they acted independently of each other, they did act at the same time in causing the damages, etc., each contributing towards it, and although the act of each, alone and of itself, might not have caused the entire injury, under the circumstances presented, there is no good reason why each should not be held liable for the damages caused by the different acts of all" (*Slater* v. *Mersereau*, 64 N.Y. 138, 146).

A case decided after *Trapp* illustrates the length to which the chain of proximate cause may be stretched (see *Matter of People [Guardian Cas. Co.]*, 253 App.Div. 360, 2 N.Y.S.2d 232, affd. 278 N.Y. 674, 16 N.E.2d 397). A taxicab collided with an automobile, as a result of which the taxicab was forced across the sidewalk and against the stone stoop of the building. The taxicab became wedged between the stones composing the stoop. The claimant's wife, some 20 minutes after the collision, was viewing the scene in order to

---

[6]*Causa sine qua non*: "A necessary or inevitable cause; a cause without which the effect in question could not have happened." (*Black's Law Dictionary*, 4th ed., p. 278.)

[7]*Causa causans*: "The immediate cause; the last link in the chain of causation." (*Black's Law Dictionary*, 4th ed., p. 278.)

ascertain the damages sustained by the laundry operated by her and her husband on the premises struck by the taxicab. She was about 20 feet away, when a stone loosened by the impact fell while a policeman and others tried to extricate the taxicab. The stone hit the claimant's wife, causing her death. The court held that the negligence of both drivers was the proximate cause of the death.

The defendant, moreover, points to *Rivera* v. *City of New York*, 11 N.Y.2d 856, 227 N.Y.S.2d 676, 182 N.E.2d 284 as precedent for the dismissal of the complaint. In *Rivera*, an infant plaintiff, standing on the edge of a bathtub and attempting to reach a light cord, lost his balance and fell into the hot water present in the tub, thereby receiving serious burns. The City of New York was alleged to have been negligent in failing to repair a leak in the hot water faucet and other defects in the plumbing, which resulted in the condition that scalding hot water accumulated in the tub. The Court of Appeals held that the failure to repair was not the proximate cause of the accident, since the intervening act of the loss of balance of the plaintiff perched on the bathtub could not have been foreseen.

The decisions in other cases serve only as examples of the process whereby the concept of proximate cause is applied. The doctrinal sweep is so broad that a flexibility of approach, almost intuitive in nature, must be used. Some helpful guidelines emerge, not as overarching principles, but simply as tools of analysis:

1. The test of status—is there an existing legal relationship between the parties? In this case, the relationship of landlord-tenant, with the concomitant statutory overlay (see Multiple Dwelling Law, §78) is present.

2. The test of temporal duration—is the occurrence of the injury tied to the claimed negligent act or omission within a reasonable lapse of time? In this case, the asserted negligent condition had endured an appreciable length of time, and it could be found that the injury occurred immediately upon contact with the condition.

3. The test of spatial relation—is the occurrence of the injury close or far in distance from the point of the claimed negligent act or omission? In this case, the injured infant plaintiff was found touching the asserted negligent condition.

4. The test of foreseeability—is the claimed negligent act or omission reasonably predictable as a cause of the occurrence of the injury? In this case, the defendant was apprised of the presence of a small child in the household and had notice of the asserted negligent condition.

5. The test of public policy—is there an identifiable policy which either protects the victim of the injury or forbids liability for the injury? In this case, the interests of public policy are embodied in the statutory command that a landlord of a multiple dwelling should maintain the premises in good repair (Multiple Dwelling Law, §78).

Surveying this case, in the posture in which it reaches us from a dismissal of the complaint at the end of plaintiff's case, we think that the combined influence of the answers to the questions posed by the suggested guidelines leads us to the conclusion that the plaintiffs produced proof enough to go to the jury. Here, the fall of the infant plaintiff did not occur from an unusual circumstance, such as in *Rivera*, where the bathtub was being used as a platform to reach a greater height—a purpose foreign to its accustomed utility. Here, the fall of the infant plaintiff occurred while he was walking or running within the apartment. As the infant was three years old—one of seven children—the defendant, in his status as landlord, could reasonably expect that falls of infants normally happen. To leave a sharp edge of a stem exposed, so that a person falling under these circumstances would be in a position to sustain injury, constituted conduct which the triers of fact might find to be negligent, and the negligence so found to be so directly connected with the injury that the requirement of proximate cause is satisfied. The issue of proximate cause is always difficult, open to the division of views, but we believe that *Rivera* is not controlling in this case.

The judgment should therefore be reversed, and a new trial granted.

FOR DISCUSSION

1. According to the evidence, what was the actual cause of the infant plaintiff's injury?
2. Could this situation reasonably be described as a "freak accident"? Explain.
3. What is the relationship between fault and proximate cause?
4. What guidelines did the court employ to determine whether defendant's conduct was the proximate cause of plaintiff's injury?
5. Do you agree with the outcome of this case? Explain.

In the following case, foreseeability is the issue that most concerns the court in making its decision. You should remember that foreseeability usually means that harm can reasonably be expected to occur as a consequence of a party's conduct, but the exact manner in which the harm occurs need not be foreseeable. Given those considerations, is the harm that occurred in this case foreseeable?

CASE **Renee McCracken Williams et al. v. Steves Industries, Inc.**
Supreme Court of Texas (1985)
699 S.W.2d 570, 55 A.L.R.4th 1087

CAMPBELL, Justice. This case arises from a collision of a truck owned by Steves Industries and a car driven by Renee McCracken Williams. Mrs. Williams was injured and her two minor children were killed in the accident. Mrs. Williams and her husband, Kenneth Williams, sued Steves Industries for personal injuries Mrs. Williams suffered as well as wrongful death and survival actions for the deaths of their two children. The Williams alleged that Steves Industries was negligent and grossly negligent in allowing its employee, Robert Robinson, to drive the truck. The jury found Steves Industries both negligent and grossly negligent and awarded $250,000 in punitive damages. The trial court disregarded the jury's findings of gross negligence and limited the award to actual damages. The court of appeals affirmed the judgment of the trial court in part and reversed and rendered in part. We affirm the judgment of the court of appeals.

On July 30, 1981, Mrs. Williams was driving her car on a four-lane segment of Interstate 35 in Austin. Her two children were riding in the back seat. The car ran out of gas and stalled in one of the center lanes. Mrs. Williams restarted the car but continued only a short distance before it stalled again. There was testimony the car was hidden from view of approaching traffic by the shadows of an overpass. Robinson, who was driving an eight-ton equipment repair truck owned by Steves Industries, hit Mrs. Williams'[s] car from behind. Mrs. Williams and her children were injured and the children died from those injuries.

The Williamses seek to recover punitive damages under a theory of negligent entrustment. The Williamses argue there is some evidence to support the jury's finding that Steves Industries was grossly negligent in entrusting the truck to Robinson. The elements of negligent entrustment are: (1) entrustment of a vehicle by the owner; (2) to an unlicensed, incompetent, or reckless driver; (3) that the owner knew or should have known to be unlicensed, incompetent or reckless; (4) that the driver was negligent on the occasion; and (5) that the driver's negligence proximately caused the accident. *Mundy* v. *Price-Slaughter Motor Co.*, 146 Tex. 314, 206 S.W.2d 587, 591 (1947).

There is, however, no evidence that Robinson had any prior speeding tickets, had caused any accidents before this one, was not experienced at driving large trucks, that Robinson was in fact an incompetent or reckless driver, or that Steves Industries had actual notice that Robinson was a dangerous driver. There are no facts to indicate that Steves Industries did not care that entrusting a large truck to Robinson endangered the rights and safety of others. Therefore, we hold that there is no evidence of gross negligence.

The Williamses also contend that there is no evidence to support the jury finding that the failure of Renee Williams to have enough gas in her car was a proximate cause of the accident. Renee Williams traveled only five miles from her home when her car stalled. After the accident, a fireman at the scene checked the gas tank for a possible fire hazard, but found no gasoline. A wrecker service employee drained the tank through a hole in the gas tank and less than a cupful of gasoline ran out of the tank. An insurance adjuster testified that he examined the car and found no gas either in the gas lines or the carburetor.

The jury found Renee Williams negligent for failing to have enough gasoline to make the trip, and found her negligence to be a proximate cause of the accident. The jury also found that her negligence contributed twenty-five percent to the collision. Renee Williams does not attack the negligence finding but contends that as a matter of law her negligence was not a proximate cause of the accident. The two elements of proximate cause are cause in fact and foreseeability. *Nixon* v. *Mr. Property Management Corp.*, 690 S.W.2d 546, 549 (Tex. 1985). We will consider each element separately.

The first issue, therefore, is whether there is some evidence that Mrs. Williams'[s] negligence was a cause in fact of the accident. If a negligent act or omission is a substantial factor in bringing about the injury and without which no harm would have occurred, the act or omission is a cause in fact of the injury. *Id.* In other words, the negligent act or omission is not a cause in fact unless "but for the conduct the accident would not have happened." *Kerby* v. *Abilene Christian College*, 503 S.W.2d 526, 528 (Tex. 1973). Had Mrs. Williams had enough gasoline in her car to make her trip, her car would not have stalled in the middle of Interstate 35. A jury could infer that had the car not stalled in the middle of the highway, Robinson would not have collided with it. Thus, we find some evidence that Mrs. Williams'[s] negligence was a cause in fact of the accident.

Finally, we turn to the question of foreseeability. "Foreseeability means that the actor, as a person of ordinary intelligence, should have anticipated the dangers that his negligent act created." *Mr. Property*, 690 S.W.2d at 550. Furthermore, the actor need only anticipate an injury of the same general character as the actual injury:

> [I]t is not required that the particular accident complained of should have been foreseen. All that is required is "that the injury be of such a general character as might reasonably have been anticipated; and that the injury should be so situated with relation to the wrongful act that injury to him or one similarly situated might reasonably have been foreseen." *Carey* v. *Pure Distributing Corp.*, 133 Tex. 31, 124 S.W.2d 847, 849 (1939.) (Cited in *Mr. Property*, 690 S.W.2d at 551.)

On the day of the accident Mrs. Williams knew the route she was taking; therefore, she knew that she would be traveling on a high traffic section of an interstate highway. The jury found that she knew or should have known that she did not have enough gas to make the trip. The jury could reasonably conclude that a person of ordinary intelligence would anticipate that if his car ran out of gas it might stall on the highway and that a stalled car on a highly traveled section of an interstate highway would create a danger of another vehicle colliding with it. Thus, there is some evidence of foreseeability.

We affirm the judgment of the court of appeals.

FOR DISCUSSION

1. Mrs. Williams did not dispute the jury's finding that she had been negligent. Explain why her conduct was negligent, using the concepts you have learned so far in this chapter.

2. According to this case, what are the elements of proximate cause?

3. Is the court here concerned with what Mrs. Williams *actually* knew about the probable consequences of making this particular trip with very little gas in her car or with what she *ought* to have known? Explain your answer.

4. Do the tests of proximate cause articulated in the previous case (*Pagan* v. *Goldberger*) help in understanding how proximate cause operates in this case? Are they relevant here?

5. It has been said that proximate cause has very little to do with "causation" and a great deal to do with duties that people owe to others not to expose them to unreasonable risks of harm that they have created. After reading this case, do you agree with this opinion? Explain your answer.

Contributory and Comparative Negligence

Traditionally, successful recovery of damages in negligence required a plaintiff to be free from fault. Contributory negligence, a failure of plaintiff's part to act with reasonable care that contributed to the injury, was an absolute bar to plaintiff's recovery. In most jurisdictions, contributory negligence was an affirmative defense to be pleaded and proved by the defendant. One way to mitigate the harshness of contributory negligence was the so-called last clear chance doctrine, which excused the plaintiff's contributory negligence in situations in which the defendant had the last clear chance to avoid the injury. The unfairness of the contributory negligence doctrine, which prevented plaintiff from recovering for even the slightest negligence on his part, led some jurisdictions to replace contributory negligence with comparative negligence. Comparative negligence is a scheme whereby plaintiff's negligence is considered and may reduce his damages proportionately to the degree of his own responsibility for the harm he suffered. Comparative negligence may exist either in statutory or case-law form, and is in force today in most of the United States.

Over time, rules were developed to protect some plaintiffs from the effects of the contributory negligence doctrine. The following case shows how the adoption of a comparative negligence standard may change established rules concerning rights and duties of actors in a particular situation.

CASE   **Ricky B. Minato v. J. E. Ferrare**
                                 Supreme Court of Oregon (1983)
                          295 Or 22, 663 P.2d 1240, 35 A.L.R.4th 1110

CAMPBELL, Justice.   Plaintiff Minato was standing in the middle of a road when he was hit by defendant Ferrare's car. The issues presented by this case are whether the worker in the road doctrine is accepted in Oregon, and if a worker in the road is a pedestrian. We hold that the doctrine is no longer necessary and reverse the Court, 60 Or.App. 122, 652 P.2d 867, of Appeals.

The facts in this case are not in dispute. Minato worked on a private survey crew. At the time of the accident his job required him to hold a plumb bob over the center line of the highway so that the surveyor in a nearby field could sight into the bob to find a section line. Ferrare did not see Minato and drove into him. Minato suffered serious injuries.

Minato asked the trial court to give the following instruction: "You are instructed that one whose duties of employment require that he work in or near a public street or highway is not required to exercise the high degree of care which might be exercised by a common pedestrian. In this regard you are to apply a standard of reasonable care to be expected of a person in such a position in the light of all the circumstances."

The trial court did not give the instruction and the plaintiff excepted.

The trial court instructed the jury concerning the rules of the road applicable to pedestrian, including an instruction that a pedestrian must yield the right of way to vehicles on the roadway, and that plaintiff had this duty. Minato excepted to these instructions, arguing that because he was a worker in the road, these general pedestrian instructions were inapplicable.

The jury assessed total damages of $113,500 and found Minato 45 percent at fault. Minato appealed, assigning as error the failure to give the worker in the road instruction and the giving of the instruction about the pedestrian rules of the road.

The Court of Appeals reversed. It held that it was not error to refuse to give the plaintiff's requested instruction concerning the worker in the road rule, although the worker in the road doctrine is accepted in Oregon, because the general negligence instruction was adequate to describe the standard of care to be applied. However, it held that the instructions regarding the rules of the road for pedestrians should not have been given, because under the worker in the road doctrine a worker is not a pedestrian and thus is not bound by the general rules. We disagree.

The Worker in the Road Instruction

The worker in the road doctrine evolved at common law, based on the recognition that a person who is necessarily in the street to do a certain job cannot do his job adequately and still maintain the standard of care required of pedestrians, especially in terms of maintaining a lookout. Because of the demands of the job and the amount of concentration the job requires, a worker in this situation is held to a lesser standard of care than the average pedestrian.

The only Oregon case to rely on the worker in the road doctrine was *Graves v. Portland etc. Power Co.*, 66 Or. 232, 134 P. 1 (1913). The Plaintiff, employed by the United Railways Company to lay street paving blocks, was struck and injured by a streetcar while he was working. Defendant claimed error in the giving of the instruction to the jury that said that a worker in the street does not need to exercise the same high degree of care required of an ordinary pedestrian. The court approved the instruction, holding that "those persons engaged in work upon the public streets are not called upon to exercise the same diligence in avoiding accidents as pedestrians who use the street merely as a medium of locomotion." 66 or. at 244, 134 P. 1. This rule was cited approvingly in *McCarty* v. *Hedges et. al.*, 212 Or. 497, 518-519, 309 P.2d 186, 321 P.2d 285 (1958), even though the doctrine was not at issue. In that case the worker was near the ditch, rather than in the road.

We believe that the worker in the road doctrine developed in order to protect workers in the road from the harsh results of contributory negligence. In 1913, when the doctrine was recognized in Oregon, if the fact finder had found that a worker was not exercising the same degree of care required of an ordinary pedestrian, the fact finder probably would have found the worker contributorily negligent. This finding would have barred the worker from recovering any damages whatsoever. Courts recognized that it would be unjust to prevent an injured worker from collecting damages because he was paying so much attention to his required employment that he could not maintain a sharp lookout. Because of this, the courts created the worker in the road doctrine, which lowered the duty of care required of the worker, and circumvented this complete bar to recovery.

This potential for injustice was eliminated when the Oregon Legislature adopted the law of comparative fault in 1971. Oregon Laws 1971, ch. 688. Since the effective date of this statute, plaintiff's contributory negligence is not a complete bar to recovery, if the plaintiff's fault is no greater than the combined fault of the persons against whom recovery is sought, ORS 18.470. We hold that because the adoption of comparative fault eliminates the previous bar to recovery created by contributory negligence, the worker in the road doctrine is no longer necessary, and is hereby no longer recognized in Oregon.

The general negligence instruction[8] adequately explains the standard of care that the jury should consider. The question that the fact finders had to decide in this case was: Did Minato act reasonably when he stood in the middle of the road as part of his job? His counsel certainly could argue that under these circumstances, Minato acted entirely reasonably.

Rules of the Road Instructions

Minato contends that the trial court erred in giving six instructions concerning the statutory rules of the road for pedestrians. He argues that a worker in the road is exempt from these rules either because of the worker in the road doctrine or because a worker is not a pedestrian.

In 1927, the legislature passed a bill to exempt workers on the road from some provisions of the motor vehicle act, including the pedestrian rules of the road. This statute was changed slightly throughout the years but workers in the road continued to be exempt from pedestrian rules until 1967. Oregon Laws 1967, Chapter 488, section 2

---

[8]"In general, it is the duty of every person in our society to use reasonable care in order to avoid damage to himself or to another person in any situation in which it would be reasonably anticipated that a failure to use such care might result in such damage.

"Reasonable care is that care which persons of ordinary prudence exercise in the management of their own affairs in order to avoid injury to themselves or others.

"Common law negligence, therefore, is the doing of some act which a reasonably prudent person would not do or the failure to do something which a reasonably prudent person would do, under the same or similar circumstances.

"The care should be in keeping with dangers, apparent or reasonably to be expected at the time and place in question, and not in the light of after effects or hindsight."

restricted this previously broad exemption to only those persons working on construction or reconstruction flowing from a governmental contract. The present form of the statute, ORS 487.045, clearly does not exempt a person working on a private survey crew from the pedestrian rules of the road.

Minato does not argue that he is exempt from the pedestrian rules of the road under ORS 487.045. He argues that he is exempt because the worker in the road doctrine not only changes the standard of care that a worker is judged by, but also exempts him from the pedestrian rules. He contends that this doctrine is judicially created law, codified in 1927 by the legislature, and was not revoked by implication when the legislature made these changes in 1967.

Minato's argument must fail, however, for he misunderstands the rationale and effect of the worker in the road doctrine. This doctrine in Oregon changed the standard of care expected of the worker. It did nothing else. It is important to note that in 1913, when the first Oregon case recognized this doctrine, there were no codified rules of the road for pedestrians. In fact, the first statutory rule applicable to pedestrians was enacted in 1921. It is unreasonable to suggest that the worker in the road doctrine made the pedestrian rules of the road inapplicable to workers, when there were no such pedestrian rules of the road at the time we recognized the doctrine. The legislature at one time chose to exempt all workers on the road from the pedestrian rules of the road. In 1967, it narrowed the class of exempt workers to only those involved in construction or reconstruction, and workers on a private survey crew were no longer exempt.

Minato's final argument is that he is not a "pedestrian" and thus the pedestrian rules of the road do not apply to him. In 1975 for the first time our legislature defined "pedestrian" as "any person afoot."[9] Minato urges us to interpret this definition as "a person afoot for purposes of locomotion." While this could be an acceptable definition of "pedestrian" were there no statutory definition, in the present case there is a clear statutory definition and we are bound by it. If our legislature had intended to exempt private survey crews from these pedestrian rules, past statutes are proof that it knew how to accomplish this. This interpretation would also allow people standing by the side of a road waiting for a ride, or children playing near or in the street to be defined as non-pedestrians, because they would not be "afoot for purposes of locomotion." We decline to resort to creative interpretation of unambiguous language.

Minato also argues that if we find workers in the road are in fact pedestrians, this leads to an absurd result. It is indeed strange that a member of a survey team, perhaps making the survey to fulfill statutory requirements, could be in violation of pedestrian statutes. However, interpreting "pedestrian" as "any person afoot for the purpose of locomotion" can also lead to an absurd result. By this interpretation, Minato would have been a pedestrian when he was walking to get to the center of the road, become a non-pedestrian when he was standing in the center of the road, and then resumed his pedestrian identity walking away from the center of the road. This result would be even more absurd.

We hold that it was not error to refuse to give the instruction describing the lower degree of care required of a worker in the road, because we hold the worker in the road doctrine is no longer necessary, and the general negligence instruction is sufficient to tell the jury the applicable standard of care it should consider. It was not error to give the instructions on the pedestrian rules of the road, and to instruct the jury that Minato, if he violated these rules, might be statutorily negligent.

The Court of Appeals is reversed and the trial court is affirmed.

---

[9]Or. Laws 1975, ch. 451 §2(13). The present statute, ORS 487.005(14), is substantially the same: "'Pedestrian' means any person afoot or confined to a wheelchair."

FOR DISCUSSION

1. How does the comparative negligence doctrine operate in Oregon? Under this doctrine, would plaintiff Minato be barred from any recovery? Explain.

2. What was the purpose of the worker in the road doctrine and why is it no longer necessary?

3. Why might the legislature choose to exempt some workers in the road from the pedestrian rules of the road and not others? Does this seem fair?

4. Adoption of comparative negligence and abandonment of the worker in the road doctrine deprives certain plaintiffs of a protection that they previously had. Does comparative negligence serve them well? Explain your answer.

5. In some states, Minato could get a proportionate recovery even if he were more negligent than the defendant(s). Would that be true in Oregon? Do you think such a result would be fair? Explain.

Despite the apparent rejection of contributory negligence in favor of comparative negligence in so many jurisdictions, strict liability[10] is one area of tort law in which the doctrine of contributory negligence apparently refuses to die, reappearing as assumption of risk or misuse of product as a complete bar to plaintiff's recovery. (This is a defense that has been used to particularly good effect in a range of cases, including those in which plaintiffs sue tobacco companies for the consequences of smoking.) In the following article, the author discusses a trend in the courts and legislatures to retain contributory negligence as part of a concept of comparative fault that will effectively retain defenses of contributory negligence in strict liability cases.

READING   **The Trend Toward Comparative Fault**
Henry Woods*

When those two great tort scholars Roger Traynor and William Prosser collaborated to draft section 402A of the *Restatement (Second) of Torts*, it was assumed that, with the help of their scholarly prestige, the swift and extensive doctrine of strict liability as they defined it in the section and comments would settle product law for at least a generation.

Comment (n) was a great step forward for the consumer. It abolished contributory negligence as a defense except for that form "which consists in voluntarily and unreasonably proceeding to encounter a known danger, and commonly passes under the name of assumption of risk." The comment was considered revolutionary because in forty-four states contributory negligence was then a complete defense to a product case based on negligence.

To complaints framed in implied warranty, contributory negligence was a defense in about half the American jurisdictions. More importantly, the warranty theory brought in its train many problems associated with the law of sales. There was the serious problem of privity, modified to some extent by the Uniform Commercial Code. There were also problems arising from the notice requirement, disclaimers, statutes of limitations, the necessity for an actual sale, and the wording of some wrongful death statutes.

---

[10]**Strict liability** in tort is liability without fault. It is a doctrine that is employed primarily in regard to extremely dangerous activities, wild or vicious animals, and defectively designed or manufactured products. Strict liability will be discussed in more detail later in this chapter.

Before the adoption of section 402A by the 1965 *Restatement*, only California and New Jersey had judicially adopted strict liability in product cases. "What has followed has been the most rapid and altogether spectacular overturn of an established rule in the entire history of torts."[11] Today, after twenty years, strict liability has been universally adopted.

DEVELOPMENT OF COMPARATIVE NEGLIGENCE

While this spectacular development was taking place in product liability law, an equally important development was occurring in tort law. The slow march of comparative negligence—Mississippi (1910), Georgia (1913), Wisconsin (1931), and Arkansas (1955)—suddenly became a quickstep. Only eight states (all in the Southeast) have now failed to adopt either comparative negligence or comparative fault.

The doctrine has developed both judicially and legislatively. The first legislative system was the "pure form," copied from the Federal Employers Liability Act. Illustrative is a recent Washington case in which the jury found the plaintiff 99 percent negligent, the defendant 1 percent, and damages as $350,000. Judgment was correctly entered for $3,500. Georgia modified the pure form by requiring that the plaintiff be less negligent. New Hampshire further refined the system by permitting a plaintiff who is 50 percent negligent to recover. This modification has proved popular with state legislatures, several of which have shifted from the Georgia to the New Hampshire system.

When the courts have adopted comparative negligence or comparative fault without waiting for legislative action, the pure form has been chosen by eight of nine jurisdictions. Only West Virginia requires the plaintiff to be less negligent. In addition to the eight states [Florida, California, Alaska, Michigan, New Mexico, Illinois, Iowa, and Missouri], New York, Rhode Island, Louisiana, Washington, Mississippi, and Arizona have "pure" comparative statutes, making a total of fourteen. No jurisdiction has adopted the New Hampshire plan judicially, but fifteen states have adopted it legislatively. Eleven states, like Georgia, require a successful plaintiff to be less negligent than the defendant in order to recover. Nebraska permits comparison if defendant's negligence is gross and plaintiff's negligence is slight. South Dakota originally adopted the Nebraska plan, but later removed the requirement of gross negligence on the part of defendant.

The parallel acceptance of two doctrines required the court to effect a synthesis. This proved difficult. Often plaintiff would sue both for a negligent failure to warn or a negligent design, and in strict liability. On the negligence counts, contributory negligence would be a defense to be compared; on the strict liability count, plaintiff's negligence would not be a defense under comment (n) to section 402A. If plaintiff was found to have assumed the risk, however, his claim would be defeated regardless of the theory pursued.

DEFINING CONTRIBUTORY NEGLIGENCE

Drawing a distinction between contributory negligence and assumption of risk was also difficult. In their fine textbook on torts, Harper and James (*The Law of Torts* [1956]) divide assumption of risk into two categories: (1) In its primary sense plaintiff's assumption of risk is only the counterpart of defendant's lack of duty to protect plaintiff. (2) In its secondary sense assumption of risk is only a form of contributory negligence. They take the position that, except for "express assumption of risk," the term should be abolished.

---

[11]Prosser, "The Fall of the Citadel (Strict Liability for the Consumer)," 50 *Minnesota Law Review* 793, n. 72 (1966).

A number of jurisdictions merged assumption of risk with contributory negligence or abolished it as a separate concept before the adoption of comparative negligence. Others used adoption of comparative negligence to achieve the same result. The Connecticut, Massachusetts and Oregon comparative negligence statutes simply abolished assumption of risk. Some jurisdictions declined to apply the defense when an employee's job required him to use the product. "In our view an employee engaged at his assigned task on a plant machine...has no meaningful choice." *Suter* v. *San Angelo Foundry & Mach. Co.*, 406 A.2d 140, 148 (N.J. 1979).

Assumption of risk, which was such an important component of comment (n) to section 402A, seemed on the verge of losing its separate identity from contributory negligence. Its application was also limited by the widespread rejection of the "open and obvious nature of the defect" as the touchstone of the defense. However, in the absence of judicial merger or statutory treatment, as in the Utah comparative negligence statute which states that "contributory negligence" includes "assumption of risk," or the New York statute, which includes "assumption of risk" in the definition of "culpable conduct," assumption of risk remained a sturdy arrow in the quiver of product defense.

Another potent arrow was "product misuse." Undoubtedly certain kinds of misuse are simply contributory negligence. However, some courts began to develop the doctrine that some misuse should be a complete defense. One of the most spurious of the "misuse" defenses was "unintended misuse." Illustrative is the case of a housewife who splashed cleaning fluid in her eye and was denied recovery on the ground that "the cleansing preparation was not intended for use in the eye." *Sawyer* v. *Pine Oil Sales Co.*, 155 F.2d 855, 856 (5th Cir. 1946). Even more pertinent is *Evans* v. *General Motors Corp.*, holding that is there was no duty to equip an automobile with a side rail perimeter frame. "The intended purpose of the automobile does not include its participation in collisions with other objects." 359 F.2d 822, 825 (7th Cir., 1966), *cert. denied*, 87 S.Ct. 83 (1966). This case formerly represented the majority view in "crashworthiness" cases but has now been overruled and repudiated. Most jurisdictions follow *Larsen* v. *General Motors Corp.*, (391 F.2d 495 [8th Cir. 1968].), which took a contrary position contemporaneously with *Evans*.

A complete defense which has persisted, however, and is now followed in many jurisdictions is "unforeseeable misuse." This defense would have been unavailing in the two cases just mentioned. While it may not be intended that cleaning fluid would splash into the housewife's eye, the possibility is foreseeable. While it may not be intended that an automobile be struck in the side by another vehicle, such an event is highly foreseeable. Some authorities take the position that, since foreseeability is a component of the definition of negligence, it should have no place in strict liability.

A Connecticut case typified the use of the unforeseeable-misuse defense. Plaintiff brought a strict liability case against the seller of a lawnmower. The misuse defense was interposed. The plaintiff demurred on the ground that this amounted to a plea of contributory negligence. The court overruled the demurrer, stating that "the use might be such that it could not have been reasonably foreseen by the manufacturer." *Gangi* v. *Sears, Roebuck & Co.*, 360 A.2d 907, 908-909 (Conn. Super.Ct. 1976).

Sometimes courts in approving the unforeseeable-misuse defense will allude to an example given in comment (h) to 402A, which says that a plaintiff cannot complain when "the injury results from abnormal handling, as where a bottled beverage is knocked against a radiator to remove the cap." This is not a very good example for either the *Restatement* or the courts. Patently, plaintiff should not recover, on the basis of simple causation. His injury did not result from a defect in the bottle or the cap, but from his own foolhardy act in striking a glass bottle against a cast iron radiator. A more appropriate example appears in another comment. When an automobile racer buys a tire for ordinary use and installs it on his racing car, according to the example, he cannot complain when it blows out during a race. But what if the blowout was caused by an unforeseeable misuse concurring with a defect in the tire? This precise issue was before the Supreme Court of Texas in *General Motors Corp.* v. *Hopkins* (548 S.W.2d 344, 351 [Tex. 1977].):

> This brings us to our case: where an unreasonably dangerous defect of the product and its unforeseeable misuse are concurring causes of the damaging event. Does the injured user recover all or none or a portion of his damages?

The court charged the manufacturer with that portion of the damages caused by the defect and the plaintiff with that portion caused by his unforeseeable misuse. The Texas Comparative Negligence Act follows the New Hampshire system of denying recovery to a more negligent plaintiff, but in this situation, the Texas court adopted pure comparative causation.

THE UNIFORM COMPARATIVE FAULT ACT

The perplexities involved in synthesizing strict liability and comparative negligence were undoubtedly a strong influence in spawning comparative fault. Why not simplify the comparison process by lumping negligence of any variety, misuse, assumption of risk, breach of warranty, and supplying a product in a defective condition under the broad definition of "fault," and then compare all the conduct of both the parties? This is the approach of the Uniform Comparative Fault Act, which defines "fault" in section 1(b):

> "Fault" includes acts or omissions that are in any measure negligent or reckless toward the person or property of the actor or others, or that subject a person to strict tort liability. The term also includes breach of warranty, unreasonable assumption of risk not constituting an enforceable express consent, misuse of a product for which the defendant otherwise would be liable, and unreasonable failure to avoid an injury or to mitigate damages. Legal requirements of causal relation apply both to fault as the basis for liability and to contributory fault.

The language of the Uniform Act has been adopted in Washington and Minnesota. The Indiana statute, effective January 1, 1985, has adopted a definition of fault that is similar. Colorado now has a comparative fault statute for product cases. The Missouri Supreme Court on November 22, 1983, adopted a comparative fault system that uses the Uniform Comparative Fault Act as a guideline.

Even before the Uniform Act, several state legislatures had opted for comparative fault. One of the first was Arkansas, which defined "fault" as follows:

> The word "fault" as used in this Act includes any act, omission, conduct, risk assumed, breach of warranty or breach of any legal duty which is a proximate cause of any damages sustained by any party. Ark. Stat. Ann., §27-1763 (1979).

The drafters of the Uniform Act seemed to have borrowed heavily from the Arkansas language. Another early state was New York, where the statute uses the term "culpable conduct" instead of negligence and specifically embraces assumption of risk as well as negligence. The term "culpable conduct" has been broadly interpreted in New York product cases to encompass strict liability, breach of warranty, and product misuse. The Maine comparative fault statute defines "fault" as "negligence, breach of statutory duty or other act or omission which gives rise to a liability in tort or would, apart from this section, give rise to a defense of contributory negligence." Me. Rev. Stat. Ann., tit. 14 §156 (1977). In a Maine diversity case, plaintiff's contributory negligence or misuse served to reduce his recovery on strict liability.

CONCLUSION

Comparative fault seems to be winning the day, although there are some stout holdouts. The scales were tipped in its favor by the promulgation of the Uniform Comparative Fault Act and the decision of the California Supreme Court in *Daly* v. *General Motors Corp.* The arguments pro and con were marshaled by the majority and dissenting opinions in this case. The attractiveness of comparative fault is its simplicity. It profits from the obvious drawback to comment (n) that it is difficult to distinguish between "failure to discover the defect or guard against the possibility of its existence" and "lack of ordinary care"; between "assumption of risk" and "contributory negligence" and "foreseeable or unforeseeable misuse."

Though one may agree with the dissenters in *Daly* and with a thoughtful article by Dean Aaron Twerski,[12] the ascendancy of comparative fault seems inevitable. There are some advantages to the plaintiff. The doctrine removes assumption of risk and misuse as complete defenses. Some disadvantages may be illusory. There has always been a proclivity for the jury to reduce damages when the plaintiff is negligent. Where contributory negligence is a complete defense, the jury will often ignore the court's instructions and apply comparative negligence, and may also ignore the court's instructions to ignore contributory negligence and award full damages.

Comparative fault works most fairly under a pure system. Under a modified system the policy of consumer protection—the *raison d'etre* of strict liability—is threatened. Surely it cannot be argued that a consumer injured by a defective product should be denied any recovery because he was 50 percent at fault. The pure principle is recognized by the Uniform Act and by *Daly*. It was also recognized emphatically when the Supreme Court of Texas in *Duncan* adopted the pure system, completely sidestepping the Texas Comparative Negligence Statute that denied recovery to a plaintiff where negligence exceeds 50 percent.

NOTES

*From 20 *Trial* 16–23. (November 1984). Reprinted with permission. Copyright © 1984 by The Association of Trial Lawyers of America.

FOR DISCUSSION

1. Why did the retention of assumption of risk as a defense in Section 402A of the Restatement (2d) of Torts nevertheless appear to be a victory for consumers?
2. What variations are possible in applying comparative negligence? Which system do you think is the fairest? Explain your answer.
3. After reading this article, can you explain the difference between contributory negligence and assumption of risk? Support your answer.

[12]Twerski, "From Defect to Cause to Comparative Fault—Rethinking Some Product Liability Concepts." 60 *Marquette Law Review* 297 (1977).

4. What is the effect on contributory negligence and assumption of risk if they become part of a rule of "comparative fault"? Does this help or hinder the consumer?

5. In a state where comparative fault is not applied to strict liability cases, what defenses might still be available to a defendant?

6. Does any state completely ignore plaintiff's fault in a strict liability case?

As the comparative fault article you have just read suggests, assumption of risk is a defense that is used often both in negligence and strict liability cases. Assumption of risk involves voluntarily exposing oneself to a known risk, the nature and extent of which is fully appreciated. Unlike contributory negligence, which involves carelessness, assumption of risk is considered to be based on consent. Therefore, actual knowledge of the risk and voluntary exposure to it are both required elements. According to *American Jurisprudence,* "Contributory negligence as a defense implies negligence on the part of both plaintiff and defendant but does not relieve the defendant from his duty to use due care. It merely prevents recovery by reason of plaintiff's own negligence. Assumption of risk, on the other hand, negates the issue of defendant's negligence by the plaintiff's previous abandonment of his right to complain if an accident occurs."[13] Whether assumption of risk is subsumed under the state's comparative negligence rule varies from one jurisdiction to the next.

The following case demonstrates traditional reasoning concerning the doctrines of assumption of risk and contributory negligence.

CASE

Lowell Foland v. Gerry Malander
Supreme Court of Nebraska (1986)
222 Neb. 1, 381 N.W.2d 914, 49 A.L.R. 4th 697

WHITE, Justice.   This is an action brought by plaintiff for injuries he suffered when he was struck and trampled by defendant's bull. Plaintiff sought special damages for medical expense and extra help hired during his recovery, and general damages for pain and suffering and permanent injury to his hand. Defendant denied any liability for plaintiff's injuries and affirmatively alleged assumption of risk and contributory negligence as bars to plaintiff's recovery. The trial court overruled plaintiff's motion for a directed verdict on the basis of strict liability but directed a verdict of negligence as a matter of law against defendant. The jury then returned a general verdict for defendant.

The incident giving rise to this suit occurred on December 29, 1980. On that date Gerry Malander, the defendant in this case, along with some family members and a hired hand, Sid Troxel, was driving a herd of approximately 80 cattle along a public road in Nance County. The herd included a 1,700 pound bull. The Malanders and Troxel were on horseback. As the drovers passed the land of Lowell Foland, one cow and the bull left the herd and proceeded toward Foland's corral. The bull then entered the corral by jumping over an electric gate.

Plaintiff, defendant, and Troxel discussed removing the bull from the corral. As plaintiff waited near the gate, defendant and Troxel entered the corral on horseback in an attempt to drive the bull out of the corral. They were successful in driving the bull toward the gate, but the bull was followed by several of plaintiff's calves. After the bull had cleared the gate, but before the calves had done so, plaintiff stepped approximately

---

[13]57A Am.Jur.2d, Negligence, §817.

15 feet behind the bull and in front of the calves, in an attempt to drive the calves back into the corral. With his back toward the bull, plaintiff made a waving motion with his hands toward the calves. The bull then turned toward plaintiff, charged him, struck him, ran over him, and stepped on his left hand.

Testimony from the record indicates that neither defendant nor his hired hand were in a position to prevent the calves from leaving the corral. Testimony also revealed that the bull was not restrained while being driven, even though defendant had a choice of methods available to him to restrain the bull.

Plaintiff alleged the following in his petition:

> That Defendant was guilty of the following acts of negligence which were the proximate cause of the injuries to Plaintiff: (a) that Defendant knew or should have known that said Simmental bull had a dangerous and vicious propensity, in that it had a propensity to attack people on numerous prior occasions, (b) that Defendant did not have said Simmental bull under proper restraint and had not taken any precautions to prevent said bull from attacking Plaintiff or other persons, (c) that Defendant permitted said Simmental bull to trespass on the Plaintiff's property where the attack on the Plaintiff took place, (d) that Defendant failed to warn the Plaintiff in any manner of the dangerous and vicious propensities of said Simmental bull.

Plaintiff also alleged injuries, that the defendant owned the bull, that the bull was of a vicious nature and disposition which was known or should have been known by defendant, and that the bull was driven along the county road and was not restrained in any manner.

In his answer defendant admitted owning the bull and denied negligence. He further claimed that plaintiff assumed the risk of his actions and that plaintiff was negligent in provoking the bull by his actions.

After carefully considering the statutes and case law, we hold that an action for the infliction of personal injury by a trespassing bull upon an occupier of land may be brought on a theory of negligence, but not on a strict liability theory. The defendant in this case drove his bull along a public road without restraining the bull in any manner. No matter how usually docile a particular bull may be, one cannot rely on it to always remain so. Although not unlawful, there are obviously dangers to driving a bull without restraint.

The plaintiff in this case clearly pled negligence on the part of the defendant. Plaintiff's assertion that the verdict was unsupported by the evidence is without merit. The jury returned a general verdict for the defendant after being instructed on the defenses of assumption of risk and contributory negligence. In order to prevail on the defense of assumption of the risk, the burden is on the defendant to prove the voluntary character of exposure to the risk, knowledge and appreciation of the danger on the part of the plaintiff, and that the injury was a proximate result of the danger. 65A C.J.S. *Negligence* §174(2), (3), and (4) (1966); *Schmidt v. Johnson*, 184 Neb. 643, 171 N.W.2d 64 (1969). One who assumes a risk in this manner is precluded from recovery for an injury resulting therefrom. *Hess v. Holdsworth*, 176 Neb. 774, 127 N.W.2d 487 (1964). Contributory negligence is conduct for which the plaintiff is responsible, amounting to a breach of the duty which the law imposes on persons to protect themselves from injury. 65A C.J.S. *Negligence* §116 (1966). It is an affirmative defense, and the burden of proving it is on the party asserting it. *Cawthra v. Shackelford*, 176 Neb. 147, 125 N.W.2d 186 (1963).

The evidence in this case clearly supports a finding by 12 jurors that plaintiff assumed a risk or was contributorily negligent when he turned his back on the bull. The jurors had heard testimony that plaintiff normally kept bulls around his farm, that he normally did not turn his back on a bull, but that he did turn his back on the defendant's bull in order to keep his calves from leaving the corral. Therefore, the trial court did not err in refusing to order a new trial.

Finally, plaintiff's last assignment of error is that the trial court erred in failing to give the jury plaintiff's proffered instructions on the rescue doctrine and strict liability. Strict liability has been dealt with above. With regard to the rescue doctrine, "A person is not relieved of the duty to exercise ordinary care for his own safety by the fact that his own or another's property is in imminent danger of loss or injury arising from the negligence of a third person." 65A C.J.S. *Negligence* §125 at 86 (1966). However, it is also a well-established rule that "when one is required to act suddenly and in the face of imminent danger, he is not required to act as though he had time for deliberation and the full exercise of his judgment and reasoning faculties." 65A C.J.S. *Negligence* §123 at 78 (1966); *Watson Bros. Transp. Co.* v. *Jacobsen*, 168 Neb. 862, 97 N.W.2d 521 (1959). The jury was properly instructed.

Finding no reversible error in this case, we affirm.

FOR DISCUSSION

1. Assumption of risk requires the plaintiff to voluntarily consent to be subjected to a known risk of injury due to defendant's actions. Based on the facts of this case, does it appear that plaintiff assumed the risk? Explain.
2. How does the court define contributory negligence?
3. Does plaintiff's action to turn his back on a bull in order to keep his calves from escaping constitute contributory negligence? Explain your answer.
4. How do the rules concerning the "rescue doctrine" quoted by the court affect the outcome of this case? Do you think that the second rule is compatible with assumption of risk? Explain.
5. Suppose Nebraska had adopted a modified comparative negligence standard. If the jury finds that plaintiff was 60 percent negligent and defendant was 40 percent negligent, can plaintiff recover any damages? Would the result be the same in a pure comparative negligence jurisdiction?
6. Which doctrine do you consider more fair, comparative negligence or contributory negligence?

In many cases, assumption of risk has been used successfully as a defense to suits involving injuries to sports spectators as well as participants. As you read the following case, you should consider whether the fact that the victim is a child makes a significant difference in the outcome. A child is generally held to a standard of care consistent with his or her age and experience. Should a child be held to assume knowingly the risk of a danger to which he or she is exposed?

CASE
Richard Benjamin, as Parent and Natural Guardian of Thomas Benjamin
v. The State of New York
Court of Claims of New York (1982)
115 Misc.2d 71, 453 N.Y.S.2d 329

THOMAS LOWERY, Jr., Judge.   In the evening of November 16, 1979, Thomas Benjamin, aged 11 years, was struck and injured by a puck while watching a hockey game at the Romney Arena, a State facility, located on the campus of the State University of New York at Oswego. Alleging that the State negligently failed to provide adequate protection for the safety of spectators seated in its arena, Thomas now seeks compensation for his injuries.

Romney Arena, as it was laid out by the State for hockey, consisted of an oblong shaped rink that ran lengthwise in a north/south direction. It was enclosed by a dasher board that was approximately three and one-half feet in height. Two players' benches had been placed along the easterly sidelines. Elevated spectator bleachers surrounded the remainder of the rink. Goals were placed at both the north and south end. To the rear of each goal and along the sidelines, a protective fence, measuring six feet and three feet in height, respectively, was mounted atop the dasher board. The fence, however, was not continuous. In front of each players' bench, a distance of approximately twenty feet, no protective fencing had been installed. Except for the dasher board, this area remained essentially open.

Thomas, accompanied by his brother and friends, had gone to the arena that evening to see a college hockey double header. The second game was to feature the "Oswego State Great Lakers," a local college team. They had paid their admission and had taken seats in the bleachers behind the south goal. Near the end of the first game, they left the area and proceeded to a concession stand which was located at the opposite end of the arena. After they purchased a drink, and while they were returning to their seats, they decided to view the remainder of the game from the sidelines. They found seats in the second or third row of the bleachers and sat down. When seated, they were behind the protective fence, ten to fifteen feet north of the nearest players' bench. While there, an errant puck found its way through the open area in front of the players' bench, passed behind the protective fence, and struck Thomas on the left side of his forehead.

The State, like any other owner or occupier of land, is only under a duty to exercise "reasonable care under the circumstances" to prevent injury to those who come to watch games played at its facilities.

In the present case, the State argues that due care required it only to provide protective seating behind the goal, where the danger was the greatest. Having done so, it argues that Thomas should have remained in his protected seat behind the goal and by choosing to do otherwise, he assumed the risk of being hit by a puck. See *Ingersoll* v. *Onondaga Hockey Club Inc.*, 245 App.Div. 137, 281 N.Y.S. 505; *Hammel* v. *Madison Square Garden Corp.*, 156 Misc. 311, 279 N.Y.S.2d 815.

The State's reasoning is somewhat flawed, however, since it undertook to provide spectators with protected seating along the sidelines, as well. In doing so, it was under a duty to make certain that such an area was reasonably safe for its intended purpose.

In determining whether the State fulfilled its duty here, the court is somewhat guided by the undisputed testimony of claimant's expert, who testified to a structural defect. He testified that in similar facilities, it was the usual and customary practice to protect the area around the players' bench. Absent such protection, it was the usual and customary practice to restrict seating to an area without the zone of danger. Since neither course of action was chosen, he opined that the State failed to provide Thomas with adequate protection that evening.

When viewing the evidence in its totality, the court finds that the absence of a fence in front of the players' bench constituted a dangerous condition that presented a foreseeable risk of injury to those spectators, including Thomas, who were seated in the protected seating area adjacent thereto. The lack of evidence that an accident of the same kind had happened before is of no moment, since such an accident was reasonably to be anticipated. In sum, the court finds that the failure of the State to provide for the safety of Thomas in the protected seating area constituted negligence and that such negligence was a substantial factor in bringing about Thomas' injuries.

In addition, the court finds that the accident and the injuries sustained by Thomas were not attributable to any culpable conduct on his part. When he took his seat in the protected area along the sidelines, he had a right to assume that every reasonable care had been taken for his safety. See *Barrett* v. *Lake Ontario Beach Improvement Co.*, 174 N.Y. 310, 66 N.E. 968. Although he admits to being aware that the area in front of the players' bench was unprotected, it cannot be said that a reasonably prudent person of Thomas' years, intelligence, degree of development, would have fully appreciated the danger and, hence, could have been said to have assumed the risk. See *Larson* v. *Nassau Electric R. Co.*, 223 N.Y. 14, 119 N.E. 92; *McEvoy* v. *City of New York*, 266 App.Div. 445, 42 N.Y.S.2d 746. Nor can it be said that such a reasonably prudent person should have been aware of the risk so as to be guilty of contributory negligence. See *Zurich General Accident & Casualty Ins. Co.* v. *Childs Co.*, 253 N.Y. 324, 171 N.E. 391.

In view of the foregoing, the court finds that Thomas has been damaged in the sum of $24,000.00 (all compensatory) and an award is made accordingly.

FOR DISCUSSION

1. What does defendant in this case claim is its duty of care to plaintiff?

2. How, according to defendant, did Thomas assume the risk of injury?

3. It has been held that when a person voluntarily assumes a duty he would not otherwise have had, he is held to the standard of the duty he has voluntarily assumed. How does that doctrine play a role in this case?

4. How does the court regard Thomas when it comes to assessing assumption of risk? Is its approach a fair and reasonable one?

5. Do you think an adult would have been found to have assumed the risk in this case? Explain your answer.

STRICT LIABILITY AND PRODUCTS LIABILITY

Although classical tort theory required that liability in tort be based on fault, it was assumed that in an earlier period persons had been liable for their actions regardless of fault, that they "acted at their peril," as Holmes described it. In recent years, there has been a resurgence of liability without fault, called either strict liability or absolute liability. Strict liability is operative in certain recognized situations, such as possession of wild or vicious animals, or practice of an abnormally dangerous or "ultrahazardous" activity. Today, injury caused by defectively designed or manufactured products is also a subject of strict liability.

Strict liability is a development primarily of the courts, as are most of the new developments in torts, such as actions for intentional and negligent infliction of emotional distress, or actions for prenatal injuries or wrongful birth. Tort is an area in which judicial activism and creativity have continually recognized and shaped new causes of action. As the next two readings demonstrate, this may be looked upon as a benefit or as a source of great danger to the legal system and society as a whole.

READING **Judicial Creativity and Tort Law**
*Cornelius J. Peck**

Much of tort law is concerned with accidental and, hence, unplanned injuries. It is, therefore, an area in which stability and predictability have less importance than is the case with the law of contracts and property; we do not take kindly to one who explains that he would have been more careful if he had known he would be held liable to those whom he has injured. Insurance companies probably have the greatest claim to a justifiable reliance on existing law for the determination of appropriate premiums, but studies indicate that the substantive law governing liability plays but a small and frequently undetectable part in fixing the total costs of providing insurance. Prospective overruling and use of dicta are available to the judiciary as means of giving advance notice that a new rule of liability will be followed in the future, affording parties the opportunity to insure against that new liability.

No empirical data are available or likely to be available with respect to some tort questions. For example, how many persons otherwise interested in doing so will be deterred from running for public office by a limitation on the right of public officers to recover for defamation? What will be the effect upon the relationship of psychiatrists with their patients if psychiatrists are held liable for failure to warn persons injured by patients' violent acts that were to some degree predictable from counseling sessions? For other problems empirical data may be available, but a court may appraise their significance as well as a legislature. Experience over time with the various factual contexts in which a problem of liability arises provides courts with a basis for determining how well the rule serves the interests of society.

Ordinarily, tort victims do not constitute a well-organized group; nor are they brought together by common interests. For example, there are no organized groups of persons injured by conduct of government employees, of employees of charities, or of land occupiers. Even if these heterogeneous groups of people were brought together, they would not be effective lobbyists. They desire redress for past injuries, not legislation addressed to the future.

Of course, the legislative approach has advantages which the judiciary cannot duplicate. Courts cannot set up the administrative machinery necessary to enforce a no-fault automobile accident reparation plan, a compulsory insurance program, or a force of inspectors to ensure compliance with safety standards. The decisions of courts may, however, catalyze legislative action to establish administrative machinery.

Some Examples   The law governing liability for injuries caused by manufactured or processed products is and has been of great importance to our society; it is and has been the subject of substantial judicial creativity. For present purposes, we start with the 1842 English decision in *Winterbottom* v. *Wright*, which required the injured person to have privity of contract with the defendant manufacturer or processor to permit recovery; there must have been a contract between them for the sale or repair of the injuring product. The exceptions that courts have been moved to develop for certain products—products characterized as imminently or inherently dangerous—permitted Justice Cardozo to write his famous opinion in *MacPherson* v. *Buick Motor Co.* Cardozo purported to do no more than precedent required, but the decision established the rule that a manufacturer may be held liable without privity of contract to a person for whose use goods were furnished because of negligence in the manufacture of the goods.

Subsequent development of a rule of strict liability was described by Dean Prosser in two articles: "The Assault Upon the Citadel (Strict Liability to the Consumer)" and "The Fall of the Citadel (Strict Liability to the Consumer)." These developments included the unjustified recognition of strict liability for food and drink as well as for products intended for intimate bodily contact, the use of res ipsa loquitur[14] approaching strict liability, and the

---

[14]**Res ipsa loquitur** ("The thing speaks for itself") is a rule of evidence under which negligence may be inferred, subject to certain limitations, without direct evidence that the negligence occurred. The rule requires that the thing that caused the injury be in the exclusive control of the guilty party and that the accident itself, and the situation in which it occurred, be such that it would not have occurred in the absence of negligence.

fictitious and strained use of the concepts of warranty. Ultimately, Chief Justice Traynor, in *Greenman* v. *Yuba Power Products, Inc.*, abandoned these camouflaging devices and stated frankly and openly that "a manufacturer is strictly liable in tort when an article he places on the market, knowing that it is to be used without inspection for defects, proves to have a defect that causes injury to a human being." 377 P.2d 897, 900 (1963).

It is significant that the case in which this announcement was made was one in which liability could have been imposed upon the defendant under the former rule requiring proof of negligence. The defect that caused the injury was the negligent design of the device used to hold wood in place on a lathe. Thus, the defendant was not subject to a new and unforeseeable liability. Judicial creativity requires something of a venturesome spirit; several years after Chief Justice Traynor wrote the decision in *Greenman*, he acknowledged that there was no single definition of defect that had proved adequate to define the scope of the manufacturer's strict liability.

Developments continued, with extension of strict liability to bystanders and to lessees and bailees of personal property. Divergent opinions developed as to whether strict liability extended to purely economic loss. Currently the courts are struggling with the problem of defining a defect. The Supreme Court of California rejects the view that a defect must make a product unreasonably dangerous, because that interpretation would involve the use of negligence standards in determining what is a design defect. The California court now prefers a definition of defect based either on consumer expectations or a reversal of the burden of proof, a reversal which requires the defendant to prove that the benefits of a challenged design outweigh the risks inherent in the design. Other problems remain, such as the role of warnings, the effect of modifications of a product, what constitutes misuse of a product, and the effect, if any, to be given to fault on the part of the injured person.

Accompanying these changes in the substantive rules governing products liability have been decisions permitting recovery for a single injury from multiple manufacturers, even though it was not possible to identify the manufacturer of the specific product that caused the injuries. Another decision permitted recovery from the current manufacturer of a line of products although the product that caused the injury was manufactured by a predecessor of the defendant for whose wrongs the defendant would not be liable under traditional rules. In this way, those who benefit from the continued use of a line of products pay for the injuries their use entails.

LEVELING THE SCALES OF JUSTICE

It is likely that in the absence of judicial activity, the change in the law of products liability would not have occurred. Injured consumers and bystanders have suffered those injuries from many different products and in many different ways. It was unlikely that they would discover a common theme to their problems. Consumers are not organized, and channels of communication are not arranged in a manner that will bring them together. Moreover, consumers have little interest in legislation directed to the future because it provides no relief to them for injuries already suffered.

Any proposed legislation imposing strict liability for defective products would have been opposed by strong lobbies. Manufacturers, retailers, wholesalers, and insurance companies have well-organized lobbies; self-interest would have dictated that they energetically oppose the adoption of strict liability. The strength of these groups has been proved in their reaction to the changes in products liability law produced by the judiciary. Largely on the basis of complaints of manufacturers about the increased rates for product liability insurance and the decreased availability of such insurance, the President's Economic Policy Board in 1976 established an Interagency Task Force on Products Liability.

One of the recommendations resulting from this study was the Department of Commerce's Model Uniform Product Liability Act. Section 104(C) of the Act rejects the consumer expectation standard and states that findings of unreasonably safe design should turn on the state of scientific and technological knowledge at the time of manufacture rather than at the time of trial. Section 110 of the Act establishes a presumption that a product has a useful life of only ten years, which would restrict rights of recovery now established in many states. The Model Act has been adopted at least in part in several states. Indeed, it has been introduced in Congress as a single and uniform law that would preempt all state product liability laws. The events prove that judicial creativity may produce legislative responses promoted by the groups that would have acted to combat the changes if they originally had been proposed in the legislatures. If they succeed, this does not mean the end to the judicial role, because—and I hope I do not sound too cynical—the language of a statute is given its meaning and application by the judiciary, and the phrases in a product liability law must of necessity be relatively general and open-ended.

CONCLUSION

Decisions have abandoned rules of sovereign immunity, charitable immunity, interspousal immunity, and parental immunity. On the other hand, recognition that severe harm may be done without the physical contact required for battery has led to new causes of action for intentional infliction of severe emotional distress, for outrageous conduct, and even for the negligent infliction of emotional distress. The California Supreme Court, leading as it so frequently does, imposed liability for the failure of psychiatrists to give warning to a person killed by a patient whose statements to the psychiatrists revealed that the patient presented a serious danger to the victim. The decision has been followed in other jurisdictions. Other decisions have imposed new duties, such as a duty of landlords to protect tenants from the criminal conduct of intruders, a duty running to fishermen from a company drilling an oil well, and a duty of a general contractor to the tenant of a building undergoing renovation to complete the work in a timely fashion.

I believe that society is better served by a judiciary that makes changes in the law than by a judiciary that leaves reform to the apparently unconcerned and often unmoved legislative process. This judicial creativity has been exercised without harm to representational democracy. If the changes had been undesirable or unsatisfactory, they could have been corrected by legislatures. There seems to be no major political movement to undo what the courts have done, however, or to prevent additional creative activity in these nonconstitutional areas of our law. The creative ventures by the judiciary have been successful.

NOTES

*From 69 *Iowa Law Review* 1 (1983). Reprinted with permission.

FOR DISCUSSION

1. What traditionally recognized purpose of tort law does not require a great degree of stability and predictability in the law?

2. Do you think Richard Posner would agree that tort law can tolerate a good measure of judicial creativity and, hence, unpredictability? Explain.

3. What characteristics of tort victims make them likely to be better served by the courts than by the legislature?

4. What is the standard of strict product liability articulated by Justice Traynor in *Greenman* v. *Yuba Power Products, Inc.*? Was strict liability actually necessary in that case?

5. If changes in the scope of liability in tort are made on a case-by-case basis by the courts, is it possible for potential defendants to have fair warning of how to act? Is it necessary that they have prior warning?

6. Why does the author favor continuation of judicial creativity in tort law? What view of legislatures does his position imply?

The following article represents the reaction of a defense attorney in tort litigation to the "explosion" of judicial creativity in tort during the past several decades. Although he concentrates on developments in Florida tort law, his concerns are representative of similar practitioners throughout the country.

READING   **"Killing the Golden Goose"**
Clifford L. Somers*

While doing my usual hasty and probably inadequate perusal of *The Florida Law Weekly* recently, I came across two cases that aroused my interest, not to mention my ire. My reaction prompted me to sit down and set my thoughts to paper with the hope of having them published, despite my pristine status as a middle-aged but unpublished lawyer. Like most of the full-time practicing civil trial lawyers I know, I have always felt I was "too busy" to be wasting my time writing articles for which I could not be paid and which all my peers would be too busy to read anyway. Nevertheless, the Supreme Court of Florida has jarred me out of that lethargy, at least briefly. I feel the need to sound off.

    One of the cases which excited this reaction is *Champion* v. *Gray*, No. 62,830 (Fla. Mar. 7, 1985), which basically destroys the "impact rule" and creates a cause of action for negligently created emotional distress and sequelae regardless of whether the plaintiff was impacted by the defendant's actions. The other is *Metropolitan Life Insurance Company* v. *McCarson*, No. 63,739, which enshrines a cause of action for intentional infliction of emotional distress in the law of Florida for all districts where the districts were split before as to whether it existed or not. It is probably not surprising that these two cases would excite the interest and the aggravation of an attorney whose primary practice is concerned with the defense of tort claims. I do not deny my reaction is the result of such feelings, but I really believe that a more important reason for my reaction lies in the fact I think these two cases are just the most recent example of the lemming-like tendency on the part of lawyers in the state to rush toward a goal which is self-destructive. The tort system of this state has been very successful at providing new and ingenious ways to compensate injured parties who have never before had the opportunity under the law to be compensated while at the same time providing a comfortable living for more and more lawyers. We seem to be haunted by the spectre of the uncompensated plaintiff. However, it seems to me that we are in great danger of succumbing to our own success and taking the present tort system down with us. This is what I mean by "killing the golden goose."

PERSONAL PERSPECTIVE

We tort lawyers seem to be particularly well insulated in our own world. What we "know" to be "true" about the law or justice tends to be highly myopic. We are very good at thinking about the technical details and the goal of compensation but not very good at understanding the larger context. We have a tendency to barge on toward our own goals and become oblivious to the fact that we are bumping our noses and other parts of our anatomy against limitations and restrictions we did not anticipate and refuse to credit as being important.

What am I talking about? Just this. For all of the second half of the 20th century the tort law has been steadily progressing toward compensating every injured plaintiff regardless of what modifications to the existing legal doctrines must be made and, more importantly, regardless of the effect on society as a whole. In this we are not unique. As our society becomes richer and better able to nurture and protect all of us, we demand and expect to be shielded from the adverse effects of nature, industry, economics and our own actions. It is the apparent unspoken goal of this trend to compensate eventually every injury, no matter how it was caused, to provide housing, clothing, food, jobs and "equal dignity" to everyone; to introduce painless dentistry and otherwise to place a cocoon around each individual which will, if not prevent harm from ever occurring, minimize that harm and compensate for it when it does occur. Whether this trend is desirable is beyond the scope of this article.

The trend exists, is "global" in its effect in our society and is reflected in our tort law. Furthermore, the evolution of the law in the last fifteen years has had the effect of employing multitudes of lawyers in the day-to-day practice of the law and in the judiciary. It has unarguably produced compensation to millions of people who might otherwise not have had it. It has unquestionably led to increased product safety and a heightened awareness in all of society with respect to safety and security of people. Described this way, it's hard to see how it could fail to be desirable to everyone. Unfortunately, there is a broader perspective.

We tend to look at tort law these days as being a vehicle for the compensation of injured parties. If we see tort law in that light, then the effects of the past 35 years have to be viewed as enlightened, progressive and highly desirable. However, it is my contention that the tort law is, and must be, larger in scope and different in emphasis from this. The tort law is a major part of our system of justice designed to provide citizens with a peaceful forum within which to resolve civil disputes. Those disputes must be resolved not only in light of the comparative equities of the parties litigating, but also in light of the good of society and its ability to cope with the resulting precedents. If the obligation to compensate the injured party grows larger than the financial ability of society at large to provide that compensation, then the law must change. It is my belief that our society is not yet rich enough to provide the cocoon toward which our law is driving us. If it is not, then our almost unrestrained drive in the legal profession toward that end must be re-examined in light of practical experience.

TORT LAW IN FLORIDA

I would like to review briefly the history of change in the tort law in the State of Florida so as to set my concluding comments in context.

One could pick any number of cases or legal precedents as illustration. I shall select some that should be familiar to any lawyer in Florida who practices tort law or knows anything whatever about it. For my purposes, Florida began to join the 20th century revolution in tort law with the decision in *Matthews* v. *Lawnlite Company*, 88 So.2d 299 (Fla. 1956). *Matthews* v. *Lawnlite* is the case in which Justice Terrell enunciated the court's departure from the requirement of privity in products liability cases. Admittedly, New York, under the guidance of Justice Cardozo, had broken the bonds of privity years before in *MacPherson* v. *Buick Motor Company*, 217 N.Y. 382, 11 N.E. 1050 (N.Y. 1916). However,

Florida was probably neither far behind nor far ahead of the rest of the states in doing this. Obviously, this decision greatly enlarged the class of plaintiffs who could sue a manufacturer for a defective product.

Another significant case was *Shingleton* v. *Bussey*, 223 So.2d 713 (Fla. 1969). As everyone knows, the Supreme Court of Florida in *Shingleton* declared that liability insurance companies were, or should be, real parties in interest in litigation between third parties and the insureds of those insurance companies and enunciated the rule that injured third parties were third-party beneficiaries of the insurance and could sue the carriers directly. It was the thesis of the Florida Supreme Court that in the enlightened era of 1969, allowing juries to know of the existence of insurance would not affect the outcome of jury verdicts. Those of us who had to live with this rule all know that, regardless of the Supreme Court's rosy view of the enlightenment of the people of 1969, the joining of insurance companies in lawsuits effectuated a remarkable increase in the size of jury verdicts.

Yet another milestone was *Hoffman* v. *Jones*, 280 So.2d 431 (Fla. 1973). In this case the Supreme Court destroyed the defense of contributory negligence and instituted the doctrine of pure comparative negligence. This allowed injured parties to collect some part of their damages even though they were in part responsible for those damages. This doesn't seem like a bad idea if they were contributing their damages to the extent of ten percent with the understanding that the ultimate award would be reduced by ten percent. Of course, because the jury is informed that this reduction will occur, it has always been the uneasy suspicion of the defense bar that the jury decides in many cases what they want the plaintiff to have and then increases it enough so that the eventual effect of comparative negligence won't hurt the outcome. Whether that suspicion is true or not, the decision in *Hoffman* v. *Jones* had a totally sweeping effect. Now every plaintiff had some chance of recovering. Put together with joint and several liability, a defendant who might be only ten percent responsible for a plaintiff's injuries could easily be required to pay the whole jury verdict if other defendants with greater responsibility happen not to be financially responsible.

The point is that in distributing the risks, the court chose to put the risk of insolvent defendants on the solvent defendants rather than on the plaintiff. Of greater significance is the fact that the court wrote a long opinion but gave the question of the overall effect of its decision relatively short shrift. Since 1973 thousands of personal injury cases of every sort in Florida have been profoundly affected by this decision. It is important to remember that the vast majority of personal injury claims are resolved far short of trial and most of them are resolved short of a lawsuit. However, very few of them are resolved without being affected in some way by the decision in *Hoffman* v. *Jones*. This one decision has made a difference to claims valuing in the billions in a 12-year span of time. That this is so, one need only consider that every claim not obviously wholly the fault of either party must be evaluated in light of comparative negligence.

"STRICT LIABILITY"

Thereafter, the court decided *West* v. *Caterpillar Tractor Company, Inc.*, 336 So.2d 80 (Fla. 1976). This is the celebrated decision in which the Supreme Court created a cause of action for "strict liability." That is, they created liability on the part of manufacturers who put products in the stream of commerce which are defective and which injure plaintiffs as a result of those defects. This doctrine makes the manufacturer liable whether the defect is the result of negligence, whether it warranted the product, whether the defect could have been said to be covered by some implied warranty or for any other reason.

Admittedly, the doctrine stops short of absolute strict liability because it does require that there be a defect in the product. However, the present trend concerning defects is mind-boggling. Even a product that was manufactured in strict compliance with the written standards and codes of the industry in question and perhaps in strict compliance with regulations of the federal or state government may be found to be defective because those standards and regulations can be determined to be "minimum standards" and if a jury decides that a reasonable manufacturer would have done something more, then the failure to do it is the production of a defect. (This all gets very confusing as to what is strict liability and what is negligence, but, let's face it, doctrine and dogma have no real requirement to be logical.)

This trend is capped in my mind by the cases of *Champion* v. *Gray* and *Metropolitan Life Insurance Company* v. *McCarson*. Neither of these two cases is seminal. There will be more. It is to be expected that the requirement of a physical effect set forth in *Champion* will be diluted almost immediately by the cases that follow. It is also to be expected that the requirement with respect to the nature of the conduct which gives rise to liability for the intentional infliction of emotional distress will be slowly modified to require less and less "outrageousness." We can also expect that what constitutes a "defect" will continue to expand as the restrictions on that definition erode. It is all heading toward the compensation of every injured party.

So far the great bastion of the defense bar has continued to be proximate cause. That is, however sloppy the definition of negligence or implied warranty or defect becomes, it is still necessary that this transgression have caused the harm suffered by the plaintiff. It is to be expected that the next attacks will come on the concept of proximate cause or "legal cause" as the jury instructions have it. The word "cause" may be fairly simple but when it is modified by the word "legal," it is subject to instant transmogrification by the courts.

An example of this trend may be found in the case of *Orlando Executive Park, Inc.* v. *Robbins*, 433 So.2d 491 (Fla. 1983). Therein, a guest of a hotel was attacked on the hotel's premises. A jury awarded compensatory damages against the owner. The district court of appeal upheld the compensatory damage award and the Supreme Court agreed. The *Orlando Executive Park, Inc.* decision turns, as most of these cases do, on the foreseeability to the owner and operator of the hotel that criminal attacks might occur. Unfortunately, the question is not that simple. Justice Boyd explains this in his dissent. He says the following:

> I must respectfully dissent because there is no evidence that the defendants' negligence actually contributed to causing the plaintiff's injuries. That is to say that even if the defendants had provided the security precautions which plaintiff's expert witnesses testified were needed, there was no evidence that such additional precautions might have deterred or prevented this particular crime. Indeed the record affirmatively shows that such additional security precautions would not have prevented the plaintiff from being assaulted. Without any proof that the defendants' negligence did in fact cause the plaintiff's injuries, the defendant should not be held liable. 433 So.2d 491 at 494.

Justice Boyd goes on to point out that plaintiff's security expert specifically stated that his hypothetical proposals for security measures would not have affected or prevented the assault on plaintiff in that case. It is obvious that to avoid the requirement for legal cause, all the court has to do is ignore it. There is a host of similar cases in the Southern Reporter, and they all concentrate on foreseeability of crime. They all tend to ignore or minimize the question of cause.

THE LAW'S TREND

The trend in the law is unmistakable. It exists in the judge-made law and is in large measure the response of the courts to the urging of counsel before them. In short, this trend is almost entirely the product of the judicial system and the practicing lawyers rather than the legislature.

It is not my contention that any one of these judge-made changes in the law is "bad" or "undesirable." I do contend the overall process has become destructive. Many of the elements of damage in a personal injury lawsuit are not true economic losses to society. That is, pain, suffering, disfigurement and the loss of capacity for enjoyment of life are not losses society need experience as economic loss. The more injuries we make compensable by the tort system, the more we transmute these losses into gold. It is not true to say society will pay for them in any event and the only question is who must pay.

It is only fair for me to point out that those of us who defend tort cases have contributed to those results ourselves. We have concerned ourselves with the technical and intellectual defenses. We have not tried to explain to the courts or the juries that there are compelling social reasons *not* to go overboard. We have not tried very hard as a group to stem the tide. Further, while we hate losing in court, we are only too well aware that the more lawsuits there are, the more business there will be for defense lawyers. (Sue my client—please!) We, who had access to the ears of large monied interests who were being bloodied, have not done enough to make them understand the process or encourage them to act effectively to change it.

The solution is probably complex. It will no doubt involve some curbs on damages. It will involve alternative dispute resolution methods, especially for smaller claims. A full solution may be beyond my skill to produce. It is certainly beyond the scope of this article. I think it is important for practicing lawyers and the judiciary to understand the system with which they are dealing. If it is driven to the point that society cannot afford it, the resolution of the issues with which it deals will be taken out of its jurisdiction. We will bump our noses on the realities of public displeasure and, more importantly, the economic facts. Neither our present tort law nor jury trials are sacrosanct. The constitution is not graven in stone. Both the state and the federal constitutions can be changed. The entire system of law can be changed if it has to be. The sentiment to "kill all the lawyers" will probably never be carried out literally in this country (I hope). However, we can commit professional suicide and we seem bent on doing it. If we can't get our consciousnesses above the level of the day-to-day fray and become instrumental in understanding the societal context, we are doomed to be shaped by it rather than contribute to shaping it.

NOTES

*From 60 *Florida Bar Journal* 9–14 (February 1986). Reprinted with permission.

FOR DISCUSSION

1. According to the author, what are the immediate and long-term dangers of the judicial trend toward compensating every injured plaintiff?
2. What is the larger goal of tort law, according to the author, and how does the concern with compensating victims affect that goal?

3. How might changes such as the one from contributory to comparative negligence, or weakening the force of proximate cause, affect cases that are settled without going to trial?

4. Which participants in the legal system bear the greatest responsibility for the great expansion of judicial activism in tort law?

5. At least one commentator has suggested that it would be better to do away with the present tort law system and enact social welfare legislation to compensate all injured victims. Do you think the author of this article would support that? Would the author of the previous article? Explain your answer.

Ultrahazardous Activity and Strict Liability

One instance in which the principles of strict liability without fault are applicable is that of abnormally dangerous or ultrahazardous activity. A traditional example of an abnormally dangerous activity is blasting in a populated area, but advances in technology have multiplied the possible ultrahazardous activities to which people and property may be exposed. A person may be strictly liable for the harm caused by an ultrahazardous activity if the harm caused is one that is foreseeable as a result of that type of activity. The theory behind strict liability in the case of abnormally dangerous activities is that these are activities that are both necessary and dangerous. In other words, the activity is not one that we can afford to prohibit, but the degree of dangerousness attached to it requires the person carrying it on to be responsible for the foreseeable harms caused by it, whether he acted negligently or not. In fact, it is assumed that such activities may cause harm even when they are carried on in the most careful manner possible. In cases involving strict liability for ultrahazardous activities, as with other strict liability situations, ordinary contributory negligence is not a defense, but assumption of risk by the victim may be a defense.

According to the *Restatement of Torts*, an activity is ultrahazardous if it (1) necessarily involves a risk of serious harm to the person, land, or chattel of another which cannot be eliminated by the exercise of utmost care and (2) is not a matter of common usage.[15] An activity may be considered ultrahazardous because of the instrumentality used in carrying it on, the nature of the subject, the condition it creates, or the location of the activity.[16] In the following case, the court considers whether transmission of high-voltage electricity by a power company can be characterized as an ultrahazardous activity. Its determination may come as a surprise.

CASE　　　　　　　**Gail Pierce et al. v. Pacific Gas and Electric Company et al.**
California Court of Appeals (1985)
166 Cal.App.3d 68, 212 Cal.Rptr. 283

SIMS, J.　In this indisputably shocking case we hold that a consumer, who was injured when a mechanical failure in an electric utility transformer sent 7,000 volts of electricity into her home, may state a cause of action against Pacific Gas and Electric Company (P.G.&E.) for strict liability in tort.

A lightning storm struck the Meridian area of Sutter County on the afternoon of November 21, 1978. Several P.G.&E. power transformers were struck and damaged by lightning, including two on plaintiffs' property. Plaintiffs' home lost its electricity.

[15]Restatement, Torts, 1st, §519.

[16]57A Am.Jur.2d, Negligence, §403.

Plaintiff Gail Pierce summoned P.G.&E., whose crew arrived at about 1:30 A.M. the morning of November 22. The P.G.&E. crew, working in the rain, removed the lightning-damaged transformers from the pole and lifted their replacements into position. One of the replacements had previously been used at another location and had been removed and stored when it was no longer needed. There was no evidence that the transformer had malfunctioned in its previous location, but the P.G.&E. crew did not test the transformer before connecting it to the power line.

The P.G.&E. crew made two of the three connections from the 12,000-volt powerline to the top of the transformers without incident, but, as a lineman attempted the third connection, the used transformer exploded in a ball of fire.

Gail observed a bit of smoke coming from the motor area of her freezer and saw a red glow in her storage shed. A fire had started in the shed. Upon closer examination, Gail saw that the fire was coming from a propane gas pipe, which had ruptured.

A P.G.&E. employee who was nearby extinguished the fire and told Gail that gas was still coming out of the pipe. He asked, "Where's the shut off valve?" Gail replied that she would go and shut it off.

As Gail grasped the propane gas tank's shutoff valve she received a terrible shock. The shock tightened her hand around the valve and she could not let go. At some point, maybe 10 or 20 seconds later, Gail fell or slid onto the propane tank, and the force of the electricity blew her hand free of the valve. Gail tumbled away from the tank and down an embankment about six feet high. She was injured.

Plaintiff's expert witness testified that the transformer malfunction had energized their house wiring, designed for 120 and 240 volts, with approximately 7,000 volts. Postaccident investigation revealed poorly insulated wiring and a ground wire unlawfully connecting plaintiffs' electrical system to the propane gas system.

Plaintiffs filed this action on August 28, 1979, alleging negligence and strict liability in tort for defective products. Plaintiffs' second cause of action for products liability alleged that P.G.&E. was "engaged in the business of designing, manufacturing, distributing, selling, leasing, renting, to the general public electrical equipment, including the electrical equipment involved in this matter." Plaintiffs' complaint did not identify the electricity itself as a defective product, P.G.&E. answered, and the plaintiffs have never amended their complaint.

The case was tried before a jury, and after plaintiffs rested, P.G.&E. moved for a nonsuit on the issue of products liability. Plaintiffs responded with a motion for a directed verdict. Plaintiffs' motion was premised on theories of (1) strict products liability, (2) absolute liability for ultrahazardous activity, and (3) breach of implied warranty of fitness for a particular purpose.

After both sides rested the trial court denied plaintiffs' motion for a directed verdict and granted P.G.&E.'s motion for nonsuit.

The case went to the jury on the negligence cause of action, and the jury found by special verdict that P.G.&E. was not negligent. Judgment was entered for P.G.&E.

I. We first consider the trial court's entry of a nonsuit on plaintiffs' second cause of action for products liability.

Plaintiffs' second cause of action was premised on the theory of strict liability in tort for defective products. Under this theory "A manufacturer is strictly liable in tort when an article he places on the market, knowing that it is to be used without inspection for defects, proves to have a defect that causes injury to a human being." *Greenman* v. *Yuba Power Products, Inc.* (1963), 59 Cal.2d 57, 62 [27 Cal.Rptr. 697, 13 A.L.R.3d 1049]. Undisputed evidence at trial established that the defective transformer was manufactured not by P.G.&E. but by Federal Electric Company, and that P.G.&E. never placed the transformer "on the market" or in the stream of commerce. P.G.&E. was, in essence, a consumer rather than a manufacturer of the transformer, and cannot be held liable in tort for the transformer's defects per se. *Price* v. *Shell Oil Co.* (1970) 2 Cal.3d 245, 258 [85 Cal.Rptr. 178, 466 P.2d 722].

Evidence presented at trial also established, however, that P.G.&E.'s electricity arrived at plaintiffs' home at nearly 60 times its intended voltage, ultimately causing Gail to suffer bodily injury. Plaintiffs contend that household electricity must be considered a product for strict liability purposes, that their evidence was sufficient to support a verdict in their favor, and that the entry of a nonsuit was therefore erroneous.

We come to plaintiffs' major contention on appeal: that the electricity P.G.&E. furnishes to its consumers is a product rather than a service.

P.G.&E. claims that electricity is merely the motion of charged ions and is not an "article" as described by *Greenman*. The courts, however, have not dwelled unduly on electricity's physical properties. Over 20 years ago the California Court of Appeal recognized that "Electricity is a commodity which, like other goods, can be manufactured, transported and sold." *Baldwin-Lima-Hamiliton Corp.* v. *Superior Court* (1962) 208 Cal.App.2d 803, 819 [25 Cal.Rptr. 798]. Although we have found no California case which has considered the issue in the strict tort liability context, the courts of other states have had little trouble in concluding that electricity delivered to homes and businesses is a "product." As the Supreme Court of Wisconsin aptly put it, "The distribution might well be a service, but the electricity itself, in the contemplation of the ordinary user, is a consumable product." *Ransome* v. *Wisconsin Elec. Power Co.*, 275 N.W.2d at p. 643.

P.G.&E. relies on *Shepard* v. *Alexian Brothers Hosp.* (1973) 33 Cal.App.3d 606 [109 Cal.Rptr. 132], and *Fogo* v. *Cutter Laboratories, Inc.* (1977) 68 Cal.App.3d 744 [137 Cal.Rptr. 417], to support its argument that provision of electricity is a service rather than a product. Both cases are readily distinguishable.

We readily acknowledge that P.G.&E.'s liability should not depend simply upon whether electricity is or is not labeled a "product." More significantly, we believe the policy justifications for strict liability in tort support its imposition in this case. This court has identified four main policy grounds for the doctrine: (1) to provide a "short cut" to liability where negligence may be present but is difficult to prove; (2) to provide an economic incentive for improved product safety; (3) to induce the reallocation of resources toward safer products; and (4) to spread the risk of loss among all who use the product. *McDonald* v. *Sacramento Medical Foundation Blood Bank* (1976) 62 Cal.App.3d 866, 874 [133 Cal.Rptr. 444]; see 50 Cal.Jur.3d, Products Liability, §17, p. 809.

Proof of negligence in cases such as this requires a plaintiff to present to a jury evidence of the inner workings of an electrical power system of vast and complex proportions. The technical operation of such systems and of electricity itself is far beyond the knowledge of the average juror. The expert witnesses who can explain such systems to the jury are concentrated within the industry itself and may be reluctant to serve as expert witnesses in plaintiff's cases. Moreover, P.G.&E. is in a much better position than a consumer-plaintiff to diagnose—and ultimately to correct—the failures which inevitably occur in systems of such magnitude.

In addition, where, as here, a huge surge of injury-causing electricity is traceable to a defective component (the transformer) in the utility's system, imposition of strict liability creates an incentive for utilities to *avoid* accidents before they occur, by investing in safer products. Although, as P.G.&E. notes, its current practices and procedures are extensively regulated by the PUC and its General Order 95, the PUC certainly has not forbidden testing transformers before they are connected to 12,000 volt powerlines. Nothing in the record suggests the PUC is of the view that electric utility procedures are incapable of being made safer.

Finally, strict liability in tort spreads the costs of personal injuries among millions of consumers instead of imposing those costs upon blameless victims chosen by chance. It is proper that those who seek to benefit from a product should bear the associated costs and should not ask the unfortunate but inevitable victims selected (literally) by accident to bear the burden unaided.

We conclude that P.G.&E., as a commercial supplier of electricity, is subject to strict liability in tort for personal injuries caused by delivery of electricity at dangerously high voltage due to a defective transformer. Accordingly, the trial court's entry of a nonsuit was error.

We emphasize that out holding is limited to cases where the electricity is actually in the "stream of commerce," and expected to be at marketable voltage. In most cases, this will mean the electricity must be delivered to the customer's premises, to the point where it is metered, although the many variations in electrical systems prevent our drawing a "bright line" at a particular point. We concur in the limitations uniformly adopted by other jurisdictions which have excluded "antenna cases" [plaintiff, installing TV antenna, accidentally touches antenna to powerline] and the "plaintiff-touches-downed-powerline" cases from liability without fault because in those cases contact with the powerline comes at a point where the electricity is not in the stream of commerce or is not in marketable form. Moreover, in such cases (as with such cases where dangerously high voltage is attributable to acts of God), the utility generally cannot prevent the accident using reasonably available means.

Nor do we have occasion in this case to examine whether a commercial supplier of electricity should be strictly liable for property damage or for any specie of damage caused by delivery of electricity at *less than* marketable voltage, i.e., damage caused by a "brownout." Those situations may well involve policy considerations not present in the scenario currently before us.

II. Plaintiffs also contend the trial court erred in denying their motion for directed verdict on the issue of ultrahazardous activity, as liability was established as a matter of law. Plaintiffs are mistaken.

The doctrine of ultrahazardous activity provides that one who undertakes an ultrahazardous activity is liable to every person who is injured as a proximate result of that activity, regardless of the amount of care he uses. *McKenzie* v. *Pacific Gas & Elec. Co.* (1962) 200 Cal.App.2d 731, 736 [19 Cal.Rptr. 628]. The doctrine of ultrahazardous activity focuses not on a product and its defects but upon an activity intentionally undertaken by the defendant, which by its nature is very dangerous. In this case it is of course true that the ultimate result of the transformer failure was very hazardous: over 7,000 volts of electricity were sent into a residential electric system designed for no more than 240 volts. However, the doctrine scrutinizes not the accident itself but the activity which led up to the accident—in this case, the maintenance of high-voltage powerlines and transformers. Thus, the issue is whether maintenance of high-voltage power systems by public utilities is an ultrahazardous activity. We conclude it is not.

Our Supreme Court has limited the doctrine of ultrahazardous activity to encompass only activities which are neither commonplace nor customary. *Luthringer* v. *Moore* (1943) 31 Cal.2d 489, 498 [190 P.2d 1]. In this case the allegedly ultrahazardous activity has become pervasive and is now entirely commonplace. We therefore join the court in *McKenzie* v. *Pacific Gas & Elec. Co.*, supra, 200 Cal.App.2d 731, in concluding that maintenance of electric power lines is not "ultrahazardous" (p. 736). The trial court's refusal to direct a verdict for plaintiffs on this issue was proper.

FOR DISCUSSION

1. According to this court, what is the rationale for holding a defendant strictly liable in tort for injuries caused by a defective product?
2. How does this court define the doctrine of ultrahazardous activity?
3. What is the difference between holding a defendant strictly liable in tort for a defective product and doing the same for engaging in an ultrahazardous activity?
4. Why does the court conclude that maintaining high-voltage powerlines is not an ultrahazardous activity? Given the court's analysis, can you explain why blasting, for instance, *is* considered ultrahazardous?
5. Do you think the court might have regarded the question of ultrahazardous activity differently if it had not already decided that defendant was strictly liable for an injury caused by a defective product? Explain your answer.

Products Liability

The most common subject of strict liability today is product liability: liability for harm caused by defectively designed or manufactured products. The law of strict products liability is predicated on the idea that, in modern society, consumers faced with increasingly complex and novel products cannot reasonably examine them to determine whether they are safe for the use for which they were marketed. The consumer is forced to trust the manufacturer and the seller that the product is safe. In that sense, products liability assumes that every manufacturer makes an implied representation that its products are safe for the use for which they are intended. If the consumer is injured by a defectively manufactured product, then it is better to make the manufacturer bear the cost of the injury, for it is in a better position to insure against the loss or redistribute the costs of increased safety to the public.

The law of product liability in the United States began with *MacPherson* v. *Buick Motor Co.*, 111 N.E. 1050 (N.Y. 1916), in which Justice Benjamin Cardozo held that a motor car was an inherently dangerous product and thus required that the manufacturer be liable to third parties for the consequences of negligent design and manufacture. Despite the *MacPherson* decision, many barriers to successful recovery had to be overcome. Was products liability a matter of negligence, or express warranty, or implied warranty? In the case of warranty, in particular, was privity of contract[17] required when the product at issue was not inherently dangerous? Did the Statute of Limitations on a product case begin to run at the time the defective product was purchased or at the time of the injury? Given these obstacles, development of products liability was very slow until the early 1960s, when the Supreme Court of California decided *Greenman* v. *Yuba Power Products, Inc.*, 377 P.2d 897 (Cal. 1963). That case held that a manufacturer was strictly liable in tort for injury caused by a defective product that he produced and sold. The *Greenman* case and its successors, many crafted by Justice Roger Traynor, justly looked on as the father of modern products liability in the United States, have made California the leader in establishing the principles of strict product liability.

---

[17]**Privity of contract** refers to the relationship between the parties to a contract. Because a warranty is a contractual promise of quality, it normally extends only to the parties to the contract, yet third-party users are frequently injured by defective products, and a requirement of privity of contract would prevent them from asserting that the manufacturer had failed to live up to the warranty of quality.

In the following case, the principles of strict products liability are applied to a situation involving an injury from what may seem at first to be a commonplace and relatively innocuous product. The analysis addresses many pertinent questions in modern products liability.

CASE

Joyce L. Payne v. Soft Sheen Products, Inc.
District of Columbia Court of Appeals (1985)
486 A.2d 712, CCH Prod. Liab. Rep. ¶ 10354, 58 A.L.R.4th 15

MACK, Associate Judge.   Joyce L. Payne, the plaintiff below, appeals from a judgment entered upon a ruling of the trial court granting the motion of defendant, Soft Sheen Products Inc. (Soft Sheen), for a directed verdict.

Joyce Payne originally brought this action against Soft Sheen and Delavell Thrower to recover damages for second degree burns sustained as a result of the application by Mrs. Thrower, a beautician, of a permanent wave product manufactured by Soft Sheen to Miss Payne's hair. The complaint alleged that the failure of the manufacturer and the beautician to warn of the product's dangers constituted breach of warranty and negligence, and in addition that Thrower had negligently applied the permanent wave solution to Payne's hair. On the first day of trial, the claims against Thrower were voluntarily dismissed, although a third-party claim by Soft Sheen against Thrower remained in the suit. The case was tried to a jury. At the close of the plaintiff's evidence, a directed verdict was granted in favor of the remaining defendant, Soft Sheen. Soft Sheen then dismissed the cross-claim against Thrower. On appeal Payne contends that the evidence adduced at trial was sufficient to warrant submission of the case to the jury, and that the trial court erred in directing a verdict. We conclude that the grant of a directed verdict was improper, and we therefore reverse the judgment of the trial court.

A. Breach of Implied Warranty and Strict Liability

In her complaint, Payne set forth two theories of liability, negligence and breach of implied warranty. Payne later asserted that a strict liability cause of action was an "implied pendant claim" under the warranty count of the complaint. This problem of pleading need not detain us, however, because in the context of a claim that the product manufacturer's inadequate warnings caused injury to a consumer of the product, the plaintiff's burden under implied warranty and strict liability is identical.

This jurisdiction recognizes both tort and warranty theories of product liability. Warranty, though it has become associated with principles of contract, originated as a tort action, similar to an action for deceit. Although the warranty action sounded in tort, the warranty itself, in early cases, invariably arose out of a contract between the two parties. Warranty therefore became inextricably linked to contract and an action on a warranty came to be considered a contract action. Standard contract concepts also became affixed to warranty actions, requiring a showing of privity of contract between the parties to an action on a warranty, allowing disclaimer of the warranty, and requiring notice by the complaining party to the manufacturer of a defect in the goods. Nevertheless, "[i]t is undisputed that the original tort form of action [in warranty]... still survives to this day, and may be everywhere maintained."[18]

---

[18]Prosser, *The Assault Upon the Citadel (Strict Liability to the Consumer)*, 69 Yale, L.J. 1099 (1960), at 1126. See also Kessler, *Products Liability*, 76 Yale L.J. 887, 900 (1967).

Recognizing that "[m]anufacturers should properly assume those burdens incident to the cost of doing business," even if they are separated by several links in the chain of distribution from the ultimate consumer, this court in *Picker X-Ray Corp.* v. *General Motors Corp.*, 185 A.2d 919 (D.C. 1962), held that warranty liability for defectively manufactured products "should no longer be dependent upon any contractual relationship between the manufacturer and the ultimate consumer or user." *Id.* at 921. This court in effect stripped the warranty action of its contractual baggage and reestablished the original tort action for warranty free of contract associations. Moreover, warranty liability was to be imposed without regard to "concepts of negligence and fault, as defined by negligence standards." *Id.* at 922. This warranty liability was instead to be a form of strict liability: a plaintiff could recover if he established, first, that the product was defective, *i.e.*, not reasonably fit for its intended purpose or not of merchantable quality; and second, that as a result of the defect, the product caused injury. *Id.*

In 1965, the American Law Institute incorporated these standards into section 402A of the Second Restatement of Torts. Comment m to section 402A made clear that

> There is nothing in this Section which would prevent any court from treating the rule stated as a matter of "warranty" to the user or consumer. But if this is done, it should be recognized and understood that the "warranty" is a very different kind of warranty from those usually found in the sale of goods, and that it is not subject to the various contract rules which have grown up to surround such sales.

This court, in *Cottom* v. *McGuire Funeral Service, Inc.*, 262 A.2d 807 (D.C. 1970), adopted the reasoning of Comment m, finding that "to a large extent [it] is true" that the "doctrines of implied warranty and strict liability in tort are but two labels for the same legal right and remedy, as the governing principles are identical." *Id.* at 808. Under either theory, the court held, "there is a liability imposed for injury caused by placing a defective product into the stream of commerce in the District of Columbia." *Id.* at 809.

In sum, in the context of this case, where no issues unique to warranty, like disclaimer or notice, are presented, a claim of strict liability in tort was effectively made out by the count in the complaint for breach of warranty.

B. Negligence and Strict Liability

In ruling on Soft Sheen's motion for a directed verdict, the trial court summarized Payne's claim as follows: "[Payne] urges that there is a defect in the manufacture of this [permanent wave product] and that the warnings were such that they were inadequate....." Payne, however, had never claimed that the defect in the product was an error in the manufacturing process, and put on no proof to that effect. Her sole claim was that the instructions contained in the manufacturer's manual were inadequate to alert the beautician, Thrower, to the danger of the product, and that this failure by the manufacturer to adequately warn Thrower resulted in Payne's injuries.

The negligence cause of action for failure to warn a consumer of a product's dangers is summarized in section 388 of the Second Restatement of Torts. That section sets forth the general rule that the supplier of a product is liable to expected users for harm that results from foreseeable uses of the product if the supplier has reason to know that the product is dangerous and fails to exercise reasonable care to so inform the user.

A plaintiff may plead a claim of manufacturer negligence in failing to warn about foreseeable harm from a product, may claim strict liability for injury derived from the same failure, or may do both. In either case, the manufacturer's duty is the same: if its product "could result in foreseeable harm [the manufacturer] has a duty to give a warning which adequately advises the user of the attendant risks and which provides specific directions for safe use." *Russell* v. *G.A.F. Corp.*, 422 A.2d 989, 991 (D.C. 1980), citing *Burch* v. *Amsterdam Corp.*, 366 A.2d 1079, 1086 (D.C. 1976). In this case we are dealing with a product which has "both utility and danger. It is well known that permanent wave solutions can never be made completely safe for all users....." *Beetler* v. *Sales Affiliates, Inc.*, 431 F.2d 651, 653 (7th Cir. 1970). Such a product is not *unreasonably* dangerous (and therefore "defective") for purposes of section 402A if it is accompanied by an adequate warning.

Payne did have the burden of proof on two issues: to show, first, that the warning on the product was inadequate, and that the product was therefore defective, i.e., unreasonably dangerous; and second, that the defect in the product proximately caused her injuries. The trial court ruled that plaintiff's proof had failed to raise facts on either of these issues sufficient to warrant submitting the case to the jury. This was error.

1. Adequacy of Warnings

It cannot be said as a matter of law that the warnings on the permanent product were adequate. It is true that the adequacy of warnings "cannot be evaluated apart from the knowledge and expertise of those who may reasonably be expected to use" the product. *Martinez* v. *Dixie Carriers, Inc.*, 529 F.2d 457, 465 (5th Cir. 1976). In this case, a warning that may be sufficient for a product distributed only through licensed beauticians, as this one was, may well be inadequate for the same product distributed through drugstores to consumers. The sufficiency of a particular warning, in light of the sophistication of its intended users, is ordinarily a question for the jury, however.

The manufacturer's warning in this case that the ammonium thioglycolate contained in the product may cause burns is included within the step-by-step instruction manual, but not under the heading "Application of Chemical Rearranger" or "Rins[ing of] Chemical Rearranger from Hair"; instead, it is found only at the very end of the manual, in small print, following the heading "Customer Care at Home." It is a jury question as to whether or not this warning was adequate under the circumstances to warn the beautician of the danger of the ammonia component of the product.

One element of an adequate warning is "a description of the precautions necessary to avoid the injury." *Ferebee* v. *Chevron Chemical Co.*, 552 F. Supp. 1293 1304 (D.D.C. 1982). The warning for the ammonia agent in the product says only that the instruction booklet must be followed carefully in order to avoid burns; and yet the instruction manual sets forth no specific instructions on this score, other than that the beautician should drape the customer and surround the scalp area with conditioning lotion.

In connection with the description of the second, "neutralizing" step of the process, the beautician is instructed, if the patron complains of burning, "to rinse area well and shampoo," and to prevent the neutralizer from dripping onto exposed skin. The beautician is also told that "the patron's safety is your responsibility." But no similar warning is given in connection with a part of the process much more dangerous, the rearranger step. In fact, although the warning at the end of the booklet states that the product contains ammonium thioglycolate, which can cause burns, at no point is the beautician informed that the *rearranger* contains the ammonium thioglycolate, not the neutralizer. The plethora of warnings surrounding the neutralizing step may well have misled the beautician into thinking that the burn-causing ammonia agent in the product is found in the neutralizer.

The plaintiff here testified that she told the beautician, Thrower, that her back was burning, and that Thrower did not know what to do. Thrower contradicted this testimony, but it was not the function of the trial court to weigh the relative credibility of Payne and Thrower.

In sum, we cannot agree that as a matter of law the directions for Delavell Thrower's use were adequate. This is a jury question, precluding a directed verdict for the defendant.

2. Causation

The manufacturer contends that plaintiff also failed to meet her burden of proof on the issue of causation: that even if the warning was inadequate, plaintiff failed to adduce sufficient evidence from which a jury could infer that it was Thrower's failure to read the inadequate warnings that proximately caused the injury.

In this case there is no dispute that the product in some cases may cause burns. Plaintiff's case was not defective because she failed to put on evidence to that effect. On the question of whether the product had proximately caused Payne's injury in this case, plaintiff's evidence was sufficient to withstand a directed verdict. Plaintiff testified that she felt a burning sensation while the beautician was working; she entered a hospital emergency room the next day, and she produced records to show that she suffered second-degree burns. Payne also supplied direct evidence: her treating physician, a burn expert, testified that an ammonia-containing product could have run down the back and caused this damage, even though it would not have burned the scalp. This evidence, and the inferences that could legitimately be drawn therefrom, were sufficient to allow the case to go to the jury.

Some courts, in keeping with the general rule that plaintiff must show that the defect proximately caused injury, have required the plaintiff to prove that it was the lack of warning that harmed the plaintiff. In other words, plaintiffs are required to show that, had an adequate warning been given, the user would have read and heeded it, and therefore, the accident would not have occurred. However, a rule requiring a plaintiff to prove not only that the failure to warn of a danger in a product made that danger unreasonable and that his injury grew out of the risk caused by that danger, but also that the failure to warn caused his injury, would impose an impossible burden on plaintiff, and would often prevent his recovery because of pure speculation on the part of the jury.

Several courts have fashioned a presumption to deal with this problem, finding a rebuttable presumption in cases of this type that the user would have read an adequate warning, and that in the absence of evidence rebutting the presumption, a jury may find that the defendant's product was the producing cause of the plaintiff's injury. We agree with this approach to the problem, and therefore hold that plaintiff here met her burden of proof on the issue of causation.

3. Misuse and Intervening Cause

Soft Sheen also argues that if Payne's injury was caused by the product because it ran down her back, then the product was "misused" by the user, beautician Thrower. It alleges further, that negligence by Thrower in allowing the product to run down Payne's back was an intervening cause of the injury. Both the alleged "misuse" of the product and the alleged negligence of Thrower as an intervening and superseding cause, they contend, as a matter of law relieve the manufacturer of liability. In granting Soft Sheen's motion for a directed verdict, the trial court appeared to agree. For the following reasons, this was error.

Product "misuse" is defined as use of a product in a manner that could not be reasonably foreseen by the defendant. Under both a negligence and a strict liability theory, the manufacturer has an obligation to anticipate reasonably foreseeable risks of harm arising in the course of proper use, and to warn of those risks. "Proper use" includes "the incidental and attendant consequences that accompany normal use." *Helene Curtis Industries, Inc.* v. *Pruitt*, 385 F.2d 841, 863 (5th Cir. 1967), *cert. denied*, 391 U.S. 913, 88 S.Ct. 1806, 20 L.Ed.2d 652 (1968). Whether the injury here arose out of proper use of the product, out of use that could reasonably have been foreseen by defendant, or out of product misuse, is a jury question and should not have been decided as a matter of law by the trial court.

Similarly, negligence by an intervening actor will not relieve the manufacturer of liability if the negligence could reasonably have been anticipated, under both negligence and strict liability theories of recovery. The manufacturer's action need not be the sole proximate cause of the injury: the manufacturer may still be held liable even though other causes proximately contributed to the injury. The question is whether the manufacturer's action was a proximate cause rather than a remote cause, and the test of proximate causation, again, is whether the result was reasonably foreseeable by the manufacturer.

The existence of an intervening cause does not alter this test. Rather, where harmful consequences are brought about by intervening, independent forces (like the beautician's actions here) whose operation could have been foreseen, the chain of causation extending from the original act (if it is established as wrongful) is treated as proximate cause. Whether the manufacturer's action here was a proximate cause of the injury, i.e., whether it could reasonably have been foreseen that a chemical product with a propensity to burn that is applied to the hair as a lotion and then rinsed off might run down a patron's back and cause burns, is a question for the trier of fact.

FOR DISCUSSION

1. According to this court, why is privity of contract no longer necessary in a case of product liability brought under a warranty theory?

2. For purposes of product liability, how does a court determine whether a product is "unreasonably dangerous" or "defective"?

3. The court concedes that a product which is "dangerous" may also be useful. What is the manufacturer's responsibility to the consumer in connection with such a product?

4. If plaintiff is to be successful in establishing defendant's liability for failure to adequately warn consumers about a dangerous product, what must be proved?

5. Can misuse of the product by the consumer or a third party relieve the manufacturer of liability for harm? What is the manufacturer's duty with respect to possible uses of its product?

In surveying the rapidly developing law of strict products liability, it sometimes appears as if we may have arrived at the point where everyone really is liable to everyone else for everything. Nevertheless, the basic principles of duty and causation have not been entirely lost, as the following case illustrates.

CASE

John Walter v. Louise Bauer et al.
New York Supreme Court (1981)
109 Misc.2d 189, 439 N.Y.S.2d 821

JOSEPH P. KUSZYNSKI, Justice.   In this motion to renew and reargue, plaintiffs John Walter as Father and Natural Guardian of Christopher Walter an Infant, and John Walter Individually, seek to amend the complaint pursuant to CPLR 3025 to increase the ad damnum clause from $125,000 to $600,000 and to add a cause of action in strict liability in tort.

The infant plaintiff, Christopher Walter, allegedly sustained injury to his eye in October 1975 at Our Lady of Pompeii School where he was a student, while performing a science experiment with a ruler and rubber bands. The experiment was described in the book

Discovering Science 4 published by the Charles E. Merrill Publishing Company. The injury resulted in two surgeries on the cataract of the injured eye with a 1977 prognosis of "Good, eye healed well. Best corrected vision with contact lenses 20/60." A later report dated in 1978 showed an improvement to a corrected vision of 20/30 and 20/40.

The action before this Court was commenced on October 2, 1978. Afterwards there was a change of trial counsel.

Analyzing the substance of the affidavit of plaintiff John Walter, it is noted that it does not show the incurrence of any additional medical expenses or a medical history which might justify the request for a change in the ad damnum clause. The condition of the infant plaintiff's eye has actually improved over that which was allegedly reported in the post-operative prognosis, upon which the cause of action was based. Requests to modify the ad damnum clause are addressed to the sound discretion of the Court. Under the circumstances, the amount requested in the original ad damnum clause should remain as is, as plaintiff had failed to show that it is inadequate or that the increase is warranted by reason of a recent discovery of additional facts.

In a novel theory, plaintiff contends that the defendant, Charles E. Merrill Publishing Company, is subject to a cause of action in strict liability in tort, because of the experiment it published in *Discovering Science 4* which allegedly led to the injury. Plaintiff maintains that "A product may be defectively designed when it represents an unreasonable risk or harm, containing dangerous design, defects and/or when there is a failure to warn about danger attendant upon the use of a product." It is claimed the experiment contained in the textbook was inherently defective because it contained an unreasonable risk or harm by placing dangerous instrumentalities of rubber bands and ruler in the hands of fourth grade students and also because the article had failed to post any warning regarding these dangers.

Plaintiffs argue that therefore the elements of strict tort liability listed in *Micallef* v. *Miehle Co.*, 39 N.Y.2d 376, 384 N.Y.S.2d 115, 348 N.E.2d 571 and *Wolfgruber* v. *Upjohn Co.*, 72 A.D.2d 59, 423 N.Y.S.2d 95, are present.

This Court concludes that the theory of action grounded upon strict liability is not applicable to the current situation. The duty to warn is an expanding area of litigation due to the growing complexity of products sold in today's market place. Strict liability in tort is meant, however, to protect the customer from defectively produced merchandise. *Discovering Science 4* cannot be said to be a defective product, for the injured plaintiff was not injured by use of the book for the purpose for which it was designed, i.e., to be read. More importantly perhaps, the danger of plaintiff's proposed theory is the chilling effect it would have on the First Amendment—Freedom of Speech and Press. Would any author wish to be exposed to liability for writing on a topic which might result in physical injury? e.g., How to cut trees; How to keep bees?

Plaintiffs' motions are denied.

FOR DISCUSSION

1. Why doesn't the failure to warn about danger attendant on the use of product apply to this case?
2. What is the intended use of a school textbook?
3. Is it possible that the injury suffered by the infant plaintiff was the result of negligence by the teacher in carrying out or supervising the experiment?
4. Is it possible that the injury was caused by a freak accident?
5. Why might the plaintiff want to add a cause of action for strict liability to his complaint?

INTENTIONAL TORTS

The subject of torts encompasses not only negligence and strict liability, but intentional harm to persons and property as well. Intentional torts to the person include assault, battery, false imprisonment, and intentional infliction of emotional distress, while intentional torts to property include trespass, conversion, fraud, and nuisance, as well as torts involving economic harm such as wrongful appropriation of a trade secret or interference with contractual relations. Another group of intentional torts lies somewhere between harm to person and property, and includes libel, slander, defamation, and invasion of privacy.

These torts are often based on activities that could also be classified as crimes, and it is possible that one event or transaction, such as a battery, can have both criminal and civil consequences. In the criminal case, the purpose is to protect society from the wrongdoer, express society's disapproval for the act, and punish him or her for the wrong committed, whereas in the civil case the purpose is to compensate the victim for the harm sustained.

In the case of intentional torts, the required intent is that the defendant not only intended to do the act that resulted in the harm complained of, but that the defendant intended the harm that resulted from the act or at least knew that the harm was substantially certain to result and acted anyway. The commonest defense to an intentional tort is consent: If the victim knowingly and voluntarily consented to the interference with his person or property, there is no tort. In other cases the law recognizes certain privileges that permit particular persons to perform otherwise tortious conduct under certain circumstances, such as self-defense or the privilege to prevent a crime. Although such privileges are available, they are very strictly regulated.

Traditional intentional torts such as battery or invasion of privacy have expanded as our technology has changed. As we gain the ability to interfere with other people's lives in ever more sophisticated ways, these causes of action have been forced to change to meet the newly perceived injuries. Changes in lifestyle, particularly those accompanying the so-called sexual revolution, have also led to new injuries and new causes of action. The following case deals with a type of harm that is likely to become ever more serious and threatening in a time when venereal diseases have reached epidemic proportions, and infection with AIDS is a real possibility for many people.

CASE

Kathleen K. v. Robert B.
California Court of Appeal (1984)
150 Cal.App.3d 992, 198 Cal.Rptr. 273, 40 A.L.R.4th 1083

HASTINGS, J. · In this action, plaintiff and appellant Kathleen K. seeks damages because she contracted genital herpes, allegedly by way of sexual intercourse with defendant and respondent Robert B. The trial court granted respondent's motion for judgment on the pleadings based upon failure to state a cause of action. We reverse the judgment.

Since judgment on the pleadings is similar to a judgment following the sustaining of a demurrer, the standard of appellate review is the same. Like the demurrer, the motion for judgment on the pleadings is confined to the face of the pleading under attack, and the allegations of the complaint must be accepted as true.

The complaint sets forth four causes of action: (1) negligence (alleging that respondent inflicted injury upon appellant by having sexual intercourse with her at a time when he knew, or in the exercise of reasonable care should have known, that he was a carrier of venereal disease); (2) battery; (3) intentional infliction of emotional distress; and (4) fraud (alleging that respondent deliberately misrepresented to appellant that he was free from venereal disease, and that appellant, relying on such representation, had sexual intercourse with respondent, which she would not have done had she known the true state of affairs).

In granting respondent's motion for judgment on the pleadings, the trial court relied upon the case of *Stephen K.* v. *Roni L.* (1980), 105 Cal.App.3d 640, 164 Cal.Rptr. 618. In *Stephen K.*, the father of a child filed a cross-complaint against the child's mother who had brought a paternity action, claiming that the mother had falsely represented to him that she was taking birth control pills. The father alleged that in reliance upon that misrepresentation, he engaged in sexual intercourse with the mother, resulting in the birth of a child which he did not want. He further alleged that as a proximate result of the misrepresentation, he had become obligated to support the child financially and had suffered emotional distress.

In affirming dismissal of the cross-complaint, the court held that the misrepresentation was not actionable: "The claim of Stephen is phrased in the language of the tort of misrepresentation. Despite its legalism, it is nothing more than asking the court to supervise the promises made between two consenting adults as to the circumstances of their private sexual conduct. To do so would encourage unwarranted governmental intrusion into matters affecting the individual's right to privacy.... ¶ We reject Stephen's contention that tortious liability should be imposed against Roni, and conclude that as a matter of public policy the practice of birth control, if any, engaged in by two partners in a consensual sexual relationship is best left to the individuals involved, free from any governmental interference." *Stephen K.* v. *Roni L., supra*, 105 Cal.App.3d 640, 644-645.

After the trial court entered its judgment, the First District Court of Appeal decided the case of *Barbara A.* v. *John G.* (1983), 145 Cal.App.3d 369, 193 Cal.Rptr. 422, (hg. den. Sept. 29, 1983). In *Barbara A.*, a woman who suffered an ectopic pregnancy and was forced to undergo surgery to save her life, which rendered her sterile, brought an action against the man who impregnated her (her former attorney), alleging that she consented to sexual intercourse in reliance on the man's knowingly false representation that he was sterile. The court reversed a judgment on the pleadings in favor of defendant and held that the complaint stated causes of action for battery and for deceit.

The court distinguished *Stephen K.*, noting that: "In essence, Stephen was seeking damages for the 'wrongful birth' of his child resulting in support obligations and alleged damages for mental suffering. Here, no child is involved; appellant is seeking damages for severe injury to her own body." 145 Cal.App.3d at pp. 378-379. We conclude that these same factors distinguish this case from *Stephen K.*, and accordingly hold that *Barbara A.* is controlling here.

Respondent, urging us to follow *Stephen K.*, criticizes *Barbara A.* in several respects. First, he argues that the viability of appellant's cause of action should not depend upon whether the injury alleged is mental or physical. However, the *Barbara A.* court did not focus solely on the type of injury involved in *Stephen K.*, but upon the fact that Stephen was alleging an injury which had significant public policy overtones: "To assess damages against the mother for false representations about birth control would have the practical effect of reducing or eliminating support from the father by way of offset. Erasing much or all of the father's financial support, to the detriment of the child, is clearly against public policy and the statutory mandate.

"Further, we think it is not sound social policy to allow one parent to sue the other over the wrongful birth of their child. Using the child as a damage element in a tortious claim of one parent against the other could seldom, if ever, result in benefit to the child." 145 Cal.App.3d at p. 379.

In the present case, as in *Barbara A.*, there is no child involved, and the public policy considerations with respect to parental obligations are absent.

Respondent also argues that it is not the business of the courts to "supervise the promises made between two consenting adults as to the circumstances of their private sexual conduct." *Stephen K.* v. *Roni L.*, *supra*, 105 Cal.App.3d at pp. 644-645.

Respondent correctly focuses on the constitutional right of privacy as the crux of this case. Courts have long recognized the right of privacy in matters relating to marriage, family and sex, *Griswold* v. *Connecticut* (1965), 381 U.S. 479, 14 L.Ed. 510, 85 S.Ct. 1678; *Eisenstadt* v. *Baird* (1972), 405 U.S. 438, 31 L.Ed. 349, 92 S.Ct. 1029, and accordingly have frowned upon unwarranted governmental intrusion into matters affecting the individual's right of privacy. The key word here, however, is *unwarranted*. The right of privacy is not absolute, and in some cases is subordinate to the state's fundamental right to enact laws which promote public health, welfare and safety, even though such laws may invade the offender's right of privacy. Examples cited by the *Barbara A.* court were the penal statutes covering both forcible and consensual sexual acts, registration of convicted sex offenders, the recently enacted criminal statute prohibiting spousal rape, and the various laws relating to the paternity of children. In each of these cases, the right of privacy is outweighed by the right of the state to protect the health, welfare and safety of its citizens. The *Barbara A.* court concluded that the right of privacy "does not insulate a person from all judicial inquiry into his or her sexual relations," and expanded the exceptions to the right of privacy to impose liability upon "one sexual partner who by intentionally tortious conduct causes physical injury to the other." 145 Cal.App.3d at p. 381.

This is precisely the type of conduct alleged in appellant's complaint. Appellant has alleged that she sustained physical injury due to respondent's tortious conduct in either negligently or deliberately failing to inform her that he was infected with venereal disease. The disease which appellant contracted is serious and (thus far) incurable. The tortious nature of respondent's conduct, coupled with the interest of this state in the prevention and control of contagious and dangerous diseases, brings appellant's injury within the type of physical injury contemplated by the court in *Barbara A.* The constitutional right of privacy does not protect respondent here.

It should be noted that several out-of-state cases, cited by the court in *Barbara A.*, have held that a woman's consent to sexual intercourse was vitiated by the man's fraudulent concealment of the risk of infection with venereal disease. *De Vall* v. *Strunk* (Tex. Civ.App. 1936), 96 S.W.2d 245; *Crowell* v. *Crowell* (1920), 180 N.C. 516, 105 S.E. 206; *State* v. *Lankford* (1917), 29 Del. 594, 102 A. 63. Respondent contends that these cases are old and, if decided today, would be dismissed under the public policy considerations outlined in *Stephen K.*, *supra*, 105 Cal.App.3d 640. He distinguishes *Crowell* and *Lankford* (involving suits by a wife against her husband for damages resulting from contraction of venereal disease) on the basis that a husband and wife occupy a confidential relationship of trust and confidence in one another which does not exist between nonmarried persons. However, a certain amount of trust and confidence exists in any intimate relationship, at least to the extent that one sexual partner represents to the other that he or she is free from venereal or other dangerous contagious disease. The basic premise underlying these old cases—consent to sexual intercourse vitiated by one partner's fraudulent concealment of the risk of infection with venereal disease—is equally applicable today, whether or not the partners involved are married to each other.

We are also unpersuaded by respondent's argument that this is really an action for seduction (which he calls "the use of deception to effect intercourse"), and is therefore barred by Civil Code section 43.5. "'Seduction imports the idea of illicit intercourse accomplished by the use of arts, persuasions, or wiles to overcome the resistance of a female who is not disposed of her own volition to step aside from the paths of virtue.'" *Barbara A.* v. *John G.*, *supra*, 145 Cal.App.3d at p. 377, citing *Davis* v. *Stroud* (1942), 52 Cal.App.2d 308, 317, 126 P.2d 409. Appellant is not complaining that respondent induced her to "step aside from the paths of virtue," and in fact she willingly engaged in sexual intercourse with him. This is an action for damages based upon severe injury to appellant's body, which allegedly occurred because of respondent's misrepresentation that he was disease-free. Such an action is not barred by Civil Code section 43.5.

In summary, we conclude that *Stephen K.* v. *Roni L.*, on which the trial court relied, is inapplicable here, and that the reasoning of *Barbara A.* v. *John G.*, in which a hearing was denied by our Supreme Court, is controlling.

The judgment is reversed.

FOR DISCUSSION

1. According to the court, how is the *Barbara A.* case different from the *Stephen K.* case?
2. Which precedent case is more like the situation complained of here, *Stephen K.* or *Barbara A.*?
3. Why does the court conclude that the precedent case involving contraception (*Stephen K.*) should not be controlling in this case?
4. Why doesn't the constitutional right of privacy prevent the state from intervening in this particular situation?
5. Does this case involve the creation of a new tort or merely hold that a certain type of behavior constitutes an already recognized tort? Explain.
6. Do you agree with the outcome of this case? Justify your answer.

LEGAL TERMS TO KNOW

assumption of risk	products liability
comparative negligence	proximate cause
contributory negligence	"reasonable man" standard
duty of care	res ipsa loquitur
foreseeability	strict liability
intentional tort	ultrahazardous activity
negligence	

ADDITIONAL QUESTIONS AND EXERCISES

1. How is the law of tort different from contract? Use the cases and readings in this chapter to support your answer.
2. You will have noticed that the term "reasonable" occurs frequently in discussions of tort duty and liability. What do you think "reasonable" means in the law of tort? Give examples from the cases you have read.
3. After reading the cases and materials in this chapter, what do you think the primary purpose of tort is? Does it accomplish its purpose successfully?
4. How does the institution of liability insurance affect the development of tort law? Is it possible to say that the existence of liability insurance encourages an expansion of liability in tort? Explain your answer.

5. It has become fashionable for commentators to say that contract is dead. Is there any evidence that tort has died? Given what you have read, is it likely to die anytime soon?

6. Some rules of tort law have the obvious purpose of limiting the actor's liability for harm he or she has caused. Which rule that you have encountered in this chapter seems to be most effective in limiting liability? Do you think that rule should be continued?

7. . What appear to be the greatest advantages of the tort system? What are its greatest disadvantages?

8. Is it possible that we are returning to the very beginnings of tort law, when "every man acted at his peril"? Use the cases and readings in this chapter to support your conclusion.

FOR FURTHER READING

1. CALABRESI GUIDO, and ALVIN K. KLEVORICK, "Four Tests for Liability in Torts," *J. Legal Stud.* 14 (1985), pp. 585–627.

2. MARKESINIS, B. S., "An Expanding Tort Law—The Price of a Rigid Contract Law," *Law Q. Rev.* 103 (1987), pp. 354–397.

3. PRIEST, GEORGE L., "The Invention of Enterprise Liability: A Critical History of the Modern Foundations of Tort Law," *J. Legal Stud.* 14 (1985), pp. 461–527.

4. RABIN, ROBERT L., *Perspectives on Tort Law*, 2d ed. Boston: Little, Brown, 1983.

5. WHITE, G. EDWARD, *Tort Law in America: An Intellectual History*, New York: Oxford University Press, 1985.

9

EQUITY

INTRODUCTION

If you ask most people in the United States what they believe the leading characteristic of the legal system should be, they will likely answer that above all they expect the system to be fair. Experience has shown, however, that the demand for fairness in the law is not always easy to reconcile with the competing demand that the law be consistent and generally applicable. In our law we rely on equity as a major means of ensuring fairness in the law. Equity is seen as a mitigating force in the operation of the legal system.

Although the word "equity" has a variety of meanings, in this chapter it refers to a body of rules, remedies, and procedures that first grew up in England to supplement, and temper the effects of, the English common law. Equity was a response to a rigid and formalized legal system that was producing too many inadequate or unacceptable results. The common law operated on the theory that no right existed if there was no remedy to enforce the right claimed. In too many situations the common law recognized no remedy for a claimed right, or the remedy available, damages, was inadequate in the circumstances of the case, or the rule applied in a particular case led to an unjust result. In these situations, equity, as administered by the Lord Chancellor of England, intervened on the petition of the dissatisfied litigant to render substantial justice on a case-by-case basis. From the beginning, equity was thought of as an extraordinary procedure—that is, it was only available in cases in which the law did not act or was ineffective. Equity was discretionary, flexible, based on fairness and good conscience, and offered procedures and remedies that were more modern than those available in the common-law courts. Over time, equity came to rival the common law in power and influence, but was eventually reconciled with it. For several centuries, England operated with two court systems, law and equity, each with differing jurisdictions, procedures, substantive rules, and remedies.

Equity came to America along with the common law and is today an integral part of the system of justice in the United States. Here, as in England, equity concerns itself with flexibility and fairness, and is present in a series of remedies and procedures of the legal system, as well as in a body of substantive rules and a particular judicial perspective that gives the doing of substantial justice priority over legal formalism.

Although in the past there were generally separate courts of law and equity in America, as there had been in England, today in most jurisdictions law and equity have been merged into one unified court system, in which litigants can have the benefit of both legal and equitable relief in a single lawsuit. This can raise several technical questions and problems, particularly with regard to the constitutional guarantee of a jury trial in actions at common law, because that guarantee does not extend to claims in equity. Despite the merger of law and equity, judges and lawyers still have to be sensitive to which claims are historically common-law claims and which are equitable claims, so that the guarantee of a jury trial may be preserved, even if it means trying some of the issues in a case before a jury and others only before a judge. These complications are a historical inheritance in a legal system that used to be two systems, each with a different set of procedures.

Today, when we think of equity, we think primarily of certain remedies: the injunction, or specialized remedies such as specific performance of a contract, or equitable devices such as the trust. We will consider some equitable remedies in more detail in Chapter 10, but in this chapter we will look at equity primarily as a perspective on doing justice and examine the role it plays in our modern legal system. In doing that, we will first look at the origin and nature of equity, and at the scope of its jurisdiction. We will also examine the nature and application of equitable principles, which are often expressed in the form of "maxims" rather than rules, even though, through precedent, the maxims have lost much of their original creativity and flexibility. We will also explore the discretionary character of equity and its role as the court of conscience—a role that has given us, among other things, the concept of unconscionability. An extremely unfair, harsh and one-sided contract that "shocks the conscience," even though it is formally valid, will not be specifically enforced by a court of equity.

As we will see, that idea of unconscionability has found its way into other situations that are governed by equity, and we will also find that certain people, such as children and incompetents, receive particular protection from equity. In fact, equity's special province seems to be protecting the powerless from unfair treatment by others with more power and resources. For that reason, equity provides devices such as the trust, arrangements by which one party holds and administers property for the benefit of another, and concerns itself with guardianships and a variety of fiduciary relationships—that is, persons who are in a position of trust and have an obligation or duty to act for another's benefit. Equity can compel a trustee to render an accounting of his activities on behalf of his beneficiary or a guardian to answer for his management of his ward's person and property. Another special concern of equity is unjust enrichment, situations in which someone has gotten the benefit of money or services to which he or she is not entitled or for which he or she may be compelled to pay.

Our modern legal system owes a great deal to equity, not only for its flexibility and mitigating influence, but also because it has provided us with many of our present-day procedures, such as pleading by complaint and answer, discovery, class actions, injunctions, and the contempt power. These "modern" procedures have made pleading and practice in our legal system more streamlined and less cumbersome than the old writ system of the common law. Nevertheless, there was a time when equity had a bad reputation for arbitrariness in its decisions that was finally overcome when the Court of equity accepted the rule of binding precedent to give consistency to its decisions, even at the sacrifice of some of its flexibility. Subsequently, equity suffered from a well-deserved reputation for slowness and delay that was satirized by Charles Dickens in his novel *Bleak House*. For many, the interminable equity proceeding of *Jarndyce* v. *Jarndyce* has become a motto for delay in the legal system. In British English, to say that a person is "in Chancery" (which was the name of the British Equity Court) is to say that he or she is in a helpless situation. Today it would be hard to say that equity moves any more slowly than any other aspect of the legal system, and at times equity can move very quickly indeed. When someone petitions for judicial assistance to prevent someone else from doing something that will irreparably affect property or other rights in dispute, a show-cause order and temporary injunction from equity can move to maintain the status quo until litigation can decide the matter once and for all.

It is a surprise to some people that equity is still so vital and active in the postmerger era, in which one might have thought that the separate identity of equity would disappear once and for all. Actually, the opposite has occurred, as societal concerns have changed. We have said that many of the traditional subjects of the common law, such as property and contract, reflect a nineteenth-century individualist, "survival of the fittest" attitude that we are no longer entirely comfortable with, and we have seen in the chapter on torts that there is an increasing emphasis on protecting and compensating victims of harm whether or not the traditional substantive law and procedure provided that protection. We have also seen there is concern about an explosion of judicial activism and judicial "creativity," in the sense of creating new rights or extending old ones, and a real concern that our society and our economy may not be able to sustain this expansion of rights indefinitely. Equity, with its emphasis on flexibility, fairness, and protection of the weak and powerless, has done its part to contribute to the expansion of rights and remedies in recent decades.

Today, equity's contributions to the legal system, such as the injunction, contempt, discovery, multiparty litigation, and class actions have made things like toxic tort litigation or business regulation or checks on perceived governmental abuses of power possible and successful. Concepts like unconscionability and remedies such as unjust enrichment and specific performance can redress the balance between parties who otherwise have greatly unequal power and resources. The injunction—that decree of the Court of Equity ordering a person to do or not do a particular thing—is a powerful weapon to prevent injustice or protect the powerless who are being treated unfairly; in the hands of an activist judge, the injunction can be used to direct the doing of all sorts of previously unheard of things, from cleaning up an oil spill to busing school children from one neighborhood to another.

Despite the merger of law and equity and the creation of unified court systems, equity has not disappeared, nor has it lost its force and vitality. Deciding legal and equitable claims in one lawsuit has, in fact, contributed to the expansion of the use of equitable remedies. As those remedies become more readily available, the traditional common-law remedy of damages seems less and less adequate. We want the court to "do something" affirmative, and often it does. Given this trend, it seems ever more important to understand where equity came from and how it traditionally works to get an understanding of where it may be going in the future. In this chapter you will see several uses of equity that bring its thinking and remedies into areas they have not been before, and you should ask yourself whether that is always a good idea and where it may lead us.

History and Nature of Equity

In the following excerpt, Charles Rembar describes how equity began and the origin of many of its basic principles. It is interesting to note how much of equity is traceable to historical circumstances rather than to a purposeful plan to add to, or reform, the existing legal system. Nevertheless, equity emerged as an enduring force in our legal system and way of thinking about the law.

READING **Equity**
*Charles Rembar**

By 1300, as we have seen, the three great courts of common law are well established. They remain, however, fingers of the royal fist. The Justices act as king's delegates. "In the name of the king" is not at first formality.

Hence petitions to remedy a wrong can bypass the Justices and be addressed directly to the throne. There they will go to the Chancellor, the premier royal aide. In the early days, sometimes called Justiciar, he was viceroy, and ruled England when the King was on Crusade or in his French dominions. In the later Middle Ages, he is more a man of words than action, but even though the clash of arms drowns out the softer voices of the time, the Chancellor retains his status and much of his former power. A simple way to define his office is to say that he handles things that have to do with writing, no small matter in the governing of a largely illiterate people to whom the written word is magic. (No small matter still, television notwithstanding.) He is the Great Clerk of medieval England.

The Chancellor and his assistants form a secretariat; it is called the Chancery. They issue the writs that start the actions in the courts of law, and it is to be expected that other legal matters will be referred to them. If you want some royal justice, these are the people you have to see.

The petitions, for something other than a royal writ, in the main, are of two sorts. In the one, petitioner asks the king to rule against himself. This is not as strange as it appears. The king has acted through his men, who may be overzealous, and the king will not lose face if he disclaims their depredations. Besides, petitioner in such cases is likely to be someone high in the social order. Typically, the royal officers have claimed escheat. They say that a vassal who held certain land directly of the king has died without heirs; hence the land must revert to the king as feudal overlord. Then petitioner appears and says it is not so: I myself am heir, a living heir. But Common Pleas, King's Bench, Exchequer—none of them can help me. Their writs do not run against the king.

It happens not infrequently. The king's men are likely to grab land any chance they get. Not likely they will incur the royal frown if they take too much rather than too little. But outraged heirs, we can assume, are for that reason too many to ignore, and some of them important. A regular procedure is developed: the Chancellor considers the petition, and if he recommends, the king sends the case to the Court of King's Bench for a trial by a jury. Escheat is a peculiarly feudal phenomenon, and these complaints die out along with feudalism.[1]

The second tapping of the reservoir of royal justice involves disputes not with the king, but between one subject and another. According to petitioner, the regular writs do not meet his crying need. The procedure is different from that of the established courts. The petition is the direct descendant of the old *querela*. It is called a "bill," like a petition addressed to Parliament. (The same word is, of course, still used for a legislative proposal.) The several governmental functions, as we have seen, are at this time not clearly differentiated. It is also called a "bill of complaint" or, later, simply "complaint."

---

[1]Escheat, though rare, still exists, and has not changed its name. When there are no heirs or will, the property goes to the state.

Here we have two branches. One we may call personal, the other institutional. In the one, the petitioner says the process of the courts is being abused or perverted. "He is poor," as Maitland puts it, "he is old, he is sick, his adversary is rich and powerful, will bribe or will intimidate jurors, or has by some trick or some accident acquired an advantage." Such cases are a large part of the Chancellor's work down through Tudor times, but in the seventeenth century they stop. They allow too much unfettered power to the Chancellor, and Parliament, finally supreme, will not permit it.

The other difficulty, the institutional, gives rise to Chancery's enduring jurisdiction. It is not that the remedies of the courts of law are being badly used, but rather that, though used at their best, they are simply inappropriate or inadequate. Perhaps there is none that suits some novel feature of the social structure. Or the closest writ is insufficient in the special circumstances, the variety of situations needing remedy having grown with the economy. Nothing in the Register will fit the case; or the kind of judgment the writ affords works poorly or not at all.

For the first hundred years of the common-law system, the Chancellor and his clerks have great freedom to design new writs or alter old ones. In the fourteenth century, as we have seen, this freedom encounters barriers. In part, they are set up by an adolescent Parliament, which, when barons hold the upper hand, resists extensions of royal power. In part, they represent a changing attitude on the part of the royal Justices. The courts of common law seem less eager to expand their jurisdiction. If the variant writ the clerks have issued seems too far out of line, the Justices will reject it. Perhaps the Justices feel overworked; business has got too good. Perhaps it is the gravity of precedent, a settling into familiar grooves. In any event, the easy entertainment of new writs slows down.

But the Chancellor, acting for the king, can if he chooses exert the underlying power. As time goes on, he chooses more and more. He may be genuinely concerned about petitioner's plight. Or he may wish to enlarge this wing of his office. Very likely both. Though arising from an institutional defect rather than a particular abuse, the petition here, like all *querelae*, is a highly personal entreaty. The bill is "couched in piteous terms." The king is begged to lend his aid, "for the love of God and in the way of Charity."

Until midway in the sixteenth century, the Chancellors are ecclesiastics; hence the church courts are the model. The Chancellor orders the person of whom complaint is made to appear before him, under pain—*sub poena*—of some punishment if he fails. The order is different from the common-law original writ, which states the gist of plaintiff's grievance. Defendant is merely told to show up, to answer the complaint. "Answer" means just that. Under oath, and sentence by sentence, defendant must stand and respond to each allegation of the bill.

It is an adversary procedure, like that in the courts of common law. But the Chancellor is a more active figure than the Justices of those courts. The Justice is essentially an umpire, though a princely one. He lets the parties draw the issues and the jury find the facts. He is bound by existing law (in theory always, and usually in practice). The Chancellor, in contrast, asks questions of the parties and finds the facts himself; there is no jury. He is not bound by fixed rules. The Chancellor will decide both what has happened and what to do about it. His disposition of the case follows conscience and good faith (in theory always, and like enough in practice).

If he decides in favor of petitioner, he will issue a "decree." It will forbid the defendant to do something he has been doing or is threatening to do. That is, the Chancellor will enjoin him. As the characteristic remedies of the courts of common law are judgment awarding seisin of land and the judgment for damages, the characteristic remedy of Chancery is injunction.

□ A fundamental difference in method between common law and equity is written into our federal Constitution and those of most of the states. The Seventh Amendment preserves the right of trial by jury "in suits at common law, where the value in controversy shall exceed twenty dollars." The draftsmen and those who voted to adopt the Bill of Rights meant common law in its narrow sense (as it is used in most of this chapter) as distinguished from what went on in Chancery. So our courts still need to know whether the issue raised is one that would in former days have been heard in one of the courts of common law, in which event either party can demand a jury, or in Chancery, in which event neither can demand a jury. With modern rules permitting joinder of various claims, occasionally a jury will be called to try one part of a case while the judge himself will try another.

The disregard of the jury was not that firm at the start; now and then the Chancellor would send a question to a court of law for a trial by jury. When that practice stopped, the Chancellor sometimes impaneled a jury himself, although he did not feel bound by its verdict; the present-day judge, dealing with a suit for equitable relief, may do the same, and, again the same, this jury's verdict is advisory, not binding.

As early as the fourteenth century, people began to speak of a Court of Chancery, apart from the rest of Chancery. Through that century and most of the next, however, the Chancellor was still acting for the King-in-Council, here as elsewhere. He acted with more and more autonomy, though, and by the year 1500 (a date convenient for historians, and not without good reason) the autonomy was complete. For his judicial work, the Chancellor had a regular staff of assistants, and he issued decrees in his own name, not the king's. By the end of the sixteenth century, Chancery was big business, and by the early seventeenth century there were more than fifteen hundred suits a year.

"Chancery" and "Equity" as the name of the court will in later years be fairly interchangeable. "Equity" will also denote the power the court wields and the body of substantive rules it eventually constructs.

As ever, improvised responses to specific occasions are gradually reined in. Procedures are fixed and principles stated. In the full development of equity, its decree will take various forms: an order to carry out an agreement, as distinguished from damages for its breach, where the subject is something deemed unique, sale of land especially ("specific performance"); the nullification or rewriting of a document which, because of fraud or mistake, does not say what the parties meant to say ("rescission," which cancels it, or "reformation," which alters it); a command to a fiduciary to tell exactly what he has done with his beneficiary's property ("accounting"); tolerance toward the delinquent mortgagor, enforced against the mortgagee ("equity of redemption"); the marshaling of the assets of an insolvent and their distribution to creditors ("equity receivership"); and order to a defendant to act rather than refrain from acting ("mandatory injunction").

The "mandatory injunction" is addressed to situations that cannot respond to negative decree. Forced inaction will not remedy the situation; defendant must be ordered to do something. Yet the injunction in the beginning was only a restraint, and so the Chancellor, until recently, felt obliged to put his decree in the traditional negative form. Hence the mandatory injunction ordered the defendant not to allow the continuance of a state of affairs he had created. An owner of waterfront property builds a wall across the beach down to the low water mark. He likes to think of the beach as his and is much disturbed by people walking by. It is not his, however. From mean high tide on down, the beach is public property. The court will enjoin the maintenance of the wall. In plainer language, the court is telling defendant to get busy and tear his wall apart. While this form of decree is still used, courts no longer hesitate to issue direct affirmative orders.

But sometimes an affirmative order will not work and a negative decree may accomplish a positive result. It happens with employment contracts. It is used not in the ordinary kind of employment, but only when the services are "unique"— that is, when a replacement will not do. Take a famous musician (classical or pop) or a famous athlete (any sport will do), a star whose appearance can be expected to draw fans to the concert hall or the ball park. If the performer, dishonoring his contract, refuses to perform, it is hard to say how many tickets will go unsold; damages are too "speculative" to support a judgment at law. So equity intervenes. But how? It cannot order the delinquent to do his job. There is an uncomfortable suggestion of involuntary servitude, even though this servitude began as voluntary and the contract will make the slave a millionaire. So equity will not command him to carry out his contract, but it will enjoin him from singing a note or swinging a bat for any employer other than the one he signed with.

☐ After a judgment in a court of law, the losing defendant had to pay the money or get off the land or return the goods. If he refused or failed, the sheriff swung into action (or crept, depending on the sheriff) armed with a "final writ" that gave him his instructions. Throw defendant off the land, distrain defendant's chattels and turn them into money that will satisfy the judgment, take the thing replevied and deliver it to plaintiff. Chancery enforced its decrees in a different way: the losing defendant must obey the Chancellor's order or go to jail. He can stay there and rot until he is ready to comply. He keeps the keys to the jail in his pocket, as the maxim has it, but he cannot draw them out until he yields.

It is said the common-law judgment operates *in rem*, it has to do with things, while the Chancery decree is *in personam*, it goes against the person. The force of the decree is aimed straight at defendant rather than his land or goods. As usual in the law, the distinction is not tidy. When the sheriff comes round with his judgment at law, the person will feel a twinge or two. And a decree of equity can for practical purposes determine ownership of land—that is, deal with the thing. But whatever the overlap may be, equity's favorite weapon, jailing for contempt, is personal *par excellence*.

Equity's ultimate place was nicely described by the nineteenth-century American Justice Story, writing at a time when Chancery courts were still separate. Schematic presentations of the law—which lawyers like so much, and laymen even more—are or should be suspect. The jurisdiction of equity, he wrote, has three parts: exclusive, concurrent, and auxiliary. Take prominent examples. As to trusts, equity has exclusive jurisdiction. Then concurrent: some kinds of fraud, not all, are covered by the common-law action of deceit; for others relief in equity is needed. Finally auxiliary, as when a party in an action at law goes to Chancery with a bill of discovery to find out what his opponent will rely on at trial. All three, since Story wrote, have been folded into our unified courts, but these remedies have only sloughed off their Chancery skin; they have kept their equitable tissue.

☐ I mentioned a maxim. Equity has a number of them. Its developed doctrines—the abstractions of principle from decided cases—often took the form of a statement not at all abstract. There is much imagery in equity. "He who seeks equity must come with clean hands." That is, defendant may have been behaving badly, but if plaintiff in their dealings has himself been tricky or overreaching, Chancery will ignore them both. "Equity will not aid those who slumber on their rights." Conversely, "Equity aids the vigilant." The specific statutes of limitation that apply to actions at law do not apply in Chancery. The Chancellors, however, impose their own demands for promptness, demands characteristically flexible and adjusted to circumstance. If plaintiff has let the state of affairs to which he objects go on too long, especially if others have been led into some action or inaction on the assumption it would continue, the Chancellor refuses to hear the complaint, though plaintiff would have won if he had brought suit promptly. "Equity will not concern itself with trifles." (Or sometimes, "Equity will not stoop to pick up pins.") Plaintiff may be altogether right and defendant altogether wrong, but the whole thing involves two shillings; don't ask the Chancellor to bother. "Equity regards as done that which ought to be done." Documents containing mistakes are ordered changed to reflect the parties' real intention; the law courts generally followed the letter of the instrument. "Equity delights to do justice, and not by halves." (Also, somewhat narrower in scope, "Equity abhors a multiplicity of suits.") Call all who have claims in the subject matter into Chancery and avoid future litigation. The old law courts heard two parties only, plaintiff and defendant, even though the situation was one where others had obvious interests and would probably start another litigation later. "Equity suffers no wrong to be without a remedy." No matter there is no precedent; if in good conscience plaintiff ought to have some help, the Chancellor will help him. This last is a bit misleading, at least from the time that equity became a system, but it is indicative. The Chancellors felt less bound by precedent than the judges at common law, and in really outrageous cases they were always willing to act. (That is, if they were proper honest Chancellors.)

These maxims are all alive today, though their expression has lost color. They are less fixed rules than guides to judgment, in cases where the remedy sought is one the Chancellors used to give.

☐ The main source of Chancery's jurisdiction, we have seen, was the grievous situation in which the courts of law refused to act because nothing in the Register of Writs applied. There were also cases in which injustice ran the other way: the law courts, tracing their geometric patterns, would render a judgment for plaintiff which in fairness they ought not to. Now it is defendant-at-law who goes to Chancery, where he becomes complainant. The injunction forbids the defendant in Chancery, who was the plaintiff in the court of law, to carry on his case at law. Here, ineluctably, there is high and mighty conflict. The Chancellor is much too polite to enjoin their Honors: he never says they must bow to his decree. But by stopping a party to the action he is actually stopping judges; the courts of common law rely on parties' energies for their motive power.

In its beginning, equity was what its name implies, and to a considerable extent it still is: "justice" as opposed to "law," a reach for fairness in the particular case as distinguished from enforcement of general rules. In other chapters I have pointed out the danger to real justice that inheres in both these concepts: the hurt done by the sharp corners of an angular legal structure, the hospitality to tyranny that lies in easy disregard of rules. Both ideas are needed—adherence to abstractions that override the inclinations (bad or good) of those who make decisions, attention to the requirements of special situations. From time to time, one or the other becomes too prominent. Then there is clamor for its counterpart.

In the reign of Henry II, system is required, and he provides it. In the fourteenth and fifteenth centuries, that system becomes both crotchety and venal. The common law is sometimes unrealistic even when its courts are honest, and all too often they are not honest. They quail before power, and they trade judgments for money. It is a time of "livery," when great lords employ armies of retainers—sometimes thousands—and tell the judges how to judge. It is also a time when sheriffs, for a few shillings, will supply juries made to order, while decent jurors are intimidated by important men who come to court and make their wishes known. Chancery offers rescue. The Chancellors are relatively honest, and the royal power is greater even than the power of great lords.

Then, in time, the balance swings the other way. The monarch rather than the aristocracy becomes the enemy of freedom, and the discretion of the Chancellor is easily abused. John Selden, the seventeenth century scholar-rebel, makes his famous statement: "Equity is a roguish thing. For law we have a measure, know what to trust to: Equity is according to the conscience of the Chancellor, and as that is larger or narrower, so is Equity." It is as though the standard of measure called the "foot," says Selden, were not a fixed length, but rather the Chancellor's foot, which will vary according to who happens to fill the office. "The Chancellor's foot" becomes the symbol of the unreliability of equity.

NOTES

*From *The Law of the Land: The Evolution of our Legal System* (New York: Simon & Schuster, 1980), pp. 272–81. Reprinted with permission.

FOR DISCUSSION

1. What is an injunction? How were injunctions traditionally worded?
2. What does the maxim that equity acts *in personam* rather than *in rem* tell us about the nature of equitable and legal remedies?
3. Why won't equity order a person to perform an employment contract? What alternative does equity offer?
4. What is meant by the equitable maxim that a person who disobeys an equitable decree "keeps the keys to the jail in his pocket"?
5. Why did equity express itself in maxims rather than rules?
6. What are some of the dangers that can be associated with using "fairness" or "justice" to decide matters on a case by case basis instead of using general rules? What is the meaning of the image of "the Chancellor's foot"?

The following case presents a classic situation for equitable relief: A woman whose claim against the insolvent estate of her deceased ex-husband is worthless turns to equity for help in recovering money to which she is entitled. This case proceeds according to the basic principles of equity to do justice where the law provides no effective remedy. In doing so, it disrupts the otherwise legally valid arrangements made by the now deceased husband to do what he should have done in the first place. You should note in particular the court's use of equitable maxims to guide its decision.

CASE **Mary Simonds v. Reva B. Simonds**
Individually and as Executrix of Frederick L. Simonds, Deceased
Court of Appeals of New York (1978)
45 N.Y.2d 233, 408 N.Y.S.2d 359, 380 N.E.2d 189

OPINION OF THE COURT

BREITEL, Chief Judge.   Plaintiff Mary Simonds, decedent's first wife, seeks to impose a constructive trust on proceeds of insurance policies on decedent's life. The proceeds had been paid to the named beneficiaries, Reva Simonds, decedent's second wife, and their daughter Gayle.

Plaintiff, however, asserts as superior an equitable interest arising out of a provision in her separation agreement with decedent. Special Term granted partial summary judgment and impressed a constructive trust to the extent of $7,000 plus interest against proceeds of a policy naming the second wife as beneficiary, and the Appellate Division affirmed. Defendant Reva Simonds, the second wife, appeals.

The separation agreement required the husband to maintain in effect, with the wife as beneficiary to the extent of $7,000, existing life insurance policies or, if the policies were to be canceled or to lapse, insurance policies of equal value. The issue is whether that provision entitles the first wife to impress a constructive trust on proceeds of insurance policies subsequently issued, despite the husband's failure to name her as the beneficiary on any substitute policies once the original insurance policies had lapsed.

There should be an affirmance. The separation agreement vested in the first wife an equitable right in the then existing policies. Decedent's substitution of policies could not deprive the first wife of her equitable interest, which was then transferred to the new policies. Since the proceeds of the substituted policies have been paid to decedent's second wife, whose interest in the policies is subordinate to plaintiff's, a constructive trust may be imposed.

On March 6, 1960, decedent Frederick Simonds and his wife of fourteen years, plaintiff Mary Simonds, entered into a separation agreement which, on March 31, 1960, was incorporated into an Illinois divorce decree granted to plaintiff on grounds of desertion. The agreement provided, somewhat inartfully: "The husband agrees that he will keep all of the policies of Insurance now in full force and effect on his life. Said policies now being in the sum of $21,000.00 and the Husband further agrees that the Wife shall be the beneficiary of said policies in an amount not less than $7,000.00 and the Husband further agrees that he shall pay any and all premiums necessary to maintain such policies of Insurance and if for any reason any of them now existing the policies shall be cancelled or be caused to lapse. He shall procure additional insurance in an amount equal to the face value of the policies having been cancelled or caused to lapse." Thus, the husband was to maintain, somehow, at least $7,000 of life insurance for the benefit of his first wife as a named beneficiary.

On May 26, 1960, less than two months after the divorce, decedent husband married defendant Reva Simonds. Defendant Gayle Simonds was born to the couple shortly thereafter.

Sometime after the separation agreement was signed, the then existing insurance policies were apparently canceled or permitted to lapse. It does not appear from the record why, how, or when this happened, but the policies were not extant at the time of decedent husband's death on August 1, 1971. In the interim, however, decedent has acquired three other life insurance policies, totaling over $55,000, none of which named plaintiff as a beneficiary. At his death, decedent had one policy in the amount of $16,138.83, originally issued in 1962 by Metropolitan Life Insurance Company, a second policy for $34,000 issued in 1967 through decedent's employer by Travelers Insurance Company, and a third policy for $5,566 issued in 1962 by the Equitable Life Assurance Society of Iowa. The first two policies named Reva Simonds, decedent's second wife, as beneficiary, and the third policy named their daughter. Hence, at the time of decedent's death he had continuously violated the separation agreement by maintaining no life insurance naming the first wife as a beneficiary.

The first wife, on March 11, 1972, brought an action against the second wife for conversion of $7,000 and to recover $13,600 in back alimony payments. This action was dismissed, essentially on the ground that the causes of action alleged could properly be brought only against decedent's estate, not against the second wife. The estate, however, is insolvent.

Subsequently, the first wife brought this action against both the second wife and the daughter seeking to impress a constructive trust on the insurance proceeds to the extent of $7,000. A second cause of action, dealing with alimony arrears, is not involved on this appeal. Special Term granted partial summary judgment to the first wife and imposed a constructive trust on the proceeds in the hands of the second wife. A unanimous Appellate Division affirmed in a thoughtful and scholarly opinion by Mr. Justice Richard D. Simons.

There is no question that decedent breached his obligation to maintain life insurance with his first wife as beneficiary. Consequently, the first wife would of course be entitled to maintain an action for breach against the estate. The estate's insolvency, however, would make such an action fruitless. Thus, the controversy revolves around the plaintiff's right, in equity, to recover $7,000 of the insurance proceeds.

Born out of the extreme rigidity of the early common law, equity in its origins drew heavily on Roman law, where equitable motions had long been accepted (see 1 Pomeroy, Equity Jurisprudence [5th ed.], §§2–29). "Its great underlying principles, which are the constant sources, the never-failing roots, of its particular rules, are unquestionably principles of right, justice, and morality, so far as the same can become the elements of a positive human jurisprudence" (*id.*, §67, at p. 90). Law without principle is not law; law without justice is of limited value. Since adherence to principles of "law" does not invariably produce justice, equity is necessary. Equity arose to soften the impact of legal formalisms; to evolve formalisms narrowing the broad scope of equity is to defeat its essential purpose.

Whatever the legal rights between the insurer and insured, the separation agreement vested in the first wife an equitable interest in the insurance policies then in force. An agreement for sufficient consideration, including a separation agreement, to maintain a claimant as a beneficiary of a life insurance policy vests in the claimant an equitable interest in the policies designated. This interest is superior to that of a named beneficiary who has given no consideration, notwithstanding policy provisions permitting the insured to change the designated beneficiary freely.

This is not to say that an insurance company may not rely on the insured's designation of a beneficiary. None of this opinion bears on the rights or responsibilities of the insurer in law or in equity.

Obviously, the policies now at issue are not the same policies in existence at the time of the separation agreement. But it has been held that mere substitution of policies, or even substitution of insurance companies, does not defeat the equitable interest of one who has given sufficient consideration for a promise to be maintained as beneficiary under an insurance policy. The persistence of the promisee's equitable interest is all the more evident where the agreement expressly provides for a change in policies, and in effect provides further that the promisee's right shall attach to the new policies.

For a certainty, the first wife's equitable interest would be easier to trace if the new policies were quid pro quo replacements for the original policies. The record does not reveal whether this was so. But inability to trace plaintiff's equitable rights precisely should not require that they not be recognized, much as in the instance of damages difficult to prove. The separation agreement provides nexus between plaintiff's rights and the later acquired policies. The later policies were expressly contemplated by the parties, and it was agreed that plaintiff would have an interest in them. No reason in equity appears for denying plaintiff that interest, so long as no one who has given value for the policies or otherwise suffered a detriment is involved. The second wife's innocence does not offset the wrong by the now deceased husband.

The conclusion is an application of the general rule that equity regards as done that which should have been done (2 Pomeroy, Equity Jurisprudence [5th ed.], §364; see, e.g., *Wallace* v. *First Trust Co. of Albany*, 251 App. Div. 253, 256, 295 N.Y.S. 769, 771). Thus, if an insured, upon lapse or cancellation of insurance, followed by replacement with new insurance, has a contractual obligation to designate a particular person as beneficiary, equity will consider the obligee as a beneficiary.

In this case, then, the first wife's interest in the original policies extended as well to the later acquired policies. The husband, upon lapse or cancellation of the earlier policies, had by virtue of the separation agreement an obligation to name her as beneficiary on the later policies, an obligation enforceable in equity despite the husband's failure to comply with the terms of the separation agreement. Due to the husband's failure to do what he should have done, the first wife acquired not only a right at law to sue his estate for breach of contract, a right now worthless, but also an equitable right in the policies, a right which, upon the husband's death, attached to the proceeds (cf. *Salinas* v. *Salinas*, 187 Misc. 509, 515, 62 N.Y.S.2d 385, 390; *McDonald* v. *Conservative Life Ins. Co.*, 292 Mich. 182, 186-188, 290 N.W. 372).

And, since the first wife was entitled to $7,000 of the proceeds at the time of the husband's death, she is no less entitled because the proceeds have already been converted by being paid, erroneously, to the named beneficiaries (see *Lengel* v. *Lengel*, 86 Misc.2d 460, 465-466, 382 N.Y.S.2d 678, 681-682). Her remedy is the imposition of a constructive trust.

In the words of Judge Cardozo, "[a] constructive trust is the formula through which the conscience of equity finds expression. When property has been acquired in such circumstances that the holder of the legal title may not in good conscience retain the beneficial interest, equity converts him into a trustee" (*Beatty* v. *Guggenheim Exploration Co.*, 225 N.Y. 380, 386, 122 N.E. 378, 380). Thus, a constructive trust is an equitable remedy. It is perhaps more different from an express trust than it is similar (5 Scott, Trusts [3d ed.], §461). As put so well by Scott and restated at the Appellate Division, "[the constructive trustee] is not compelled to convey the property because he is a constructive trustee; it is because he can be compelled to convey the property that he is a constructive trustee" (*id.*, §462, at p. 3413).

More precise definitions of a constructive trust have been termed inadequate because of the failure to recognize the broad scope of constructive trust doctrine. As another leading scholar has said of constructive trusts, "[t]he Court does not restrict itself by describing all the specific forms of inequitable holding which will move it to grant relief, but rather reserves freedom to apply this remedy to whatever knavery human ingenuity can invent" (Bogert, Trusts and Trustees [2d ed. rev., 1978], §471, at p. 29).

Four factors were posited in *Sharp* v. *Kosmalski*, 40 N.Y.2d 119, 121, 386 N.Y.S.2d 72, 74, 351 N.E.2d 721, 722. Although the factors are useful in many cases constructive trust doctrine is not rigidly limited. For a single example, one who wrongfully prevents a testator from executing a new will eliminating him as beneficiary will be held as a constructive trustee even in the absence of a confidential or fiduciary relation, a promise by the "trustee," and a transfer in reliance by the testator (see, e.g., *Latham* v. *Father Divine*, 299 N.Y. 22, 26-27, 85 N.E.2d 168, 169–170). As then Judge Desmond said in response to the argument that a breach of promise to the testator was necessary for imposition of a constructive trust (at p. 27, 85 N.E.2d at p. 170), "[a] constructive trust will be erected whenever necessary to satisfy the demands of justice.... [I]ts applicability is only limited by the inventiveness of men who find new ways to enrich themselves unjustly by grasping what should not belong to them."

It so happens, as an added argument, if it were necessary, that the four factors enumerated in *Sharp* v. *Kosmalski* are perceptible in this case: a promise, a transfer in reliance on the promise, the fiduciary relation between decedent and his first wife, and the "unjust enrichment" of the second wife. Because decedent and plaintiff were husband and wife, there is a duty of fairness in financial matters extending even past the contemplated separation of the spouses. Hence, a separation agreement based on one party's misrepresentation of financial condition is voidable. A similar rule applies in Illinois, where the instant separation agreement was made. Thus, at the time of the separation agreement, decedent and plaintiff remained in a confidential or fiduciary relationship.

It is agreed that the purpose of the constructive trust is prevention of unjust enrichment (*Sharp* v. *Kosmalski*, 40 N.Y.2d 119, 123, 386 N.Y.S.2d 72, 76, 351 N.E.2d 721, 24, *supra*; Restatement, Restitution, §160; 5 Scott, Trusts [3d ed.], §462.2).

Unjust enrichment, however, does not require the performance of any wrongful act by the one enriched. Innocent parties may frequently be unjustly enriched. What is required, generally, is that a party hold property "under such circumstances that in equity and good conscience he ought not to retain it"(*Miller* v. *Schloss*, 218 N.Y. 400, 407, 113 N.E. 337, 339). A bona fide purchaser of property upon which a constructive trust would otherwise be imposed takes free of the constructive trust, but a gratuitous donee, however innocent, does not.

The unjust enrichment in this case is manifest. At a time when decedent was, certainly, anxious to remarry, he entered into a separation agreement with his wife of 14 years. As part of the agreement, he promised to maintain $7,000 in life insurance with the first wife as beneficiary. Later he broke his promise and died with insurance policies naming only the second wife and daughter as beneficiaries. They have collected the proceeds, amounting to more than $55,000, while the first wife has collected nothing. Had the husband kept his promise, the beneficiaries would have collected $7,000 less in proceeds. To that extent, the beneficiaries have been unjustly enriched, and the proceeds should be subjected to a constructive trust.

The issues in this case should not generate significant controversy. The action is in equity, and the equities are clear. True, some courts have decided the issues differently. Those cases, however, rely heavily on formalisms and too little on basic equitable principles, long established in Anglo-American law and in this State and especially relevant when family transactions are involved. "A court of equity in decreeing a constructive trust is bound by no unyielding formula. The equity of the transaction must shape the measure of relief" (*Beatty* v. *Guggenheim Exploration Co.*, 225 N.Y. 380, 389, 122 N.E. 378, 381 [Cardozo, J.], *supra*).

Accordingly, the order of the Appellate Division should be affirmed, with costs.

FOR DISCUSSION

1. How does the court apply in this case the equitable maxim "Equity regards as done that which should have been done"?
2. What is a constructive trust, and what is it supposed to accomplish?
3. Why does a constructive trust express the conscience of equity?
4. What is unjust enrichment? If the second wife appears to be an innocent third party, how can she be unjustly enriched?
5. Why is decedent's first wife entitled to $7000 of the insurance proceeds? Do you think the court arrives at a fair outcome?
6. How does the equitable maxim "Equity regards substance and intent rather than form" apply to the fact that decedent specifically named his second wife and daughter as the sole beneficiaries of his insurance policies in violation of the separation agreement?

Equity Jurisdiction

Because equity is considered an extraordinary proceeding, it is left to the court's discretion to determine whether to exercise jurisdiction over a matter. One of the most famous of the equitable maxims is "Equity follows the law," and that maxim means, among other things, that equity may only intervene in a matter when the petitioner has no adequate remedy available at law. That may mean that the petitioner has a legally recognized right, but the law does not offer an effective means to enforce it. It can also mean, as was true in *Simonds* v. *Simonds*, that the petitioner has a legally enforceable right, but circumstances have made it useless. What good is a claim for damages against an estate that is insolvent?

Another possibility is that the remedy of damages, although available, is inadequate in the particular situation. This idea underlies the special equitable remedy of specific performance of a contract. In some situations people have contracted about property that is unique and that cannot be adequately replaced by mere money damages. This was first used with respect to agricultural land, which was considered to be unique, but has been extended to other forms of "unique" property as well. One thing that the court may no longer do in deciding whether to exercise its equitable jurisdiction is to create new rights, even though at one time equity freely did just that, despite the maxim that "Equity follows the law." One of the concessions that led to a reconciliation of law and equity was that the Court of Equity would no longer expand the list of rights that it would help to enforce but would restrict itself to situations in which an already existing right lacked an adequate legal remedy. Today, therefore, decisions about whether to exercise equitable jurisdiction are made according to careful analysis of already existing legal rights and remedies to determine whether the case is an appropriate one for equitable intervention. The judge must consider the interests of the competing parties as well as the demands of the legal system and the interests of the public in deciding whether to exercise jurisdiction.

The following case illustrates a situation in which equity, exercising its discretion, refuses to take jurisdiction over a matter because the petitioner has an adequate legal remedy.

CASE

Sharon Gerety v. J. Leo Poitras
Supreme Court of Vermont (1966)
224 A.2d 919

KEYSER, Justice.   The defendant appealed from the order of the chancery court denying his motion to dismiss plaintiff's petition for specific performance. The appeal is by permission of the court below before final decree under 12 V.S.A. §2386.

Since the motion to dismiss attacks the sufficiency of the petition, it is in the nature of a demurrer and consideration of the motion depends entirely upon the facts stated in the petition.

On January 24, 1964, the plaintiff entered into a written agreement with the defendant to purchase a ranch home owned by said defendant located on George Street in Montpelier, Vermont. The sale was consummated in accordance with the agreement on February 6, 1964.

The agreement contained the following provision: "The seller also agrees that if any major water problem should arise regarding the spring under the cellar floor he would do what is necessary to make the cellar useable for general use. This agreement is for two years from date of purchase."

On or about October 14, 1964, the plaintiff notified the defendant that a major water problem had arisen as the result of the spring under the cellar floor of her home. The plaintiff also sent the defendant a copy of a letter from a contractor whom she had engaged to examine the premises. In his letter the contractor set forth in detail what was necessary to be done to make the cellar usable for general uses. The defendant has refused to make the repairs plaintiff claims are necessary.

The plaintiff alleged she is without an adequate remedy at law and asked the court to order specific performance of the agreement in question. Defendant's motion to dismiss challenges this allegation and claims plaintiff has an adequate remedy for damages.

The defendant in his brief also argues that the petition should be dismissed because a court of equity will not undertake to enforce specifically a contract for construction or repair. This point was not raised by defendant's motion to dismiss and is not for consideration here.

Where the inadequacy of damages is great, and the difficulties not extreme, specific performance will be granted and the tendency in modern times has been increasingly to grant relief, where under the particular circumstances of the case damages are not an adequate remedy. 5 Williston on Contracts, Rev.Ed., §1423. Of course, in a particular case, the remedy at law may be adequate and specific performance will be denied for that reason.

Since the plaintiff seeks the special equitable remedy of specific performance, she has the burden to allege and demonstrate in the complaint why money damages will not furnish an adequate remedy.

Equity will not afford relief where there is a plain, adequate, and complete remedy at law. *Union Pac. R. Co.* v. *Board of Com'rs of Weld County*, 247 U.S. 282, 38 S.Ct. 510, 62 L.Ed. 1110, 1117. And if the complainant does have such remedy, and the main cause of action is of a legal nature, equity has no jurisdiction. *United States* v. *Bitter Root Development Co.*, 200 U.S. 451, 26 S.Ct. 318, 50 L.Ed. 550, 560. To the same effect, *Schoenthal* v. *Irving Trust Company*, 287 U.S. 9, 53 S.Ct. 50, 77 L.Ed. 185, 188.

This is the test according to the great weight of authority including this jurisdiction. 19 Am.Jur., Equity, §101; *Smith* v. *Pettingill*, 15 Vt. 82, 40 Am.Dec. 667; *Smith* v. *Thibault*, 122 Vt. 256, 259, 168 A.2d 729.

In *Smith* v. *Thibault,* 122 Vt. 256, 259, 168 A.2d 729, 731, the pleadings presented only a case of breach of contract, nothing more. We held it was error for the court below to transfer the case to equity, saying: "(E)quity affords relief where the law does not furnish a remedy. Ordinarily, if the law affords a remedy that is adequate, a case may not be made the basis of a suit in equity."

The record shows no peculiar circumstances exist in the case at bar. It is clear from the facts alleged in the petition that at most only a breach of contract is involved. The plaintiff's main cause of action is of a legal nature and her available remedy is in a court of law for the recovery of damages. The existence of this situation removes any doubt or uncertainty that the plaintiff does not have a plain, adequate, and complete remedy. The ruling of the court below was error.

The order denying defendant's motion to dismiss is reversed; plaintiff's petition is dismissed.

FOR DISCUSSION

1. According to the court, what considerations determine whether the equitable remedy of specific performance will be granted?
2. What is plaintiff's adequate legal remedy?
3. Is there any good reason why defendant should personally undertake to make the repairs to the cellar instead of reimbursing plaintiff for the cost of repairs?
4. How did the court exercise its discretion in this case and what factors guided its decision?
5. Do you think the outcome is fair? Explain.

In the next case, a California appeals court considers whether it was appropriate to grant the plaintiff equitable relief in the particular circumstances of the case. You should pay particular attention to the court's reasoning process concerning whether an adequate legal remedy was available to the plaintiff.

CASE   Bernard Halperin v. Clarence A. Raville et al.
                              (California Court of Appeal (1986)
                              176 Cal.App.3d 765, 222 Cal.Rptr. 350

STONE, Presiding Justice.   The issue for resolution on appeal is whether the evidence
was sufficient to support the trial court's decision that appellant/defendant (son) received
the benefit of monies loaned to appellant's father (father) by respondent/plaintiff (plaintiff) and is therefore obligated, along with father, to repay plaintiff. Civ.Code, §3521.[2]
Applying the usual standards of appellate review, we conclude there was sufficient evidence
permitting application of this rule in equity. Accordingly, the judgment below is affirmed.

    Facts   The facts are stated in the light most favorable to the judgment. Plaintiff moved
to California from New York after retiring from the United States Postal Service in 1971. In
California, plaintiff worked part-time as a typist for Jay Vasquez who owned a small financial
consulting business. In 1979, Mr. Vasquez introduced plaintiff to father and son at Caraville
Arms, the family gun manufacturing business, explaining to plaintiff before the meeting that
father was in dire financial circumstances and needed a loan.
    Plaintiff and father soon developed a close friendship. They often went gambling together
at the horse races and plaintiff frequented Caraville Arms on a regular basis. Several months after
their introduction and for the next several years, plaintiff provided money to father at varying
intervals and for varying amounts of $250 to $5,000. Father would complain to plaintiff that he
needed to borrow money or he would go bankrupt. Plaintiff wanted to help out because he
admired father's skill as a craftsman and they were friends. Later, plaintiff advanced money to
father for fear that the business would collapse and he would lose the money he had already
loaned father. Plaintiff's continuous loans consisted solely of his life savings.
    On one occasion, father told plaintiff he needed $20,000 to pay off a debt on a piece of
machinery at Caraville Arms. This request came after son had taken an active role in helping
plaintiff sell plaintiff's AT&T stock for $48,000. Son had contacted the stockbroker on plaintiff's
behalf and had gone with plaintiff to meet with the stockbroker for the first time. Son even forged
plaintiff's deceased mother's signature on the stock in order to assist plaintiff in selling them.
The stockbroker testified that both plaintiff and son seemed anxious to get the highest possible
price for the stock. Son had identified himself to the stockbroker as the owner of Caraville Arms
and stated that plaintiff was interested in investing capital in the company. On another occasion,
son assisted plaintiff in completing the paperwork to sell plaintiff's oil lease. Plaintiff received
$13,000 from this sale of which $10,000 was loaned to father for business purposes.
    Plaintiff asked for all the money back he had loaned father after plaintiff was rebuffed
by son one day. Father refused.
    Father testified he is the sole owner of Caraville Arms. Son "helps out" at Caraville
Arms and father pays him as a machinist and gunsmith, but son is not a company employee.
Son had his own business next door to father's.
    Son stated he has worked for father since 1966. He described his status with Caraville
Arms as that of a subcontractor. When testifying, son always referred to Caraville Arms as
"our" (meaning father and son) company. At one point, son identified it as a "father/son
business." All monetary transactions between plaintiff and father were referred to by son as
transactions between plaintiff and "us." Son further stated that Caraville Arms uses ma-

    [2]Section 3521, part of a number of equitable maxims contained in the Civil Code, reads: "He who takes the
benefit must bear the burden."

chinery and equipment purchased by son. Son had also loaned father money from son's business on a monthly basis to keep Caraville Arms solvent. Eventually, son's company assets were sold to pay the debts of Caraville Arms.

A past employee of Caraville Arms testified that the company was father's business but that son "was in there, working with father" and father and son "contributed equally in Caraville Arms." He had worked with son in making gun parts. He denied son was an owner of Caraville Arms.

Proceedings Plaintiff's complaint against father and son and Caraville Arms for breach of contract, common counts[3], and fraud, was filed in 1983. The complaint alleged that Caraville Arms was a corporation, partnership or other form of business entity. It further stated that, pursuant to an oral agreement, plaintiff loaned money to the defendants in the amount of $80,000 which the defendants refused to repay. Father and son filed a joint answer. They denied the allegations and raised the defense that the funds provided by plaintiff were a gift. The answer admitted that Caraville Arms was a partnership. It also referred to the company as a "family operation."

After a court trial, judgment was entered against father and son in the amount of $78,315.45. The court issued a statement of decision which declared that, as to the issue of whether the monies father received from plaintiff were a gift or a loan, logic dictated that a person "does not tender life savings to any individual without anticipation of said funds being returned." The statement contained a list of findings pertinent to this issue and findings supporting the court's conclusions that son was unjustly enriched by the transactions between father and plaintiff and therefore was individually liable to plaintiff. Civ.Code §3521.

Only son appeals the judgment. He attacks the judgment on the ground that the findings relating to his involvement in the matter were without evidentiary support in the record. Son does not dispute the amount of judgment or the conclusion that the monies provided by plaintiff constituted a loan.

Discussion

Without reviewing the sufficiency of every finding challenged by son, we note son's primary contention that there was no factual basis for concluding he was unjustly enriched by plaintiff's loans because there was no evidence showing son had an ownership interest in Caraville Arms. Plaintiff claims the judgment against son is amply sustained by evidence of son's partnership with father in Caraville Arms and son's subsequent liability as a partner for the company's debts.

In urging the court to adopt his partnership theory, plaintiff tells this court that we can adopt any legal theory applicable to support the judgment and not necessarily the one used by the lower court. However, because we agree with son that no evidence was presented below of son's legal interest in Caraville Arms, the only possible theory of law applicable to the case is the equitable one adopted by the trial court.

Therefore, both plaintiff and son are misguided in approaching the issues on appeal. The question for review is not whether son was a joint-owner or partner in Caraville Arms, but whether he benefited from plaintiff's monetary assistance to that company and so became liable to plaintiff under equitable principles. According to traditional appellate review

[3]This refers to an equitable action for recovery of money on the basis of an implied contract or unjust enrichment. Plaintiff is claiming that defendant should return money that he should not in good conscience and justice be allowed to keep.

standards, we must look at the evidence supporting the judgment and disregard contrary evidence, resolving all conflicts in favor of the prevailing party.

Son testified Caraville Arms was a "father/son business." He also referred to it as "our" business. Son further stated that he continuously transferred funds from his separate company to Caraville Arms to keep the latter business solvent, and eventually sold his company to accomplish this objective. The inference that Caraville Arms had the utmost personal significance to son was even further strengthened by evidence of son's active participation in the company's affairs, including his daily employment there and his aggressive efforts to secure business funds from plaintiff through the sale of plaintiff's stock and oil lease.

We point out initially that it was entirely proper for the trial court to apply the equitable maxim contained in Civil Code section 3521 to this case. Code of Civil Procedure section 187 provides that a court with jurisdiction over a matter is given all the means necessary to carry out its jurisdiction and that "any suitable process or mode of proceeding" may be employed to effectuate it. "The business of the courts is to administer justice as nearly as may be in accordance with fixed rules of law and procedure, aided wherever and whenever proper and necessary by established and governing principles which relate to equity jurisprudence." *Estate of Kline* (1934) 138 Cal.App.514,520,32 P.2d 677.

In addition, the term "remedy" signifies the judicial means for enforcing a cause of action or redressing a wrong. 3 Witkin, Cal. Procedure (3d ed. 1985) Actions, §2, p. 34 citing Civ. Code, §3523 declaring that "[f]or every wrong there is a remedy." "[A] remedy may be entirely created by judicial decision where statutory procedure for the enforcement of a right is lacking." *Id.*, §3, p. 34.

Section 3521 requires a reasonable interpretation. It is readily apparent that the trial court was reasonably justified in concluding that, due to son's personal relationship to Caraville Arms, son benefitted from plaintiff's loans. No person can be permitted to adopt that part of an entire transaction which is beneficial to him/her, and then reject its burdens.

Consequently, a showing that a person had the use and benefit of money raises the obligation to pay for the value received. *Brown v. Brown* (1930), 104 Cal.App. 480, 489, 285 P.2d 1086. Moreover, where several people may be liable to a plaintiff on the same claim, there is only one right and no inconsistency in seeking its enforcement against all of them. 3 Witkin, Cal. Procedure (3d ed. 1985) Actions, §146, p. 176. "'A party may pursue any number of consistent and concurrent remedies against different persons, until he obtains satisfaction from some of them'; ..." *Ibid.*

Certainly, inferences can be drawn that son was a partner in Caraville Arms because of his contribution in time, loans and equipment. Indeed, the trial judge stated that son's testimony tended to show joint ownership in father's business. Nevertheless, the issue of son's alleged status partnership in Caraville Arms was not litigated in the trial court and appeared not to concern plaintiff in that proceeding. Plaintiff did not plead that son was a partner of Caraville Arms nor did he present proof at trial of a partnership between father and son. His theory of son's liability at trial was son's involvement in the receipt of various loans from plaintiff and son's own loans to Caraville Arms. A party is not permitted to adopt a new and different theory on appeal. Therefore, a ruling by this court that a partnership could be inferred from the evidence would deny father and son their day in court relative to this issue.

Furthermore, on appeal, plaintiff relies solely on statements of witnesses at trial to support his *inference* of a partnership. The establishment of a partnership is a mixed question of law and fact. Such a question must be addressed to the trial, not the appellate, court. Thus, son's point that the term "family operation" is not the legal equivalent of a partnership has merit, at least in the present case. The only thing that is certain from the testimony is that father depended upon son to provide labor for the company, that is, to actually manufacture the gun parts.

Without evidence of a partnership, the record reveals that son had an important role in the company and a direct personal stake in the survival of Caraville Arms. Based on this degree of son's involvement to that entity, it would be unjust for this court to conclude that the trial court erred in applying section 3521.

The judgment is affirmed. Costs on appeal are awarded to plaintiff.

FOR DISCUSSION

1. Explain how the equitable maxim "He who takes the benefit must bear the burden" relates to the facts of this case.
2. If plaintiff can prove that son is an owner-partner of Caraville Arms, what legal remedy would be available to him?
3. Why does plaintiff fail to prove that son is a legal owner of Caraville Arms?
4. Do you think, given his role in this affair, that son bears a moral responsibility for plaintiff's predicament?
5. Why does the court conclude that the money plaintiff gave to father and son was a loan rather than a gift? Do you agree?
6. Has son been unjustly enriched by plaintiff's loans? If so, what does that say about son's *actual* relationship to Caraville Arms?
7. How does this case differ from *Gerety* v. *Poitras*?
8. What statutory rule gives the court possible jurisdiction over this case? How does the discussion of that rule add to your understanding of the operation of a "merged" system of law and equity?

Equity as Protector of the Rights of Incompetent Persons

One of equity's traditional functions is to protect the rights of incompetent persons, particularly children and the mentally disabled. This includes establishment and management of trusts, appointment and supervision of guardians, and oversight of the activities of fiduciaries with respect to their responsibilities to their beneficiaries or wards. A principal guideline for the Court of Equity is the so-called best interests test. Equity will do what is in the best interests of the incompetent and holds the trustees and guardians to the same standard.

The next case deals with a doctrine that is somewhat different from the traditional "best interests" test: substituted judgment. "Best interests" is obviously paternalistic, doing what is "best" for the incompetent even if it is against his or her preferences, whereas substituted judgment assumes that the court will put itself in the place of the incompetent and do exactly what he or she would do if he or she were able, whether it is the "best" thing to do or not. That doctrine poses some serious problems, both conceptually and practically, as the following case demonstrates.

CASE

In Re Guardianship of Richard Pescinski, Incompetent
Janice Pescinski Lausier v. Richard Pescinski
Supreme Court of Wisconsin (1975)
67 Wis.2d 4, 226 N.W.2d 180

WILKIE, Chief Justice.   Does a county court have the power to order an operation to be performed to remove the kidney of an incompetent ward, under guardianship of the person, and transfer it to a sister where the dire need of the transfer is established but where no consent has been given by the incompetent or his guardian *ad litem*, nor has any benefit to the ward been shown?

That is the issue presented on appeal here. The trial court held that it did not have that power and we agree. The appellant, Janice Pescinski Lausier, on her own petition, was appointed guardian of the person of her brother, the respondent, Richard Pescinski. In 1958, Richard was declared incompetent and was committed to Winnebago State Hospital. He has been a committed mental patient since that date, classified as a schizophrenic, chronic, catatonic type.

On January 31, 1974, Janice Pescinski Lausier petitioned for permission to Dr. H. M. Kauffman to conduct tests to determine whether Richard Pescinski was a suitable donor for a kidney transplant for the benefit of his sister, Elaine Jeske. Elaine had both kidneys surgically removed in 1970 because she was suffering from kidney failure diagnosed as chronic glomerulonephritis. In order to sustain her life, she was put on a dialysis machine, which functions as an artificial kidney. Because of the deterioration of Elaine, the petition contended that a kidney transplant was needed. Subsequent tests were completed establishing that Richard was a suitable donor, and a hearing was then held on the subject of whether permission should be granted to perform the transplant. The guardian ad litem would not give consent to the transplant and the county court held that it did not have the power to give consent for the operation.

At the time of the hearing Elaine was thirty-eight and her brother Richard was thirty-nine. Evidence was produced at the hearing that the other members of the Pescinski family had been ruled out as possible donors on the basis of either age or health. The father, aged seventy, and the mother, aged seventy-seven, were eliminated as possible donors by Dr. Kauffman because, as a matter of principle, he would not perform the operation on a donor over sixty. A similar rationale was applied by Dr. Kauffman as to all of the six minor children of Elaine, the doctor concluding that he "would not personally use their kidneys" as a matter of his "own moral conviction." Mrs. Jeske's sister, Mrs. Lausier, was excluded as a donor because she has diabetes. Another brother, Ralph Pescinski, testified that he was forty-three years old, had been married twenty years and had ten children, nine of whom remained at home. He is a dairy farmer and did not care to be a donor because there would be nobody to take over his farm and he felt he had a duty to his family to refuse. He further testified that he had a stomach disorder which required a special diet and had a rupture on his left side. He had been to see Dr. Capati at the Neisville Clinic, who told him he should not get involved and that his family should come first.

The testimony showed that Richard was suffering from schizophrenia-catatonic type, and that while he was in contact with his environment there was a marked indifference in his behavior. Dr. Hoffman, the medical director at the Good Samaritan Home, West Bend, Wisconsin, testified that in laymen's terms Richard's mental disease was a flight from reality. He estimated Richard's mental capacity to be age twelve. No evidence in the record indicates that Richard consented to the transplant. Absent that consent, there is no question that the trial court's conclusion that it had no power to approve the operation must be sustained.

"A guardian of the person has the care of the ward's person and must look to the latter's health, education, and support." 39 Am.Jur.2d, Guardian and Ward, p. 60,§68. The guardian must act, if at all, "loyally in the best interests of his ward." *Guardianship of Nelson* (1963), 21 Wis.2d 24, 123 N.W.2d 505, 509. *Cf.* §880.19(5)(b), Stats. There is absolutely no evidence here that any interests of the ward will be served by the transplant.

As far as the court's own power to authorize the operation, we are satisfied that the law in Wisconsin is clearly to the contrary. There is no statutory authority given the county court to authorize a kidney transplant or any other surgical procedure on a living person. We decline to adopt the concept of "substituted judgment" which was specifically adopted by the Kentucky Court of Appeals in *Strunk* v. *Strunk* (Ky. 1969), 445 S.W.2d 145. In that case, the Kentucky court held a court of equity had the power to permit the removal of a kidney from an incompetent ward of the state upon the petition of his committee who was also his mother. Apparently a committee in Kentucky is like a guardian in this state. The Kentucky Court of Appeals authorized the operation based on the application of the doctrine of substituted judgment. However, the court also held that neither the committee nor the county court had the power to authorize the operation, in the absence of a showing that the life of the ward was in jeopardy—only the Court of Appeals had the power. In the instant case the county court had no power to authorize the procedure, and the question is whether this supreme court can by using the doctrine of substituted judgment.

As the dissenting opinion in *Strunk* v. *Strunk* points out, "substituted judgment" is nothing more than an application of the maxim that equity will speak for one who cannot speak for himself. Historically, the substituted judgment doctrine was used to allow gifts of the property of an incompetent. If applied literally, it would allow a trial court, or this court, to change the designation on a life insurance policy or make an election for an incompetent widow, without the requirement of a statute authorizing these acts and contrary to prior decisions of this court. *Kay* v. *Erickson* (1932), 209 Wis. 147, 244 N.W. 625; *Van Steenwyck* v. *Washburn* (1884), 59 Wis. 483, 17 N.W. 289.

We conclude that the doctrine should not be adopted in this state.

We, therefore, must affirm the lower court's decision that it was without power to approve the operation, and we further decide that there is no such power in this court. An incompetent particularly should have his interests protected. Certainly no advantage should be taken of him. In the absence of real consent on his part, and in a situation where no benefit to him has been established, we fail to find authority for the county court, or this court, to approve this operation.

Order affirmed. No costs on appeal.

DAY, Justice (dissenting).

I would reverse the decision in this case. The majority of the court holds that in the absence of a showing of "benefit" to the incompetent in this case or proof of consent on his part, the trial court and this court lack authority to authorize a kidney transplant operation to be performed on him to save the life of his sister. I disagree.

I think the court as a court of equity does have authority to permit the kidney transplant operation requested in the petition of the guardian of Richard Pescinski. I agree with the reasoning of the Court of Appeals of the state of Kentucky wherein that court said:

> The specific question involved upon this appeal is: Does a court of equity have the power to permit a kidney to be removed from an incompetent ward of the state upon petition of his committee, who is also his mother, for the purpose of being transplanted into the body of his brother, who is dying of a fatal kidney disease? We are of the opinion it does. *Strunk* v. *Strunk* (Ky. 1969), 445 S.W.2d 145, 35 A.L.R.3d 683.

That case involved the authorization of a transplant from a 27-year-old incompetent to his 28-year-old brother. The court in that case did find, based on the testimony of a psychiatrist, that while the incompetent had the mental age of six, it would be of benefit to him to keep his brother alive so that his brother could visit him on occasion; I would regard this as pretty thin soup on which to base a decision as to whether or not the donee is to be permitted to live. In the case before us, if the incompetent brother should happily recover from his mental illness, he would undoubtedly be happy to learn that the transplant of one of his kidneys to his sister saved her life. This at least would be a normal response and hence the transplant is not without benefit to him.

The guardian *ad litem* for the incompetent in this case has interposed strong objection to the transplant from Richard Pescinski to his sister, who at the time of the determination was a 39-year-old mother of six minor children and who, as we were informed on February 24th at the time of the oral arguments, in attempting to live on a bi-weekly "washing" of her blood through a kidney dialysis machine has now deteriorated to the point of confinement in a wheelchair. We were advised that without a kidney transplant death for her is quite imminent. The brother, on the other hand, the incompetent is in good health. The medical testimony is that the removal of one of his kidneys would be of minimal risk to him and that he would function normally on one kidney for the rest of his natural life, as do thousands of others in similar circumstances. The guardian *ad litem* argues strenuously that for us to permit this transplant is to bring back memories of the Dachau concentration camp in Nazi Germany and medical experiments on unwilling subjects, many of whom died or were horribly maimed. I failed to see the analogy—this is not an experiment conducted by mad doctors but a well-known and accepted surgical procedure necessitated in this case to save the life of the incompetent's sister. Such a transplant would be authorized, not by a group of doctors operating behind a barbed-wire stockade but only after a full hearing in an American court of law. To avoid the concerns expressed by the guardian *ad litem*, there are certain definite standards which could and should be imposed. First of all, a strong showing should be made that without the kidney transplant the proposed donee or recipient stands to suffer death. This is certainly the evidence here. Secondly, that reasonable steps have been taken to try and acquire a kidney from other sources and the record is clear that such attempt was made here. Because of the fact that the donee has had six children, she has built up certain chemical resistance to the receipt of foreign tissue into her body which can be overcome only by a transplant from one close to her by blood such as a brother or sister. The testimony showed the impracticality of acquiring a kidney from either her other brother or her sister. No suitable kidney from a cadaver has been found since her kidneys were removed in 1970. The next showing that should be made is that the incompetent proposed-donor is closely related by blood to the proposed donee, such as a brother or sister, which of course is the case here. Showing should be made that the donor, if competent, would most probably consent because of the normal ties of family. Here, the trial court specifically found "...the conclusion would appear to be inescapable that the ward [the incompetent proposed-donor] would so consent and that such authorization should be granted." (The trial court concluded, however, that such an authorization would be analogous to giving away an incompetent's property and since there was no "benefit" to him the court had no authority to act.) Another showing should be that the proposed-incompetent-donor is in good health and that was shown here. And lastly, that the operation is one of minimal risk to the donor and that the donor could function normally on one kidney following such operation. The medical testimony is all to the effect that the donor would undergo minimal risk and would be able to function normally on one kidney. In fact, the testimony is that a person can function on as little as one tenth of a normal kidney.

With these guidelines the fear expressed that institutions for the mentally ill will merely become storehouses for spare parts for people on the outside is completely unjustified. I agree with the trial court that if the brother here were competent in all probability he would be willing to consent to the transplant to save his sister's life. For him it would be a short period of discomfort which would not affect his ability either to enjoy life or his longevity.

The majority opinion says there is no showing of consent by the incompetent. Dr. William C. P. Hoffman, medical director of the Good Samaritan Home where the incompetent is a patient, testified that one with the mental condition of the incompetent has no lucid intervals and that his reasoning is completely impaired in making decisions. The doctor testified the incompetent would not be aware of what the proceeding involved and testified the incompetent is "insane seven days a week." From such a record it is difficult to see how one could ever get a meaningful "consent" from the incompetent in this case.

The majority opinion would forever condemn the incompetent to be always a receiver, a taker, but never a giver. For in holding that only those things which financially or physically benefit the incompetent may be done by the court, he is forever excluded from doing the decent thing, the charitable thing. The British courts have not so held. Two British cases cited in *Strunk* permitted the estate of an incompetent to provide a pension for a faithful servant in one instance and in another to help an indigent brother—this by the device known as "substituted judgment" where the court in effect does for the incompetent what it is sure he would do for himself if he had the power to act. This approach gives the incompetent the benefit of the doubt, endows him with the finest qualities of his humanity, assumes the goodness of his nature instead of assuming the opposite.

The equities in this case favor taking the action which may save this mother's life.

FOR DISCUSSION

1. Why is the court concerned about whether the kidney transplant operation will benefit the incompetent ward? Does "benefit" have to be physical? Is any other type of benefit possible in this case?

2. Under what circumstances, if any, would the court authorize a kidney transplant operation for Richard Pescinski?

3. According to the court, what is the connection between the maxim "Equity will speak for one who cannot speak for himself" and the doctrine of substituted judgment? Why won't the court accept the doctrine of substituted judgment for the State of Wisconsin?

4. Why does the court conclude that substituted judgment is inappropriate in this situation in particular? Is there anything about the facts in *Pescinski* that makes it substantially different from the situation in the precedent case of *Strunk* v. *Strunk*?

5. How does the dissenting judge propose to safeguard the interests of the incompetent ward while still permitting the doctrine of substituted judgment to be used? Do you think the proposed safeguards are adequate?

6. What are the dangers of the use of substituted judgment in situations like this one? Do you think the dissenting justice's dismissal of the dangers is justifiable? Explain.

7. The dissenting justice assumes that the incompetent, although "insane seven days a week," according to testimony, would nevertheless consent to the surgery because of family ties and argues that the majority is robbing the incompetent of the opportunity to be generous and charitable. Is there anything in this case to suggest that family members are not always so self-sacrificing?

8. Do you think the court comes to the right decision? Support your answer.

Although the Supreme Court of Wisconsin rejected the doctrine of substituted judgment in *Matter of Pescinski*, substituted judgment has become increasingly important in dealing with the medical treatment needs of incompetent patients. In many cases, however, it is clear that the overriding concern is the physical benefit to the patient, but that need not be so. In 1976, the New Jersey Supreme Court cited *Strunk* v. *Strunk*, the precedent rejected in *Pescinski*, as support for its decision in the *Matter of Karen Ann Quinlan*, that under the doctrine of substituted judgment the Equity Court could authorize the withdrawal of extraordinary treatment measures for a patient in an irreversible coma. 70 N.J. 10, 355 A.2d 647, 666. In that case, it was assumed that withdrawal of a respirator would result in the incompetent patient's death, although, in fact, it did not.

The *Quinlan* decision and the doctrine of substituted judgment have subsequently been used in a line of "right to die" or "death with dignity" cases throughout the country. Not surprisingly, some see this as a vindication of the incompetent patient's rights, whereas others see it as an excuse to terminate the lives of helpless persons who have become an inconvenience to their families or to society. The following essay describes how substituted judgment has been used in the courts of one state.

READING   ## Medical Decisionmaking for Incompetent Persons: The Massachusetts Substituted Judgment Model
Sean M. Dunphy and John H. Cross*

In his book, *The Silent World of Doctor and Patient* (1984), Professor Jay Katz describes the apparently ingrained belief of physicians that patients are unequal partners in the medical decisionmaking process. Professor Katz contends that this insistence on authority has stifled any serious exploration of whether doctors and patients can interact with one another on the basis of greater equality. "Thus the idea of informed consent—of mutual decisionmaking—remains severely compromised" (p. 87).

A related context is that of medical decisionmaking for incompetent persons. In the next few pages, the authors will explore this area in terms of Massachusetts law focusing particularly on extraordinary treatment situations. We believe that physicians' insistence on authority creates additional and unnecessary obstacles to meeting the legitimate treatment needs of incompetent patients. This traditional attitude on the part of the medical community, coupled with the continuing confusion on the part of both doctors and lawyers regarding the substituted judgment doctrine, poses the risk of seriously compromising the civil rights of incompetent persons.

Judges, in making substituted judgments for incompetent persons, are in an analogous position to that of competent patients in relation to their physicians. The judge's duty is to discover and implement the incompetent person's own values and preferences and not to defer to physician authority as a conditioned response. Judges, like patients, can benefit from Professor Katz's model of effective, respectful conversation, albeit within the confines of a formal judicial proceeding.

I. THE *SAIKEWICZ* DECISION

A. *Significance of the Decision*

In 1977, the Massachusetts Supreme Judicial Court issued its landmark decision regarding potentially life-prolonging medical treatment for an incompetent person—*Superintendent of Belchertown State School* v. *Saikewicz* (373 Mass. 728, 370 N.E.2d 417 [1977]). Factually, the case involved the question of whether chemotherapy should be administered to a mentally retarded person who suffered from leukemia and who was incapable, due to his profound mental retardation, of making a medical treatment decision.

The *Saikewicz* opinion rejected the idea that such decisionmaking responsibility should be delegated either to doctors or family members or guardians. Instead, the supreme judicial court held that the trial court should make a so-called "substituted judgment" determination by substituting itself for the ward and attempting to ascertain his actual interests and preferences. In essence, the supreme judicial court fashioned a judicial decisionmaking model to be applied in cases involving the question of whether life-prolonging treatment should be administered to incompetent persons.

The reaction of the medical community to *Saikewicz* was extremely negative. As one physician wrote, "[t]his astonishing opinion can only be viewed as a resounding vote of 'no confidence' in the ability of physicians and families to act in the best interests of the incapable patient suffering from a terminal illness."[4]

The supreme judicial court, however, did not view its decision as a "gratuitous encroachment on the domain of physicians." *Saikewicz*, 373 Mass. at 759, 370 N.E.2d at 435. From the authors' perspective, too much of the discussion of this judicial decisionmaking model has been couched in terms of lawyers or judges usurping the traditional role of physicians. Such narrow perspective misses the important considerations which underlie the *Saikewicz* opinion and the decisions following *Saikewicz* which have extended the substituted judgment doctrine to other areas of medical care and treatment. A review of the basic tenets of these decisions underscores the important but different roles of the court, the medical community, and other players in extraordinary treatment cases.

B. *Judicial Analysis and Reasoning*

According to *Saikewicz*, one of the underlying principles of the substituted judgment doctrine is the constitutional right of an individual to privacy, a guaranty which encompasses the right to accept or refuse medical treatment. This fundamental right extends "not only to competent patients but also to incompetent persons because the value of human dignity extends to both." *Id.* at 745, 370 N.E.2d at 424, 427.

It is important to note that a substituted judgment determination cannot be made until there is a judicial determination of incompetency by reason of an individual's minority, mental illness, or mental retardation. A person is presumed to be capable of handling his or her affairs unless shown by evidence presented to be incompetent. The law protects an individual's right to accept or reject medical treatment, whether that decision is wise or unwise. As set forth in the *Saikewicz* decision, once a determination of incompetency has been made, the role of the court is to substitute itself as nearly as possible for the incompetent person and to act on the same motives and considerations as would move the incompetent person. The court's role as substitute decisionmaker is subjective in nature—that is, the goal is to determine with as much accuracy as possible the wants and needs of the individual involved. This may or may not conform to what is thought wise or prudent by most people. The problems of arriving at an accurate substituted judgment in matters of life and death vary greatly in degree, if not in kind, in different circumstances.

The *Saikewicz* court, in essence, forced conversation between the physician and the trial court about the incompetent's medical and nonmedical wants and needs. In doing so, the court established a formalized variant of Professor Katz's goal of self-reflective conversation between doctor and patient. Both models are designed to eradicate a silent relationship between doctor and patient. Professor Katz proposes a decisionmaking process in which the parties concentrate on conscious and unconscious values affecting their positions on treat-

---

[4]Relman, "The Saikewicz Decision: Judges as Physicians," *N. Engl. J. Med.*, 298 (1978), 508, 509.

ment, with hope leading both to recognize previously unspoken bases for the final decision (pp. iii–4, 150–55). Professor Katz's model addresses a silent world in which one party dominates and refuses to communicate to the other; the *Saikewicz* court addresses a silent world in which the parties cannot communicate with each other because of one's disability.

The supreme judicial court has established a process which seeks information similar to that Professor Katz wished to realize in his own model: the trial court and the doctor attempt to discover how the incompetent person would view the treatment options, with the court deciding which facts are important and using them to make a final decision. The *Saikewicz* court also demonstrated the same respect as Katz does for the sanctity of the patient's final decision, whether or not the decision seems reasonable to doctors or other similarly situated patients. As Professor Katz stated, "although [respecting patients' ultimate decisions] may mean bowing at times to 'foolish' choices, they must be honored to protect the process of thinking about choices ..." (p. 154). Katz and the *Saikewicz* court seem to agree that preserving a patient's right to self-determination begins with protection of the method through which the patient's wishes and needs are best expressed, regardless of the outcome.

Respect for the outcome in substituted judgment determinations, however, is not absolute until the final participant—the state—determines that the incompetent person's interests do not conflict with its own interests in the decision. The court must balance the individual's interests against potentially countervailing state interests, which have been defined as "(1) the preservation of life; (2) the protection of the interests of innocent third parties; (3) the prevention of suicide; and (4) maintaining the ethical integrity of the medical profession." *Id.* at 741, 370 N.E.2d at 425. In *Saikewicz*, the supreme judicial court found no state interest or combination of interests strong enough to override the patient's decision, as determined by the court, to decline life-prolonging treatment.

C. *Cases Following Saikewicz*

At this juncture, it is appropriate to underscore two related comments made by the supreme judicial court in cases following *Saikewicz*. First, a substituted judgment decision is distinct from a decision by doctors as to what is medically in the "best interests" of the patient. *In Re Roe*, 383 Mass. 415, 435, 421 N.E.2d 40, 52 [1981]. Secondly, medical advice and opinion are to be sued for the same purposes and to the same extent that the incompetent individual would, if he or she were competent. *Id.* at 435, 421 N.E.2d at 52; *Rogers* v. *Comm'r of Dept. of Mental Health*, 390 Mass. 489, 500, 458 N.E.2d at 317. These comments and the *Saikewicz* decision clarify the respective roles of the trial judge and the treating physician. The judge is to probe the individual's values and preferences, while the physician is to present and explain treatment options. As Professor Katz commented:

> no single right decision exists for how the life of health and illness should be lived. Medical advances have led to a proliferation of treatment options and a better understanding of their benefits and risks. Alleviation of suffering can be accomplished in a variety of ways and alternative choices must be explained. Physicians alone cannot decide which treatment is best. The patient must be consulted. (p. 102)

In cases of extraordinary medical treatment for incompetent persons, the court, in effect, stands in the place of the patient for the purpose of considering medical advice and opinion. Beyond this, the court must balance the patient's individual interests against potentially countervailing state interests.

From the authors' point of view, the role of the physician is neither diminished nor reduced in this process—unless one perceives such role as including ultimate decisionmaking responsibility for incompetent persons. In the case of *Rogers* v. *Commissioner of Department of Mental Health*, the psychiatric profession argued that if a substituted judgment is to be required before there can be forcible administration of antipsychotic medication to involuntarily confined, incompetent patients, the decision as to substituted judgment should be made by a physician and not a judge. The supreme judicial court rejected this procedure, the so-called medical model, citing, among other things, the likelihood of conflicting interests on the part of physicians. Doctors, according to the opinion, are not only attempting to treat psychiatric patients but also to maintain institutional order. Thus, "the temptation to engage in blanket prescription of such drugs to maintain order and compensate for personnel shortages may be irresistible." *Id.* at 504, 458 N.E.2d at 318, n. 19. As Professor Katz comments, "The idea that doctors know what is in their patients' interest and therefore can act on their behalf without inquiry is so patently untrue that one can only marvel at the fervor with which the notion has been defended" (p. 98). The supreme judicial court has repeatedly rejected any delegation of decisionmaking responsibility away from the court in extraordinary treatment situations.

In the aftermath of *Saikewicz*, there have been a number of cases involving life-prolonging treatment issues. The supreme judicial court and appeals court consistently have applied the substituted judgment doctrine on behalf of mentally incompetent persons or minor children. The supreme judicial court and appeals court have also extended the substituted judgment doctrine and judicial decisionmaking responsibility to other areas of extraordinary medical care and treatment, including sterilization, antipsychotic medication, and artificial maintenance of nutrition and hydration. In dicta, Massachusetts courts have also included electroconvulsive therapy and psychosurgery.

II. THE JUDGE'S ROLE

In *The Silent World of Doctor and Patient*, Professor Katz commented on the tendency of patients to defer to doctors with "unquestioning compliance, unilateral trust, and verbal silence" (p. 100). There is a similar tendency on the part of trial judges, when confronted with a substituted judgment determination, to question their own roles in making such a decision. A not infrequent comment on the part of judges is, "I'm not a doctor. I have no business making a medical decision." This perspective misses the critical point that the trial judge's role is to stand in the place of the ward and attempt to ascertain the incompetent person's actual values and preferences.

The *Saikewicz* line of decisions now provides both guidance and instruction for the trial court judge. For example, in the *Roe* opinion, the supreme judicial court identified six factors to be considered by the judge in making a substituted judgment decision. These include: "(1) the ward's expressed preferences regarding treatment; (2) his religious beliefs; (3) the impact upon the ward's family; (4) the probability of adverse side effects; (5) the consequences if treatment is refused; and (6) the prognosis with treatment." *Roe*, 383 Mass. at 444, 421 N.E.2d at 57. This criteria is not exclusive, but rather provides a basic framework for the judge's inquiry. The *Roe* decision also states, "In this search, procedural intricacies and technical niceties must yield to the need to know the actual values and preferences of the ward." *Id.*

In the *Moe* decision, the supreme judicial court developed detailed and specialized criteria for the court to apply in sterilization cases. The supreme court stressed that the judge must exercise the utmost care in reviewing all of the evidence presented. "The judge must enter detailed written findings indicating those persuasive factors that determine the outcome. We are persuaded that the conscientious judge … will give serious and heedful attention to all stages of the proceeding," *Moe*, 385 Mass. at 572, 432 N.E.2d at 724.

In *Saikewicz*, the supreme judicial court indicated that the trial judge may, at any stage of the proceedings, "avail himself or herself of the additional advice or knowledge of any person or group," including medical experts or medical ethics committees or panels. *Saikewicz*, 373 Mass. at 757-58, 370 N.E.2d at 434. Although such information may be considered by the court whenever available and useful, the judge may not delegate to any individual or group the ultimate decisionmaking responsibility. According to the supreme judicial court, "such questions…seem to us to require the process of detached but passionate investigation and decision that forms the ideal on which the judicial branch of government was created." *Id.* at 759, 370 N.E.2d. at 435….

VII. THE BROPHY DECISION

Recently, the supreme court issued its opinion in the controversial and highly-publicized case of *Brophy* v. *New England Sinai Hospital, Inc.*, 398 Mass. 417, 497 N.E.2d 626 [1986]. The *Brophy* decision is a further example of the Massachusetts substituted judgment model. In this case, the supreme judicial court decided that food and water may be withheld from a patient who is in a persistent vegetative state but not terminally ill. The court's balancing of Mr. Brophy's individual interests and preferences against specifically identified state interests is worth reviewing in some detail.

At the trial court in *Brophy*, the presiding judge found that if Mr. Brophy were competent, his choice would be to forego the provision of food and water and thereby terminate his life. Despite this finding, the trial court concluded that the state's interest in the preservation of life outweighed Mr. Brophy's individual interest and preference to decline treatment. The trial court also concluded that it would be "ethically inappropriate to cause the preventable death of Brophy by the deliberate denial of food and water, which can be provided to him in a noninvasive, nonintrusive manner which causes no pain and suffering…." *Brophy* v. *New England Sinai Hosp., Inc.*, No. 85E0009G1 [Norfolk Division, Probate and Family Court Department, Oct. 21, 1985].

In reversing the trial court decision, the supreme judicial court balanced Mr. Brophy's substituted judgment to reject treatment against three potentially countervailing state interests: (1) the preservation of life, (2) the prevention of suicide, and (3) the maintenance of the integrity of the medical profession. Regarding the state's interest in the preservation of life, the supreme judicial court indicated that "the State's interest in life encompasses a broader interest than mere corporeal existence. In certain, thankfully rare, circumstances the burden of maintaining the corporeal existence degrades the very humanity it was meant to serve. The law recognizes the individual's right to preserve his humanity, even if to preserve his humanity means to allow the natural processes of a disease or affliction to bring about death with dignity." *Brophy*, 398 Mass. at 434, 497 N.E.2d at 635. Thus, the supreme judicial court concluded that the state's interest in the preservation of life did not overcome Brophy's right to discontinue treatment.

The supreme judicial court also rejected the state's interest in the prevention of suicide as an applicable consideration. The court noted "[a] death which occurs after the removal of life sustaining systems is from natural causes, neither set in motion nor intended by the patient." *Id.* at 439, 497 N.E.2d at 638.

Finally, regarding the ethical integrity of the medical profession, the supreme judicial court concluded that as long as the defendant hospital was not forced to withhold food and water from the patient, the integrity of the medical profession was not violated. The supreme judicial court noted that there is substantial disagreement in the medical community over the appropriate medical action. The supreme judicial court remanded the case to the trial court for a new judgment to be entered ordering the hospital to assist the guardian in transferring the patient to a different facility or to his home where the patient's wishes could be effectuated.

CONCLUSION

Professor Katz urges that "[a]bove all, physicians and patients must learn to converse with one another" (p. xxi). In cases of extraordinary medical treatment for incompetent persons, Massachusetts has created a judicial model which, in effect, forces conversation between the physician and the trial court regarding a patient's medical needs and individual preferences. Throughout the article, we have tried to convey what we consider to be the fundamental principle underlying the Massachusetts substituted judgment model—that of individual autonomy and the "emphasis away from a paternalistic view of what is 'best' for a patient to a reaffirmation that the basic question is what decision will comport with the will of the person involved....." *Brophy*, at 431, 497 N.E.2d at 633. As participants in this symposium, we have been fascinated by the numerous parallels between Professor Katz's thesis and many of the basic tenets expressed in the *Saikewicz* line of decisions.

NOTES

*From 9 *Western New England Law Review* 153–61; 165–67 (1987). Reprinted with permission.

FOR DISCUSSION

1. The authors say that under the doctrine of substituted judgment the judge is supposed to "discover and implement the incompetent person's own values and preferences." Would that have been possible in the case of someone like Richard Pescinski?

2. How is the situation in the *Saikewicz* decision different from that of *Pescinski*? Does it make sense to use substituted judgment in the *Saikewicz* situation? Explain.

3. How does the constitutional right of privacy relate to the doctrine of substituted judgment?

4. What is meant by the authors' description of substituted judgment as subjective in nature? Do you see any problems in using such a standard?

5. What process of decision making using substituted judgment was established by the court in *Saikewicz*? What demands does this process place on the various participants in the legal proceeding?

6. What are the state's interests in a substituted judgment decision involving medical treatment? Given the cases described in the article, do the state interests provide an effective check on the results of substituted judgment decision making?

7. According to the authors, how is substituted judgment different from the "best interests" standard? Are the authors saying that one standard is superior or preferable to the other?

8. Why have the courts of Massachusetts rejected the so-called medical model of decision making for incompetent patients?

9. What factors must a judge consider in making a medical treatment decision for an incompetent patient under the Massachusetts substituted judgment model? Do you think these factors provide adequate protection for the incompetent?

10. In the *Brophy* case, Paul Brophy had been a competent adult before the stroke that left him in a persistently vegetative state and had expressed his personal views on extraordinary life-prolonging treatment. How is this situation different from *Pescinski*, *Strunk*, or *Saikewicz*? Do you think the *Brophy* case is a good precedent to use in all situations regarding extraordinary life-prolonging treatment for incompetents?

Equitable Maxims

By this time we have already seen several equitable maxims in operation. The common law relied on precedents, whereas equity operated by general principles called maxims. Today, however, equity, too, obeys the rule of *stare decisis* or binding precedent, but nevertheless equitable maxims still have great force as a context for equity decision making. These maxims act as general guidelines for decision and are of several different types. Many maxims refer to equity jurisdiction or provide guidance for court action. These include the following.

> Equity follows the law.
> Equity will not suffer a wrong to be without a remedy.
> Equity acts *in personam*, not *in rem*.
> Equity is equality and equality is equity.
> Equity regards as done that which ought to be done.
> Equity regards substance and intent rather than form.
> Equity imputes an intent to fulfill an obligation.
> Equity abhors a forfeiture.

Other maxims are applicable to litigants. These include the following.

> Equity aids the vigilant and diligent.
> He who seeks equity must do equity.
> He who comes to equity must come with clean hands.

The following case deals with one of the best-known equitable maxims, "Equity delights to do justice, and that not by halves." This maxim refers to the spirit of fairness, right dealing, and substantial justice that underlies equity as a whole. In this case equity literally comes to the rescue of the weak and powerless—two little boys—to ensure that they are dealt with fairly by an older person in a dispute over abandoned property.

CASE   **Eugene Edmonds, Jr. an infant, and Pat Fava, an infant**
v. Antoinette Ronella, an infant,
New York Supreme Court (1973)
73 Misc.2d 598, 342 N.Y.S.2d 408

FREDERIC E. HAMMER, Justice.   The court has been called upon to determine the respective rights to found property, viz., $12,300 in cash. The story unfolded in the courtroom at the trial of the action that on the 19th day of September 1971, little Eugene, then aged 12, and little Pat, then aged 9, were on their way home from attending church. As little children are wont to do, the two boys passed the parking lot of an A & P supermarket located at Rockaway Boulevard and 84th Street, in Ozone Park. Rummaging around, the children discovered a manila envelope (in a bag) containing a large bankroll of cash, amid the trash and the discarded clothing located in said parking lot. The young children became excited, confused and, in their immature way, sought the assistance of friends to determine what disposition should be made of this "treasure trove." Some friends, also on their way home from church, including the defendant in this case, Antoinette, a grown young lady then 15 years of age, came to their aid and assistance. Subsequently, the envelope in the bag was picked up by Antoinette and taken to her house for parental advice. The boys tagged along. On the way, by means of the sense of touch, a gun was also found in the envelope.

The children arrived at Antoinette's home. Antoinette, with the loot, went into the house. The little boys were told to wait outside. Sometime later, two police officers arrived at the house and the children were then advised to go to their respective homes—that Antoinette's family would take care of the entire problem. There was some testimony by the defendant, Antoinette, that the boys disclaimed any interest in the money and wished to sever any relationship they had to the money. This, however, was denied by the two little boys.

While the boys were still present in front of the house, the police officers arrived and thereafter, together with the defendant, Antoinette, and her mother, left the house and went to the station house. The money was there deposited with the police and receipt was given to Antoinette as the "sole" finder of this money. The little boys, wishing to share in the bonanza found, commenced, through their parents a declaratory judgment action. The Police Department listed young Antoinette as the "finder."

Equity delights to do justice, and *that* not by halves. *Black's Law Dictionary*, 4th ed., *Tallman* v. *Varick*, 5 Barb 277, 280.

The established common law principle is that a finder of property acquires a right in the found chattel or goods against the entire world except the true owner. A finder has been defined as the person who first takes possession of lost property. An intention or state of mind with reference to the lost property is an essential element to constitute a legal finder of such property.

Equity in its broadest and most general signification denotes the spirit and the habit of fairness, justice and right dealing which would regulate the intercourse of men with men, the rule of doing to all others as we desire they should do to us; or, as it is expressed by Justinian, "to live honestly, to harm nobody, to render to every man his due." It is, therefore, the synonym of natural right or justice, but in this sense its obligation is ethical rather than jural, and its discussion belongs to the sphere of morals. It is grounded in the precept of the conscience.

With these rules as our guideposts in equity and upon the testimony given at trial, it is the determination of this court that the lost money was not found, in a legal sense, until the plaintiffs and the defendant had, together, removed it from the parking lot. Having thus obtained possession jointly, the court finds that each of the parties is entitled to an equal share of the money. Prior case law of this point, though meager, clearly establishes that if several persons participated in a finding, they are joint finders with equal rights in the property found.

In each of these decisions, although each presents different factual situations, the courts appear to have been governed "by those practical considerations of fairness and conceptions of common right which influence just and thoughtful men in the ordinary affairs of life and which are in harmony with the principles of equity and not discountenanced by rules of law." *Weeks* v. *Hackett*, 104 Me. 264, at p. 275, 71 A. 863. In reaching the conclusion that the parties were joint finders of the $12,300, entitling each to a one-third share, the court has similarly been governed by these considerations.

The judgment to be settled hereon shall provide that upon the expiration of the statutory period for the retention by the Police Property Clerk of the $12,300, the money should be delivered to each infant plaintiff and the infant defendant in equal shares of one third each, at which time title shall vest in each of them, and said shares shall be held in a depository subject to the order of this court until each of said infants shall attain the age of 21 years.

FOR DISCUSSION

1. Suppose the law regarding found property stated that a "finder" is the person who knowingly takes possession of the property and reports the finding to the proper authorities. Would the two boys be finders in that case?

2. Suppose the law stated that a "finder" is the person who actually discovers and takes initial possession of the property. Would Antoinette be a finder in that case?

3. How does deciding to divide the property equally among the three children show fairness and substantial justice? Do you think that this is the proper outcome?

4. Does the court's decision here agree with the definition of a legal finder set forth in the case? Another important equitable maxim is "Equity follows the law." Is that maxim adhered to by the court in this situation?

By far one of the most famous of the equitable maxims is "He who comes to equity must come with clean hands." This maxim refers to equity's role as the court of conscience and its discretionary character. Equity, as an extraordinary proceeding, is not required to grant relief in a case in which the plaintiff is not an innocent party in the transaction complained of. The following excerpt explains the concept of clean hands in more detail.

READING　　　　　**The Use of the Clean Hands Doctrine**
William J. Lawrence III*

A. THE CLEAN HANDS DOCTRINE: DEFINITION AND RATIONALE

The clean hands doctrine demands that a plaintiff seeking equitable relief come into court having acted equitably in that matter for which he seeks remedy. Inequitable conduct alone does not prevent a plaintiff's recovery, but generally only conduct related to the plaintiff's claim. The inequitable conduct which causes the doctrine to be invoked must be wilful, and usually involves fraud, illegality, unfairness or bad faith.

The clean hands doctrine, however, is not "a license to destroy the rights of persons whose conduct is unethical,"[5] nor is it a "judicial straitjacket."[6] The doctrine is a matter of sound discretion for the court, and should never prevent a court "from doing justice."[7] Thus, if allowing an "unclean" plaintiff to recover serves one of the fundamental rationales of the doctrine, that plaintiff should recover.

[5] D. Dobbs, *Remedies* §2.4 (1974).
[6] *Smith v. Marzolf*, 81 Ill.App.3d 59, 66, 400 N.E.2d 949,954 (1980).
[7] *Id.*

The three fundamental rationales that form the basis for the clean hands doctrine are judicial integrity, justice, and the public interest. First, the doctrine protects judicial integrity. Allowing an unclean plaintiff to recover would not only abet him in his inequitable conduct, but would also raise doubts as to the justice provided by the legal system. Thus, the court must close its door to the unclean plaintiff and "refuse to interfere on his behalf,"[8] allowing the court to remain above inequity.

Second, the clean hands doctrine promotes justice. Courts use the doctrine to ensure a fair result. Where the plaintiff's conduct is such that it would be unjust to allow him a remedy, courts can use the doctrine as a bar to remedy. Therefore, withholding assistance from the unclean plaintiff allows courts to prevent "a wrongdoer from enjoying the fruits of his transgression."[9]

Third, the clean hands doctrine promotes the public interest. Courts can use the doctrine where a suit involves a public right or issue. The Supreme Court of the United States has stated that, in cases involving the public interest, the "doctrine assumes wider and more significant proportions."[10] Thus, in suits involving the public interest, a court may not only prevent a wrongdoer from benefitting from his transgressions, but avoid injury to the public.

Morton Salt Co. v. *G. S. Suppiger* (314 U.S. 488 [1942]) illustrates this concern for the public interest. In *Morton Salt*, the Supreme Court denied a patentee equitable relief because the patentee had used his patent to unnecessarily restrict competition. The plaintiff not only came into court with unclean hands, but he infringed upon the public interest by restricting competition.

Finally, the clean hands doctrine must be distinguished from the doctrines of *in pari delicto*, and "he who seeks equity must do equity." Often, the clean hands doctrine has been misunderstood and confused with these two doctrines.

In pari delicto, potier est conditio defendentis means that where the acts of the plaintiff and the defendant are equally inequitable, the plaintiff will not be allowed to recover. This doctrine is closely related to the clean hands doctrine, but is narrower in application. *In pari delicto* usually applies only where the parties have entered into a fraudulent, illegal, or inequitable transaction. In its most conventional form, *in pari delicto* condemns a party if "by participating in the illegal [or fraudulent] transaction he is guilty of moral turpitude."[11] Thus, while *in pari delicto* focuses on the transaction and its possible illegality or fraudulence, the clean hands doctrine looks at the plaintiff's inequity and its connection with the matter at issue. It is entirely possible for a party to have unclean hands in a transaction that is lawful and not violative of public policy.

The second major difference between the clean hands doctrine and *in pari delicto* is that *in pari delicto* requires the plaintiff to have been "in equal fault"[12] with the defendant, while clean hands is not concerned with the parties' relative fault. Thus, while courts considering the clean hands doctrine may weigh the parties' relative fault, courts may properly refuse the plaintiff relief on a clean hands theory even if the plaintiff's wrongdoing is not as serious as the defendant's.

The clean hands doctrine must also be distinguished from the maxim that "he who seeks equity must do equity" (seek-do). While the clean hands doctrine denies the plaintiff relief if his conduct has been inequitable, the "seek-do" maxim denies him relief unless he makes an affirmative effort to aid the defendant. The "seek-do" maxim is best exemplified

---

[8]*Keystone Driller Co.* v. *General Excavator Co.*, 290 U.S. 240, 245 (1933).

[9]*Precision Instrument Mfg. Co.* v. *Automotive Maintenance Mach. Co.*, 324 U.S. 806, 815 (1945).

[10]*Id.*

[11]*Truitt v. Miller*, 407 A.2d 1073, 1079 (D.C. App. 1979).

[12]*Tarasi v Pittsburgh Nat'l Bank*, 555 F.2d 1152, 1157 (3d Cir. 1977).

in a case where the defendant builds a house on the plaintiff's land, honestly claiming title. There, the court may expect the plaintiff to "do equity" by paying for the house before equity will quiet title in his name.

B. CURRENT USE OF THE CLEAN HANDS DOCTRINE WHERE EQUITABLE REMEDIES ARE SOUGHT

By the twentieth century, the clean hands doctrine was well established as an important equity principle. In addition to extensive scholarly treatment, an "astonishing number" of decisions turned on the doctrine.[13] Courts apparently found the doctrine's broad scope an attractive feature.

Today, the clean hands doctrine may arise in any suit where the plaintiff seeks an equitable remedy, such as specific performance, rather than a legal remedy, usually damages. The defendant normally raises the doctrine as a defense, and in some jurisdictions the court may raise it *sua sponte*. Ordinarily, it may not be raised on appeal for the first time, unless a party shows very strong grounds for doing so.

The clean hands doctrine commonly arises in eighteen different types of actions. The categories include actions for specific performance of a contract, tort actions by persons charged with a crime and actions to protect copyrights, patents, and trademarks. Note that in all of these categories the plaintiff could sue for equitable relief or damages. However, only if the plaintiff seeks one of the remedies developed in the equity courts will he generally be subject to a clean hands defense.

NOTES

*From 57 *Notre Dame Lawyer* 673 (April 1982). Reprinted with permission. Copyright © 1982 by the *Notre Dame Law Review,* University of Notre Dame.

FOR DISCUSSION

1. What considerations provide a basis for the clean hands doctrine?
2. How does the clean hands doctrine differ from *"in pari delicto"*?
3. How does the clean hands doctrine differ from the "seek-do" maxim?
4. How is the clean hands doctrine generally employed in modern equity cases?

In the following case, the plaintiff is permitted to recover even though he does not have clean hands. You should pay particular attention to the court's reasoning with respect to why it grants relief to a plaintiff who is not an innocent party in the transaction.

CASE

Saleh M. Nizamuddowlah v. Bengal Cabaret, Inc.
New York Supreme Court, Trial Term (1977)
92 Misc.2d 220, 399 N.Y.S.2d 854

JOSEPH S. CALABRETTA, Justice.   This is a case of novel and current interest, since it involves the question of employment of certain aliens and the practical problems it represents, especially in these times of high unemployment in our State and Nation. We

[13]Z. Chafee, *Some Problems of Equity*, (1950).

have before us the plaintiff, a citizen of Bangladesh, and now a resident alien in the United States, seeking to recover from the defendants for working here, based upon an agreement made by both with the obvious intention of circumventing and disobeying the United States Immigration Law. The plaintiff claims ignorance of such law, and the defendants claim that the plaintiff did not work, and even if he did, such work contract was illegal and therefore, he has no right to recover.

The facts as found by the court relate an oft-repeated story and warrant serious consideration. Plaintiff had met defendant Shamsher Wadud (the principal owner of the Nirvana Restaurant) in August of 1972 in Bangladesh, at which time and place, the defendant offered to employ plaintiff at his restaurant in New York City. The agreement called for plaintiff to serve an apprentice period of about three months without salary, at the end of which time he would receive a waiter's salary, and eventually, become the manager of the restaurant. It is conceded by both sides that defendant Wadud did make all visa and travel arrangements.

Plaintiff came to this country at the expense of defendant Shamsher Wadud, arriving on September 17, 1972, and thereafter, resided at defendant Wadud's home for at least two to three months, and slept and ate at defendant's restaurant for an additional two months.

During this time and continuing through May of 1974, plaintiff worked as a waiter in the restaurant, and after so working for a few months, made several demands for payment of wages, but all to no avail. The plaintiff had also made frequent inquiries of defendant regarding his resident visa (commonly called a "green card"), which defendant had promised to obtain for him through his attorney. But, defendant persistently stalled him through devious tactics, until finally, the plaintiff managed to obtain his resident visa at his own time and expense.

The court must now come to grips with the crucial issue in this case, and that is, whether or not an alien possessing a visitor's visa may recover wages under a contract of employment. It is well-settled law that:

> Generally, a party to an illegal contract cannot recover damages for its breach. But as in the case of many such simplifications, the exceptions and qualifications to the general rule are numerous and complex. *Gates* v. *Rivers Construction Co., Inc.* Alaska, 515 P.2d 1020, 1021.

At bar, the dilemma is compounded by conflicting public policies and equitable doctrines. Plaintiff does not come into court with "clean hands" as he clearly violated the Immigration Laws by working after his arrival until the date he was issued his "green card"; and, although he acted out of a strong desire to emigrate to the United States, he willingly fell in with the defendant, thus making him in effect a coconspirator. This type of conduct poses serious economic problems for our citizenry.

> Employment of illegal aliens in times of high unemployment deprives citizens and legally admitted aliens of jobs; acceptance by illegal aliens of jobs on substandard terms as to wages and working conditions can seriously depress wage scales and working conditions of citizens and legally admitted aliens; and such employment of illegal aliens under such conditions can diminish the effectiveness of labor unions. *De Canas* v. *Bica*, 424 U.S. 351, 356-357, 96 S.Ct. 933, 937, 47 L.Ed.2d 43.

Additionally, the court cannot give credence to plaintiff's claim of ignorance. As stated in *Londono* v. *Immigration and Naturalization Service*, 2. Cir., 433 F.2d 635, 636:

> The petitioner was warned in his application for a visitor's visa that gainful employment in the United States would constitute violation of visa conditions, and he agreed, in making that application, to abide by all the terms of his admission.

However, the court finds that it is the defendant who is the main perpetrator, intent on evading and taking advantage of the Immigration Laws. It appears that plaintiff was not the first "friend" that the defendant has manipulated into working for his restaurant with grandiose promises but without remuneration, and, unless this court takes action to prevent its continuance, will not be the last.

The cases cited by the defendant in support of his motion to dismiss merely establish that if an alien on a visitor's visa is employed in this country in violation of the Immigration Laws, he is subject to deportation. However, aliens do have certain rights under our laws and access to our courts to redress certain wrongs.

Prior to 1952, the Immigration Law (8 U.S.C., §141) expressly made work contracts entered into "previous to migration" by undocumented aliens "void and of no effect." "Apparently, Congress determined that the exclusion of certain aliens from admission to the United States was a more satisfactory sanction than rendering their contracts void, and thus unjustifiably enriching employers of such alien laborers." *Gates* v. *Rivers Construction Co., Inc., supra*, 515 P.2d p. 1023. It therefore repealed and replaced that section with 8 U.S.C., §1182(a)(14). This court must agree with the court in *Gates* that "permitting employers knowingly to employ excludable aliens and then with impunity to refuse to pay them for their services" (*supra*, p. 1023) does not safeguard American labor from unwanted competition. Furthermore, even under the repealed section, it has been held in New York that an alien could recover for a work contract entered into *after* entering the United States, since the statute forbade only work contracts entered into "previous to migration." *Dezsofi* v. *Jacoby*, 178 Misc.2d 851, 36 N.Y.S.2d 672. The present statute may not be construed to prohibit all work contracts entered into by undocumented aliens. In addition, to deny an alien such redress would, in the court's opinion, violate his right to equal protection under the Fourteenth Amendment to the Constitution.

New York State does not have any effective statutory prohibition against an employer knowingly hiring illegal aliens. The Federal law, which makes it a felony to harbor illegal entrants, does not encompass employment. Therefore, the only equitable alternative available to this court is to allow the employee to recover based on the theory of unjust enrichment. Defendant was well aware that a party to an illegal contract cannot ask the court to help him carry out his illegal objective, and being quite knowledgeable about the Immigration Laws, has managed to run his enterprises without fairly compensating his employees.

This court holds that plaintiff's violation is overshadowed by defendant's entire course of deceptive conduct and, therefore, plaintiff is entitled to payment under the New York State Labor Law of the minimum wage then in effect for the period from January 1, 1973, to May 13, 1974, amounting to $6,629.60 (the initial 15 weeks constituting the period of plaintiff's apprenticeship), plus liquidated damages of $1,657.40, equal to 25%, totalling $8,287. In addition, defendant shall pay the sum of $1,500 as and for reasonable attorney's fees.

However, in arriving at any monies due to the plaintiff, credit must be given to the defendant for (a) the fair and reasonable value for room and board provided by the defendant in the sum of $2,400; (b) the payment of $450; and (c) air fare to New York in the sum of $688.

All motions made during the trial of this action, and upon which the court reserved decision, are decided in accordance with this decision.

Accordingly, judgment shall be entered for the plaintiff in the sum of $6,249, plus interest, costs and disbursements.

FOR DISCUSSION

1. What acts of the plaintiff cause him to have "unclean hands"?
2. Why can't the plaintiff recover on his contract of employment?
3. Is the remedy of unjust enrichment appropriate here? Explain.
4. Which party to the proceeding is the court more concerned about punishing, plaintiff or Wadud?
5. Is there a strong public interest at stake in this case? Do you think the outcome might be different if citizens of New York were actually being deprived of jobs?

Laches

Laches is an equitable principle that denies equitable assistance to a person who has been guilty of an unconscionable delay in asserting his right to relief. Ordinarily laches is a defense against an equitable claim rather than a means of seeking affirmative equitable relief; that is, in the words of a maxim, laches is a "shield rather than a sword." The point of laches is that the Court of Equity, in its discretion, will withhold relief when the petitioner's delay will cause harm or prejudice to the defendant. Laches is seen as the opposite of "vigilance and diligence"—the plaintiff has neglected to pursue his rights in a timely way and has thereby caused harm to the adverse party. Laches is predicated on the assumption that the other party has changed his circumstances in reliance on the claimant's failure to assert his claim and would now suffer a disproportionate harm if the claim were asserted. It is based on the maxims "He who seeks equity must do equity" and "He who comes to equity must come with clean hands" and is concerned to prevent the injustice that might be caused by allowing someone to pursue a claim that has become "stale" through the neglect or omission of the claimant.

A similar doctrine is that of **equitable estoppel**. That doctrine operates in situations where one party allows another party to act or fail to act in reliance on a material fact which is untrue or mistaken. In such a case the first party, who knew the true state of affairs but nevertheless allowed or induced the other party to rely on the mistaken fact to his detriment, is barred from pleading or proving the truth because, owing to his own action or inaction, he allowed the other party to order his affairs in reliance on the untrue situation. Again, the basis of this doctrine is "He who seeks equity must do equity," and its purpose is to prevent injustice by forbidding one to speak against his own act or words to the detriment of one who reasonably relied on either. Thus the doctrine is based on morality and fair dealing and serves the ends of justice. Unlike laches, which may be based on neglect rather than deliberation or willfulness, the main target of equitable estoppel is fraud.

CASE

In the Matter of Harry Vickery v. Village of Saugerties
New York Supreme Court, Appellate Division (1984)
106 A.D.2d 721, 483 N.Y.S.2d 765

MEMORANDUM DECISION. The procedural history of this matter is somewhat complex. Petitioner was a police officer with respondent, the Village of Saugerties located in Ulster County, in May, 1972. On May 31, 1972, he was charged with misconduct; i.e., taking property at 12:20 A.M. on May 29, 1972, from Saugerties Coal and Lumber

Company without permission. On July 25, 1972, after a hearing, the Village of Saugerties Board of Trustees (board) found him guilty of misconduct and discharged him from the police force. On October 6, 1972, the Ulster County Civil Service Commission affirmed the finding of misconduct, but recommended that the penalty be modified from suspension to discharge without pay from May 29, 1972, to September 19, 1972. Thereafter, the village commenced a CPLR article 78 proceeding, and the decision of the Civil Service Commission was annulled on March 1, 1973, by the Supreme Court of Ulster County and a new hearing was ordered. On June 21, 1974, petitioner moved to modify the Supreme Court's order. Nine months later, on March 12, 1975, an order was entered on the motion to modify which directed the board to hold a hearing within 30 days. On October 31, 1975, after two days of hearings, the appointed hearing officer recommended that the charges against petitioner be dismissed. Three years later, by petition dated October 10, 1978, petitioner commenced a CPLR article 78 proceeding against respondent seeking reinstatement and back wages.

On April 12, 1979, the Supreme Court of Ulster County rendered a decision on the October 10, 1978, petition, denying the petition without prejudice[14] and remitting the matter again to the board for appropriate findings and compilation of a record within 20 days of service of the order. The decision expressly directed petitioner to submit an order in accordance with the decision.

Four years later, on April 27, 1983, petitioner finally submitted the order in accordance with the April 12, 1979, decision, which was signed and subsequently entered on April 29, 1983. Petitioner now claims that he has acted diligently in the matter and that his former attorney, now deceased, is to blame for the four-year delay.

On May 26, 1983, respondent moved to vacate the April 1983 order, *inter alia*, on the ground of laches. Respondent alleges that it has been prejudiced by the four year delay because records of the event are now missing and witnesses to the misconduct no longer live in the area.

Before a decision was made on the motion to vacate, petitioner filed a second CPLR article 78 proceeding on May 31, 1983, again requesting, *inter alia*, reinstatement and back pay. Respondent then made a second motion to dismiss the second proceeding on the grounds of laches, CPLR 9802, and the Statute of Limitations. Special Term denied both motions. Special Term did, however, grant leave to appeal from the order entered April 29, 1983, which remitted the matter to the board for appropriate findings and dismissed the petition without prejudice. This court, by order dated July 2, 1984, granted respondent permission to appeal to this court from so much of the order of Special Term, entered May 3, 1984, as denied respondent's motion to dismiss the second CPLR article 78 proceeding.

Respondent claims that petitioner should have been barred by laches from having the order dated April 27, 1983, signed and entered. We agree. Laches is an equitable doctrine which bars recovery where a party's inaction has prejudiced another party, making it inequitable to permit recovery. *Matter of Sheerin v. New York Fire Dept. Arts. 1 & 1B Pension Funds*, 46 N.Y.2d 488, 414 N.Y.S.2d 506, 387 N.E.2d 217. Petitioner delayed four years in submitting the order, an act which should have taken a few days. Although petitioner has attempted to place all of the blame on his former attorney, the excuse is not entirely convincing, as petitioner has produced little evidence to support his claim that he has endeavored to move this litigation along. Indeed, the evidence which petitioner has produced merely tends to demonstrate that petitioner was active during the last year of the four-year dormancy. A significant problem with petitioner's excuse is that the four-year delay in question began with a written decision by Justice Klein, which referred the matter to the

---

[14] A dismissal without prejudice is not a dismissal based on the merits of the case and allows the litigant to recommence the action if he so desires.

board for appropriate findings to be completed within *20 days* of service of the order. If, as petitioner claims, he was in touch with his former attorney, and maintained even the slightest familiarity with the case, petitioner should have known that new findings were to be made within a few weeks of the decision, not a few years. The facts simply do not support petitioner's bald assertion that he was diligent in asserting his rights. Moreover, respondent has demonstrated prejudice. It appears that critical documents are now missing and that it will not be able to reconstruct an adequate record.

In sum, the four-year delay without a valid excuse in procuring an order which should have been submitted within a few weeks, together with prejudice, leads unmistakably to the conclusion that petitioner was guilty of laches. The order entered April 29, 1983, should therefore be vacated, and the subsequent petition dated May 26, 1983, dismissed.

FOR DISCUSSION

1. In this case, the petitioner asserts that he acted with "due diligence" in pursuing his remedies. Why doesn't the court agree with petitioner's assertion?

2. According to this decision is delay alone sufficient to warrant dismissal on the ground of laches? If not, what more is needed?

3. Respondent claims it will be hampered in defending itself after so much time because certain critical documents have been lost. Why does the court consider that to be significant? Couldn't the loss of the documents merely be regarded as negligence on respondent's part?

4. Do you consider the outcome of this case to be fair? Does it fit in with what you have learned in this chapter about the equity system?

LEGAL TERMS TO KNOW

clean hands	laches
constructive trust	maxim
contempt	specific performance
equity	substantial justice
estoppel	substituted judgment
fiduciary	unconscionable
injunction	unjust enrichment

ADDITIONAL QUESTIONS AND EXERCISES

1. After reading the cases and materials in this chapter, explain what is meant by rendering "substantial justice." Choose a case from the chapter that best illustrates your understanding of substantial justice and use it to support your answer.

2. Equity is considered to be an "extraordinary" remedy. What does that mean and why is it so? Do you think equitable remedies should be more widely available? Explain.

3. Do you think there is a substantial difference between equitable maxims and other legal rules? Does equity give judges too much discretion? Using the cases in this chapter, give examples of exercises of discretion and indicate what the limits of that discretion appear to be. Are the limits observed?

4. Equity is sometimes known as the "Court of Conscience." Which case in this chapter best exemplifies that concept? Do the principles of equity that you have learned in this chapter have a necessary role to play in the legal system? Explain.

5. Sometimes people treat law and justice as if they were identical. Does your knowledge of equity suggest that law and justice are always the same thing? Give examples.

6. Suppose you were reluctant to entrust judges with the degree of discretion necessary for Equity. Can you think of ways of insuring fairness and flexibility in the legal system without resorting to the equity system?

FOR FURTHER READING

1. BLACK, EUGENE F., "A Brief for Resurrection of Equity Jurisprudence," *Mich. B. J.* 60 (1981), pp. 381–389.

2. KERSHEN, DREW L., "Commentary: Facts, Law and Equity," *Okla. L. Rev.* 35 (1982) pp. 117–125.

3. SAMPEN, DON R., "Law and Equity, the Right to a Jury Trial, and Equal Protection," *Ill. B. J.* 70 (1982). pp. 376–387.

4. WEINBERG, LOUISE, "The New Meaning of Equity," *J. Legal Educ.* 28 (1977), pp. 532–541.

10

REMEDIES

INTRODUCTION

Remedies are the means available in the legal system to enforce a legally recognized right or redress a legally cognizable injury. Remedies are of central importance in our common-law legal system. In fact, the traditional statement "Remedies precede rights" suggests that remedies were the driving force of the early common law, a system dedicated to resolving particular disputes and offering concrete relief rather than articulating rights and duties in the abstract. Not surprisingly, as our society has developed, the demand for remedies to address new, complex problems has resulted in an expansion of remedies, as well as in the legally recognized rights that entitle people to a remedy.

In the early days of the common law, the basic remedy in civil lawsuits was **damages**, monetary compensation for harm caused by the defendant to the plaintiff. With the advent of equity, the remedy of the **injunction**, an order of the court directing a person to either do or refrain from doing something, became available. In essence, these remain the core remedies of our legal system, even though they have been refined and diversified over time. Today, we look to judicial remedies to compensate (**damages**); to prevent unjust enrichment (**restitution**); to order persons to do or refrain from doing on pain of contempt (**injunctions**); or to determine a person's legal rights in a particular situation (**declaratory judgment**). We still categorize remedies as either legal or equitable in nature, and that classification determines both the nature and availability of a particular remedy in a given situation, as well as the availability of a jury trial in the matter. Sometimes plaintiffs must choose between available remedies, but on other occasions a plaintiff may ask for both a legal and an equitable remedy, such as damages and an injunction, to obtain full relief.

Even though "remedies precede rights," according to the old saying, the type of right a plaintiff claims determines, in large measure, what relief is available. In most cases in property, contract, and tort, for example, the established remedy is damages, but equitable remedies such as injunctions and specific performance (a specialized form of injunction) are increasingly in demand and increasingly granted in situations in which damages used to be the only available remedy.

Because we discussed the basic scope and rules of equity in Chapter 9, our examination of equitable remedies in this chapter is limited and somewhat technical, concerning itself mainly with the nature and limitations of two equitable remedies, the injunction, and specific performance. The main focus of the chapter, however, is on the legal remedy of damages. What is the purpose of the damages remedy and how is it awarded? Damages, too, have their specialized categories, and we will examine compensatory, nominal, liquidated, and punitive damages in an effort to assess the range of this time-honored remedy, as well as gain an insight into its possible limitations. The final remedy we will consider is the declaratory judgment and its place in our justice system.

We will also encounter once again a series of questions that build a kind of recurring theme in this text: Is the civil justice system "out of control"? Are judicial and statutory remedies too readily available? Are aggressive litigants and activist judges going too far in expanding the rights that give rise to remedies and the scope and availability of those remedies? Are juries adequate to the task of assessing damages in ever more complex and often emotionally charged circumstances? Can our society, and particularly our economy, afford the costs of the ever-expanding availability of monetary and other forms of relief to more and more legally recognized "victims"? No doubt these questions have been raised continually ever since the Royal Courts of Justice opened for business at Westminster at the beginning of the common law in England, but the urgency with which these questions are being raised in the United States today suggests that many regard our legal system as being in a state of crisis, and remedies are just one aspect of that crisis.

EQUITABLE REMEDIES

In the broadest sense, any remedy other than damages is considered a form of equitable relief. As we saw in Chapter 9, Equity provides flexible remedies designed to do substantial justice in situations in which damages are unavailable or are inadequate to enforce the particular right or redress the particular wrong complained of by the plaintiff. Remedies such as **restitution** (defined previously), **reformation** (which is the rewriting of a contract in a situation where the written provisions do not express what the parties actually agreed to), **rescission** (the cancellation of a fraudulent or unfair and unconscionable contract), and **declaratory judgment** today occupy a kind of border area between law and equity, although they all began as equitable remedies.

Today, when we think of equitable remedies, we think first and foremost of the injunction, the decree of specific performance, and specialized equitable relief such as the **accounting** (discussed in chapter 9), **partition** (an action to divide real property owned by more than one person), the **trust**, or the **constructive trust**. As you will recall, equitable remedies are considered to be **extraordinary remedies**—that is, to obtain equitable relief, a litigant must demonstrate the following: (1) that there is no adequate remedy available at law; (2) that the plaintiff has clean hands; (3) that the plaintiff has not engaged in delay that will cause adverse effects on the defendant (laches); and (4) that the remedy requested is capable of practical enforcement in a given situation. Because the granting of equitable remedies is in the discretion of the court, such remedies will not be granted if the plaintiff cannot meet these requirements.

Injunctions

An injunction is a court order telling a person to do or not do something. It is directed toward the **prevention of future harm** rather than to the redressing of past injuries, which can be dealt with through damages. Generally, in order to obtain an injunction, a plaintiff must show that no other form of relief is adequate in the situation and that he or she will suffer otherwise uncompensable injury if the injunction is not granted.

Over time, various forms of injunctions have developed. The **temporary (or preliminary) injunction** is used to maintain the status quo or preserve the subject matter of a dispute until the parties' rights can be determined through litigation. The **permanent injunction** is a permanent (or at least long-term) order respecting a right that has been established through litigation. As we discussed in Chapter 9, injunctions were originally negative in character (**prohibitory injunction**); that is, they ordered persons not to do certain things. Over time, the **mandatory injunction**, an order directing a person to affirmatively do a certain thing, was developed. An offshoot of the injunction is the **temporary restraining order** (often referred to as a **TRO**), which is an **ex parte order** (granted without prior hearing, on minimal notice to the other party) requested to prevent immediate irreparable harm until such time as a temporary or permanent injunction can be applied for. Because TROs are ex parte orders, they are only granted in situations of real emergency when immediate relief is necessary to prevent irreparable harm. The application for a TRO is generally accompanied by an **order to show cause**, which summons the other party to a hearing to determine whether more permanent relief should be granted.

In deciding whether to grant an application for an injunction, the court must exercise its discretion. That means, in addition to considering the four factors required for any equitable relief (mentioned earlier), that the judge must also examine and balance the competing interests of the plaintiff and defendant with respect to the injunction. If preventing harm to the plaintiff will result in disproportionate harm to the defendant or to the public, the injunction may not be granted. As we saw in Chapter 9, the issue of the public interest is of great concern in equity, and often public interest issues may be decisive in cases involving injunctions. For example, suppose a group of homeowners seeks an injunction to prevent a corporation from expanding its operations in a way that will harm the value of their property and their ability to enjoy it. The court will consider all the competing issues such as (1) the character of the area in which the dispute arises; (2) the value of the property and the degree of harm suffered by the plaintiffs; (3) the degree of harm to the defendant if the injunction is granted; and (4) the consequences to the public. If the corporation employs a great many people and contributes significantly to the economy of the area, and if the granting of the injunction will cost jobs and adversely affect the local economy, the court may well decide not to grant the injunction and compel the plaintiffs to make do with damages for the harm they have suffered. Such matters are within the sound discretion of the court, and decisions of this type are not infrequent.

In the following case the plaintiff is seeking an injunction against his employer to prevent continuing injury to his health due to smoking by co-workers in the workplace. You should pay particular attention to the court's analysis of the appropriateness of injunctive relief in such situations, particularly with respect to "potential" or future injuries in contrast to those permanent injuries which have already occurred.

CASE   Paul Smith v. Western Electric Company
                              Missouri Court of Appeals (1982)
                              643 S.W.2d 10, 37 A.L.R.4th 473

DOWD, Presiding Judge.   Plaintiff appeals from an order dismissing his petition on the ground that it fails to state a claim upon which relief can be granted.

The petition seeks an injunction to prevent plaintiff's employer from exposing him to tobacco smoke in the workplace and from affecting his pay or employment conditions because of his medical reaction to tobacco smoke. The petition alleges that by allowing smoking in the work area, defendant permits its employees to be exposed to a health hazard and thereby breaches its duty to provide a safe place in which to work.

Plaintiff contends that the trial court erred in dismissing his petition in that it invokes legal principles entitling him to relief and shows that injunctive relief is appropriate. Plaintiff further contends that federal law does not preempt state common law in this case.

In reviewing this petition for failure to state a claim, we grant the petition its broadest intendment and liberally construe its averments. We accept as true all factual allegations and their favorable inferences. If the averments thus viewed invoke principles of substantive law upon which relief can be granted to plaintiff, the petition is not subject to dismissal. Any reasonable doubt with regard to the petition's sufficiency is resolved in favor of plaintiff.

The petition includes the following allegations. Plaintiff has been employed by defendant since 1950 and has worked in defendant's Missouri branch since 1967. He is a nonsmoker sharing an open office area with other employees, many of whom smoke tobacco products as they work. In 1975 plaintiff began to experience severe respiratory tract discomfort as a result of inhaling tobacco smoke in the workplace. A subsequent medical evaluation determined that plaintiff suffers a severe adverse reaction to tobacco smoke. His symptoms include sore throat, nausea, dizziness, headache, blackouts, loss of memory, difficulty in concentration, aches and pains in joints, sensitivity to noise and light, cold sweat, gagging, choking sensations, and light-headedness. After a sufficient period of non-exposure to smoke, plaintiff's symptoms abate somewhat. The symptoms have become increasingly severe over the years, however. Doctors evaluating and treating plaintiff have advised him to avoid contact with tobacco smoke whenever possible.

The petition further alleges that plaintiff first complained to defendant about the tobacco smoke in the workplace in 1975. Defendant thereafter moved plaintiff to different locations within the plant, but no improvement resulted because each location contained significant amounts of tobacco smoke. In 1978 plaintiff was informed that he should no longer submit complaints about the smoke through defendant's anonymous complaint procedure since defendant would not process them. In response to recommendations of the National Institute for Occupational Safety and Health, defendant adopted a smoking policy in April 1980. The declared policy was to protect the rights of both smokers and nonsmokers by providing accommodations for both groups and by making a reasonable effort to separate the groups in work areas. Because defendant has failed to implement its policy by making such a reasonable effort, improvement of the air in the workplace has not resulted.

According to the petition, in August 1980 plaintiff filed with defendant a Handicapped Declaration Statement that he was handicapped by his susceptibility to tobacco smoke. Refusing to segregate smokers or to limit smoking to non-work areas, defendant informed plaintiff he could either continue to work in the same location and wear a respirator or apply for a job in the computer room (where smoking is prohibited). The latter option would entail a pay decrease of about $500 per month. Defendant thereafter provided plaintiff with a respirator that has proven ineffective in protecting plaintiff from tobacco smoke.

The petition states that plaintiff has exhausted all avenues of relief through defendant; he has no adequate remedy at law; he is suffering and will continue to suffer irreparable physical injuries and financial losses unless defendant improves working conditions. The petition alleges that defendant is breaching its common law duty as an employer to provide plaintiff a safe place to work, and that defendant has available reasonable alternatives to avoid the continuous breach of duty, as demonstrated by defendant's ability to protect its computer equipment from tobacco smoke. The petition further states that, although "second-hand smoke" is harmful to the health of all employees, defendant is permitting them to be exposed in the workplace to this health hazard which is neither related to nor a necessary by-product of defendant's business.

Construing these allegations favorably to the plaintiff, we must determine whether they invoke principles of law entitling him to relief.

It is well-settled in Missouri that an employer owes a duty to the employee to use all reasonable care to provide a reasonably safe workplace and to protect the employee from avoidable perils. Whether the employer has fulfilled its duty depends upon the facts of each case. For example, in *McDaniel* v. *Kerr*, 258 S.W.2d 629 (Mo.banc 1953), the employer had failed to provide a safe workplace where the employee's inhalation of dust on the job caused damage requiring removal of his lung. In *DeMarco* v. *United States*, 204 F.Supp. 290 (E.D.N.Y. 1962), the court found a negligent failure to provide a safe working environment where the plaintiff was injured when he fainted and fell after complaining about gasoline fumes in an unventilated work area.

The allegations of the instant case, taken as true, show that the tobacco smoke of co-workers smoking in the work area is hazardous to the health of employees in general and plaintiff in particular. The allegations also show that defendant has the authority, ability, and reasonable means to control smoking in areas requiring a smoke-free environment. Therefore, by failing to exercise its control and assume its responsibility to eliminate the hazardous condition caused by tobacco smoke, defendant has breached and is breaching its duty to provide a reasonably safe workplace. As stated in *Thompson* v. *Kroeger*, 380 S.W.2d 339, 343-44 (Mo.1964) (quoting *Gatzke* v. *Terminal Railroad Ass'n of St. Louis*, 321 S.W.2d 462, 466 (Mo.1959):

> the exercise of due care requires precautions which a reasonably prudent employer would have taken in given circumstances, even though other employers may not have taken such commensurate precautions. What usually is done may be evidence of what ought to be done, but what ought to be done is fixed by a standard of reasonable prudence, whether it is usually complied with or not.

If plaintiff's petition establishes defendant's failure to provide a safe place for plaintiff to work, we must next consider whether injunctive relief would be an appropriate remedy. An injunction may issue "to prevent the doing of any legal wrong whatever, whenever in the opinion of the court an adequate remedy cannot be afforded by an action for damages." §526.030 RSMo. 1978. Injunctive relief is unavailable unless irreparable harm is otherwise likely to result, *see City of Grandview* v. *Moore*, 481 S.W.2d 555, 558 (Mo.App.1972), and plaintiff has no adequate remedy at law. See *State ex. rel. Taylor* v. *Anderson*, 242 S.W.2d 66, 72 (Mo.1951).

The petition alleges that plaintiff's continuing exposure to smoke in the workplace is increasingly deleterious to his health and is causing irreparable harm. Assuming the allegations and reasonable inferences therefrom to be true, we think it is fair to characterize deterioration of plaintiff's health as "irreparable" and as a harm for which money damages cannot adequately compensate. This is particularly true where the harm has not yet resulted in full-blown disease or injury. Money damages, although inadequate, are the best possible remedy once physical damage is done, but they are certainly inadequate to compensate permanent injury which could have been prevented. Plaintiff should not be required to await the harm's fruition before he is entitled to seek an inadequate remedy. Moreover, the nature of plaintiff's unsafe work environment represents a recurrent risk of harm that would necessitate a multiplicity of lawsuits. Finally, the petition states that plaintiff has no adequate remedy at law and alleges facts indicating that prior to this action plaintiff unsuccessfully pursued relief, both through his employer's in-house channels and through administrative agencies. Viewing the petition favorably, as we must to determine its sufficiency, we find that injunction would be an appropriate remedy.

Defendant contends the trial court lacks jurisdiction to provide relief, and therefore the petition fails to state a claim upon which relief can be granted, because the subject matter of this case is preempted by the Occupational Safety and Health Act (OSHA), 29 U.S.C. §§ 651–678 (1970). The Act specifically states, however, that it does not affect the common law regarding "injuries, diseases, or death of employees arising out of...employment." §653(b)(4). The Act also declares that it does not prevent a state court from asserting jurisdiction over an occupational safety or health issue for which no OSHA standard is in effect. §667(a). We are unpersuaded by defendant's argument that §653(b)(4) refers only to the common law pertaining to workers' compensation laws. In addition, defendant has not directed our attention to any OSHA standard which would appear to cover tobacco smoke. No such standard figured in the opinions of other courts considering OSHA and tobacco smoke. Furthermore, defendant conceded in oral argument that a court may retain jurisdiction in the absence of an OSHA standard.

The judgment is reversed and the cause is remanded.

FOR DISCUSSION

1. According to the court, what conditions must be fulfilled for injunctive relief to be appropriate?

2. What is the court's understanding of the term "irreparable injury"? Does plaintiff's situation fit the court's definition?

3. What purpose is served by awarding damages? What different purpose is served by granting an injunction?

4. Why is it particularly inappropriate to limit the plaintiff in this case to an award of damages?

5. What facts in this case support the court's conclusion that providing a smoke-free work environment is not an unreasonable or burdensome demand to place on this employer? Do you agree?

Specific Performance

Specific performance is an order directing a person to actually perform as agreed under a contract. Because this equitable remedy is only available in situations in which damages is not an adequate remedy, specific performance is generally granted when the subject matter of a contract is unique. That is, in most cases a person whose contract is breached can replace the item or service contracted for in the open market and then sue the other party for any damages suffered as a result of the breach. But if the thing contracted for cannot be replaced, then damages is not an adequate remedy.

Specific performance originated in cases involving contracts for sale and purchase of real property, because land is considered to be a unique and irreplaceable item. Gradually other unique items have been recognized and made the subject of specific performance, such as a work of art or a valuable antique. Ordinarily fungible goods, (goods that are mass produced and interchangeable, such as most consumer goods) cannot be unique goods for purposes of specific performance, but occasionally an otherwise interchangeable item can become unique because of scarcity or association with a famous person or event. Thus, President John F. Kennedy's rocking chair or a Cadillac belonging to Elvis Presley may be considered a unique item, the sale of which could be compelled by specific performance.

As we discussed in Chapter 9, specific performance is not available in contracts of employment, because forcing a person to work is too much like slavery, not to mention the fact that the quality of the work under such circumstances is not likely to be very good. In employment cases involving unique services (such as a famous athlete or entertainer), instead of specific performance a court may issue an injunction prohibiting the person from performing for anyone else during the period of the contract that he or she breached.

In the following case, the main issue is the appropriateness of specific performance as a remedy in this particular situation. A second key issue involves provision of services as a part of the original deal and how that affects the request for specific performance.

CASE   DeBauge Bros., Incorporated v. G. C. Whitsitt
                Supreme Court of Kansas (1973)
                212 Kan. 758, 512 P.2d 487, 82 A.L.R.3d 1095

OWSLEY, Justice.   Defendants appeal from the trial court's order sustaining plaintiff's motion for summary judgment directing specific performance of a contract for sale of defendant's business.

Defendants are G. C. Whitsitt and Bernica R. Whitsitt, owners of the Emporia Coca Cola Bottling Company. In the Fall of 1970, Whitsitt was negotiating a sale of his plant and franchise rights with Robert Wagstaff of the Kansas City Coca Cola Bottling Company. He refused Wagstaff's proposal, considering the offered price too low. DeBauge Brothers, Inc., an Emporia corporation, contacted Whitsitt on December 11, 1970, and offered to buy the plant and franchise for $172,000. Whitsitt accepted, and DeBauge's attorney prepared a contract for sale and presented it to Whitsitt the following day. After some changes suggested by Whitsitt, it was signed by the parties on December 17, 1970. The transfer and sale were subject to approval of the Coca Cola Corporation, and Whitsitt agreed as part of the contract to make immediate application for that approval. Other terms of the contract provided for sale of real and personal property, franchise, and good will for $100,000. Inventory was not included in the sale price. DeBauge Brothers, Inc. agreed to employ Whitsitt and/or his sons as consultants for six years at $1000 per month. The $72,000 to be paid for consulting services constituted the balance of the purchase price and the parties agreed to execute a separate contract setting forth in detail the terms of the consulting service. Payments on the purchase price were to be escrowed until Coca Cola approved the franchise transfer.

Whitsitt received a letter from Wagstaff on December 29, 1970, containing another offer to buy the plant and franchise for $150,000 cash. Whitsitt testified he began to feel the DeBauge deal of $100,000 cash, plus $72,000 in deferred payments as salary for consulting services, was not as advantageous to him as Wagstaff's second offer. He concluded the deferred payments made to him as salary would be reduced considerably by social security and income tax.

DeBauge Brothers, Inc. made the agreed payments to escrow, $5,000 at the time of signing and $45,000 on January 1, 1971, and took possession of the plant on that date. Later that month, despite a letter from Coca Cola agreeing to meet with DeBauge and Whitsitt on January 14, 1971, and approve transfer of the franchise, Whitsitt told DeBauge that Coca Cola would not accept them as franchisee, the deal was off, and he wanted the keys back. They surrendered the plant to him.

DeBauge Brothers, Inc. filed this suit for specific performance and $200,000 damages for lost rents and profits on March 25, 1971. Defendants admitted their refusal to deliver abstracts to the real estate and admitted they did not make formal application to Coca Cola for approval of the franchise transfer as provided in the contract. They admitted execution of the contract, but alleged defendant G. C. Whitsitt did not have capacity to enter into a valid contract due to his age and infirmity. Defendants further alleged the contract was not subject to specific performance since it contained provisions for personal services.

Plaintiff moved for summary judgment, for specific performance, and for damages for loss of rents and profits. Wagstaff's offer of December 29, 1970, and the Coca Cola company's letter of December 30, 1970 offering to meet with DeBauge and Whitsitt to negotiate transfer of the franchise, were entered into evidence along with depositions of the parties, briefs of counsel, and oral arguments on the motion. The court sustained plaintiff's motion for summary judgment, ordered specific performance of the contract for sale, and an evidentiary hearing on the amount of damages due plaintiff for loss of rents and profits.

On appeal, defendants assert the court erred in ordering specific performance because the contract contained provisions for personal services and was unenforceable since it provided for making a separate contract for those services. They also claim specific performance was not necessary because plaintiff had an adequate remedy at law for damages.

We find no merit to these contentions. Plaintiff had no adequate remedy in money damages since the real and personal properties to be conveyed were unique and were not available to plaintiff from any other source. Land conveyances are frequently the subject of specific performance due to the unique properties of each parcel which cannot be duplicated. Franchises are by their very nature unique and exclusive, which is the source of their value to the possessor. A contract for sale or transfer of such a retail franchise, along with the real property necessary to operate the business, is a proper subject for specific performance.

Defendants further contend the court erred in ordering specific performance because the contract included provisions for personal services and, to be complete, required execution of an additional contract for those services. It is our conclusion that the provisions for personal services of defendants were only incidental to the intent of the parties. It is clear that services of this kind by the defendants have some monetary value, but the payment provided for them in the contract is clearly out of proportion to such value. In an equitable proceeding for specific performance of a contract, the court looks to the real intent of the parties and enforces the contract accordingly. Consulting services might be temporarily valuable following change of ownership, but it is obvious that after an initial period of operation, much less than six years, these consulting services will grow valueless as vendee's experience in the manufacture, sale and distribution of beverages increases. We conclude the real purpose of the payment of $12,000 per year was not for consulting services, but was a method of enforcing the agreement not to compete for that period. Had the contract not provided for these services, consideration for the sale of the business would have been the same, $172,000. It is apparent that the purchaser was willing to continue the deferred payments, even in the event of the death of the seller, G. C. Whitsitt, indicating payment was not dependent upon his performance of consulting services. The purchaser indicated in its brief that payment of the total consideration, including the deferred payments, was not dependent upon consulting services of the seller; and in argument before this court stated its willingness to pay the whole purchase price regardless of the availability of such services. It is a recognized principle of equity that a vendee, in an action brought by him for specific performance of a contract, may waive the performance on the part of the vendor of portions of his contract, and may elect to take a partial performance if he himself is willing to perform fully. *Wallerius* v. *Hare*, 200 Kan. 578, 438 P.2d 65.

Defendant claims the court erred in granting specific performance because there is no mutuality of remedies. The argument has no merit as a matter of law. Mutuality of remedy does not require identical remedies. The granting or refusal of the decree is not to be determined by whether the remedy of specific performance is mutually available to both parties to the contract. Specific performance at the instance of one party will not be denied merely because that remedy is not available to the other party against whom specific performance is sought. This court has long been committed to the view that many valid contracts afford one party a remedy by an action for recovery of money, either upon a specific promise to pay or in an action for damages, while the other party may be entitled to specific performance.

Defendants' assertions of procedural errors in sustaining plaintiff's motion for summary judgment are without merit. They contend in their answer that G. C. Whitsitt had no capacity to contract due to his age and infirmity, and that this question of fact was at issue. The depositions of all interested parties were before the court. We find no indication in any of the testimony that Whitsitt did not understand the provisions of the agreement at the time of its execution. There was no complaint of fraud, overreaching, undue influence, or any other factor which, combined with his age, would indicate that it was not Whitsitt's intention to sign the contract as written. The test of mental capacity to contract is whether the person possesses sufficient mind to understand in a reasonable manner the nature and effect of the act in which he is engaged. *Mills* v. *Shepherd*, 159 Kan. 668, 157 P.2d 533. Since the testimony of all interested parties was before the trial court and there was a complete absence of any claim of lack of understanding of the effect of the contract, we conclude there was no genuine issue of fact as to his mental capacity. Summary judgment should be rendered forthwith if the pleadings, depositions, answers to any interrogatories, and admissions on file, together with the affidavits, if any, show there is no genuine issue as to any material fact. K.S.A. 60–256. The trial court was justified in granting summary judgment for specific performance.

Affirmed.

FOR DISCUSSION

1. According to the defendant, why was specific performance an inappropriate remedy in this case?
2. Did the plaintiff have an adequate remedy at law? Would he be fully compensated by an award of damages? Explain.
3. What is a franchise? Why might a franchise be considered a unique item?

4. In the opinion of the court, did the contract in this case really involve provision of personal services? What was plaintiff trying to accomplish by contracting for defendant's services as a consultant?

5. Is the outcome in this case fair? Justify your answer.

LEGAL REMEDIES

In this section we will examine the legal remedy of **damages**. Damages is monetary compensation for harm caused by the invasion of a legal right or for a legally cognizable injury. The rights and legally recognized harms, of course, are found in the substantive law of torts, contracts, or whatever other legal subject is involved in the particular incident. The remedy of damages is principally intended to restore the injured party to the position he would have occupied had the injury not occurred. There are, however, other possibilities. In this section we will consider nominal, compensatory, liquidated, and punitive damages, each of which has a different purpose and different underlying philosophy.

Although damages is a time-honored remedy in our law, there has been considerable criticism in recent years about the way damages are awarded. Often we read in the newspaper of multimillion (today even multibillion) dollar damages awards and are frequently warned by the insurance industry, in particular, that excessive damages awards are becoming the ruin of the civil justice system. All actors in the legal process are criticized in connection with this problem, but much of the blame is heaped on the juries that render enormous damages verdicts. In the following article, the authors offer statistical evidence that sheds a different light on the claims about excessive jury awards.

READING   ## Civil Jury Awards Are Not Out Of Control
Stephen Daniels and Joanne Martin*

It is by now a maxim, which few have dared challenge: The nation is facing an insurance crisis of unprecedented proportion. The allegation is that the civil system has run amok, that traditional legal standards have eroded and that the number and amount of jury awards made to plaintiffs have reached unprecedented levels. From this perspective, the only choice available to us, if we are to have affordable premiums, is to institute civil justice reform. Thus, legislatures in at least 40 states have enacted some kind of civil justice reform since early 1985.

However, claims about jury behavior that are typically used to illustrate a malfunctioning civil justice system as a justification for reform have little basis in fact. Our findings suggest that jury awards are not, generally speaking, out of control. Thus, the alleged causes and remedies for the insurance crisis need to be critically evaluated. Many of the proposed reforms—which are being promoted by a multi-million dollar public relations campaign and by a concerted, organized lobbying effort—would involve substantial changes in the civil justice system. As Kenneth Jost, editor of the *Los Angeles Daily Journal*, a legal newspaper, reminded his readers at the end of the *Journal*'s series of stories on the crisis, "[t]he current tort reform movement seeks not neutral efficiency-enhancing procedural changes, but substantive legal revisions to rewrite the rules more in their [the reformer's] favor."

This article will be limited to an examination of civil jury verdicts and awards, which have been identified as one of the principal causes of the insurance crisis. It will first briefly discuss the place of civil juries in the policy debate; and then it will review some of the findings of a 43-site survey of civil jury awards in state trial courts. The information from this survey may have some direct, practical implications for judges who are called upon to render civil awards from the bench and who are asked to reassess jury awards.

JURY VERDICTS AND THE POLICY DEBATE

About one issue there is little debate—the immediate problems of availability, affordability, and adequacy of certain lines of insurance and the effect of this on the provision of goods and services by those who need to be covered to operate. Rather, the debate centers on the causes of and remedies for these problems. The reformers perceive that the insurance crisis is caused by factors external to the insurance industry and to the affected parts of the economy. It is only a symptom and consequence of a more fundamental crisis in the civil justice system.

Probably the most visible and symbolically important example of this perspective is the U.S. Justice Department's *Report of the Tort Policy Working Group on the Causes, Extent and Policy Implications of the Current Crisis in Insurance Availability and Affordability*. It identifies four major causes for the insurance crisis. The first is the erosion of the idea of "fault" and the increasing use of various no-fault approaches (such as strict liability that allow plaintiffs to establish a cause of action against defendants who are not directly and immediately at fault). Second, and related, is the attenuation and erosion of the idea of causation through doctrines such as joint and several liability which force defendants to pay far beyond their alleged contribution to the injury (the "deep pockets" idea). Third is alleged explosive growth in the number and size of damage awards made by juries, especially for non-economic damages like pain and suffering awards and punitive damages. The final cause is the increasing level of transaction costs in the tort system—legal fees and the like which ultimately are not paid to plaintiffs. According to one insurance industry trade journal, the Justice Department *Report* "...strongly supports insurance industry positions on the causes of current availability and affordability problems and on civil justice reform."

Having identified the causes of the crisis, the *Report* also presents a number of specific reform proposals. Among them are: retention of fault as the basis for liability and elimination of the no-fault concept; express limitation of non-economic damages, with the strong implication that punitive damages should be abolished; elimination of joint and several liability; and limitation of contingency fees for plaintiffs' attorneys. The reform proposals offered by the insurance industry and business interests are essentially the same as those presented in the *Report*. They also include recommendations for a modified or 50 percent comparative negligence system; specific proposals related to jury instructions, pretrial discovery procedures, and the standards and defenses to be used in professional malpractice and product liability cases.

While not always cast as the sole cause of the current crisis in the affordability, availability, and adequacy of insurance, civil juries are portrayed as at least being among the primary causes. The *Report* is typical in this regard. Though the line of causation is never explicitly laid out, the *Report* concludes that "[t]he increase in the number of tort lawsuits and the level of awarded damages (or settlements) in and of itself has an obvious inflating effect on insurance premiums." Jury awards are also a regular target of the insurance industry and business interests, and are often used as both an illustration and as proof of the crisis and the need for substantial civil justice reform.

In characterizing jury awards as a primary cause of the insurance crisis, the reformers cite evidence for alleged trends in jury awards—for awards generally, as well as for particular types of cases such as medical malpractice and product liability—that show rapidly increasing award sizes in recent years. The implication is that jury awards across the country are presently "skyhigh" for all kinds of cases. In other words, the problem is pervasive and national in scope. This is what justifies the call for sweeping and fundamental reform in the civil justice systems of nearly every state.

DATA ON JURY VERDICTS

In this section some of the findings of a study of jury verdicts in 44 counties in 10 states will be presented. Thirty-one local jury verdict reporters covering all or part of 20 states were examined and the data in Tables 10 –1 and 10 –2 are drawn from 12 of these which are chosen on the basis of their accuracy, comprehensiveness, and regional balance. Each of the reporting services used includes information on the county and court in which the case was heard; the date the verdict was rendered; the names of the parties and the attorneys; a short description of the facts of the case; the jury's verdict and the amount of the damages, if awarded; the apportionment of liability, where appropriate; and a breakdown of the award into components such as compensatory, punitive or other exemplary damages.

For each of the sites included in the analysis, all reported jury verdicts in state courts involving a money damage award are included. The data generally cover the years 1981 to 1985 and are presented in combined totals (all years for each site combined); in some cases the number of years is fewer because the data are not available for the entire period. All dollar amounts are reported in 1985 dollars.

Table 10 –1 reports the total number of jury verdicts and the number and percentage of cases in which the plaintiff is successful in being awarded damages in the amount of $1 or more in 44 counties in 10 states being studied. The overall success rates vary considerably from a high of 78.9 percent in Skagit County in Washington to a low of 39.7 percent in Westchester County, New York. In most sites it appears that plaintiffs fare reasonably well; only in four sites (Fresno County, California; San Diego County, California; Nassau County, New York; and Westchester County, New York) were the success rates below 50 percent.

While Table 10–1 shows the variations in success rates among sites in different states, the more interesting figures are the intrastate variations. Some interstate variation may be attributable to deficiencies in legal rules such as negligence systems, but this factor does not provide an intrastate explanation for variations. In some states the range of fluctuation in success rates is very narrow—less than 10 percent. In other states, such as California, New York and Washington, the range of difference is greater. New York exhibits the widest variation—from a 71.9 percent success rate in Bronx County to 39.7 percent in Westchester County. Although the identification of the specific causes of these intrastate variations is beyond the scope of this article, it is possible to speculate on some of the issues involved. Although specific causes behind such wide intrastate variations (where major legal rules are held constant) is beyond the scope of this short essay, there are some clues.

Part of the explanation for unusually high or low success rates might be found in difference in mix of business. A number of studies have shown that different types of cases are more likely to go to trial than others and that plaintiffs are more likely to win in cases involving certain causes of action rather than others. This may explain the very high success rate in Skagit County (78.9 percent) where 52.6 percent of the verdicts are in vehicular accident cases which in turn have a 90 percent success rate in that county. But it is not a useful method for explaining the unusually high success rate in Bronx

Table 10–1 Reported Money Damage Verdicts, Plaintiff Success Rates, and the Range of Awards

	VERDICTS			AWARDS (1985 $)		
	Reported N	PF Wins $ N	PF Wins $ %	Percentile 25th	Percentile 50th	75th
ARIZONA (Superior Court)						
Maricopa (1981–85)	1,765	1,024	58.4%	$ 7,098	$ 20,702	$ 71,600
CALIFORNIA (Superior Court)						
Alameda (1981–84)	269	155	57.5%	$ 17,373	$ 60,020	$212,380
Fresno (1981–84)	120	59	49.2%	$ 32,306	$122,580	$269,532
Los Angeles (1981–84)	2,229	1,243	55.8%	$ 20,720	$ 78,218	$295,750
Sacramento (1981–84)	301	169	56.1%	$ 13,368	$ 51,800	$172,800
San Diego (1981–84)	369	179	48.5%	$ 16,710	$ 65,040	$169,774
San Francisco (1981–84)	534	318	59.6%	$ 21,600	$ 64,961	$207,200
GEORGIA (Superior Court)						
Fulton (1982–84)	539	315	58.4%	$ 6,734	$ 20,720	$ 55,700
DeKalb (1982–84)	239	139	58.2%	$ 2,986	$ 8,433	$ 27,000
Cobb (1982–84)	90	58	64.4%	$ 4,144	$ 11,074	$ 34,631
ILLINOIS (Circuit Court)						
Cook (1981–85)	4,181	2,431	57.9%	$ 3,342	$ 10,382	$ 50,000
DuPage (1981–85)	436	242	55.5%	$ 5,090	$ 12,800	$ 41,440
Kane (1981–85)	171	104	60.8%	$ 8,624	$ 24,920	$ 75,000
Lake (1981–85)	295	179	60.7%	$ 6,603	$ 23,290	$ 75,674
McHenry (1981–85)	61	33	54.1%	$ 4,530	$ 16,145	$ 54,850
Will (1981–85)	290	179	61.7%	$ 6,510	$ 16,841	$ 62,175
Winnebego (1981–85)	148	88	59.5%	$ 3,941	$ 11,830	$ 42,778
KANSAS (District Court)						
Johnson (1981–85)	310	165	53.2%	$ 2,700	$ 9,687	$ 37,696
Wyandotte (1981–85)	286	175	61.2%	$ 4,388	$ 12,477	$ 42,588

Jurisdiction					
MISSOURI (Circuit Court)					
Clay (1981–85)	104	62	59.6%	$ 4,142	$ 17,933	$ 58,195
Jackson (1981–85)	894	496	55.5%	$ 2,958	$ 11,855	$ 50,000
Platte (1981–85)	47	28	59.6%	$ 5,180	$ 13,505	$ 54,001
NEW YORK (Supreme, Civil, County)					
Bronx (1981–84)	363	261	71.9%	$ 77,700	$216,000	$699,744
Erie (1983–84)	134	72	53.7%	$ 18,648	$ 68,770	$155,400
Kings (1981–84)	739	448	60.0%	$ 51,800	$103,600	$463,618
Monroe (1983–84)	92	57	62.0%	$ 10,360	$ 24,840	$108,000
Nassau (1981–84)	595	261	43.9%	$ 15,432	$ 50,316	$130,130
New York (1981–84)	1,025	668	65.2%	$ 46,620	$131,357	$486,000
Onondaga (1983–84)	65	40	61.5%	$ 7,184	$ 27,684	$118,800
Queens (1981–84)	439	234	53.3%	$ 16,710	$ 54,850	$175,557
Richmond (1981–84)	84	51	60.7%	$ 35,490	$ 71,799	$445,600
Suffolk (1981–84)	398	220	55.3%	$ 14,196	$ 40,467	$103,600
Westchester (1981–84)	239	95	39.7%	$ 16,710	$ 46,181	$135,546
OREGON (Circuit Court)					
Multnomah (1984–85)	285	172	60.4%	$ 7,438	$ 25,900	$ 82,817
TEXAS (District, County)					
Bexar (1982–84)	574	302	52.6%	$ 5,400	$ 14,916	$ 49,474
Dallas (1981–85)	2,106	1,071	50.9%	$ 6,684	$ 19,172	$ 63,976
Harris (1981–85)	2,012	1,116	55.5%	$ 4,419	$ 16,787	$ 66,840
WASHINGTON (Superior Court)					
King (1983–85)	416	254	61.1%	$ 7,770	$ 23,289	$ 95,000
Pierce (1983–85)	131	81	61.8%	$ 6,600	$ 17,719	$ 55,000
Skagit (1983–85)	19	15	78.9%	$ 13,000	$ 64,800	$ 81,000
Snohomish (1983–85)	114	68	59.6%	$ 6,216	$ 21,669	$ 55,944
Spokane (1983–85)	122	83	68.0%	$ 11,448	$ 36,260	$ 85,150
Yakima (1983–85)	73	46	63.0%	$ 11,551	$ 30,047	$ 75,498

County and the unusually low success rate in Westchester County. Though not identical, the respective mixes of business for these two counties are relatively similar, but with the exception of some contract cases, the success rates for different types of cases are consistently and dramatically higher in Bronx County. This suggests that substantial intrastate variations in success rates may also be due to fundamental environmental (including attitudinal) differences.

Table 10–1 also displays data on the size of jury awards—the median and interquartile ranges in 1985 dollars. These data show four important things: that award sizes vary by site; that *median* awards (50th percentile when awards are ranged lowest to highest) in most sites are modest (below $50,000); that most interquartile ranges (from the 25th to 75th percentile) are not large with the 75th percentile below $100,000; and that in only a few sites awards are unusually high (medians above $100,000 or interquartile ranges exceeding $250,000).

The size of awards varies dramatically among the 43 sites. Medians vary from a low of $8,433 in DeKalb County, Georgia to a high of $216,000 in Bronx County. The 25th percentile ranges from a low of $2,700 in Johnson County, Kansas to a high of $77,000 in Bronx County. The 75th percentile ranges from $27,000 in DeKalb County to $699,744 in Bronx County. Even with the kind of variation among sites, awards in most sites are modest. Medians in 29 of the 43 counties are $50,000 or less, and just over half (23) are below $25,000. The interquartile ranges are also modest for most sites. The 75th percentile is below $100,000 in 26 sites, and the interquartile range itself is less than $100,000 in almost two-thirds (28) of the sites, indicating that most awards fall within a well-defined and relatively narrow range. Still, there are a few sites in which awards are unusually high in terms of their medians and the widths of their interquartile ranges (the range for Bronx County, for instance, is over $600,000); but they are the exception and not the rule.

Fourteen sites have medians above $50,000 and four are over $100,000. With the exception of Skagit County, all of these high award sites are in New York and California. Part of the reason for the higher awards in the California sites can be traced to the fact that the jury verdict reporter for these sites covers only the superior court, the highest level of trial court. For most of the period covered (1981–84) these courts heard only the money damage cases involving $15,000 or more. Cases involving lesser amounts of money typically went to the municipal courts, and reasonably comprehensive data for those courts are not presently available. In addition, superior court cases under $25,000 may have been diverted to arbitration, especially in Los Angeles County. If the municipal court data were included, we would expect the California medians to be lower and more in line with most other sites.

New York also provides for arbitration in cases involving lesser amounts of money, but the data used *include* verdicts from the lower level courts. This means that the higher awards in New York, primarily in the five counties making up New York City, are especially and unusually high compared to the other sites in the study. The larger dollar award counties (Bronx, Kings, New York and Richmond) also have dramatic ranges, and their respective 25th percentiles are higher than the medians in most other sites.

The reasons for these unusually high awards are unclear. Our first reaction might be to look at legal rules, but the intrastate differences among the New York sites suggest that this will not provide a full explanation. The medians in the upstate counties of Monroe and Onondaga are more similar to those in sites in Texas, Illinois, or Washington than to those around New York City. This suggests, again, that a major part of the explanation for differences in awards may be found in environmental factors. While the two high award states — California and New York

—have wide variation among sites in award sites, in contrast the awards in most states fluctuate within a much narrower range even for quite different counties within the state. This suggests that legal factors may have some importance but only in combination with environmental factors. How much effect is attributable to legal factors alone remains unknown.

Table 10–2 disaggregates the award data and presents median awards (again in 1985 dollars) for seven different types of cases. First are vehicular accident cases, which comprise the largest proportion of reported money damage verdicts in every site. Though typically about one-third of these are accident cases, in some sites they account for as much as one-half or more of all verdicts. Next are medical malpractice and product liability cases which have played such a highly visible role in the policy debate. They comprise only a small proportion of the verdicts. Product liability verdicts are less than 10 percent of the reported money damage verdicts in all sites, and less than 5 percent in 80 percent of the sites (35 of 44). Medical malpractice verdicts are generally less than 10 percent except for the metropolitan New York City area where the percentage goes as high as 17.6 in Kings County. Street hazard cases (against governmental units) and premises liability cases are included in Table 10–2 because they are two types of cases particularly important for discussing issues concerning the availability, affordability, and adequacy of property-casualty insurance. Street hazard cases typically comprise a small proportion of reported verdicts, less than 5 percent except for Bronx County (7 percent) and Snohomish County, Washington (6 percent). Premises liability cases make up a larger proportion of verdicts than street hazards—generally 15 percent or less except for Bronx County (18 percent), Erie County, New York (20 percent), Onondaga County, New York (22 percent), and Skagit County (16 percent).

As Table 10–2 shows, the median awards vary considerably by type of case. Generally speaking, awards in vehicular cases are relatively low, and the success rates of these cases tend to be high (in 77 percent of the sites these success rates are higher than the overall success rates in Table 10–1). The medians for these cases are $40,000 or lower in three-quarters of the sites, and below $20,000 in one-half of the sites. The higher medians occur in Fresno County, California, Skagit County, and the five counties of New York City.

Awards in premises liability cases also tend to be modest, with the exception of metropolitan New York City. Awards for street hazard cases, in contrast, seem to vary considerably, ranging from no award in six sites (even though each—Johnson, Kansas; Monroe and Richmond, New York; Bexar and Dallas, Texas; and Spokane, Washington—had reported street hazard verdicts) to $756,000 in San Diego County, California. Thirteen sites had median awards in excess of $100,000. These cases, however, tend to involve serious personal injury, disability, or death. Success rates for both types of cases vary considerably.

The awards in product liability and medical malpractice cases, in contrast, are generally much higher than those based upon other causes of action. These two types of cases, as noted earlier, make up small proportions of reported verdicts, and tend to have lower plaintiff success rates. In all but three sites the success rates for product liability are lower than the overall success rates, and each of these three sites had fewer than three reported product liability cases. Except for Clay County, Missouri, which had four reported verdicts, the success rates for medical malpractice are lower than overall success rates. Forty-one sites had at least one reported product liability verdict, and over 85 percent of these sites (34 to 41) have median awards in this type of case of over $100,000; six have medians over $1,000,000 (Bexar County, Texas and Bronx, Kings, Monroe, New York and Richmond Counties in New York). Forty-two sites reported at least one medical malpractice verdict, and nearly 70 percent of those sites (29 of 42)

Table 10–2 Median Awards in Selected Types of Reported Tort Cases (Plaintiff Wins $1.00 or more)

Site	Vehicular Accidents	TYPE OF TORT CASE Product Liability	Median (1985 $) (n) of successful verdicts Medical Malpractice	Street Hazard	Premises Liability
ARIZONA (Superior Court)					
Maricopa (1981–85)	$ 13,368 (415)	$135,320(26)	$ 68,000 (15)	$111,400 (11)	$ 16,381 (48)
CALIFORNIA (Superior Court)					
Alameda (1981–84)	$ 28,190 (55)	$263,542(11)	$151,710 (8)	$ 25,900 (3)	$ 89,836 (14)
Fresno (1981–84)	$111,202 (25)	$ 91,140 (1)	— (0)	$ 46,264 (1)	$ 41,613 (6)
Los Angeles (1981–84)	$ 31,136 (422)	$428,121(93)	$155,400 (76)	$ 81,000 (23)	$ 59,150(134)
Sacremento (1981–84)	$ 22,280 (57)	$250,422 (2)	$260,818 (6)	$253,800 (1)	$ 28,964 (21)
San Diego (1981–84)	$ 40,370 (79)	$255,226 (6)	$135,908 (16)	$756,000 (3)	$ 63,529 (24)
San Francisco (1981–84)	$ 36,517 (102)	$591,556(11)	$248,640 (14)	$ 72,015 (2)	$ 51,974 (26)
GEORGIA (Superior Court)					
Cobb (1982–84)	$ 13,500 (17)	$ 12,150 (1)	$ 3,240 (1)	— (0)	$ 216 (1)
DeKalb (1982–84)	$ 7,935 (44)	— (0)	$111,418 (5)	— (0)	$ 5,400 (9)
Fulton (1982–84)	$ 13,976 (81)	$508,680 (5)	$ 48,376 (16)	$ 1,209 (1)	$ 18,715 (38)
ILLINOIS (Circuit Court)					
Cook (1981–85)	$ 5,698(1,500)	$278,570(46)	$215,000 (45)	$ 29,733(133)	$ 25,900(161)
DuPage (1981–85)	$ 11,357 (151)	— (0)	$ 17,280 (5)	$123,146 (4)	$ 19,954 (15)
Kane (1981–85)	$ 12,611 (51)	$156,498 (2)	$ 33,420 (3)	$154,000 (3)	$ 35,640 (13)
Lake (1981–85)	$ 20,003 (104)	— (0)	$ 66,840 (9)	$ 81,972 (2)	$ 17,490 (14)
McHenry (1981–85)	$ 11,140 (17)	$207,200 (1)	$ 97,340 (2)	— (0)	$ 13,205 (5)
Will (1981–85)	$ 13,084 (107)	$219,806 (1)	$152,980 (4)	$ 23,154 (4)	$ 38,439 (18)
Winnebago (1981–85)	$ 13,548 (38)	$ 37,980 (2)	$401,824 (2)	$ 3,904 (1)	$ 7,690 (11)

390

KANSAS (District Court)

Location (Year)					
Johnson (1981–85)	$ 5,184 (67)	$ 159,419 (6)	$ 280,800 (8)	— (0)	$ 21,116(13)
Wyandotte (1981–85)	$ 8,872 (93)	$ 331,415 (2)	$ 810,000 (5)	$ 19,996 (4)	$ 16,576 (7)

MISSOURI (Circuit Court)

Location (Year)					
Clay (1981–85)	$ 4,144 (17)	$ 854,700 (2)	$ 300,000 (3)	— (0)	$ 17,989 (4)
Jackson (1981–85)	$ 5,570 (142)	$ 270,732(14)	$ 69,850(10)	$ 2,958 (5)	$ 37,318(22)
Platte (1981–85)	$ 30,680 (8)	— (0)	— (0)	— (0)	$ 54,001 (1)

NEW YORK (Supreme, Civil, County)

Location (Year)					
Bronx (1981–84)	$139,949 (87)	$1,068,129(10)	$ 698,859(22)	$161,542(20)	$150,887(53)
Erie (1983–84)	$ 67,340 (31)	$ 274,144 (2)	$ 907,868 (2)	$116,550 (5)	$ 32,400(13)
Kings (1981–84)	$ 76,895 (206)	$4,158,263 (3)	$ 369,845(60)	$257,476(13)	$ 78,734(61)
Monroe (1983–84)	$ 24,840 (19)	$4,325,300 (2)	— (0)	— (0)	$ 32,634 (6)
Nassau (1981–84)	$ 53,354 (109)	$ 987,825 (4)	$ 250,609(30)	$591,500 (3)	$ 35,490(25)
New York (1981–84)	$118,300 154	$1,131,980(17)	$ 259,005(76)	$164,550(29)	$104,715(97)
Onondaga (1983–84)	$ 36,260 (9)	$ 288,156 (2)	$3,643,234 (1)	$369,852 (1)	$ 27,000 (9)
Queens (1981–84)	$ 41,405 (98)	$ 147,875 (5)	$ 156,070(32)	$ 26,026(14)	$ 42,660(31)
Richmond (1981–84)	$143,760 (34)	$2,590,000 (1)	$3,135,069 (2)	— 0	$445,600 (3)
Suffolk (1981–84)	$ 39,368 (120)	$ 131,378 (6)	$ 113,960(12)	$562,425 (4)	$ 45,674(23)
Westchester (1981–84)	$ 46,160 (43)	$ 16,710 (1)	$ 389,900 (7)	$ 45,360 (1)	$142,032 (9)

OREGON (Circuit Court)

Location (Year)					
Multnomah (1984–85)	$ 13,550 (71)	$ 116,275 (8)	$ 183,000 (9)	$ 73,302 (2)	$ 81,800(14)

TEXAS (District, County)

Location (Year)					
Bexar (1982–84)	$ 6,348 (62)	$1,092,490 (6)	$ 499,870 (2)	— (0)	$ 21,665(11)
Dallas (1981–85)	$ 8,423 (143)	$ 252,013(12)	$ 54,000 (9)	— (0)	$ 12,700(30)
Harris (1981–85)	$ 11,140 (376)	$ 351,869(31)	$ 455,600(13)	$ 15,379 (9)	$ 42,361(77)

WASHINGTON (Superior Court)

Location (Year)					
King (1983–85)	$ 14,599 (138)	$ 198,042(10)	$ 90,500 (8)	$135,864 (5)	$ 78,840(21)
Pierce (1983–85)	$ 15,000 (40)	$ 500,000 (3)	$1,133,100 (2)	$ 55,000 (1)	$ 37,500 (5)
Skagit (1983–85)	$ 72,500 (9)	— (0)	— (0)	— (0)	— (0)
Snohomish (1983–85)	$ 15,000 (37)	$ 865,130 (1)	$ 172,800 (1)	$ 25,500 (6)	$ 31,080 (5)
Spokane (1983–85)	$ 21,589 (53)	$ 504,003 (3)	$ 321,160 (3)	— (0)	$ 85,150 (9)
Yakima (1983–85)	$ 15,102 (22)	$ 142,968 (1)	$ 102,564 (3)	— (0)	$ 51,800(21)

have a median award of over $100,000. Three sites have medians over $1,000,000 (Onondaga and Richmond in New York and Pierce in Washington). Although these two types of cases make up small proportions of the reported verdicts, the size of the awards made in these cases has given them a visibility far beyond their numbers. It must be kept in mind, however, that the verdicts in these cases typically involve awards for serious personal injury, long-term or permanent disability, or even death. Lost wages or support, the medical costs, and the costs for long-term or lifetime care predictably drive up the size of these verdicts.

Table 10–2 also shows considerable variation among the sites in the median awards for different types of cases, and the intrastate variations may be as great as the interstate variations. For example, the range for vehicular accidents in New York goes from $24,840 in Monroe County to $143,760 in Richmond County, and in California the range goes from $22,280 in Sacramento County to $111,202 in Fresno County. The greatest intrastate variations are found in product liability and medical malpractice cases. In Washington the range for product liability goes from $142,968 in Yakima County to $865,130 in Snohomish County; and for medical malpractice the range goes from $102,564 in Yakima to $1,133,100 in Pierce County. The widest intrastate variations, as might be expected, are in New York. For product liability the range goes from $16,710 in Westchester County to over $4,000,000 in Kings and Monroe Counties; and for medical malpractice the range goes from $0 in Monroe and $113,960 in Suffolk County to over $3,000,000 in Onondaga and Richmond Counties. Such intrastate variations should caution against too much reliance on identifying legal rules as the major explanatory factor affecting award sizes in individual types of cases.

CONCLUSION

Is there a crisis in the civil justice system? Are ever-increasing numbers of plaintiffs going to court and successfully garnering large awards with such regularity that the death knell of the current civil justice system should be tolled? The data gathered in the study show that plaintiff success rates tend to fall within a well-defined range and awards are generally modest. Awards for some kinds of cases, such as product liability and medical malpractice, may be high, but these cases comprise only a small proportion of the reported verdicts and plaintiffs are less likely to make a successful case based on such causes of action. Additionally, because of the nature of the injuries involved in such cases, higher damage awards should be expected. On the other hand, there are some sites, particularly in the counties of New York City, that are quantitatively different. Awards are generally much higher here than they are in other jurisdictions. While there may be problem sites as defined by the reformers, this does not mean there is a general system failure. The situation is like a weather map that shows conditions to be generally fair to partly cloudy with just a few areas of inclement weather.

The empirical connections for the causal logic linking jury verdicts and awards to the current insurance crisis are elusive, and systematic data have been scarce at best. Perhaps it is the lack of much empirical data that has given the crisis rhetoric its strength. Characterizing the insurance crisis as being caused by a more fundamental civil liability crisis may well be a matter of arbitrary labeling defined on the basis of purely symbolic benchmarks. Our findings suggest that in reality, the patterns in jury verdicts across the country are not as the reformers claim. There is some reason, then, to be skeptical about the efficacy of the current round of civil justice reform as a remedy for the insurance crisis. This skepticism should lead us to a closer examination of the crisis rhetoric itself and to consideration of alternative explanations for the insurance crisis.

NOTES

*From 26 *Judges' Journal* 10 (1987). Reprinted with permission.

FOR DISCUSSION

1. What is the standard explanation for the crisis in availability and affordability of liability insurance?
2. What reforms are advocated by the insurance industry and its supporters?
3. According to the authors' survey, where are jury awards the highest? Is there any explanation for high awards in particular locations?
4. What type of cases make up the majority of jury verdicts? Do these cases support the notion of a "crisis" in the justice system?
5. What types of cases garner the highest jury verdicts? What reasons do the authors give for this phenomenon?
6. What do extreme intrastate variations in jury awards indicate about the need for substantive legal reform to address the insurance crisis?
7. Do the data on street hazard and premises liability cases support the claims of the reformers with regard to the insurance crisis? Explain.
8. After reading this article, do you think that civil jury awards are contributing significantly to the insurance crisis? Did the data in the article change your mind about this problem in any way?

Nominal Damages

Nominal damages are token damages that are awarded in cases in which the plaintiff's legal rights have been violated, but there has been no significant or material loss or injury that can be compensated. Sometimes nominal damages are awarded when the plaintiff can show a legally cognizable injury but cannot adequately prove the nature and/or extent of the damage suffered. In such cases, the small sum of money awarded (often one dollar) serves as a symbol rather than as actual compensation. If there are actual damages that can be awarded, nominal damages are not available.

In the following case, the court concludes that the plaintiff has, in fact, suffered a violation of her legal rights, but the actual harm suffered is not real or substantial, a classic case for nominal damages.

CASE
Eliza W. Stevenson v. Economy Bank of Ambridge
Pennsylvania Supreme Court (1964)
413 Pa. 442, 197 A.2d 721, 4 A.L.R.3d 1450

ROBERTS, J. Appellant, Eliza W. Stevenson, instituted an action in trespass in the Court of Common Pleas of Beaver County against appellee, Economy Bank of Ambridge, for conversion of the contents of a safe deposit box, leased by appellee to Doctor W. B. Carson, appellant's brother-in-law, who died testate April 17, 1961, and to appellant as co-tenants.

The complaint charged appellee-bank in the first count with conversion of $450,000, the value of the contents of the safe deposit box, to which appellant claimed she was entitled to possession under the terms of the safe deposit lease. This consisted of stock certificates registered in the name of the decedent alone, valued at $367,000, and cash in the amount of $82,300. Not in dispute was $4,825 in currency clearly identified as appellant's. The second count alleged conversion of the $82,300 in cash, which appellant claimed was her property and to which she had right of possession under the terms of the lease. Prior to trial, appellant withdrew the claim alleged in the first count and summary judgment was accordingly entered for appellee. From that judgment no appeal was taken. Thus, appellant has limited her claim to the $82,300 as set forth in the second count of the complaint.

At the conclusion of all the evidence, both sides presented points for binding instructions. The trial court refused appellant's request, granted that of appellee, and directed a verdict in appellee's favor. This appeal followed from the refusal of the court en banc to grant appellant's motions for judgment *non obstante veredicto* or, in the alternative, for a new trial and from the entry of judgment on the verdict.

The relevant facts from which this controversy arises and on which it must be determined are not in dispute. Decedent and his wife, for many years prior to her death (October 17, 1955), were co-lessees of the safe deposit box. On November 16, 1955, shortly after his wife's death, Doctor Carson substituted the name of appellant, his wife's sister, for that of his deceased wife as co-lessee. The lease for the safe deposit box was signed by both decedent and appellant and two keys were issued. Each lessee retained a key, but appellant never exercised her right of access during Doctor Carson's lifetime. Appellant testified that at the time Doctor Carson had her sign the lease, he gave her one of the keys. He also told her that the purpose of having her sign the lease was to make her co-owner and that she could enter the box at any time she desired.

Decedent's will, dated September 4, 1959, was prepared by his attorney and, at decedent's death, was in the possession of the scrivener. Testator bequeathed his residence and half of his approximately $490,000 estate (after $6000 of pecuniary legacies) to appellant and designated his attorney as executor. On the day following decedent's death, appellant and decedent's attorney together sought and obtained access to the safe deposit box for the sole purpose of learning whether it contained a will of later date. No other will was found, and the box, with its contents intact, was returned to the vault. Appellant, on this occasion, had provided her key for entry to the box. Testator's counsel read a part of decedent's will to appellant and informed her and the president of the bank that the safe deposit box could not be opened until the will had been probated and that nothing could be removed until a proper inventory of the contents had been completed. The record does not disclose that appellant voiced any objection, nor did she express a desire to remove anything from the box at that time.

On the next afternoon (April 19), following decedent's funeral, appellant, accompanied by the funeral director, went to the bank and requested access to the box for the purpose of removing the contents in order to take the cash for herself and deliver the stock certificates and other papers to testator's executor. Appellant was advised by the bank employee in charge of the vault that she was not permitted into the box and was refused permission to sign an entry slip. Shortly thereafter, the named executor entered the bank and, upon being informed of appellant's purpose, again stated that access to the box was not to be permitted. He repeated his direction that the box should remain closed until after the probate of decedent's will and the granting of letters testamentary. It was on the basis of these instructions that appellee-bank refused appellant entry that afternoon.

The executor advised appellant that he intended to probate the will the next day (April 20) and requested her to meet him at the bank on the succeeding day (April 21) to open the box and make an inventory of its contents.

The following day, April 21, at the appointed time, appellant and her adult son came to the bank; present also were the president of the bank, the executor, and a representative of the Pennsylvania Department of Revenue (whom the executor requested to be present). Appellant furnished her key, she and the executor together signed the entry slip, and the box was removed from the vault and opened. The contents were inventoried and written copies of the list were signed by appellant, her son, the executor, the bank president, and the representative of the Department of Revenue. A packet containing $4,825 in currency and marked "Property of Mrs. Eliza Stevenson" was delivered to her.

Additional cash in unmarked envelopes, amounting to $82,300, was counted by all those present, including appellant's son. To those assembled, appellant stated that decedent had told her that she should have the money. The executor, however, denied her possession and claimed it as an asset of the estate. Appellant could make her claim to the money before the Orphan's Court of Allegheny County, he added. The box also contained stock certificates, deeds, life insurance policies, and other documents, all in the name of decedent. Upon completion of the inventory, the executor took possession of the entire contents of the box except the $4,825 in bills marked as the property of appellant and previously delivered to her.

After the box had been cleared of all contents, appellant, at the request of the bank president, agreed to surrender the box so that the executor could place the stock certificates and other papers in it. She then signed the printed form at the bottom of the lease, certifying that all the property in the box had been safely withdrawn and that the box was surrendered. The executor, in the name of the estate, immediately executed a new lease for the box and placed into it everything but the currency. This he deposited with the appellee-bank in an account in the name of the estate.

The parties concede—as, indeed, they must under prevailing statutory and decisional authorities—that the issue of title to the cash found in the safe deposit box is exclusively within the jurisdiction of the Orphan's Court of Allegheny County. Only that forum is legally competent to make that initial determination. Since that adjudication is yet to be made, it is appropriate to observe that our disposition here is not intended to influence and should not be regarded as indicating or influencing the result here to be reached.

In this trespass action, the principal issue is not title to the cash at decedent's death, as it would be in the Orphan's Court, but rather appellant's right to possession of the cash on April 19 under the terms of the lease and whether the bank's refusal to grant her access to the box two days after decedent's death constituted a conversion of the cash contents, so as to entitle her to recover damages in that amount.

Appellant's basic contention is that the written rental lease, by its specific language, gave her the right to enter the safe deposit box on April 19, as she requested. The lease provided: "A rental contract, signed by two or more lessees constitutes a separate rental to each, and either of them shall have access, free from liability of the lessor for misappropriating any of the contents thereof.... In all cases of joint lessees, it is hereby declared that each of them has such interest in the entire contents of said box as to entitle him or her to the possession thereof, without liability to lessor for misappropriating same...." It is argued that appellant, having the right of access to the box and being known to the bank as a co-lessee, could not legally be denied access to the rented box, and that the refusal of access constituted a conversion of the cash in the box.

Appellant further contends that the bank, in refusing her access, could not have been motivated by a concern for possible liability arising from conflicting claims between the co-lessees because the lease, by its express terms, provided that the lessor shall not be liable for misappropriation of the contents by either co-tenant.

Appellee's primary contention is that the Orphan's Court has exclusive jurisdiction to determine both ownership and possession of the cash and that appellant's right of access to the box pursuant to the lease did not, in any way, fix the ownership of its contents. In the absence of proof of appellant's ownership, the bank urges, appellant is not entitled to a judgment in the amount of the cash found in the box.

Appellee further contends that it was legally justified in deferring appellant's access to the box for two days pending probate of the will and a proper inventory of the contents, and that such reasonable delay did not constitute a conversion of the cash. Moreover, appellee points out that on the second day, access to the box and to its contents were made available to appellant and the executor and that on that occasion appellant surrendered the box and signed the bottom of the printed form lease. It is contended that she thereby released the bank from any claim against it for conversion. We do not view this occurrence or appellant's signature to the form as a waiver or release by her of any claim she may have acquired for conversion. The transaction was merely the termination of the lease agreement and the physical surrender of the rented box, nothing more.

It is also urged that should appellant's claim for conversion prevail, a bank would be required, in situations of conflicting claims, to determine, at its peril, ownership of the contents of the box. If it should turn the property over to claimant-co-lessee, the bank argues it would expose itself to an action for conversion by the decedent's estate, whereas if it acted as it did here, under appellant's rationale, it would be liable for conversion to her for the full value of the contents. This argument lacks validity in view of the precise provisions of the lease specifically absolving the lessor from liability for safe deposit box property misappropriated by a co-lessee.

"A conversion is the deprivation of another's right of property in, or use or possession of, a chattel, or other interference therewith, without the owner's consent and without lawful justification." *Gottesfeld* v. *Mechanics and Traders Insurance Co.*, 196 Pa. Super. 109, 115, 173 A.2d 763, 766 (1961). Prosser states that "conversion is an act of interference with the dominion or control over a chattel...Conversion may be committed by:... (c) Unreasonably withholding possession from one who has a right to it." Prosser, Torts §15 (2nd ed. 1955). Since title to the cash is for determination by a tribunal other than the court below appellant's action for conversion, if it is to prevail, must be based upon her right of access to the box and to possession of its cash contents. Was the bank, as appellant contends, obligated under the terms of the lease to give appellant, at her request, access to the box; or was the bank, as it urges, justified in denying her entry until the executor qualified? This fundamental aspect of the controversy must be resolved by resort to the provisions of the lease agreement.

The pertinent portions of the lease, already quoted, specifically and unmistakably conferred upon appellant, as co-lessee, the right of access to the box both before and after her co-lessee's death. The express language "either of them shall have access" and the further declaration that "each of them has such interest in the entire contents of said box as to entitle him or her to the possession thereof," do not restrict or limit her right of entry and possession only to those occasions when she is accompanied by her co-lessee or by his personal representative in the event of his death.

Were we to accede to appellee's argument, we would, in effect, expand the language of the lease by reading into it conditions and limitations upon the right of entry not contained in its terms. A construction of the lease which permits lessor to deny or delay access for the reasons asserted by it and upon grounds not recited or otherwise implied in the lease is to add to that writing restrictions not contained in the contract itself. To do so would be an obvious violation of the parol evidence rule. See *Caplan* v. *Saltzman*, 407 Pa. 250, 180 A.2d 240 (1962).

Careful consideration of the lease satisfied us that appellant had a contractual right of access to and entry into the box on April 19, and that the bank was without legal authority or justification to preclude her from exercising that right. Its refusal to admit appellant to the box was a willful interference with her right of possession of the contents and constituted an act of conversion. Allowing her access with the executor two days later did not bar the action of conversion which she acquired on April 19. We conclude, therefore, that the court below, in the light of the undisputed facts, erred in refusing appellant's request for binding instructions.

It seems clear to us that in no event, on the record before us could appellant's recovery against the bank reach $82,300. If it be determined that the funds in question are assets of the decedent's estate, appellant, as a fifty percent residuary beneficiary under the will, would receive, in the normal administration of the estate, half of that sum, less state and federal taxes. If she succeeds in establishing her ownership of the cash, she receives the entire amount.

Appellant concedes that if she obtains a judgment against the bank in the amount of $82,300, and she subsequently establishes her ownership of the entire fund in the Orphan's Court, she would be entitled to only one satisfaction and payment. She would not be entitled to payment of the judgment in this action as well as an award of that amount in the Orphan's Court.

Appellant's claim to damages equal to the full value of the cash in the box is based primarily upon her contention that the withholding of possession from her adversely affects her position as a litigant or claimant in the Orphan's Court. We are unable to accept this speculative circumstance as a basis for awarding real or compensatory damages in this proceeding. The asserted loss of a procedural or evidentiary advantage in another and independent legal action is too conjectural and unreliable a basis on which to assess substantial damages. This Court has held repeatedly that a claim for damages must be supported by a reasonable basis for calculation; mere guess or speculation is not enough. Is it not entirely too speculative to base a computation of damages on the assumption that appellant will prevail in the Orphan's Court if she has actual, physical possession of the funds? And is it not equally speculative to base the calculation on the assumption that she will not be successful without such possession?

On the record presented, appellant has not established her entitlement to damages in the sum of $82,300, or in any other substantial sum. All that she has proved is that she was denied possession of the funds. No acceptable evidence was offered as a basis for fixing compensation for that deprivation of possession, nor did appellant prove real, special or other compensatory items of damages. In the absence of such proof, appellant's recovery for the technical and temporary interference with her right of access and possession must be limited to a vindication of that right by an award of nominal damages.

Since we are directing the entry of a judgment for appellant for nominal damages only, something should be said concerning damages of that nature. Blackstone defines nominal damages as "a shilling or nominal sum," *Commentaries*, Book 3. Ch. XI, at 600 (Gavit ed. 1941). Courts throughout the nation have made awards for this type of recovery in amounts ranging from six cents to one dollar. Nominal damages represent the award of a trifling sum where there has been a breach of duty or infraction or invasion of a right, but no real, substantial or serious loss or injury has been established. See *Bigham* v. *Wabash-Pittsburg Terminal Railway Co.*, 223 Pa. 106, 113, 72 A. 318, 320 (1909); *R. & B. Electric Co.* v. *Leventry*, 102 Pa. Super. 353, 156 A. 581 (1931); 11 PLE Damages §3 (1958).

In view of the nature of nominal damages and the purpose of such recovery, there is no reason why modern courts should continue to make awards in terms of English coinage translated into American values. The basic unit of American money is the dollar, and, in the future, when nominal damages are awarded in our courts, one dollar shall be the measure thereof.

The judgment of the court below is reversed; the court below is directed to enter judgment for the plaintiff-appellant in the amount of one dollar.

FOR DISCUSSION

1. What legal right of the plaintiff's was violated and what was the source of that right?
2. Did violation of plaintiff's right result in an actual loss to her of $82,300? Explain.
3. Plaintiff alleges that the violation of her rights by the bank has prejudiced her claim to ownership of the $82,300. Does the court accept her argument? Does it offer support for her claim of actual damage as a result of the bank's wrongful conduct?
4. What does the court mean when it says that plaintiff's claims of actual harm are "too speculative"? Do you agree?
5. According to the court, what is the purpose of awarding nominal damages to the plaintiff in this case?

Compensatory Damages

Compensatory damages is the most frequently sought and awarded legal remedy. As we have noted previously, the purposes of such damages is to make the injured party whole, to restore him or her to the position he or she would have been in had the injury not occurred. Sometimes damages of this type are fixed by statute, but most often they are a subject of decisional law that has grown up over many years in response to many different circumstances. Assuming the plaintiff has established his or her right to the remedy of damages, the measure of damages in a particular case must still be assessed. As you will see, there are different elements of damages that may be available in different cases. One thing is clear, however: The damages must be real, direct, and substantial, not remote or speculative in nature. The burden is on the plaintiff to produce satisfactory proof of the elements of damages he or she is seeking.

Personal Injury   You may think that money damages is a grossly inadequate remedy in cases of physical injury, particularly those involving substantial physical impairment, disfigurement, or death. Nevertheless, there is no other remedy that can even begin to make the plaintiff whole in such cases, so damages must suffice.

Physical injury cases may involve several different elements of damages. Compensation may be had, on production of satisfactory proof, for physical impairment, mental impairment, pain and suffering (both physical and mental), medical expenses, loss of time and earnings, and impairment of earning capacity. In certain cases, interest and attorneys' fees may also be available.

Proof of some elements of damage in personal injury cases may be very difficult. How does one actually prove mental anguish, for example? (In fact, mental anguish, or mental pain and suffering, is not available as an element of damages without an actual injury or an intentional, willful or reckless act by the defendant that caused the mental suffering.) Moreover, even when the existence of an injury is proved, the extent of the damage and the amount of compensation that is appropriate are difficult to calculate.

The following case presents a claim for compensation for a kind of intangible harm: loss of enjoyment of life. The situation is further complicated by the fact that the comatose victim lacks conscious awareness of her condition. The claim raises many difficult issues, such as the possibly speculative nature of the harm, the victim's inability to make use of the award, and the problem of duplication of damages awards.

CASE

Emma McDougald v. Dr. Sara Garber et al.
New York Supreme Court, Appellate Division (1988)
135 A.D.2d 80, 524 N. Y.S.2d 192

SULLIVAN, Justice.   This appeal presents the question of whether loss of enjoyment of life is an element of damages separate and distinct from conscious pain and suffering, and compensable even without the injured party's cognitive awareness of his physical condition. The issues appear never to have been directly addressed by an appellate court of this state. Mindful but wary of the precedent which will be established, we find that loss of enjoyment is a damage element separate and distinct from pain and suffering, for which compensation may be awarded despite the injured party's lack of cognitive awareness.

On September 17, 1978, while undergoing an elective caesarean section and tubal ligation at New York Infirmary, plaintiff Emma McDougald, then thirty-one years of age, became anoxic (oxygen deprived) and suffered severe diffuse brain damage after being delivered of her second child, a girl, born healthy. Plaintiff lapsed into a comatose condition and has since remained in a vegetative state. She is a permanent spastic quadriplegic with incontinence of urine and feces. In this lawsuit, she and her husband, suing derivatively, charged the defendants, the obstetrician/gynecologist-surgeon at the subject procedure, the anesthesiologists and the hospital, with various acts of malpractice. The jury returned a verdict in their favor in the amount of $11,150,102.00, collectively, which was reduced by the trial court to $6,296,728.00. Liability is unchallenged on appeal, except for a claim by one of the defendants, Dr. Garber, the surgeon, that plaintiff was permitted to offer proof of fault on theories never raised in the complaint or bill of particulars. All the other issues relate to the question of damages.

One of the sharply contested factual issues at trial was whether plaintiff had any cognitive awareness of her condition. It is undisputed that she is unable to communicate or respond to verbal commands. She breathes through a trachesostomy, an opening into the trachea, and is fed through a nasogastric tube. Most of the time her neck is extended, her back arched and knees straight, her ankles and feet pointed, and her wrists turned inward.

The jury awarded plaintiff damages in the sum of $9,650,102, including $1,000,000 for conscious pain and suffering and $3,500,000 for loss of pleasures and pursuits of life. Her husband was awarded $1,500,000 on his claim for loss of services. In their posttrial motions the defendants asserted a claim of error in the court's submission of loss of enjoyment of life as an item of damages separate and distinct from pain and suffering, and further that plaintiff could not recover for pain and suffering or loss of enjoyment of life because she was not cognitively aware of her circumstances. The court reduced plaintiff's damages to $4,796,728, striking the entire award of $2,353,374 for future nursing care as not supported by the evidence and diminishing, as excessive, the awards for conscious pain and suffering ($1,000,000) and for loss of enjoyment of life ($3,500,000) to $2,000,000 collectively. The derivative award to the husband was not disturbed. Plaintiff has stipulated to the court's reduction of the damage award, and judgment was entered accordingly.

Plaintiff has appealed from those parts of the order and the judgment which reduced damages, while the defendants seek a further reduction, and specifically seek elimination of the award for loss of enjoyment of life. They also challenge the propriety of allowing a recovery for loss of enjoyment of life separate and in addition to an award for pain and suffering.

We affirm and take this opportunity to address the questions of whether separate awards may be made for conscious pain and suffering and loss of enjoyment of life, and whether cognitive awareness is a prerequisite to a recovery for the latter. We note at the outset that our exploration of these issues is not to be construed as a finding that, as a matter of law, plaintiff does not have any cognitive awareness. In support of the jury's finding on that issue we think sufficient is found in the record. Dr. Kaplan's opinion evidence, as well as the husband's testimony that plaintiff's eyes followed him as he moved from one side of the bed to the other, and the attending nurses' notes, which found her "responsive" and "alert" on numerous occasions, provide a foundation for the verdict.

Loss of enjoyment of life as an element of damage in a personal injury action was discussed in New York, at least as long ago as 1857, when the Court of Appeals stated: "The law guarantees to every person the right of personal security, which includes the uninterrupted enjoyment of his life and limbs, of his health and reputation; and he who, by a wilful or by a culpably negligent act, deprives him of these blessings, or interferes with the full enjoyment of them, subjects himself...to the liability of making compensation in damages to the aggrieved party." *Ransom* v. *N.Y. Erie R.R. Co.*, 15 N.Y. 415, 416. Subsequent authority in New York is, however, sparse, although two recent Second Department cases dealt with the issue in dicta. In *Ledogar* v. *Giordano*, 122 A.D.2d 834, 505 N.Y.S.2d 899, in discussing the damages for pain and suffering which would be awarded to a child severely injured at birth, the court stated, "it is not necessary for the infant to be able to fully appreciate the consequences of his injury or to verbalize his pain." The court further noted, "Also, the jury may properly consider the effect that the plaintiff's injuries had on the normal pursuits and pleasures of life as part of the pain and suffering component of damages." In *Kavanaugh* v. *Nussbaum*, 129 A.D.2d 559, 514 N.Y.S.2d 55, the court reemphasized the point:

> In addition, we note that, although there is no evidence that the infant plaintiff is capable of fully appreciating the consequences of his injuries, or that he is presently conscious of pain, an award for pain and suffering may be based upon the effect that the injuries had upon the infant plaintiff's ability to enjoy the normal pursuits and pleasures of life.

There can be little doubt that loss of enjoyment may be measured in damages in New York as an element of pain and suffering. A host of cases have discussed the issue tangentially, usually in the context of defending awards for pain and suffering.

In one of the few instances where a state's highest court has spoken on the subject, *Flannery* v. *U.S.*, W.Va., 297 S.E.2d 433, loss of enjoyment of life was placed in the category of a separate element of damages, in the nature of a permanent injury. In considering the propriety of allowing an award for "the plaintiff's permanent disability resulting from his loss of capacity to enjoy life…," the West Virginia Supreme Court of Appeals noted: "Just as a jury may consider the nature, effect and severity of pain when fixing damages for personal injury, or may consider mental anguish caused by scars and disfigurement, it may consider loss of enjoyment of life." *Id.* at 438.

Other courts, without discussing its conceptual basis, have recognized loss of enjoyment of life as a separate and distinct claim. Some have noted that a separate award has the advantage of facilitating judicial review as to the excessiveness of the total award. Those which have been wary in permitting loss of enjoyment of life to stand separate from pain and suffering have indicated a concern for the possible overlapping of awards.

The confusion between pain and suffering and loss of enjoyment of life has prompted one commentator to note:

> Despite the distinctions between pain and suffering and loss of enjoyment of life, the two concepts are often equated with one another. This result is derivative of at least two factors; the intangible nature of each concept, and the similar circumstances under which both types of damages may arise. *Loss of Enjoyment of Life as a Separate Element of Damages.* 12 Pacific L.J. 965, 973 (1981).

Clearly, as amorphous as the concepts may be, pain and suffering and loss of life's enjoyment are nevertheless distinguishable from one another. The award of damages for pain and suffering compensates the victim for physical discomfort and anguish, while loss of enjoyment, as the Pacific Law Journal article observed, concerns "the impairment of one's capacity to enjoy life." *Id.* at 972. While perhaps pain and suffering is somewhat more tangible an element of damage and thus easier to recompense than loss of enjoyment, both are measurable, as well as distinguishable from each other.

In a leading tort text on the subject, Minzer: *Damages in Tort Law*, it has been noted: "The injuries are not unrelated, and often are discussed as though they were synonymous or closely associated with items of damages in personal injury litigation. A number of jurisdictions treat loss of enjoyment as an element to be assessed in arriving at an award for pain and suffering. This approach can blur the distinctions which should guide careful analysis." *Id.*,sec. 8.10, pp. 8–13. Minzer further notes: "Basically, the problem is nothing more than one of definition. As with any other item of damage, the elements unique to a loss of enjoyment claim should be carefully identified. In jurisdictions which permit a separate award for loss of enjoyment, the injury so claimed should be distinguished in its crucial aspects from those falling in the separate category of pain and suffering." *Id.* at p. 8–15.

In 3 *Personal Injury Actions: Defenses on Damages*, sec. 3.04[5], p. 296, Messrs. Frumer and Friedman write: "The possible overlapping between an enjoyment or inability to lead a normal life claim and a pain and suffering claim is considerable. Some jurisdictions treat these items of damages separately while a number of jurisdictions treat loss of enjoyment as an element considered in arriving at an award for pain and suffering. In either case, the elements unique to loss of enjoyment, the damage claimed, must be distinguished in its unique respects from the separate category of pain and suffering." The authors also note: "The difficult issue arising from loss of enjoyment claims is whether the injuries compensable via the element of loss of enjoyment of life are distinguishable from other compensable items of injury. The majority rule is in the affirmative." *Id.* at p. 301.

Thus, as these commentaries indicate, loss of enjoyment of life is conceptually different from pain and suffering. Furthermore, as those courts which have sanctioned their use point out, separate awards have the utility of facilitating appellate review as to the excessiveness of the total damage award.

Of course, the real issue in a case involving a comatose patient, which the jury in this instance factually resolved in the plaintiff's favor, is whether recovery may be had for loss of enjoyment of life absent cognitive awareness. The defendants, citing *Flannery for Flannery* v. *U.S.*, 4th Cir., 718 F.2d 108, cert. den. 467 U.S. 1226, 104 S.Ct. 2679, 81 L.Ed. 874, argue that loss of enjoyment is an inseparable component of pain and suffering and therefore not compensable absent a conscious awareness on the plaintiff's part of his/her condition. In *Flannery,* the Court of Appeals for the Fourth Circuit expressly rejected separate awards for both the permanency of plaintiff's injuries as an element of pain and suffering and loss of enjoyment of life as an "impermissible duplication of damages." *Id.* at 111.

The precedential value of the Fourth Circuit's holding in *Flannery* has been seriously undercut, however, by a recent decision of the Court of Appeals for the Second Circuit in *Rufino* v. *United States*, 829 F.2d 354, which, after our Court of Appeals refused to accept certification of two questions involving the right of recovery in a loss of enjoyment of life case, and based primarily on the "well-reasoned opinion" of the trial justice in this case, allowed a comatose plaintiff without any cognitive awareness to recover for loss of enjoyment of life. In so doing, the court predicted that "in this evolving area of the law, New York will in due course recognize the loss of enjoyment of life as a separately compensable item of damages." *Id.* at 362.

Several English cases, which appear to be precisely on point, have also adopted an objective standard, that is, that the victim's ignorance of his/her loss is irrelevant, in determining the viability of a loss of life's enjoyment claim. In *Wise* v. *Kave* ([1962] 1 Q.B. 638, *mod. on other grds* [1962] 1 All E.R. 257), the plaintiff, a passenger injured in an automobile collision, had remained unconscious from the time of the accident three and one-half years earlier to the time of trial. By reason of the deep and extensive brain injury she had sustained, she could not see, talk or hear and was deprived of every faculty, except the ability to breathe and digest enough sustenance to survive. The trial judge had awarded her a sum for loss of enjoyment of life, known as "loss of amenities." Rejecting many of the same arguments as are made here, namely that the plaintiff was incapable of personally enjoying such an award, which would likely not to be used to maintain her, but ultimately pass to her next-of-kin, the court disposed of the lack of awareness argument as follows: "I am not apprised of any branch of our law which permits a person who is known or believed to be alive to be treated as if he or she were dead.... [A]s long as the plaintiff lives her damages in my view fall to be considered as damages to be awarded to a living person and no living person could have lost more of the use of limbs and faculties." *Id.* at 654.

In *H. West & Son, Ltd.* v. *Shepard* ([1963] 2 All E.R. 625), the House of Lords, in considering the claim of a patient who, not unlike plaintiff herein, was conscious "to a slight degree," made the following observation, "The fact of unconsciousness is therefore relevant in respect of, and will eliminate, those heads or elements of damage which can only exist by being felt or thought or experienced. The fact of unconsciousness does not, however, eliminate the actuality of the deprivations of ordinary experiences and amenities of life which may be the inevitable result of some physical injury." *Id.* at 633.

We conclude that there is a conceptual difference between pain and suffering and loss of enjoyment of life, and that the latter is a separate element of damage to which cognitive awareness or the ability to spend the award of damages is irrelevant. A loss of enjoyment of life claim should, therefore, consonant with the purpose and spirit of CPLR 4111(d), which requires an itemization of malpractice awards, be submitted as a separate item of damages, even though it is not explicitly listed therein as an element, while pain and suffering is. It should be noted that the section's listing of damage elements is expressly stated to be non-inclusive. Moreover, in this case, the separate submission of the loss of enjoyment claim has the advantage of facilitating appellate review of the issue of excessiveness of damages and segregating the claim, which does not require a showing of cognitive awareness, from conscious pain and suffering, which does.

FOR DISCUSSION

1. What is the difference between pain and suffering and loss of enjoyment of life as separate items of damages?
2. If loss of enjoyment of life were to be considered an element of pain and suffering, would cognitive awareness be required? Explain your answer.
3. What are the disadvantages of allowing these two types of damage to be considered separately? Does the court see any advantages in treating them as separate and distinct?
4. Why does the court consider loss of enjoyment of life to be an objective type of damage, which does not require cognitive awareness, while pain and suffering is subjective and does require it? Does the court offer adequate support for this distinction?
5. In the torts chapter (Chapter 8), one commentator complained that the law is being extended—or distorted—to compensate every victim for every possible injury. Would you consider this case to be an illustration of that complaint? Explain your answer.

Contracts   Cases involving damages for breach of contract naturally focus on economic (or pecuniary) harm to the plaintiff rather than physical injury. Elements of damages in contract cases may include loss of profits, expenses, and interest. In some cases, attorneys' fees may also be recoverable. In contract cases (as well as in many other cases involving pecuniary losses), the injured party is limited in his or her recovery by certain time-honored principles of damages. For example, damages sued for may not be speculative. Especially where lost profits are concerned, the losses must be real and ascertainable. The point of damages in such cases is to make the plaintiff whole, not to reward him. Moreover, plaintiffs in breach of contract cases have a duty to mitigate their damages; that is, to do what is reasonable to limit damages suffered and not aggravate the harm caused by the breach. The traditional measure of damages in such cases is the comparison of the plaintiff's position after the breach with his position had the contract been performed as agreed. Where contracts involving purchase and sale of goods are concerned, damages are frequently measured by subtracting the contract price of the goods from the fair market price of the same or similar goods at the time of the breach. Where damage to property is involved, the traditional measure of damages is the fair market value of the property before the injury less the fair market value after the injury.

In the following case, the main dispute is over how damages in a breach of contract case should be computed. In considering that question, the court gives its attention to questions involving the purpose of damages awards in such cases.

CASE

Bruce Adams v. Lindblad Travel, Inc.
U.S. Court of Appeals, 2.Circuit (1984)
730 F.2d 89

CARDAMONE, Circuit Judge.   In this breach of contract case plaintiff obtained a jury verdict for $7,650 in damages against defendants in the United States District Court for the Southern District of New York (Metzner, J.). Plaintiff has appealed claiming principally that the trial court's charge on the issue of damages incorrectly limited the amount he was entitled to recover.

I. Background

Bruce Adams, d/b/a Southwest Safaris, is in the business of designing and conducting adventure tours. A comfortable chartered bus is not part of this tour package. For those who subscribe to Adams' tours of the Four Corners Region—where the states of Colorado, New Mexico, Arizona and Utah meet—travel is by more imaginative means. Taking groups of five or less, Adams utilizes a helicopter, horse, jeep and river raft to show his clients America's Southwest. Defendant Lindblad Travel, Inc. is a prominent wholesaler of adventure tours, and its subsidiary, defendant Special Expeditions, Inc., promotes such tours within the United States. Since its beginnings in 1979, Special Expeditions has been managed by its president, defendant Sven Olof Lindblad.

Defendants sought out Adams in 1978 with a proposal for a joint business venture. According to the terms and conditions of an agreement reached in the fall of 1979, the parties were to develop a number of air tour programs to the Four Corners region to be conducted in 1980 and 1981. These programs, known as Special Expeditions' American Wing Safari, featured Adams as tour operator. Defendants, meanwhile, were to promote, market and sell the tours and pay Adams a set price per planeload of passengers (which in 1980 was $5,700 for "lodge" trips and $4,030 for "camping" trips). The specific itineraries, dates and prices of all tours would be mutually agreed upon by the parties in advance of sale, and it was agreed that the identity of Bruce Adams as founder of Southwest Safaris would be mentioned in all advertising and marketing materials.

During 1980 the American Wing Safari program ran smoothly. Defendants did in fact market and sell several five-passenger safaris, four of which actually departed. At the outset of negotiations for 1981, defendants expressed their dissatisfaction with the four-to-five passenger format. They insisted that each tour be increased to 20 passengers to make the venture more profitable. By letter to Adams of December 29, 1980, defendants proposed an itinerary for September 16, 1981, which required Adams to accommodate 20 passengers in groups of five passengers each. Adams rejected it. He asserted that safety considerations related to hazardous flying conditions at the South Rim Airport on the edge of the Grand Canyon resulting from its high altitude (thin air) and dangerous turbulence precluded an itinerary that required tightly scheduled landings with a fully loaded aircraft, i.e., the itinerary proposed by defendants. It soon became clear that the parties were nearing an impasse.

During the last week of January 1981 defendants sold their version of the September 16 itinerary to Eli International, Inc., a branch of the Yale University Alumni Association. The sale took place without Adams'[s] prior knowledge or consent and violated the parties' earlier agreement that Adams and Lindblad mutually agree on itineraries, dates and prices in advance of sale. By letter dated January 30, 1981, defendants informed Adams that they had sold the September 16 itinerary exactly as presented in their December 29 letter. On February 6 Adams telephoned Special Expeditions demanding an explanation. Since Sven Lindblad was out of the country, his executive secretary, Pamela Fingleton, spoke to Adams. She acknowledged the need for a quick resolution of the parties' differences and assured Adams that Lindblad would return his call.

Because of their need to assure an itinerary for Eli International, defendants had already begun to search for another tour operator. On February 4, 1981, Ms. Fingleton wrote to Patrick Conley, President of Wild & Scenic Inc., and requested details as to that company's ability to conduct tours of the Four Corners. Negotiations with Wild & Scenic continued through March 4 when Lindblad offered Conley the American Wing Safari tour, identical to the proposed September 16 itinerary he was still discussing with Adams. Meanwhile, defendants continued to take advantage of Adams' expertise and reputation. Specifically, they mailed out more than 11,000 newsletters on March 2, 1981, promoting the American Wing Safari, emphasizing that Adams, with extensive knowledge of the Southwest and a 10-year perfect flying safety record, would be conducting the aerial tours. In addition, and contrary to the original agreement, the newsletters failed to mention that Adams founded Southwest Safaris.

Because of defendants' sale of the September 16 itinerary without his knowledge and their insistence that he fly that itinerary with 20 passengers, Adams terminated the business relationship on March 5, 1981. As a result, he found himself in difficulties with respect to the 1981 season. Having relied entirely on defendants' agreement to promote his business, Adams was faced with the prospect of putting together a marketing campaign at the last minute. Consequently, from 1980 to 1981 the number of passengers he carried dropped drastically—from 134 to 57. Meanwhile, defendants continued blithely to appropriate the information and itineraries obtained by them from Adams and through Wild & Scenic conducted their own aerial tours of the Southwest. The proof at trial showed that during the summer of 1981 defendants carried 34 passengers they otherwise would have referred to Adams.

From this background the present litigation ensued in district court. Adams made a number of claims, including breach of contract, misappropriation of business information, unjust enrichment and breach of fiduciary duty. The district judge dismissed the fiduciary breach claim at trial as well as all claims against Sven Lindblad personally. It also ruled that the evidence produced was insufficient to support Adams'[s] claim in *quantum meruit*. The trial court submitted the breach of contract and misappropriation of business causes of action to the jury. In response to special interrogatories, the jury found that defendants breached their contract with Adams, but did not misappropriate business information. Accordingly, it awarded Adams $7,650 as damages for breach of contract. This amount was the top limit imposed by the court's charge. On appeal Adams argues that the district court erred by: refusing to allow an award of pre-judgment interest; refusing to charge the jury on his claim in *quantum meruit*; and holding as a matter of law that he could not collect damages on an agency theory. We find merit only as to the first two contentions and remand this case to the district court for reconsideration solely on the issue of damages. In all other respects, the judgment is affirmed.

II. Contract Damages

Since defendants do not dispute the jury finding that defendants had breached the contract they had with Adams, liability is not an issue on appeal. With respect to damages, Adams claims that the district court's charge placing a ceiling of $7,650 on his contractual recovery was erroneous. The way in which the district court arrived at this figure was to make the following calculations:

(1)	$57,000	Adams'[s] actual 1981 gross revenues (57 passengers carried by Adams at $1,000 each)
(2)	+ 32,060	Adams'[s] lost revenue (8 planeloads at $4,060 each — mathematical error should be $32,480)
(3)	89,060	Adams'[s] projected gross revenues but for the breach
(4)	- 24,000	Average fixed costs
(5)	65,060	
(6)	- 44,530	Variable costs (one-half of gross revenues) divided by 91[*](7)
	$20,530	passengers + $225 net profit / per passenger × 34 passengers = $7,650 lost profits

[*]91 passengers are the 57 Adams actually carried in 1981 plus the 34 referred to Wild & Scenic by defendants.

In essence, the district court was attempting to determine how much Adams would have profited from handling the eight additional planeloads (or 34 customers) referred by defendants to Wild & Scenic in 1981.

Adams challenges the court's figures on several grounds. First, he argues that the district court should have instructed the jury to award Adams the difference between his profits in 1979—the year prior to his agreement with defendants—and his losses in 1981. Second, he claims that the formula used by the court was flawed because it mistakenly took into account Adams'[s] fixed costs. Finally, he asserts that the numbers the trial court plugged into this formula are erroneous.

The general rule for measuring damages for breach of contract has long been settled. It is the amount necessary to put the plaintiff in the same economic position he would have been in had the defendant fulfilled his contract. Therefore, Adams improperly seeks damages based on his 1979 profits. Even were the defendants to have fulfilled their 1981 contractual obligations, there is no reason to believe that such would have guaranteed Adams the same success he had enjoyed two years earlier. Too many variables, apart from the breach, could have caused a discrepancy between Adams'[s] 1979 and 1981 profits. That is to say, the 1979 economy might have been more conducive to domestic travel, or Adams'[s] potential market might be finite and his pool of possible customers might diminish each year.

Even more important for our purposes is the fact that Adams'[s] lost revenues can readily be measured in terms of the business taken from him by defendants. With profit as the incentive, defendants promoted the tours conducted by Wild & Scenic just as vigorously as they would have promoted tours conducted by Adams. Further, defendants used Adams'[s] name in their March 1981 newsletter, as they would have done had Adams agreed to conduct the tours. Thus, Adams cannot successfully argue that he lost any more business in 1981 than that represented by the eight planeloads (or 34 passengers) handled by defendants.

Having established the basis for computing Adams'[s] lost revenues, it is relatively easy to find the proper formula for his lost profits. But for the breach, Adams'[s] lost profits equal the revenues he would have received from the 34 additional passengers (*i.e.*, additional revenues) minus the additional costs he would have incurred in handling those passengers (*i.e.*, additional costs). The district court's error was in considering Adam'[s] "fixed costs." Simply stated, fixed costs represent the total dollar expense that occurs regardless of output and include such "overhead" items as an enterprise's commitments for rental and maintenance, depreciation and the like. Adams had already paid his fixed costs for 1981 and by definition would have paid the same amount of fixed costs regardless of whether he carried

57 passengers, 91 passengers, or even zero passengers. Thus, he would not have incurred any additional fixed costs handling 34 extra passengers. What he would have incurred are "variable costs," such as expenses for additional fuel and supplies.

We restate the correct damage formula as follows:

(1)   Additional Revenues from carrying 34 extra passengers
(2) - Additional Costs incurred in carrying 34 extra passengers (i.e., additional variable costs)
_____
(3)   Additional Profits Adams would have made but for the breach.

The remaining task is to determine what numbers should be plugged into this formula. "Additional revenues" equal the number of additional passengers (34) times the tariff Adams would have received from each passenger. If the evidence shows that Adams would have collected per planeload, as urged by plaintiff, rather than per passenger, as stated in defendants' brief, then additional revenues equal the number of additional planeloads he would have flown times the tariff he would have received from each planeload. These are questions of fact, and on remand the parties should be permitted to present to the jury any evidence that might bear on them. Similarly, the parties should present evidence as to the additional costs Adams would have incurred in handling the extra passengers. Additional costs equal either the number of extra passengers times the variable costs per passenger or, under a planeload approach, the number of extra planeloads Adams would have handled times the variable costs per planeload. If, for example, Adams proves that the breach cost him 34 passengers, that each passenger would have paid him $1000 and that each would have cost him an additional $500, the jury must award him $17,000:

(1) $34,000 revenues (34 passengers @ $1000)
(2) - 17,000 costs (34 passengers @ $500)
      $17,000 profits

III. Prejudgment Interest

Adams further contends that the district court erred in refusing to grant him prejudgment interest. Since federal jurisdiction in this case is premised on diversity and the right to interest on a cause of action qualifies as a substantive right, we must look to New York law. The applicable state statute provides, in pertinent part: "Interest *shall* be recovered upon a sum awarded because of a breach of performance of a contract...." N.Y.C.P.L.R. §5001(a) (McKinney 1963) [emphasis supplied in original]. Under the law of New York, therefore, prejudgment interest is normally recoverable as a matter of right in an action at law for breach of contract. *Julien J. Studley, Inc.* v. *Gulf Oil Corp.*, 425 F.2d 947, 950 (2d Cir.1969).

Despite the fact that Adams neglected at trial to ask the district court for an award of prejudgment interest, he is not precluded from doing so on remand. In *Lee* v. *Joseph E. Seagram & Sons, Inc.*, 592 F.2d 39, 42-44 (2d Cir.1979), we held that in some circumstances the failure to request prejudgment interest either in the complaint or at trial constitutes a waiver of the statutory entitlement. This is not such a case. More instructive is *Newburger, Loeb & Co., Inc.* v. *Gross*, 611 F.2d 423 (2d Cir.1979). Here, as in *Newburger*, the policies of "finality and repose" underlying the *Lee* decision are not present. *Id.*at 432–33. Since we are remanding this case for a redetermination of damages, the parties have no legitimate expectation that the issues relating to the ultimate award have been finally decided.

Moreover, the district court on remand will have ample opportunity to determine such a necessary issue as when the cause of action accrued. Thus, Adams can and should receive prejudgment interest pursuant to N.Y.C.P.L.R. §5001.

IV. *Quantum Meruit* and Agency Claims

Although he has succeeded in obtaining damages for breach of contract, Adams insists that he is also entitled to recover on theories of *quantum meruit* and breach of fiduciary duty. His *quantum meruit* claim alleges that defendants were unjustly enriched because they took and used for their own benefit his advice, information and itineraries. Adams'[s] agency claim asserts that defendants were his agents and, as such, breached a duty of good faith and loyalty by engaging in a competitive business. For these infringements, Adams seeks damages for the value of his services, recovery of any profits defendants might have realized from conducting competitive air tours and all damages naturally resulting from defendants' unauthorized actions.

We need not deal with these claims in any detail for they are wholly without merit. As the record clearly shows, Adams' purported causes of action in *quantum meruit* and agency merely duplicate his contract claim. The ultimate goal underlying each of these theories of recovery is to make the injured party whole. In this case, Adams is made whole once he is placed in the same economic position he would have occupied but for the defendants' breach. As already discussed, contract damages for his lost profits will restore Adams to that position. To accept Adams'[s] arguments and grant him full recovery under three alternative theories would in effect award the same damages three times. There is no legal or equitable basis to afford plaintiff such a windfall.

Accordingly, the judgment is reversed and remanded for a redetermination of damages. Additionally, the district court should award plaintiff prejudgment interest pursuant to N.Y.C.P.L.R. §5001. The judgment of the district court in all other respects is affirmed.

FOR DISCUSSION

1. According to the court, what is the general rule for measuring damages for breach of contract?
2. Based on the proof at trial, the number of passengers plaintiff carried dropped from 134 in 1980 to 57 in 1981. Why shouldn't he be compensated for the loss of 77 passengers instead of only 34? Do you think this is fair?
3. What error did the trial court make in computing the financial losses suffered by plaintiff as a result of defendants' breach of contract? Does it appear, given the new formula for computing damages, that plaintiff's lost profits were significantly greater? Explain.
4. The court finds that under New York law plaintiff is entitled to prejudgment interest as an element of damages. For what injury to plaintiff does prejudgment interest compensate?
5. Why does the court reject plaintiff's *quantum meruit* and agency claims? What would be the result if the plaintiff were compensated on the basis of each of the three theories of recovery he advances?

Liquidated Damages

Liquidated damages is an amount agreed on in a contract as the damages recoverable in the event of a breach of the agreement. Liquidated damages can be a benefit to either the breaching party or the injured party, depending on the circumstances, because liquidated damages guarantees the plaintiff a certain amount of compensation, but it also fixes the defendant's maximum liability in the event of a breach of contract. Liquidated damages clauses are enforceable when the amount of liquidated damages is a reasonable, good faith approximation of the actual damages that would be suffered if the contract were breached. Conversely, if a clause fixing liquidated damages bears no reasonable relationship to actual damages and appears to be a deterrence of, or punishment for, a breach of the contract, the liquidated damages provision is regarded as a penalty and is not enforced.

In the following case, the court must determine whether a provision in a contract for the sale of land allowing the seller to keep the down payment in the event the buyer defaults on the contract is enforceable as liquidated damages.

CASE
Larry R. Bando v. Esther M. Cole and Leo H. Cole
Supreme Court of Nebraska (1977)
197 Neb 722, 250 N.W.2d 651, 4 A.L.R.4th 987

BOSLAUGH, Justice.   This is an action to recover the downpayment made pursuant to a contract for the sale of real estate. The action was tried to the court which found generally for the defendants. The plaintiff has appealed. The assignments of error allege in substance that the plaintiff was entitled to judgment as a matter of law.

The facts are for the most part undisputed. Where there are conflicts in the evidence, they must be resolved in favor of the defendants. In determining the sufficiency of the evidence to support the judgment it must be considered in the light most favorable to the defendants, all conflicts must be resolved in their favor, and they are entitled to the benefit of every inference that may be reasonably adduced from the evidence.

The record shows that on January 19, 1972, the plaintiff, Larry R. Bando, and his father, Ralph H. Bando, inquired of the defendants, Esther M. Cole and Leo H. Cole, concerning the sale of their 160-acre farm in Otoe County, Nebraska. The parties arrived at an agreement for the sale of the land to Larry R. Bando for the sum of $80,000. The sum of $12,000 was to be paid at the date of the execution of the contract with the balance of $68,000 to be paid on March 1, 1972.

The parties met at the office of Vantine A. James that afternoon to execute a written agreement. A contract was prepared by James on a printed form which was signed and acknowledged by the plaintiff and the defendants. The contract, which is exhibit 2, provided specifically that if the purchaser did not consummate the purchase upon the terms set forth, all right or claim of the purchaser under the agreement might be terminated at the option of the sellers "in which case the purchaser shall forfeit all payments made."

At the time exhibit 2 was executed James cautioned the plaintiff and his father several times that if they did not complete the contract they would forfeit the $12,000 downpayment. Ralph replied to the effect there was no problem with financing because he could obtain the money from several sources.

After exhibit 2 had been executed by the parties, Ralph wrote out checks to the defendants totalling $12,000. The plaintiff then produced a printed form for an "Option to Purchase Real Estate" prepared by the Farmers Home Administration (FHA). The plaintiff explained that he needed to have this form executed so that he could obtain a loan from the FHA. James made several changes in the form at the request of the defendants and filled in the necessary information. The option agreement, which is exhibit 1, was then executed and acknowledged by the plaintiff and the defendants.

Exhibit 1 recited that the consideration for the option was $12,000 and other valuable consideration. It further provided the option was given to enable the buyer to obtain a loan insured or made by the FHA; that the buyer's efforts to obtain a loan constituted part of the consideration for the option; and in the event a loan could not be processed by the FHA or obtained from another source, any downpayment would be refunded.

The plaintiff and his father were unable to obtain financing so the purchase was never consummated. This action was commenced on July 8, 1974, to recover the downpayment of $12,000.

The petition pleaded only the option agreement, exhibit 1, and alleged the facts concerning the inability of the plaintiff to obtain financing. The answer of the defendants pleaded the contract, exhibit 2, and alleged the parties intended for it to govern the sale of the property. The answer further alleged that the option agreement, exhibit 1, was executed solely as an accommodation to the plaintiff in order to enable him to obtain financing through the FHA.

The plaintiff's principal contention is that the option agreement, exhibit 1, superseded the contract, exhibit 2, because exhibit 1 was executed after exhibit 2 was executed.

Generally, in the absence of anything to indicate a contrary intention, instruments executed at the same time, by the same parties, for the same purpose, and in the course of the same transaction, are legally one instrument and will be construed together as if they were as much one in form as they are in substance. *Pike* v. *Triska*, 165 Neb. 104, 84 N.W.2d 311. Generally, parol evidence is admissible for the purpose of explaining and showing the true nature of the transaction between the parties. *Olds* v. *Jamison*, 195 Neb. 388, 238 N.W.2d 459.

Exhibit 1 and exhibit 2 were executed by the parties at approximately the same time and as part of the same transaction. They are in conflict as to whether the downpayment should be refunded or forfeited. Exhibit 2, the sales contract, provides that all payments will be forfeited if the purchaser fails to complete the contract. Exhibit 1, the option agreement, provides that the downpayment will be refunded in the event the purchaser is unable to obtain financing.

The evidence sustains a finding that the parties understood the $12,000 would be forfeited by the plaintiff if he was unable to complete the contract and the option agreement was intended only as an accommodation to the plaintiff so that he could obtain financing through FHA. The defendants demanded the 15 percent downpayment because they were required to deliver possession of the property on or before March 1, 1972. To perform the contract, the defendants were required to move out of their house and sell their farm equipment. They offered evidence to show they had disposed of their farm equipment and were ready to perform on March 1, 1972.

The plaintiff did not notify the defendants that he was unable to complete the transaction until on or about May 28, 1972. The defendants offered evidence to show they had difficulty in finding a tenant by that time and suffered heavy crop losses due to the resulting delay in planting the land.

The plaintiff also contends the forfeiture provision in the contract was not enforceable because the amount exceeded the damages the defendants sustained as a result of the plaintiff's failure to perform. This issue was not raised in the pleadings in the District Court, and the plaintiff objected to the evidence offered by the defendants to show the damages they had sustained as a result of the plaintiff's failure to perform.

Ordinarily a sum paid in part performance of a contract, with a provision that it shall be forfeited in the event of a default, if not excessive, and if the actual damages are not calculable in advance, will be regarded as liquidated damages. *Growney* v. *C. M. H. Real Estate Co.*, 195 Neb. 398, 238 N.W.2d 240. A liquidated damages provision is enforceable if the amount stipulated is either a reasonable estimate of the probable damages or is reasonably proportionate to the actual damages caused by the breach.

The evidence shows the plaintiff and his father went to the defendants' home and solicited the sale of the property. The defendants were unwilling to sell unless they received their price and 15 percent of the price was paid in advance. In reliance on the contract they disposed of their farm equipment and prepared to vacate the farm property on March 1, 1972. When the plaintiff finally conceded that he could not perform, the normal planting dates were past and it was difficult to find a tenant. The defendants offered to prove that because of late planting they received a yield of only 15 bushels per acre as opposed to an average yield of 89 bushels per acre.

While evidence on this phase of the case is not as complete as would ordinarily be required, the plaintiff in this case is in no position to complain because he did not raise the issue in the District Court and prevented the defendants from proving in greater detail the damages they actually sustained. Under these circumstances we believe the judgment for the defendants should be affirmed.

FOR DISCUSSION

1. According to this court, under what conditions might the forfeiture of a downpayment on a real estate sales contract be classified as liquidated damages?
2. Under what conditions is such a liquidated damages provision enforceable?
3. The court is very concerned that the amount of liquidated damages bear some reasonable relationship to the amount of actual damages. Can you give any reasons why this might be so?
4. Given the facts of this case, is it believable that defendants were harmed in an amount approaching $12,000? What factors did the court weigh most heavily?

Punitive Damages

Punitive damages are awarded not as compensation to an injured plaintiff but as a punishment to the defendant. Because the purpose of punitive damages (also called **exemplary damages**) is to punish for past wrongdoing and deter future wrongdoing, the focus is not on the extent of injury to the plaintiff but on the outrageousness of defendant's conduct. Punitive damages can only be awarded where the defendant has demonstrated malice, a term that has a variety of definitions, but that involves willful, wanton conduct and reckless disregard for the rights of the others. Assessing punitive damages is a way to show society's disapproval for defendant's actions, which distinguishes punitive damages from ordinary damages, whose purpose is to make the plaintiff whole. In fact, the plaintiff is regarded as a kind of inadvertent beneficiary of damages that are meant more as a penalty or fine than anything else.

In the following article, the authors severely criticize the institution of punitive damages and offer several recommendations for reform. As in the article concerning civil jury awards, both substantive law and the behavior of juries is examined and criticized.

READING   **Punitive Damages and the Tort System**
Griffin B. Bell and Perry E. Pearce*

I. INTRODUCTION

From 1763, when the doctrine of punitive damages was first articulated, the concept has become almost commonplace in jury awards. Not only have punitive damage awards grown commonplace, they have also grown excessive. All too frequently we read about large punitive damage awards bearing no reasonable relationship to the actual damages. For example, in Georgia this year, a jury awarded a construction company $5 million in punitive damages for $53,000 of property damage to a bulldozer where the bulldozer merely hit a petroleum line that was not buried deep enough! Such awards have given rise to the criticism that punitive damages are one of the major problems in tort law.

Reforming the doctrine of punitive damages is necessary if our tort system is to remain viable. One possible reform is a cap on punitive damages. The cap could be based on a reasonable relationship to the compensatory damage award, such as a 2-to-1 ratio, or on the amount of the fine for the most comparable crime in the penal code. Another approach is to allow the jury to award actual damages and to find whether the plaintiff has proved malice. The court would then set the amount of punitive damages. A third possibility for reform is to require the defendant to pay all or a percentage of the punitive damage award to the federal or state governments, depending on whether the award comes from a federal or state court.

Until such reform is enacted into law, judges should not hesitate to use their remittur power if they find that the punitive damages awarded by the jury are excessive. Recently, in *Kemp* v. *Ervin*, 651 F. Supp. 495 (N.D. Georgia 1986), the court ordered a remittur[1] and reduced the $2.3 million jury award of punitive damages to $400,000, finding the original award "shockingly excessive." The court explained that it did not want to financially destroy the two defendants and determined that a reasonable amount of punitive damages was twice the amount of damages awarded by the jury for mental anguish. If judges used their remittur power more often to insure that a punitive damage award bears a reasonable relationship to the award of actual damages, there would be less criticism of punitive damages....

III. CRITICISM OF THE CONCEPT OF PUNITIVE DAMAGES

A. *Punishment versus Deterrence*

The concept of punitive damages has been criticized since its inception. The overwhelming majority of jurisdictions that authorize the recovery of punitive damages espouse the theory that punitive damages serve two functions: (1) to punish past wrongful conduct; and (2) to deter future wrongful conduct. Both theories of punishment and deterrence are criticized for being inconsistent with each other and for being inconsistently applied by the courts in particular cases.

Historically, the objective of civil law has not been to confer a profit or a windfall upon an injured party, but rather to make the injured party whole. Payment of punitive damage awards to the state or federal government rather than to the plaintiff seems a more sensible way of accomplishing the deterrence or punishment function, while at the same time remaining true to the basic objective of the law of damages.

B. *Double Jeopardy*

Some commentators charge that the award of punitive damages violates the rule against double jeopardy by imposing a double punishment for the same crime. This criticism arises from the situation where the defendant can be assessed punitive damages in a civil action for the same acts for which he can be fined in a criminal action. The punishment inflicted in both cases may exceed what is sufficient to deter or punish the defendant.

[1]**Remittur** refers to the judge's authority to reduce an excessive verdict by the jury.

This problem is exacerbated by the inability of the civil and criminal justice systems to recognize their mutual interest in punishing or deterring a wrongdoer. For instance, in sentencing, the judge in the criminal court may not consider the punitive damages awarded by a civil jury. Similarly, a civil jury may not be told that the defendant has been or could be subjected to criminal prosecution for the same acts. Thus, both courts might punish the defendant for his malice or wrongdoing. In light of this problem, perhaps the civil plaintiff's burden of proof on the issue of malice should be heightened to correspond with that required in the criminal courts. Such a provision might also be effectively coupled with a requirement that punitive damages be related to penal fines.

C. *Relation to Compensatory Damages*

The most often repeated criticism of punitive damages is that the jury has unfettered discretion to award any amount of punitive damages even if the amount bears no relationship to the "actual" damages. For example, in *Aetna Life Insurance Co.* v. *Lavoie*, 470 So.2d 1060 (Ala. 1984) *vacated*, 106 S.Ct. 1580 (1986), an Alabama jury awarded $3.5 million dollars in punitive damages against an insurance company for its bad faith refusal to pay a $1,650.22 hospital bill. Although some jurisdictions require a reasonable relationship between the actual and punitive damages, the Alabama courts do not require such a correlation.

One of the questions presented to the United States Supreme Court on appeal was whether the award of punitive damages violated the excessive fines clause of the Eighth Amendment. Unfortunately, the Court did not reach this question. Instead, the Court vacated and remanded the case on the grounds that an associate justice of the Alabama Supreme Court should have disqualified himself from participation in the decision because he had filed a similar insurer bad faith claim.

The Supreme Court recently noted probable jurisdiction in another case raising the issue of whether a punitive damage award violates the excessive fines clause. In *Bankers Life and Casualty Co.* v. *Crenshaw*, 483 So.2d 254 (Miss. 1985) *prob. juris. noted*, 197 S.Ct. 1367 (1987), the Supreme Court of Mississippi upheld a jury award of punitive damages against an insurance company that had refused to honor a claim. The jury awarded $1.6 million in punitive damages in addition to $20,000 actual damages. In its appeal to the Supreme Court, the insurance company contended that the punitive damages award violates the excessive fines clause of the Eighth amendment.

The majority of jurisdictions allowing punitive damages require actual or compensatory damages as a prerequisite to an award of punitive damages. However, the amount of actual or compensatory damages required is not specifically defined, and nominal actual damages will often suffice. Factors to be considered in fixing punitive damages include: (1) the nature of the defendant's acts; (2) the amount of the compensatory damages awarded; and (3) the wealth of the defendant. In addition, some jurisdictions require the amount of exemplary damages to be reasonably related to the amount of actual damages. This "reasonable relationship" rule allows an appellate court either to overturn a punitive damage award, or to order remittur if the court concludes that a reasonable relationship between the compensatory damages and punitive damages does not exist. Other courts do not require a reasonable relationship between actual and punitive damages but rely instead on the judge's remittur power to control grossly excessive awards. Finally, some courts allow evidence of a defendant's financial net worth so that the jury may set the punitive damages award at a level sufficient to punish or deter.

Allowing the jury to decide only whether there is sufficient malice to support an award of punitive damages is another way to curtail excessive punitive damages awards. The problems that occur when juries decide the amount of punitive damages to be awarded are revealed by the following jury charge, which was approved on appeal by the Fifth Circuit in *Martin* v. *Texaco, Inc.*, 726 F.2d 207 (5th Cir. 1984). The trial court instructed the jury on the standard for measuring punitive damages under Texas law as follows:

> The appropriate ratio will vary from case to case, depending on such factors as the character of the wrongful conduct, the extent to which the defendant is involved in the conduct, and the extent to which that conduct offends the public sense of justice and propriety.

> A very recent court decision listed five relevant factors for reviewing a jury's award of punitive damages, as follows:

(1) the nature of the wrong;
(2) the character of the conduct involved;
(3) the degree of culpability of the wrongdoer;
(4) the situation and sensibility of the parties;
(5) the extent to which defendant's conduct offends the public sense of justice and propriety.

The subjectivity of these factors, which are frequently found in jury instructions, illustrates the advantage of having the trial court fix the amount of punitive damages to be awarded. This would avoid the aberrant jury awards that are increasingly found in the crazy quilt of the tort system.

D. *Mass Tort Cases*

Repeated punitive damage awards against the same defendant in multiple product liability suits are another major problem on the litigation front. Judge Friendly recognized this problem in *Roginsky* v. *Richardson-Merrill, Inc.*, 378 F.2d 832 (2d Cir. 1967), explaining that repetitive punitive damage awards in mass products liability cases would subject a defendant to vastly excessive damage awards when viewed in their entirety.

Large companies are forced into bankruptcy to avoid successive awards of large punitive damages and the prospect of more such awards. Thousands of punitive damage suits have been filed against manufacturers because of a single defective product. A company's total exposure for a product can far exceed any fine for a criminal violation.

The legal community must find a way to reduce subsequent punitive damage awards by amounts previously paid. This could be accomplished by a jury instruction or by remittur. The rules of the federal multi-district litigation panel should be amended to permit trials in one or as few federal or state courts as possible in mass tort cases. A fund could be created in which all claimants would share after compensatory damages have been awarded or settlements made. The current system favors plaintiffs getting judgments before the defendant company enters bankruptcy and encourages a race to the courthouse. Plaintiffs with pending cases or injuries that become apparent much later are deprived of any punitive damages.

In sum, the power vested in juries to assume the public role of imposing the equivalent of the criminal fine may be misplaced. Allowing juries virtually unfettered discretion to make punitive damage awards on an ad hoc basis smacks of vigilante justice. The jury is transformed into a roving commission to punish and deter wrongdoing by transferring wealth. Putting the net worth of the defendant in evidence to relate the punitive award to the total worth of the defendant exacerbates the problem and is an open invitation for outrageous awards against companies with substantial assets.

IV. RECOVERY OF PUNITIVE DAMAGES

A. *Legal Standards*

Punitive damages have been awarded in a myriad of factual situations involving disparate legal theories. Reliance by the courts on various legal bases for punitive awards has resulted in subtle changes in jury instructions and articulations of the burdens of proof. Thus, the jurisdiction in which the plaintiff brings his action often dramatically affects whether and to what extent punitive damages may be awarded.

Most jurisdictions focus on outrageous or aggravated conduct by the defendant rather than on the nature or extent of harm to the plaintiff. Courts usually require "circumstances of aggravation or outrage such as spite or malice or a fraudulent or evil motive on the part of the defendant, or such a conscious and deliberative disregard of the interests of others that the conduct may be called willful or wanton." Prosser, Law of Torts, §2, at 9-10 [5th ed. 1984]. Mere negligence is not enough, though some courts expand gross negligence to include "conscious indifference to consequences" as a justification for punitive damages. At least one jurisdiction has ruled that punitive damages may be recovered for gross negligence where that gross negligence is shown by violation of a statute. Another court has ruled that gross negligence will not support an award of punitive damages.

Courts have espoused various standards in analyzing the type of wrongful conduct which will justify punitive awards. For example, a Florida appellate court in *Jacmar Pacific Pizza Corp.* v. *Huston*, 502 So.2d 91 (Fla.Dist.Ct.App. 1987), ruled that a plaintiff must establish "that the conduct of the defendant was tantamount to willful, intentional and wanton disregard for others and that the character of negligence required to support a punitive damages award is the same as that required to support a manslaughter conviction." Using somewhat different language, the Supreme Court of Florida held in an earlier case that the negligent conduct necessary to support and award of punitive damages must be of a "gross and flagrant character, evincing reckless disregard of human life" or "which shows wantonness or recklessness, or a grossly careless disregard of the safety and welfare of the public, or that reckless indifference to the rights of others...." *American Cyanamid Co.* v. *Roy*, 498 So.2d 859, 861-2 [Fla. 1986].

By comparison, an appellate court in Missouri held in one case that punitive damages could be awarded "upon a showing of either actual or legal malice." *Guirl* v. *Guirl*, 708 S.W.2d 239 [Mo.Ct.App. 1986]. The test offered by the court was "whether the actor did a wrongful act intentionally without just cause or excuse." In another appellate decision, a Missouri court developed this test more fully, ruling that in order to recover punitive damages the plaintiff must establish that the defendant acted "at the least, with legal malice." The court further explained that "[l]egal malice is shown by the intentional, knowing commission of a wrongful act without just cause or excuse, and in contravention of, or reckless disregard for, the rights of others." *Collet* v. *American Nat'l Stores*, 708 S.W.2d 273, 287 [Mo.Ct.App 1986].

B. *Particular Actions*

In addition to the courts' use of different standards and language to support punitive damage awards, there is also a great deal of confusion over which actions will support a punitive award. For example, tort actions for personal injuries arise from a variety of actual situations ranging from automobile accidents to product liability actions. Once again, the jurisdiction where the case is brought is often critical. For example, only eighteen states allow punitive damages in wrongful death actions. Typically, the rationale is that the legislative intent of wrongful death statutes is compensation, not punishment.

Courts apply different standards in determining whether juries can award punitive damages for assault and battery. For example, in Alabama courts require that "particularized circumstances of aggravation or insult" be shown before punitive damages will be awarded. *Peete* v. *Blackwell*, 504 So.2d 222, 223 [Ala. 1986]. Other courts hold that punitive damages are justified when there is "implied malice" or when there is "malice, or oppression, or gross and willful wrong, or a wanton and reckless disregard of plaintiff's rights." Nominal damages alone are usually sufficient to support an award of exemplary damages in an assault and battery action. Some jurisdictions, however, require that actual damages be proved before punitive damages can be awarded.

Punitive damages are awarded in actions for false imprisonment in some jurisdictions where there is malice or where the wrongdoer acts willfully, wantonly or in a reckless disregard of the rights or safety of others. The amount of punitive damages for false imprisonment varies widely as evidenced by the store detention cases where customers have been unlawfully detained on suspicion of shoplifting.

Plaintiffs bringing defamation suits must prove actual damages as well as actual malice or reckless disregard for the truth before punitive damages may be awarded. The United States Supreme Court in *Gertz* v. *Welch, Inc.*, 418 U.S. 323 (1974), held that the Constitution prohibits awards of punitive damages even to a private figure plaintiff unless he proves actual malice. The *Gertz* decision also limited "defamation plaintiffs who do not prove knowledge of falsity or reckless disregard for the truth to compensation for actual injury." 418 U.S. at 342.

A recent report by the Rand Corporate Institute for Civil Justice finds that the upward trend in awards of punitive damages springs not from personal injury and products liability cases, but primarily from litigation involving business disputes. The growth of punitive damages in business and contract cases has resulted in part from the evolution of the so-called "bad faith" cases. The verdict in *Pennzoil Co.* v. *Texaco, Inc.*, 107 S.Ct. 1519 (1987) [judgment in excess of 11 billion dollars upheld], is an example of the large punitive damage awards that may be made in this type of litigation. Punitive damages have been awarded for interference with business relations in a variety of situations where aggravated circumstances and malice are shown. The general rule in this country is that damages for breach of contract are limited to pecuniary loss and punitive damages are not recoverable. There are exceptions to this general rule, however. For example, in those cases where the complaint alleges that an independent willful tort accompanies or underlies the breach of contract, the plaintiff may recover punitive damages upon proof of malice, wantonness or oppression.

Punitive damages have also been awarded through arbitration. The first case in federal court challenging an award of punitive damages by an arbitration panel arose from a construction contract. The general contractor cancelled his contract with a subcontractor for the construction of a roof after altering the requirements for the roof. The subcontractor sued for compensatory and punitive damages, alleging breach of contract, fraud, misrepresentation and violation of the requirement of good faith and fair dealing. The general contractor stayed the lawsuit for arbitration pursuant to a contract provision that required arbitration of all disputes arising out of the contract. After the arbitration panel awarded the subcontractor $108,908 in punitive damages and $41,091 in compensatory damages, the general contractor argued to the federal district court that the arbitration panel lacked the authority to award punitive damages. The district court rejected this argument and the Eleventh Circuit affirmed.

Injury to property is another area of the law where courts have restricted awards of punitive damages. For example, most jurisdictions allow the recovery of punitive damages in trespass actions only when the defendant's trespass was malicious and willful. Punitive damages may not be recovered when the defendant acted in good faith without wrongful intent. Punitive damages have been allowed in connection with a wide variety of nuisances. Usually, conduct which could be considered willful, wanton or malicious as well as actual damages must accompany the alleged nuisance before punitive damages can be awarded.

In addition to the torts discussed above, punitive damages have been awarded in cases involving special duty relationships between plaintiffs and telephone, telegraph and utility companies, attorneys, insurance companies, fiduciaries, and landlords.

Although the various tort actions discussed above are based on different legal theories, the usual focus with regard to punitive damages is the defendant's conduct, not the harm to the plaintiff. Unfortunately, the standards incorporated into jury instructions are usually confusing and often do not reflect this focus. Those of us who encourage reform in the area of punitive damages should advocate a more stringent and definite legal basis for allowing such awards. We can begin by drafting clear, understandable and precise jury instructions....

VII. RECOMMENDATIONS

Excessive punitive damages awards have become a national problem. Legislation by the states providing for caps on punitive awards or requiring a fixed formula or a reasonable relationship between compensatory and punitive damages will help solve the problem. Legislation that would give the trial court alone the power to determine the amount of a punitive damages award after the jury has determined that the defendant's malicious conduct justified such an award is a better solution. In the interim and pending full legislative solutions, the courts should not hesitate to accomplish this same result by using their remittur power in appropriate instances.

Abandoning punitive damages altogether is not a sound idea, since there will always be the unusual case where punishment is warranted or deterrence is necessary. But under current law and practice, punitive damages are awarded far too easily, far too often and far too excessively. State legislators and judges alike must recognize the dangers inherent in the current system and take steps to correct what is fast becoming the most serious flaw in our tort system today.

NOTES

*From *University of Richmond Law Review* 22 (1987). pp. 1–17. Reprinted with permission.

FOR DISCUSSION

1. What are the purposes of punitive damages? Do the authors think these purposes are being fulfilled?

2. According to the authors, what are the major problems associated with punitive damages awards?

3. How can the trial judge limit an excessive award of punitive damages?

4. How are juries traditionally instructed with respect to punitive damages? Why are the authors critical of these jury instructions?

5. What is malice? Do you think there should be a standard definition of malice for the entire country? What would it be?

6. After reading this article, what do you consider to be the most significant criticism of punitive damages? Which of the suggested reforms would you most like to see instituted?

The following case considers the questions of who should be liable for punitive damages and what the standards for awarding punitive damages should be.

CASE

Timothy Wilson v. City of Eagan et al.
Supreme Court of Minnesota (1980)
297 N.W.2d 146, 8 A.L.R.4th 1277

WAHL, Justice. Eagan, Minnesota, Ordinance No. 5, §5.05 (March 2, 1976) and Minn.Stat. §35.71, subd. 3 (1978) require that before an impounded animal can be destroyed, the animal must be held for five business days, with certain exceptions not applicable in this case. In direct contravention of the ordinance and statute, Eagan animal warden Cary Larson and police officer Robert O'Brien, in performance of their duties, intentionally killed Timothy Wilson's pet cat on the same day it was properly impounded. Wilson sued the City of Eagan, the warden, and the police officer for compensatory damages and the warden and the officer for punitive damages. The deputy police chief, Jay Berthe, was joined as an additional defendant on the second day of the three day trial. The court ruled at the close of the trial that the defendants were all liable for compensatory damages as a matter of law because they had at least negligently violated the statute and because Wilson was free from contributory negligence. The jury awarded compensatory damages of $40 and punitive damages of $5,000 against the three individual defendants: $2,000 against Larson; $500 against O'Brien; and $2,500 against Berthe. The court dismissed Berthe as having been improperly joined. The court then ruled that Minn.Stat. §466.04, subd. 1a (1978) prohibits an award of punitive damages against municipal employees acting in performance of their duties. The trial court also held that if this court interprets the statute to allow punitive damages, the awards should be reduced to $500 each against Larson and O'Brien. We affirm in part and reverse in part.

The issues raised by the appeal belie the humble origins of the case.

(1) Does Minn.Stat. §466.04, subd. 1a (1978) preclude an award of punitive damages against municipal officers and employees?

(2) Does the conduct of Larson, the animal warden, and O'Brien, the police officer justify an award of punitive damages against either of them?

(3) Did the trial court err in reducing the punitive damages awarded by the jury?

(4) Was Berthe improperly dismissed from the suit?

(5) Did the trial court err in directing a verdict as to negligence?

1. Appellant argues that Minn.Stat. §466.04, subd. 1a (1978) does not preclude an award of punitive damages against municipal officers and employees, thus raising a question of first impression.

Minnesota Statutes §466.04, subds. 1, 1a (1978) provide:

MAXIMUM LIABILITY. Subdivision 1. Limits: punitive damages.
Liability of any municipality on any claim within the scope of sections 466.01 to 466.15 shall not exceed
(a) $100,000 when the claim is one for death by wrongful act or omission and $100,000 to any claimant in any other case;
(b) $300,000 for any number of claims arising out of a single occurrence.
No award for damages on any such claim shall include punitive damages.
Subd. 1a. Officers and employees. The liability of an officer or an employee of any municipality for a tort arising out of an alleged act or omission occurring in the performance of duty shall not exceed the limits set forth in subdivision 1, unless the officer or employee provides professional services and also is employed in his profession for compensation by a person or persons other than the municipality.

Whether subdivision 1a prevents an award of punitive damages against municipal officers and employees as well as limiting the amounts recoverable as compensatory damages, cannot be determined from the face of the statute. If the preclusion of an award of punitive damages is considered a *limit* on the liability of the municipality as "Limits" is used in the heading of subdivision 1, then the provisions in subdivision 1a that "[t]he liability of an officer or employee ... shall not exceed the limits set forth in subdivision 1" could be interpreted to mean that punitive damages cannot be awarded against municipal officers and employees.

The contrary interpretation is equally plausible. Subdivision 1 has two sentences. The first limits monetary liability for tort claims against municipalities. The second precludes punitive damages entirely. The first sentence states: "Liability...shall not exceed" certain dollar amounts. Subdivision 1a reads: "The *liability* of an officer or employee...*shall not exceed* the limits set forth in subdivision 1" [emphasis added]. The same language of limitation is used in both subdivisions. There is no mention of punitive damages in subdivision 1a. Because both interpretations are plausible, the statute is ambiguous. Therefore, we must turn to legislative intent and rules of construction to interpret the statute.

In 1962, the Minnesota Supreme Court prospectively overruled the sovereign immunity of municipalities. During the 1963 session of the legislature, the legislature enacted Minn.Stat. §466 (1963), establishing dollar limits on municipal liability for compensatory damages and precluding the award of punitive damages against municipalities. Minn.Stat. §466.04 (1978). The statute did not affect the personal liability of municipal employees and officers who continued to be liable for unlimited compensatory damages and for punitive damages.

In *Douglas* v. *City of Minneapolis*, the plaintiffs claimed that the city illegally paid the punitive damages imposed against Minneapolis police in federal district court for actions of the police which violated the civil rights of private citizens attending a fund-raising party for a political cause. We noted that despite the fact that punitive damages could not be awarded against a municipality directly under Minn.Stat. §466.04 (1978), the municipality was empowered by Minn.Stat. §471.45 (1978) to indemnify municipal employees and officers for punitive damages awarded against them "if it deems it 'fitting and proper to do so,' assuming that the actions of the officer or employee which lead to the judgment occur in the performance of duty and do not arise as a result of malfeasance in office or wilful or wanton neglect of duty." 304 Minn. 259, 270, 230 N.W.2d 577, 585 (1975).

Defendants argue that the legislature intended to change the *Douglas* holdings by the 1976 amendments to Minn.Stat. §466.04 (1978), which added subdivisions 1a and 1b and which increased the dollar limits of subdivision 1. Had the legislature intended to preclude the award of punitive damages against municipal officers and employees, it could have done so expressly. Had *Douglas* been the specific target of the amendments, the legislature could have enacted a statute plainly preventing punitive damage awards or plainly preventing the indemnification of employees for punitive damages. The use of the word "limits" is not the best means to achieve both liability ceilings and punitive damages preclusion. The failure of the legislature to address the holdings in *Douglas* in more specific language indicates that the legislature did not intend to change our decision in *Douglas*. Therefore, the amendments appear to have been directed only at dollar limits.

Policy arguments also favor the allowance of punitive damages. First, sovereign immunity is an exception to the general tort rules that one should be liable for the harm one causes and for punitive damages in the appropriate case. Consequently, sovereign immunity should be treated restrictively so that the underlying purposes and philosophy of our tort law, including the provisions for punitive damages, can be given effect. Thus, the statute should be read restrictively, not expansively. Second, the potential for abuse of power by municipal officers and employees in ways that could cause harassment, invasion of privacy, or injury to property low in value is great. Although such abuses are presumably rare, when they occur compensatory damages are likely to be small and will not function to deter similar conduct. Furthermore, citizens and attorneys are not likely to take action to redress the wrongs where the actual compensatory damages would be low. Punitive damages are, therefore, appropriate for such cases.

We are aware that municipalities may ultimately pay the punitive damages. We are also aware that the legislature made the indemnity provisions mandatory, Minn.Stat. §466.07, subd. 1a (1979), rather than discretionary, Minn.Stat. §466.07, subd. 1 (1978). However, allowing punitive damages awards against municipal officers and employees does not circumvent the clear intent of the legislature that municipalities not be subject to punitive damages awards because municipalities are prohibited from indemnifying officers and employees in cases of "malfeasance in office or wilful and wanton neglect of duty." Minn.Stat §466.07. subds 1a (Supp. 1979), 2 (1978).

We construe Minn.Stat. §466.04, subd. 1a (1978) to allow punitive damages against municipal employees.

2. We consider next the propriety of the punitive damages awards in this case. Punitive damages are allowed only where the harm complained of is the result of conduct done in malicious, willful, or reckless disregard for the rights of others. *Huebsch* v. *Larson*, 291 Minn. 361, 364, 191 N.W.2d 433, 435 (1971). Whether punitive or exemplary damages are appropriate under the particular facts of this case is within the discretion of the jury. The weight and force to be given evidence relating to punitive damages is exclusively a jury question.

A review of the record shows that animal warden Larson received a phone call from the owner of a day care center complaining that a cat was being a nuisance in her yard. By the time Larson arrived, the cat had returned across the street to an apartment patio of the apartment complex in which Wilson and his cat resided. Larson captured the cat and put it in a cage. After a brief conversation with the tenant of the apartment adjacent to the patio where the cat was caught, and after a cursory search for the owner, Larson returned to the city hall with the lawfully impounded cat.

Because the city had no facilities to care for the cat and had no contract or arrangement with any kennel or agency to care for impounded cats, Larson attempted to find a city employee or other local citizen who would volunteer to take care of the cat for the required five days. He was not successful. At around 2:30 P.M. Larson met with Jay Berthe, the deputy chief of police, and they agreed the cat should be killed. After attempts to asphyxiate the cat were unsuccessful, Larson and police officer O'Brien took it to the rifle range and shot it three times with a shotgun.

Minnesota Statutes §35.71, subd. 3 (1978) expressly states: "All animals seized by public authority *shall be held* for redemption by the owner for a period *not less than five regular business days* of the impounding agency..." [emphasis added]. The relevant city ordinance also requires impounded animals to be held for five days. In direct contravention of the Minnesota statute and the city ordinance, the defendants intentionally killed the cat on the same day that it was impounded.

Larson did not act with malice toward the plaintiff; he did not know who the cat's owner was. Nevertheless, the award of punitive damages was appropriate because Larson's conduct in killing the cat within hours of its impoundment evinces a willful disregard for both the law and the property rights of private citizens.

There is no evidence in the record, however, that O'Brien, the police officer who did the actual shooting, knew how long the cat had been impounded. Assuming that he had a duty to inquire before killing the cat, breach of that duty is negligence. It is not the type of malicious, intentional or willful disregard for plaintiff's rights that would support punitive damages. O'Brien is liable for compensatory damages only.

3. The issue of the appropriate amount of punitive damages in cases involving infringement of the rights of private citizens by public officials and employees is troublesome. As noted above, the potential for abuse of authority by public officials and employees in ways that can cause harassment, invasion of privacy, or injury to property low in value is great. Such wrongs against citizens are likely to go unredressed if the costs of trial are greater than the amount the injured party could hope to recover. In determining whether punitive damages are unreasonably excessive, the court should consider, among other factors, the degree of malice, intent, or willful disregard, the type of interest invaded, the amount needed to truly deter such conduct in the future, and the cost of bringing the suit. *See* Minn.Stat. §549.20, subd. 3 (1978). We find no error in the court's ruling that the jury award of $2,000 against Warden Larson be reduced to $500.

4. Appellant challenges the dismissal of defendant Berthe from the suit. Rule 15 of the Minnesota Rules of Civil Procedure allows a party to amend pleadings after a responsive pleading has been served only by leave of court or by written consent of the adverse party. Minn.R.Civ.P. 15.01. Where the amendment would add a defendant, the proposed defendant must consent or the court must give leave to amend. Berthe did not consent.

Leave to amend "shall be given freely when justice so requires." Minn.R.Civ.P. 15.01. Whether leave should be given in a particular case depends upon a number of factors, including, in particular, prejudice to the adverse party. Prejudice to the adverse party can be weighed against prejudice to the moving party if leave is denied. Where the plaintiff seeks to add a new defendant, the relationship between the new and old defendants and whether the proposed defendant had notice of the suit are important factors. Berthe would have been prejudiced in several ways had the dismissal not been granted. He had not been present at trial for most of the testimony; he had no opportunity to decide whether he wanted a lawyer other than the lawyer representing the city and other defendants; he had no opportunity to examine or prepare to examine witnesses already called; and he had no meaningful opportunity to present his own evidence. The prejudice to the plaintiff that resulted from not adding Berthe was minimal because the statute of limitations had not run, and, therefore, a separate suit could have been initiated against Berthe.

Berthe was properly dismissed from the suit after having been improperly joined where he did not have notice that he would be a defendant and where he had no opportunity to prepare his defense.

5. We find the verdict directed against defendants on negligence to be proper. The killing of a cat by public employees on the day they impounded it, when the statute and ordinance require it to be held for five days, is at least negligence.

The defendants argue that Wilson was contributorily negligent in supervising the cat. The wandering of the cat may have caused its impoundment, but the cat's being allowed to wander is not a cause of its being killed by the animal warden and a police officer in violation of a statute on the same day it was impounded. The trial court did not err in refusing to submit the issue of contributory negligence to the jury.

Affirmed in part; reversed in part.

FOR DISCUSSION

1. Can you think of any reason why public officials and employees should be exempted from paying punitive damages?

2. According to the court, why is it a good idea for public officials and employees to be liable for punitive damages, even though the municipality itself is not?

3. What legal standard for liability for punitive damages is articulated in this case? How does this standard compare with those described in the preceding article on punitive damages?

4. What behavior of defendant Larson is considered to have justified an award of punitive damages? Do you agree?

5. Do you think it was appropriate that the punitive damages award against defendant O'Brien was overturned? If Deputy Chief Berthe had been properly joined as a defendant, do you think the punitive damages award against him would have been sustained? Explain.

6. The court approved the reduction of the punitive damages award against Larson from $2000 to $500. Was this appropriate? Do you think the authors of the punitive damages article you read would have agreed? Explain.

DECLARATORY JUDGMENT

A **declaratory judgment** is a decree by a court articulating the legal rights of the parties before it in a particular case. A declaratory judgment, standing alone, does not require that anything further be done; it only renders a binding ruling about the question or questions of law presented. This is not the same as an advisory opinion, however, because the court is declaring the parties' rights within the context of a real case or controversy. Declaratory judgment originated in equity, but it is no longer regarded as strictly an equitable remedy. In many jurisdictions, the declaratory judgment remedy is established and controlled by statute.

The remedy of declaratory judgment can be and is used in a variety of different situations, but one of the most frequent uses of declaratory judgment is by insurance companies who wish to establish in advance of the main lawsuit whether they are obligated to cover their insured in a particular situation. The following case presents a somewhat less frequent situation: Here an insured is attempting to establish whether an insurance company must provide coverage for her in an accident situation in which she was apparently at fault.

CASE   **Patricia Hollander v. Nationwide Mutual Insurance Company**
                       New York Supreme Court, Appellate Division (1978)
                       60 A.D.2d 380, 401 N.Y.S.2d 336

DENMAN, Justice.   While operating a vehicle owned by her sister and insured by defendant, plaintiff was involved in a serious accident giving rise to extensive potential liability. Plaintiff's own automobile was also insured with defendant under a policy which provided excess coverage for operation of non-owned vehicles, provided that such other vehicle:

> (i) is not owned by…any member of the same household…;
> (ii) is not furnished for regular use to…a member of the same household;

On the date of the accident, plaintiff was living at the home of her parents with her sister. Plaintiff obtained declaratory relief determining that the clause excluding coverage of non-owned vehicles when owned by a "member of the same household" did not apply in the circumstances presented here. We affirm that determination.

Preliminarily, defendant urges that commencement of this action was premature inasmuch as the policy in question provides excess coverage only and the liability actions pending against the plaintiff have not yet proceeded to judgment in excess of the primary coverage under her sister's policy. "[T]he policy in this State has been to deny the declaratory judgment where the matter in dispute can be determined in the basic negligence action but to permit the action when the dispute is such that it depends on matters outside of the negligence action or will not arise in the negligence action as part of the lawsuit." *Nationwide Mut. Ins. Co.* v. *Dennis, 14 A.D.2d 188, 189, 217 N.Y.S.2d 680, 681.* The matter in dispute here requires judicial interpretation of an exclusionary provision which will not arise in the pending negligence actions. Furthermore, where resolution of the matter in dispute is determinative of the insurer's liability to its insured for potential judgments, declaratory relief is appropriate. This is true even where, as here, the insurance company is an excess liability insurer. Resolution of the disputed clause here should not wait adjudication of the principal actions.

The disputed phrase "member of the same household" is not defined in the policy but defendant relies on the facts that plaintiff had been living at her parents' home with her sister prior to the accident; that at the time of the accident she had not established a new residence; and that she indicated in a motor vehicle accident report and in a conversation with defendant's adjuster that her home address was that of her parents. Defendant argues that she was still a member of her sister's and parents' household when the accident occurred, and is thereby excluded from the excess coverage.

Physical presence in the home alone is insufficient to establish a residence, particularly where, as here, plaintiff had previously established other legal residences. The record indicates that, except for a period of a few months, plaintiff had not been a member of her parents' household for at least two years prior to the accident. While she stayed with her parents, she continually sought another apartment. A few days prior to the accident, she had signed a lease for an apartment and had obtained permission to move in earlier than the date provided in the lease. She had had telephone service installed in that apartment and, on the morning of the accident, paid her first month's rent, obtained the keys to the apartment and commenced moving. At the very time of the accident, she was engaged in moving her belongings to the new apartment. She was self-supporting at this time and received no money from her parents.

The questions of whether a person is a member of the same household as another is a question of fact for the trier of the facts. On these facts it was certainly competent for the trial court to determine that plaintiff was not a member of her parents' household and had established a different legal residence.

Moreover, the rule of construction applied to ambiguous terms in insurance contracts strongly favors the insured. "Where an insurer attempts to limit liability by use of an ambiguously worded term which is subject to more than one reasonable construction, the courts will construe it strictly against the insurer." *Sperling* v. *Great American Indemnity Co.*, 7 N.Y.2d 442, 447, 199 N.Y.S.2d 465, 469, 166 N.E.2d 482, 484–485. This principle holds particularly true in cases where the ambiguity is in an exclusionary clause.

With regard to the second exclusionary clause, defendant argues that plaintiff's sister's car was "furnished for regular use" to plaintiff but this is not supported by the record. The evidence clearly establishes that plaintiff had used her sister's car only three times in the three-month period prior to the accident. Such use could only be considered occasional and thus would not fall within the exclusionary clause.

The judgment should be affirmed.

FOR DISCUSSION

1. According to the court, when is a separate declaratory judgment action concerning insurance coverage appropriate?
2. What exactly is the court being called on to do in this lawsuit?
3. What is the rule in New York concerning interpretation of exclusionary clauses in insurance contracts? Does this rule make sense?
4. What did the plaintiff accomplish in this lawsuit? Do you think it was worthwhile? Explain.

LEGAL TERMS TO KNOW

compensatory damages	permanent injunction
damages	prohibitory injunction
declaratory judgment	punitive damages
ex parte	remedy
liquidated damages	remittur
mandatory injunction	temporary injunction
mitigation of damages	temporary restraining order
nominal damages	unique goods

ADDITIONAL QUESTIONS AND EXERCISES

1. In this chapter there are several criticisms of the jury's role in awarding damages. What do you see as the advantages of having a jury assess damages? What are the disadvantages? Should juries continue to do this job?

2. Some commentators have complained that damages awards, both compensatory and punitive, have escaped their bounds and become devices for transferring wealth from the rich to the poor (or at least to the victimized). Can you think of examples from this text, or from other sources you are familiar with, that would support this charge? Explain.

3. Other critics have commented that damages is a way of giving people permission to create harm in exchange for the payment of a fee. Is there any truth to this criticism? Can you think of examples that would support it?

4. To what extent do the types of remedies available in the civil justice system reflect society's concerns with respect to controlling harmful behavior? How does the institution of insurance influence the effectiveness of available remedies?

5. We started this chapter with the saying "Remedies precede rights." After reading the materials in this chapter, do you think the character of available remedies places limits on the rights people have? Give examples from this chapter to support your answer.

FOR FURTHER READING

1. BRODER, IVY E., "Characteristics of Million Dollar Awards: Jury Verdicts and Final Disbursements", *Just. Syst. J.* 11 (1986), pp. 349–359.

2. CORBOY, PHILIP H., "The Impact of Economic Theory on the Determination of Damages in a Wrongful Death Case." *Forum* 20 (1984–85), pp. 606–626.

3. DANIELS, STEPHEN, and JOANNE MARTIN, "Jury Verdicts and the 'Crisis' in Civil Justice," *Just. Syst. J.* 11 (1986), pp. 321–348.

4. MURIS, TIMOTHY J., "The Costs of Freely Granting Specific Performance," *Duke L. J.* 1982, pp. 1053–1069.

5. TREECE, ROBERT S., and RICHARD D. HALL, "When Do You File a Declaratory Judgment Action?" *Ins. Counsel J.* 53 (1986) pp. 396–400.

6. WOLF, SUSAN M., "Enforcing Surrogate Motherhood Agreements: The Trouble With Specific Performance," *N.Y.L.S. J. Hum. Rts.* 4 (1987), pp. 375–412.

INDEX